Badiou

Badiou

a subject to truth

Peter Hallward

Foreword by Slavoj Žižek

University of Minnesota Press   Minneapolis / London

Published by the University of Minnesota Press
111 Third Avenue South, Suite 290
Minneapolis, MN 55401-2520
http://www.upress.umn.edu

Library of Congress Cataloging-in-Publication Data

Hallward, Peter.
    Badiou : a subject to truth / Peter Hallward ; foreword by Slavoj Žižek.
    p.   cm.
    Includes bibliographical references and index.
    ISBN 0-8166-3460-2 (HC : alk. paper) — ISBN 0-8166-3461-0 (pbk. : alk. paper)
    1. Badiou, Alain.   I. Title.
    B2430.B274 H35 2003
    194—dc21

                                                                    2002015357

Printed in the United States of America on acid-free paper

The University of Minnesota is an equal-opportunity educator and employer.

12 11 10 09 08 07 06 05 04 03   10 9 8 7 6 5 4 3 2 1

All things proceed from the void and are borne towards the infinite. Who can follow these astonishing processes?

—Pascal, *Pensées,* §84

There is no science of man, since the man of science does not exist, but only its subject.

—Jacques Lacan, *Ecrits*

Today the great majority of people do not have a name; the only name available is "excluded," which is the name of those who do not have a name. Today the great majority of humanity counts for nothing. And philosophy has no other legitimate aim than to help find the new names that will bring into existence the unknown world that is only waiting for us because we are waiting for it.

—Alain Badiou, "The Caesura of Nihilism"

The subject is rare because, contrary to contemporary opinion, it cannot simply coincide with the individual. It falls to us to preserve the form of this rarity, and we shall succeed insofar as the God of the One has died. . . . We who are summoned by the void, we who intervene so as to decide the undecidable, we who are sustained by the indiscernible truth, we who are finite fragments of that infinity which will come to establish that there is nothing more true than the indifferent and the generic, we who dwell in the vicinity of that indistinction in which all reality dissolves, we, throws of the dice for a nameless star—we are greater than the sacred, we are greater than all gods, and we are so here and now, already and forever.

—Alain Badiou, *Une Soirée philosophique*

Contents

f o r e w o r d

Hallward's Fidelity to the Badiou Event
Slavoj Žižek

According to Richard Dawkins's well-known formulation, "God's utility function" in living nature is the reproduction of genes, that is, genes (DNA) are not a means for the reproduction of living beings, but the other way round: living beings are the means for the self-reproduction of genes. Ideology should be viewed in the same way, and we should ask the following question: What is the "utility function" of an ideological state apparatus (ISA)? The materialist answer is this: The utility function of an ISA is neither the reproduction of ideology qua network of ideas, emotions, and so on, nor the reproduction of social circumstances legitimized by this ideology, but the self-reproduction of the ISA itself. The *same* ideology can accommodate itself to different social modes, it can change the content of its ideas, and so on, just to "survive" as an ISA. However, from time to time something emerges that cannot be reduced to this placid logic of survival and reproduction: an *event*, an engagement for a universal cause that inexorably follows its inherent necessity, disregarding all opportunistic considerations.

So what does Alain Badiou aim at with his central notion that philosophy depends on some truth event as its external condition? When Deleuze, Badiou's great opponent-partner, tries to account for the crucial shift in the history of cinema from *image-mouvement* to *image-temps*, he makes a surprisingly crude reference to "real" history, to the traumatic impact of World War II (which was felt from Italian neorealism to American film noir). This reference is fully consistent with Deleuze's general anti-Cartesian thrust: a thought never begins spontaneously, out of itself, following its inherent logic; what provokes us to think is always a traumatic, violent encounter with some external real that brutally imposes itself on us, shattering our established ways of thinking. It is in this sense that a true thought is always decentered: one does not think spontaneously; one is forced to think. And, although with a slightly different accent, Badiou would agree with Deleuze: an authentic philosophical thought does not spin its web out of itself, following an "immanent conceptual necessity"; it is rather a reaction to the disturbing impact of some external truth event (in politics, science, art, or love), endeavoring to delineate the conditions of this event, as well as of a fidelity to it.

Badiou—a founding member, together with Jacques-Alain Miller, Jean-Claude Milner, Catherine Clément, Alain Regnault, and Alain Grosrichard, of the pathbreaking Lacano-Althusserian *Cahiers pour l'analyse* in the mid-1960s—is a supremely charismatic intellectual figure. He combines in a unique way rigorous mathematical knowledge, authentic philosophical passion, artistic sensitivity (he is not only the author of remarkable analyses of Mallarmé and Beckett, but also himself a noted playwright), and radical political engagement, which started with his "Maoist" activity in the 1960s and went up to supporting publicly, in a letter to *Le Monde,* the Khmer Rouge regime against the Vietnam invasion in 1978. What more should one want than an author who combines the three great Ms of scientific, aesthetic, and political revolutions: mathematics, Mallarmé, and Mao? But Badiou starts to look even more impressive when one resists this fascination by his person and seriously immerses oneself in his work.

Komar and Melamid, the two former Soviet painters who emigrated to the West in the mid-1970s, in the early 1990s made two paintings, the "best" and the "worst," on the basis of an opinion poll they conducted of a representative sample of the average American population. The worst painting, of course, was an abstract composition of sharp-edged triangles and squares in bright red and yellow à la Kandinsky, while the best was an idyllic scene, all in blue and green, of a clearing, with George Washington taking a walk near the bank of a river running through it and a Bambilike deer timidly observing him from the wood. During the past several years, they expanded this project, producing the "best" and the "worst" paintings of Germany, Italy, France, and other countries. This ironic experiment perfectly renders what Alain Badiou is opposed to when, in an unrepentant old Platonic way, he rejects today's rule of "tolerance," which tends to dismiss the very notion of someone's sticking to truth against the pressure of others' opinions as intolerant, Eurocentric, and so on. That is to say, today's predominant liberal political philosophers relegate politics to the domain of opinions (tastes, preferences, etc.), rejecting the conjunction of politics and truth as inherently "totalitarian"; is it not "evident," they might insist, that if you insist on the truth of your political statement, you dismiss your opponent's view as "untrue," thus violating the basic rule of tolerance?

Badiou not only passionately advocates a return to the politics of truth, but turns against all other predominant "postmodern" political and philosophical mantras. Although his thought is clearly marked by the specific French politicophilosophical context, the way it relates to this context (his critical rejection not only of the predominant pseudo-Kantian democratic liberalism, inclusive of its self-complacent criticism of "totalitarianism," but also his penetrating critique of the stances that are allegedly more "Leftist," from philosophical "deconstructionism"—which he dismisses as a new form of sophism—to "politically correct" multiculturalist identity politics) also makes its intervention in the present Anglo-Saxon theoretical scene extremely important and productive. The point is not only that Badiou serves as the necessary corrective to the still predominant identification of "French" thought with "deconstructionism" (this empty container into which Anglo-Saxon academia throws authors who, if dead, like Lacan, would turn over in their graves if informed of this insertion), presenting us with thought that clearly eludes all received classification: he is definitely not a deconstructionist or a post-Marxist, and is as clearly opposed to Heidegger as to the "linguistic turn" of analytical philosophy, not to mention that he shows disdain for liberal-democratic "political philosophy" along the lines of that espoused by Hannah Arendt. A perhaps even more important point is Badiou's critical rejection of the predominant form of today's Leftist politics, which, while accepting that capitalism is here to stay as the "only game in town," instead of focusing on the very fundamentals of our capitaloparliamentary order, shifts the accent to the recognition of different cultural, sexual, religious, and other lifestyles, endorsing the logic of *ressentiment:* in today's "radical," multiculturalist, liberal politics, the only way to legitimate one's claim is more and more to present oneself as a victim. Against the politically correct identity politics that focuses on the "right to difference," Badiou emphatically insists that the justification of any political demand by the substantial features that define the contingent particularity of a group ("We want some specific rights because we are women, gay, members of this or that ethnic or religious minority," etc.) violates the fundamental democratic axiom of principled equality, that is, the right to be defended today is not the "right to difference," but, on the contrary and more than ever, the right to Sameness.

Most of today's Left thus succumbs to ideological blackmail by the Right in accepting its basic premises ("The era of the welfare state with its free spending is over," etc.). Ultimately, this is what the celebrated "Third Way" of today's Social Democracy is about. In these conditions, an authentic act would be to counter the Rightist stir apropos of some "radical" measure ("You want the impossible. This will lead to catastrophe, to more state intervention, etc.") not by saying, defensively, that this is not what we mean, that we are no longer the old Socialists, that the proposed measures will not increase the state budget, that they will even render the state expenditure more "effective," give a boost to investments, and so on, but by saying, resoundingly, "Yes, this, precisely, *is* what we want!" When the status quo cynics accuse alleged revolutionaries of believing that everything is possible, that one can change everything, what they effectively mean is that *nothing at all* is really possible, that we cannot *really* change anything, since we are basically condemned to live in the world the way it is.

One is therefore tempted to apply Badiou's notion of event to his philosophy itself: in today's philosophical scenery, in which the old matrixes (analytical philosophy, Heideggerian phenomenology, deconstructionism, the "communicative" turn of the late Frankfurt School) appear more and more saturated, their potentials exhausted, its impact is precisely that of an event that intervenes in this constellation from the point of its "symptomal torsion," questioning as the indisputable background of its endeavor the series of preferences accepted by today's deconstructionism—the preference of difference over Sameness, of historical change over order, of openness over closure, of vital dynamics over rigid schemes, of temporal finitude over eternity.

With regard to this book of Peter Hallward, one is again tempted to resort to Badiou's own categories: if Badiou's recent work is *the* event of contemporary philosophy, Hallward's book bears the greatest fidelity to this event—fidelity, not dogmatic allegiance and blind repetitive résumé. Philosophical fidelity is not fidelity to all that an author has written, but fidelity to what is in the author more than the author himself (more than the empirical multitude of his writings), to the impulse that activates the author's endless work. So, with a breathtaking vigor, Hallward traces the consequences of the Badiou event, pointing out not only Badiou's tremendous achievements, but also local inconsistencies, deadlocks to be resolved, tasks that await further elaboration. Of course, although Badiou recognizes Lacan as one of his masters, his critical differences with regard to Lacan's "antiphilosophy" (to which antiphilosophy I subscribe) are well documented in Hallward's book. With regard to these differences, I can only turn around the standard phrase and say, With "enemies" like this, who needs friends? Because Badiou was engaged in a Maoist political group two decades ago, let me invoke Chairman Mao's well-known distinction between nonantagonistic contradictions within the people, to be resolved by patient argumentation, and antagonistic contradictions between the people and its enemies: the gap that separates Badiou from Lacan is definitely a nonantagonistic contradiction.

Furthermore, the fact that an English-speaking author has written a book on a French philosopher has had the rare, miraculous result of bringing together the best in the English and in the "continental" philosophical tradition: what we have here is the almost impossible intersection of clear analytic argumentation and "continental" philosophical speculative reflection. The only apprehension I have about Hallward's book is that, on account of its very excellence, it will—contrary to the author's intention, of course—contribute to the recent deplorable trend toward preferring introductions to the works of original authors themselves. So, although I am sure that Hallward's book will enjoy well-deserved success among philosophers, mathematicians and logicians, political theorists, and aestheticians, I hope its very success will also contribute to the growing interest in the writings of Badiou himself.

Acknowledgments

I am grateful to Bruno Bosteels for his meticulous and trenchant reading of an earlier version of this book, and to Gilbert Adair, Daniel Bensaïd, Ray Brassier, John Collins, Sam Gillespie, Brice Halimi, Keith Hossack, Eustache Kouvélakis, Sinéad Rushe, Daniel Smith, and Alberto Toscano for their various comments and support. Andrew Gibson and Todd May wrote helpful reviews of the full manuscript when it was at a particularly cumbersome draft stage.

Were it not for Alain Badiou's own encouragement and readiness to engage in an argument that has now gone on for more than seven years, this would have turned into an altogether different book.

I dedicate this book to my father, John.

Notes on Translation

Although it is often difficult to convey the remarkable concision of Badiou's prose (to say nothing of the power of his voice), to translate Badiou is not fundamentally problematic. Unlike Heidegger or Derrida, say, he makes no appeal to a mysterious "gift of language." On the contrary, as a matter of firm principle he insists that "the transmission of thought is indifferent to language," as he wrote in "De la Langue française comme évidement." Most of Badiou's key terms—*truth, truth process, generic procedure, void, event, subject, being, situation, site, fidelity*—can be translated literally, even when (as occasionally with *void* and *fidelity*) these translations jar somewhat with normal English usage.

As is well known, the English language cannot easily distinguish the French verb *être* (to be, or being) from the French noun *un étant* (a being). When the word *être* is meant to evoke this verbal dimension more than its substantial dimension (as, for example, in the phrase *être-en-tant-qu'être*), I occasionally remind readers of the gerundial form by translating it as "be-ing."

After some indecision I have had recourse to the rather clumsy neologism "evental" to translate Badiou's use of the word *événementiel*, which has little to do with either the conventional meaning of "factual" or the connotation made famous by Fernand Braudel and the *Annales* approach to historiography. To my mind the more natural choice of "eventful" by Norman Madarasz and Louise Burchill in their respective translations of Badiou's *Manifesto* and *Deleuze* invites misleading associations (plenitude, bustle, familiarity).

To draw attention to Badiou's peculiarly rigorous understanding of *représentation* as an ontological category, I have generally hyphenated the translation as "re-presentation" (on the model, for instance, of *L'Etre et l'événement*, p. 100). The term *véridique*, which unlike *vérité* is a qualification of knowledge *(savoir)*, is most clearly distinguished from truth if it is translated as "verifiable." Where it has been too awkward to translate Badiou's neologism *déliaison* (to unlink, to unrelate or separate), I have left it in the original French.

Abbreviations

AM	*Abrégé de métapolitique* (Badiou)
B	*Beckett: L'incrévable désir* (Badiou)
BW	*Basic Writings* (Heidegger)
C	*Conditions* (Badiou)
CD	*Casser en deux l'histoire du monde?* (Badiou)
CM	*Le Concept de modèle: Introduction à une épistémologie matérialiste des mathématiques* (Badiou)
CT	*Court traité d'ontologie transitoire* (Badiou)
D	*Gilles Deleuze: "La clameur de l'Etre"* (Badiou)
DI	*De l'idéologie* (Badiou)
DO	*D'un désastre obscur (Droit, Etat, Politique)* (Badiou)
DP	*Monde contemporain et désir de philosophie* (Badiou)
E	*L'Ethique: Essai sur la conscience du mal* (Badiou)
EE	*L'Etre et l'événement* (Badiou)
EL	*"L'Etre-là: Mathématique du transcendental"* (Badiou)
LM	*Logiques des mondes* (Badiou)
LS	*Le Siècle* (Badiou)
MP	*Manifeste pour la philosophie* (Badiou)
NN	*Le Nombre et les nombres* (Badiou)
PM	*Petit manuel d'inésthétique* (Badiou)
PP	*Peut-on penser la politique?* (Badiou)

RT	*Rhapsodie pour le théâtre* (Badiou)
S1	*Le Séminaire I* (Lacan)
S2	*Le Séminaire II* (Lacan)
S3	*Le Séminaire III* (Lacan)
S7	*Le Séminaire VII* (Lacan)
S11	*Le Séminaire XI* (Lacan)
S17	*Le Séminaire XVII* (Lacan)
S20	*Le Séminaire XX* (Lacan)
SP	*Saint Paul et la fondation de l'universalisme* (Badiou)
T	"Topos, ou logiques de l'onto-logique: Une Introduction pour philosophes, tome 1" (Badiou)
TA	"Théorie axiomatique du sujet: Notes du cours 1996–1998" (Badiou)
TC	*Théorie de la contradiction* (Badiou)
TS	*Théorie du sujet* (Badiou)

A New Philosophy of the Subject

Badiou's philosophy of the event is itself undoubtedly one of the great events in recent French thought. Badiou is perhaps the only serious rival of Deleuze and Derrida for that meaningless but unavoidable title of "most important contemporary French philosopher," and his major treatise, *L'Etre et l'événement* (1988), is certainly the most ambitious and most compelling single philosophical work written in France since Sartre's *Critique de la raison dialectique* (1960). It is only appropriate, moreover, that his work at this stage remain so emphatically *new* to English-speaking readers, since Badiou's entire philosophy is geared to the rigorous description of innovation as such. His work is an elaborate engagement with a relatively small set of essential questions: How can something entirely new come into the world? What sorts of innovation invite and deserve fully universal affirmation? How can the consequences of such innovation be sustained in the face of the world's inevitable indifference or resistance? And how can those who affirm these consequences continue their affirmation?

Although Badiou has himself encountered no small degree of such resistance over the course of his long and unusually varied career, today he occupies a prominent though still controversial place in French philosophy. For many years a professor at the University of Paris VIII at Vincennes / Saint Denis, he was appointed head of the philosophy department at the Ecole Normale Supérieure in 1999. His public lectures at the Collège International de Philosophie continue to draw hundreds of listeners. A committed Maoist in the 1970s, he retains an assertive voice in radical politics and is directly involved in a number of campaigns concerning immigration, labor issues, and political justice in the broadest sense. Along with a dozen books of philosophy, he has published a number of novels and plays and explored the conceptual implications of several of the most intensely debated domains of contemporary mathematics. Badiou is more than conventionally unclassifiable. His work ranges across a bewildering diversity of fields—number theory, psychoanalysis, modern poetry, political theory, theater, and performance theory. His allegiance extends, in different ways, to Cantor, Cohen, Lacan, Mallarmé, and Lenin. In particular, and perhaps more than any other contemporary French philosopher, he demonstrates the obsolescence of any clear-cut distinction between analytic and continental philosophy. Guided by mathematics though critical of mathematized logic, he is as familiar with Frege, Wittgenstein, and Gödel as he is with Hegel, Nietzsche, and Deleuze. His conception of philosophy rejects the qualifiers "analytic" and "continental" as much as it refuses its division into distinct and relatively autonomous spheres (political, aesthetic, epistemological, etc.).

If Badiou's work has yet to gain the recognition won by his more celebrated contemporaries,[1] this is very largely because it is so firmly at odds with every dominant philosophical orientation in both the French and the Anglo-American domain. Badiou is nothing if not polemical, and his list of targets is long and varied. He refuses to accept that Nietzsche was the last metaphysician, or that an educated use of ordinary language can dissolve all philosophical "non-sense," or that Plato, Hegel, and Marx were the precursors of totalitarianism, or that Auschwitz demands a complete transformation of philosophy, or that Stalin's crimes compel a return to republican parliamentarism, or that cultural anthropology must replace the universalism of concepts, or that recognition of "whatever works best" should replace the prescription of principles, or that philosophy must be sacrificed to an ethics of the altogether Other. His ontology breaks with the entire neo-Heideggerian legacy, from Levinas and Derrida to Nancy and Lacoue-Labarthe. His assertion of an absolute ontological multiplicity excludes any covertly theological recourse to the unity of being (Deleuze) or a One beyond being (Lardreau, Jambet). His measured fidelity to Plato is a challenge to the modern triumph of sophistry (Nietzsche, Wittgenstein, Lyotard). Though faithful to the militant atheism of the Enlightenment, his peculiarly post-Lacanian realism is a principled refusal of pragmatism in all its forms. Badiou has never accepted that "twilight of radical universalism" now condoned by so many once-Marxist intellectuals,[2] but his singular conception of the universal sets him apart from Kant and the transcendental tradition. His hostility to communitarianism is even stronger than his contempt for merely procedural conceptions of justice or morality. His insistence on the rigorous universality of truth aligns him with the scientific and rationalist tradition against the linguistic or relativistic turn in all its forms, but his conception of the subject marks a break with the Althusserian as much as with the conventionally empiricist conception of science. Last but not least, Badiou's work condemns in the strongest terms the emergence, since the late 1970s, in both French philosophy and Anglo-American cultural criticism, of an ethics oriented to the respectful recognition of (cultural, sexual, moral, political, and other) differences. Badiou's proximate targets here, though seldom mentioned, are those who used to be called the *nouveaux philosophes,* but his argument extends to a confrontation with positions as diverse as those of Levinas and Rawls, along with much of what is called "cultural studies" in North America.[3]

It is probably not much of an exaggeration to say that Badiou's work is today almost literally unreadable according to the prevailing codes—both political and philosophical—of the Anglo-American academy. Badiou accepts, sometimes flaunts, the consequent marginalization without hesitation: "Since Plato, philosophy has always been a break with opinion. . . . For the philosopher, everything that is consensual is suspect" (AM, 90).

The fundamental and immediately striking move in Badiou's philosophy, the move that sets him starkly apart from his contemporaries, is his affirmation of the strict, uncompromising universality of truth, and his consequent subtraction of this truth from the legislation of judgment or interpretation. Perhaps the most basic of Badiou's assumptions is that whatever else it may be, "truth" can be reached only through a process that breaks decisively with all established criteria for judging (or interpreting) the validity (or profundity) of opinions (or understandings). This assumption has two main implications. On the one hand, if and when we can speak about the truth of a situation, this truth will concern not its most clearly identifiable and distinctive elements but its most indiscernibly or "evasively included" groupings of elements (EE, 313). The truth of a situation will always concern whatever is most indistinct or "generic" about that situation. On the other hand, the process whereby such groupings might be assembled will itself take place in violation of all the usual ways in which elements are grouped. A truthful or generic grouping is something that must occur as a break with the status quo.

Badiou's whole conception of philosophy is inspired by the "simple, powerful idea that any existence can one day be transfigured by what happens to it, and can commit itself from then on to what holds for all" (SP, 70).

It is a conception that holds firmly to Lacan's austere prescription "The important thing is not to understand but to attain the true."[4] In this respect Badiou is the untimely descendant of a long line of interventionist thinkers whose central insight is that access to truth can be achieved only by going against the grain of the world and against the current of history—a group of thinkers that includes Saint Paul, Pascal, and Claudel (for whom the "way of the world" can never lead to God[5]) as much as Descartes, Cantor, and Hilbert (for whom sensual intuition can never provide for the secure foundation of knowledge), not to mention Lenin, Lukacs, and Breton (for whom merely objective historical trends will never enable a genuine break with the inertia of the past). In each case the truly decisive moment—the "indefensible" wager on God's existence, the formal elaboration of "undefinable" mathematical axioms, the "unjustifiable" commitment to political or aesthetic revolution—is abruptly inventive. Such decisions are quite literally founded upon nothing. Nothing—no knowledge, no familiarity with the rules, no "feel for the game," no understanding of habitus or tradition—will allow for the deduction of the decision from "the way things are" or indeed from any operation (rationalization, clarification, extrapolation, exaggeration, variation, derivation, etc.) performed upon the way things are. Each such decision begins as a principled *break* with the way things are. Insistence upon the consequences of this affirmation, however, can promise the radical transformation of our conception of things, a thorough revaluation of the world, or of intuition, or of history.

Nothing is more exceptional today than a genuinely inventive as opposed to a merely nostalgic commitment to so unabashedly zealous and partisan an understanding of truth. For, obvious differences aside, what all three of the great currents of twentieth-century philosophy—the analytical philosophy descended from logical positivism and the later Wittgenstein, the hermeneutics variously inspired by Dilthey, Heidegger, and Gadamer, and the poststructuralism developed by Derrida and Lyotard—have in common, in addition to a shared commitment to language as the fundamental medium of philosophy, is a profound suspicion of the very word *truth*. Modern philosophy has embraced a kind of generalized sophistry. In response, Badiou's work represents a decidedly contemporary effort to take another step in the ancient tradition that links philosophy with the discrimination of the clear and distinct from the uncertainties of opinion and meaning. By "contemporary" I mean that Badiou's philosophy of truth is anything but a simple return to Platonic or Cartesian procedures. As we shall see, Badiou presents his philosophy as conditioned in a very precise sense by the particular truths that characterize *our* time.

What, then, does Badiou mean by truth *(vérité)*? The essential thing to grasp is that, as Badiou conceives it, *a* truth is something that *takes place* (from time to time). Like Marx, Badiou knows that "the question whether human thought achieves objective truth is not a question of theory but a *practical* question," that genuine thought changes the world more than it understands it.[6] A truth is something we *make*. It is declared, composed, and upheld by the subjects it convokes and sustains. Both truth and subject are occasional, exceptional. When they emerge, they emerge together, as qualitatively distinct from the opposing categories of knowledge and the object.

This distinction pervades Badiou's entire enterprise. There is, on the one hand, an enduring realm of objectively specified knowledges, of positive identities or differences, of clearly established interests—a realm of orders and places within orders. And on the other hand, there come into existence, every now and then, without order or continuity, fully singular, strictly subjective truths (in the plural). These truths escape the specifying action of the first, objective realm, through a kind of subtraction from the particularity of the known. Badiou's philosophy of truth asserts a rigorous coherence without objectivity. In every case, he asserts, "what is true (or just—as it happens they are the same thing) cannot be referred back to any objective set, either with regard to its cause or to its destination."[7] Badiou's work, we might say, splits apart the two adjectives linked by the familiar platitude "tried and true." Every truth pushes the subject into the realm of the untried, and for that reason, "tries" (is the trial of) the subject. Or again: every subject "believes something without knowing why" (TA, 9.1.97).

Truths are materially produced in specific situations, and each begins from an event or discovery that eludes the prevailing logic that structures and governs those situations. Badiou agrees with Lacan: "All access to the real is of the order of an encounter."[8] As a rule, every "singular truth has its origin in an event. Something must happen, in order for there to be something new. Even in our personal lives, there must be an encounter, there must be something which cannot be calculated, predicted or managed, there must be a break based only on chance."[9] Such an encounter or event has no objective or verifiable content; it takes place in a situation but is not "of" that situation. A truth persists, then, solely through the militant proclamation of those people who maintain a fidelity to the uncertain event whose occurrence and consequences they affirm—those people, in other words, who become subjects in the name of that event. Although any individual can become a subject, merely individual existences are generally caught up in the preservation of some sort of objective routine. But any such routine can be broken by an encounter with something that does not fit with the prevailing regime of re-presentation—a moment of pure surprise, a crisis of some kind, to which the individual as such cannot react (something he or she cannot easily re-present). Confronted with such an event, an individual is liable to deny or suppress it: anyone can, however, make of this suspension of routine an opportunity for the invention of something new. Individuals become subjects in Badiou's sense of the word if and only if this invention, conceived as a new criterion for action, is further consistent with a properly universal principle—that is, only if it is an invention with which *everyone* can in principle identify. Only such a principle can become the truth of a new sequence.

Truth is thus a matter of *conviction* first and foremost, and every subject demonstrates "what a conviction is capable of, here, now, and forever" (SP, 31). The word truth *(vérité)*, as Badiou uses it, connotes something close to the English expressions "to be true to something" or "to be faithful to something." What Badiou calls subjectivization essentially describes the experience of identification with a *cause,* or better, the active experience of conversion or commitment to a cause—a cause with which one can identify oneself without reserve. "Either you participate, declare the founding event, and draw the consequences, or you remain outside it," he writes. "This distinction without intermediary or mediation is entirely subjective" (SP, 22). The identity of the subject rests entirely, unconditionally, on this commitment. *I am, because I am (or we are) struggling* (for a new society, a new art, a new scientific order, etc.). It is only in such rare moments of pure engagement, Badiou suggests, that we become all that we can be, that is, that we are carried beyond our normal limits, beyond the range of predictable response. Only in this unpredictable domain, this domain of pure action, is one fully a subject rather than an object. Frantz Fanon's incisive account of the irreducibly militant process of decolonization provides a good illustration of the sort of engagement Badiou has in mind: under the constraints imposed by a divisive and oppressive regime, "decolonisation transforms spectators crushed with their inessentiality into privileged actors, with the grandiose glare of history's floodlights upon them." As with every truth procedure, such "decolonisation is the veritable creation of new people."[10]

Truth, subject, and event are all aspects of a single process: a truth comes into being through the subjects who proclaim it and, in doing so, constitute themselves as subjects in their fidelity to the event. "Our path toward truth," as Žižek puts it, "coincides with the truth itself."[11] This shared fidelity is the basis for a subjective community or being-together with no other criteria of inclusion than fidelity itself. That such a truth is always singular means that nothing "communally or historically established lends its substance to its process," that no "available generality can account for it, or structure the subject who maintains it." Deprived of an established place, a truth is open and "offered to all" (SP, 15). Any singular truth, in other words, is necessarily generic or indiscernible, indifferent, the stuff of a radically egalitarian homogeneity.

Badiou's own examples include, in characteristically diverse registers, Saint Paul's militant conception of an apostolic subjectivity that exists only through proclamation of an event (the resurrection) of universal import but of no positive or established significance; the Jacobin or Bolshevik fidelity to a revolutionary event that exceeds, in its subjective power and generic scope, the particular actions that contributed to its occurrence; a pair of lovers' conception of themselves as loving subjects, grounded only in a shared fidelity to the ephemeral event of their encounter; an artistic or scientific fidelity to a creative line of inquiry opened up by a discovery or break with tradition. Further political examples might include the Palestinian Intifada and the Burmese student movement of 1988, and, more recently, Mexico's Chiapas rebellion and Brazil's Movimento dos Trabalhadores Rurais Sem Terra: each sequence has succeeded in mobilizing, in the most subjectively assertive terms, precisely those people who for decades have been the most invisible, the most unrepresentable, in their respective situations.

For reasons that will become clear, Badiou lists as the four modes of truth "revolution, passion, invention, and creation," which correspond to the four domains of truth—politics, love, science, and art (D, 97). In each of these domains the subject is the subject of a truth that is itself both singular (in its occasion and originality) and universal (in its scope). Philosophy itself produces no active truth in this proper sense. Instead, it seeks to identify and group together, when they exist, the contemporary products of these four domains, as the "truth of its time." Such truths make up what, of this time, is properly eternal.

The four modes of truth thus provide the literal "conditions" of philosophy— that from which philosophy comes to be. Philosophy is always under the condition of events of thought that are external to it. Outside these conditions, or "generic procedures," there prevails only what Badiou diagnoses as our *abjection contemporaine*: the supervision of established differences and distinctions, the dominance of inherited privileges and prejudices, the proliferation of identitarian claims coordinated solely by market mechanisms and justified only by a dose of negative "ethical" constraint formulated in the cynical terms of human rights or humanitarian obligation.[12] Such is the nature of a world confirmed, in its daily operations, as "hostile to philosophy" (DP, 8–9)—a world of specified interests, relative judgments, and measured calculations. This is why, for Badiou no less than for Pascal or Claudel, every subject and every proclamation of truth risks a break with the world as it is, an end to business as usual.

Badiou's revival of the category of the subject is to be scrupulously distinguished, therefore, from other recent returns to the subject. His subject is firmly antinormative and antimoralist. "Empty, riven, a-substantial, nonreflexive," Badiou's subject is perfectly consistent with the "death of Man" declared by Althusser and Foucault.[13] True subjectivation is indifferent to the legal or communitarian norms of social consensus, and there is no escaping the fact that every affirmation of truth "can always be perceived as being a demoralization of the subject" (TA, 6.11.96). Asocial and acultural, Badiou's subject is just as firmly antipsychological. It can never coincide with the cultivation of conscious experience, and its foundation is always, in a certain sense, unconscious or at least other than conscious. Strictly speaking, "there can be no experience of the subject."[14] The subject of truth is no more a function of (neo-Cartesian) reflexivity than it is of (neo-Hegelian) negation or totalization.[15] Above all, it is indifferent to the tangled business of self-deferral and self-distancing generally central to those post-Sartrean resurrections of a subject whose very being is mediated through the categories of difference and the Other—the notion of "oneself as another" variously explored by Merleau-Ponty, Irigaray, and Ricoeur. The truth that splits a subject in Badiou's post-Lacanian sense simultaneously subtracts this subject from all merely textual or symbolic deferral. Badiou's subjects are no less self-contained than those deconstructed by Derrida and Bhabha, say, but this is because they have escaped the logic of *différance* and withdrawn from all "secret" interiority,[16] so as to exist entirely in the present externality of their affirmation. Sustained only by the force of their own inventive conviction, Badiou's subjects are essentially without other, without vis-à-vis.

It is thanks to the widely shared commitment, however diversely expressed, to such a "subject without vis-à-vis" (MP, 74), to a singularity without specificity, that Badiou today looks forward to "a possible regrouping of Lacan, Sartre and myself, on the one hand, and on the other, of the Heideggerians and, in some ways, Deleuze and Lyotard . . . —a somewhat unexpected formal regrouping of the philosophy of these last thirty years."[17] Badiou's own philosophy of a "generic" singularity is perhaps the most rigorously argued, the most exacting, and certainly the most original contribution to this emerging configuration. It links in the strictest possible terms a philosophy of the extraordinary—of the event—with a philosophy of the unspecifiable or aspecific; it is a philosophy of the extraordinary under the Platonic sign of the Same. The connection enables Badiou to salvage reason from positivism, the subject from deconstruction, being from Heidegger, the infinite from theology, the event from Deleuze, revolution from Stalin, a critique of the state from Foucault, and, last but not least, the affirmation of love from American popular culture. He asserts a philosophy of the subject without recourse to phenomenology, a philosophy of truth without recourse to adequation, a philosophy of the event without recourse to historicism. It is a remarkable enterprise. Badiou's mature work provides the most powerful alternative yet conceived to the various postmodernisms that still dominate the humanities, without yielding an inch to the neoliberal, neo-Kantian "pre-postmodernisms" that have recently emerged in response.

The central concept of Badiou's philosophy is the concept of the generic. A generic truth proceeds in terms that remain indiscernible or unrecognizable from within the situation as it stands. Subtracted from the supervision of differences and the supervision of distinctions, the composition of a generic truth attests, very much against the contemporary grain, the "primacy of the Same over the Other, the rejection of Difference as a principle of classification (for the generic is difference reduced to almost nothing, that is, to being of the same situation or presentation). A truth is the wandering of the Same."[18]

According to Badiou, the great events of our time are precisely those instances in which thought, be it political, mathematical, scientific, or loving, has most inventively explored a fully generic conception of reality. These inventions determine the conditions of a truly contemporary philosophy:

> The generic, at the conceptual core of a Platonic gesture turned toward the multiple, is the basis for the inscription of philosophy as for the compossibility of its contemporary conditions. Of today's creative politics, when they exist, we have known at least since 1793 that they can only be egalitarian, anti-state; that they trace, through the accumulated layers of history and the opacity of the social, a human genericity and the deconstruction of strata, the ruin of differential or hierarchical representations, the assumption of a communism of singularities. Of poetry, we know that it explores an undivided language, offered to all, non-instrumental, a use of language which founds the genericity of language itself. Of mathematics, we know that it grasps the multiple stripped of all presentable distinction, the genericity of multiple-being. Of love, finally, we know that beyond the encounter, it declares itself faithful to the pure Two that it founds, and that it makes a generic truth of the difference between men and women. (MP, 91–92)

More specifically, Badiou develops the consequences of the following events: in mathematics, the formalization of set theory from Cantor to Cohen; in politics, a sequence of militant popular uprisings that began with the Cultural Revolution in China and May 68 in France; in poetry, the works of Mallarmé, Pessoa, and Celan; in love and desire, the exemplary work of Lacan.[19] Badiou's work is to be read as an effort to establish the "compossibility" of these events.

In a recent book devoted precisely to an exploration of the truths characteristic of the twentieth century, Badiou argues that what these and other equally generic declarations have in common is their "passion for the real" and their faith in the resources of pure "formalization" as the sole medium adequate to such passion. The real, as Badiou understands it, in terms adapted from Lacan, is nothing other than an active encounter with the generic as such. Grasped in the full "heat of the moment," experienced in the violent urgency of the here and now, indifferent to the promise of ideal expectations, inaccessible to any moralizing judgment, subtracted from every trace of particularity, the consequences of a passionate encounter with the real can be sustained only through the invention of formal means that leave literally nothing to negotiate or interpret. We might say that Badiou's great achievement is to have reconceptualized for our times the relation between the real (of immediate action or declaration) and the ideal (of formal consistency), where the latter is composed, over time, as the consequences of the former. Generic formalization directly presents its terms in such a way as to block their possible re-presentation: that which is accessed through pure formalization cannot be attained by any other means. The generic can be rendered only in terms that are indifferent to any "specifying" signification, which is to say indifferent to any signification *tout court*. All of the great initiatives of Europe's most violently ambitious century—the formalization of mathematical procedures from Hilbert to Bourbaki; the elaboration of a party discipline as the exclusive form of politics from Lenin through Mao; the development of a thoroughly formal or antihermeneutic analysis of sexuality from Freud through Lacan; the invention, from Mallarmé, Schoenberg, and Picasso through Beckett, Webern, and Pollock, of artistic forms detached from the limitations of content or meaning—have had as their ultimate purpose the attempt to devise transparent, self-regulating forms of thought whose only occasion, in the absence of any object that they might represent or interpret, is an encounter with the generic nudity of the real as such. Every claim to re-present "reality," by contrast, and with it every reference to semantic depth, social complexity, or material substance, amounts only to an invitation to participate in the interpretation and negotiation of meanings, opinions, and impressions. Like Althusser and Lacan before him, Badiou equates reality in this sense with ideology pure and simple. And since it is always "reality that gets in the way of the uncovering of the real" (LS, 53), the first task of any generic practice of thought is the "subtraction" of whatever passes for reality so as to clear the way for a formalization of the real.

As everyone knows, this became ever more difficult in the closing decades of the twentieth century, a time of radical reaction organized precisely around the aversion to any encounter with the real, a time notable for its willingness to accept "objective reality," to adopt the dismal imperative of laissez-faire as its universal motto. Generic thought must renew, in terms that engage effectively with this thoughtless resignation, the fundamental wager of our revolutionary century. It must affirm "the univocity of the real over the equivocity of semblance" and thereby take another step in the ancient struggle that opposes formalization to interpretation, and with it, the implacable clarity of the Idea to the vague uncertainties of appearance, the flash of the event to the inertia of tradition, the integrity of rebellion to the docility of acceptance—an "immortal intensity," in each case, against the (in)significance of survival (LS, 132).

Thus defined, the generic is synonymous with a certain kind of "purity." The generic is attained through the "purification" *(épuration)* of the specific or specifiable, the evacuation of all that makes relative or particular. The generic is pure, essentially, of relationality itself. In keeping with one of the most profound convictions of his revolutionary century, Badiou everywhere affirms "the end to relations *[liens]*, the absence to self of the unrelated" (LS, 75).

Lien is the word Badiou usually uses for relation in general: it connotes the physical restriction of a bond or link, as much as the more flexible dynamics of community and rapport. As far as Badiou is concerned, the two are symptoms of a single delusion. Whatever is true is essentially unrelated or autonomous, self-constituent and self-regulating, while "the idea of the link *[lien]*, or of relation *[rapport]*, is fallacious. A truth is unlinked *[déliée]*, and it is toward this local point where a link is undone that a truth procedure operates" (PM, 56). Truth is nothing other than the local production of a freedom from all relation, a situated production of radical autonomy or self-determination. As far as its subjects are concerned, access to truth is thus identical to the practice of freedom pure and simple. Ordinary individuals are constrained and justified by relations of hierarchy, obligation, and deference; their existence is literally bound to their social places. True subjects, by contrast, are first and foremost free of relation as such, and are justified by nothing other than the integrity of their own affirmations. Pure subjective freedom is founded quite literally on the absence of relation, which is to say that it is founded on nothing at all. Pure freedom, in short, will always risk proximity to what Hegel called "absolute freedom."[20]

This is where we might usefully make the link between perhaps the two most important concepts that Badiou adapts from his philosophical inheritance: Sartre's conception of radical subjective freedom as *being* nothing, as an objective nothingness, or *néant*—that is, a freedom that determines its existence at each moment, as an ongoing "creation ex nihilo"[21]—and Marx's conception of the proletariat as *having* nothing, "nothing to lose but their chains." From Sartre, Badiou retains the notion of a subjective freedom that effectively invents itself from the void, in the absence of any objective support or social justification. From Marx, Badiou retains the force of a subjective intervention adequate to a process—capitalism—that puts an end to all "feudal, patriarchal, and idyllic" relations, an intervention that goes on to formalize, "above and beyond the merely negative force of Capital, an order without relation, an un-related collective power." As with Marx, this power is nothing other than the revolutionary conversion of an absolute proletarian impoverishment to the restoration of equally absolute human "creativity" (LS, 75; cf. EE, 425). Simply, Badiou subtracts Sartre's freedom from its ontological justification (i.e., from its structural link to the faculty of imagination) and cuts Marx's *déliaison* away from its historical specification (i.e., from its structural link to the development of a mode of production). Badiou's freedom is neither an ontological attribute nor a historical result but something that occasionally comes to pass, from time to time. His concept of freedom is not a condition to which we are condemned but an activity we must labor to sustain. The ontological foundation of this evental alternative will turn, as we shall see, on a topological or situation-specific conception of the void, or *néant*.

Founded upon nothing other than its own axiomatic integrity, thought attains "the Pure" by purging itself of all relational confusion (C, 119). Every attempt to formalize the generic "at the level of the real *[au ras du réel]*" draws exclusively upon the consequences of its own postulations (LS, 130). By thus freeing its adherents from all inherited ties or bonds, a truth takes place as the unrelating of its initially related proponents (TA, 13.11.96). Inspired by Mallarmé, Badiou's affirmation of the pure can serve as the guiding thread for an interpretation of his work as a whole: "Purity is the composition of an Idea such that it is no longer retained by any relation *[lien]*, an idea that grasps from being its indifference to all relation, its isolated scintillation . . . , its coldness, its disjunction, its virginity. . . . That which the purity of the Notion brings forward, designates above all, is the unrelated solitude of being, the ineffective character of every law, of every pact that links and relates. Poetry [and with it the other truth procedures] states that the condition of being is to be in relation with nothing."[22] Such is our "modern ascesis: to expose thought to *déliaison* pure and simple . . . : everything diverges" (D, 123). This *déliaison* underlies both the extraordinary ambition of Badiou's philosophy, its unflinching determination, and its own peculiar difficulty—the difficulty it has in describing *any* possible relation between truth and knowledge, any dialectic linking subject and object. Rather than seek to transform relations, to convert oppressive relations into liberating relations, Badiou seeks subtraction from the relational *tout court*. So long as it works within the element of this subtraction, Badiou's philosophy forever risks its restriction to the empty realm of prescription pure and simple.

A book of this kind is doomed by definition to simplify complex phrasings, to reroute convoluted trains of thought, to suggest continuities where none exist, and generally to smooth out some of the conceptual wrinkles that are bound to appear in the fabric of so varied a philosophical project as Badiou's. Badiou is the first to warn of the danger posed by the "obscuring devotion of fanatical disciples."[23] I hope to have avoided at least some of these dangers through occasional reference to the questions implied at the end of the previous paragraph.

If the eclectic range of Badiou's work disconcerts, it should be stressed that the mixture is anything but arbitrary or haphazard. Badiou situates himself squarely in the Enlightened tradition: "Always, in order to crush the infamy of superstition *[pour écraser l'infâme de la superstition]*, we have had to call upon the solid, lay eternity of the sciences" (C, 164). Badiou has always maintained that the "systematic vocation of philosophy is inevitable and part of its very essence."[24] "Philosophy is always systematic"[25] because, as we shall see, its foundations are ultimately grounded on a strictly axiomatic or unconditional point. The most obvious immediate consequence is the special privilege accorded to that most axiomatic discipline: mathematics. Badiou maintains, as did, in different ways, Plato, Descartes, Leibniz, and Kant, that mathematics is an essential condition of philosophy—which is not to say that Badiou, any more than Plato, writes a philosophy *of* mathematics. The mathematically illiterate should not be put off; Badiou's demonstrations assume no prior knowledge, and my own explanations take up only the most elementary and most consequential points. (Nevertheless, readers with no background in the principles of modern mathematical logic might find it useful to read the appendix to this volume before starting the main body of the text.)

Precisely because of its highly systematic rigor, however, Badiou's work is not easy to summarize quickly. Each component makes sense only according to its place in the system as a whole—and even Deleuze and Guattari, no strangers to complication, testify to the "extreme complexity" of Badiou's system.[26] Philosophy demands "patience," its "concepts must be grasped slowly," and it is fitting, says Badiou, that overhasty readers be discouraged by a "rocky" textual terrain and a slightly "foreign vocabulary that must be learned as [they] go along. . . . The time of philosophy, protected by its writing, excludes all haste." At the same time, however, Badiou insists on the univocal rigor of philosophical presentation, which must "struggle against equivocation, must adjust the pattern until its core, its essence, has been purified of every circumstantial variation, of every contamination by the haphazard choices of its exposition."[27] And this exposition itself, of course, has much evolved and continues to evolve. Badiou's philosophy has been and will remain for some time very much a work in progress. A full presentation of Badiou's mature work, as proposed in *L'Etre et l'événement* and as developed in a variety of fields in his more recent books, must begin with an assessment of the (partial) transformation of his work, from its early emphasis on the historical and the partisan to the later emphasis on the ontological and the true. It should also include an awareness of what remains to be done, of where things may lead. Only then will we be in a position to consider how Badiou's system works, to what ends and at what cost.

What follows aims to provide a relatively thorough introduction to all of the major components of Badiou's philosophy. The first chapter situates Badiou's project in terms of its principal "friends and foes": it presents what is at stake in his critique of sophistry and "antiphilosophy," and describes how he positions his contribution to the ongoing project of a "laicization of the infinite." This project is first and foremost a political one. So chapter 2 traces the political motivation of Badiou's philosophy, as it has evolved from his initial Maoist commitment to the recent elaboration, via L'Organisation Politique, of a "politics without party." Chapters 3 and 4 tackle Badiou's mathematical conception of ontology and his axiomatic conception of the infinite as the sole dimension of human experience. Chapter 5 is the central chapter of the book: it proceeds systematically through the components of Badiou's theory of the subject. Chapter 6 considers the conception of truth that corresponds to this theory, and distinguishes it briefly from its major philosophical competition (intuitionist, Kantian, Spinozist, Hegelian, and Deleuzian). Chapters 7 through 10 explore the concrete operations of truth in each of the four dimensions Badiou identifies as the "generic procedures" or "conditions" of philosophy (love, art, science, and politics), while chapter 11 moves on to summarize what can be said of philosophy per se. The next chapter considers how Badiou tackles the ethical problems associated with the "evil" corruption of truth. My penultimate chapter then does what, I think, any study of a living philosopher should do: it points to several problems with the existing configuration of things, and frames a couple of the issues likely to be raised in Badiou's subsequent writing. Might it be possible, in partial competition with Badiou's conception of the generic, to develop a notion of the *specific* as an emphatically subjective orientation—but one that is, precisely, specific to (rather than specified by) those objectifying conditions that enable it to exist? The last chapter jumps ahead to look at Badiou's current work in progress, and ponders his response to a question that will come up, in one form or another, throughout my own exposition of his thought—the question of relation in the broadest sense. An appendix, finally, provides easily digestible background information about the mathematical theory of sets that plays such a crucially important role in all aspects of Badiou's philosophy.

Along the way we will touch on materials ranging from Badiou's earliest articles to still unpublished drafts. In addition to the major tome that is his *L'Etre et l'événement* (1988), his oeuvre includes three or four works that we might qualify as "early," that is, as prior to the systematic connection of subject and event (*Le Concept de modèle: Introduction à une épistémologie matérialiste des mathématiques* [1972], *Théorie de la contradiction* [1975], *De l'idéologie* [1978], and *Théorie du sujet* [1982]); two political tracts (*Peut-on penser la politique?* [1985] and *D'un désastre obscur (Droit, Etat, Politique)* [1991]); a short book entitled *L'Ethique: Essai sur la conscience du mal* (1993); monographs on theater, Beckett, Deleuze, and Saint Paul; four volumes of essays (*Conditions* [1992], *Court traité d'ontologie transitoire* [1998], *Abrégé de métapolitique* [1998], and *Petit manuel d'inésthétique* [1998]); a series of meditations on the philosophically distinctive attributes of the twentieth century (to be partially published in the forthcoming bilingual volume, *Le Siècle* [2003]); a couple of recent unpublished bundles of lecture notes ("Théorie axiomatique du sujet: Notes du cours 1996–1998" and "L'Etre-là: Mathématique du transcendental" [2000]) containing, in still tentative form, material to be reworked in the forthcoming second volume of *L'Etre et l'événement: Logiques du monde*. This already substantial bibliography regrettably excludes, for lack of space, Badiou's several novels and plays. By way of compensation I have frequently drawn on our correspondence and conversations to elucidate issues that his published work has yet fully to address. At the risk of repeating certain essential points, I have tried to explain things as clearly and as thoroughly as space permits, assuming no prior familiarity of his work. Badiou's writing is often abstract and demanding, but it is rarely abstruse. Its *systematic* coherence demands patience more than specialist expertise.

The book's prevailing tone, I hope, is one of a sometimes skeptical respect. As will become clear, my skepticism concerns Badiou's partial equation of the singular and the specific—his fundamental distrust of relationality—and its various consequences. But it should already be obvious that I believe Badiou's work to be among the most significant of his generation, and that its significance has grown more rather than less compelling with time. No philosopher is more urgently needed, in this particular moment, than Badiou. We live in supremely reactionary times. Ours is a moment in which inventive politics has been replaced with economic management, in which the global market has emerged as the exclusive mechanism of social coordination. Ours is a moment in which effective alternatives to this mechanism find expression almost exclusively in the bigotries of culturally specified groups or identities, from ultranationalism in Germany and France to competing fundamentalisms in Israel and Algeria. Among contemporary thinkers, Badiou stands alone in the uncompromising rigor of his confrontation with these twin phenomena, the most characteristic of our age.

part I

Matters of Principle

Chapters 1 through 3 provide essential background materials. The first chapter surveys various direct influences on Badiou's thought, and introduces the polemical aspect of his work, his campaigns against constructivism, sophistry, and hermeneutics. This allows for a preliminary presentation of Badiou's thought in terms of more familiar figures (aligned with Plato, Descartes, and Lacan; against Wittgenstein, Heidegger, and Lyotard). The second chapter isolates the main features of Badiou's early, primarily political, work (from the late 1960s to the early 1980s). The third prepares the ground for his later equation of ontology and mathematics, and explores the implications of the move that will inspire all of Badiou's mature thought—what he calls the "laicization of the infinite."

chapter 1

Taking Sides

Badiou presents his enterprise as another step taken in the ancient struggle of philosophy against dogmatic prejudice or *doxa*. Badiou's philosophy is militant in its very essence. At its core, his philosophy involves taking a principled stand, distinguishing between claims for and against. He likes to quote Mao's dictum "If you have an idea, one will have to divide into two" (E, 31; cf. TS, 131). He has no interest in a merely deliberative resolution of differences or a merely procedural concept of justice. This is not to say that he advocates a kind of generalized agonism based on the dubious incommensurability of language games or cultural orientations. Indeed, his position has nothing to do with perspective as such. But like any position worth the name, it does separate its rivals into groups according to what they contribute or threaten, inspire or discourage.

Badiou is fond of distinguishing dominant philosophical trends according to a number of different criteria, as so many sets of rival claims made with respect to ontological multiplicity, the relation of truth and meaning, the status accorded to the event, to the undecidable, or to the inaccessible. All of these schemas of distinction provide variants on what is a generally consistent division of the partisans of affirmative truth from their rivals, namely the partisans of structure, continuity, meaning, language, or knowledge.

First and foremost, what Badiou calls the "great philosophical war" is the argument that separates those who, like Spinoza and Leibniz, identify eternity and necessity (and thereby promote effectively subjectless philosophies) from those who, like Plato and Descartes, link "eternity and contingency." The latter grant eternity itself the evental status fundamental to Badiou's conception of truth. (Descartes's God is contingent, since "he *creates* eternal truths," whereas Nietzsche's eternal return and Deleuze's fold, by contrast, because ultimately caught up in notions of repetition and continuity, locate them in the first camp.)[1] As regards the relation of meaning and truth, there are three logical possibilities: the assertion of a "rigorous continuity between truth and meaning," which Badiou identifies with religion; the assertion of the "unilateral supremacy of meaning" over truth, or sophistry; and the assertion of a "meaningless *[insensé]* primacy of truth as the annulment of meaning" (CD, 23–24), which is the basis of Badiou's own position. As regards, finally, "the essential identity of thinking and being" (D, 117), Badiou again divides the field into three broad camps. There are those who seek to sustain this identity with reference to what happens, with reference to events and the decisions they give rise to; there are those who seek to elucidate a structural articulation of being and thought via the mediation of language and linguistic criteria of coherence and construction; and there are those who insist that this identity can be grounded only in an ultimately inarticulable, ultimately mysterious, first principle—this is typical of the orientation that Badiou calls "antiphilosophy." Badiou himself always defends the first option, against every variant of the linguistic turn and every invocation of transcendence.

Taking Another Step

Badiou follows in the tracks of many, above all in those of the most influential of philosophers and those of that most influential of antiphilosophers: Plato and Lacan, respectively. Between them lies what Badiou understands to be the major intellectual effort of modernity itself: the attempt, guided by science and mathematics, to arrive at a full "laicization of the infinite." The preliminary steps taken by Galileo and Descartes came to fruition, as far as Badiou is concerned, with Georg Cantor (1845–1918) and the elaboration of contemporary set theory. Other, quite different, steps in roughly parallel directions—in each case toward the radical distinction of subject from object and truth from knowledge—have been taken with the assistance of Pascal, Rousseau, Mallarmé, Sartre, and Althusser.

Each of these steps has presumed perhaps the most far-reaching insight of broadly post-Romantic thought: the understanding that our conventional notion of the subject—the subject conceived as the subject of consciousness, or experience—is fundamentally an illusion born of habit, ideology, neurosis, or *ressentiment*. At every stage of his work, Badiou has confirmed the dissociation performed by Marx, Freud, and Nietzsche, and radicalized by their most inventive descendants (Althusser, Lacan, Foucault, and Deleuze), of genuine, active subjectivity from normal conscious experience. The merely apparent subject of such experience is in each case a product rather than a producer, the product of an ideology designed precisely to normalize relations of class struggle, or of a neurosis designed to normalize relations of unconscious struggle, or of reactive forces designed to disavow struggle between active forces. And a genuine subject can arise, through the intervention of a new form of critical or analytical practice, only to the degree that political actors become aware of their historical agency (after Marx), or that desiring actors become able to sustain their unconscious drive (after Freud), or that thinking actors are able to plug into assemblages of active forces and creative expression (after Nietzsche). Or, as Badiou will say, to the degree that decisive actors affirm a truth.

Plato

First and foremost, Badiou's mature work takes up "the banner of Plato."[2] To this day, Badiou remains firmly "convinced that the questions around which Plato structures what would become known as philosophy are the right ones, and that the world of truths has, all things considered, changed only a little since this invention."[3] As far as philosophical genealogy is concerned, Badiou writes, "there is no doubting the validity of the proverb: 'tell me what you think of Plato, and I will tell you who you are'" (D, 148). Badiou's allegiance to this unlikely forbear is a defiantly anticontemporary gesture, and its polemic dimension should not be forgotten. All of the major trends in recent Western philosophy have been hostile to Plato: Nietzsche and Heidegger most obviously, but equally Wittgenstein and Popper, the analytic and the pragmatist traditions, the poststructuralisms associated with Derrida and Deleuze, the neo-Kantian moralism of the "nouveaux philosophes"—even Soviet historical materialism.[4] Badiou's own loyalty is partial, and partly strategic or provocative. But the influence is nonetheless profound and revealing.

From Plato Badiou has taken three things in particular. First, the belief that philosophy proceeds only when provoked by things or events beyond its immediate purview, outside the conceptual homogeneity of its own domain—an encounter with a friend or lover, an argument, a political debate or controversy, the demonstrations of mathematics or science, the illusions of poetry and art. These "conditions of philosophy" are what push the philosopher to reflection. Philosophy, in other words, lacks the pure independence of a system of "total knowledge . . . ; for Plato, philosophy doesn't begin thinking in relation to itself, but in relation to something else."[5]

Second, Badiou upholds the essential Platonic commitment to the true or Ideal, as distinct from the merely apparent or prevalent. For both Badiou and Plato, to think means to "break with sensible immediacy." Thought does not begin with representation or description but with a "break (with opinion, with experience), and thus a decision."[6] (And since mathematics is the most perfect example of a science purged of opinion and experience, a virtually infallible sign of a Platonic orientation is *some* kind of privilege accorded to mathematical thought as exemplary of truth.)[7] Commitment to the necessarily "eternal" nature of truths, however, need not compel their characterization as transcendent or aloof. Badiou never flirts with the kind of transcendence associated with those Forms famously expounded in the *Phaedo* and the *Republic*. As Badiou reads him, "Plato's fundamental concern is to declare the immanent identity, the co-belonging, of the known and the knowing mind, their essential ontological commensurability,"[8] more than it is to preserve the transcendence of the former over the latter. What is true as opposed to false, what is real as opposed to unreal, is always clear and distinct, always ideal in the sense that any thinking subject can participate in the discovery of its consequences, as its co-inventor or "co-worker."[9]

With Plato, finally, Badiou asserts the emphatically universal dimension of philosophy as the only dimension consistent with truth. Whenever "we abandon the universal we have universal horror" (TS, 197). The operation of truth will be subjective and immanent rather than transcendent, but truth it will be, every bit as universal and eternal as it is in Plato. It follows that both philosophers have seen the major external challenge to their discipline as posed by sophistry in all its forms. Philosophy's main critical task, likewise, concerns the distinction it must establish between its own truthful legitimacy and the false, disastrous manipulations of its simulacra—a problem Badiou analyzes in due course as the very essence of evil.

The Real Death of God

Pursuing the logic developed to opposite ends by Pascal, Badiou maintains that "the category 'God' has subjective power only insofar as we start out from the misery of man," that is, from man's mortality or finitude (and it is a short step from here to Badiou's conclusion that any development of "existentialist" reflections on finitude and being-for-death is a "disguised form of the preservation of God, whatever name we use for him"[10]). A genuinely atheist philosophy, then, must begin with a denial of human finitude, or, more positively, with an affirmation of infinity as the ordinary and thoroughly secular dimension of existence. Badiou identifies such an affirmation with the thrust of distinctly "modern" thought. Modern thought dislocates the attribute of infinity from its traditionally divine location, from its as-sociation with an immeasurable, inconceivable Wholeness or Unity. Badiou assumes that this dislocation is now fully complete, and that this justifies the bald assertion that "our time is without any doubt that of the disappearance without return of [all] gods."[11]

No one, perhaps, has taken the death of God as seriously as Badiou. He aims to take Nietzsche's familiar idea to its absolute conclusion, to eliminate any notion of an originally divine or creative presence (however "inacces-sible" this presence might remain to the creatures it creates), and with it, to abolish any original intuition of Life or Power. In the absence of God, what there *is* is indeed, as we shall see, purely and simply the void.[12] Since there is no God, if the conventionally divine attribute of an "actual infinity" applies to anything at all, it must apply, very simply, to *all* that is. The death of God implies not a disillusioned or postenchantment acceptance of the human condition but rather the rigorous affirmation of our *own* infinity. No longer are we to consider ourselves finite creatures whose particularity emerges in the pathos of our relation to a transcendent infinity. Instead, we already exist in an "absolutely flat" infinity. The infinite is here and now, and "here" is the only place we will ever be (CT, 23).

For the premoderns, of course—the Greeks as much as the medieval philosophers—the infinite was an attribute of the divine alone, of the wholly Other, and they believed that all that exists in the worldly sense, all that *is,* is finitely (including even God, in his *being*). Modern thought as Badiou conceives it thus begins with the laicization of the infinite, the assertion of an endless multiplicity of infinities, demonstrated in the absence of any *One* Infinite (or, as a mathematician might say, any one "set of all sets"[13]). "Modernity defines itself through the fact that the One is not."[14] For the moderns it is ordinary being itself, cut off from its ancient mythical associa-tions with substantial plenitude and transcendent mystery, that is infinite. In short, "the only really contemporary requirement for philosophy since Nietzsche is the secularisation of infinity."[15] The essential thing to under-stand is that this secularization can be achieved in only one way: by (axiom-atic) prescription. Granted the incoherence of a "great whole" (demonstrat-ed by Kant), of one all-inclusive "self-belonging" (demonstrated by Cantor), "the thesis of the infinity of being is necessarily an ontological decision, that is to say, an axiom. Without this decision, it will always remain possible that being is essentially finite" (EE, 167).

Galileo, Descartes, and Cantor mark the decisive steps in this cumulative effort. Galileo in particular, and the scientific revolution in general, stand at the doorway to Badiou's atheist modernity. The medieval universe had been centered on the intermediary position of Man in the closed hierarchy of a great chain of being: Galileo and his collaborators then revived the Platonist conception of an open, endless universe ruled by the indifferent universality of mathematical principles, a book of nature "written in the language of mathematics, ... without which one wanders in vain through a dark labyrinth."[16] The mathematization of science eliminates at a stroke the tangled neo-Aristotelian interpretation of qualitative essences (hardness, lightness, smoothness, and so on) in favor of the anonymous, asignificant variables of quantity and motion. For the next two centuries, mathematics and physics were to belong to essentially one and the same logic of explanation, a formal order of deductive thought directly articulated with the rational order of materiality itself.[17] At the same time, the subjects of this new science were to find themselves isolated and bereft of a clearly ordained place at the center of creation.[18] What Badiou has retained from the great movement of the scientific revolution and the subsequent Enlightenment campaign against parochial superstition is this conjunction of an isolated, self-grounding subjectivity and an indifferent mathematized rationality as the only fully adequate vehicle of truth.

This conjunction is especially significant, of course, in Descartes's philosophy. For Descartes as much as for Badiou, mathematics provided the one truly reliable guidance to philosophical speculation. Badiou applauds Descartes's conception of philosophy as the introduction of order and clarity into the realm of tacit assumption or outright confusion, and endorses (after laicizing) Descartes's unambiguous assertion of the priority of the actually over the merely potentially infinite.[19] More precisely, anticipating Lacan and Sartre, Descartes connected being and truth through the axiomatic assertion of an impersonal subjectivity. The Cartesian subject provides for its own ontological foundation, after the subtraction of all (doubtful) knowledge, in the self-grounding *activity* of thought.[20] And what enabled Descartes's "mathematization of extension," his affirmation of a "power of literalization" as the very medium of science, was their foundation on "the empty point of the Subject as sole 'delivery' of being *[unique "envoi" de l'Etre]*."[21] As Heidegger understood full well, the *essentially* mathematical orientation of modern thought is bound up with such a foundational subjectivity: the first or "unconditional" principle of the axiom is indeed "*I* think."[22] So Badiou is happy to confess, "Deep down, I am Cartesian: the idea of founding anything at all in a passive immediacy (such a German idea ...) is foreign to me."[23] Badiou's concept of the subject "is obviously rooted in Descartes's transparency and *centration*,"[24] just as his notion of purity is grounded in the Cartesian clear and distinct.[25]

Badiou's own, more precise concept of ontological truth develops the relatively recent mathematical assertion of an actual or "completed" infinity (as opposed to a merely potential infinity of succession)—the assertion associated with Georg Cantor's pathbreaking work in transfinite set theory. Set theory conceives a multiplicity "made" of nothing but multiples of multiples, in such a way that the traditional or premodern distinction of finite and infinite dissolves in a single homogeneous dissemination, in excess of any closure and in violation of any definitive order. I consider aspects of this theory in some detail in chapters 3 and 4. For now it is enough to know that Cantor's work stands for Badiou as *the* philosophical event of our time: our "century is secretly governed by the radical invention which is attached to the name of Cantor. He laicized infinity by a literalization of unprecedented daring," a literalization that breaks through "the religious veil of meaning" and orients us toward a "thought still to come, a thought summarised by a single phrase: every situation, insofar as a number is its real *[pour autant qu'un nombre est son réel]*, is essentially infinite."[26] Because these infinities cannot coherently be collected together in a single Unity, the consequences of Cantor's theory confirm the essential point, that "God is really dead" (MP, 85).

In this respect, a contemporary philosophy still has some way to go before it will catch up with the material movement of history itself, which in the form of unmitigated capitalism has long since declared the immediate theoretical consequences of the divine death. As Marx was the first to understand, whether we like it or not, capital has already forced the "general desacralization" of our experience, and "it is within this very element of desacralization," Badiou accepts, that we have to rejoin the true "vocation of thought"[27]:

> It is indisputable that our time is based on a kind of generalized *atomistique*, since no symbolically sanctioned relation *[lien]* is capable of resisting the abstract power of capital. That everything which is connected indicates that it is disconnected in its being, that the reign of the multiple is the groundless ground of all that is presented, that the One is only the result of transitory operations—such are the unavoidable effects of the fact that all of the terms in our situation are to be located in the circulating movement of a generalized monetary equivalence. [... This] is obviously the only thing we can and should applaud in capital: it reveals the purely multiple as the ground of presentation, it denounces every effect of the One as a merely precarious configuration. (MP, 35, 37)

Such is the nature of our situation, and rather than turn back or away, any truly emancipatory politics must confront its challenge directly. On this point, Badiou's Marxism is perfectly orthodox: "Marx accepted that there were formal similarities between the ambitions of emancipatory politics and the workings of capital. Because we can never go back on universalism. There is no earlier territoriality calling for protection or recovery. . . . We are rivals to capital, rather than merely reacting against it. It is a struggle of universalism against universalism, and not of particularism against universalism."[28]

French Connections

Among the many heroes of modern thought, Badiou regularly turns to the inspiration offered by a select group of his fellow countrymen: Pascal, Rousseau, Mallarmé, and, up to a point, Sartre and Althusser. Like Plato and Descartes, all work to eliminate the sphere of re-presentation as such, all strive to move beyond that which mediates (obscurely) between subject and idea and thereby confirm the sufficient purity of the idea—respectively, faith, the general will, the poem, science, or class struggle. In each case, what conditions the subject is the radical, active elimination of a relation to an object of any kind.

Rousseau forbids political re-presentation: his social contract establishes itself by itself, without reference to its constituent "elements" (PP, 86; EE, 384–85). Likewise, "for Pascal, God is not representable in philosophy. Nothing in the world leads to God." On the contrary, "the subjective relation to God lies in the aleatory movement of a wager," and nowhere else.[29] There can be no adequate proofs of a God whose existence is affirmed only as immanent to that act of faith by which this existence is declared. The chooser is a function of the choice. With Mallarmé, finally, the poem has no mimetic, semantic, or figural relation either to an object or an author, but composes, in the void of such relations, its own ideal integrity. His poetry demonstrates that "what is at stake in a modern poem is the pattern [motif] of an idea," a pattern subtracted from the mediation of interpretation as such. In his *Coup de dés* in particular, Mallarmé composed a poem patterned on the very idea of an event as such (EE, 443; PP, 86).

Drawing on more contemporary sources, Badiou's Marxism can perhaps be most economically described as a partial combination of the apparently incompatible doctrines of Althusser and the later Sartre, the last great revolutionary voices in recent French philosophy. Badiou shares Sartre's firmly subject-centered approach, but Badiou's subject is endowed with precisely that self-regulating autonomy Althusser attributes to science. On the one hand, against Althusser's understanding of history as a "process without a subject" and of science as a "discourse without a subject," Badiou celebrates Sartre's active "exactitude in revolt."[30] Like Sartre, Badiou defends an idea of the subject as fundamentally isolated, as *délié*—a subject that becomes "authentically" subject to the degree that it shakes off the forces that objectify and compromise. Like Sartre's subjects, each of Badiou's must begin its subjective life with a solitary decision, made in the absence of clearly established criteria. Every true subjectivation, every genuine freedom from objective determination or re-presentation, must proceed very literally "ex nihilo." On the other hand, Badiou agrees with Althusser that "philosophy has no object" and consequently "no history." He accepts that "Althusser indicated just about everything we need to emancipate philosophy," to establish it, that is, as an "activity of thought *sui generis* that finds itself under condition of the events of real politics."[31] What Badiou manages to privilege in both thinkers is a refusal of the merely objective in favor of an essentially principled, essentially militant intervention.

Badiou situates his own writing, moreover, within the long tradition of French philosophical populism whose roots can be traced from Descartes through Voltaire, Rousseau, and Comte to Bergson and Sartre, if not Foucault and Deleuze. Each of these philosophers has sought to be both fully contemporary (and thus close to the literary language of their time) and fully democratic (and thus anti-Academy, anti-Sorbonne). Each has drawn upon a language as incisive and prescriptive as it is seductive and persuasive—a form of language addressed, so to speak, to "women and the proletariat," to an audience on the fringes of the establishment. In line with a self-description long affirmed by French grammarians, Badiou defends the philosophical use of French in terms that privilege syntactic clarity over semantic profundity, logical order over sensual suggestion, affirmation over interrogation, conviction over reverie, abstraction over complication, and univocity over polyvocity. Eschewing German depth and resonance along with English subtlety and nuance, his writing is designed to *cut*.[32] It is sharp, compressed, decisive, consequential. He writes in order to compel assent.

Lacan

Badiou has had no particular experience of psychoanalysis as such. He never attended Lacan's famous seminars, and with the partial exception of *Théorie du sujet*, the form of his work bears little resemblance to Lacan's. The psychoanalyst's approach is even an especially important example of what Badiou criticizes as "antiphilosophy" (more on this below). Nevertheless, of all contemporary thinkers it is Lacan who left the deepest mark on Badiou, and his name, along with Žižek's, will recur frequently throughout this study. Lacan—"my master Jacques Lacan," as Badiou calls him (C, 85), "the greatest of our dead" (MP, 7)—figures here as "the educator of every philosophy to come." Badiou proclaims: "I call contemporary philosopher him or her who has the courage to cross through, without faltering, the antiphilosophy of Lacan."[33]

The main things Badiou has picked up from his own crossing through Lacan include the latter's campaign against an Imaginary identification with the status quo, his evacuation of the subject of desire, his eventual articulation of subject and truth, his recognition of the formal integrity of mathematical transmission, and his conception of the real as the "impossible" of a situation. (Badiou also builds directly on Lacan's notions of sexuality and ethics, matters discussed in chapters 7 and 11, respectively.) It may be worth going over these points very quickly, one at a time.

Badiou adopts much of the spirit behind Lacan's major critical offensive, his crusade against the illusions of Imaginary fixation, against the temptations of a passive conformity to what goes literally without saying. No more than Lacanian analysis, philosophy as Badiou understands it never serves to reinforce the individual ego or to adapt individuals to the needs and nature of society. Like Lacan, Badiou presumes a strict distinction between the genuine subject and the mere individual or ego, "seat of illusions" and "imaginary object."[34] The goal of analysis is not so much therapy or cure as the articulation of truth, that is, the disruptive truth of one's unique desire.

By "subject" Lacan means the subject of the unconscious—the subject split by its incorporation into the symbolic order and sustained as a gap in the discourse of that collective Other whose desires structure this unconscious.[35] Badiou's subject, by contrast, is in a certain sense consciousness in its purest forms: decision, action, and fidelity. Nevertheless, several characteristic traits of Badiou's subject can be more or less directly attributed to Lacan. For starters, the subject is clearly not an object: "What do we call a subject? Quite precisely, what in the development of objectivation, is outside of the object."[36] There is no more powerful imperative in Lacan's writing than the command "Do not objectify the subject." Analysis is founded on a respect for the subject qua subject, in his or her unique singularity. At the same time, Lacan's theory "reinforces to an incredible degree the denudation of the subject" (S11, 160/142), and Badiou's philosophy of truth persists in the certainty that "the subject has no substance, no 'nature,'" that "there exists no norm upon which we might found the idea of a 'human subject'" (E, 8). Badiou accepts that "the being of the subject *is* the coupling of the void and the *objet a*,"[37] that is, the coupling of a gap in the established symbolic order (the state of the situation) and an always already missing object of desire or inspiration (an event).

More important, Lacan's subject, however split, however divided from an absolute self-knowledge, retains an irreducible relation to truth. Lacan's subject is closely related to the subject of science, the subject who, closing the avenues of intuition and imagination, resolutely accepts the austerity of reason as the exclusive avenue of insight.[38] Like Badiou after him, Lacan defended a notion of truth that remains firmly distinct from knowledge or "exactitude" (S3, 175–76/155), as forever singular or unique to each subject (S7, 32–33/24), and as always underway, as something built up over the course of an analysis (*Ecrits*, 144). The goal of analysis is "the advent of a true speech and the realization by the subject of his history"[39]; in this fidelity over time, as process or project, Lacan's subject "announces himself—he will have been—only in the future perfect."[40] Badiou has adopted an almost identical formula.

A more peculiar Lacanian contribution is the principle of the matheme. Badiou quotes Lacan with approval: "Mathematical formalization is our goal, our ideal. . . . Only mathematization attains a real [*atteint à un réel*]."[41] The matheme is the symbolic made pure, purged of image and intuition.[42] Only in mathematics can science realize its goal of an "integral transmission" of knowledge (S20, 100). Lacan's enduring conviction that "the question of the real is commensurable with the question of language" led Lacan, as Badiou observes, to identify "mathematization as the key to any thinkable relation to the real. He never changed his mind on this point." With far more systematic rigor than his mentor, Badiou has argued in his turn that "the grasp of thought upon the real can be established only by the regulated power of the letter," a regulation that only mathematics can perfect.[43]

It is this notion of the real, finally, that has most influenced Badiou—in particular, Lacan's later conceptions of the real as the result of "an essential *encounter*" (S11, 64/53), as what *"ex-sists"* (as essentially *apart*) rather than exists (as recognizable).[44] What Badiou finds most important in Lacan's teaching is "the distinction he makes between the real and reality, which is not the same as the classical metaphysical distinction between appearance and reality, or between phenomenon and noumenon. And in particular, this conception of the real as being, in a situation, in any given symbolic field, the point of impasse, or the point of impossibility, which precisely allows us to think the situation as a whole, according to its real."[45] Lacan's own most emphatic example is the famous impossibility of a sexual relationship: it is this impossibility, this absence of rapport, that structures the *situation* of the sexes, that is, their division into the purely symbolic positions of man and woman.[46]

The real is never real in itself. An element is always real *for* a situation; it is that which the situation's normal supervision of possibilities is precisely designed to obscure or foreclose. Purely for the sake of analysis, it may be helpful to think of the real as having two dimensions, static and dynamic. On the one hand, the real does not itself structure the situation: void for the situation, it is that around which the situation structures itself. To anticipate terminology explained in chapter 4, the real is that "foundational" or "singular" element, an element that is present but unrepresentable, around which a situation is organized. It is an element whose own elements cannot be distinguished as such, cannot be known, from within that situation. Rejected from any stable assignation of place, the real thereby calls into question the prevailing regime of place and placement as a whole (SP, 60). The proletariat, for instance, is that unrepresented element upon which the capitalist situation is built, just as the *sans-papiers* (undocumented immigrants) occupy the absent center of current debates on the nature of France as a political community.

On the other hand, the real is the element of action undertaken at precisely this unknowable point, action that converts the impossible into the possible. Action pursued at the "level of the real" is action in its most inventive and most dangerous sense, a kind of rigorous improvisation pursued in the suspension of every moral norm and every academic certainty. Only such action can access the real in its structural sense. This is why my heuristic distinction of "dimensions" is misleading, and can be sustained only in the comfortable abstraction of analysis. The "stasis" of the real—the real as that which always remains in its place—can be encountered, very precisely, *only* by moving it. Participation in a truth procedure is nothing other than a fundamental shift in the regime of possibility that structures a situation, and it is only from within this participation, from within the militant declaring of a truth, that the real of a situation can be situated at all: "The real declares itself more than it makes itself known" (CT, 39). What Badiou calls a "passion for the real"—the driving force, as he sees it, for the revolutionary projects of the twentieth century—is a passion for "what can be *done,* here and now," in the material urgency of the present (LS, 48). Every encounter with the real "is always a tearing away from reflection, a plunging into the immediate, into the instant" (LS, 136 n. 14). In keeping with his activist conception of the real, what Badiou calls "emancipatory politics always consists in making seem possible precisely that which, from within the situation, is declared to be impossible"[47]—the empowerment of the proletariat, the legalization of immigrants, and so on.

The essential thing to understand is that this making possible is always an exceptional process. This is what distinguishes Badiou's subjective or activist conception of the real from Lacan's ultimately more structural or passive conception.[48] As Bruno Bosteels points out with particular force, it is only the subject who, by affirming the apparently impossible consequences of an event that the situation cannot recognize, can truly act on the level of the real.[49] Such is Badiou's most basic article of faith: truly autonomous subjective action, if founded only on an event, can indeed touch its own real—which is to say, can achieve the impossible.

More precisely, both what Badiou calls an event and its situational "site" are real in some of the Lacanian senses, the first as traumatic encounter,[50] the second as structural remainder or mirage. What he conceives as truth, however, transcends Lacan's antiphilosophical typology altogether: "The truth is not itself the real; it is the process whereby the regime of the real is modified. It is an active transformation of the real, a moving of the real" (TA, 14.1.98), that is, the rigorous and internally consistent transformation of the rules that govern what seems logical or possible in the situation. Just as Badiou's notion of the subject does not comply with Lacan's structural emphasis on language and the signifier, so too does his notion of the real refuse its early Lacanian associations with horror, brute materiality, mystery, and fixity. All the same, like his contemporaries Žižek, Milner, Lardreau, and Jambet, Badiou can fairly claim to have arrived at a reconstruction of philosophy—that is, a reasoned articulation of subject, truth, and real—that passes through rather than around the challenges posed by Lacan's ambivalent engagement with the Cartesian tradition.

On the Offensive

Contemporary "philosophy is ill, this is not in doubt" (DP, 26), and much of Badiou's work is devoted to protecting it from further corruption and disease. He opposes all forms of pseudophilosophical speculation that delegate its autonomy to a relation with another dimension, be it historical, transcendent, linguistic, poetic, communal, or cultural. This effort takes place with comparable urgency on four overlapping fronts: against sophism, against the hermeneutic interpretation of Presence, against antiphilosophy, and against worldliness in the most general sense. Badiou's use of these terms is idiosyncratic, and can be all the more confusing in that certain figures double on occasion as both sophist and antiphilosopher (Nietzsche, Wittgenstein) or as both sophistic and religious-hermeneutic (Heidegger). The campaign against antiphilosophy, moreover, provides Badiou with some of his closest allies, including Saint Paul, Pascal, and Lacan. But it is clear that all four of the influences against which he battles are, in the end, variants of a single error: an attachment to the *mediate* as such, a commitment to the realm of language and *meaning* in either the semantic / historical or the religious / ineffable sense (for Badiou the difference is slight).

As Badiou presents them, the major currents of contemporary philosophy (logical-analytic, hermeneutic, and postmodern) all share, beyond a negative resistance to Plato and a suspicion of the metaphysics of truth generally, a positive commitment to *language* as the vehicle of "a plurality of meaning."[51] All are more or less descriptive of and complicit with our fragmented world of meanings and communications (DP, 22). Badiou's resistance to these currents turns precisely on the question of whether there may "exist a regime of the thinkable that is inaccessible to this total jurisdiction of language."[52]

Against Sophism

Sophistry privileges rhetoric over proof, the seductive manipulation of appearance over the rigorous demonstration of a reality, and the local contingency of rules over the deduction of universal principle (CD, 18–19). By Badiou's criteria, most of what passes for "contemporary 'philosophy'" is only a generalized sophistry ... : language games, deconstruction, weak thought *[pensée faible]*, radical heterogeneity, differend and differences, the collapse of Reason, the promotion of the fragment": all this is typical of a sophistic line of thought (C, 76). Sophism sets in once philosophy is reduced to the level of mere discourse or conversation, that is, when it is cut off from the active prescription of its conditions and so considered "as detached from its act." As soon as it is reduced to propositions or a discursive regime, philosophy is sophistic. For the "essence of philosophy lies in the *act* of grasping truths, and not in the rhetorical montage of its linguistic operation."[53]

In Badiou's various polemics, three modern sophists stand out: Nietzsche, Wittgenstein, and Lyotard. Nietzsche figures as "supreme sophist," the "prince of modern sophistry" (C, 77; CD, 6). The relentless enemy of Socrates, Nietzsche proclaimed the dislocation of eternal truth in favor of an essentially historical genealogy, had recourse to the "substantial" categories of life and power, and privileged a rhetoric of parables, metaphors, aphorisms, and the like (C, 77 n. 6; cf. MP, 82). Nietzsche cultivated a "veritable hatred of universalism," and looked forward to the despicable resurrection of "national Gods" (SP, 66). His campaign against the categories of philosophical truth was waged on the basis of sophistry's two founding "axioms": first, the determination to refer every statement back to the question Who speaks?, to read every statement in terms of its constituent interests and orientation; and second, the insistence that "what can be thought is necessarily a fiction." Although Badiou accepts Lacan's idea that certain kinds of truth can ever be presented only *as* a fiction, he firmly rejects the equation of fiction and thought as the first step toward a merely "conventionalist conception of thought" (CD, 18).

Badiou believes that the later "Wittgenstein is our Gorgias" (C, 60–61), the great inspiration of precisely such a conventionalist conception. Wittgenstein assumed that "rules are the 'ground' of thought, inasmuch as it is subject to language." Philosophy can then do little more than make sure that we speak by the rules, as they should be used, in keeping with the underlying "form of life" that they express and reinforce—that is, that we use words as they should be used. The basic assumption here is already explicit in the *Tractatus:* whatever does not refer back to the unsayable act of pure (divine) goodness is simply a matter of descriptive and ultimately valueless pragmatics.[54] True speech, then, becomes a contradiction in terms: "The power of the rule is incompatible with truth, which becomes nothing more than a metaphysical Idea. There is, for the sophists, nothing beyond conventions and relations of power. And for Wittgenstein, there is nothing beyond language games."[55]

Lyotard and postmodern philosophy generally stand condemned by the same judgment. Badiou is brusquely dismissive of "the whole package of 'modern' deconstructivist paraphernalia."[56] For Lyotard no less than Wittgenstein, philosophy is "a discourse in search of its own rules," and, thanks in part to this unexpected conjunction of the continental and analytical lines of thought, "the anti-systematic axiom is today axiomatic" (MP, 46, 45). According to Lyotard's language-based ontology, what *is* is simply the heterogeneous variety of "phrases"; "what happens" and "what there is *[ce qu'il y a]*" are phrases, "event phrases" whose intrinsic incommensurability exceeds all generic qualification (all subsumption within one genre of discourse). The subject or speaker figures here merely as the effect of certain phrase linkings. Philosophy's only specific task is then to guard the intrinsic incommensurability of phrases against the hegemony of any particular genre of phrasing. Among other things, Badiou objects to Lyotard's recourse to the judicial register (judgment, differend, tort) and his reference to an ultimately inarticulable (and thus antiphilosophical) "sentiment" or "passibility" as principal defense against evil, against tort; toward the end of this study, however, we will see that Badiou himself has trouble answering Lyotard's countercharge of a radical "decisionism" without recourse to an explicitly unsayable limit of his own, a limit he calls the unnameable *[l'innommable]*.

Against Heidegger and Hermeneutics

Truth in Badiou's sense proceeds as a subtraction from meaning. What a truth declares is not mediated by what that declaration means to those whom it affects. The political truth asserted by the Declaration of the Rights of Man (1789), for example, does not pause to consider the meaning of its prescription. It does not ask, "What is a person?" or "What does it mean to be human?" The categories of meaning are external to the principle of its construction. Rather, the declaration is axiomatic and thus unqualified in its effect. Its truth applies to all, immediately, and without asking who "all" might be or what they are like.

Meaning is itself, Badiou argues, the religious concept par excellence: "I call 'religion' the desire to give meaning to everything that happens" (B, 42). For what provokes interpretation, ultimately, is always a (quasi-divine) inscrutability: "God's designs are impenetrable, and for this reason we can negotiate, to infinity, our being-in-the-world, interpret traces, and interpret the interpretations. In other words: the foundation of Meaning being itself inaccessible, there are only interpretations."[57] Whether this foundation is divine or profane, religious or humanist, makes little difference to Badiou. Religion subordinates the articulation of truth to a reverence for the *One* meaning of meaning (D, 60).

We know that modernity opened with the gradual acceptance of the death of God, the end of any transcendent One. Negatively, then, pursuit of the modern campaign against the One involves a relentless suspicion of those reactionary thinkers who resist, more or less explicitly, the passing of this Unity. Badiou thought Hegel was the first major culprit: "Hegel will try to show that the Whole is the history of the One" (TS, 23), whereas "that truth and totality are incompatible is certainly the decisive—or post-Hegelian—teaching of modernity."[58] Hegel anticipated the eventual fusion of being and truth, or (and it amounts to the same thing) a notion of truth as itself Subject. It is Heidegger, however, the Heidegger who looked back to the original union of being and truth, who stands accused as the great contemporary prophet of semantic Reaction. Heidegger's obsessive question, endlessly reworked, was precisely, "What does Being *mean*?"[59] All of his work presumes a primordial, prephilosophical (presocratic) source of meaning, a meaning forgotten by philosophy and then actively obscured by modernity. In other words, Heidegger refused to accept the full desacralization of being: he deconstructed the rational, empty God of Aristotle, onto-theology, and the metaphysical tradition, only in order to proclaim the imminent truth of that other, fundamentally mysterious, God "who alone can save us"—the God of poetic inspiration, the God of a pure Creation.[60] Heidegger preserved the religious paradigm by translating it into rigorously ontological terms, such that "only from the truth of Being can the essence of the holy be thought. . . . Only in the light of the essence of divinity can it be thought or said what the word 'God' is to signify."[61] Heidegger, in short, wrote the ultimate religious challenge to a properly philosophical sovereignty, traced back to its own (Greek) roots. What Badiou calls a "contemporary atheism" is first and foremost a break with this configuration, to the exclusion of *all* gods (CT, 20). What Badiou has come to present as the pure logic of presentation is "the exact contrary" of Heideggerian "presence" (EE, 35).

To be sure, Badiou's project invites comparison with Heidegger's in a number of respects. Like Badiou, Heidegger began with the elimination of all mediation or "covering" of being (EE, 142). Like Badiou, Heidegger and his privileged poets have worked for "the destitution of the category of the object . . . and of objectivity, as necessary forms of presentation" of being-as-being—and, like Badiou, they know that whatever else it is, being is not something we can *know*.[62] More important, Heidegger understood that "truth is never gathered from things at hand, never from the ordinary." His truth *[aletheia]* is "an occurring," an exceptional "happening."[63] Like Badiou, finally, Heidegger related the event of truth to a certain priority of the void, or nothing, a "nothing" that is "more original than the 'not' and negation" and that acts as the subjective gateway to a grasping of the situation (of Being) as a whole.[64] Every Heideggerian composition of truth demands "resolution" in the face of the void.

Nevertheless, these similarities are only superficial. The fundamental orientation of Heidegger's philosophy is, of course, to "the appearing, or the opening up of being itself, the coming-to-be of its presence" (EE, 141). Especially in its post-Nazi "humility," Heidegger's thought is essentially a matter of contemplation, if not resignation. It is a thought organized around the imperatives of dwelling, revealing, and listening, around the command of that "clearing *[Lichtung]*" opened through the primordial giving that is Being beyond beings: "to let be."[65] There is no conviction more antithetical to Badiou than Heidegger's insistence that "truth is the truth of Being."[66] Heidegger deliberately equated ontology and truth. Heidegger's truth is a matter of "being attuned" to the mysterious "errancy" of Being, to being revealed *[aletheia]*, in a rapt awareness that precisely leaves "all subjectivity" behind.[67] However absent for us, Heidegger's ontology is directed toward that primordial presence of the One refused by the whole thrust of modern thought.[68] Badiou thus reads Heidegger's philosophy as nothing more than a "nostalgia for the sacred" in its purest form (MP, 33–34; EE, 15), a kind of "speculative totalitarianism" (MP, 9). The medium of this speculation, of course, is again language. Language is itself the clearing in which being *is*. Since "language alone brings beings as beings into the open for the first time," so the essence of thought is itself a matter of articulation and poesis.[69] As for Heidegger's romantic references to the "historical destiny of a people" and "the silent call of the earth,"[70] they are to be interrupted once and for all by precisely that philosophical initiative blocked by this jargon of authenticity: the matheme. To Heidegger's nostalgic evocation of an elusive presence, Badiou opposes his subtraction from all presence, an operation based only on the self-constituent validity of the axiom or Idea (EE, 143). Badiou lends this polemic a starkly gendered poignancy: against the "soft" "temptation of presence," he asserts the virile "rigor of the subtractive," the cold austerity of the empty set, "the hard novelty of the matheme," the unemotional, non-affective fidelity of deduction.[71]

Anti-antiphilosophy

The difference between religion and antiphilosophy is slight. Antiphilosophy is a rigorous and quasi-systematic extrapolation from an essentially religious *parti pris.* Antiphilosophy is religion in philosophical guise, argued on philosophical terrain. (Heidegger himself, of course, is most easily read as an antiphilosophical thinker.) The antiphilosophical label, borrowed from Lacan's self-description, can be applied to several of Badiou's own sources of inspiration: Heraclitus, Saint Paul, Pascal, Rousseau, and Lacan himself, as well as Kierkegaard, Nietzsche, and the early Wittgenstein.

Antiphilosophy proclaims an ineffable, transcendent Meaning, grasped in the active refutation of philosophical pretensions to truth. To use Pascal's phrase, to mock or "dismiss philosophy is to be a true philosopher."[72] Since (divine) truth is a function of the heart, a matter of faith and direct intuition, Pascal concluded that "the final achievement of reason is the recognition that there are an infinity of things that surpass its power."[73] True value here holds itself aloof in a pure, supraphilosophical event or act, in "a thinking more rigorous than the conceptual,"[74] in a "silent, supra-cognitive or mystical intuition" (D, 31). Every "antiphilosophy culminates in a moral theology, or an aesthetic one (it is the same thing)," whose sole "theoretical" declaration is that only the redemptive act or intuition can interrupt the futile chatter of theory.[75] Saint Paul, for example, evacuated (Greek) philosophy through the invention of a new discourse of Life, a new conception of reality, based on a pure act of redemptive grace (SP, 62). More contemporary antiphilosophers tend to inscribe their version of the "event-real within the sphere of effective truths: the 'great politics' for Nietzsche, the arch-scientific analytical act for Lacan, mystical aesthetics for Wittgenstein" (SP, 62). Antiphilosophical truth *is* once and for all; it is typically apocalyptic or metahistorical. Nietzsche's Life or "active" force (against the "theoretical" *ressentiment* of the philosopher-priest); Pascal's *charité* (against rational and institutional intellect); Rousseau's candor (against the science of Voltaire and the *Encyclopédistes*); Kierkegaard's redemptive choice (against Hegel's synthesis); Wittgenstein's inarticulable, other-worldly Meaning—these are all so many efforts to set transcendent value against mere theory, a genuine Act against the feeble abstractions of philosophy. Showing here prevails over saying: antiphilosophy reveals, where philosophy explains. As Badiou puts it, "The antiphilosophical act consists of letting become apparent 'what there is' to the degree that 'what there is' is precisely that which no proposition is able to say."[76]

Like the sophists, antiphilosophers write a "linguistic, logical, genealogical critique" of philosophy's pretensions to *systematic* clarity. It is no accident that they generally compose fragmentary interventions rather than systematic books—Paul's letters, Lenin's pamphlets, Nietzsche's aphorisms, Wittgenstein's lectures, Lacan's seminars, and so on. An equally characteristic antiphilosophical symptom is the subjective guarantee of meaning by the declared sincerity or inspiration of the author. Whereas "philosophy has never been possible without accepting the possibility of an anonymous statement" and the authority of statements that compel examination in their own right (CD, 17), the antiphilosopher looks first to the integrity or authenticity of the speaker: Badiou can point to Rousseau's frankness in the *Confessions*, Kierkegaard's obsessive relation with Regine, Nietzsche's insistence upon his own genius, Paul's "election" ("By the grace of God I am who I am").[77]

Take the case of Lacan, whose own insistence on the element of speech as the sole dimension of truth is more than usually emphatic. For all his influence on Badiou *philosophe*, for all his privileging of *erklären* over *verstehen*, Lacan's subject is derivative of some deeper, ultimately inaccessible (unconscious), force—first desire, then drive. In either case, he has famously declared, "Whatever it is, I must go there, because, somewhere, [the] unconscious reveals itself" (S11, 41/33). Because Lacan's subject is primarily that which flickers through flaws in the mechanics of social consensus and psychological normalization, his theory can easily stagnate in little more than contemplation of the perverse particularity of the subject (as a gap in the Other, as the phantom puppet of an *objet a*, as *driven* by its own jouissance).[78] Unlike Badiou, Lacan holds that "the dimension of truth is mysterious, inexplicable" (S3, 214/214), that desire is constitutively elusive (S20, 71), that the real is essentially ambivalence and loss, that analysis is steeped in the *tragic and horrific* dimensions of experience. Lacanian insight, in other words, is not so much a function of clarity and hope as it is an endurance of radical abjection.

Much of Badiou's recent work, including a four-year sequence of lectures given at the Collège International de Philosophie (1992–96), has involved an elucidation and critique of the great antiphilosophers. Antiphilosophy is both a more worthy and a more insidious opponent of philosophy than sophism. Heraclitus against Parmenides, Pascal against Descartes, Rousseau against the *Lumières*: the great antiphilosophers are, in a sense, the simulacra of the great philosophers, as well as a temptation the philosopher must confront and surpass. "In the end," Badiou says, "my theory is that philosophy should always think as closely as possible to antiphilosophy."[79] What will forever block the transformation of this proximity into complicity, as might be expected, is the challenge posed by mathematics: "The simple question 'Is mathematics a form of thought?' organizes, subterraneously, the debate between philosophy and antiphilosophy. Why? Because if mathematical propositions *think*, this means that there exists a saying *[un dire]* without experience of an object, an asubjective, regulated access to the intelligible. That being is not necessarily foreclosed to all proposition. That the act is perhaps even of a theoretical nature. Antiphilosophy challenges all this absolutely."[80] Resistance to mathematics provides the most concise way of indicating the ground common to that most unlikely pair of antiphilosophical thinkers: Wittgenstein, for whom the pretensions of mathematics amounted to a kind of philosophical *sin*, and Heidegger, for whom the modern turn toward scientific mathematization culminated in the thoughtless domination of technology.[81]

Thus far, Badiou has considered three cases of antiphilosophy in particular detail: Nietzsche's last writings, Wittgenstein's early *Tractatus,* and Guy Lardreau's *La Véracité.* The arch-sophist Nietzsche was also a "prince of contemporary 'antiphilosophy'" (CD, 24). For all the vehemence of his critique, Badiou preserves a kind of "distant tenderness for this hero" of antiphilosophical thought, and is careful to distinguish his position from that of rival, reactionary, anti-Nietzscheanisms (CD, 5–6). According to Badiou's reading—unlike those, say, of Heidegger or Deleuze—Nietzsche's originality lies less in the invention of alternative values or concepts than in his insistence upon a "senseless and worthless dimension to the vital act" (CD, 9), the absolute singularity of apocalyptic revaluation itself. In his last writings and letters Nietzsche anticipated an ultimate "rupture" or "explosion," a revolution "without concept or program" destined to smash the history of the world in two and to transform humanity as a whole.[82] Simply, lacking any sustained historical engagement, this absolute break begins to blend imperceptibly with its own declaration. Nietzsche's madness, according to this reading, was nothing more than the effort to create a new world from scratch, turned inward upon its exceptional creator. Like all purely antiphilosophical gestures, Nietzsche's great Event opened only onto hysterical conflagration and eventual silence. In the end, Nietzsche was consumed in his own divine annunciation (CD, 15–16; cf. SP, 94).

Wittgenstein's *Tractatus* provides Badiou with a more measured instance of a comparable sequence.[83] Wittgenstein's aim was to demonstrate that philosophy's pretension to answer questions of genuine value is "absurd" and "meaningless." Philosophy does not touch the problems of life (*Tractatus,*

6.52). If the "meaning of life, in other words the meaning of the world, can be called God," philosophy must accept that "God does not reveal himself in the world."[84] Access to God must pass through the ineffable act of revelation itself, a pure showing most adequately conveyed by music and scripture. Wittgenstein's effort was to isolate this mystical reality from the invasive approximations of thought, and entrust it to the guardianship of a pure devotion.[85] Thought, he believed, is to be confined to meaningful but merely fortuitous propositions about contingent happenings in the world on the one hand—propositions whose "truth" is a matter of empirical confirmation alone—and to necessary but therefore meaningless logical propositions on the other: "Outside logic all is accident *[Zufall]*" (6.3), but "the propositions of logic are tautologies" and "say nothing" (6.1, 6.11). There cannot be propositions that are both about the world and rigorously coherent.

Guy Lardreau provides a final, more contemporary, example of antiphilosophy, all the more interesting because his work has been so close in many respects to Badiou's own work. Like Badiou, Lardreau is a confirmed *soixante-huitard*, was once a strong Maoist, and still cuts a striking if eccentric figure on the radical fringes of organized politics. Again like Badiou, Lardreau counts among his central points of reference Plato (more specifically the neoplatonism of Plotinus and Proclus, along with the various mysticisms they inspire) and the later Lacan: his work can be thought of as an attempt to think, through neo-Kantian categories, the concept of a One beyond being together with a radical conception of the *réel* as pure *déliaison*, pure resistance to representation. After attracting some attention for his early book *L'Ange* (1976, written with Christian Jambet), Lardreau is chiefly known today for his cryptic neo-Kantian treatise on negative ontology, *La Véracité* (1993). Badiou admires much about this difficult book—its systematic rigor, its uncompromising radicalism, its productive confrontation with Lacan. But he is strongly critical of Lardreau's peculiar melancholy, the symptom of a "postromanticism tempted by exile."[86] Lardreau's *La Véracité*, rather like Lyotard's *Le Différend*, is organized around a bearing witness to the "unsayable real" beyond all logic or discourse. Veracity affirms the exclusively negative and inarticulable "right of the real within discourse." The imperative of philosophy is thus to pick out and defend in any discourse that real point which the discourse cannot incorporate.[87] Concretely, this means, by domain: in politics, the celebration of pure, sublime revolt, revolt for its own sake *("pour deux sous")*; in morality, a counterbalancing pity for the other as victim, a pious respect for all suffering; in aesthetics, a sensitivity to sensual particularity. Badiou has little difficulty showing that this and other comparably eclectic collections of prescriptions amount only to a respectful passivity that leaves the status quo more or less intact.[88]

Against Worldliness

Badiou's campaign against antiphilosophy, religion, and sophistry is part of a still broader struggle against interpretation in general. "I am profoundly convinced," he writes, "that the current situation of philosophy is organized around the decisive opposition between truth . . . and the question of meaning," where meaning is "supposed to be the question that comes forward, in modernity, once the classical question of truth is closed" (DP, 16). Only a fully literal, that is, fully formal (as opposed to empirical or interpretable), discourse can be adequate to the truth, and to ontological truth in particular. Truth interrupts all relations with an object or meaning: "Philosophy is not an interpretation of the meaning of what is offered to experience, [but] the operation of a category inaccessible to presence. And this operation, which grasps truths . . . , interrupts the regime of meaning. This point, in my opinion, is crucial. . . . Philosophy separates itself from religion because it separates itself from hermeneutics" (C, 69; cf. DP, 16). In every case, "truths have no meaning," and come to be through the "failure of meaning" (C, 237).

If philosophy has no relation to meaning, how does it proceed? A truth is composed by its subject, point by point and step by step; each step, however, escapes modulation by any intermediate force. Philosophy is immediately conditioned by truths: "The relation of (philosophical) Truth to scientific, political, artistic, or amorous) truths is a relation of grasping [saisie]. In 'saisie' we imply capture, taking, and also being seized, surprise. Philosophy is that place of thought in which (nonphilosophical) truths are seized as such, and seize us" (C, 68). Such grasping does not pass through knowledge. It is not filtered through the mechanisms of re-presentation. True thought does not represent, narrate, or relate; it interrupts a chain of re-presentations (PP, 88). Consider, for example, the symptomatic method of Freud and Lacan: it begins by rejecting conscious re-presentations as mediations, as cover-ups, so as to focus on certain suggestive gaps or lapses, indicating the real unconscious thought "underneath." Likewise Pascal: he rejected our worldly knowledge or self-valuation as mere confinement in human misery, in favor of an unqualified openness to Grace as the only possibility of salvation. Or Mallarmé, who, against all forms of communication as such, asserted "the ability of language to exhibit, on the ground of nothingness, the essence of the thing" in its ideal sufficiency (PP, 89). In every domain, Badiou's true "thought of the same . . . excludes all hermeneutics of meaning," just as a generic "politics excludes all interpretation" (C, 250).

At the root of this whole polemic is a refusal of what might be called the worldly condition in the widest sense. "To be of the world ... means to act without Idea" (C, 218). Badiou's philosophy is infused with that same contempt for worldliness characteristic of the great antiphilosophers, most obviously Saint Paul and Pascal. The world, as such, is defined for Badiou by the imperatives of communication and interest, of communal relations or links, of a mere "preservation in being" (E, 42). As developed at some length in a recent book, Badiou's assessment of our world, our present situation, is unequivocal. Two defining trends emerge. First, as we might expect, is the "progressive reduction of the question of truth (and so of thought) to the linguistic form of judgment, a point on which Anglo-Saxon analytical ideology and the hermeneutic tradition coincide [and which] culminates in cultural and historical relativism." This cultural relativism recognizes no other form of truth than the lived particularity of specific, designated groups, in particular groups made up of passive "victims" of one kind of another, duly specified according to language, race, nation, religion, or gender. Second, the only unifying mechanism behind this collection of "subsets of the oppressed" is the "false universality of monetary abstraction," the undivided rule of capital (SP, 7). There is no place for truth in such a world: culture takes the place of art, technology replaces science, management replaces politics, and sexuality replaces love. The resulting cluster, culture-technology-management-sexuality, is perfectly homogenous with the market it feeds (SP, 13). Such pseudovalues, Badiou concludes, define nothing other than a being-for-death, or mere life as judged by the transient trivia of its desiring mortality.

"The world," as Badiou conceives it, "never offers you anything other than the temptation to yield" (TS, 334). Philosophy, then, when and where it exists, is as a matter of course in essential conflict with the world. Philosophy is in the world only to change it (TS, 335). If philosophy is a kind of "logical revolt," a "wager" on the universal (DP, 5–6), it is blocked by our world at every step. The world blocks revolt with the illusion of (a merely commercial) freedom; it disarms logic, for it is governed by the "illogical" business of communication, the incoherent transmission of images and opinions; the world inhibits every genuine wager, for it works to ensure itself from chance, to affirm the "necessary calculation of security"; and it opposes the universal, for ours is a "specialized and fragmented world," a bundling together of specific communities and knowledges (DP, 8–9; cf. E, 46–47). Trapped within the exclusive medium of a global financial market, "communitarian, religious, and nationalist passions" have expanded to fill the void left by the collapse of any viable universalist political project (DP, 29; E, 12).

This last point is especially urgent. Every invocation "of custom, of community, works directly against truths" (E, 67; cf. PP, 19). Badiou rejects categorically the idea that true understanding is a function of belonging to a given community. This idea results in "catastrophic statements, on the model: only a homosexual can 'understand' what a homosexual is, only an Arab an Arab, etc." (SP, 13). No community, be it real or virtual, corresponds to philosophy, and all genuine philosophy is characterized by the "indifference of its address," its lack of explicit destination, partner, or disciple. Mindful of Heidegger's notorious political engagement, Badiou is especially wary of any effort to "inscribe philosophy in history" or identify its appeal with a particular cultural tradition or group (C, 85, 75–76). Philosophy and communal specificity are mutually exclusive: "Every particularity is a conformation, a conformism," whereas every truth is a nonconforming. Hence the search for a rigorously generic form of community, roughly in line with Blanchot's *communauté inavouable,* Nancy's *communauté désoeuvrée,* and Agamben's *coming community,* so many variations of a pure presentation without presence.[89] The only community consistent with truth would be a "communism of singularities," a community of "extreme particularity."[90] Nothing is more opposed to the truth of community than knowledge of a communitarian substance, be it French, Jewish, Arab, or Western. As Deleuze might put it, philosophy must affirm the necessary deterritorialization of truth. "I see nothing but national if not religious reaction," Badiou writes, "in the use of expressions like 'the Arab community,' 'the Jewish community,' 'the Protestant community.' The cultural idea, the heavy sociological idea of the self-contained and respectable multiplicity of cultures . . . , is foreign to thought. The thing itself, in politics, is acultural, as is every thought and every truth."[91] What may distinguish Badiou's critique of the communal is the rigor with which he carries it through to its admittedly unfashionable conclusion: "The whole ethical predication based upon recognition of the other must be purely and simply abandoned. For the real question—and it is an extraordinarily difficult one—is much more that of recognizing the Same."[92] An ontology of infinite multiplicity posits alterity—infinite alterity—as the very substance of what is. So, "differences being what there is, and every truth being the coming to be of that which is not yet, differences are then precisely what every truth deposes, or makes appear insignificant." Difference is what there is; the Same is what comes to be, as truth, as "indifferent to differences" (E, 27). True justice is either for all or not at all.

The critique of any communal or "humanist vision of the *lien,* of being together" (AM, 76), is thus basic to any political truth procedure. Since true political sequences are precisely "excepted" from the social, the first task of a political process is "to disengage itself from the prescription of relation *[lien]* or rapport."[93] This disengagement has no properly anthropological limit. From the beginning, Badiou has said that his philosophy "does not bring together, but separates, that is, opposes, the operations of life and the actions of truth."[94] Any truth procedure distinguishes a properly immortal disinterest from an abject, properly "animal" assemblage of particular interests.[95]

An essential preliminary to truth is thus the admission that "we are indeed animals lodged in an insignificant world loaded with excrement" (B, 22). For Badiou as for Saint Paul, the worldly way of the flesh is simply another name for death itself. The human in its "animal substructure," conceived simply as a living creature, is very exactly a "being-for-death," and nothing more. Its interests are "neither more nor less estimable than those of moles or tiger beetles" (E, 13–14, 52). "Man," in short, is that peculiar being that generally "prefers to represent himself in finitude, whose sign is death, rather than know himself traversed, and surrounded, by the omnipresence of the infinite" (EE, 168). Or again: "man" can become subject, can become a being worthy of philosophy, only through participation in those projects or procedures that necessarily appear, from the perspective of the world as it is, as "inhuman" and "immortal."[96]

Since Badiou agrees with Saint-Just that "corruption is the opposite of Virtue,"[97] he summarizes his crusade against our contemporary world as a resistance to its reenactment of Thermidor. "Thermidorian" connotes a situation of thought conditioned by the end of a truth procedure, by the restoration of the status quo and the primacy of calculable interests. Whereas Jacobin "virtue is an unconditioned subjective prescription that refers back to no objective determination," the Thermidorian state—the state that prevails over the postrevolutionary reaction—is founded upon an objective, measured notion of social interest. Thermidor effects the equation of interest and property. It asserts "the idea that every subjective demand has an interest at its core," and so declares the category of Virtue irrelevant to politics. Whereas a Jacobin politics refers back to the act of insurrection as the ultimate measure of its legitimacy, Thermidor inspires a politics of order and *tranquillité*. Whereas the Jacobin asserts the dissolution of hierarchy in the sovereign unity of the nation, "a Thermidorian is constitutively (as subject) in search of a position *[une place]*."[98] Not surprisingly, Badiou finds in today's triumph of liberal republicanism a prime example of Thermidorian reaction. It began with the collapse of the Maoist political procedure (active in France from 1966 to 1975), and it has proceeded through reaffirmation of the state of the situation; it has accelerated a process of "parliamentarization" designed to include philosophical and academic institutions, to the exclusion of all principled prescription (60–62).

Philosophy can have no distinctive purpose if thought is not conceived as a creative practice that resists, in its essence, specification by an object, interest, or identity. Thought cannot be reduced to the passivity of consumption or representation. This is an assumption Badiou shares with the otherwise divergent projects of Heidegger, Foucault, Lyotard, and Deleuze, to mention only those. My own question is simply this: What kind of despecification does thought involve? Does it involve subtraction not only from the positively, objectively specified—the realm of animal instinct as much as of acquired habit—but from the properly specific as well, in the sense of being specific to but not determined by something? Should we not distinguish a specified realm of definition or classification from a properly relational realm of the specific per se? This is a distinction Badiou is generally reluctant to make; we will come back to it in the last two chapters of this book.

chapter   2

From Maoism to L'Organisation Politique

The question of the internal coherence of Badiou's work is a fairly complicated one. The few published accounts of his philosophy often assume that he
began writing in the mid-1980s. There is indeed a sense in which his books up
to and including *Théorie du sujet* (1982), the summa of his early work, have
become partially obsolete by his own subsequent criteria. The break between
the overtly Maoist works of the 1970s and the more serenely argued books of
the 1980s and 1990s—the break in argument and priority, as much as in tone,
style, and presentation—is obvious enough. On several occasions Badiou al-
ludes, rather discreetly, to his early *"égarement,"* his misguided emphasis on
"destruction," and his effective equation of philosophy and politics.[1] The evolution of his relations to both Althusser and Deleuze certainly gives a colorful
measure of how far his position has shifted from the days when he labeled the
former "arrogant, idealist, irresponsible, hypocritical and metaphysical" and
the latter a *"petit professeur de l'embuscade désirante."*[2]

The principal motor and medium of Badiou's evolution has been political
through and through. Radical political engagement is both the great constant
of Badiou's life and the field in which the slow transformation of his position
is most obvious, from his earliest adherence to a Sartrean Marxism through
his fully fledged Maoism in the decade following 1968 to the difficult elaboration of a post-Maoist "politics without party," a politics coordinated by the
Organisation Politique, which Badiou founded, in 1984–85, with his friends

29

Sylvain Lazarus and Natacha Michel. The Organisation Politique is currently engaged in a number of precise campaigns concerning immigration, housing, and the political status of work and workers. The practical promotion of these campaigns absorbs much of Badiou's energy and conditions his philosophy in the most literal and emphatic sense. They testify to a clear shift in Badiou's conception of the role of the state, of the party, and of social class, a shift that bears some limited comparison with the post-Marxisms variously defended by Alain Touraine, Ernesto Laclau, and Chantal Mouffe.

It would be a mistake, however, and one Badiou would be quick to condemn, to assume that these shifts imply a fundamental change in his underlying notion of political commitment itself. What should be stressed is that Badiou's properly decisive concepts—concepts of the pure, the singular, and the generic—are themselves at least relatively constant. Judged according to this consistency, the evolution of his thought begins to look more strategic than substantial. Certainly, for every disclaimer of "early excesses" there have been many suggestive symptoms of a global continuity, at least from May 68 to the present. Badiou's mathematical orientation, set theory and all, preceded his specifically Maoist engagement.[3] The radical "courage" affirmed in the early *Théorie du sujet* was reaffirmed in the later *Conditions* and *Rhapsodie pour le théâtre* (C, 286; RT, 95); the "communist invariants" celebrated in *De l'idéologie* and *L'Echarpe rouge* return in *D'un désastre obscur*. Althusser, Lacan, Cantor, and Mallarmé have been constant points of reference. The literally pivotal notion of "the Two" *(le Deux)* as the dimension of real subjective antagonism was inspired as much by Mao as by Lacan, and figures as prominently in *Le Siècle* (2003) as in *Théorie de sujet* (1982). And so on.

The precise evolution of these concepts demands careful attention. Whatever else it is, Badiou's early work is not the hesitant, embryonic version of a subsequently finished product. It is not the first or primitive stage of a dialectical culmination. *Théorie du sujet* is by any criteria the most difficult to approach of Badiou's books, and his early work as a whole stands as a more or less self-sufficient system in its own right.[4] It represents a first effort to impose his philosophy of the subject. If Badiou was soon forced to retreat and reconsider, this obligation was in a sense, at least at first, pushed on him from without, by the historical collapse of the Maoist and Leninist projects and the rise of the so-called *nouvelle philosophie*—the renewal, inspired by both Solzhenitsyn and Kant, of the liberal discourse of human rights and ethical guarantees. This new situation called for a different sort of philosophical response. When the time came, Badiou addressed the challenge posed by the crisis of Marxism full on, while retaining as much of the essential thrust of his first engagements as possible.

For all these reasons, a summary of Badiou's early and arguably less original work is an essential prelude to the assessment of his mature system. This system should be read, I think, as a reaction to the failed promise of Maoism—as an effort to salvage Mao from history as such. Badiou's mature work is very much a response to (rather than a dogmatic denial of, or nostalgic evasion of) the defeat of the revolutionary inspiration of Europe's most violent century. Badiou is virtually alone among his contemporaries in his proud insistence, "Not for one instant have I ceased to be a militant.... [I am] one of the few philosophers known—and surely reviled—for having never yielded, neither to the sirens of conversion to capitaloparliamentarism, nor to the rule of the abandonment of all principle that has, [since the late 1970s], devastated the French intelligentsia."[5] What must be assessed, in short, is the flexible but determined persistence of Badiou's work, his refusal to yield while accepting the need to adapt.

Badiou's Early Work: Party and *Épuration*

Even if we were to ignore Badiou's subsequent rise to prominence, his early work would still deserve attention as a major contribution to the still fragmentary history of French Maoism.[6] Here I include as "early" the Potemkin pamphlets and Maspero books published in the Yenan collection, which Badiou edited along with his friend Sylvain Lazarus, and his *Théorie du sujet* (Seuil, 1982). From 1970, Badiou belonged to the radical Union des jeunesses communistes de France (marxistes-léninistes), and like other Maoists at the time, was—and unlike most of these others, remains—an active campaigner in factories and among workers' groups across the country. Throughout Badiou's early work, we see that "today's political subject [is] that of the Cultural Revolution, the Maoists" (TS, 247). The early Badiou was convinced that "there is only one great philosopher of our time: Mao Zedong."[7] Everything in his early work is organized in view of "the victory of armed popular struggle, in the strategic perspective of the total collapse of imperialism . . . , backed up by China, the steady rear guard of the global revolution."[8] Marxism, as Badiou here affirms it, calls not simply for the establishment of a society without classes or a destruction of the state, but for the destruction of the agent of this first destruction, the consummation of the organized proletariat itself in its own ongoing "fading away *[évanouissement]*."

Badiou's Earliest Work

Only with his discovery of Maoism in the wake of May 1968 did Badiou begin to develop a systematic philosophy. He began writing, however, well before this discovery. Some of the positions he promoted in his pre-Maoist articles suggest themes more rigorously argued in his post-Maoist work, and so provide us with a first and fundamental point of reference—a first sub-traction from relation, a first version of the Pure.[9]

In the wake of his earliest publications—the novels *Almagestes* and *Portulans,* issued with considerable acclaim by Seuil in 1964 and 1967, respectively—Badiou's first theoretical writings turned on the question of *autonomy,* both aesthetic and scientific. Badiou had already been familiar with Lacan's teach-ings for more than a decade. For the novelist, he thought, "the aesthetic effect is certainly imaginary; but this imaginary is not the reflection of the real, since it is the real of this effect."[10] Moving beyond Macherey's notion that literature is ideology become visible, that literature is ideology's *"mise-en-oeuvre,"* Badiou maintained (in a highly compressed argument) that the "autonomy of the aesthetic process forbids our thinking of it as *rapport. . . . * The problem of the passage from ideology to art cannot be posed [as such]" (81). Art is not *redoublement* but *retournement,* and "this turning back does not reproduce the real; it realizes its reflection" (81).

Science makes a still more radical claim to autonomy: "Science is what relates only to itself, the multiple outside. No signifying order can envelop the strata of its discourse."[11] The earliest Badiou was broadly in line with his then teacher Althusser in conceiving of science as a purely formal logic whose self-regulating rigor is maintained in the absence of any reference to an external object: "Neither the thing nor the object has a chance of acceding here to any more existence than their exclusion without trace. . . . The Leibnizian require-ment of self-identity, upon which the security of truth depends, is intralogi-cal (theoretical) only if it concerns the identity of inscriptions *[marques].* It is science as a whole that maintains self-identity, not as the predicate of the object, but as the predicate of its inscriptions. This rule certainly holds for the written artefacts of Mathematics. It also holds for the inscriptions of energy in Physics. . . . Science is pure space, without underside or mark or place of that which it excludes."[12] Scientific notations are perfectly "substitutable with each other," and the nonsubstitutable is excluded from science by definition. The earliest Badiou concluded, as a result, that "there is no subject of science" (161). Science proceeds without that gap or *"recul"* basic to a properly *subjec-tive* perception, a subjective "difference." As readers of Althusser's texts of the time will know, the subject is rather "a defining feature of ideology."[13] At this point, then, philosophy per se is limited to the merely negative revelation of science: "Let's call 'philosophy' that region of ideology that is specialized in science." And because science is sufficient in itself, "that which, in philosophy, declares itself as science, is inevitably the lack of science. . . . Philosophy car-ries and insists on the mark of its lack."[14]

Force, Place, Evanescence

What are still known as the *events (les événements)* of May 1968 blew these first pretensions to a discrete autonomy apart. As Badiou was to write seven years later, "I admit without any reticence that May 68 was for me, in the order of philosophy as in everything else, a genuine road-to-Damascus experience" (TC, 9; cf. DI, 24). That May revealed once and for all that "it is the masses who make history, including the history of knowledge" (TC, 9). Again: "May 1968 was for us first and foremost a formidable lesson. We felt ourselves woken up, contested, by the immense collective anger of the people.... After May, nothing is or should be 'as before.'"[15] The great task became "the ideological preparation of the masses," "a vast campaign of ideological rectification, so as to guarantee the progressive preponderance of Marxism-Leninism." Ideological questions became "questions of *life and death*."[16]

In place of that distinction of realms proposed in his earliest articles, Badiou now sought a single epistemological-ontological framework coordinated by the explosive subjective emergence of a rigorously proletarian logic. His early ontology united what would become the later concepts of being and event in one shared field—in Mao's phrase, "All reality is process *[processus]*" (TC, 51). This process has two and only two terms: *force* and *place*. Process is the priority of force over place, of revolutionary movement over established order, where consolidation of "the one is the loss of the other.... This is Marx's great discovery" (TS, 188).

Up to a point, Badiou's early ontology was an adaptation of the ancient Greek arrangement of void, atom, and clinamen. Atoms—objective reality in general—exist in and according to their place, while the void exists as "outside-place" *(hors-lieu)*. Force, then, is what displaces the placed. It draws place toward the void. And if atoms behave objectively in this schema, it is "the clinamen that is subject" (TS, 77). The clinamen, or what Badiou more generally calls the "vanishing term" *(terme évanouissant)*, relates static atoms and the fixity of place to the void that alone underlies being. Were it not for the clinamen, the atoms would remain forever suspended in absolute stasis, forever in their place (TS, 74, 81). Self-constituent, self-propelling, the clinamen is the sole condition of change and innovation, the exclusive source of energy as such. "The clinamen is aspecific, beyond necessity, absolutely out of place *[hors-lieu]*, unplaceable *[inesplaçable]*, unfigurable: chance *[le hasard]*" (TS, 77). Wholly singular, its purely erratic movement "marks the void.... Hardly has it taken place than the clinamen must absent itself from all its effects without exception. Hardly has it marked the void in the universe of atoms than it must be the absolute void of this mark" (TS, 76, 79). As soon as it has acted, the clinamen vanishes—in this sense, at least, it anticipates the later concept of event. It can never be encountered in thought. It is because it is fully consumed in its effects that these effects are properly unlimited, that is, unlimited by the "separate" persistence of their cause. The essence of the vanishing term is "disappearance" by definition, "but it is at the same time that which exists the most—as Whole, cause of itself" (TS, 82, 87). For if the vanishing term can never be encountered as object, it can be made to consist as subject: "The subject follows, step by step, the fate of the vanishing term" (TS, 152). This is the organizing principle of Badiou's Maoism: "the trajectory of a thorough-going materialism can be read from the real as cause [i.e., as vanishing term] to the real as consistency [i.e., as political subject]" (TS, 243).

The clinamen, or vanishing term, as such is thus subtracted from presence, but nevertheless retains a kind of substantial force, which is nothing other than the movement of history itself. "The movement of the masses is the vanishing term of history," according to Badiou, and history is simply "a result, whose possibility, invariably, emerge[s] from the fading fury of the veering masses—that is to say, aroused, in the unpredictable storm of their revolt against the figure of the state" (TS, 81). The great task of the Maoist is to lend a minimal "consistency" to this ephemeral power—to remain calm within the storm, so to speak, so as to increase its force. Every political enterprise persists in the vanishing movement of the masses, taken as sole foundation for a new (non-)organization: "The masses are the only antistate force; this defines them. The masses erupt in history only in destructive excess over the state. . . . We call 'masses' historical interruption as such, the real of the cut. . . . The masses are neither thought, nor thinkable. The 'there are the masses' [le 'il y a les masses'] is the vanishing mode of the historical real, which can be perceived only thanks to some defect, some break, in the armor of the state. . . . At the same time, we must recognize that the masses are the only principle of political consistency" (TS, 190, 244).

The distinction of subject and object is thus nearly as absolute in Badiou's early work as in his later. In the early work, this distinction obtains above all in the (still dialectical) movement from the working class (as object) to the proletariat (as subject): the former is a function of "structural" relations and rivalries of place; the latter is the agent of unending "historical" displacement and struggle (LS, 45). Insofar as they are conditioned by their well-defined social and economic *place,* the working classes are the mere object of history, not its subject or motor.[17] As a class in the ordinary sociological sense, the workers lack any political "consistency"; they are confined within the static "algebra" of place, within the inert isolation of the "object" (TS, 252–53). As a unionized class the workers become capable of action, but of action confined to the cautious, subservient pursuit of an equilibrium within the existing structural arrangement of places. The workers become subject only when, guided by the party, they explode this arrangement. The subjective, or historical, "topology" of partisan antagonism explodes the static algebra of class. "In the proletariat, the working class has disappeared," writes Badiou. "Realized as vanishing cause, it consists in the party, whose existence has no other purpose than to suppress that which enabled this causality" (TS, 254). Whereas every object stays in its place, every subject violates its place, "inasmuch as its essential virtue is to be disoriented. Subjectivation operates in the element of force whereby place . . . finds itself altered" (TS, 54, 271). Before they erupt as masses, workers are classed as objects; subjectivation is then what purges class of its structural inertia. Mao's proletariat, the singular subject of history, "exists in purifying itself [of place]" (TS, 148). The proletariat is not that class which seeks an improvement of its place and, still less, that aims to usurp the place of the bourgeoisie; it is that force beyond class whose coming into existence destroys the very concept of place in general. The proletariat is the unique historical subject that overcomes and destroys its objective basis.[18]

The Party

In Badiou's early work, the mechanism of this subjectivation is exclusively political. At this stage, "every subject is political" (TS, 46). Only the political pursuit of class struggle can lead to classlessness (DI, 111). Through struggle, object becomes subject. Badiou reminds us that Marxism, less than an objective science of History, "is the discourse that supports the proletariat as subject. This is a principle we must never abandon."[19]

The precise agent of this support here remains the party, meaning the Maoist version of a communist party. (Badiou never had anything but scorn for the established French Communist Party, the party that betrayed the barricades of May 68—to say nothing of neo-Stalinist state-based parties.) In the most general sense, Badiou's early Marxism was the "systematization of a partisan experience/experiment" (TC, 16), one conditioned by "the great Maoist principle 'Be confident in the masses, be confident in the party'" (DI, 128). The only real political question then becomes "What is the organic link between the masses in revolt—the decisive historical actor—and the Party, as constituted political subject?"[20] Badiou's early answer to this question was organized, broadly speaking, in terms of the distinction between (partisan) form and (massed) content: "The political subject is the class party" (TS, 259), or, more exactly, "the party supports the complete subject, whereby the proletariat, erected upon the working class, seeks the dissolution of the algebraic framework in which this class is placed" (TS, 254). It is only through the party that the (objectively) working class becomes revolutionary Subject, and it is *"the distinctive essence of Marxism to be, openly, a party philosophy"* (DI, 15, Badiou's emphasis). Through the party, pure subjective catalyst, the all-powerful but ephemeral power of the masses becomes conscious of itself, becomes the actual rather than simply the effective subject of history. The masses make history, but as vanishing or ephemeral; the party makes this very vanishing *consist* and endure. The party is precisely that which "consists in its cause." For example, through Lenin the ephemeral "cause" that was the Paris Commune was made to consist in the success of the October Revolution, and persist as a contribution to the eventual "consistency of a prolonged proletarian politics." Like the crucified Christ, the Commune thereby "consist[ed], for having disappeared" (TS, 245–47).

Through the party, the working class abstracts itself from the relations defining its social place. The decisive moment of subjectivation, in all phases of Badiou's work, is one of purification. Here the party effects a double purification of the masses: it concentrates their intrinsic potential energy into an effectively focused strength, and thereby enables them, at the same time, to isolate themselves from the established order as a whole. The proletariat is the result of this "purification and concentration" (DI, 126). More, "to concentrate force constitutes the very essence of Leninist work" (TS, 63). Mao went one step further, declaring that "the party *is* purification" (TS, 56; cf. LS, 44). In Badiou's work, both early and late, a politics of disciplined purification prevails over a politics of alliance and negotiation. Following Lenin, Badiou believes that "a minimal, purified political heterogeneity is a hundred times stronger than an armada of represented struggles."[21] The political subject, in short, is that process which concentrates its represented or "objective" content to zero, toward an absolutely Ideal purity. And if only the proletariat is adequate to the criteria of the Ideal, it is because only it fully "exists in purifying itself" (TS, 148).

Why only the proletariat? Because it has been the first exploited class to form itself as *revolutionary subject* (DI, 18, 72). All revolutionary movements throughout history, from Spartacus through Münzer to Saint-Just, have adhered to what Badiou calls the "communist invariants"—they pursue the dissolution of the state, of private property, of domination, and so on. But the proletariat does more than repeat the invariant; it "masters its realization" (DI, 74). The proletariat is the first exploited class that has, and can have, no specifiable class interest. The proletariat is the result of both an objective dispossession (performed by capitalist polarization) and a subjective divestment or rejection of objectivity itself (guided by the party). In the universality of its coming to be, the proletariat redeems the whole of preceding revolutionary history and formulates "the first form of universal thought,"[22] that is, the first form of rigorously logical revolt. "When all is said and done," writes Badiou, "everything boils down to this maxim: we must dare to struggle; we must dare to revolt,"[23] and "Marxism simply says: revolt is reason, revolt is subject" (TC, 21). Strictly speaking, no-thing justifies revolt. Revolt justifies itself, on the basis of nothing, through its evacuation of the objective as such.

This irreducibly destructive moment played a role in all of Badiou's early work.[24] At this stage, "To destroy ... is the necessary proletarian statement."[25] Consequently, the polemic thrust of his Maoism was directed in the first place against all forms of revisionist deviation away from this revolt-destruction, this uncompromising struggle against the state—which is to say, against the legal, reformist institutions of the French Communist Party (PCF) and its trade unions, along with the "false working-class left, the inheritor of anarchosyndicalism" (i.e., the Gauche prolétarienne).[26] Badiou has always refused a parliamentary or electoral framework for politics. He has always asserted a "principled anti-electoralism," where the initial goal has been not to "reform the PCF but to abolish it."[27]

But this is not yet the whole story. Even the dictatorship of the proletariat remains, of course, a form of the state. If the advent of the proletariat destroys the class basis of capitalist society, a further process must effect the destruction of this destroyer itself. The proletariat qua proletariat must eventually consume itself, leaving only justice and equality in its wake. In the end, it must be possible to say, adapting Mallarmé's phrase, that literally "nothing took place but the Revolution" (TS, 146). The singularly true retrospectively eliminates the merely specific circumstances of its advent. The vanishing cause comes to consist in the party, but the party itself consists only in order to vanish. How exactly do we move from the first destruction (of classes) to the second (of the proletariat itself)? The first destruction has a structural, historical logic to it, the necessity carried by mass revolt; the second, however, requires a more deliberate, more purely willful element. The subject is precisely what provides this element. The subject of the second destruction is more than a double negation: "The lack of the lack ... is not twice the lack. ... It requires something more," something that evades any logic of necessity or place. "I provisionally name 'subject' this unpredictable bifurcation," Badiou declares. "Every subject is a forced exception, which comes in a second moment" (TS, 106). This is the moment, so to speak, where consistency returns to its original vanishing. The subject, in this early definition, is that minimal, open consistency required to maintain an on-going dissolution. In other words, the party consists only so as to dissolve itself, and to keep on dissolving itself. Badiou's early commitment to the party is unqualified, to the degree that the party is precisely that thing which works to eliminate itself (TS, 263): "The party's activity must be relentless, perfect, exhausting,"[28] but "the party has no proletarian reality other than in the tumultuous history of its own termination [résiliation]."[29]

The question is then: What is the possible *limit* of this dissolution or auto-suppression? By his own subsequent admission, more or less, in his early work Badiou failed to devise a sustainable answer to this question. The attempt, however, is instructive. What he provided is a schema with four subjective components (anguish, superego, justice, and courage), which can, under slightly different names, be easily recognized in his later works. They allow the vanishing term to become first consistent in itself, then "consistent" in its own vanishing. The superego effects a preliminary self-purification: "The superego makes destruction something consistent" (TS, 174, 308). Anguish sets in through "submersion in the real, the radical excess of the real" over the symbolic means of the situation (164). Anguish is a necessary price to be paid for truth: "No subject preexists anguish," but nothing can "live" or persist in pure anguish (172–73). So if the superego and anguish are the two traumatic conditions of the subject, justice and courage make subjectivation bearable. Justice is an egalitarian "recomposition" of forces external to the state of the situation (311–12), while courage, finally, is what ties this whole system together. Courage is the courage to wager on Pascal's model, a radical "wager on the real" (310). It is not simply an attribute of the subject, but its very "intrinsic process." To sum up: in anguish, place collapses; courageously, the subject then "assumes the real that divides the place. . . . Courage has no other definition: exile without return" (177, 185).

The essential criteria to emerge from this early configuration of the subject, I think, are close to those of the absolute itself—the imperative of an absolute radicality, an absolute refusal of the relational or specific in all its forms. The subject, here as everywhere in Badiou, is that which constitutes itself in the absence of *liens*, as pure singularity: "The more radical the revolution can be . . . , the more it operates in the courageous toppling over of destruction, in the just audacity of recomposition, and the more it indicates that it is the act of a people, of which the proletariat does nothing other than name the One, as political One" (TS, 189). It is no accident, then, that the critical operation of a becoming-subject is here an essentially auto-constituent "confidence [*confiance*]," where "the essence of confidence is to have confidence in confidence" (TS, 341). Mere "belief" (*croyance*), by contrast, is a function of its object. Belief is belief in something that can in principle be verified (or falsified); confidence, on the other hand, is indifferent to all contrary evidence. Confidence is a subjective or self-referential attribute. Hence, Badiou stated, very rigorously, "I have confidence in the people and in the working class in proportion to the degree to which I do not believe in them."[30] Such is the conclusion of Badiou's early work: "The fundamental concept of the ethics of Marxism is confidence," as expressed in a tight sequence of imperatives: "confidence is belief in the outplace *[horlieu]*"; "be confident in the masses"; "be confident in the Party."[31] In short: "To be confident in oneself in the mode of the destructive division of local constraints [is what] generalizes the process of the subject" (TS, 341).

The Retreat from History

The apparent impasse of Badiou's early work, then, is easily explained. His confidence was insufficiently detached from its object. His confidence remained, despite everything, contaminated by belief in a minimally "objective" telos, mediated by an irreducibly dialectical process. In a word, the movement of history failed to live up to Badiou's *confiance.*

Badiou's early effort was precisely to equate the subjective process of becoming confident in oneself with the global process of historical struggle itself, as aspects of a single logic. The proletariat was to be the vanishing yet consistent vehicle of this logic. Badiou's early work was conceived as a contribution to the ongoing *victory* of the proletariat: the subjective power of Marxism springs precisely from actually "victorious Leninism" (TS, 144), not from abstract theoretical prescriptions. (This is why, in his early work, there is properly "only one subject" [TS, 160, 148].) His later work, by contrast, begins with an acknowledgment that Marxism and historical victory present, at least in the current state of things, a contradiction in terms (PP, 27). The error of classical Marxism as a whole, the later Badiou concludes, was to have mistaken object for subject: "It thought the working class as the class of *workers*," that is, as a sociological category. Since it "simultaneously declared itself to be political truth—militant, faithful—*and* knowledge of History, or of Society, so Marxism eventually died." It died because it was unable to free itself from the "fluctuations" of social categories and objects (EE, 368; my emphasis).

When Badiou comes to reconsider the communist project with the tense mixture of undiminished admiration and rueful self-criticism that characterizes his recollection of *Le Siècle* (2003) as a whole, he locates the root cause of its collapse in the political determination to maintain a relation, however disjunctive it might be, between pure subjective will and implacable historical necessity. He sees Lenin, Stalin, and Mao as united in their determination to align the revolutionary renewal of humanity itself ("to change the very essence of Man") with the objective vitality of Life or History as such. Their question remains "What must be *willed* of Man so as to bring him into line with the Historical movement toward absolute justice and peace?" However heroic the attempt, Badiou now sees this effort as doomed from the start. The attempt to align subjective will and objective development can lead only to terror (LS, 14–15; 27). Unterrorized, the subjective commitment to History can never be objectively guaranteed. Violence alone can close the gap between subject and object.

The lesson Badiou drew from this experience is straightforward: it is essential, in any truth process, to preserve the absolute integrity of this gap, to avoid any direct articulation between subjective will and objective necessity. Rather than attempt to impose our will upon what happens, the real task is actively to yield to what happens—to commit unreservedly to what happens—by maintaining a kind of "intense indifference" to what might happen. It is only by remaining aloof from all that is likely to happen (all that is predictable, established, settled, comfortable) that it is possible to throw oneself entirely into what actually does happen (LS, 21).

Communism's historical mistake, in other words, was to assume "the mutual belonging together of the community and the truth of the collective." One after another, the progressive principles that motivated the various liberation struggles of the 1960s have dissolved in the face of American imperialism, market pressure, Soviet corruption, state terrorism, and communal chauvinism (C, 219; SP, 8). After the fact, Badiou has been able to date the historical turning point fairly precisely: the year 1977, the year in which popular mobilization for radical change began to be integrated within the pacifying consensus of *Mittérandisme* and the corresponding "intellectual regression" from which the French intelligentsia has yet to recover. Glucksmann's *Les Maitres penseurs,* inaugural text of the subsequent "intellectual counter-revolution," was published in 1977 and set the tone for the posttotalitarian "repentance" and liberal respect for human rights that came to define *la nouvelle philosophie.* Abroad, the failure of the Cultural Revolution in China marked "the last effort to reformulate the revolutionary capacity of the masses from within a 'classical' socialist state." The war between the liberators of Vietnam and Cambodia signaled the end of a united struggle against imperialism, and the interstate maneuverings between Egypt and Israel (Sadat visited Israel in November) brought the first and most militant stage of popular mobilization to an end in Palestine. Meanwhile, in France domestic policy began to gravitate around the supremely apolitical question of employment. This shift coincided with and confirmed a new anti-immigrant campaign: the right to reunite the families of foreign workers was suspended on 27 September 1977, the first move in a reactionary strategy that would persist through the Pasqua laws of 1993 to Jospin's crackdown against the *sans-papiers* (1997–98).[32] Over the last two decades, in short, "monsters have prospered in the space left empty by progressive and inventive politics."[33]

So began Badiou's "long search for a political path that would this time be entirely original, without any state reference of any kind . . . , measured exclusively against the experiences of thought and action of which we are capable."[34] Today, Badiou accepts that "the era of revolutions is closed" (TA, 26.11.97). Already in *Théorie du sujet,* in a declaration dated November 1977, he admitted that "to defend Marxism is today to defend something weak" (TS, 198). By 1985, he had to acknowledge that Mao is "a totally forgotten character,"[35] that "Marxism is historically defeated" (PP, 48), that it has lost all its historical points of reference, be they in China, Vietnam, or the industrialized working class (PP, 42–48). By the time Badiou wrote *D'un désastre obscur* (1991) it was clear that the "'proletarian we' that every ideal community poses above itself as historical axiom"—"we, faithful to the event of October 1917"—no longer existed, and had in fact been "inoperative for more than twenty years" (DO, 7). In short, Marxism's historical ambitions had been "destroyed" in their turn.[36] In Badiou's subsequent work he would strive to rise to the challenge posed by this destruction, a challenge that effectively compelled the invention of a way out of the confines of history as such. Or to put it another way: Badiou began to write what he would later recognize as genuine philosophy—as distinct from a theoretical discourse sutured to politics—at the very moment when what he would remember as the true revolutionary twentieth century ended (LS, 8).

Transition: Remembering Sartre

Matters of historical contingency aside, it would be impossible to locate in a single point what has been evidently a gradual process of transformation in Badiou's own work. With his pamphlet on Sartre, however, written immediately after his mentor's death in 1980, Badiou provides us with a remarkable description of the move that he was about to make: the move toward a definitive renunciation of a party-based conception of politics and the institutional weight or continuity that party entails. This pamphlet offers a uniquely suggestive way to approach Badiou's later work.

We know that almost from the moment Sartre published *L'Etre et le néant* (1943), his great effort was to shift from his early "private" existentialism, the anguished solitude affirmed in that book as much as in his novel

La Nausée (1938), toward a militant collective conception of praxis. Like many of Sartre's readers, Badiou notices the lack of any sustainable "rapport with the other" in the early work of Sartre, who was doomed thereby to oscillate between a sadistic objectification of the other and a masochistic objectification by the other: the mere reversibility through which antagonistic "liberties flee from each other provides no ground for a reciprocity, for a fighting solidarity."[37] Here only individuals are active, and are active precisely in their flight from others, from all "objectification." With his turn to Marxism in his *Critique de la raison dialectique,* Sartre retained the notion of an individual subjective praxis as sole productive principle, but attempted to integrate it with "the organized discourse of collective activity" (6). What praxis produces, however, limits its ongoing production; socialized praxis tends to congeal to form a "practico inert," meaning new forms of objective (habitual, institutional...) constraint. The task of an existentialist Marxism, then, was to conceive of a social energy that could overcome this inertia. This was achieved by what Sartre called a "group in fusion." The group in fusion comes into existence as an "apocalyptic" dissolution of a merely passive or serial objectivity. Rather than remain one among others, "in the group in fusion, the unity is immediately here and now," Sartre wrote, "in me and in all the others. . . . The Same is everywhere" (10). Within the group, what Sartre called the position of *"le tiers regulateur"*—the subjective catalyst of the group—is anonymous and indifferent, open to everyone. Crucially, "this character has no institutional or external status. It is anybody at all, through whom everyone becomes the possible mediator of the reciprocity of all" (10). The question then arises, of course, as to how the coherence of the (inherently unstable) group in fusion is to be maintained. The group risks a constant betrayal, a return to the normal, passive, serial state of sociality. The group requires some minimal institutional integrity, some ultimately punitive recourse against corruption or betrayal. To provide this is the task of a political organization or party, but the risk is always that through its reliance upon a party, praxis will once again become inert.

The still mostly Maoist Badiou of 1980 adopted much of the logic of this analysis—the critique of the social, the refusal of the objective, the affirmation of a collective subject without domination—but with a significant twist. Unlike Sartre, Badiou continued to believe that "History [itself] is oriented toward the increasing liquidation of passivity" (13), and that what enables this forever more active activity to persist is the political coherence of the party as rigorous incarnation of a proletarian logic. History remains the driving force, but it is liable to slacken and tire; only the party can achieve the full transition from the History of class struggle to the Politics of a communism beyond class. The definitive end of history cannot itself be fully achieved "by" history. In this sense, Badiou remains fully consistent with his positions of the previous decade. The party is that agent, produced in history, by which history overcomes itself as history, that is, by which history becomes political logic. For the Maoist it remained crucial to maintain, first and foremost, the "continuity of the proletarian politics" through the institutional durability of the party (15). For the Sartre of the *Critique*, by contrast, the authentic collective praxis active in the group in fusion was *essentially* ephemeral, discontinuous. Genuine "Man exists only in flashes, in a savage discontinuity, always absorbed, eventually, in inertia." Collective activity is reserved purely for the moment of revolt as such. Everything else follows inevitably from our essential passivity, our animal "inhumanity." True Sartrean "humanity" emerges only in the ephemeral, occasional dissolution of passive anonymity (13–15).

What has happened in Badiou's subsequent work is that he has slowly adopted, while struggling to maintain his strictly political principles, a perspective similar to Sartre's historical-ephemeral pessimism. The further from party Badiou has moved, the more his conception of politics has come to resemble a politics of the "flash," a politics grounded in the revolutionary but ephemeral moment in which a serial inertia can be suspended with only minimal recourse to an institutional stability of any kind. But whereas Sartre was able to move beyond the ephemeral only by equating an ultimate historical coherence with a global political coordination—which accounts for the failure of the second volume of his *Critique* to move beyond Stalin as the apparent end of history—Badiou's determination to avoid this alternative has driven him ever further toward the radical subtraction of politics from history altogether.

Politics without Party: The Organisation Politique

An adequate survey of Badiou's more recent conception of politics can come only toward the end of our exposition of his mature thought as a whole. The characteristic traits of his post-Maoist political practice, however, have been clearly established since the mid-1980s, when he helped found the Organisation Politique, an organization dedicated to the pursuit of a "politics without party."[38] The group remains small, relying on several dozen committed activists to coordinate its various interventions and campaigns, ranging over issues of health and education, the status and representation of work and workers, and the treatment of undocumented immigrants, or *sans-papiers*.

What changed between the early 1970s and the early 1990s is obvious enough. Badiou emphasizes three major points of evolution: party, class, and state. As a matter of urgent principle, the Organisation Politique refuses the concept of party as the source and driving force of politics, preferring to conceive of political sequences as specific to particular issues in particular situations (AM, 85). The political mode whose "central theme is the party" is now equated with Stalinism (DO, 61 n. 6). As regards class, Badiou has become ever more vehemently critical of "the idea that politics *represents* objective groups that can be designated as classes. . . . There may exist emancipatory politics or reactionary politics, but these cannot be rendered immediately transitive to a scientific, objective study of how class functions in society." As regards the state, for so long the major target of Badiou's political work (and still, in many ways, the principal target of his *philosophy*), Badiou today acknowledges that at least some forms of political change must proceed through demands made upon the state, rather than through a radical subtraction from the state. The state can no longer be considered solely as "the external adversary." He now accepts that it is occasionally "a matter of requiring something from the state, of formulating with respect to the state a certain number of prescriptions or statements."[39]

What Badiou has relinquished, in other words, is nothing less than the historical realization of the communist ideal itself. The "generic communism" described in Marx's *1844 Manuscripts* anticipated "an egalitarian society of free association between polymorphous workers, in which activity is not governed by status and technical or social specializations but by the collective administration of necessities." The demise of the state was to bring about a "pure presentation" and the "undivided authority of the infinite, or the advent of the collective as such" (AM, 91). But precisely this pure "democracy" is now recognized to be a "Romantic" dream, a "fraternity terror" tending toward populist dictatorship (AM, 101): "Communism was the idea of a collective mastery of truths. But what then happened, everywhere, was that a Master rose up, since the truth was no longer separated from mastery. And in the end, to love and will the truth meant to love and will this master" (PM, 85). So Badiou now proposes an "altogether different hypothesis," that of democracy as a function of "political prescription itself" (AM, 103). He envisages a politics for which "equality would be, precisely, an axiom and not a goal." True equality must be "postulated rather than willed" (AM, 126). Universal equality is not an objective state to be accomplished or approximated, but the guiding principle of a purely subjective mobilization.

Today more than ever before, in order for such mobilization to continue it must retain a fundamental "distance" from the inevitably particularist, inevitably corrupt manipulation of interests that defines institutionalized politics:

It's simply not true that you can participate in a system as powerful and as ramified as parliamentarism without a real subjective commitment to it. In any case, the facts speak for themselves. *None* of the parties which have engaged in the parliamentary system and won governing power, have escaped what I would call the subjective law of "democracy," which is, when all is said and done, what Marx called an "authorised representative" of capital. And I think that this is because, in order to participate in electoral or governmental representation, you have to conform to the subjectivity it demands, that is, a principle of [cross-party] continuity, the principle of the *politique unique*— the principle of "this is the way it is, there is nothing to be done," the principle of Maastricht, of a Europe in conformity with the financial markets, and so on. In France we've known this for a long time, for again and again, when left-wing parties come to power, they bring with them the themes of disappointment, broken promises, etc. I think we need to see this as an inflexible law, and not as a matter of corruption. I don't think it happens because people change their minds, but because parliamentary subjectivity compels it.[40]

The price to be paid for this uncompromising rectitude is of course a certain marginality. In the present circumstances, Badiou writes, "What I call political is something that can be discerned only in a few, fairly brief, sequences, often quickly overturned, crushed, or diluted by the return of business as usual."[41] It is a matter of making the most of the few opportunities that do open up, of exploiting the few chinks in the established armor, without yielding to the temptations of political rearmament. The break with party is definitive but not disabling.

Persistence of the Two

The concept of the Two has remained implicit in our discussion thus far. Fundamental to the difficult logic of *Théorie du sujet*, it remains very much at the center of Badiou's ongoing work: as Lacan understood, "once one makes two, there is no going back."[42] This concept is also, it must be said, one of the most elusive aspects of Badiou's thought. The term applies to a bewildering diversity of concepts, drawn from classical logic (p = not-not-p), Manichean dualisms, Lacan's doctrine of the sexes, and Marx's polarization hypothesis.[43] "Nothing is more difficult than the Two," Badiou writes, "nothing is more subject, simultaneously, to both chance and faithful work. The highest duty of man is to produce, together, the Two and the thought of the Two, the *exercise* of the Two" (MP, 72). Again, in a more oratorical vein: "The real that is ours depends only on this: there are two sexes; there are two classes. Busy yourselves with this, you subjects of all experience!" (TS, 133).

However eclectic its occasions, what is involved here is always "the possibility of a Two that is not counted as one, nor as the sum of one plus one," that is, an immanent two, a two experienced as pure bifurcation.[44] At its most abstract, it is this notion of a pure two, without the third element that would be the relation *between* the two, that lies at the heart of Badiou's alternative to a dialectical or relational philosophy. At its root is Mao's principle "If you have an idea, one will have to divide into two" (TS, 131; E, 31). It is not a matter, Badiou insists, of engendering two from one. On the contrary: that "one divides into two means there is no identity other than split. Not only is reality process, but the process is divided. . . . What comes to be is what disjoins" (TC, 61–62). The political two is not the duality of a class relationship—"there are no class relations *[rapports de classe],*" just as there are no sexual relations—but their active disjunction, or "nonrapport" (TS, 145). This disjunction does not precede and condition the existence of the proletariat, the advent of the proletariat is itself what splits society for and against revolution, leaving no space for compromise. Badiou's philosophy, early and late, refutes the possibility of any "third way." The two implies, very literally, *le tiers exclu:* the excluded middle. Political struggle takes place between "opposites," pure and simple.[45]

However, if the proletariat divides from the bourgeoisie in the process of coming to be, the revolutionary subject of this division, of course, is itself one. More, it is the *one* one, the unique one—Hegel's *das Eine Eins.* It exemplifies another of Mao's principles, that "nothing essential divides the working class," and so this "class, in its socially divided but sometimes eruptive existence, is the One from which can proceed, as politics, the party, the One One" (TS, 26, 228–29). The Two is that process through which the eventual One comes to be. The One comes to exist by splitting in two that which pre-exists: "It is the Two which gives its concept to the One, and not the reverse" (TS, 23; cf. TC, 80).

In Badiou's later philosophy, it is the eruption of an event that splits a situation in two. The subjects of an event divide the elements of their situation into two subsets, those that are connected to the event and those that are not (Christian or not Christian, Bolshevik or not Bolshevik, loving or not loving). The two cohere here as the "divided effect of a decision" (EE, 229). In its post-Maoist guise, the Two becomes a category of the subject alone, cleansed of all relations to an object, all substantial incarnation. Whereas for the Maoist "politics was thinkable only insofar as the movement of History was structured by an essential Two" (MP, 71), the later Badiou has recognized that "the real Two is an eventual production, a political production, and not an objective or 'scientific' presupposition."[46]

The essential thing to remember is that the configuration of a two always eliminates relations *between* two elements. Such relations are indeed, as Badiou argues, describable only from the position of an implicit third element. The "between" is external to the two. As pure splitting, the two has no discernible terms in the strict sense; such terms come to exist as a consequence of the two, as the result of a true decision, itself made as a choice between strictly "indiscernible" elements (C, 190–91). The two of a truth will divide its situation between those who are for or those who are against, but this division is always a *result:* before the two, the situation was governed by the false unity of consensus, by the apparent identification of elements with their situational place.

The revolutionary twentieth century, the century that lasted from 1905 to 1977, was first and foremost a century of war. It was dominated from start to finish by a "combative conception of existence," by a shared belief in the *decisive* nature of social conflict (LS, 31–32). Its fundamental number was the Two of pure struggle rather than the One of harmonious reconciliation or the Multiple of diversity and equilibrium. Anchored in the decade of Malraux and Jünger, of Stalin and Hitler, it was a century indifferent to compromise.

That century came to an end, Badiou recognizes, more than twenty years ago. Profound antagonism remains the real principle of politics, but war can no longer provide the paradigm for its varied and contemporary forms of expression. How are we to think the shift from war to peace, without giving up on the struggle for truth (without confusing demilitarization and "demobilization")? How are we to move from the aggressively fraternal "we" of the warlike epic to the peaceful "we" of the disparate collectivity, without compromising the principle that "we" must remain *truly* we? "I, too," Badiou admits, "exist in this question" (LS, 79). The remainder of this book is an engagement with his attempt to answer it.

c h a p t e r 3

Infinite by Prescription: The Mathematical Turn

The impasse of Badiou's early work, we saw, lay in its partial delegation of philosophical autonomy to historical development. His early conception of truth, like that of Hegel or Marx, was *ultimately* cumulative, ultimately coordinated with the singular movement of History as a whole. The expression of confidence, though maintained as a militant "confidence in confidence," was still filtered through an at least partially substantial or objective mediation. In short, Badiou had yet to develop a fully subtractive theory of the subject.

In the wake of 1968, Badiou was determined not to repeat the mistakes of ultraleft "dogmatists" such as the Maoists of the Gauche prolétarienne, who in identifying themselves with the popular movement had persisted in their misplaced belief that "political consciousness was coextensive with the brute, purely 'objective' reality of revolt." When the movement faltered in the late 1970s such ultraleft convictions faltered along with it. "What allowed me and my friends to avoid this kind of intellectual liquidation," Badiou explains, "was our conception of politics, not as an activism carried by the transitory objectivity of a movement, but as subjectivity, as thought, as prescription."[1] Although they do not add up so as to lend a continuous meaning or direction to History,[2] sequences of such thought or commitment retain an "eternal" force even in the absence of any objective consequence. From now on *confiance dans la confiance* will be carried by the rigor of a self-sustaining prescription with a minimum of direct historical mediation. For a more

49

conventionally materialist ontology, Badiou has substituted the mathematical manipulation of the void, which has become the exclusive basis for his
articulation of a be-ing without substance, without constituent relation to
material existence; for a historical eschatology, he has substituted a "politics
of the impossible," a politics purged of dialectical *liens*.[3] Truth is what happens in history, but as a subtraction from history. What can thus be read in
one sense as a retreat from ambitious historical claims can in another sense
be read as proof of an ambition too grandiose and too discontinuous for history itself.

The most obvious and most telling characteristic of Badiou's post-Maoist
work is the equation of mathematics with the ontological situation. For readers with little or no background in mathematics, it is no doubt this particular
move that is most likely to complicate their appreciation of Badiou's thought.
The present chapter considers with some care some of the wider philosophical issues at stake; chapter 4 will then work through the precise components
of Badiou's actual ontology.

In keeping with a tradition that goes back to Aristotle (via Heidegger, Wolf,
Duns Scotus, and others), Badiou defines ontology as what is "sayable of being
as be-ing" (CT, 38; EE, 14), that is, what can be articulated of being exclusively
insofar as it *is*, in the absence of all other qualities including the contingent
quality of existence itself. Consider any random object, any particular being
(*étant*) in the substantial sense of the word—say the pen that I am writing
with now. Like any being, it has a whole range of qualities, including weight,
shape, purpose, color, accumulated accidental characteristics, and so on. It
has the qualities of being blue, being plastic. It also has the quality of *be*-ing
(*être*) as such, in the dynamic or verbal sense of the word. The pen is blue, it is
smooth, it is made of plastic, and it also *is*, purely and simply. Ontology is the
science that concerns itself with this last and seemingly elusive quality, which
is not properly a quality at all: the be-ing (in the verbal sense) of beings (in the
substantial sense). Over the centuries, philosophers have suggested a whole
host of answers to the question of what is, simply insofar as it is: Ideas for
Plato, substances for Aristotle, God for Spinoza, synthetic intuition for Kant,
the will to power for Nietzsche, pure Being for Heidegger, vital energy for
Deleuze. Badiou's own answer is perhaps the most surprising: "Mathematics
is the science of all that is, *insofar as it is*" (EE, 13). It is not that things or beings are themselves mathematical forms, of course; Badiou's concern is with
what can be thought or presented of pure be-ing, rather than with the (variable and empirical) substance of beings or presented things (EE, 14). All the
same, he can fairly present this concern as consistent with

a very old and somewhat inevitable ontological programme, which is that ontology always gathers up what remains to thought once we abandon the predicative, particular determinations of "that which is presented." We might conclude that there remains nothing at all. This was the idea that dominated the whole nineteenth century, the whole post-Kantian theory, according to which, in this case, there would remain only the unknowable, and eventually nothing. Or we might conclude that there actually remains everything, which was after all Heidegger's guiding inspiration; that is, if we put to one side the diverse singularity of the existence of the existent [*étant*], we come to a thought of being that is itself suspended or deferred in fairly problematic fashion. As for me, I conclude that what remains is mathematics. I think it's a fairly strong thesis.[4]

To make this thesis plausible we need first to understand why any answer to the question of be-ing can be founded only in a decision. Next we will review the two most basic decisions any ontology must make, concerning the priority of numbers or things on the one hand, and the priority of the one or the multiple on the other. We will then be in a position to see why, though being in itself is neither one nor multiple, what can be said of be-ing is purely and exclusively multiple; that this multiplicity is a multiplicity without units or unity; that the "substance" of such unitless multiplicity is indistinguishable from nothing, or the void; that the very multiplicity of this multiplicity, consequently, cannot be perceived or verified but must be proclaimed multiple through an inaugural inscription or proper name.

Numbers or Things?

Since be-ing is not a quality, the question of what be-ing is cannot be answered by empirical investigation or experimental falsification. Philosophies that equate be-ing with what science can reliably tell us about particular beings—such as philosophies that belong to the Anglo-American tradition of analytic philosophy, for instance—naturally tend to dismiss the question of be-ing as meaningless and incoherent. But even this answer shares an essential characteristic with other answers to the question of be-ing: since the brute facts of existence cannot settle the issue, the answer must properly be a *decision*, rather than an investigation or perception. In the end, whatever is to be thought of as *pure* being as be-ing proves to be indistinguishable from the very be-ing of thought itself. As a general rule, "to think being, being-as-being, requires the determination of the axioms of thought in general" (CT, 183), and there is no deriving this determination from the analysis of a faculty, or a nature, or an evolution. Or, in Badiou's terms, the discourse of ontology is itself a truth procedure, and like any truth procedure, it involves a fundamental choice that cannot be referred back to a more primitive objectivity.

The most fundamental decision of ontology appears, abruptly, as an answer to the deceptively naive question "what comes first, things or numbers?" The answers to this question lead one off along two very general paths that Badiou associates, again in keeping with a long tradition, with Aristotle and Plato, respectively. Each path foregrounds a different conception of multiplicity (things or numbers), and grounds a different understanding of the major categories of philosophy—"difference, the void, excess, infinity, nature, decision, truth, and the subject" (CT, 56). The fundamental choice was already clearly presented in one of Badiou's earliest articles, in which he summarized "the two tendencies that have struggled against each other, according to Lenin, since the beginnings of philosophy . . . , the struggle between the [scientific] materiality of the signifier and the [ideological] ideality of the Whole":

> Quality, continuity, temporality, and the negative: the enslaving categories of ideological objectives.
> Number, discretion, space, and affirmation, or better: Mark, Punctuation, Blank [Blanc], and Cause: the categories of scientific processes.[5]

What is rigorously consistent about the whole of Badiou's work is his commitment to the second of these two tendencies, to Plato over Aristotle, to the subtractive austerity of Number over the seductive plenitude of Nature. The immediate consequence of Badiou's own choice is a break in the ancient connection between philosophy and being: by reserving questions of being qua being to mathematics, philosophy itself becomes something firmly distinct from any sort of ontological speculation.

Aristotle (and after him Leibniz, Bergson, Deleuze, and others) presumes an originally material or *natural* complication as the foundation of what *is*—things, that is, before numbers. Aristotle begins with the substantial equivocity or uncertainty of things (and the corresponding confusion of the senses). He then brings in the whole apparatus of logic—the principle of noncontradiction, the principle of the excluded middle, and so on—from the epistemological outside so as to reduce this "initial equivocity of being," and thereby guide the philosophical movement from apparent confusion to analytical clarity. According to Badiou, this "choice of the equivocal as the immediate determination of beings grasped in their being excludes, for Aristotle, the ontological pretensions of mathematics" (CT, 185). Since substance alone is, logicomathematical distinctions can serve merely as useful fictions, imposed after the fact upon preexistent materials. Indeed, it is *because* logic is uncontaminated by or cut off from the tangled confusion of reality that, although without any ontological reality of its own, it can usefully order our perception of this reality. Logic, and with it mathematics, is here a matter of *applied clarity.* It is no accident that Aristotle sees mathematical discourse as oriented toward the Beautiful rather than the True, or that this path would lead, ultimately, to the twentieth century's linguistic turn. In Badiou's judgment, it has provided the spontaneous philosophy for every reactionary era that, like the late twentieth century, has retreated to the presumption that things are best left to follow their natural course, that the task of thought is not a matter of doing or acting *(faire)* but of "letting be" *(laisser-faire)* (LS, 81).

Badiou's own neoplatonic option, then, implies (at various stages of the argument) the destitution of the categories "substance," "thing," "object," and "relation"; the ontological primacy of mathematical over physical reality; the distinction of mathematics from logic and the clear priority of the former over the latter. In this Platonic tradition, that mathematics is a form of thought means, first of all, that it "breaks with sensory immediacy," so as to move entirely within the pure sufficiency of the Ideal (CT, 97). Badiou refuses any cosmological-anthropological reconciliation, any comforting delusion that there is some deep connection (such as that proposed by Jung and his followers) between our ideas or images and the material world we inhabit. Indeed, there is no distinct place in Badiou's work for a philosophical anthropology of any sort.[6] His ontology everywhere presumes the radical cut of symbolic representation from the nebulous cosmos of things and experiences that was first proposed by Descartes and subsequently given a particularly strident formulation by Lacan, who insists again and again that we "can only think of language as a network, a net over the entirety of things, over the totality of the real" (S1, 399/262). According to the Lacanian perspective championed by Badiou and the other contributors to *Les Cahiers pour l'analyse* in the mid-1960s, "Reality is at the outset marked by symbolic *néantisation,*" and as Badiou confirms, every *"truth is the undoing, or dé-fection, of the object of which it is the truth."*[7] In particular, "all scientific progress consists in making the object as such fade away," and replacing it with symbolic-mathematical constructions.[8] Whatever else they are, numbers are not objects, and true mathematical multiplicity cannot be assembled from elementary units, or intuited as some kind of primordial essence or attribute (NN, 261; EE, 13). Instead, mathematics formally presents or enacts multiplicity—its axioms *decide* it.

A Platonist, then, equates mathematics with ontology itself, whereas for the Aristotelian the essence of mathematics is merely a matter of logical coherence. Where the Aristotelian seeks to formulate "the *protocol* of legitimation," the Platonist looks for "*principles* of rupture." The Aristotelian is concerned with the demonstrable integrity of mathematical forms and their application to empirical realities, that is, with the supervision of *constructions* (geometric, in the sphere of representations; algebraic, in the sphere of calculations). The Platonist, on the other hand, is more interested in what cannot be controlled or what exceeds construction. The Aristotelian position, exemplified in Leibniz's monadology, leads to a "pluralist perspectivism" whose inaccessible summit is the possibility of mutually contradictory worlds. The Platonist, by contrast, insists that although the One is not, nevertheless "being is One as regards its localization [. . . ;] there is only one situation of being" (PM, 73). In short, the Aristotelian tradition presumes a fundamental equivocity and explores (with Leibniz, Bergson, and Deleuze) the complex folds of a dynamic nature, of a vital and creative energy or élan; Badiou's Platonism, by contrast, presumes the empty univocity of pure multiplicity as the sole province of ontology.

Of course, there is nothing particularly unusual about a close articulation of philosophy and mathematics. Their mutual implication is one of the most long-standing and most fruitful constants of the Western metaphysical tradition from Parmenides to Husserl, through Spinoza, Leibniz, and Kant. Badiou's insistence that any philosophy is necessarily conditioned by what is going on in the mathematics of its day would have been as acceptable to Plato or Descartes as it is self-evident to Russell or Quine. When Badiou writes that "outside mathematics, we are blind,"[9] what he means is, in the first instance, broadly compatible with the general current of scientific opinion since Galileo and Newton.[10] In the field of contemporary French philosophy, Badiou's general approach extends that of thinkers who, like Brunschvicg, Lautman, and Cavaillès, believe that only mathematics or forms of reasoning modeled on mathematics can serve as the vehicle for "rational purity and universality."[11]

But Badiou's ontology does more than reiterate the familiar virtues of scientific precision. Badiou does not simply say that "mathematics coincides with all that is exact in science."[12] He does not just confirm the uncontroversial fact that so much of the "real world" (from radio waves to subatomic particles) is not what our senses perceive but what our mathematical theories allow us to model or reconstruct. He says that mathematics articulates be-ing itself. Mathematics does not describe, represent, or interpret being, but is, in itself, what can be thought of being *tout court*: "The apodicity of mathematics is guaranteed directly by being itself, which it pronounces" (EE, 13). Badiou's ontology is similar to that of his great rival Deleuze in at least this one respect: both set out from the classical or non-Kantian presumption that thought engages directly with true reality or being, rather than supervise the orderly analysis of phenomena or appearance. Or, as Badiou puts it in his book on Deleuze, "Not only is it possible to think Being, but there is [ontological] thought only insofar as Being simultaneously formulates and pronounces itself therein" (D, 33; cf. D, 69). The analysis of number, then, is not merely a matter of formal representation: "It is a matter of realities. . . . A number is neither part of a concept, nor an operational fiction, nor an empirical given, nor a constituent or transcendental category, nor a syntax, nor a language game, nor even an abstraction from our idea of order. Number is a form of Being."[13]

Only a mathematical ontology, Badiou believes, can answer some of the oldest questions in philosophy: Why does reality conform so precisely to mathematical description? Just how do we *know* the reality of mathematical objects—and, in particular, of infinite objects?[14] The most familiar responses to these questions effectively evade them. Mathematical constructivists insist that finite minds and infinite ideas cannot really relate in any demonstrable sense at all, while formalists reduce this relation to something resembling a meaningless game. The indispensability argument proposed by Quine and Putnam accepts that although we must indeed assume this relation if we are to make sense of well-known characteristics of our empirical world, we cannot rigorously account for it; Gödel and other realists, by contrast, rely on a somewhat mysterious kind of mathematical intuition or "sense," which allows us to perceive mathematical objects in much the way our other senses perceive physical objects. All of these approaches are couched in terms of a problematic relation between the subject of mathematical knowledge and its objects. By contrast, Badiou simply brackets this relation altogether, so as to affirm the immediate articulation of being in mathematical thought. Mathematical forms are not objects at all; they never "face" a subject. We think mathematical forms simply because they express, without recourse to linguistic approximation, what can be thought of as being as be-ing. Mathematics is not caught up in a problematic relation (of representation, or figuration, or approximation) with being; it *is* "being thought" as such. Consequently, mathematics is the purest and most general form of thought, the thought of the pure be-ing of thought, or thought in its most freely creative form, unconstrained by the mediation of any external corporality, materiality, or objectivity.[15] Mathematics is the thought of *nothing but* pure being as be-ing. Badiou's ontology thus sets off in exactly the opposite direction from that of Adorno, say, whose project begins with the deliberately humbling assumption that philosophy must abandon its belief that "being itself is appropriate to thought and available to it."[16]

To make proper sense of Badiou's position, it may be worth comparing it briefly with the celebrated analysis of a similar logic by another of his great ontological rivals: Heidegger. For what Heidegger recognized as distinctive about modern or post-Cartesian thought was precisely its *mathematical* aspect, understood in its etymological sense as that awareness presumed by any focused "grasping of things," that basic coherence we assume when "we take up things as already given to us."[17] Through mathematics, "the basic blueprint of the structure of every thing and its relation to every other thing is sketched in advance," and within this field, "bodies have no concealed qualities, powers, and capacities," that is, no qualities resistant to precise and immediate measurement (292). The triumph of mathematical reasoning and a mathematized science is thus bound up with a transformation in the very perception of what is—a transformation associated, for both Heidegger and Badiou, with the general desacralization of reality that began with the end of the Middle Ages. The triumph of mathematics presumes a critical distance from all inherited tradition and habit, the adoption of a new sort of "freedom" and mental discipline, conceived as "a binding with obligations that are self-imposed. . . . According to this inner drive, a liberation to a new freedom, the mathematical strives out of itself to establish its own essence as the ground of itself and thus of all knowledge" (296). The axiomatic and the subjective orientations of post-Cartesian philosophy are rigorously reciprocal, bound together in a decisive, aggressively atheist conjuncture: "Only where thinking thinks itself is it absolutely mathematical,"[18] and thought thinks itself only when its activity is exhausted by reference to an abstract "*I* think." Only a mathematical conception of reality allows for an abstract, self-positing subjectivity as foundational of objectivity itself. After Descartes, Heidegger went on, "the Being of beings [was] determined out of the 'I am' as the certainty of the positing" alone, and, as Kant and Husserl were eventually to confirm, only to a purely *subjective* reason can "things themselves become 'objects'" for impartial science (302–3). The upshot confirms mathematics as the final "court of appeal for the determination of the Being of beings, the thingness of things" (305).

This outcome, disastrous according to Heidegger, is nothing less than an emancipation for Badiou. All of Badiou's philosophy presumes the justice of this court of appeal. Along the way, the ancient question concerning the exact correspondence of epistemology to ontology disappears. Mathematics is not simply that discourse which most emphatically disregards the empirical realm of existence. It actively brackets, in its operation, the very distinction of the existent and the merely possible or potential. It is for precisely this reason, as Badiou reminds us, that "people have always debated the status of mathematical idealities [i.e., numbers and their relations], the status of their reality. Are they real, do they exist somewhere, are they merely possible, are they linguistic products . . . ? I think we have to abandon these questions, simply because it is of the essence of ontology, as I conceive it, to be beneath the distinction of the real and the possible. What we will necessarily be left with is a science of the multiple in general, such that the question of knowing what is effectively presented in a particular situation remains suspended."[19] To put it another way, Badiou equates ontology with mathematics because mathematics isolates the pure gesture of presentation as such, that is, the presenting of something such that the question of what exactly this presented thing is, let alone what it re-presents, never comes up. Numbers differ from one another, clearly, only in terms of multiplicity (and not "in" something else). "Arithmetic," as one historian of the discipline observes, "considers only one single property of things, namely their individuality, that is to say, their identity with themselves and their distinction from each other." The number three is clearly different from the number four or the square root of two, but these distinctions are internal to the operation of quantitative distinction itself, the pure presentation of multiplicity in its own right. This is why "mathematics presents, in the strict sense, nothing . . . except presentation itself" (EE, 13). In short, mathematics provides Badiou with a language for describing the general situation of all conceivable situations, regardless of their particular contexts or contents.

By the same token, of course, such an ontology can say nothing about the substantial being of any particular situation or any particular object. What can be said of a being as a be-ing says nothing about its material qualities (its shape, purpose, history, and so on).[20] The discourse that claims to present presentation in general must withdraw from any constituent relation with what is presented. Or again, it must present nothing other than presentation. Every nonontological situation, of course, presents precisely something rather than nothing. Any such situation presents some collection of particular beings (stars, pens, apples, people, impressions, and so on). All such beings are presentable in principle as so many groupings of units, however obscure or hard to pin down these units might be. Badiou characterizes the multiplicity of such collections as contingent or "impure," since it depends upon how the particular situation in which they appear is structured—for instance, in the case of a collection of stars, upon whether it is structured in such a way that it includes many stars, or, like our own solar system, just one star. Unlike pure multiplicity, whose criterion, as we shall see, must remain implicit and axiomatic, every impure multiplicity is counted or arranged according to an explicit and definite structure. Badiou's subtractive conception of ontology must be indifferent to every such definition and every such particularity. The founding axioms of mathematics must be arranged in such a way that it will never encounter impure multiplicity, or even define what such impurity might "be" (EE, 38). Even at its most abstract point—the point where substantial being can be considered indifferent matter in the broadest sense—the precise relation between mathematics and physical existence is thus a problem that exceeds the specifically ontological situation.[21] However the world happens to be, whatever happens to be the case, Badiou refuses to delegate properly ontological authority to the essentially contingent categories of material existence.

This does not mean, however, that Badiou's ontology has nothing to say about material or nonmathematical situations. For if ontology suspends the question of what is presented in any presentation, nevertheless "each time we examine something that is presented," Badiou explains, "from the strict point of view of its objective presentation, we will have a horizon of mathematicity, which is in my opinion the only thing that can be clear." This horizon emerges as soon as we try to think about the situation, that is, to conceive the situation with any degree of genuine precision. Most obviously,

> everyone can see that the investigation of matter, the very concept of matter, is a concept whose history shows it to be at the edge of mathematicity. It is not itself mathematical, but on the border of the mathematical, since the more you decompose the concept of matter into its most elementary constituents, the more you move into a field of reality which can only be named or identified with increasingly complex mathematical operations. "Matter" would simply be, immediately after being, the most general possible name of the presented (of "what is presented"). Being-as-being would be that point of indistinction between the possible and the real that only mathematics apprehends in the exploration of the general configurations of the purely multiple. Matter, in the sense in which is at stake in physics, is matter as enveloping any particular presentation—and I am a materialist in the sense that I think that any presentation is material. If we consider the word "matter," the content of the word matter, matter comes immediately after being. It is the degree of generality immediately co-present to ontology. The physical situation will then be a very powerfully mathematised situation and, in a certain sense, more and more so, the closer it comes to apprehending the smallest, most primordial elements of reality.[22]

Though matter itself is clearly not mathematical, there is nothing here about the be-ing of matter that might somehow resist mathematical (i.e., onto-logical) description, other than the current inadequacy of that description itself. And though mathematics is indifferent to all the myriad qualities of an existence, Badiou believes that these qualities present no significant chal-lenge to mathematization, and that they are in fact dramatically limited by comparison with the truly dizzying wealth of mathematical forms. He is fond of countering the commonplace idea that existences are somehow richer or more profound than mathematical "abstractions," by analogy with the argument that existences confined to three or four dimensions make up an altogether minuscule fraction of the realm of being explored in post-Euclidean geometries. Badiou certainly rejects any claim that a mathematical ontology cannot, for instance, grasp the creative diversity of, say, the sensual and the organic. Mathematics, he insists, is "always richer in remarkable de-terminations than any empirical determination."[23] Take that most elusive of examples, the experience of touch itself. Badiou compares, unfavorably, the imprecise sensual notions of "brushing against" or "fleeting contact" with the exact calculus of tangents to the curves of continuous functions, that is, an infinitesimal approaching or connection in one extensionless point. What is more, true mathematical invention begins only where such intuitive analogies end: he goes on to note the completely counterintuitive demon-stration (again in the wake of non-Euclidean geometries) of continuous functions that elude *any* such tangential touch. Indeed, it turns out that these paradoxical or metaintuitive functions are in fact the mathematical norm, thereby confirming a kind of "general law, that wherever mathematics comes close to experience, pursuing its own movement to its end, it discov-ers a 'pathological' case that absolutely defies the initial intuition—only to confirm that this pathological case is in fact the rule, and that the intuitable case is the exception" (8).

Stripped of its inaugural reference to the mysterious aura of appearances or things, purified of any quasi-sacred, quasi-poetic investment in the pleni-tude of nature, Badiou's ontology thereby adheres to at least one essential premise of modern analytic philosophy: it deprives traditional metaphysical speculation of its ultimate justification, the mandate it inherited both from the presocratic poem and from a postsocratic theology, namely, its preten-sion to coordinate its judgments directly with an intuition of the profound nature of being. What can be said of be-ing as such is not the business of phi-losophy per se. So Heidegger's own version of the question of Being—Being as precisely that which cannot be incorporated through mathematization,

Being as that which cannot be grasped, or can be grasped only by letting be, by passive exposure to the "clearing" in which things can be glimpsed in their "unconcealment"—cannot even be posed within the contours of Badiou's philosophy.[24] Badiou's ontology evacuates it and its various (aesthetic, ethical, political) implications in advance, just as it reinvigorates a general conceptual resistance to Romanticism, broadly understood. This is no coincidence: Romanticism began precisely when Hegel, against Descartes and the rationalist tradition, divided mathematics from philosophy (C, 159, 172–73): "The Romantic project implies the dismissal of mathematics, since one of its aspects is to render philosophy homogeneous with the historical power of opinion," with the dialectical movement carried by "the 'spirit of the age'" (C, 168). Badiou's ontology does nothing less than deprive this whole movement of its very foundation in being.

In much the same way, Badiou's ontology severs the old dialectical relation of the in-itself and the for-itself. In an essay on Sartre dated 1990, Badiou explains that "for a long time" he had followed his mentor's conception of pure being as in-itself *(en-soi)*, as "the painful opacity of the chestnut tree's root [in *La Nausée*], as massivity, as the 'too much,' the practico-inert," an impenetrable backdrop to the actively negating for-itself *(pour-soi)* of free consciousness, forever wrestling with the tempting passivity of bad faith. "What allowed me to escape all this—and woke me from my Sartrean slumber," he declares, "was an interminable meditation on set theory." The new approach at once dissolved the problem of an anguished authenticity confronted with the viscous opacity of the in-itself. No more was an empty and indeterminate freedom to be faced with the "absolute plenitude and unadulterated positivity" of being.[25] From then on, *both* subject and be-ing would be based on that "nothing" or absence of positivity that is the medium of pure thought. By the same token, whereas Sartre's in-itself remained ultimately unthinkable, deprived of any raison d'être, by confiding being to mathematics "we expose it, on the contrary, to the most subtle, most ramified form of thought there is, even as we subtract it, at the same time, from all experience."[26]

In other words, since a mathematical materialism is immediate to being—and this is its great advantage over a dialectical or historical materialism—it is entirely subtracted from the operations of perception and description, just as it is indifferent to all matters of opinion or social action.[27] The forms, succession, and operations of be-ing are all intrinsic features, consequences of its own nature.[28] Mathematics is thus "the only discourse that 'knows' absolutely what it is talking about," because it is withdrawn from the irreducibly dubious relation between subject and object. Deprived of an object and constituted entirely through itself, literally ex nihilo, mathematics is the only discourse to have "a complete guarantee, and the criterion, of the truth of what it says" (EE, 15).

Such is indeed the exclusive privilege of a purely literal discourse (C, 286; cf. MP, 56–57). As Lacan used to say with evident admiration, "Mathematics uses a language of pure signifiers," a language free from any "signifying mythology" (S3, 258/227). And Badiou's equation of mathematics with the literal articulation of multiplicity is no doubt the most striking philosophical illustration of Lacan's thesis that "the signifier doesn't just provide an envelope, a receptacle for meaning, it polarises it, structures it, and brings it into existence ..." (S3, 295–96/260). Mathematical formalization is the closest approximation of a "pure" or nondialectical writing, that is, a writing without any constitutive or figurative reference to an object. Mathematical forms are nothing other than pure inscriptions, because pure inscriptions are nothing other than being thought. Being cannot be intuited (Bergson), phrased (Lyotard), or actualized (Deleuze). At most, being can be inscribed, subtractively, without presence, in the formal presentation of mathematical writing.[29]

The One or the Multiple?

So much for the question of numbers or things. No sooner have we accepted the ontological priority of number, however, than a second and no less fundamental question arises: Which sort of number comes first, the one or the many, unity or multiplicity? Ever since Plato's *Parmenides,* Badiou maintains, classical metaphysics has been unable to reconcile these two categories. For if be-ing is one, that which is not one—that is, the multiple—must not be. But the beings we can present to our minds are presentable precisely as multiple and variable beings: presentation itself is clearly multiple. If be-ing is one, it appears that presentation itself must somehow not be. On the other hand, if be-ing is multiple, it would seem impossible to conceive of a presentation as *a* single presentation, that is, as one be-ing. Badiou's way out of this conceptual quagmire is to accept that be-ing is not one, while recognizing nevertheless that ones are made to be: *"L'un n'est pas"*—There is no be-ing of the one—but *"Il y a de l'Un,"* a statement whose meaning might be best rendered as "There is a One-*ing*." The one is not, but there is an operation that "one-ifies" or makes one. There is no one; there is only an operation that *counts* as one (EE, 31–32). And if the one is not, only the multiple is.

As we might expect, this conclusion is not so much justified by way of a neo-Aristotelian investigation of reality (in order to verify its actual multiplicity) as it is decided from the outset (in order to found any subsequent investigation). It is perfectly possible, of course, to make the opposite choice. What Badiou calls the "ontology of Presence" (as distinct from an ontology of presentation) turns on the assumption that beyond the multiplicity that mathematics presents there lies the One, cloaked in an aura and vested with an intensity that no reasoned concept or presentation can convey. All the same, since the being of this One is itself unpresentable, since it must be a One beyond being in the broadly neo-Platonic sense, both ontological approaches agree that its status must depend upon a decision rather than upon a perception or demonstration. And both decisions agree, in their own way, that if it is at all, this One must in a certain sense be a nothing, or not-be. As we shall see, "above" or "behind" the structured presentation that is the mathematical situation, the mathematician, like the metaphysician, can acknowledge only the nothing of pure inconsistency, the characteristic of quantities that cannot coherently be considered *quantities* at all (such as the unthinkable quantity that would include every possible quantity). It is perhaps no accident that the same man who invented the theory of consistent sets, Georg Cantor, also fervently believed that the inconsistent quantities that elude any coherent quantification point directly, in a sort of metamathematical confirmation of negative theology, to the absolute infinity of a transcendent God.[30]

Badiou, for his part, contents himself with the realization that if we decide that ontology exists, we cannot consistently invest nonbeing with any quality other than nonbeing pure and simple. And he thereby concludes, once and for all, that God does not exist, and that there is no concept of infinity other than that which Cantor himself called the merely transfinite, or mathematically infinite. As soon as we accept a mathematical rather than a metaphysical or "ethical" conception of infinity, the very notion of a (divinely) inclusive "One-All" is made irredeemably incoherent: there can be no largest possible number, for any attempt to specify such a number leads immediately to paradox and the derivation of ever larger numbers (through multiplication or addition, for instance). Badiou's philosophy, we might say, is ontologically atheist. The only genuine alternative is indeed, as Levinas understood with particular clarity, to accept instead that ontology itself is incoherent and so cannot fulfill the role of first philosophy—a move that prepares the way for an effective dismissal of philosophy by religion.

L'Etre et l'événement begins, then, with the decision that the one is not, and once we have made this decision it follows that multiplicity is "the general form of presentation" (EE, 31, 550). Why does it follow? Because if the one is not, only what is not one, or multiple, can be. What is, insofar as it is, must purely and simply be multiplicity, that is, multiplicity "reduced, in the absence of immanent unification, to the sole predicate of its multiplicity"

(CT, 34). Nevertheless, it remains the case that every presentation of multiplicity is indeed *a* presentation: multiplicity, which is the being of presentation, is always presented as *a* multiplicity, as a multiplicity that has been "put into one," or "counted as one." The one is not, but every presented multiplicity is presented as one-ified. Such one-ification does not affect the be-ing of what it counts, which remains pure (or "inconsistent") multiplicity. But it constrains, and constrains absolutely, every presenting of be-ing. Nothing can be presented that is not presented as one. And conversely, whatever is thus presented as one—whatever can thus be counted as one—shows itself for that very reason to be not one, that is, multiple. The one is not, precisely because ones, unifications, come to be as *results*.

Now if every unity or one is conceived as the result of an operation, it seems plausible to conclude that the undefined, intraoperational "stuff" upon which this operation operates must itself be multiple. This is all very well, the skeptical reader may object, but how can we demonstrate that whatever is not one actually *is* multiple? Badiou is quite happy to admit that we cannot. Pure multiplicity cannot be defined, precisely because it is not accessible as a unity. Moreover, though such mathematical multiplicity characterizes what can be said of being as be-ing, we cannot thereby conclude that being itself (what is presented) is multiple, since "the multiple is a characteristic of presentation alone." Be-ing is multiple, so to speak, insofar as it is presented to thought. But though we can certainly decide that what is presented of being is multiple, we cannot say that substantial being itself "is either one or multiple" (EE, 32). And this for the simple reason that actual beings are clearly not themselves numbers. Badiou's ontology is not a fanciful return to Pythagorean speculation. The substantial being of beings (pens, pigs, trees, stars, etc.) cannot meaningfully be considered either one or multiple, since these categories apply only to mathematical forms. Badiou's point is that the qualities of such a substantial being put no constraints on what can be presented of its pure be-ing, that is, on what can be said of this being as a one-ified multiplicity. His ontology stands or falls on the validity of this distinction. (A philosopher like Deleuze, by contrast, who makes the opposite ontological choice, must resist this opening move: as Deleuze understands it, the strict univocity of being requires us to think the pure be-ing of a tree, say, along with and in the same sense as all the other qualities or affects expressed by such a being: its green-ing, its wooden-ing, its sway-ing, and so on.)

"Multiple of Nothing": The Proper Name of Being

Substantial being itself, then, is indifferent to every counting as one, that is, to every structured presentation. This certainly implies that "being has no structure" (EE, 34). It does not mean, however, that ontology itself has no structure, and thus that only a metastructural intuition of being will allow access to the hidden or chaotic intensity of its presence. Pursuit of this option, which culminates in mysticism and negative theology, is barred by Badiou's insistence that, though being itself has no structure, what can be presented of being itself must be a situation, where a situation is defined as a "structured presentation of multiplicity" (EE, 34–35). Structured means to be presented according to a consistent process of one-ification, a coherent counting as one. And multiplicity describes, as we know, the be-ing of what is thus counted. Since this quality of be-ing cannot be derived from the substantial nature of beings, however, we come back to our central point: the multiplicity of be-ing must be asserted or postulated: "The precise relation of mathematics to being is entirely concentrated—for the era to which we belong—in the axiomatic decision that authorizes set theory" (EE, 12). Badiou can take comfort, however, in the necessity of this axiomatization: "Because it must think the purely multiple without recourse to the One, ontology is necessarily axiomatic."[31] Only nothing, strictly speaking, can be presented as not one, or as pure multiplicity. Once again, since nothing has no qualities, the attribution of unity or multiplicity cannot be derived from an inspection of the nothing. So what mathematics must do, very precisely, is impose this attribution, and it can do so only by literally *calling* the nothing multiple—by giving be-ing the proper name of "the multiple of nothing."

How are we to make sense of this seemingly perverse piece of reasoning? Bear in mind the following points. First, whatever is presented must be presented as one, that is, it must be structured in such a way that it can be counted as a one: Badiou defines a situation, in the most general sense, as the result of any such structuring or counting operation. To exist is to belong to a situation, and within any situation there is normally no chance of encountering anything unstructured, that is, anything that cannot be counted as a one. Second, we know nonetheless that this operation is a result, and that whatever was thus structured or counted as one is not itself one, but multiple. Although the being of what was thus counted cannot be presented as the inconsistent multiplicity that it is, its multiplicity continues to hover like a shadowy "phantom" or remainder on the horizon of every situation (EE, 66). But because it is unpresentable, this multiplicity must figure from within the situation purely and simply as nothing. As far as any situation is concerned, there is simply nothing that resists the operation of the count, nothing that cannot be presented as a one, as a particular person or thing.

All the same (and this is a third point), this nothing cannot amount to a mere absence of being, since its positive existence, over and beyond the horizon that circumscribes the situation, is a necessary implication of the (counting or structuring) operation that makes the situation what it is. It is perfectly coherent, then, to affirm the being of the nothing. The nothing *is;* it is not mere nonbeing. As a nothing, however, this being clearly cannot be described or defined. The nothing can never be identified in a situation; it cannot belong to a situation as one of its elements or places (as nothing, it clearly cannot itself be counted as a one). A situation simply implies its indiscernible existence, as in some obscure sense indistinguishable from the very "stuff" structured and discerned by that situation, but which in itself remains unstructured and uncounted (EE, 67–68). This nothing, which Badiou calls the "void *[vide]* of a situation," is the unpresentable link that connects, or "sutures," any situation to its pure be-ing. The void is what connects any particular counting operation (any particular situation) to the ungraspable inconsistency that it counts. Or again, the void is the normally inaccessible access to the pure inconsistent being of a situation, an access that can never normally be presented within the situation, never identified, one-ified, or located. (What Badiou will then go on to argue is that access to this void can become exceptionally—and always retrospectively—possible in the wake of an *event,* where an event is defined as something uncountable or non-one-ifiable, a sort of "ultra-one," which disrupts the normal counting operations that structure the situation.)

The void is thus all that can be presented, within a situation, of pure, inconsistent multiplicity, or be-ing. And since ontology is the presentation of presentation, it can just as well be redescribed as the presentation of the unpresentable, or as the presentation of nothing. This is what Badiou means when he calls his a "subtractive" ontology: what can be said of being as be-ing can be said only insofar as being is held to be inaccessible to the categories of presence, perception, intuition, or experience.[32] Being can be articulated only insofar as we can assume, very literally, that nothing is all we can say about the substance of being. Indeed, were ontology to present something other than nothing, it would require some means of distinguishing this otherness from nothing, that is, some means of counting or distinguishing the nothing as such. Since this is impossible, ontology must be arranged in such a way that all the elements it presents are "made" pure and simply of nothing, that they figure as so many compositions of the void. Only by counting multiples of nothing is it possible to avoid the alternative, of counting multiples of ones (which, we know, are not).

In this way we come back to our previous conclusion: if the multiplicity of be-ing cannot be positively presented, if multiplicity as such can be presented only as nothing, the multiplicity of this very nothing must be declared or assumed. It is the active presenting of the nothing that must proclaim itself as multiple. The nothing, which is itself neither one nor multiple, must be given a name that establishes it as multiple. And since it is indeed nothing that is being named in this way, the name must be a proper name in the strictest sense of the term. It must be a name that invents, literally ex nihilo, the characteristic (multiplicity) that it names, without distinguishing this characteristic from any other and without pretending to subsume the being named in this way within the conceptual extension of this characteristic (since this would restore the one, in the form of this very characteristic). The naming must present the unpresentable as multiple without its ceasing to be unpresentable: the name must remain the name of precisely nothing. Which is to say that ontology can begin only with the "pure uttering of an arbitrary proper name," a wholly implicit name that, "indexed to the void," can provide us with the true "proper name of being" (EE, 72). This name presents the void as multiple. It presents a multiple of nothing—or, in set-theoretic terms, an empty set. As we shall see, every presentable set is always a multiple of multiples, a collection of pure multiples: the empty or unpresentable set, written Ø, is thus a set that has the unique characteristic of collecting nothing, of being the multiple of nothing.

To sum up, we have established that while every presented multiple must indeed be *a* multiple, that is, a consistent multiple, a multiple coherently counted as one, nevertheless the true ontological foundation of any multiple being is not its "consistency—and thus its derivation from a procedure that counts as one—but its inconsistency, that is, a multiple deployment that no unity can assemble" (EE, 53). Though it can only be presented within any situation *as* nothing or void, pure inconsistent multiplicity is irreducible to mere nonbeing. The void is just the name of inconsistent multiplicity within a situation: "nothing" names all that any situation can directly present of inconsistency. Inversely, whatever names inconsistency or be-ing for a situation must remain nothing for that situation. Nothing is presentable about this name, other than the necessary implication of its referent (inconsistent multiplicity) beyond or behind the horizon of the situation (EE, 109).

Actual and Potential Infinity: Cantor's Intervention

Before moving on to consider the details of Badiou's ontology (in the next chapter), this is perhaps the best time to introduce in their own right the two most general consequences of his mathematical turn—his commitment to an infinity both actual and axiomatic, and his campaign against any constructionist or intuitionist conception of truth. This will require a brief detour into the ontological universe opened for exploration by the undisputed founder of modern mathematics, Georg Cantor. This opening is perhaps the single most important "condition" of Badiou's philosophy as a whole, and it demands careful (though minimally technical) attention.

That "every singular human life is an uncountable infinity" (SP, 10) can mean one of two things. That we are substantially infinite, infinite in the intensity or plenitude of our tangible experience, in our perception of reality, or in our appreciation of nature is of course an old Romantic motif and one that mainly belongs to an aesthetic orientation (Van Gogh's "vertigo of the infinite," Miro's "Towards the Infinite," and so on).[33] Its great modern locus is the sublime, and its logic is consistent with ultimately religious notions of transcendence (the dreadful infinity of the divine beyond). By contrast, a purely subtractive conception of the infinite implies no such intuition or experience. That we are subtractively infinite simply means that what we do as subjects, without any reference to an object, has infinity as its dimension. We are infinite because we think infinitely.[34] We are infinite, most obviously, because we can think mathematically, that is, because we can think the being of infinite quantities or sets.

But what is the existential status of such infinity? Is it best described as real or ideal? Is it the actual dimension of an actual process, or can it only indicate the virtual limit of any actuality? It is precisely the achievement of post-Cantorian mathematics to have finally answered, at least up to a point, the ancient question of the relation between "actual" and "potential" conceptions of infinity, and with it, the relation of the finite and the infinite more generally. While speculative metaphysicians had long invested actual infinity in something "supremely adequate, autonomous, all-transcending"[35]—the divine One beyond being of the *Parmenides* and the *Aenneads,* along with all its theological variants—Aristotle's refusal to accept the existence of anything actually infinite (or "nontraversable") in physical nature conditioned the expectations of mathematicians for centuries to come. Mathematicians restricted themselves to the more prosaic conception of the infinite as a pure horizon indicated, beyond the limits of number, by the succession of "one thing after another" $(1, 2, 3 \ldots n)$. Descartes summed up the pre-Cantorian consensus: "Since we are finite, it would be absurd for us to determine anything concerning the infinite, for this would be to attempt to limit it."[36] Philosophers from Zeno to Bergson, as Russell noted in the immediate aftermath of Cantor's work, had "based much of their metaphysics upon the supposed impossibility of infinite collections."[37] This impossibility had conditioned Kant's division of pure from practical reason, for instance (a division transcended only through the sublime presentation of the unpresentable), just as it had Hegel's distinction of a "good" (or metaphysical) from a "spurious" (or mathematical) infinity.

The metaphysical tradition as a whole was then thrown into question with Cantor's "definite solution of the difficulties" associated with the infinite, his "precise definition of infinity." Almost "all current philosophy," Russell wrote, "is upset by the fact (of which very few philosophers are as yet aware) that all the ancient respectable contradictions in the notion of the Infinite have been once and for all disposed of."[38] For the first time in history, Cantor proposed "an exact science of the infinite," thereby conquering "for the intellect a new and vast province that had been given over to Chaos and old Night." His achievement, Russell declared, was "probably the greatest of which the age can boast."[39]

Badiou—and the balance of modern mathematical opinion—endorses Russell's enthusiastic assessment. Cantor's axiom of infinity has "nothing obvious about it," Maddy notes, but it was this "bold and revolutionary hypothesis that launched modern mathematics."[40] Cantor's was "a wildly radical and altogether unprecedented step."[41] His accomplishment, another commentator writes, "was monumental: he made the study of infinity precise. ... His work went so counter to the ideas of the time—infinity is out there where you cannot get at it, there is only one infinity, and nothing infinite can truly be said to exist anyway—that he was bitterly fought by philosophers, mathematicians, and even theologians."[42] As David Hilbert (the leading mathematician of the immediately post-Cantorian generation) put it, Cantor's transfinite set theory was "the finest product of mathematical genius and one of the supreme achievements of purely intellectual human activity." No one, he famously concluded, "will succeed in driving us from the paradise Cantor created for us."[43]

The technicalities of Cantor's theory need not concern us here. What matters is that he found a way of conceiving the infinite not simply as "the indefinitely growing" but "in the definite form of something consummated, something capable not only of mathematical formulation but of definition by number."[44] He was able to demonstrate the existence of different infinite numbers, that is, different *sizes* of infinity, conventionally written $\aleph_0, \aleph_1, \aleph_2. \ldots$ In particular, he showed that the infinite set of all "denumerable" numbers (i.e., all the natural numbers and fractions), or $\aleph_0$, was dwarfed by a still larger set made up of these along with real (irrational and transcendental) numbers, written c. The real numbers play a fundamental role in physical science, since they allow for the calculus of motion and continuous variation: the set of all real numbers c is the set mathematical convention ascribes to a complete numerical description of the so-called geometric continuum (the "set of all points on a line"). The size of the continuum can thus be shown to be infinitely larger than the infinite set of all natural and rational numbers. At the same time, from our first, denumerably infinite set, it is an apparently simple matter to construct a further infinite series of ever larger sets, each one exponentially larger than its predecessor: starting from the denumerable set of all natural numbers, $\aleph_0$, we can generate an endless sequence of ever-larger infinite numbers:

$$\aleph_0, 2^{\aleph_0}, 2^{2^{\aleph_0}} \ldots$$

Perhaps the most famous of Cantor's proposals—and the most crucial for Badiou's philosophy—concerns the precise relation between these two orders of magnitude. In a celebrated proof, Cantor was able to demonstrate that c is equal to $2^{\aleph_0}$. Might, then, this number c, the number of all real numbers, itself be equal to $\aleph_1$, that is, the number defined as the next largest infinite number immediately after $\aleph_0$? Cantor was convinced this must be so, and what is known as his "continuum hypothesis" (or CH, for short) states that the size or cardinality of the second, next largest, infinity $\aleph_1$ must be nothing other than the cardinality of the power set of the first, denumerable, infinity. If CH is true, then $\aleph_1 = 2^{\aleph_0}$.

This apparently abstruse conjecture has vast ontological implications. It asserts an orderly, well-defined relation between the conventional measuring system of mathematics (the numerical hierarchy of alephs) and the real numbers of physical science.[45] If this continuum hypothesis were true, not only would there be (*pace* Bergson) a precise, measurable link between physical continuity and number, but everything within the transfinite universe could be thought of as in its appropriate place, as occupying degrees in a clearly ordered hierarchy. The power set sequence $\aleph_0, 2^{\aleph_0}, 2^{2^{\aleph_0}} \ldots$ would coincide with and exhaust the transfinite numerical sequence $\aleph_0, \aleph_1, \aleph_2 \ldots$. The numerical universe in which CH holds true would be, so to speak, the smallest, most rigorously ordered transfinite universe possible (an implication eventually confirmed by Gödel). On the other hand, if CH cannot be proved, there is at least one infinite number, $2^{\aleph_0}$, that cannot be assigned a definite place in the cumulative hierarchy. Looking at the equation the other way around, if CH is not true, the smallest infinite power set ($2^{\aleph_0}$) is in a kind of pure, immeasurable excess over the set $\aleph_0$ itself. A universe that denies CH would thus accept a constituent degree of ontological anarchy. It would tolerate the existence of sets that could not be assigned any clear place in an order that would include them.[46]

Cantor himself was unable, to his growing despair, to prove CH. After decades of speculation, in 1963 Paul Cohen confirmed that CH is indeed independent of the basic axioms of set theory, if not (as Cohen himself suggested) "obviously false."[47] Mathematics itself thus points directly to an irreducible excess of being beyond "objective" measurement, and a further theorem, formulated by Easton in 1970, confirms the virtually absolute radicality of this excess: $2^{\aleph_0}$ *may* be equal to $\aleph_1$, but it may just as well be equal to $\aleph_{18}$ or $\aleph_{\aleph_{18}}$ ... (EE, 307–9, 559). In short, the science of number points to a fundamental discrepancy between pure being as being, on the one hand, and, on the other, what any science of being can measure or number. The problems associated with measuring the continuum (or with numbering $2^{\aleph_0}$) figure as an "intrinsic obstacle" to mathematical formalization, as its own internal and irreducible point of impasse. Or, in Lacanian terms, the seeming impossibility of measuring the numerical continuum is the real of mathematical measurement itself.

It was Badiou's laborious engagement with the implications of this real, as he explains, that first led him to the equation of ontology and mathematics (EE, 11). Along with Cantor's initial discovery, Badiou includes Cohen's result among the great conceptual events of our time, and it was perhaps the single most important event to have shaped the composition of *L'Etre et l'événement*.[48] As far as Badiou is concerned, "Cohen's theorem completes ... the modernity opened by the distinction between thought and knowledge" (C, 203). In Cohen's own words, his work demonstrates that CH is "a very dramatic example of what might be called an absolutely undecidable statement."[49] CH cannot be deduced from more primitive assumptions: it is a matter of pure and unguided choice. After the work undertaken by Cohen, Gödel, and Easton, among others, we know that at infinity—more precisely, at the point numbered $2^{\aleph_0}$—"we must tolerate the almost completely arbitrary situation of a choice.... That quantity, this paradigm of objectivity," Badiou affirms, "leads to pure subjectivity, this is what I would happily call the Cantor-Gödel-Cohen-Easton symptom" (EE, 309).

It may be worth emphasizing, for readers unfamiliar with this material, that Badiou's position here is anything but idiosyncratic. The precise implications of the power set axiom—the axiom that takes us from $\aleph_0$ to $2^{\aleph_0}$—have been the subject of vehement and unresolved controversy ever since Cantor first introduced it as a solution to the problem of conceiving the real numbers (the continuum) as a coherent set. It is a strange and remarkable fact, that no-one has yet figured out a way of relating this new quantity to a well-defined numerical scale. Since its introduction, all manner of proposals have been put forward so as to limit the size of this new set of subsets (and with it, the size of the consistent set-theoretic universe as a whole). But as the most thorough account of this effort concludes, "The extent of an infinite power-set is indissolubly linked to the *unlimited* extent of the [mathematical] universe."[50] No limitation of size, no principle of constructibility, serves to measure its consequences. Indeed, if CH cannot be confirmed, "we have no positive reason to assume that even only *one* application of the power-set axiom to an infinite set will not exhaust the whole [numerical] universe." In other words, we seem compelled to accept that "the power-set axiom is just a mystery. Axiomatic set theory was constructed as much to capture the structure of Cantor's transfinite number-scale as it was to capture 'classical' mathematics. Yet we are still no closer to knowing how these domains fit together. Indeed, given the effort and ingenuity expended *since* Cantor's time, one has to say that the mystery is deeper today than it ever was."[51] This "objective" mystery is precisely Badiou's own subjective opportunity. In ontological terms, it situates what he calls the real "impasse" of being—and with it, the *"passe"* of the subject (EE, 469).

Badiou's philosophy stakes a properly fundamental claim to "the famous [Cantorian] 'paradise' of which Hilbert spoke" (CT, 37). It is this claim that grounds the full laicization (or numeration) of the infinite, and a consequent end to the Romantic or Heideggerian investment of finitude. In the wake of Cantor's intervention, it is the finite that must be defined as a derivative limitation of the infinite, and not the other way around: even if the cumulative hierarchy of numbers is built up from 0 through 1, 2, 3 . . . , it is only retroactively, in the wake of the decision that asserts the existence of an infinite number, that we can describe the sequence of finite numbers *as* finite, that is, as a limitation of the infinite sequence that leaves them behind (EE, 179). Finitude is not the natural attribute of being, but a secondary restriction that unusual circumstances sometimes force upon being. At a stroke, the pathos of a finite creature confronted with the infinite indifference of the cosmos, the heroic resolution of a Dasein facing its being-for-death, is made literally out of date. No more will it be possible to say, with Nietzsche, that "there is nothing more awesome than infinity,"[52] or, with Jaspers, that our "infinite possibilities" stem from a mysterious, transcendent source, an "inaccessible One Truth."[53] Post-Cantorian mathematics enables, we might say, an exact refutation of antiphilosophy (which is nothing other than an investment in our inability to *think* the infinite). At the same time, true thought ceases to be constrained by the confusion of objects, by the finite plurality of competing claims to knowledge: it operates in the essentially simple medium of the purely infinite or indifferent, at an absolute distance from merely statistical confusion.[54]

Formalism, Realism, Intuitionism

My account so far has been flagrantly incomplete in at least one significant respect: I have yet to describe in what sense an infinite sequence of numbers

quasi-Kantian mathematical formalism

actually can be held to form a finished totality or set. Cantor certainly showed that *if* the infinite can be considered in this way, it follows automatically that numerical distinctions apply to the realm of the infinite every bit as much as to the realm of the finite. But what is involved in this "consideration"? It is no exaggeration to say that this seemingly innocuous question has been, and to some extent remains, the major point at issue in the elaboration of the three great schools that have long divided the philosophy of mathematics. For it was quickly pointed out—in part by Cantor himself, and most famously by Cantor's great admirer, Russell—that a naive consideration of sets as so many "collectings of objects into wholes" leads to insoluble paradox, both at the upper end of the scale (as regards the impossibility of a set of all sets, or largest possible number) and at the very heart of collecting itself (as regards the set of all sets that do not include themselves). Realism, formalism, and intuitionism—the three major philosophical approaches to the foundations of mathematics—evolved in the first decades of the twentieth century as so many ways of coping with these paradoxical implications. In a striking corroboration of Badiou's association of mathematics and ontology, they divide precisely over the question of mathematical existence, over what kind of mathematical objects can be accepted as in some sense real or accessible. And for all three positions, as Maddy observes, "set theory is the ultimate court of appeal on questions of what mathematical things there are, that is to say, on what philosophers call the 'ontology' of mathematics."[55]

It is indispensable to revise very quickly the essential orientation of each position, so as to be able to make some sense of Badiou's own unusual combination of realism and formalism in what might be called an "axiomatic realism." For a formalist like David Hilbert—"the champion of axiomatics," and according to many critics "the foremost mathematician of our age"[56]—Cantor's discovery was decisive but should be limited to a purely heuristic status. "Nowhere is the infinite realised," Hilbert maintains, and the mathematically infinite is simply a necessary ideal, a quasi-Kantian regulatory concept that helps guide mathematical practice, nothing more.[57] Rather, then, than make any reference to being or existence, formalism limits itself to the rigorous manipulation of mathematical symbols, symbols whose "reality" is in turn grounded only in their own internal logical consistency. Mathematics begins with axioms justified not by their self-evident truth or approximation to reality, but by their utility, simplicity, and consistency with other equally useful and primitive postulates. Formal axioms are asserted, purely and simply.

In formalist or axiomatic set theory, consequently, a set is regarded not as an actual bundle of objects collected into a unity, but "simply as an undefined object satisfying a given list of axioms."[58] The most popular list (and the version adopted by Badiou himself) is known as the Zermelo-Fraenkel system. These axioms assert the existence of an empty set and the legitimacy of those operations (the subset axiom, the power set axiom, the axiom of infinity, and several more) that allow for the generation of the entire numerical universe from this one exclusive foundation. Among other things, these axioms preclude the existence of sets belonging to themselves and thereby avoid Russell's paradox. Thus axiomatized, set theory as such refers to nothing outside its own internal and purely abstract consistency; its subsequent, and perfectly legitimate, application to other (physical) domains is not itself considered properly mathematical at all. The price axiomatic set theory pays for this coherence is the loss of any clear sense of just "what" a set actually is. One consequence is the suspension of claims to truth and reality in the familiar sense. Within formalism, as one popular account puts it, "one cannot assert that a theorem is true, any more than one can assert that the axioms are true. As statements in pure mathematics, they are neither true nor false, since they talk about undefined terms. All we can say in [formalist] mathematics is that the theorem follows logically from the axioms."[59]

Mathematical realists, by contrast, insist that mathematical objects retain some kind of existence beyond what is required for their internally consistent manipulation. Mathematical operations are performed upon a domain whose reality may never be exhausted by these operations. Orthodox mathematical Platonists hold that a theorem is actually true or false, independent of the available means of proving it so. For instance, Kurt Gödel, the most celebrated Platonist of recent times, defends the self-evident quality of the set theory axioms, grasped via an assumed faculty of mathematical intuition every bit as basic and reliable as sensual perception.[60] That we are able, then, to conceive of apparently undecidable situations (such as Cantor's continuum hypothesis) is simply proof of how far we have to go before our powers of understanding catch up with reality. The actual infinity of this reality is here assumed as a matter of course.

Intuitionists propose a very different approach to the paradoxes of set theory. Constructivists in general (and intuitionists in particular)[61] accept as valid only those propositions that can be directly verified. The only mathematical objects with any defensible claim to reality are those that can be produced or constructed in a series of clearly defined steps: "Only by virtue of an effective construction, an executed proof, does an existential statement acquire meaning."[62] Intuitionists insist that we can know only what we have made or could in principle make. They reject, then, all formalist or classical theorems based on indirect proof (via the law of the excluded middle). The most obvious example of something that cannot be directly constructed or produced in this way is precisely an actually infinite totality, or infinite set. On this point, intuitionists adopt a version of the old empiricist approach: "Whatever we imagine is finite."[63] Beginning with Kronecker and Brouwer, intuitionists set themselves resolutely against Cantor's theory, and they still deny the existence of transfinite numbers altogether. According to Dummett, for instance, the notion of a completed infinite is one that "destroys the whole essence of infinity."[64] An archconstructivist like Wittgenstein sees in Cantor's demonstration of the nondenumerability of the real numbers a demonstration of the possible existence of some unnumbered numbers, but nothing approaching the completion of an infinite number as such.[65] As for the controversial CH, constructivists tend to conclude, again like Wittgenstein, that it is simply a badly formulated question, a question whose apparent undecidability is the consequence only of an initial confusion (the attribution of meaning and existence to meaningless, nonexistent things).

Now it should be emphasized that "*all* points of view that have been put forward as a philosophical basis for mathematics involve serious gaps and difficulties."[66] Realists cannot explain how mathematical perception works, formalists cannot explain why meaningless mathematical statements apply so conveniently to physical reality, and intuitionists cannot explain why so much of classical mathematics seems reliable and coherent. Not only are there problems with each position, but there is nothing within mathematical practice itself that can decide unambiguously which position is most legitimate. It remains, in other words, a matter of taking sides. It is precisely this taking sides that underlies what is distinctive about Badiou's own understanding of contemporary mathematics, just as it sets him firmly apart from any neo-Heideggerian form of receptivity or passivity.

A first approximation of Badiou's ontology might describe it as an amalgam of the formalist and realist positions, arranged explicitly against all intuitionist restrictions. From formalism he has adopted the strictly self-constituent character of mathematical rigor. But whereas formalists claim that "the natural numbers are mere figments of our imagination"[67] and thus deprived of any ontological significance, Badiou maintains that it is precisely our imagination or thought—a thought purified of image—that alone sheds light on the nature of pure being as being. From realism he has adopted the belief that what is at stake in Number is indeed a matter of reality, a reality whose radically "inconsistent" or disruptive power far exceeds our ability to construct and represent it. But whereas realists hold that actual mathematical objects exist in some sense independent of our ability to conceive them, Badiou equates being and thought. In the wake of axiomatization, the primordial terms "set" and "belonging" remain entirely undefined, and, as Hallett puts it, "What is left is rather the bald claim that sets exist."[68] Badiou's unprecedented move has been to erect this prescribed existence as the foundation for an articulation of be-ing as such.

Badiou's mature ontology is established, then, on the basis of three fundamental decisions. First, there is the preliminary (or "preontological") decision that opts for numbers over things: this decision prepares the way for the general equation of mathematics and ontology. Second, there is the central decision that opts for the multiple over the one: this decision is the condition for a truly modern (or "posttheological") ontology, an ontology pursued in the absence of any One beyond being. Since the multiple qua multiple cannot be presented as a one, since pure multiplicity can be presented only as nothing or void, this second decision, if it is to be rigorously maintained, requires the consequent attribution of multiplicity to the void: to choose the multiple over the one implies, in the end, the active naming of be-ing as "the multiple of nothing." This naming provides a mathematical ontology with its one and only existential link to being: as we shall see, on the basis of this one name ("multiple of nothing," or $\emptyset$), set theory develops the whole unending universe of mathematical forms. The decision to name the void as multiple (what set theory calls the null set axiom) is all that mathematics needs in order to ground these forms in existence.

A further decision is required, however, to establish that the unending universe of mathematics is indeed actually infinite. Only this third decision (what set theory calls the axiom of infinity) ensures that "every situation is ontologically infinite" (AM, 157; cf. EE, 260, NN, 75). Certainly no mathematician would be willing "to base assertions concerning the existence of infinite structures on physical considerations."[69] Actual infinity cannot be perceived as the attribute of an empirical existence: after all, even the estimated number of particles in the currently observable universe amounts to the admirably compact number of only around 10 to the power of 88. In strictly mathematical terms, infinity must be decided, because the simple construction of successive ordinal numbers (0, 1, 2, 3 . . .) can never be said to *reach* an actually infinite number.[70] If there is an infinite number, it must be imposed as a break in the continuity of numerical succession, as what set theorists call a limit ordinal. However we approach it, "the thesis of the infinity of being is necessarily an ontological decision, that is to say, an axiom" (EE, 167).

This last decision need not compel disagreement with the fact that, in Adrian Moore's words, "we *know* that we are finite." We know that as individuals we are limited in a universe that exceeds us, that remains forever "other than us."[71] We know this finitude, Badiou acknowledges, just as we know the finitude, say, of a work of art (PM, 25). Every subject, Badiou accepts, is finite. We must represent ourselves as finite: we exist, like everything else, as counted for one. But we can assert the *truth* of our infinity, we can present the infinity of what we think, precisely as a subtraction from such knowledge. Unlike the Romantics—and unlike Cantor, Wittgenstein, or Moore—Badiou does not make of the knowledge of our structured finitude a motive for reverence of an infinity that exceeds us. Such knowledge is not the spur to something else but the material through which truth will emerge. In the absence of any objective knowledge of infinity, the truth of infinity is available only to its subject.

What links all the aspects of Badiou's ontology—his formalist axiomatics, his realist claims to verification-transcendent existence, and even his insistence on the unending development of ontology itself—is thus its triply decisive foundation. At the operational foundations of Badiou's ontology we find neither revealed word nor reconstituted thing but the subject in its purest form. What comes first is the decision and its decider, the subject who asserts the axiom: the subject who decides questions beyond proof, who affirms the inconsistent medium of being, and who takes another step in the (endless) pursuit of ontological consistency.

It is thanks to this explicitly subjective orientation that Badiou has been free to make of the most flagrant problem confronted by modern mathematics his own great opportunity. This is the problem posed by the increasingly obvious partiality of mathematical knowledge. For centuries, mathematical truths had provided philosophers with their most apparently irrefutable examples; Descartes and Spinoza, for example, referred to elementary relationships in Euclidean geometry as the very paradigm of self-evident truth; Copernicus and Kepler defended the heliocentric theory with the argument that God's creation should conform to the most mathematically economical solution; both Newton and Leibniz grounded the applications of calculus on the immanent unity of a divine rationality and physical reality; and so on. As an eminent historian of the discipline reminds us, "The Greeks, Descartes, Newton, Euler, and many others believed mathematics to be the accurate description of real phenomena and they regarded their work as the uncovering of the mathematical design of the universe. Mathematics did deal with abstractions, but these were no more than the ideal forms of physical objects or happenings."[72] Over the nineteenth century, however, this comforting symmetry began to break down, beginning with the conception of purely mathematical objects, that is, objects beyond ordinary intuition, such as so-called complex numbers and geometric figures in more than three dimensions. More than anything else, the invention in the first decades of the nineteenth century of elaborate counterintuitive and non-Euclidean geometries, capable of describing properties of space as accurately as the "self-evident" Euclidean system, suggested that mathematical relationships are imposed upon rather than derived from nature.[73] As Kline observes, "The introduction of quaternions, non-Euclidean geometry, complex elements in geometry, n-dimensional geometry, bizarre functions, and transfinite numbers forced the recognition of the artificiality of mathematics . . . ; by 1900 mathematics had broken away from reality . . . , and had become the pursuit of necessary consequences of arbitrary axioms about meaningless things."[74] In other words, "there is not just one, but several different mathematics, perhaps justifying the plural 's' with which the word has been used for centuries."[75] According to many commentators, the overall effect of post-Cantorian set theory "has been to demonstrate once again the relative nature of mathematics" and to accelerate the gradual retreat from the "belief that set theory describes an objective reality."[76] The axioms that condition any given mathematical field have been widely recognized to be "arbitrary to a considerable extent."[77] In the wake of non-Euclidean geometries and post-Cantorian set theories, most philosophers have responded by shifting the focus of mathematics away from ontology (which asserts the inherently mathematical nature of reality) to epistemology (whose focus is the ultimately arbitrary nature of human knowledge). Most authorities seem to agree that "when one is engaged in pure mathematics in the modern vein, nothing is further from one's mind than ontology."[78]

Those who would invest mathematics with an essentially objective universality—rather like those *soixante-huitards* who put their faith in the historical objectivity of the popular movement—can only be dismayed by this outcome. Since what this story confirms is precisely "the subjective nature of mathematical ideas and results,"[79] however, Badiou's philosophy can at the very least make a strong claim to be conditioned by a truly contemporary conception of mathematics. Rather than seek (as did Frege, Hilbert, or Russell) to overcome the apparently irreducible partiality of modern mathematics, Badiou strives in his ontology to rise to the challenge of this partiality and confront its implications head on—to confront them, that is, through the independent creativity of axiomatic decision itself.

Before going any further, two elementary misreadings of Badiou's mathematical ontology should be dismissed out of hand. First, a "vulgar" Heideggerian reading: Badiou's recourse to mathematics has little to do with what is understood by Heidegger under the name of science or technology.[80] Badiou's recourse to mathematics cannot be diagnosed as an investment in beings at the expense of Being. Pure mathematics is supremely indifferent to the instrumental manipulation of mere objects as such. Embracing a mathematical ontology is a space-clearing gesture even more radical than Heidegger's own.

Second, Badiou's orientation is anything but sympathetic to some kind of statistical or quantitative method of analysis. Badiou cannot be accused of complicity in what Davis and Hersh, among others, attack as the unthinking "mathematisation of the world" and "the social tyranny of number."[81] On the contrary: the static mathematical description of being presents, precisely, that which any true philosophy of the subject must transcend: "What we must get beyond . . . is being, insofar as it is being."[82] Badiou readily accepts that whatever can be numbered has no real value (NN, 264), and that "the passage of a truth is signaled by its indifference to numericity."[83] The merely numerical domain is what defines the world as such, the world of opinion polls, stock options, and market research. Within the world, all that matters can be counted in terms of dollars or votes. In the end, only capitalism applauds "the rule of thoughtless numerical slavery."[84]

What has true value, by contrast, always begins with an event, or "that-which-is-not-being-as-being [ce-qui-n'est-pas-l'être-en-tant-qu'être]" (EE, 193). Every event is "absolutely supernumerary with respect to all that we are in the habit of counting, to all that we believe 'counts.'"[85] An event is something that cannot be recognized as a "one" within a situation; it is the (necessarily ephemeral) presentation of unpresentable inconsistency in a situation: an event thus reminds us of what we truly *are*, i.e., of what it is that numbers count. Our day-to-day knowledge of numbers depends upon ignorance of the truth of Number. The socioeconomic rule of number "imposes the fallacious idea of a link between numericity and value, or truth. But Number, which is an instance of being as such, can support no value, and has no other truth than that which is given in mathematical thought" (NN, 263).

Being and Truth

The next three chapters outline the central components of Badiou's mature philosophical system. Chapter 4 goes over the details of Badiou's ontology, his general theory of "situation." It includes a summary of the basic concepts of set theory, and an explanation of the crucial distinctions between belonging and inclusion, consistent and inconsistent notions of multiplicity, presentation and re-presentation, and the structure and state of a situation. Chapter 5 is concerned with the intervention, in a situation, of a subject and the truth she or he sustains. This chapter provides a comprehensive analysis of each stage of a truth procedure, from its inaugural decision (the naming of an indiscernible event) to its eventual restraint (with respect to an unnameable). Chapter 6 then more closely considers the precise axiomatic status of truth, before moving on to evaluate Badiou's response to his major philosophical rivals: Kant, Spinoza, Hegel, and Deleuze.

Badiou's Ontology

The only possible ontology of the One, Badiou maintains, is theology. The only legitimately posttheological ontological attribute, by implication, is multiplicity. If God is dead, it follows that the "central problem" of philosophy today is the articulation of "thought immanent to the multiple" (D, 12). Each of the truly inventive strands of contemporary philosophy—Badiou mentions Deleuze and Lyotard in particular, along with Derrida's "dissemination" and Lacan's "dispersive punctuality of the real"—have thus presumed the "radical originality of the multiple," meaning pure or *inconsistent* multiplicity, multiplicity that is ontologically withdrawn from or inaccessible to every process of unification, every counting-as-one.[1] For Lyotard and Deleuze, of course, such multiplicity is caught up with (the neo-Aristotelian) substantial or intensive connotations of difference, fragmentation, and incommensurability. We know that Badiou's innovation is to subtract the concept of multiplicity per se from any such reference, however implicit, to the notion of substantial differences between multiples, indeed from the very medium of the "between." Instead, "what comes to ontological thought is the multiple without any other predicate other than its multiplicity. Without any other concept than itself, and without anything to guarantee its consistency" (CT, 29).

Since the concept of the multiple is subtracted from any constituent reference to unity or units, its only conceivable foundational point must be void pure and simple, a none rather than a one. The multiple must have literally no limit, or, to put it another way, its limit must be void from the beginning. This is precisely the step that Badiou—unlike Bergson or Deleuze, for instance—has been only too happy to take. Only on this condition, only as founded on nothing or nothing but itself, can the concept of multiplicity be made properly absolute. Were the multiple to be founded on something (else)—an *élan vital*, a primordial agonism, a Creative or chaotic principle, an elementary unit or "atom"—its multiplicity would to some degree be constrained by this thing beyond its immanent logic. The multiplicity of elements in our physical universe, for example, however vast, is certainly constrained in a number of ways, not least by its origin in an inaugural Bang.

At both ends of the scale, then, Badiou's pure multiplicity must have no limit to its extension, neither intrinsic nor extrinsic, neither from above nor from below. Any such limit would reintroduce a kind of One beyond the multiple or reduce the sphere of the multiple itself to a kind of bounded unity. Pure multiplicity must not itself be made to consist. Badiou needs, in short, a theory that both confirms the multiple as unlimited self-difference and "bases" it only on the absence of a limit, that is, on the sole basis of an original nothing or void. Both requirements are fulfilled, very neatly, by contemporary set theory. As prescribed by set theory, the multiple is neither cobbled together from more elementary particles nor derived from a (divisible) totality, but multiplies (itself) in pure "superabundance."[2] Even a relatively dry textbook on the history of mathematics enthuses about set theory as "indescribably fascinating," and no one has made more of the theory's philosophical potential than Alain Badiou.[3]

The Elements of Set Theory

Badiou himself, to be sure, is a philosopher rather than a mathematician, and *L'Etre et l'événement* is a work of philosophy rather than of mathematics. If every new piece of mathematical research makes a direct contribution to the extraordinarily ramified discourse of ontology, Badiou's own philosophical project, though conditioned by this research, is concerned with the properly "metaontological" task—that is, the active identification of mathematics *as* ontology (since there is nothing within the discipline of mathematics itself that affirms this identity) and the elucidation of those properly fundamental principles that shape the general "site" of every work of ontological research (since most such research takes these principles for granted).[4] Badiou is happy to admit that set theory is now far from the cutting edge of most truly inventive ontological work, but it retains an exemplary philosophical or metaontological value as that branch of mathematics which expressly considers the nature of its objects and terms, that is, what they *are* or how they are made.[5] A survey of set theory is absolutely essential to any discussion of Badiou's work, and in working through it we shall be only reconstructing the first, elementary, stages of the abstract argument of *L'Etre et l'événement* itself. Badiou himself provides the patient reader with all of the technical knowledge required, and the initiated can certainly skip the following outline. Here, for the mathematically illiterate—those readers like myself, whose mathematical education ended in secondary school—I summarize the most basic aspects of the theory in deliberately analogical style. It is a risky technique and is certain to annoy (or worse) those familiar with the pure mathematics involved. We already know that all analogies with substantial objects or situations are in a very real sense wholly inappropriate, and can serve only to convey the basic gist of the logic involved. The analogies presented here are intended as strictly disposable pedagogical aids. What set theory itself provides is precisely a way of describing terms whose only distinguishing principle is distinction itself—the distinction inscribed by an arbitrary letter or proper name (EE, 36).

Badiou sees in set theory's nine canonical axioms nothing less than "the greatest effort of thought ever yet accomplished by humanity" (EE, 536). These axioms—of extensionality, of subsets, of union, of separation, of replacement, of the void or empty set, of foundation, of the infinite, and of choice—postulate, by clearly defined steps, the existence of an actually infinite multiplicity of distinct numerical elements.[6] Any particular set, finite or infinite, is then to be considered as a selection made from this endless expanse. At its most basic level, the modern exercise of "mathematical thought requires the presumed infinity of its place" (C, 162; cf. EE, 59). If we accept the coherence of this presumption—and this coherence is what the axioms are designed to establish, in purely immanent fashion—what a set *is* is a collection of these previously given elements, considered as a completed whole.[7] As one textbook puts it, "In set theory, there is really only one fundamental notion: the ability to regard any collection of objects as a single entity (i.e., a set)."[8] The precise number of elements involved in any such collection is strictly irrelevant to the definition, and infinite sets actually figure here as much simpler than large finite ones.[9] The elements thus collected are always themselves sets, however far we go down the scale toward the infinitely small. The sole limit or stopping point of such regression is what is defined as a purely memberless term (or "urelement"). In the strictly ontological, set-theoretic, situation, the only such term is the void or empty set, whose own existence is postulated pure and simple.[10] That the void is alone foundational means there is no elementary mathematical particle, no indivisible or "smallest possible" number: the empty set is never reached by a process of division.[11]

If all elements are sets and thus equally multiple in their being (i.e., are multiple in the "stuff" that their elements are made of, the stuff that these elements count as one), what distinguish different sorts of elements or sets are only the sets to which they in turn belong. In ontological terms, we can declare the existence of a multiple only insofar as it belongs to another multiple: "To exist as a multiple is always to belong to a multiplicity. To exist is to be an element *of*. There is no other possible predicate of existence as such."[12] As a rough analogy, consider the set of all galaxies, with its many millions of elements. Each galaxy may be said to exist as an element of this set, that is, it counts as one member of the set. "In itself," of course, what makes up a galaxy is a very large set of physical components: stars, planets, parts of planets, and so on, down to subatomic collections of electrons and quarks. But as far as set theory is concerned, such substantial realities are of no consequence: "There is only one kind of variable . . . : everything is a multiple, everything is a set" (EE, 55). Questions of scale do not apply: "Neither from below nor from on high, neither through dispersion nor by integration, the theory will never have to encounter a 'something' heterogeneous to the purely multiple" (EE, 77–78). In terms of their organization as a *set*, a set of galaxies, a set of nations, a set of algebraic letters or of molecules will be treated in exactly the same way. This is how set theory meets the ontological requirement reviewed in the last chapter, that the unity or oneness of an element be considered not an intrinsic attribute of that element but a result, the result of its belonging to a particular set. To pursue our analogy: a galaxy exists as a galaxy (as distinct from a mere group of stars) to the degree that it belongs to what we define as the set of galaxies, to the degree that it fits the rules by which that set counts or recognizes its elements.[13] Remember that what *is* is inconsistently multiple and eludes all presentation, but whatever can be presented consists as counted as one in some set (or sets).

The elements of set theory as such are not galaxies or anything else, but pure bundles of multiplicity, distinguished only by arbitrary notations. Given a set called S made up of three elements called x, y, and z, for the purposes of set theory the only thing that separates these elements is the literal difference of the letters themselves. What the letters might represent is of no consequence whatsoever. They represent, very literally, nothing at all. There is no relation of any kind between the one produced by a counting for one in a set and the "intrinsic" qualities of such a one—this very distinction has no meaning here, since the word "'element' designates nothing intrinsic" (EE, 74). Consequently, "the consistency of a multiple does not depend on the particular multiples it is the multiple of. Change them, and the one-consistency, which is a result, stays the same" (EE, 78). Take, for instance, the set defined by a national population whose elements include all of those counted for one in a particular census. The fact that an individual belongs to this set has strictly nothing to do with the particular nature or idiosyncratic experiences of the individual as such. The individual citizen belongs to the nation precisely as an arbitrary number (on an identity card, on an electoral roll, etc.). In other words, the only form of predication involved here is belonging itself. A given element either belongs or does not belong to a given set. There can be no partial or qualified belonging, and since to exist is to belong to or be presented by another set, it is impossible for an element to present itself, that is, to belong to itself. Belonging (written ∈) is the sole ontological action or verb (EE, 56).

Now then, although to belong (to a set) is the only form of predication, it is immediately obvious that those elements which belong to a set can, if we so choose, be variously grouped into distinct *parts* (or subsets) of that set, that is, distinct groups of belongings. A subset p of a set q is a set whose own element(s) all belong to q. A part or subset is said to be *included* in its set. The distinction between belonging and inclusion—and thus between member and part, element and subset—is crucial to Badiou's whole enterprise. Elements or members belong to a set; subsets or parts are included in it. (The most inclusive of these subsets—the whole part, so to speak—clearly coincides with the set itself.) For example, it is possible to establish, within the set of galaxies, an altogether astronomical number of subsets or parts of this set: for example, galaxies grouped according to shape, number of stars, age of stars, the presence of life forms, and so on. The elements of a national set can be distinguished, in the same way, according to the subsets of taxpayers or prison inmates, social security recipients or registered voters, and so on. The elements of these subsets all belong to the national set, and in their "substance" remain indifferent to the count effected by any particular subset. To belong to the subset of French taxpayers has nothing to do with the substantial complexity of any individual taxpayer as a living, thinking person. Such elemental complexity is always held to be infinitely multiple, nothing more or less.

The whole of Badiou's admittedly complex ontology is based upon this simple foundation. Before reviewing his terminology in more detail, however, it is worth pointing provisionally to three especially important theoretical consequences, which concern matters of selection, of foundation, and of excess.

In the first place, axiomatic set theory decides the basic ontological question "What is a set?" in terms of a strictly extensional (rather than what used to be called intensional) principle of selection. This was once a matter of some debate. An intensional notion of set presumes that a set is the collection of objects that are comprehended by a certain concept. The sets of prime numbers, of red things, of people living in London, are intensional in this sense. Versions of intensionality were defended by Frege and Russell.[14] In today's standard version of set theory, however, "the guiding idea is that the members of a set enjoy a kind of logical priority over the set itself. They exist 'first.'"[15] The first and most widely endorsed of the theory's axioms, the axiom of extensionality, simply declares that "a set is determined solely by its members." Under the axiom of extensionality, sets y and z are the same if they have the same elements, regardless of how these elements might be related or arranged.[16] (By the same token, every difference between two beings is "indicated in one point . . . : every difference proposes a localization of the differing."[17]) Relations between elements have no place in the set-theoretic universe as such. Considered as a set, the set {a, b, c} is exactly the same as the set {b, a, c}. As Cantor points out, we can begin talking about the mathematically relevant features of a set M, such as its size or cardinality, only "when we make abstraction from the nature of its various elements m and of the order in which they are given."[18]

This extensional or combinatorial conception of set ensures the entirely open-ended character of the set-theoretic universe. Since the only requirement for the construction of a set or collection is the presumed "priority" of collectible elements, as Penelope Maddy confirms, "every possible collection can be formed, regardless of whether there is a rule for determining which previously given items are members and which are not."[19] Sets are determined solely by their elements. Just how these elements are brought together, in the extensional conception of set, is a perfectly open question: the possibilities can include, as a matter of principle, every conceivable intensional selection, as well as purely haphazard selections made without reference to any concept at all. The extensional selection may conform to a property or may be determined by a completely random choice.[20] Mary Tiles suggests a useful illustration: "Faced with a page of print one cannot say how many objects there are on it. One needs to know whether to count letters, words, sentences, lines, etc."[21] An intensional approach to the enumeration of the sets included on such a page would seek to specify the (vast) range of definitions distinguishing letters, words, sentences, and lines, before "counting" the elements that fall under each definition—say the number of words beginning with e, the number with three letters, the number with Latin etymologies, and so on. An extensional approach would accept the validity of any sort of "combinatorial" approach to collections—every possible intensional selection, as well as purely arbitrary collections, such as the set of words enclosed by a rough circle drawn on the page.

Relative tolerance of such an open conception of "being-with" is a characteristic indication of the differences between Badiou's classical approach to mathematics and the intuitionist approach he so staunchly opposes. Intuitionists refuse to accept a purely extensional understanding of infinite sets, just as they deny many applications of the axiom of choice.[22] An intuitionist conception of set requires a well-defined principle of construction, that is, clear criteria for members' belonging. But intuitionism is resisted (for compelling reasons) by the great majority of working mathematicians, and it is Badiou's conviction that people, like numbers, are not constructible in the intuitionist sense. Seen through Badiou's ontological lens, the human universe is one where absolutely no criteria of membership or belonging apply. Badiou's ontology recognizes no constraints (social, cultural, psychological, biological, or other) as to how people are grouped together. It remains the case, clearly, that at this particular moment in history our dominant groupings are indeed national, religious, ethnic, or otherwise communal, but—from the ontological point of view—this dominance is strictly contingent. There is nothing about people, Badiou presumes, to suggest that they should be grouped in one way rather than another. As a rule, the most truly "human" groupings (i.e., those most appropriate to a purely generic understanding of humanity) are those made in the strict absence of such communal or social criteria.

In the second place, for any particular set to be "founded" means, in set-theoretical terms, that it has "at least one element which presents nothing of which it itself presents" (NN, 93). The foundational term of a situation is that element to which, as seen from within the situation, nothing belongs (i.e., has no members in common with the situation). As an apparently nondecomposable term, this term figures as the most elementary or basic element of the situation, the term upon which all recognizable or situated belonging is based: as far as the situation is concerned, it cannot be broken up into still more fundamental constituent parts. In a situation made up of sets of books, a single book would serve as this foundational term: so would a single musical note in situations made up of sequences of notes. The set of living things offers another example. This set includes elements on several levels of complexity, from ecosystems and species to organisms, to the organs and cells of the organism, and perhaps to certain components of the cell (mitochondria and so on), but at a certain point of cellular organization there are elements (mitochondria, say) whose own elements (proteins, membranes, biochemical structures) are not themselves elements of the set of living things. Such biochemical structures are *fundamental* to the set of living things—they are that upon which living elements are built, but are not themselves living (NN, 92–93). In the case of mathematical entities, only the postulated empty set can play this foundational role. Since the empty set has no elements by definition, any set that includes the empty set is founded in this sense: it includes something with which it has nothing (no elements) in common.

A direct ontological consequence of this principle is that no (founded) set can belong to itself. The set of whole numbers, for instance—which is certainly well founded—cannot itself be a whole number (EE, 51, 59). A "normal" or ontologically acceptable set cannot be self-founding.[23] (As we shall see in the next chapter, what this ontological prohibition makes illegal is nothing other than an event as such.) To put things a little more formally, what is known as the axiom of foundation (addressed in mediation 18 of *L'Etre et l'événement*) states that, given a set x, there is always an element y of x, such that y has no elements in common with x. This means that, starting out from a given collection of members, we are blocked from counting indefinitely down from that set to a member of the set and then to a member of that member. Eventually, we must reach something that belongs to the set but that itself has no members that can be discerned from within that set—the empty set, or "urelement." In the metamathematical applications of ontology, this member or urelement can be anything at all, so long as it is defined as having no members in common with the set. Elementary particles might act as urelements in certain physical situations; so could an individual phoneme, say, in linguistic situations made up of sets of phonemes.

Finally, the number of possible ways of grouping together the elements of a set—the number of parts, or subsets of the set—is obviously larger than the number of elements themselves. As a consequence, and no matter what kind of situation we might consider, "it is formally impossible that everything which is included in it (all subsets) belongs to the situation. There is an irremediable excess of subsets over elements."[24] It would be hard to exaggerate the importance of this excess in Badiou's philosophy. There must always be more subsets than elements, because these subsets include not only each individual element, considered as the sole element or "singleton" of its own private subset, but also every possible combination of two or more elements—say, to stick with our national analogy, elements combined according to civil status, tax rates, criminality, levels of education or salary, or indeed according to any arbitrary criterion ("everyone with black hair," "everyone living east of the Seine," etc.). The combination of all these parts—the set made up of the subsets of a set—is in massive excess of the set itself. More precisely, given a finite set with n elements, the number of its subsets or parts is 2 to the power of n. For example, the set α with three elements, x, y, and z, has eight parts (2^3), as follows: {x}, {y}, {z}, {x, y}, {x, z}, {z, y}, {x, y, z}, and {Ø} (this last, empty, subset {Ø}, for reasons I will explain in a moment, is universally included in all sets). A set with nine members has 512 (i.e., 2^9) parts.

But with an infinite set—and all human situations are infinite—the excess of parts over elements is, thanks to the undecidability of the continuum hypothesis, properly immeasurable. So are the ontological consequences Badiou draws from this excess. This gap between α (a set that counts as one its members or elements) and the set of its subsets p(α) (a set that counts as one its included parts or subsets) indicates precisely "the point at which lies the impasse of being" (EE, 97; cf. 469). This point, whose measurement or specification is ontologically impossible, is thus the real of being-as-being.[25]

To give a rough sense of the kind of excess involved here, consider the set made up of the letters of the English alphabet, a set with twenty-six elements. Excluding repetitions, we know that these letters can be arranged in 2^{26} different ways. Allowing for repetition, they can be arranged in any number of "words," a small portion of which are listed in the most comprehensive English dictionaries available. Moving from the combination of letters in words to the combination of words in sentences, we move into a still vaster combinatorial range, a tiny fraction of which is covered by the history of the English language and the various ways it has been used. The sort of over-abundance Badiou has in mind here is a bit like that of the excess, over the relatively small collection of letters at our disposal, of all that has ever been or could have been said. Thanks to this *immanent excess* of parts over elements, Badiou—unlike Bergson or Deleuze—has no need to invoke a cosmic or chaotic vitalism in order to secure "the principle of an excess over itself of pure multiplicity," nor does he need to explore the virtual dimensions of an "indetermination or undecidability that affects all actualisation. For it is *in actuality* that every multiple is haunted by an excess of power that nothing can measure, other than . . . a *decision*."[26]

Precisely this excess of parts over members locates the place of ideology in Žižek's clear and compelling sense: "At its most elementary level, ideology exploits the minimal distance between a simple *collection* of elements and the different *sets* one can form out of this collection."[27] More specifically, the ideology of a situation is what organizes its parts in such a way as to guarantee the structural repression of that part which has no recognizable place in the situation—that part which, having no discernible members of its own, is effectively "void" in the situation. Such, Žižek continues, is "the

basic paradox of the Lacanian logic of *pas-tout:* in order to transform a collection of particular elements into a consistent totality, one has to add (or to
subtract, which amounts to the same thing: posit as an exception) a paradoxical element which, in its very particularity, embodies the universality of
the genus in the form of its opposite."[28] This element is what Žižek calls the
symptom of the situation.[29] For example, Hegel's rational-constitutional state
requires the irrational exception of the proletarian "rabble" as "an element
within civil society which negates its universal principle." Likewise, the
anti-Semitic situation requires for its coherence the phantasmatic figure of
the Jew as its intolerable Other, just as the contemporary liberal-capitalist
consensus is built on the marginalization of the variously "excluded" (the
unemployed, the homeless, the undocumented, and so on). Such symptomal
elements—rabble, Jew, immigrant—are perceived within the situation as
"absence embodied."[30] Hence Žižek's most concise "definition of ideology: a
symbolic field which contains such a filler holding the place of some structural impossibility, while simultaneously disavowing this impossibility."[31]

What Badiou calls the "site" of an event plays almost exactly the same role
in his own system, and Žižek's terminology fits it nicely: the site, or symptomal real, is both that around which a particular situation is structured (i.e., its
foundational term), and "the internal stumbling block on account of which
the symbolic system can never 'become itself,' achieve its self-identity."[32]

Consistency and Inconsistency

The distinction of consistent from inconsistent multiplicity may remain one
of the most confusing in all of Badiou's work for first-time readers, and it is
well worth going back over the essential points again here. We know (from
the previous chapter) that pure or inconsistent multiplicity is the very being of being: consistency is the attribute of *a* coherent presentation of such
inconsistent multiplicity as *a* multiplicity, that is, as a coherent collecting of
multiplicity into a unity, or one. Mathematics presents only consistent multiplicities (multiplicities collected into ones), but what these multiplicities
are ("what" is thus collected) is itself inconsistent. Mathematics is nothing
other than a (consistent) presentation of pure (inconsistent) multiplicity.[33]
And mathematics is the one and only such presentation: axiomatic set theory
is the only theory we have that allows us coherently to think inconsistent multiplicity as such. If we do not make use of this theory, we will always be forced
back to Plato's conclusion in his *Parmenides:* pure dissemination, pure oneless
multiplicity, must be unthinkable pure and simple. Only set theory can present inconsistency (EE, 44). It is this operational quality of pure multiplicity,
the fact that the presumption of inconsistency is internal to consistent presen-

tation itself and thus independent of any extramathematical "preponderance of the object," that sharply distinguishes Badiou's inconsistency from, say, Adorno's theory of the nonidentical, no less than from Heidegger's theory of Being or Deleuze's theory of intensity.

Now since mathematics works only with consistent multiples, the presentation of inconsistency as such must remain entirely indirect. Nevertheless, we know as a matter of necessary implication that since every existent one has come to be merely as the effect of some particular counting for one, what *is* (what is thereby counted) must be not-one, that is, purely or inconsistently multiple. Though it cannot be directly perceived as such, pure or inconsistent "multiplicity is the inevitable predicate of what is structured, since structuration, i.e., the counting for one, is an effect. . . . Inconsistency, as pure multiplicity, is simply the presumption that, prior to or above the count, the one is not" (EE, 32, 65). This presumption is necessary, but its necessity does not authorize us to say anything about inconsistency as such. All we can ever *know* is that "every inconsistency is in the final analysis unpresentable, thus void" (EE, 71). Strictly speaking, we cannot even know that inconsistency is actually multiple at all. Hence the unavoidable primacy of that naming of the void (which is all we can present of pure or inconsistent be-ing) as multiple, even if the void, since it is "composed of nothing, is in reality diagonal to the intrasituational opposition of the one and the multiple. To name it multiple is the only permissible solution if we cannot name it as one" (EE, 72).

The point to remember from all this is that what Badiou calls a truth or "generic procedure" is precisely a way of approaching a situation in terms of strictly inconsistent be-ing. By definition, "a truth does draws its support not from consistency, but from inconsistency. It is not a matter of formulating correct judgments, but of producing the murmur of the indiscernible."[34] Truth is irreducible to knowledge: truths will be maintained of those inconsistencies about which we *know* we can know nothing. (We are thus already in a position to anticipate three of the necessary conditions of any such truth: Since ontology can present or know nothing of inconsistency as such, a truth must first interrupt the discourse of ontology: any truth must break with what can be said of being as be-ing. Since there is normally no access to what remains void or inconsistent in a situation—since everything that is demonstrably *in* a situation is by the same token counted as one—access to this void must be both exceptional and nondemonstrable: the void will be indicated only by something that violates a situation's normal way of counting or recognizing its elements, and the actual existence of this something [this event] in the situation must depend on a decision rather than a perception or demonstration. Since only the void of a situation is nothing other than inconsistency, the only way of approaching a situation in terms of its inconsistency will be to refer its elements back to this void, that is, to test them to see if they "connect" with the exposure of its void. A collection of elements that pass this test will be one whose sole criterion is the simple be-ing of these elements themselves.)

There is one last point to be made here before we can move on. Badiou's identification of inconsistent multiplicity with the banal be-ing of all being is what guarantees the strictly secular and immanent nature of his conception of infinity, and what eliminates the transcendent connotations of the concept explicitly affirmed by Cantor himself and still widely defended today. Since the basis of this identification remains a decision, however, there can be no question of refuting or disproving the alternative approach. A full century after Cantor's discoveries, Adrian Moore's important study of the infinite (1990) reaffirms his quintessentially antiphilosophical conclusion: although we can point toward the infinite, it remains an insight "to which (we find) we cannot properly give voice."[35] Moore's response is precisely to cut the infinite off from ontological speculation altogether: "We are shown that the truly infinite exists, though in fact (as we are bound to say) it does not. It does not exist because what does exist, in other words what is, is finite. What is is what can be encountered, addressed, attended to, grasped, managed, known, defined. . . . It is what can, in some way or another, be limited. It would be an abrogation of the very concept of infinity to apply it directly to anything of this kind."[36] Moore concludes—as much like Cantor as like that great anti-Cantorian, Wittgenstein—with a quasi-reverential respect for this uncertain something beyond being, a truth beyond precise articulation or mathematization.

This is obviously a conclusion that Badiou *philosophe* must refute at all costs. Cantor was indeed right, he says, to see in inconsistency the true orientation of being. But it is wrong to conceive of inconsistency as the inaccessible limit to numerical consistency. Inconsistency is instead the "stuff" of every consistent presentation in precisely the *same* way that it lies "beyond" any such presentation. At the limits of being there is only inconsistency, that is, nothing. In other words, there simply is no limit. And since there is no limit, it must be *all* being that is inconsistent. In the absence of any God, any Outside, any absolute transcendence, being simply multiplies in an open, infinite dissemination, as if in confirmation of Lucretius's "acosmism" (CT, 36). Rather than mute testimony of a divine beyond, Badiou sees in unpresentable inconsistency the very "substance" of every consistent structure. The whole effort of Badiou's philosophy (as distinct from his ontology) has been to equate this unpresentable inconsistency or no-thing with the very be-ing of every consistent situation, but to reserve the articulation of this equation to the subject of a truth procedure. Access to inconsistency can be only subjective: though it can never be grasped as the object of knowledge, it is occasionally possible to affirm its truth.

What may remain a matter of some debate, no doubt, is the degree to which Cantor—or, for that matter, Moore, or Hallett, or even Jambet and Lardreau—would recognize the absolutely infinite as a *one* in any sense of the term. They present it instead as that inconceivable horizon of thought where all distinctions between the one and the multiple collapse. In what precise sense is the neoplatonic One beyond being, the deity of Plotinus or Suhrawardî, "one" or even one-all, rather than an indication of the limit of our ability to conceive of unity?[37] Badiou's firmly axiomatic treatment of the problem, moreover, deploys what some readers might see as effectively absolute powers of its own, that is, the exceptional power of a constitution that creates the very medium of its existence. After all, is there any more "divine" a power than that which creates consistency out of a pure inconsistency— through a mechanism that can be referred to only as a pure proper name?

Situation, State, Void

Having considered the more abstract implications of Badiou's equation of mathematics and ontology, we can move on now to detail what this equation allows him to do in practice—what it allows him to say about the elements, structure, and state of a situation in general. The simplest thing is to review the basic terms as they come up.

A Situated Theory of Situation

In *L'Etre et l'événement*, Badiou writes: "I will maintain—it is the wager of this book—that ontology is a situation," that is, that ontology is itself a "structured presentation" (EE, 35). The object of this presentation, we know, is simply the immanent logic of presentation itself. Because it is itself structured, or situated, Badiou can refuse the traditional ontotheological conclusion that what is "revealed" in the pure presentation of presentation is only a quasi-divine beyond—inconceivable plenitude, or creativity, the clearing or letting be of Being—which defies structured, systematic exploration. Badiou's fully systematic presentation of presentation is instead entirely unspecified by its content, be it divine or mundane. As a rule, "all thought supposes a situation of the thinkable, that is to say, a structure, a counting for one, whereby the presented multiple is consistent, numerable" (EE, 44). But other, non-ontological discourses (starting with physics, at the edge of mathematicity) always begin with some kind of criteria that limit what is presented, that is, what qualifies for inclusion in the situation they describe (EE, 13, 209). Such discourses begin by situating their material in a restricted sort of way. Only ontology—since it proceeds without any reference to what is situated—can claim to present a general theory of situation as such.

Situation

Like most "interventionist" thinkers (Marx, Freud, Sartre, Žižek, among others), Badiou maintains that "the singularity of situations is the obligatory beginning of all properly human action" (E, 16). Here the term "situation" is synonymous with an infinite set, such that to be presentable as existent means "to belong to a situation."[38] We know that all situations are infinite by prescription, that infinity is simply "the banal reality of every situation, and not the predicate of a transcendence.... In fact, every situation, inasmuch as it is, is a multiple composed of an infinity of elements, each one of which is itself a multiple" (E, 25; cf. E, 72). The "extraordinarily vague" notion of a situation is thus defined only by the fact that it has an infinite number of distinct components. These might include "words, gestures, violences, silences, expressions, groupings, corpuscles, stars, etc."; it is of no ontological consequence.[39] We know, moreover, that since "nothing is presented that is not counted [as one], from the inside of a situation, it is impossible to apprehend an inconsistency inaccessible to the count" (EE, 65). Whatever is presented in a situation is indeed governed by Leibniz's principle: "What is not *a* being is not a *being*" (in EE, 31, 66).

The Structure of a Situation

The structure of a situation is what specifies it as a particular situation, that is, what ensures that it presents these elements and not those. It is what distinguishes its elements as its *own* elements. A situation is simply the result of such a structuring (EE, 33). What Badiou rather loosely calls the "structure of the situation" is "the existing mechanism of the counting-for-one that qualifies the situation as being this particular situation."[40] The structure of life, for example, is made up of those operations that distinguish the elements of the set of living things from the elements (which make up living elements) of the set of nonliving, biochemical elements; the structure of the nation is whatever guarantees the belonging of its own elements while excluding the rest, and so on. As opposed to truth *(vérité)*, what Badiou calls the "merely verifiable" *(véridique)* is always a function of "structure and knowledge" *(savoir)*, that is, a correct application of the rules by which a situation identifies its elements and classifies its parts: "Of the structural statements admissible in the situation, we will never say that they are true, but only that they are verifiable *[véridiques]*. They are a matter not of truth, but of knowledge."[41]

The State of a Situation

The role of the state is a little more complicated. For both the early and later Badiou, "the state is the serious issue, the central question. . . . Every vast revolt of the workers and the people sets them against the state, invariably,"[42] and every genuine "thought is nothing other than the desire to finish with the exorbitant excess of the state" (EE, 312). Even if Badiou's most recent thinking mitigates his once unqualified determination to pursue the withering away of the state, reducing it to a minimum and foreclosing it from the properly subjective realm remain high on the list of principles that guide his philosophy.

We know that the number of parts or subsets of a set always exceeds the number of its elements, and that for an infinite set this excess is wildly immeasurable. The mere structure of a set provides no order to this excess of parts over elements. What Badiou calls the "knowledge" (savoir) operative in a situation does supply the means of arranging these parts. Knowledge is "a classifier of subsets"; its task is to discern or "name the subsets of a situation" (C, 200–201). But knowledge by itself provides no global organization to these arrangements: "Nothing is more disruptive [errant] than the general idea of a 'part' of a set" (CT, 146). Since it cannot be ordered in any obvious way, the excess of parts over elements is properly anarchic and immediately dangerous. It risks, so to speak, the introduction of an elementary disorder. Moreover, in the midst of this disorder there is nothing to ensure that the foundational void of the situation—that is, that unstructurable "something" that haunts the situation, from beyond its unpresentable horizon, as an indication of the very "substance" of its being—might not somehow erupt into the situation itself, precisely as something uncountable, anarchic, threatening. The classic historical emblem of such eruption is an uprising of the masses (EE, 127). Such breakdowns in law and order are possible in principle from within any unstructured point of a situation. And there is at least one such point in every situation, since the structuring operation that shapes a situation is unable to structure itself. The structure is not itself counted for one as an element within the situation that it structures: its existence is exhausted in its operational effect. In other words, there is always a risk that the void could somehow emerge, as the collapse or absence of structure, through the very operation that structures a situation (EE, 110–11).

The specter of the void, consequently, can be exorcized only through the operation of a second structuring principle, a sort of re-presentation or metastructuring—a structuring of the structure. This further operation will unify or count as one the operation that structures the situation itself, and it will do so by structuring every possible way of arranging its elements. That

(state classifies*

is, it will count as one not the elements of the situation but the way these elements are grouped into parts or subsets of this situation. The state or meta-structure of a set ensures that the counting as one "holds for inclusion, just as the initial structure holds for belonging."[43] The state—and Badiou uses the term in both its political and its ontological senses simultaneously—is what discerns, names, classifies, and orders the parts of a situation. In our national example, the state is of course what organizes the parts of its situation as legal residents, taxpayers, soldiers, social security recipients, criminals, licensed drivers, and so on. The state's concern is always with the parts or subsets of a situation since, elements being simply what they are, it is only the configuration of a situation's parts that can open the way to a radical transformation of that situation. In particular, though the void can certainly never appear as an element of the situation, it could always appear as an indeterminate, "inexistent" part or subset of the situation; the state is what ensures that this inexistent but universally included part will remain merely inexistent. A set-theoretic ontology thus confirms, as a fundamental law of be-ing, a central insight of the Marxist analysis of the state: the state's business relates not to individuals per se (to elements) but rather to groups or classes of individuals, and this insofar as the elements of these classes are already presented by the situation itself. That the state is always the state of the ruling class means that it re-presents, or arranges, the existing elements of its situation in such a way as to reinforce the position of its dominant parts (EE, 121–23).

The state is thus a kind of primordial response to anarchy. The violent imposition of order, we might say, is itself an intrinsic feature of being as such. The state maintains order among the subsets, that is, it groups elements in the various ways required to keep them, ultimately, in their proper, established places in the situation. The state does not present things, nor does it merely copy their presentation, but instead, "through an entirely new counting operation, re-presents them," and re-presents them in a way that groups them in relatively fixed, clearly identifiable, categories.[44]

Because the state is itself the immeasurable excess of parts over elements made ordered or objective, under normal or "natural" circumstances there is a literally "immeasurable excess of state power" over the individuals it governs (namely, the infinite excess of $2^{\aleph_0}$ over $\aleph_0$). Within the situational routine, within business as usual, it is strictly impossible to know by how much the state exceeds its elements. In normal circumstances, there can indeed be no serious question of resisting the "state of things as they are." This excess is essential to the efficient everyday operation of state business. By the same token, the first task of any political intervention is to interrupt the indetermination of state power and force the state to declare itself, to show its hand—normally in the form of repression (AM, 158–60). From a revolutionary perspective, if the excess of the state appears "very weak, you prepare an insurrection; if you think it is very large, you establish yourselves in the idea of a 'long march.'"[45] Today, of course, the power of the state is chiefly a function of the neoliberal economy. As far as any given individual or group of individuals is concerned, the blind power of capital is certainly more than immeasurable, and so "prevails absolutely over the subjective destiny of the collective" (AM, 164). One thing that any contemporary political intervention must do, then, is to keep the economy at a principled distance from politics as such.

Whatever the circumstances, the struggle for truth takes place on the terrain first occupied by the state. It involves a way of conceiving and realizing the excess of parts over elements in a properly revolutionary (or disordered, or inconsistent) way, a way that will allow the open equality of free association to prevail over an integration designed to preserve a transcendent unity. So while the distinction between structure and metastructure, or between presentation and re-presentation, might suggest that analysis begins with the first term in each pair, in actual practice (i.e., from within any given situation) the members of a situation always begin with the second term, with the normality regulated by state-brokered distinction and divisions. From within the situation, it is impossible immediately to grasp the "intrinsic," presented individuality of particular elements belonging to the situation. If any such grasp is to have a chance of success, the state's mechanisms of classification and re-presentation must first be suspended.

There are many different kinds of states. The communist-totalitarian state, for instance—in this respect like the state of the ancien régime—is one that organizes the way it counts its parts around the explicit interests of one particular privileged part, the party (or aristocracy). Our liberal état de droit, by contrast, counts without direct reference to a privileged part per se, but rather according to a perspective that works indirectly but efficiently in the interests of such a part (C, 239–40; DO, 45). The state can re-present only what has already been presented, but it does so in a certain way. In a capitalist society, of course, the state represents its elements—including and especially its "laboring elements"—as commodities, in the interests of those who own commodities. The chief task of such a state, then, is to arrange these commodity-elements into parts whose relations are governed as much as possible by the rules that preserve and regulate the ownership of property. What such a state counts is only capital itself; how people are in turn counted or re-presented normally depends upon how much they themselves *count* (in terms of capital or property). Like all states, the liberal-capitalist state defends itself against any attack on its way of arranging parts, that is, it is designed to foreclose the possibility of an uprising against property. The true alternative to our state, then, is not the invention of (or regression to) prestate forms of social ties or community, but the dissolution of all links specifically based on a binding respect of property or capital: "The state is founded not on the social bond *[lien]* that it would express, but on unbonding *[dé-liaison]*, which it forbids" (EE, 125). The *dé-liaison*, or unbonding, forbidden by the state, is itself the very operation of a truth.

It is in this way that Badiou's mature work has continued the Maoist war against the state by other, more measured, means: "To *think* a situation *[penser une situation]* is always to go toward that which, in it, is the least covered or protected by the shelter the general regime of things provides." For example, in contemporary France, the political situation (the situation that structures the nature of a specifically *French* democracy) is to be thought from the point of view of the vulnerability of the *sans-papiers* (D, 126); in Israel, the political situation must be thought from the point of view of the dispossessed Palestinians. "To count finally as One that which is not even counted [in a situation] is what is at stake in any genuinely political thought" (AM, 165). But we know, too, that Badiou is no longer waging a struggle for the strict elimination of the state. *L'Etre et l'événement* provides a properly ontological reason for Maoism's historical defeat: the state is co-original with any situation. It is objectively irreducible. If "there is always *[toujours]* both presentation and representation" (EE, 110), the task is indeed to find an alternative to this *toujours*, this everyday. Simply, such an alternative can no longer be a once-and-for-all transformation, a destructive redemption from historical time, so much as a rigorous conception of the exceptional as such, a basis for a notion of time that transcends, without terminating, the *toujours* and the *tous-les-jours*.

Badiou's goal, early and late, has been to "outline in the world an imperative that is able to subtract us from the grip of the state."[46] What has always been "invariant" about the communist ideal is precisely the "conflict between the masses and the state" (DI, 67; cf. DO, 15–19). Marxists have always sought "the end of representation, and the universality of simple presentation," an egalitarian counting for one and the unrestricted reign of the individual qua individual (EE, 125–26). To this day, "the heart of the question is indeed the reaffirmation of the state *[réassurance étatique]*," "the disjunction between presentation and representation" (EE, 149). But the whole point is that this disjunction can be tackled only subjectively and not objectively. Badiou's project persists as the "destatification of thought *[désétatisation de la pensée]*," the subtraction of subject from state.[47] For as long as his philosophy remains a philosophy of the subject, it will remain a philosophy written against the state.

Badiou summarizes the ontological distribution of terms as follows:

Structure / Situation	Metastructure / State of the Situation
Element	Subset/part
Presentation	Representation
Belonging	Inclusion
The counting for one	The counting as counted for one

Normality, Excrescence, Singularity

The relation between situation and state, or between presentation and re-presentation, can logically take one of three forms (EE, 115–17).

What Badiou calls "normality" applies when presentation and re-presentation effectively coincide: a normal element is one that is both presented and re-presented in the situation. Not only does a normal element belong to the situation, but all of its own elements also belong to the situation. Consider the example of an ordinary army platoon: the platoon belongs to its (military, or national) situation, and so do the individual soldiers who make up the platoon. The platoon is a normal subset of its situation. An entire situation is fully normal if every member of its every subset is duly recognized and classified by its state.

What Badiou calls an "excrescence" *(excroissance)* is a term that is represented but not presented in the situation. An excrescence usually corresponds to a state institution in the purest sense. Military and bureaucratic institutions provide the clearest examples (EE, 125): they are certainly included in modern historical situations and play a central role in the ways such situations are governed, but they cannot be said to be ordinary members of such situations. To take the most extreme case, if our normal army platoon was given fully covert or "special operations" status, it would continue to be included in the state but would become effectively invisible to the ordinary members of the situation. The status of excrescence also applies, exceptionally, to the initial stages of a truth procedure (EE, 377).

What Badiou calls a "singularity," finally, is a term that is presented in the situation but not represented in it. Such a term would continue to belong to the situation—its lack of re-presentation does not itself deprive it of existence—but as a fundamental anomaly, as something or someone strangely out of place, as a violation of the way things should be. Such a term can no longer be organized as a proper part of the situation. It cannot be arranged in a stable, recognizable way with other elements of the situation. The components of such a term cannot be directly confirmed or classified by the state, and the term thereby eludes its complete re-presentation. In the case of our army platoon, if one member of the platoon were to go AWOL, the state would no longer be able to count him as a part of the platoon. Such a platoon would then become a singularity in Badiou's sense, in that not all of its own members would continue to be visible in the situation to which it itself belongs (cf. EE, 194). The status of a singularity applies, as we shall see, to the inhabitants of what Badiou calls a situation's "evental site."

The Place of the Void

"The central idea of my ontology," Badiou explains, is "the idea that what the state seeks to foreclose through the power of its count is the void of the situation, and the event that in each case reveals it" (AM, 134). Before we can address the process of this revealing, we will need to go back over and complete our review (begun in chapter 3) of the void as such, which is certainly the most crucial—and most elusive—term in Badiou's system.

We know (from chapter 2) that Badiou's ontology is founded, in the set-theoretic sense of the term, exclusively and sufficiently upon the void, or, more precisely, the void as it is named or "presented" in set theory (and, in a universe in which all existence is defined in terms of sets, the void is naturally presented as an empty set). Everything that exists belongs to a situation, and everything present in a situation is counted as one; since it is not a one, a unit, the void itself can never be counted; it can never be presented. Instead, the void, or nothing, is that absent "no-thing" upon which any conceivable count or presentation is effected. Unpresentable, the void is "the very being of multiple presentation" (EE, 68, 103–4). It is thus perfectly true to say that in "a certain way, the void alone 'is.'"[48]

It remains no less true that nothing can be presented of nothing. The void can be presented not as *a* being, but only as the unpresentable link or "suture" of a situation to its be-ing (EE, 68–69; cf. CT, 158). Once again, since it is unpresentable as a being, all that the void can present is its name. It is the void as name that provides ontology with its presentable foundation, its "absolutely initial point" (EE, 59). If God is indeed dead, in the beginning there was quite simply the naming of the void, and nothing else: "There is no God. Which also means: the One is not. The multiple 'without-one'—every multiple being in its turn nothing other than a multiple of multiples—is the law of being. The only stopping point is the void."[49] That this stopping point can never normally be grasped or "reached" is simply a consequence of its being nothing. Since only nothing is not presented or counted for one in a set, we will never *find* an empty set. (Nor will we ever find, as Badiou often reminds us, the proletariat or the unconscious.) It is the pure assertion of the empty set that grounds its existence.[50]

In set-theoretical terms, the naming of the void is accomplished through what is known as the null set axiom. This axiom simply postulates the existence of a set (a multiplicity) that has no elements. From this existence all mathematical things derive, except itself.[51] While most of the other axioms of set theory govern the manipulation of already existing sets, the axiom of the void is exceptional in that upon it and it alone rests the whole derivation of presentation as such. All multiples are multiples of multiples, with the one exception of this "multiple of nothing." In other words, though to exist is to belong to a set, the axiomatic foundation of existence is itself the exception that establishes this rule: the null set axiom states, in effect, that "there exists that to which no existence can be said to belong." There exists a presentation of the unpresentable, and this unpresentable is nothing other than the very be-ing of (all other) presentation. Or again, in terms that will please readers with a taste for paradox: "Being allows itself to be named, in the ontological situation, as that whose existence does not exist" (EE, 80–81).

To put this another way, if inconsistency itself can never be presented (can never belong to a situation), what can be presented of inconsistency is just the *mark* of its unpresentability, that is, its name. Every naming takes place under the structural constraints of that place. In the fully depoeticized set-theoretical situation itself, that "the void is what can only be said or grasped as pure name" (PM, 167) means that the void is simply an empty sign or letter—by convention, the letter Ø. In terms of the theory, this letter indicates the existence of an empty set, and its own literal existence, its existence as a letter, is exhausted by this indication. Ø is thus not properly the name of inconsistency "in itself," but the name of inconsistency *according to* a particular situation, that is, as it is presented in ontology (EE, 68). The only privilege of this particular name, the ontological name, is that it presents the be-ing of naming at its most subtractive or abstract. Ontology demonstrates that, considered in its be-ing, and whatever the situation, the name of the void is a name normally deprived of all meaning and resonance, a name for anonymous namelessness as such.

By thus founding his ontology on the letter Ø, Badiou can fairly claim to fulfill Lacan's great program: "It is in this *instance de la lettre*, to use Lacan's expression, an agency *[instance]* indicated here by the mark of the void, that unfolds thought without One.... Thus is accomplished the equivalence of being and the letter, once we subtract ourselves from the normative power of the One."[52] Through the nonmediation of the letter Ø, the imposition of an empty mark, so indeed "being and nothingness are the same thing" (B, 37). On this condition, a fully univocal ontology—an ontology without any reference to the transcendent and without any reliance on figural approximation—can absorb the finite within the infinite, can be entirely "actual," and can fully absolve itself from any "poeticization." We need only accept that "the *sole* power that can be aligned with that of being is the power of the letter *[puissance de la lettre]*."[53] In its quite literal insistence on the void, Badiou's ontology is perhaps the only consistent formulation of Lacan's purely symbolic register, in which "nothing exists except on an assumed foundation of absence. Nothing exists except insofar as it does not exist."[54]

Now since it cannot be counted as one, the void clearly belongs to no situation. But—and this is an essential difference—it is for the same reason *included* in every situation. As the suture to its being, the void is an empty but universally included subset or part of any set. Why? Remember that to be included in a set, that is, to be a part or subset of a set, is to have no elements that are not themselves included in the set. So, if set F is not a part of another set, E, it must be because there are elements of F that are not elements of E. But the empty set has no elements. It is thus impossible for it *not* to be a part of E: "The empty set is 'universally' included, because nothing in it can block or prevent such inclusion."[55] Containing nothing, with no belongings or "roots" of its own (nothing underneath it, nothing supporting it), the void is thus a kind of ontological vagrant. The void is "the without-place of every place" (CT, 200); it is "neither local nor global, but scattered everywhere, in no place and in every place." It is precisely as nothing, as void, that "inconsistency roams through the whole of a situation" (EE, 68, 71). And, by the same token, while the void itself is not one-ifiable, it is certainly "unique. One void cannot differ from another, since it contains no element (no local point) that might indicate this difference."[56] Inconsistency is not only everywhere; it is the being of everything.

The essential point is this: the void is included in every part of a situation, but since it can never belong anywhere in a situation, what is "in" the void can never be known or presented within that situation. A situation cannot encounter its own void. Set theory itself cannot in any meaningful sense know what lies "under" the proper name Ø: an axiom provides only an implicit definition of what it establishes. The normal regime of a situation is structured in precisely such a way as to preserve an essential ignorance or "unconsciousness" *[inconscience]* of its void. And it is impossible, Badiou insists, to combat this structural ignorance so long as the situation is dominated by business as usual, however apparently compassionate or democratic that business might be: "The void of Being can only occur at the surface of a situation by way of an event" (D, 115), and we shall see that "what allows a genuine event to be at the origin of a truth, which is the only thing that can be for all, and that can be eternally, is precisely the fact that it relates to the particularity of a situation only from the bias of its void, [which] is the absolute neutrality of being" (E, 65).

The Generation of "Nature," or the Succession of Ordinals

It is now a relatively simple matter to demonstrate how set theory "draws a Universe from the sole void." I will proceed, all the same, as gently and as carefully as possible. The critical thing, again, is that any unit is not an object or element of being per se but the element of a *set,* that is, the result or effect of a counting for one. There is nothing prior to the count, but this inconsistent nothing is nevertheless "what" is counted (C, 338; EE, 67).

The axioms of set theory demonstrate that "it is the essence of the multiple to multiply itself in immanent fashion," based only on the void (EE, 43; cf. 414). How does this work, exactly? All we need do is assume this void or empty set (i.e., the number zero) and prescribe one basic operation that enables us to consider any given term, or group of terms, starting with zero itself, as a collection or set. From these two assumptions "we may construct all of the sets required in mathematics."[57] Crossley suggests a helpful metaphor.[58] Imagine numbers as lines or queues of other numbers, each of whose final member is obligingly identified as the sum total of all preceding numbers in the queue: should we then want to compare our numerical queues, we need only read off the number identifying the final member in each queue. An empty queue, a queue with no members at all, corresponds to zero: zero is defined as having no numerical predecessors. Since such an empty queue does not properly "exist" at all (an empty queue is surely a contradiction in terms!), we simply have to posit its existence. Call it Ø. The number that now comes after zero, the number 1, corresponds to the queue that has precisely Ø as its one and only predecessor: whereas Ø itself has no elements, 1 corresponds to the set that has Ø as its single element, that is, the set {Ø}. The next largest number is defined as the queue of these two predecessors {Ø, {Ø}}, and so on. Such is the sequence of what is known as "ordinal" numbers: first, second, third, and so on. Since it quickly becomes very tedious to write our numerical queues out longhand in this way, we adopt the familiar shorthand

$$0 = \emptyset$$
$$1 = \{\emptyset\} = \{0\}$$
$$2 = \{\emptyset, \{\emptyset\}\} = \{0,1\}$$
$$3 = \{\emptyset, \{\emptyset\}, \{\emptyset, \{\emptyset\}\}\} = \{0,1,2\} \ldots$$

Thus begins, as Badiou observes, "the unlimited production of new multiples, all drawn from the void, through the combined effect of the axiom of subsets—for the name of the void is part of itself—and of the putting into one."[59] This unlimited production governs the succession of "normal" (or "transitive") sets, known technically as Von Neumann ordinals: each one is literally a "part" of its successors. As we have seen, a "normal" set is one where what is presented is also represented: all of its elements are also included as parts.[60] Between two successor ordinals, there is no intermediary ordinal. There is no ordinal between 2 and 3.

This seamless derivation of ordinals provides Badiou with his very concept of "Nature."[61] Nature is everywhere all it can be, a universal plenitude. The natural (or ordinal) network of sets is interlocking and exhaustive: "Every natural multiple is connected to every other, by presentation [itself]." Or again, "Every ordinal is a 'piece' of another" (EE, 155–56). Natural multiplicities thus fill the universe without remainder. But because no natural set can belong to itself, so *la Nature*—one all-inclusive Nature—cannot exist: we know that the irreducible excess of parts over elements ensures that there cannot be one infinitely large set whose elements would include all of its parts (EE, 160).

The naturally finite is thus that which extends itself in a potentially infinite displacement. But it must be emphasized again that this multiplication alone, though indefinitely repeatable, cannot be said to produce an actually infinite number of sets. However many times the procedure is repeated, the largest resulting set will always be finite. The simple succession of ordinals—itself an endless counting to infinity—does not by itself provide effective access to the infinite as such. As Russell accepts, "It cannot be said for certain that there are in fact any infinite collections in the world."[62] The production of an actually infinite set requires an additional axiom, an axiom of infinity. Such an axiom simply states that the infinite exists, "without operational mediation," or, more technically, that there exists a "limit ordinal" (written ω_0), an ordinal that does not succeed from another ordinal (EE, 175–76; cf. C, 297–98). Whereas nothing (the void) separates one successor ordinal from another, "between the finite ordinals—those that belong to ω_0—and ω_0 itself there is an abyss without mediation."[63] Literally beyond mediation, the infinite is always decided, and decided alone.

It is no exaggeration to say that the consequences of its axiomatic foundation determine the whole orientation of Badiou's later philosophy. The axiom guarantees an original break with the merely given, inherited, or established. It ensures a foundation before or beyond the worldly. (It is precisely because the axiom cuts itself off, so to speak, from an objective reality external to it, that pure mathematics is often held to be a discipline without "truth" in the conventional sense.)[64] Axioms "pose the problem of a 'nonworldly' or nonfortuitous existence. . . . Within infinity, it is doubtful that we can refer existence back to 'what is the case,' to what allows it to be 'recorded' as fact."[65] The axiom is alone adequate to the decision of the radically undecidable. The axiom, ultimately, is the sole condition and exclusive medium of the subject: Badiou thus claims that true "decisions (nominations, axioms) suppose no subject, since there is no subject other than as the effect of such decisions."[66]

But at what cost? The skeptical reader may still be wondering, How exactly does the mathematical discourse relate or apply to the actual, material situations it purports to describe? How precisely do we move from the purely void-based multiples presented in ontology, which are all "qualitatively very indistinct" (EE, 270), to the qualitative variety of historical situations? To be sure, we know that Badiou "in no way declares that being is mathematical, that is, composed of mathematical objectivities" (EE, 14). Nevertheless, his conviction is that the substance of material or historical situations offers no significant resistance to their mathematization, and that insofar as they can be thought, all situations are to be subtracted from the uncertain domains of substance, perception, and the object. He takes a further step when he argues—against Kant's foreclosure of the void, against Kant's insistence on the conjunction of object and concept in the orderly perception of "hetero-geneous existence"—that the void or "nothing, rigorously (mathematically) subsumed under a concept, is precisely what upholds *the heterogeneously existent*." Such, for instance, is the ontological path opened "by Epicurus and Lucretius, for whom the void is the first name of the heterogeneously exis-tent, splendidly indifferent both to subjects and to gods."[67]

Now while Badiou might easily dismiss as simplified forms of intuition-ism the perception or imagination-dependent conception of mathematics held by thinkers like Deleuze or Merleau-Ponty, it is less clear that the onto-logical dispute per se is so easily resolved. Both Deleuze and Merleau-Ponty would no doubt retort that pure mathematics leaves mainly untouched the great problem of ontology as they understand it, namely the relation between abstract being and concrete existence. However immediately it may think the be-ing of being, mathematics proceeds at an irreducible methodological dis-tance from our experience of beings, from what phenomenology famously dubs our "return to the things themselves." This return, as Merleau-Ponty puts it, is always a return "to that world which precedes knowledge, of which knowledge always *speaks,* and in relation to which every scientific schemati-zation is an abstract and derivative sign language, as is geography in relation to the countryside in which we have learned beforehand what a forest, a prairie, or a river is."[68] From the outset, Badiou banishes from ontology precisely this general "feel for the world" as no more than an invitation to sensual and ideological confusion. The question is whether the resulting clarity can ever adequately move beyond its operational abstraction.

We have already seen how Badiou aligns the purely material situation along the mathematical frontier with being as being (the frontier of a mathematized physics). But can the same logic apply, in the same way and without further modulation, to all human situations in general? In what meaningful sense can set theory account for the fundamental *structure* of, say, biological or psychological situations? In what pertinent sense can set theory claim to articulate the be-ing of such situations, whose most elementary characteristics are inconsistent with the axioms of extensionality and replacement? Indeed, once we admit that all aspects of a particular situation that might resist mathematization are of no relevance to ontology, some readers may conclude that such an ontology is of little relevance to particular situations. Questions regarding how situations are structured, how what is presented relates to what is represented, and so on, may require essentially different answers depending on whether we are referring to mathematical, physical, biological, psychological, or historical situations. Answers to such questions may require, beyond an extensional theory that defines a situation exclusively in terms of the elements that belong to it, a still more fundamental account of how the elements in any particular situation might relate to each other.

chapter 5

Subject and Event

We arrive now at the dynamic core of Badiou's system, the dynamism that moves beyond the objective normality enforced by the state of a situation. "It is vain to suppose," Badiou writes, "that we can invent anything at all—and all truth is invention—if nothing happens, if 'nothing takes place but the place'" (PM, 24). A truth is something that *happens,* something both exceptional and universal, both punctual in its origin and for all in its implication.

With the concepts of subject and event Badiou has broken out of the merely "natural" confines of being as being. His ontology provides a negative but exact description of that which exceeds it: an event is precisely "that which is not being as being" (EE, 193). What a truth process composes is indeed the truth of a situation, but its composition requires something more than the situation itself can provide. For instance, in order to reveal the proletariat as the foundation of the capitalist situation, politics first requires a revolutionary intervention that is itself strictly outlawed from that situation. Likewise, it is an exceptional encounter, or recollection, or association, that can alone allow the subjects of psychoanalysis to penetrate the repression that conceals the truth of their situation. In each case, the event—the uprising, the encounter, the invention—breaks fundamentally with the prevailing routine: "Every radically transformative action has its origin in one point."[1] Through the subject who proclaims it, a truth that is thus ephemeral in its occasion thereby comes to consist as generic in its substance. Badiou adopts

107

Cohen's notion of "forcing," finally, to describe the process by which such a consistent truth may eventually produce verifiable components of a new knowledge, a new way of understanding the parts of the situation.

In this chapter I consider these three notions in sequence: event, subject (intervention-fidelity-connection), and forcing; in the next chapter I will provide a more synthetic analysis of the general criteria of truth as such. The guiding thread is provided, as always, by the notion of the generic or aspecific. Badiou maintains that "a single concept, that of the generic procedure, subsumes both the disobjectification of the truth and that of the subject, by making this subject appear as a simple finite fragment of a postevental truth without object" (MP, 75). The systematic coherence of this concept demands the patience of an extended exposition. The elements, dimensions, and pitfalls of such generic procedures must be assembled carefully, piece by piece, over the next six chapters.

Three Examples

Perhaps the simplest way to start is to consider what are perhaps Badiou's most compelling and certainly his most insistent examples: Christianity according to Paul and Pascal, and the French Revolution according to Saint-Just and anticipated by Rousseau. An event is always a historical entity, what Badiou now calls the very essence of the historical (EE, 199). Cantor's invention of transfinite set theory provides another pertinent illustration, one that Badiou himself does not develop but whose effect resonates throughout his work.

The Gospel according to Saint Paul

Badiou quotes Lacan's aphorism: "If no religion is True, Christianity comes the closest to the form of truth."[2] Only in Christianity does the "essence of truth suppose an eventual ultra-one," such that "to relate to this truth is not a matter of contemplation—or immobile knowledge—but of intervention" (EE, 235). The (Pauline) Christian does not so much cultivate inner peace or worship a supreme being as remain faithful to the event of Christ's resurrection.

Badiou's militant atheism does not prevent him from acknowledging that "all the parameters of the doctrine of the event are thus laid out in Christianity" (EE, 235). What Badiou terms the "eventual site" is here marked by the flesh, the human experience taken, through suffering and death, to the very edge of its void. What he calls the event—here, the death and resurrection of God—was a wholly ephemeral passing that cannot be assigned to any stable element of the situation in which it took place. The Christian version of the Two was effected through the "splitting of the divine One" as Father and Son. The state or metastructure—the Roman imperial state—dismissed the event as the mere conjunction between a site (Palestinian uprisings) and the nullity of a particular singleton (the execution of another fanatic). What Badiou calls a subjective intervention then proclaimed the event as the decisive turning point between a before (Adam's sin) and an after (the Last Judgment); it established the event as the beginning of a time oriented toward universal redemption. "The political time of the universal Church, of which Saint Paul was the bilious and inspired Lenin, founds the Incarnation retroactively as fact. Understand: as the discursive fact of this militant, conquering apparatus" (TS, 143). Finally, Christianity established an "institutional fidelity"—"the Church, the first institution in human history to aspire to universality"[3]—in order to maintain and organize a genuine connection to the event, as distinct from false, heretical connections.

In *L'Etre et l'événement*, Pascal figures as the most eloquent representative of this version of a Christian subjectivity. Pascal eliminates a worldly rapport to Christ. Pascal knows that nothing in or about the world leads to God. Rather, a relation to God can be established only, subjectively, as a gamble on God's existence (PP, 87). Confronted with a modern scientific skepticism, Pascal abandons all traditional proofs of God so as to restore the purely evental force of faith, conceived as "a militant vocation" whose only foundation is properly "miraculous" and extralegal. And "since the heart of truth is that the event from which it originates is undecidable, the choice, with respect to this event, is ineluctable. . . . The true essence of the wager is that we *must* wager."[4]

In Badiou's more recent book *Saint Paul et la fondation de l'universalisme* (1997), Paul's exemplary logic finally gets the detailed attention it deserves. Looking for material to inspire a "new figure of the militant," Badiou turns to Paul as one of the first political or religious leaders to "subtract the truth from the grip of the communal, whether it be a people, a city, an empire, a territory, or a social class" (SP, 2, 6). Paul was the only apostle not to have known Jesus in his lifetime, and he showed little interest in that intimate or personal relationship to God that was to become such a constant preoccupation of later Christianity. Of all the apostles, Paul's conversion (from persecutor to martyr) was the most decisive and extravagant. Following the revelation on the road to Damascus, Paul did not join Peter and the other apostles preoccupied with the internal transformation of the Jewish community in Jerusalem but headed out on his own into the Arabian desert, before spending most of the next two decades traveling as an itinerant preacher, choosing to work mainly among non-Jews, encouraging the formation of small militant congregations in the far-flung cities of Corinth, Ephesus, Rome, and elsewhere. Written some twenty years before the four canonical gospels, Paul's letters say almost nothing about Jesus the man, the miracle worker, the teller of parables: they are confined to matters of urgent principle, and turn in their compressed complexity on a few fundamental points of doctrine (life, death, sin, law, desire, faith, hope, love).

With Paul, Badiou emphasizes four cardinal qualities of truth. First, "the Christian subject does not preexist the event he declares (the resurrection)." What he was before that declaration is of no importance. In light of the resurrection, "there is no such thing as Jew or Greek, slave or free man, man or woman . . . , for you are all one person in Jesus Christ."[5]

Second, "the truth is entirely subjective," a matter of pure conviction, rather than of conformity to an immemorial (Jewish) law nor to a cosmic (Greek) coherence. For Paul "the figure of knowledge is itself a figure of slavery" (SP, 63), and the Law (the Commandments) is merely a law of death, a law regulating the management of desires oriented toward death (27). Both Greek philosophy and Jewish prophecy or law—the two rival discourses to Christianity—are figures of "mastery," the discourses of a universal order or signifying "Father," whereas Paul conceives the event (of the resurrection) as neither cosmic nor legal, as "the sign of nothing" (45), and thus as the basis for a discourse of the Son. By proclaiming the truth of the event, we become the *children* of God, "co-workers with God" (64). Again, to be such a co-worker has nothing to do with any sort of cultural or communal peculiarity. All "children" are made equal through the "dissipation of paternal particularity" (63).

Third, truth is a process and not an illumination. It takes much time and much effort. To be sustained it requires "conviction" (or faith), "love" (or charity), and "certainty" (or hope). It does not require, however, proof in the form of confirmed knowledge or corroboration.

Fourth, truth is "indifferent to the state of the situation"—here, the Roman state or the Jewish religion. Christ's resurrection certainly took place in the Jewish situation but was not of it, as Saul the Pharisee knew full well. Truth springs from a moment of grace, defined as "that which comes to pass without being the basis of any predicate, that which is translegal, that which happens to everyone without any ascribable reason" or justification (SP, 80–81). To become adequate to the truth, oriented by truth, involves indifference to knowledge of the world as it is. Paul urged his followers: "Adapt yourselves no longer to the pattern of this present world, but let your minds be remade and your whole nature thus transformed. Then you will be able to discern the will of God, and to know what is good, acceptable and perfect" (Rom. 12:2).

Rousseau and Robespierre

Robespierre and Saint-Just stand for what was "most intense, most inventive in political thought"[6] prior to Marx, Lenin, and Mao. The Jacobins were those subjects whose revolutionary intervention preserved a fidelity to the self-constituent sovereignty prescribed by Rousseau. The Revolution itself was that ephemeral event whose occasion was deemed "impossible" from within the assumptions of what was to become known, in its wake, as the ancien régime. The elements of its evental site include what historians generally consider the immediate causes of the Revolution: the Estates General, the peasants of the Great Fear, the *sans-culottes,* the public debt, and so on. What sets a limit to this dissemination of causal factors is "the mode whereby the Revolution becomes an axial term of the Revolution itself, that is to say, the way the consciousness of that time—and the retroactive intervention of our own—filters the whole site through the 'one' of its evental qualification" (EE, 201). The event of the revolution takes place as that imperceptible moment of transition after which the groups of people involved conceive themselves precisely no longer as members of this or that group but as so many subjects of the revolution itself (which suspends the *political* pertinence of any group qua group, or "faction"). As proclaimed, the Revolution became an element of itself, constituent of the revolutionary process as such (the universal declaration of human rights, the abolition of privilege and slavery, the assertion of a national or popular sovereignty, etc.). Revolutionary truth then persisted through those groups who preserve a fidelity to this event and these declarations.

It was Rousseau who first formulated the logic of a Revolutionary politics— that is, a self-founding politics, one based on the event of its own assertion: "Rousseau establishe[d] once and for all the modern concept of politics" because he declared that the political as such always begins with an event rather than a structure. Rather than emerge from any sort of social bond, politics begins all at once with an effectively axiomatic "contract," where contract is the "evental form that we must presume if we want to think the truth of this aleatory being that is the body politic" (EE, 380; cf. PP, 13). The subject here is Rousseau's famous legislator. The legislator names the event, the social contract, from a position outside it, from the "void" of an unspecifiable space. Rousseau's legislator is the very prototype of "an interventionist avant-garde," which is to say of the subject in general. The social contract is not a naming, after the fact, of an already constituted people, but the constitution of a people through this self-naming itself. The consequent political or subjective (or "general") will is subtracted from the mediation of particular wills: "The evental self-belonging that governs it, under the name of the social contract, makes of the general will a term inaccessible to *[soustrait à]* all distinction" (EE, 384–85). The sovereign general will is indivisible by definition; it cannot be broken into more elementary units or interests. It exists precisely as the active process that transcends such division, that transcends the operations of the state. Or again, the political is that which cannot be represented. Politics is primarily concerned not with policy or administration but with the militant constitution of a people, "a local and fragile creation of collective humanity" (EE, 380): its most pressing imperative is to *continue* or persist in this creation. Simply, Rousseau failed to go far enough in the direction of a practically generic *désétatisation*: Rousseau was not quite Marx.

Cantor's Commitment

We already know the gist of Cantor's theory, but it is worth recalling the circumstances of its assertion since they are typical of those involved in any scientific truth procedure. The immediate situation in which Cantor set to work was conditioned by the reaffirmation of a strictly potential as opposed to an actual or "completed" notion of the infinite, an affirmation associated with the great effort to establish the purely arithmetic foundations of mathematical analysis undertaken by Cauchy, Weierstrass, and others over the middle decades of the nineteenth century. By 1870, commitment to a potential conception of the infinite and a suspicion of the confused "metaphysical" notions of the actually infinite or infinitesimal was orthodox in every mathematics department in Germany. In these circumstances, Cantor's proposal was, as one survey describes it, nothing less than an "act of rebellion," in "direct opposition to the doctrines of the greatest mathematicians of the time . . . : the storm that was about to lash out exceeded in its fury anything that had been seen before."[7] Like Copernicus and Galileo before him, Cantor was vigorously attacked by almost the entire mathematical establishment of his day, led by the powerful protointuitionist Leopold Kronecker.[8]

Cantor's theory began with the active assertion and naming of an actually infinite set, and developed as the stream of consequences to be drawn from this inaugural act. Like all truths, it took shape as a kind of logical revolt: although Cantor did not at first set out to establish a theory of "the completed infinite," this theory was, he wrote, "logically forced upon me, almost against my will since it was contrary to traditions which I had come to cherish in the course of many years of scientific effort."[9] Blocked from promotion and widespread recognition by established figures in Berlin and Göttingen, confined to a minor post at the University of Halle, he was to face years of discouragement and an eventually clinical depression. But against Kronecker's "keen and relentless opposition," Cantor held to his own position as "absolutely the only true theory possible." Writing in 1888, he declared, "My theory stands as firm as a rock; every arrow directed against it will return quickly to its archer."[10] And, almost at once, this theory did indeed force mathematicians to take sides, for or against. As early as 1892, Frege recognized the question of the actually infinite as "the battlefield where a great decision will be made," "the reef on which mathematics will founder."[11] On the one hand, Poincaré joined Kronecker in condemning set theory as "pathological," as a "disease" from which future generations would eventually recover;[12] Wittgenstein and the more extreme constructivists were to follow suit in due course. On the other hand, Cantor's idea was taken up and refined by a whole legion of set theorists (Zermelo, Fraenkel, Von Neumann, Bernays, Skolem, Gödel, Cohen, and others); their fidelity to Cantor's original declaration has shaped much of contemporary mathematics. Not only did this declaration change the scope and orientation of mathematical inquiry; it changed the very concept of mathematical truth itself: "Cantor's set theory had brought mathematicians to a frightening and perilous precipice. Cantor's infinite had shaken the traditional faith in mathematics' everlasting certitude."[13] We know that this crisis of faith deepened with the interventions of Gödel and Cohen. Badiou himself has struck another blow in support of Cantor's innovation, by accepting this loss of certitude as the very condition of a contemporary philosophy of *truth*.

The enterprise of Cantor's greatest intellectual contemporaries, Darwin, Marx, and Freud, might be understood in a similarly eventual way. Following the event of the *Beagle*'s voyage (1831–36), Darwin's enterprise developed the consequences of a single insight, albeit one that immediately ran up against the most profound certainties of his age (the stability of nature and the fixity of species, organized around the eternal centrality of man): an explanation of diversity and change in terms of natural selection. By the same token, Marx was the first political thinker to draw the rigorous consequences of those unprecedented events that were the working-class uprisings in the most reactionary years in the history of European capitalism, the 1830s and 1840s. And Freud's great achievement, as Badiou sees it, was the "eventalization" of childhood, that is, an understanding of childhood not as an innocent parenthesis (a simple "before" adulthood) or a moment of training and development (of *"dressage"*), but rather as a sequence of events whose consequences are duly assumed by the unconscious subject. This allowed for an analysis of childhood as an unfolding process of creative thought, that is, of thought able to transform itself. Freud's most essential insight was "Something has happened, it cannot be erased, and the constitution of the subject depends on it" (TA, 14.1.98). In each case, and always in the face of massive institutional opposition, those who constitute themselves as scientists or activists or analysts in the name of these most anticonsensual insights (those who, at least in an initial moment, identify themselves as "Marxists," or "Darwinians," or "Freudians"), are the people with the courage and tenacity to continue the elaboration of these truths, the exploration of as yet unproven consequences. The moment of verification or falsification, Badiou would say in response to Popper, always lags comfortably after the initial affirmation.

The Event and the Instance of Chance

The question of how to relate the status of an event to a general ontology of the multiple, Badiou believes, is "the principal question of all contemporary philosophy." It was the question at issue in Heidegger's shift from *Sein* to *Ereignis* and in Lacan's shift from the interpretation of the symbolic to the mathematization of the real—from a "supposed knowledge" to a fully transmissible "truth." It was Nietzsche's final question when he asked how we might "break the history of the world in two." It was Wittgenstein's original question: How can an Act yield access to the silent "mystical element" if all meaning is captive to the empty form of the proposition? And it is Deleuze's question: How can the process of actualization (the movement from virtual to actual) be thought of as a process of "differen*t*iation," as introducing difference into what exists?[14] In each case, the question is much the same: How can the merely reflective discipline of philosophy grasp what happens or what has value in all its urgency and activity? "Is truth what comes to being, or what unfolds being?" (CT, 59). Since the event is what demonstrates that not all is ontological, must we then accept, with Deleuze, a heterogeneity of the multiple, an original dualism of the intensive and the extensive? Badiou's commitment to a radical ontological univocity precludes this option. The only alternative is to develop "the argument that in any case the truth itself *is* only a multiplicity," but an *exceptional* multiplicity, a multiplicity put together in an exceptional way (CT, 59).

What is an event? For Badiou, first and foremost, an event is "purely haphazard *[hasardeux]*, and cannot be inferred from the situation" (EE, 215). An event is the unpredictable result of chance and chance alone.[15] Whereas the "structure" of a situation "never provides us with anything other than repetition," every event is unprecedented and unexpected (C, 189; DO, 11). Only the event enables the assertion that there can be genuine "novelty in being" (EE, 231; cf. EE, 444–45). It is its eventfal origin that ensures that true innovation is indeed a kind of creation ex nihilo, a chance to begin again from scratch, to interrupt the order of continuity and inevitability. For what is encountered through an event is precisely the void of the situation, that aspect of the situation that has absolutely no interest in preserving the status quo as such. The event reveals "the inadmissible empty point in which nothing is presented" (PP, 115; cf. EE, 227), and this is why every event indicates, in principle, a pure beginning, the inaugural or uncountable zero of a new time (a new calendar, a new order of history): "It is not from the world, in however ideal a manner, that the event holds its inexhaustible reserve, its silent (or indiscernible) excess, but from its being unattached to it, its being separate, lacunary."[16] In this Badiou follows in Paul's footsteps: an event comes from beyond, undeserved, unjustified, and unjustifiable. From within the situation, the occurrence of an event always resembles an instance of grace, a kind of "laicized grace."[17] It is thus futile to wait for, let alone try to anticipate, an event, "for it is of the essence of the event not to be preceded by any sign, and to surprise us by its grace."[18] We must instead accept that "everything begins in confusion and obscurity": the emergence of clarity is always the result of an active and never-ending clarification.[19]

It is not that the event itself is nothing. It has the same (inconsistent) being-as-being as anything else. An event can be only a multiple, but it is one that counts as nothing in the situation in which it takes place. If everything that exists in or belongs to a situation is numbered or counted for one in that situation, an event is "supernumerary" (EE, 199): it is "something" that evades the count. As something that cannot be recognized as one in a situation, an event is the (necessarily ephemeral) presentation of inconsistency in the situation. Though it thus indicates the true being of the situation, an event must for that very reason count as nothing for this situation.

As a result, from within the situation, the existence of an event cannot be proved; it can only be asserted. An event is something that can be said to exist (or rather, to have existed) only insofar as it somehow inspires subjects to wager on its existence (EE, 214). An event can be only "evanescent,"[20] though what is subsequently done in its name may transcend time altogether, or rather, may provide the basis for an altogether new time. Since the event has no present and leaves no durable trace, the temporality of the event as such is necessarily confined to the time of a future anterior: thanks to a subsequent subjective intervention, the event "will have been presented" (EE, 217). The event cannot itself provide this intervention, upon which its very existence depends, with any compelling justification or reason. If Mallarmé's *Coup de dés* provides Badiou with "an absolute symbol of the event," it is because the poem demonstrates that, since the "essence of the event is to be undecidable as regards its effective belonging to the situation, so an event whose content is the eventality of the event (and such is precisely the dice throw thrown in 'eternal circumstances') can have only indecision as its form" (EE, 215). Being purely undecidable, an event can be affirmed only through equally pure subjective decision; by the same token, truly decisive or subjective action can continue only insofar as it grounds itself upon nothing other than this inconsistency. Celan thus wrote what is for Badiou "the central maxim of every interventionist thought" (which I will not dare to retranslate): "Sur les inconsistances / S'appuyer."[21]

Where exactly lies the ontological peculiarity of the event? Unlike all normally structured or well-founded multiples, an event belongs to no already existent set. Insofar as it "exists" at all—and remember that to exist means to belong to a set—the event simply belongs to itself. It is, as an occurrence, self-founding, which is to say that it is properly unfounded. Self-founding and unfounded are indeed one and the same thing, because in order for a set to be founded it must contain an element with which it has nothing in common, that is, whose own elements do not also belong to that set. What happens with an event is thus the "collapse of foundation, i.e., the insurrection of the unfounded," or a "destabilization of the ordinary universe" (TA, 23.4.97). In set-theoretic terms, an event is exceptional because it does not comply with the axiom of foundation, that is, the axiom proposed (by Zermelo in 1906) precisely in order to block the paradoxical possibility of sets belonging to themselves. Because it violates the axiom of foundation, "the event is forbidden; ontology rejects it" (EE, 205). What truly happens is always unfounded, but once it has happened, "foundation closes around the event like water" (TA, 23.4.97). And since it is because a normal set cannot belong to itself that "set theory is essentially hierarchical in nature," that is, built up in succeeding collections,[22] we might say that an event, by violating this fundamental rule, is indeed the basis for an exceptional egalitarian break within what passes for "normal" or "natural" hierarchy.

On the Edge of the Void: The Evental Site

The event is "unpresented and unpresentable," and its belonging to the situation is "undecidable" from within the situation itself (EE, 199, 202). Since the laws of ontology will not recognize its existence, only subjective intervention will be able to determine if the event really belonged to the situation or not. But in order for this belonging to be possible at all, the event must first be shown to have its own site within the situation, what Badiou calls a *site événementiel.* A foreign invasion, say, cannot count as an event for the obvious reason that it cannot belong to the situation itself. It is a condition of any genuine event that "its evental site be counted within it. It is a strict condition of immanence, since the site is a part of the situation."[23]

It is this evental site that guarantees the specificity of a truth procedure, its location within the situation that it transforms. Thanks to its site, an event can always be located precisely in a situation, in a specific "point" of the situation, and to begin with each event concerns precisely this point (EE, 199). For example, the site for the event of Christ's resurrection was his mortality and death: the resurrection was situated in the element of death. The event of the resurrection certainly could not be inferred from death as such (on the contrary), but Christ's acceptance of death, his assumption of human mortality, ensured that this event "will have been destined to human beings" (SP, 74). We might say that every event is specific to, but not specified by, its site. In science, for instance, the sites of unpredictable truths to come are indicated by those points of apparent impasse or resistance to formalization—points indicated, perhaps, by isolated theorems whose underlying theoretical justification has yet to be established. In art, likewise, sites are located at the limits of currently available formal resources—for instance, at the saturation of the tonal system in Wagner's *Tristan*, composed at the edge of what is recognizable as "music": to push any further toward dissonance would have been to leave the classical tonal system altogether (which was precisely the decision taken, eventually, by the subject Schoenberg and his collaborators).[24]

Like the void whose "edge" it defines, the role played by the evental site is one of the most important and most slippery aspects of Badiou's philosophy of truth. We have anticipated some of the strictly ontological issues in the previous chapter, but are now in a position to present the full concept with the systematic attention it requires.

However it takes place, we know that it is "the event [that] reveals the void" of a situation, and "a truth always begins by naming this void" (PM, 88). Revealed or hidden, the void as such remains universally included in every part of the situation, and for that very reason remains unpresentable, ungraspable. The evental site is not itself void but that element of the situation which is located "at the *edge* of its void."[25] The void that sutures a situation to its being is, by the same token, radically aspecific and asituational: it is scattered everywhere throughout that situation. Whatever lies along the edge of the void, however, is always precisely located in the situation. The edge of the void is locatable even if the void itself is not.

What is void in any human situation, for instance, is simply generic humanity as such, a pure be-ing human considered without reference to any criterion of hierarchy, privilege, competence, or difference. We can *know* nothing of such pure humanity, even if it is—as it is, of course—"included" in every human individual by definition. What we can usually know about individuals will depend upon the sorts of qualities that count for a situation, for instance, occupation or status, education or wealth, skills or interests, and so on. The orderly distinction of individuals in terms of these qualities is the daily business of the state and the matter of its various knowledges. Nevertheless, in every human situation there are certain groups of individuals who, as judged by the dominant criteria of the situation, seem devoid of any such distinction.[26] As far as "normal" inhabitants of the situation are concerned, these groups seem to have nothing in common with the other groups that populate the situation—they seem, precisely, to have nothing but their own be-ing. In contemporary France, for example, to say that the *sans-papiers* are located at the edge of the void means that they occupy the place in this situation in which it is possible, by pursuing the consequences of their militant subjectivation, to approach the situation from the bias of its indistinct or generic humanity. The group known as *sans-papiers* certainly belongs to this situation, but as an anomaly: its members are in the French situation as non-French, that is, at the edge of that indistinct humanity that itself would be precisely neither French nor non-French.

An evental site is thus an element of a situation that, as inspected from a perspective within the situation, has no recognizable elements or qualities of its own (no elements in common with the situation). As a collective group this element belongs to the situation, but the situation has no means of meaningfully individuating particular members of this element. The members of those situations structured as anti-Semitic, for instance, cannot meaningfully see *individual* Jews but can see only an indistinct gap in the normal social fabric, the living lack of all "positive" (Aryan) characteristics; in much the same way, the members of situations that define themselves as a "soft touch for asylum seekers" cannot truly individuate the people they consequently detain or exclude. Likewise, gays are clearly an element of predominantly homophobic situations, but not—not in any really substantial sense—as particular men and women engaged in particular relationships. Consider again the event of the French Revolution. The elements of its site included all the things not re-presentable according to the old situation of the ancien régime. These were presentable elements (the peasants, the *sans-culottes*, the guillotine, etc.) whose own elements were not presentable. The peasantry was certainly a presented category of the ancien régime, "but not *these* peasants of the Great Fear, who [took] over castles" (EE, 202). The guillotine was perfectly presentable, but not *this* guillotine (the one that cut off the king's head). The canonical example, of course, is the evental location of the proletariat—the name Marx gave to "the central void of early bourgeois societies" (E, 61–62)—in the site defined by the exploitation of waged laborers. Having nothing other than its own being (i.e., having nothing other than its chains), the proletariat is the void that sutures the capitalist situation to its be-ing; it is the one fragile link between this situation and the general in-consistency of human be-ing as such. As defined by Marx, the working class inhabits the evental site of this situation because there is nothing between it and the explosive void of humanity that is the revolutionary proletariat. Or again, the proletariat is itself the without-place of the capitalist configuration of place, but it is from a particular (laboring) place that a proletarian subject may rise up to transform that configuration.[27]

Since a site has nothing in common with the rest of the situation (i.e., since there is nothing between the evental site and the void), it provides that situation with what we have called its "foundational" element (see the first section of this chapter). What does this mean, exactly? Remember that ordi-nary or nonfoundational elements are always made up of further elements of their own, that is, they can always be decomposed into their constituent parts. A foundational element, then, is simply one that has no distinguish-able parts at all. Since it is presented in such a way that nothing belonging to it is also presented, the existence of such an element in the situation cannot be the result of a combination of other still more elementary elements. It follows that "the evental sites block the infinite regression of the combina-tions of multiples. As they are on the edge of the void, we cannot think what is beneath their being presented. It is thus legitimate to say that the sites found the situation, since they are its absolutely primary terms" (EE, 195). Extrapolating from this logic, Badiou concludes that "any element of a situa-tion that is not rooted in that situation can enter into an evental site" (TA, 14.5.97), that is, into the foundation of that situation.

This does not mean that every founded situation necessarily contains an evental site. Within the ontological situation itself, we know that normal sets (or ordinals) are founded exclusively upon the empty set $\emptyset$, for the obvious reason that nothing belongs to $\emptyset$: $\emptyset$ can have nothing in common with any other set, even though all other sets are nothing other than compositions of $\emptyset$. It is clearly impossible for any material or nonontological situation to be founded upon the literal (or mathematical) void $\emptyset$ as such. There is an essential difference however, between nonontological situations endowed with the same sort of foundational stability that ontology attributes to the succession of ordinal numbers, on the one hand, and, on the other hand, nonontological situations deprived of any such stability. Badiou calls the former "natural" (or "normal") and the latter "historical" (or "abnormal"). A historical situation contains an evental site; a natural one does not.

This last point should come as no surprise. We know from chapter 4 that set theory defines the situation of nature as a universal dissemination of inter-locking transitive sets, that is, as a set of elements all of whose own elements also belong to that set. A natural nonontological situation, then, contains no element whose own elements elude presentation in the same situation, no element that itself seems (as seen from within the situation) to be founded on nothing (EE, 146). A normal or natural situation contains no element that lacks respectable "roots" in the situation, nothing that threatens its fundamental stability and continuity (EE, 210). A normal material situation (a lump of metal, say) simply contains ever more divisible material elements all the way down toward the absence of matter, or zero matter—precisely until that point where it encounters the apparently abnormal limit of indivisible particles (the limit where it approaches the ontological or mathematical situation pure and simple). A "historical" situation, by contrast, is thus a situation characterized by the presence of at least one abnormal or "singular" element, that is, an element that is presented but not fully re-presented (EE, 193–98). As far as other inhabitants of the situation are concerned, there is nothing in or "beneath" such an element that might tie it to the rest of the situation, no trail of belongings or roots that might determine its proper place in the situation.

What distinguishes a historical from a natural situation, in other words, is thus a purely structural (rather than an anthropological or a psychological) matter: the presence of at least one evental site. Such a site concentrates the "historicity" of a situation, since it is from there that true structural transformation is possible (EE, 199–200: unlike Deleuze, say, Badiou maintains that no merely natural movement, however convoluted or convulsive, can be the vehicle of genuine change). The evental site is the place from which radical innovation can take place, innovation beyond the normal means of the situation to interpret, classify, and forget. Every truth thus proceeds from that point in a situation where all recognizable differences are at their most imperceptible, at that place where, according to the criteria of distinction operative in the situation, there is "almost nothing."[28] Every truth begins in the place that the situation represents as desert or wasteland, a place devoid of what the situation recognizes as of value and promise (AM, 83).

An evental site, then, is certainly in a situation, but it belongs to it as something uncertain, something whose own contents remain indiscernible and mysterious, if not sinister and threatening. The state of the situation is secure so long as the inhabitants of its evental site(s) can be safely dismissed under a collectively sanctioned label ("inhuman terrorists," "unreasonable fundamentalists," "enraged protesters," "hysterical feminists," "backward primitives," and so on). Each situation is structured in such a way as to be incapable of analyzing these inhabitants in any meaningful way: even to attempt to do so is already to risk the stability of the situation itself. Any genuinely sustained or international investigation of the Palestinian site within the Israeli situation, for instance, must immediately throw the established understanding of that situation into question (i.e., the understanding established on the basis of illegal settlements, of a refusal of the refugees' right of return, etc.). Again, any searching encounter with the claims of indigenous people in settler nations such as Canada, Australia, or Mexico can only put the very identity of such nations in doubt.[29] The same applies to the claims of immigrants from the Third World to the First World: to consider them in ways that avoid facile recourse to the dismissive label of "asylum seeker," or that take seriously the violence that creates an "economic migrant," is already to call into question the cardinal principle that underlies political normality in the so-called advanced countries—the belief that the unrestricted pursuit of profits is a benevolent or at worst a neutral force of progress in the world.

The state of the situation is ordinarily capable of blocking or evading all such investigation. It requires an event (the Intifada, Mabo, Saint Bernard, etc.) to suspend this blockade. Badiou's entire project turns on the conviction that only through a truth procedure is it possible to see what belongs to an evental site, what is normally known only as unknowable, for what it genuinely is: an indifferent collection of particular, infinitely variable individuals. Only the militant subjective composition of a truth, in the wake of an event, will expose what had been hidden in this place of "internal exile." In the wake of an event (say, in Palestine, the Intifada that began in 1987, or, in Ireland, the Troubles that began in 1968), certain elements belonging to these situations (Palestinians, Catholic nationalists), elements that were not previously counted, come to appear as needing to be counted as individuals in the situation: "It is only through this discovery that there irrupts a gap between what is counted as one in the situation and the intrinsic one that the element is. Retroactively, we will have to declare that this something which appears, eventually, as needing to be counted, did indeed belong to the situation."[30] We are not far from Lacan's famous aphorism: "What is refused in the symbolic order returns in the real."[31]

By the same token, that every event is sited means that the initial consequences to be drawn from the declaration of its existence will concern the particular elements of its site, or those that are nearest to them. The actual arrangement of a site, the way its inhabitants are brought together, is entirely variable, and is what distinguishes the movement of the *sans-papiers*, say, from the organization of the Soviets, or of the Intifada, or of Brazil's landless workers' movement. In other words, what an event will force is a decision that first attests to the positive and thoroughly individuated presence of what has remained, thus far, indiscernible or unindividuatable. An event will give rise to implications of the type "Gays are not in the closet," "Immigrants are not clandestine," "Palestinians are not landless migrants," "Atonal music is not noise," and so on. And in order for this to happen, in order for the "indistinguishable" members of the site to become true individuals in their own right, the entire situation must change.

We know that the void as such can never be presented in a situation, while an edge of the void is presented in a situation as a element without any recognizable elements of its own; by contrast, the void can take on a meaningful *name* in the situation only through the process of subjectivation itself, since, as we shall see, subjectivation is nothing other than a particular "occurring" of the void, or "the proper name in a situation of this general proper name" (EE, 431). In the capitalist situation, for instance, the void as such is, as in any human situation, purely generic humanity; the edge of the void is inhabited by the working class; and the name of the void is "proletariat" in the political sense, that is, a name that is normally mere "nonsense" but that can become a true subjective name in the wake of a revolutionary event.

Intervention, Connection, and Fidelity

An event is "incalculable," but the truth it enables is not instantaneous or miraculous. Truth does not descend from on high, a ready-made revelation. If its occasion is indeed—for its subjects—experienced as a kind of grace, still "only the work that declares it constitutes it" as truth (SP, 53–55). Truth is sparked by an event, but bursts into flame only through a literally endless subjective effort. The truth is in no sense the void made present. Of the void, "there can be no experience, for what results from its—invariably evental—convocation is only the laborious work of a procedure, a procedure of truth."[32] The truth is constructed, bit by bit, *from* the void. As a result, a truth and the subjects it supports will indeed be the truth of this particular situation, but will not be recognizable as one of its state-sanctioned parts: as exceptions, subjects are always in literal excess of their situation, but they are exceptional only in and with regard to that situation. In Badiou's compressed phrase, "The universal is only that which is in immanent exception."[33]

A subject, then, is something quite distinct from an individual in the ordinary sense. In any truly revolutionary process, as Rosa Luxemburg reminds us, its subjects do not direct it from afar, at a safe distance, but constitute themselves *as* revolutionary subjects through the process itself.[34] A subject is an individual transfigured by the truth she proclaims. The individual, strictly speaking, hardly survives this transfiguration: "It is only by dissipating himself in a project that exceeds him that an individual can hope to direct himself to some subjective real *[réel]*," and thereby contribute to the constitution of a true collective subject. From the moment of this commitment, the "'we' that this project constructs is alone truly real, that is, subjectively real for the individual who carries it." The real subject of truth is this new collective "we," which comes to be at precisely the point where the self is lacking: "The individual is thus, in his very essence, the nothing that must be dissipated in a we-subject"—a we that is itself immortal, eternal, indifferent to any perishable nature or mortality (LS, 82).

Why, we might ask, does so rigorously subjective a philosophy need anything like a concept of the event at all? Are not the political agents of any given sequence themselves responsible for what happens? Considering the example of May 1968, Badiou acknowledges that

> yes we were the genuine actors, but actors absolutely seized by what was happening to them, as by something extraordinary, something properly incalculable.... Of course, if we add up the anecdotes one by one, we can always say that at any given moment there were certain actors, certain people who provoked this or that result. But the crystallisation of all these moments, their generalisation, and then the way in which everyone was caught up in it, well beyond what any one person might have thought possible—that's what I call an evental dimension. *None* of the little processes that led to the event was equal to what actually took place ... ; there was an extraordinary change of scale, as there always is in every significant event.... Lin Piao—someone rarely mentioned these days—once said, at the height of the Cultural Revolution, that the essential thing was to be, at a revolutionary conjunction, both its actor and its target. I quite like this formula. Yes, we are actors, but in such a way that we are targeted by, carried away by, and struck by *[atteint par]* the event. In this sense there can undoubtedly be collective events.[35]

An event is the hinge in this transition from calculation to the incalculable, and every crisis of calculation means precisely that an answer to the question "What is to be done?" can be not discerned but only decided, as Lenin well knew. An event cannot dictate its own consequences. To fall in love does not determine the ensuing relationship as loving. The French Revolution need have ended in neither Terror, nor Thermidor, nor Empire. Christ's death suggested no intrinsic valorization of human suffering (SP, 69), any more than his resurrection itself effected an automatic, all-inclusive redemption from death. It is precisely the evental orientation of Badiou's philosophy, in other words, that determines its strictly subjective basis.

The operation of a truth can be divided into a number of closely related moments: the naming of the event; the intervention that imposes this name and makes it stick; the division of those elements of the situation that affirm or fit the name from those that do not; the establishment of an enduring fidelity to this name. The subject is the agent or instance of this process as a whole, a process that bears some comparison to what Benjamin described, in often-quoted words, as a moment of deliberate crystallization, "singled out by history at a moment of danger.... Where thinking suddenly stops in a configuration pregnant with tensions, it gives that configuration a shock, by which it crystallizes into a monad. A historical materialist approaches a historical subject only where he encounters it as a monad."[36] Badiou's subjects are always solitary, singular, always endangered, in something like Benjamin's sense.

Nomination and Implication

First the name. Since the name must be drawn from the void of the situation, "the event will have as its name the nameless" as such. Any event will carry the name of its "Unknown Soldier" (EE, 227), but of *its* particular unknown solider—the soldier of its site.[37] With Mallarmé and against Heidegger, Badiou reserves the legitimate meaning of the term "poetic" for this nomination. Poetry is language directed to the expression of the void, language used without object or reference. Poetry is the language of pure invention as such. In a particularly forceful illustration of what Kripke calls an antidescriptivist use of language, eventual nomination is the creation of terms that, without referents in the situation as it stands, express elements that will have been presented in a new situation to come, that is, in the situation considered, hypothetically, once it has been transformed by truth (EE, 436–37). The names "Proletariat," "Christian," and "Revolutionary" are terms that incant their eventual referents, insofar as Proletariat is not the working class, Christian is not a particular kind of Jew or Roman, and Revolutionary is not merely an advocate for the Third Estate. The same goes for individual proper names: as eventual, the names Haydn, Schoenberg, Picasso, and Grothendieck refer to a process that, from the point of its presumed completion, converts an insignificant anonymity into the inspiration of a universal truth.[38]

In his most recent work, Badiou has revised this conception of the name of the event somewhat. The risk of the configuration proposed in *L'Etre et l'événement* itself is that the name might effectively operate as just that sort of eventual trace that the axiom of foundation so rigorously forbids. It is essential to maintain that "there can be *no* ontological remnant of the event."[39] So, rather than somehow leave its name "behind," Badiou explains that an event simply *implies* a statement, the "eventual statement." All that belongs to the event disappears, and all that remains is the eventual statement (say, "I love you," or "The revolution has begun," or "Christ is risen"). This eventual statement is ontologically fully "detached" from the event itself. The evental declaration "I love you" is not properly a name of the evental encounter, but an "implicative remnant of the encounter." Only the encounter is properly real: the declaration is not itself the real, but its direct implication. The connection between an event and an evental statement can thus be expressed as an explicitly logical connection (as an implication, precisely), and the consequences of a decision to affirm the statement can be described more exactly as a transformation of the rules of logic currently operating in a situation.[40] According to the logic that governs the status quo, the evental statement will simply make no acceptable sense at all ("That cannot be right," "I cannot possibly be in love with this person," "No revolution could take place *here*"). The initial affirmation of the statement is thus a matter of anguished confusion pure and simple. The anguish eventually recedes as the truthful consequences of the statement begin to transform the existing rules of logic, so as to force explicit acknowledgment of the statement ("Yes, I am indeed in love"; "Yes, the world does move around the sun"; "Yes, Jesus was truly resurrected").

Intervention

The term "intervention" describes both the courage to name the event (or to affirm its implication) and the determination to make this implication apply. Without any relation to an already existing object or situation, the implication intervenes but does not figure, represent, or interpret. "There is no interpretation in this business," writes Badiou, "there is a name, by which it is decided . . . that the event belongs to the situation. . . . I call intervention every procedure by which a multiple is recognized as event."[41] Or again: "The axiom of truth is always of the form, 'This took place, which I can neither calculate nor demonstrate'" (C, 190). Intervention is purely a matter of yes or no, it did happen or it did not happen, and this yes or no applies only to the existence of the event rather than to its alleged (and always debatable) "meaning" or manner. It is simply a matter of deciding that the revolution or breakthrough has indeed taken place, that we did indeed fall in love, and so on. Conversely, to refute a truth is not to argue with what it means but instead to deny that it ever took place at all, that is, to deny the reality of its founding event. Thermidor, for instance, reduces the Revolution to a passing moment of popular disorder, and thereby reduces the subject of *Vertu* to the agent of Terror. To "refute" *la pensée 68* is again to say, first and foremost, that *les événements* were only an assertion of sexual freedom and self-indulgence. Likewise, the definitive breakdown of a relationship comes with the declaration "I never really loved you."

What Badiou retains from Lenin as much as from Saint Paul is the supreme importance of an active (rather than reactive) intervention. Lenin's "The Crisis Has Matured" of September 1917 provides an exemplary illustration of how such an intervention should be done: Lenin was not content to postpone action until the circumstances "dictated" change but was determined to force change when the moment for intervention was ripe. Although the decision to intervene presumes a carefully reasoned assessment of what might become possible in the situation, there can be no question of waiting for the permission or approval of the situation as it is.[42] From any established perspective, intervention always takes place as "illegal and anonymous" (EE, 254), an unreasonable gamble or leap of faith—faith in Christ, faith in the party, faith in the Revolution, faith in abstract painting, faith in this unknown stranger. From the perspective of the situation to come, however, the consequences of the decision are a matter of implacable rigor, pure deductive fidelity *en acte.* And what matters is precisely the act of decision itself. Just what is decided, the content of the decision, is by definition immanent to the situation as it stands; it is the decision itself, as act, that changes the situation as a whole. For example, the mere content of the 1789 Declaration of the Rights of Man was certainly made up of principles widely discussed over the latter half of the eighteenth century. Nothing new there. But that a constituent assembly took the step of proclaiming these principles to be at the constitutional basis of the nation as a whole was a revolutionary act that abolished the very basis of the ancien régime in a single sweep. It was precisely the Declaration that counted.[43]

Investigation and Connection

Confrontation with the name or evental implication will force the elements of a situation to take sides: for or against the event. In the wake of intervention, subjectivation proceeds through the slow accumulation, point by point, of inquiries or "investigations" *(enquêtes)* undertaken to determine the relation each element of the situation might entertain with the event. Investigation is a militant rather than a scholarly process. It is an attempt to win over each element to the event; it is a matter of "enthusiasm" and "commitment" rather than of knowledge or interpretation (EE, 364–65). In the early Christian situation, for instance, each sermon, each conversation with the unconverted, was an investigation; rallies, demonstrations, and canvassings play a similar role in political procedures, as does the production of new experimental works in an artistic procedure. In an amorous sequence, investigations will explore "the existential episodes" (experiences, places, objects, memories, etc.) that the loving couple might explicitly associate with their love (EE, 374).

The result of an investigation will be either a positive or a negative "connection" *(connexion)* to the event. A negative connection means that the element investigated remains indifferent to the event, unaffected by or hostile to its consequences. Depending on the situation, a positive connection might amount to a conversion, a commitment, a renewal, a successful experiment. In keeping with a strictly classical conception of logic, an investigation can recognize "only two values, connection and disconnection *[la connexion et la disconnexion]*" (EE, 364). The "middle" is excluded in advance. Only rigorous converts can maintain a truth, and conversion in this half-Pauline, half-Leninist sense leaves little room for modulation or discussion, let alone for skeptical or distanced admiration (terms that can be consistent here only with indifferent disconnection pure and simple).[44] The truth is an all-or-nothing deal.

It is only so, however, one element at a time. In each case the sequence of elements investigated is entirely random, the result of a series of chance encounters. In order to sustain this haphazard consolidation after the immediate postevental confusion, a truth procedure will have to invent ways of inspiring, organizing, and disciplining its "operators of connection"—for example, the party after the Revolution, or the Church after the apostles. The laborious pursuit of investigations undertaken by this operator will, in turn, give rise to finite sets of positively (+) or negatively (-) connected elements, and the truth itself, considered in its multiple being, will be nothing other than the infinite set that "regroups all the terms of the situation that are positively connected to the name of the event" (EE, 370).

In the ontological terms that prove crucial to the difficult definition of a "generic set" in meditations 33 and 34 of *L'Etre et l'événement,* an investigation (which in Badiou's system is the process that gives rise to what Cohen himself calls a "condition") can thus be formally expressed as a sequence of elements $\{x_1, x_2, x_3 \ldots x_n\}$, where each element is marked as positively or negatively connected to the event—say, for instance, $\{x_1(+), x_2(-), x_3(+) \ldots\}$. An investigation thus has a double ontological status, both as a simple collection of *elements* $\{x_1, x_2, x_3 \ldots\}$ that themselves belong to the situation and that it leaves, qua multiples, unaltered, and as a collection of *judgments,* or classifications (+ or -), through which it encodes a certain amount of information about these elements. In this latter capacity it resembles an operation of knowledge, and the great challenge confronting a properly generic set theory will be to conceive of these investigations or conditions in such a way as to subtract their truthful operation of classification (or their "gathering into a subset") from the ordinary, discernible classifications of knowledge. More on this in a moment.

Fidelity

Fidelity is the virtue required to sustain a literally endless sequence of investigations (or, an investigation is a "finite stage" of a fidelity to truth [EE, 364]). In the simplest terms, "to be faithful to an event is to move within the situation that this event has supplemented, by *thinking*... the situation 'according to' the event" (E, 38). To take the most obvious case: two lovers remain faithful to the event of their encounter insofar as they preserve its various consequences as the basis for a new understanding of their shared situation. Along the same lines, Berg and Webern are among the composers who have worked in fidelity to Schoenberg's initial break with tonal harmonies, just as the political practice of French Maoists between 1966 and 1976 was conceived in terms of a "fidelity to two entangled events: the Cultural Revolution in China, and May 68 in France."[45] Whatever the procedure, fidelity is what lends it an enduring, eventually institutional, stability or solidity, without yielding to an internal objectification. The subjects of love, art, and politics all discover, in their different domains, that "fidelity is the opposite of repetition" or routine.[46]

The essential thing to understand is that only those who remain actively faithful to the implications of an event can grasp them at all. To "perceive" an event as an event is in no sense to appreciate it at a safe distance (as Kant admired the French Revolution, say). The truth is true only for its subjects, not for its spectators: as Žižek notes, all "subject-language involves the logic of the shibboleth, of a difference which is visible only from within, not from without."[47] This is again most obvious in the case of love. A third person looking in on a loving couple may be charmed or irritated, but is unlikely to share in the experience of love itself; those whose subjective *parti pris* is to treat love as sentimental delusion, moreover, will of course see only the semblance of genuine emotion. The same with modern art: those whose vision is limited to realist perspectivism will see in modern abstraction only a kind of practical joke played by the art market. We know, too, what Schoenberg sounds like to those brought up on Bach and Mozart. Politics is no different. The Revolution qua revolution—that is, as distinct from a political crisis, disturbance, or disorder—will appear as such only to those who in some sense adopt its cause as their own.[48] In short, "it will remain forever doubtful if there really was an event, except for those who, by intervening, decided that it belonged to the situation" (EE, 229).

Remember though that if, as the name implies, to be *fidèle* is properly a matter of faith, this does not at all mean that fidelity is a matter of blind or arbitrary faith. On the contrary, Badiou's model of fidelity is the "adventurous rigor" of mathematical deduction itself.[49] We know that mathematics cannot establish the existential foundation of its constructions—the void and the infinite—otherwise than through their axiomatic declaration or nomination. The careful, step-by-step deduction of proofs from the presumption of these terms is authorized, in the end, "only by a prescription that nothing founds."[50] By the same token, there is nothing private or introspective about fidelity. Fidelity is, by definition, ex-centric, directed outward, beyond the limits of a merely personal integrity. To be faithful to an evental implication always means to abandon oneself, rigorously, to the unfolding of its consequences. Fidelity implies that, if there is truth, it can be only cruelly indifferent to the private as such. Every truth involves a kind of antiprivatization, a subjective collectivization. *In truth,* "I" matter only insofar as I am subsumed by the impersonal vector of truth—say, the political organization, or the scientific research program.

On the other hand, the collective dimension of a fidelity need not imply uniformity or orthodoxy: "In the same situation and for a same event there may exist different criteria of connection that define different fidelities" (EE, 258). There are clearly many ways of maintaining a fidelity to Christ, Marx, Freud, or Schoenberg, for instance, and there was nothing about the event of October 1917, say, that implied the inevitable triumph of a Stalinist approach to fidelity. It is in order to distinguish a truth procedure from ephemeral or disastrous distortions of fidelity that Badiou distinguishes the generic criteria of connection that characterize an indiscernible collection from "spontaneous" criteria of connection on the one hand (whereby only those elements directly involved in an event are deemed to be truly connected to it), and from "dogmatic" criteria of connection on the other (whereby all elements in the situation are presumed to be connected to the event as a matter of course).

The more general questions remain open. Do certain types of event or certain sorts of intervention appeal to particular sorts of fidelity (spontaneous, dogmatic, or generic)? Can the general rules of a fidelity be deduced from the nature of the evental conversion itself? How far, for instance, can we make sense of the differences between French and American politics in terms of the ways these nations maintain a fidelity to their founding revolutions? Such questions have profound theoretical implications. If the subject is "the very process that sustains the link between the event (and thus the intervention) and the procedure of fidelity (and thus its operator of connection)," then, Badiou suggests, most philosophical systems will adopt, as their fundamental organizing principle, "a theoretical proposition regarding this link" (EE, 264). The more substantial the link, the more its effects will be conditioned by stability, continuity, and consistency with the remainder of the situation; the less substantial the link, the more dramatic and disruptive will be its effect. Neither extreme is sustainable: pure continuity eliminates the very possibility of an event, while pure disruption suggests that any post-evental intervention must itself proceed as a second event.

The Generic Subset

Since the evental origin of a truth aligns it precisely with what is not being as being, ontology has strictly nothing to say about the active process of truth. What can be said of truth qua truth and being qua being, *pace* Hegel and Heidegger, can never be said in one and the same discourse. Thanks to Cohen's revolutionary elaboration of a *generic* set theory, however, the disjunction of these discourses does not amount to a genuine contradiction. Although mathematics has nothing to say about the production and imposition of a truth, it can at least demonstrate the ontological form of its accumulation. After Cohen, we know that being and truth are at least "compatible," that is, that mathematics can indeed describe the being of truth—even if a truth, in both its operation and development, is irreducible to its being (EE, 391). More precisely, Cohen's work tells us that the being of a truth (a generic set) is to be situated in the very space opened by the im-passe of ontology, that is, the impossibility of measuring the infinite excess of inclusion over belonging, which is to say, in the space normally occupied by the state of a situation. This impasse, whose "*truth* cannot be thought or grasped within the field of ontology itself," is the point through which a subject may pass, since only a subject is capable of the "indiscernment" that being itself indicates as its real. Only a subject is capable of those decisions that force a path through the impasse of number, thanks precisely to their evental foundation in the supernumerary.[51]

Ontologically, what a truth is, is a particular subset or part of the situa-tion, one that collects, to infinity, all the positively investigated elements of the situation. A truth is what counts as one all the elements that investiga-tions have connected to the name or implication of the event (all those who take up the cause of the Revolution, of Christ, of Schoenberg, etc.): "A ge-neric set is the multiple being of a truth" (EE, 373). Subsets qualify as generic or "indiscernible" if they evade all of the criteria of discernment operative in the situation in which they are included. The be-ing of a truth is composed as a generic subset, since the sole criterion of its assembly is the unpresent-able be-ing of its elements: although it is never possible to present the pure inconsistency that we are, a generic subset is one that adopts this inconsistency, which is "the very being of that which is," as its sole raison d'être.[52] Or, in other words, though the being of every situation is inconsistent, and though "being as being is itself simply the multiple composition of the void, it follows from the event alone that there can be truths of this empty [or inconsistent] foundation" (D, 132).

The precise mathematical description of generic sets is, without a doubt, the most complex and most intimidating aspect of *L'Etre et l'événement,* and there can be no question of working through it in any detail here. For the benefit of those readers who might otherwise skip the final meditations of Badiou's book altogether, however, I provide an analogical outline of the logic here, along with a highly simplified version of Cohen's own procedure in the final pages of my appendix. Four points are especially significant.

1. As a subset of any given situation S, a truth operates in an effectively "statelike" way: it is collected as a *part* of S. Simply, whereas the state orders the arrangement of all officially sanctioned parts, a truth part gathers together those elements that connect to a particular, paradoxical multiple: the event (EE, 258–62). Remember that since an event evades the "counting for one" that structures a situation, since it is "supernumerary" and not presentable in the situation, its membership in the situation cannot be verified (it will have to be decided) (EE, 199). Localizable in S but not necessarily belonging to it, an event is initially included in S as a subset whose own elements—that is, itself and the elements belonging to its site—have nothing in common with the elements belonging to S. A truth thus begins as a pure excrescence, as defined in chapter 4: it is included or represented in S without belonging to it, without being presented in it (EE, 377). It begins as a pure evental name with no referent. The set-theoretic version of such a name is, by convention, G (for generic); Badiou himself, for reasons his Lacanian readers may guess, uses the symbol ♀ in its place (EE, 392).

2. To begin with, ♀ will be a subset to which, as far as an inhabitant of the situation S is concerned, nothing at all belongs (and that includes nothing other than an empty name and the indistinguishable inhabitants of the evental site). What a truth does, then, is proceed to flesh out the referential space to which it lays its initially meaningless claim: element by element, investigation by investigation, it will add to ♀ those elements of S that connect positively to the event's implications, and it will do so in such a way that these new

groupings of elements evade classification by the existing mechanisms of discernment available to the state of S. Since the resulting subset will be indiscernible and unpresentable in S, it will of course be hard to say exactly "what" it is. Set theory's most fundamental axiom, however—the axiom of extensionality—makes at least the concept of such a generic procedure intuitively plausible: since a set is defined solely by its members without any explicit reference to exactly how these members are assembled, it seems reasonable in principle to talk about sets made up of infinitely many members that share no common characteristic and conform to no common rule. The axiom justifies the *possibility,* as one commentator puts it, of joining "entirely disparate sets together in unnatural union."[53] The direct implication is that if a generic procedure is not to have recourse to some overarching principle of classification or construction, the only way it can proceed is by considering or "investigating" each element of the situation, one at a time. (The point, again, is that only a militant truth procedure will allow this possibility to become an actuality.)

3. What a truth procedure adds to the generic set ♀ are thus the results of such investigations, that is, finite groups of elements that connect positively to the event. (In set theory proper, what Badiou calls "investigations" are referred to as "conditions" [EE, 376].) In the Christian situation, for instance, such groups of "conditions" will consist of names of individuals who have affirmed the Resurrection. As they accumulate—at a rate that depends entirely on the evangelical zeal and haphazard trajectory of the subjects of this truth—these names will be arranged in ever more inclusive lists. A more inclusive list is said to "extend" or "dominate" the lists it includes. At any finite point of its extension, however, it is at least theoretically possible that the names included in such a list might be re-presented in terms that the situation will continue to recognize—say, as a group of "fanatics," or "religious reformers," or "disaffected Jews," or "people excluded Roman citizenship." Remember that there can be no "holes" in the language of a situation as such: as far as the ordinary members of S are concerned, the state's re-presentation of what is presented in S will always appear to be complete and definitive. Every finite subset of S falls under the count of its state, so if the truth is to take place at all, it is the truth itself that will have to punch a hole in the language of S.[54] (The underlying principle be-

hind this point is just the simple idea that we can have no objective knowledge of love, or of artistic creation, or of scientific invention, because what can be said about these procedures as inventive improvisations is quite distinct from what can be said about any limited collection of their products or results. The very attempt to treat procedures of love, or of art, in terms of demonstrable certainties or "interpretative keys" destroys them as a matter of course.)

4. For a set to qualify as generic, then, it must be *unending* and thus open in principle to any number of new inclusions (EE, 367), and these inclusions must avoid classification within the encyclopedia of knowledges operative in S. A subset avoids classification by a given property if it contains some elements that exhibit that property and others that do not: a subset avoids *all* classification, then, if for every distinct principle in the encyclopedia it contains some elements that fit that principle and others that do not. In the pre-Christian situation whose elements are re-presented in subsets or parts distinguished in terms of Jew and Gentile, Roman citizens and Roman subjects, free individuals and slaves, men and women, and so on, the new Christian subset remains indiscernible insofar as it comes to include elements from all of these categories (both Jew and non-Jew, both free and enslaved, etc.). In terms of the "extended" lists of conditions it might include, the Christian version of ♀ will thus be one that embraces, in ascending order, implications such as "can include free male Jews," "can include male Jews," "can include Jews," "can include Jews and non-Jews," "can include people of any religious background," and finally (for this is the ultimate condition of any generic set), "can include anyone." The result will be a subset that, by intersecting with every possible extension of its conditions, includes "a little of everything" belonging to S. It will be a subset about which, using the resources of the situation, we can say nothing distinct or particular, other than that it simply is a set. What such a set is, is thus nothing other than the "truth of the situation as a whole, since what it means to be indiscernible is to demonstrate as a one-multiple [i.e., as a set] the very being of that which belongs to it, inasmuch as it *belongs* to it," pure and simple (EE, 374). A generic set, in other words, is an inclusion (a re-presentation) whose only property is to expose belonging (presentation) in its purest state— an exposure that the state of the situation is precisely designed to foreclose.

The investigations or conditions that belong to ♀ are thus distinct from other multiples in S because their inclusion in ♀ brings with it a certain amount of cumulative information about these elements—such is its "knowledgelike" dimension (EE, 370). As it is assembled, the generic subset will provide both the raw material (the elements) of a truth and the conditions of its "intelligibility," since "the conditions that the indiscernible must obey so as to be indiscernible [within S] will be materialized only by certain structures of the given situation" (EE, 393). In the generic procedure defined by modern painting after the Cézanne event, for instance, a condition or investigation will be made up of both those elements—those works of art—in the artistic situation that in some sense qualify as "post-Cézanne" (as distinct from pre-Cézanne, anti-Cézanne, or indifferent to Cézanne), along with an implicit recognition of the test they passed in order to qualify as such. Such painting will qualify as properly generic if and only if there is no way of characterizing the cumulative set of investigations that coincides with premodern criteria of classification—that is, as it comes to include subjects from all discernible genres and perspectives, to explore both the figural and the abstract, to emphasize both line and color, and so on. Likewise, in their fidelity to the encounter, two lovers will come to explore their situation "in such a way as to find out what is related or unrelated or difficult to relate to this primordial event. In so doing they will trace a subset of the situation, little by little over time—because the extraordinarily ramified activities of love necessarily circumscribe a particular time. The subset is generic and therefore, indiscernible. This means that the lovers cannot discern the truth that they themselves constitute. It's in this sense," Badiou concludes, "that I'd say they are its subject."[55]

To sum up: a generic subset is an infinite and unconstructible subset that evades all available means of classification, that collects the most indifferent or anonymous qualities of the situation, that is thus "both immanent to the situation and indistinguishable in thought from its being." What Badiou calls a truth process or a generic procedure is, ontologically, "the coming to be of this subset, through the succession of finite investigations that 'test' the elements of the situation with respect to a supplementary element, which is the trace in the situation of the vanished event. A subject is in a sense the active face, the 'naturing nature' of these explorations, materially indiscernible from their existence."[56]

Forcing: *Vérité* and *Véridicité*

The last major step or component of a truth procedure is the operation whereby a truth changes the situation in which it is included, so as to impose or "force" its recognition in a transformed version of that situation. Forcing is the process whereby the truth that was initially collected as an indiscernible and anonymous part (or inclusion) of the situation S comes to belong as an element or member of S (EE, 377). Unlike nomination, intervention, or fidelity, forcing is thus "a relation that is verifiable by knowledge" (EE, 441), a relation that allows for the eventual *confirmation* of a truth—that allows the effects of a vérité to become *véridique* (verifiable).

Like the mathematization of a generic subset, the logic of forcing (again adapted from Cohen) is both too tricky to summarize in any detail and too important to be passed over altogether. The gist of the sequence is as follows.

1. Although an ordinary inhabitant of S can understand the *concept* of a generic set (i.e., one that intersects every possible extension of the conditions belonging to S), nevertheless he or she will not be able to see such a set in S. Since it can never belong to S, it will always seem that a generic collection ♀ could exist only in another world. From within S, it will always seem, so to speak, that "only God could be indiscernible" (EE, 410). Insofar as it is confined to ♀, a truth remains, for the remainder of S, a matter of promise pure and simple: a prophecy of imminent revolution, the announcement of a new art to come, or something along such lines.

2. In order for this promise to be converted into something more substantial, ♀ must be made to *belong* to the situation in which it has been initially included. This will require reorganizing S as a whole so as to make room for ♀. S will have to be altered in such a way that it becomes possible to add ♀ to a new version of S, the "generic extension" of S, written S(♀). This might involve changing the art world (producers, galleries, consumers, and so on) so as to make room for modern art, or changing society so as to make room for the consequences of a political revolution. However disruptive such transformation might be, still S(♀) will remain, in its being, almost indistinguishable from S itself. The extension will add no new "information" about S. (In strictly set-theoretical terms, it will, for instance, contain no new ordinals, meaning that the "natural" part of S(♀) will remain the same as that of S itself—which is another way of confirming that the generic concerns what is least natural, least ordered, or least stable about being [EE, 422].)

Just how it is possible to add something indiscernible to a situation is a very delicate problem. The solution, roughly speaking, is initially to modify not S itself but the "language" of S, so as to make it capable of naming the still hypothetical elements of its generic extension. Because the new subset is precisely indiscernible, we cannot simply construct it in keeping with a distinct, recognizable definition. But if we can manage to rework terms in S that might serve to *anticipate* future knowledge about these elements, we will at least be able to refer to them before we quite know what they are (i.e., before we can verify what actually belongs to them). Such terms will allow us to name what these still unknown elements will become in the generic extension of S, S(♀). Since ♀ itself will remain indiscernible in this extension, we will not be able to say exactly which element of S(♀) will be identified by a given name in S, but it is possible to prove, at least from the position of "general ontology" (i.e., a set-theoretical perspective that includes our situation S as one among many other, larger sets), that every element must have such a name, and that the manipulation of these names will indeed allow us to specify the essential features of S(♀) (EE, 394; cf. 410–12). It will then become possible for an inhabitant of S to say: "If there were to be a generic extension of our situation S, then such-and-such a name that exists in S will come to designate this particular part of the extension." Creating the extension is a matter of "naming that which is precisely impossible to discern," a process in which "it is indeed the name that creates the thing" (EE, 415).

Consider, for instance, the invention—or rather, since they must already belong to S, the "reworking" *(bricolage)*—of names such as "faith," "charity," "sin," and "salvation" (for Paul), or "discipline," "revolution," and "politics" (for Lenin): despite being recognizable as words in the existing language of S, as new names these terms have no referents in the initial situation at all, but serve rather to designate terms that will have been presented in the new situation S(♀), once its advent has been accomplished (EE, 435–36). In Badiou's compressed phrase, the names proposed by the subject, in the absence of all recognizable signification, are "empty only for being full of what is sketched of their own possibility."[57] The more visible this sketch becomes in the extended version of the situation, so "to be an element of the extension S(♀)" will mean "to be the referential value of a reworked name of S." Hence the apparently "nominalist" quality of S(♀): for an inhabitant of S (though not for the "general ontologist"), the elements of the generic extension will be "accessible only through their names" (EE, 418). Moreover, access to these elements will remain limited in this way until the structures of language and knowledge in the new extension change in their turn; if they do not, it will never be possible to verify the claims made by a truth.

3. The anticipated referential value in S(♀) of the new names in S will depend upon the information encoded by the "conditions" (or "investigations") included in the truth ♀. Remember that investigation is what determines whether a term is or is not positively connected to an event. The positive investigation of a term then "forces" a statement made with the newly reworked names of S if the connection of this term to the event, that is, its belonging to ♀, ensures the imminent truthfulness of that statement in the new, extended situation S(♀). More precisely, that "a term x belonging to the situation forces a statement of the subject language means that the verifiability of this statement in the situation to come is equivalent to the belonging of this term x to the indiscernible part ♀ that results from the generic procedure" (EE, 441; cf. 450). Once it has been forced, it will become possible to know the truthfulness of this statement in the transformed, postevental situation. What will remain forever unverifiable by knowledge, of course, is whether the term that forced the statement does indeed belong to ♀, since this is a matter of its militant investigation alone.

Badiou offers a couple of compressed illustrations, beginning with a "caricature" of Newtonian astronomy. The declaration made in the new "subject language" of Newtonian physics that "the gravitational pull of an as yet undiscovered planet is affecting the orbits of certain other planets" clearly cannot be verified in the scientific situation as it then is. Its eventual verification will depend on whether future investigations, undertaken in fidelity to the event of Newton's discoveries, will be able to connect (here, through the combination of calculation and observation) a hitherto invisible term of the situation (here, the solar system) with the implications of this event. Clearly, if this "new" planet can be shown to exist—that is, if its eventual connection qualifies it for membership in ♀—the declaration will have been truthful in the new extended universe that will become the solar system supplemented by scientific astronomy (EE, 440). Pending the investigation and connection of such a "forcing" or validating term, however, the truthfulness of the declaration is suspended: its verification can be anticipated but not confirmed.

Along the same lines, consider a simple declaration made in the subject language of a post-Maoist fidelity to the events of May 68: "The factory is a political place." This means that a factory is irreducible to the logic of corporate profits, on the one hand, and to that of the parliamentary supervision of moderate trade union demands, on the other. The validity of such a statement is undecidable in our currently depoliticized situation. The situation will have to be investigated through the organization of militant meetings and rallies at factories. The investigation of a positively connected ("won-over," "rallied") group of workers will force the statement to become verifiable in any new situation in which such an as yet indiscernible political mobilization has been established. And if such a factory or group of workers has yet to be encountered, the only conclusion the subject of this procedure can draw is that the investigations must continue until the truthfulness of the statement can be confirmed (EE, 443).

So while a truth always remains heterogeneous to knowledge, forcing ensures that truths are "also the sole known source of new knowledges" (E, 62). More precisely, "forcing operates at the point where a truth, however incomplete it might be, authorizes anticipated knowledge, not about what is, but about what will have been if the truth comes to its completion" (C, 206; cf. PM, 40). Marx, for example, confronted by the intolerable "nightmare of history," the senseless accumulation of millennia of toil and suffering, forced it into intelligibility as the story of class struggle, in anticipation of a society in which that struggle will have been resolved.[58] Likewise Galileo, at the outset of a preliminary mathematization of nature, anticipated its eventually total mathematization and a consequently "total" physics. Such speculations are not strictly internal to the truth process itself, which simply continues step by step, through the investigation of one element after another. To explore them involves the transformation of what can be *known* of the situation to come. "This is what Plato had already anticipated," Badiou explains, "when he indicated that the duty of those who escape from his famous cave, dazzled by the sun of the Idea, was to return to the shadows and to help their companions in servitude to profit from that by which, on the threshold of this dark world, they had been seized. Only today can we fully measure what this return means: it is that of Galilean physics back toward technical machinery, or of atomic theory back toward bombs and nuclear power plants. The return of disinterested interest toward brute interest, the forcing of knowledges by a few truths" (E, 53).

4. Since it is the truth of S and not the "absolute beginning of a new situation," the addition of ♀ will not alter the profound being qua being of S (EE, 456). What it enables, authorized by the indiscernible set of conditions that come to belong to it, is the verification in S(♀) of truthful statements that were previously undecidable in S. It is in this way that "art, science, and politics change the world, not by what they discern in it, but through what they indiscern *[par ce qui'ils y indiscernent]*." These procedures change the way things are named, so as to reveal, in its inconsistent unnameability, that "unnameable being that is the very being of that which is" (EE, 377).

5. As far as the discourse of ontology itself is concerned, the paradigm of an undecidable statement is Cantor's continuum hypothesis (CH). Cohen developed the technique of forcing precisely in order to demonstrate the independence of CH from the basic laws of set theory (i.e., the axioms that normally decide the verifiability of statements in the situation of set theory) by showing that $2^{\aleph_0}$ can be forced into a one-to-one correspondence with just about any transfinite cardinal, be it $\aleph_1$ or $\aleph_{101}$. This unmeasurable ontological gap between belonging and inclusion provides a general description of the being of what all subjects do (in ways that vary, of course, according to their situations). This is why the "impasse of being as being" locates, ontologically, the "*passe* of the Subject." We know that in a normal situation the gap between belonging and inclusion (between $\aleph_0$ and $2^{\aleph_0}$) is covered over by the re-presentations of its state, and that it can be exposed only through an exceptional rent in the fabric of being, that is, in the wake of an event. Thus exposed, the impasse of being is the point where a subject is "summoned to decide" its measure—both to set a limit upon the normally exorbitant excess of the state, and to "measure himself," what he is capable of, in this pure space of presentation, the space that was liberated from re-presentation through an evental "convocation of the void."

The Subject

We are now in a position to understand more exactly what Badiou means when he defines a subject as "any local configuration of a generic procedure by which a truth is sustained" (EE, 429). Negatively, this definition precludes conceiving of the subject as:

a substance (since the procedure evades the counting for one that determines existence);

an empty point (since the procedure clearly "proceeds" as a multiplicity rather than a point, and since the void itself is "inhuman and asubjective");

the transcendental organizing mechanism of an experience (since the word "experience" can refer only to what is presentable or countable in a situation, whereas the evental sequence eludes the count; it is supernumerary or "ultra-one");

the seat of meaning (since a truth remains indiscernible and thus devoid of any meaning that the situation might recognize);

a structural principle (since evental procedures are invariably rare and exceptional);

simply autonomous, or indifferent to that to which it is subject (since every faithful subject emerges as the subject *of* a truth, for example, of a political or artistic sequence);

an origin or result (since the procedure is always underway, in excess of the situation's resources);

the consciousness of truth (since every subject is local, or finite, and is not in a position to know or count out the unending subset collected by a truth).[59]

More positively, the subject as "local configuration of a generic procedure" will be the connection, through the insignificant void of a proper name (Paul, Lenin, Cantor, Schoenberg) of an intervention (that imposed the name of the event) with an operator of fidelity (that makes its implications stick). Lenin qua subject, for instance, is both the October Revolution (in his evental aspect) and Leninism (as fidelity to the attempt to generalize that revolution). Cantor is both the inspired inventor of infinite numbers and the slow process that strives, in fidelity to this invention, to reconstruct the entire language of mathematics (a process that has run from Zermelo to Bourbaki). It is because an intervention concerns a situation-specific exposure to the void that is the name of being in general that subjectivation can be described as "an occurrence of the void."[60]

Badiou's definition suggests a number of distinct though overlapping ways of describing the roles played by a subject in the elaboration of a truth. Listing these allows us to review the whole sequence of a generic procedure.

1. What an event exposes is the void of a situation S, that is, the pure being of what it presents (what it counts as one), in the suspension of all re-presentation. The subject is, first and foremost, a response to this exposure, an attempt to articulate its implications. If "the event reveals the void of the situation, . . . it is from this void that the subject constitutes himself as fragment of a truth process. It is this void that separates him from the situation or the place, inscribing him in a trajectory without precedent. . . . The subject is he who chooses to persevere in this distance from himself inspired by the revelation of the void—the void, which is the very being of the place" (PM, 88).

2. A truth proceeds as the collecting together of all those elements in the situation that respond or "connect" positively to this revelation of its void. These connections are established by a subject in fidelity to the event. The subject undertakes the finite sets of investigations that a truth then collects (as the elements of that generic subset ♀ that defines the being of a truth). But the subject is not itself to be identified with any particular set of investigations; he is "'between' the terms that the procedure collects"; his only "substance" is that combination of persistence and chance that leads him to encounter and test this term or that term, one after another. Strictly speaking, "chance, from which is woven every truth, is the matter of the subject."[61] We might say, then, that the subject is separated from the generic subset—the truth itself—by "an infinite series of chance encounters" (EE, 434–37).

3. What an event implies cannot be said in the language of a situation S as it stands. By definition, the situation as such can say nothing of its void. This is why the subject who intervenes to name the event (or draw its implications) is also the active principle behind the forcing of new knowledges (EE, 439). By definition, no finite subject is in a position to know an infinite truth—the very attempt implies a truth's termination. Instead, by testing the elements of S with respect to the event, a subject can predict what a situation transformed by the implications of that event will be like. Over the course of his investigations, the subject will rework terms of the language of S in order to anticipate the implications of the event. In the process, such words—for instance, "painting," "perspective," and

"form" for the subject Picasso, or "sexuality," "superego," and "drive" for the subject Freud—will be both stripped of a discernible referent in S and then used to force the verification of statements made about new elements that "will have been" presented in the transformed situation. The testing of such terms in an endless sequence of evental investigations will ensure that they evade every principle of classification recognized in S (technically, they will intersect with every consistent extension of the conditions distinguishable in S), clearing a referential space that "will have been filled if the truth comes to be in the new situation." For instance, when the subject Galileo declared the principle of inertia, he anticipated by several decades its eventual verification within the new order of knowledge formulated by Descartes and Newton: Galileo could only wager that by reworking the terms he had at hand ("movement," "equal proportions," etc.) he would name a principle that would become verifiable in the situation that the indiscernible, unending subset we call "rational physics" would transform. Unable to know a truth, what drives the subject of truth (as opposed to subsequent users of knowledge) is instead a form of rigorous faith, or "confidence" (*confiance*)—a confidence that the endless, haphazard pursuit of investigations is not in vain (EE, 437–39).

4. Strictly speaking, it is thus a truth that "induces" its subjects, and not the other way around. Truths are infinite accumulations; subjects amount only to finite "points" of a truth (E, 39–40): "The subject is nothing other, in its being, than a truth grasped in its pure point; it is a vanishing quantity of truth, a differential eclipse of its unfinishable infinity" (C, 286). The inventive truth that is tonal music or transfinite mathematics infinitely exceeds the finite investigations (musical works, theorems) made by those subjects called Schoenberg or Cantor, even though what this truth amounts to at any finite stage of its accumulation will be made up solely of the collection of these works or theorems (EE, 433).

5. Since every truth is exceptional, the subject must be firmly distinguished from an ordinary individual. What Badiou calls an ordinary "someone" (*quelqu'un*) is simply an indifferently infinite element already presented in a situation. By contrast, a subject in no way preexists the truth process that inspires him: subjectivation is the abrupt conversion of a someone. Although all someones *can* become subjects, Badiou offers no grounds for accepting the moralizing

presumption that "every human animal is a subject" (TA, 6.11.96). Unlike those "ethical" ideologues preoccupied with the nebulous administration of human rights, Badiou is determined to distinguish the attributes of true humanity from the ultimately quantifiable sufferings of ordinary animality. For Badiou no less than for Lacan or Žižek, subjectivation is essentially indifferent to the business and requirements of life as such.

6. That it is truth that induces its subjects ensures, moreover, that there is nothing private or capricious about Badiou's "subjective" conception of truth. Although "what is addressable to all is so only if it is absolutely gratuitous" (SP, 81), those who "answer the call" live it as absolute necessity. Starting out from the radical obscurity of the evental site, the subject is precisely the imposition of clarity and certainty in circumstances of initial uncertainty and confusion.[62] As a rule, "he who is a militant of truth identifies himself, like everyone else, on the [sole] basis of the universal," and knows that he is "justified [justifié] only to the degree that everyone is" (SP, 117, 103). Badiou's subject is always *anybody*. "Subjective," here, means impersonal, rigorous, and universal—never introspective or idiosyncratic. All truths are singular, but "no truth is solitary, or particular." Since every true subject is "deprived of all identity," there is no choice to be made here between subjective or universal. "Subjective" simply means: indifferent to objective differences (SP, 95).

In this way an evental truth procedure rescues, as actually universal, the One initially banished from ontology. The one is not, yet the one can come to be as "for all."[63] The only possible Pauline correlate to the resurrection is humanity as a whole, just as the immediate political dimension of the Jacobin sequence must be "Man" in general. As Simone de Beauvoir has observed, mediocrity is reserved for those who do not feel "responsible for the universe" as a whole.[64]

We are now in a position to confirm the important differences between Badiou's and Lacan's conceptions of subjectivation. Both thinkers understand that "the subject is decentred in relation to the individual," or the ego (S2, 17/9). It is simply regarding the nature of this ex-centricity that the two differ. For the analyst, the subject as subject of the unconscious is structurally or systematically ex-centric, thanks to the unconscious agency of the signifier, the play of distinction and "polarization" that allows the subject to speak. As Žižek notes, "The Lacanian 'subject of the signifier' is not a positive, substantial entity persisting outside the series of its representations: it coincides with its own impossibility; it 'is' nothing but the void opened up by the failure of its representations. . . . In Lacanian theory the subject is *nothing* but the impossibility of its own signifying representation—the empty place opened up in the big Other by the failure of this representation."[65] For Badiou, by contrast, this impossibility is simply what can be *known* of the subject from within the existing situation. Becoming a subject is in every case exceptional, the result of an operation in which language and signification enjoy no special privilege.

In the extraordinarily compressed critique of Lacan that closes *L'Etre et l'événement,* Badiou distinguishes his evental conception of the subject—the subject that emerges from the supernumerary "ultra-one" of an event—from the essentially void-based subject of Descartes and Lacan. In order to preserve the subject of truth from imaginary or sensual delusion, Descartes and Lacan believe they must "hold the subject in the pure void of its subtraction if the truth is to be preserved": only an evacuated subject can be perfectly traversed by the integral transmission that is scientific logic.[66] Lacan thus persists in thinking of the subject as a structure (as an empty set), as opposed to the consequence of an event. Only by cutting the link between subject and structure (and thereby suspending the mediation of language) is it possible to complete the dissociation of truth from what Lacan himself calls, with justifiable contempt, "exactitude" or "adequation."

Moreover, when the later Lacan does make some moves in this direction (toward the "other side" of fantasy), it is only to identify with that most antiphilosophical of configurations: the drive. Unlike desire, the drive "never comes to an impasse. . . . The drive knows nothing of prohibition and certainly doesn't dream of transgressing it. The drive follows its own bent and always obtains satisfaction."[67] Only the drive is truly independent of the Other, but this independence is trapped within the effectively thoughtless pursuit of inarticulate *jouissance.*[68]

What Badiou proposes, in short, is the liberation of truth from the drive.

Toward a Topological Understanding of the Subjective Space

In his seminars over the last few years, Badiou has begun to provide a more nuanced understanding of the process of subjectivation. The transformation of an individual into a subject is starting to look like a less insistently immediate process. Badiou realizes that an event can evoke a range of possible subjective responses (TA, 26.11.97). Rather than speaking of just "one operation of the subject" (as was the case in *Théorie du sujet*) or just four applications of this operation (as is still effectively the case in *L'Etre et l'événement*), he now speaks of the familiar subject of fidelity in permanent tension with other rival though equally subjective figures: the "reactionary" and the "obscure." Rather than insist that the subject is simply decided into existence, more or less instantaneously, he now believes that the subject *"appears"* over time, over the course of a more articulated process, as an "inscription in a subjective space" (TA, 12.11.97). He now sees each effect of truth as raising the possibility of a countereffect, no longer considered as simply external to the process of subjectivation, but as internal to the subjective space itself. In short, he now considers the subjective realm precisely as a *space*—as something that no one figure can fully occupy and determine, as something that every subject must traverse.

Although it is too early to evaluate these new developments properly, it is certainly worth summarizing Badiou's two main innovations. First, by replacing the literal connection between an event and its name with the implicative connection of an event and its "evental statement" (see "On the Edge of the Void" in this chapter) Badiou ensures the ontological independence, or "detachment," of this statement (TA, 5.3.97). The statement is not ontologically but logically related to the event. The truth of the statement itself will not be marked by any ontological trace of the subject position of whoever first declared it, just as any true scientific result, even if originally arrived at by accident or coincidence, will stand up independently of its haphazard occasion. The declaring implies a series of detachable consequences more than it enfolds them in a proximity to its "insight." Hence a further difference of Badiou from Descartes, whose *cogito* remains coextensive with the subjective position that declares it, and from Marx, for whom there is a direct link between the identification of the subject of history and the truth of this history itself. To lend the event an implicative dimension is already to submit the process of its affirmation to a kind of logical mediation, as distinct from the immediacy of a pure nomination.

More important, Badiou now carves up the process of subjective intervention to accommodate the possibility of five distinct subjective figures, but without thereby diluting the direct connection each maintains with the evental statement. (To dilute this connection would be to reduce the subject into the passive, impotent agent of "memory" or "interpretation.") The first figure, adapted from Lacan's matheme of hysteria, coincides with an immediate, unprocessed expression of the evental statement. The hysterical assertion is always a variant of "Something has happened," and this something is too urgent, too catastrophic, to put into ordered words. "Every irruption of truth is hysterical," Badiou writes, and the hysterical figure inspires or energizes each of the successive figures of the subject (TA, 4.12.96).

The second position conforms to the figure of the "master." Mastery belongs to the subject of fidelity, the subject who puts the hysterical assertion to work. While the hysteric is entirely caught up in the declaration and effectively paralyzed by it, the master is able, at a distance from the immediate circumstances of the declaration, to draw out the consequences of the declaration and make them apply.[69] Freud was himself the master who "put the speech of the hysteric to work," just as Marx was the master who drew the consequences of the hysterical uprisings of the 1830s and 1840s (TA, 9.1.97; TS, 148). Mastery is an attribute of the self-sacrificing militant, of the adherent to the revolution, who sees the continuation of a truth as a task to be undertaken methodically here and now. If the hysteric speaks in the urgency of the evental instant, the master lives in the unfolding *present* of its consequences. The figure of the master clearly corresponds to Badiou's own subjective self-description.

With the third figure we enter the realm that Badiou has previously condemned as antisubjective pure and simple. This is the figure of reaction, which consists in the active denial of the event. The reactionary figure can be considered "subjective" insofar as its position remains entirely derivative of its relation to the eventual statement. Simply, this relation is a negative one. Reactionary figures may be defined, for instance, by their belief that the revolution was pointless or that their once consuming love was in fact an illusion. Every reactionary is a relativist, unable or unwilling to distinguish truth from matters of opinion, that is, from the diversity of "more or less." This is why "the reactive figure implies the democratization of truth," its dissolution in the bland coordination of consensus (TA, 3.12.97).

The fourth figure also entertains a negative relation to the present consequences of an eventual statement. This is the figure of obscurity, *le sujet obscur,* who refuses to recognize the possibility of truth *en acte.* The obscurantist devalues an ongoing (and thus unproven or unapproved) fidelity in favor of a rigid conformity to the absolute past of an allegedly original event or revelation. Such, for example, is the figure of religious orthodoxy, for whom the certainty of inherited knowledge regarding a past definitive event stifles any subjective capacity to proclaim a truth in the here and now. The obscure subject "mortifies" every present (and thus divided, open-ended) subject in the name of a definitive Truth attributed to an originally sufficient Law (TA, 19.3.97.) For such an obscure subject all that is clear is the past, a past that has since become clouded in the present. Religious fundamentalism is thus the obscure form of the declaration "God is dead," that is, that God no longer lives in the present, or that the present must be mortified "in honor" of the divine past. Likewise, Stalinism is an obscure form of revolutionary politics, one that abandons an active fidelity to a particular event (October 1917) in favor of a dogmatic insistence upon invariable historical laws. Other examples include an obscurantist resistance to scientific discoveries, an iconoclastic hostility to art, a conservative political traditionalism, and, in the realm of love, a morbidly possessive jealousy (one that attempts to "hold" the beloved to an unchanging guarantee or promise of love, or—for it is the same thing—that pretends to enfold love into the institutional confinement of marriage and the family).[70] In each case, the obscure figure takes the disastrous step of substantializing the truth, of confusing the true with the verifiable (with a doctrine or a revelation).

Finally, Badiou raises the possibility of a fifth figure, which is nothing other than a figure who has returned to a position of mastery and fidelity. Such is the figure who revitalizes a truth and restores the present as a time of consequence. (Badiou draws here on Husserl's notion of desedimentation.) Every truth is, in principle, renewable. Badiou cites the return to Archimedes and Greek mathematics during the Renaissance; the consolidation of neoclassicism as opposed to an obscure academism; the renewal of love, in its anarchic "nudity," as an escape from the restrictions of family (TA. 28.1.98).

Taken together, and given the initial declaration of the hysterical figure, the four subsequent figures correspond, respectively, to the production, the denial, the repression, and the resurrection of truth. This new "axiomatic theory of the subject" is thus a "topological theory," a theory of the transformations of the subjective space, which is to be analyzed as the system linking these various figures of the subject: faithful, reactionary, obscurantist, and renewed.

The cycle of these correlations can be summarized in the following diagram (simplified from TA, 18.3.98):

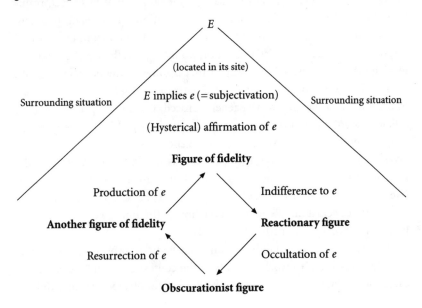

The diagram can be read as follows. Everything begins with an event, which is precisely sited but ontologically unfounded (i.e., which takes place at the edge of what is rootless or belongingless in the situation). The event implies an evental declaration, e (say, "I love you"). The initially hysterical affirmation of e will give rise to a figure of fidelity ("'I' am who I am, because I hold true to this love"). Indifference to e will give rise to a reactionary figure ("I, who once cared about love, now insist that it was all a mistake"). Occultation of e would give rise to the obscurantist figure ("I am entitled to possess you entirely, since you once promised to love me forever"). The resurrection of e (the rebirth of love) would allow for the renewal of the faithful figure, or the creation of another such figure.

Having completed our survey of Badiou's general conception of the subject, we are now in a position to address directly one of the most serious objections yet put to this conception: Žižek's suggestion that it is fundamentally a form of ideological identification. "The first thing that strikes the eye of anyone who is versed in the history of French Marxism," Žižek argues, "is how Badiou's notion of the Truth-Event is uncannily close to Althusser's notion of ideological interpellation." Žižek sees Badiou's "knowledge" as taking the place of science in Althusser's opposition of science and ideology, thereby aligning truth with ideology.[71] He supports this argument by emphasizing the fact that "Badiou's ultimate example of the Event is religion"—indeed, the very religion epitomized by the same Saint Paul who plays such a prominent role in Althusser's discussion of interpellation: "This event, precisely, does *not* fit any of the four *génériques* of the event Badiou enumerates (love, art, science, politics)." Christian religion would appear, then, to be "Badiou's own 'symptomal torsion,' the element that belongs to the domain of Truth without being one of its acknowledged parts or subspecies. . . . With regard to Badiou's own classification of generic procedures in four species, does not religious ideology occupy precisely [the] generic place? It is none of them, yet precisely as such it gives body to the generic as such" (141, 144). Žižek even suggests that Badiou might be "read as the last great author in the French tradition of Catholic dogmaticists from Pascal and Malebranche on (we need only recall that two of his key references are Pascal and Claudel)" (142). His conclusion: "Religious revelation is the unavowed paradigm of Badiou's notion of the Truth-Event" (183).

This accusation is certainly not one that Badiou—who from the beginning has presented his work in terms of the contest between "the enslaving categories of ideological objectives (quality, continuity, temporality, and the negative)" and the true "categories of scientific processes (number, discretion, space, and affirmation)"[72]—can afford to ignore.

There are three good reasons, however, why Žižek's argument here does not hold up. First and most important, he pays virtually no attention to the foundational role of mathematics in Badiou's thought. In particular, he disregards the decisive consequence of that axiom of infinity presumed by every component of Badiou's system: the ruin of any elementary conception of the One, and thus the definitive proof of God's "nonexistence." Rather than "profoundly Christological,"[73] Badiou's thought must be characterized, first and foremost, as post-Cantorian—which is to say, rigorously atheist. The model for Badiou's fidelity is not religious faith but mathematical deduction pure and simple.[74]

Second, Žižek does not fully acknowledge the well-defined place of antiphilosophy in Badiou's system. Although he concedes that Paul figures in Badiou's account as "the antiphilosophical theoretician of the formal conditions of the truth-procedure," he nevertheless goes on to ask

> how it was possible for the first and still most pertinent description of the mode of operation to a Truth-Event to occur apropos of a Truth-Event that is a mere semblance, not an actual Truth? From a Hegelian standpoint there is a deep necessity in this, confirmed by the fact that in our century the philosopher who provided the definitive description of an authentic political act (Heidegger in *Being and Time*) was seduced by a political act that was undoubtedly a fake (Nazism). So it is as if, if one is to express the formal structure of fidelity to the Truth-Event, one has to do it apropos of an Event that is merely its own semblance.[75]

This is to encourage the confusion, which Badiou has been at great pains to avoid, of the legitimate antiphilosophical rival to truth and its merely "disastrous" simulacrum.[76] Badiou has always insisted that philosophy should "work as closely as possible" to antiphilosophy,[77] while firmly defending itself against corruption and evil *(le Mal)*.

It is, finally, only because Žižek ignores the foundational role of mathematics in his system that he can attribute to Badiou the inversion of Althusser's categories of science and ideology. This is at best a highly misleading suggestion. Badiou's subject is in several respects inspired by "the precise consciousness of the theory of scientificity,"[78] very much as Althusser defines it. Althusser's science is emphatically a practice that asserts "its own criterion and [that] contains in itself definite protocols with which to validate the quality of its product, i.e., the criteria of the scientificity of the products of scientific practice. . . . Once [the sciences] are truly constituted, they have no need for verification from external practices to declare the knowledges they produce to be 'true,' i.e., to be knowledges."[79] If Althusser famously presents science as a "subjectless discourse,"[80] this is mainly because *he*—more like Žižek than Badiou—was unable to conceive of the subject in anything other than ideological terms. This is not to say that Badiou's subjectivation is in any way reducible to Althusser's theoricism, which was for years one of the main targets of Badiou's polemics. But, more recently, Badiou himself has come to acknowledge his debt to his former teacher, recognizing that, thanks to his uncompromising insistence on the rationality of thought, "Althusser was indeed *the* philosopher [of his generation], contrary to Lacan, Foucault, or Derrida, all antiphilosophers." Badiou's most recent reading even finds in Althusser glimpses of a subjective register (albeit one "without the subject"), thanks to the irreducibly militant dimension of his work (AM, 74–75).

It is indeed because Žižek's own perspective is so close to Badiou's that their differences emerge with such striking and suggestive clarity. Žižek has explicitly allied himself with Badiou's campaign against the "new sophists" of postmodernity, at least since 1993.[81] A self-declared "Paulinian material-ist,"[82] Žižek, like Badiou, recognizes that "subjectivity and universality are strictly correlative": he says, "I become 'universal' only through the violent effort of disengaging myself from the particularity of my situation."[83] Kant, Hegel, and Schelling, after Lacan, have provided his primary points of refer-ence. For all these reasons, nowhere is the distinction between philosophy and antiphilosophy more pertinent today than between Žižek and Badiou. Like most antiphilosophers, Žižek tends to write in episodic, often repetitive fragments, governed by the same driving obsessions from book to book. In typically antiphilosophical style, Žižek favors elusive, paradoxical formula-tions over systematic elucidation, circling endlessly around that "'repressed' kernel of the Real which philosophy is never able to confront."[84] Žižek's version of Hegel's absolute knowledge implies an equally antiphilosophical "impossibility of accordance between knowledge and being."[85] As opposed to Badiou's reasoned wager on immortality, Žižek's work is guided by an ultimately morbid "fascination with a lethal Thing," a profoundly pessi-mistic conception of "man [as] 'nature sick unto death.'"[86] As Bosteels has suggested with particular force, Žižek—like Laclau and Lacan—again op-poses an effectively static or structural conception of the real to Badiou's essentially interventionist or activist approach. Whereas Badiou maintains that the symptomal real that literally founds a situation is accessible only to those subjects who actively affirm the implication of an event that took place at its edge, Žižek's belief that critique can simply reflect upon the real (albeit as the kernel that resists reflection) or recognize the real (albeit as the gap that resists recognition) reduces thought to an ultimately passive and at best therapeutic form of engagement with the real.[87] Perhaps all that such thought can do, in the end, is acknowledge and affirm the real as drive and identify with its "mindless jouissance," with the "utter stupidity . . . of presymbolic substance in all its abhorrent vitality."[88] In the end, all "drive [is] ultimately the death drive."[89] And death, we know, is one occurrence that never qualifies as an event.

chapter 6

The Criteria of Truth

The most familiar conceptions of truth define it in terms of coherence, correspondence, or confirmation. A coherence model of truth, variously advocated by Gadamer, Davidson, Rorty, and Foucault, frames it in terms of the ultimately harmonious integration of discursive "regularities" (to use Foucault's term) with a specific context or location. If the word *truth* means anything, Rorty might say, it means something like "this is how we do things around here." Truth as coherence downplays any sharp distinction between the statement of truth and its reference—between nature and its "mirror."

By contrast, according to a correspondence or realist theory—versions of which are defended by Gödel, Maddy, Bhaskar, and Norris—truth remains a function of the relation between an assertion and the extralinguistic reality it describes or refers to. Since there is no reason why such assertions should exhaust the full truth "out there" in reality, "one definitive aspect of correspondence theories is that what it takes for a sentence to be true might well transcend what we are able to know."[1] Given some disputed statement, Dummett has famously characterized realism as "the belief that statements of the disputed class possess an objective truth value, independently of our means of knowing it: they are true or false in virtue of a reality existing independently of us."[2]

Dummett's own antirealism—an understanding of truth in terms of confirmation—thus "opposes to this the view that statements of the disputed class are to be understood only by reference to the sort of thing which we count as evidence for a statement of that class."[3] Though not strictly reducible to verificationism, antirealism demands a direct proof or demonstration before accepting a statement as true. Antirealism thereby implies the possibility of statements that are neither true nor false (i.e., that violate the principle of bivalence).

Badiou's conception of truth is not only not reducible to any one of these three alternatives; it undercuts the basis for their distinction *tout court.* Badiou's truth certainly surpasses what can be known or proved, but it does so only because it links its assertion with the method of its verification. A truth sets its own conditions, more rigorous than those of any correspondence, coherence, or confirmation. Truth is not knowledge, but neither is it independent of us. It is we who make truth, but precisely as something that exceeds our knowing. So Badiou's truth coheres, in the sense that a generic procedure must group an internally consistent set of investigations or conditions; it is expressly founded on the real of the situation and implies the unrestricted application of bivalence; and it is effectively self-verifying, composed over time in a laborious series of incremental steps. Subjectivation itself provides, in the absence of an object, the confirmation of its own truth.

Badiou believes that there is no truth in general; there are only particular truths in particular situations. But precisely as the truth of its situation, each truth, in its essential inconsistency, is an exposure of the "Sameness" of being. A situation counts its elements, and its state counts groups of these elements as one: only a generic procedure, by contrast, exposes the truth of what is counted in a situation, that is, its inconsistent being. Generic procedures reveal that which is counted, or presented, "in the indifferent and anonymous equality of its presentation" (C, 248). Badiou maintains, "Since the being of the situation is its inconsistency, a truth of this being will present itself as indifferent *[quelconque]* multiplicity, anonymous part, consistency reduced to presentation as such, without predicate. . . . A truth is this minimal consistency (a part, an immanence without concept) which indicates in the situation the inconsistency that it is" (MP, 90). Each truth "represents, in sum, what is most anonymous, or least specified, in the situation (whose truth it is)."[4] True theater, for instance, is one whose audience must represent "humanity in its very inconsistency, its infinite variety. The more it is united (socially, nationally) . . . , the less it supports, in time, the eternity and universality of an idea. The only audience worth the name is generic, an audience of chance" (PM, 116).

Having looked at the mechanics of subjectivation in chapter 5, in this chapter we review the more general characteristics of Badiou's conception of truth: truth is a matter of acts rather than words, of axioms rather than definitions; truth is very exactly "the conjunction *[noeud]* of thought and being," but this conjunction is neither essentially temporal nor grammatical; it escapes the supervision of "anthropological rules, the logical rules of language or culture" (CT, 120). The chapter then moves on to consider Badiou's critique of constructivism (the explicit antithesis of any generic conception of truth) and his elaboration of a "subtractive" alternative to militant "destruction" before concluding with a brief evaluation of his response to the more philosophically substantial challenges posed, respectively, by Kant, Spinoza, Hegel, and Deleuze.

Axiom or Definition?

That the truth is axiomatic, or decided, means precisely that it cannot be defined. An axiom in no sense describes what it prescribes. Those who live and assert the truth of love or art, say, are not likely to be in a position to *define* art or love to the satisfaction of those who deny its truth.

If the substantially existent is ontologically primary, as the neo-Aristotelian ontological tradition maintains, it makes sense to begin with definitions of existence: "Definition is the linguistic mode of the establishment of the preeminence of the existent *[étant]*" over the empty univocity of being as being. Dialectics, for example, the manipulation of "successive delimitations," proceeds by definitions, qualifications, and counterdefinitions: it begins and ends with the One (CT, 31). But we know that for Badiou, the existent or *étant* is always a result, the effect of a particular structuring or count. The existent is something that comes to be through its belonging to a situation. What thus comes to belong can itself be only purely inconsistent multiplicity. The pair "definition and existence" cannot be primary. In a far more rigorous way than certain philosophers of difference or *différance*, Badiou insists that "there can be *no* definition of the multiple" (CT, 31), no matter how differentiated or convoluted such a definition might be. It is the inconsistency of multiple being that is primary, even though only an exceptional procedure can expose this inconsistency, from time to time, for what it truly is.

Badiou's approach is post-Gödelian in at least this familiar sense: a truth always says more than can be defined or proved, or, as Hofstadter puts it, "Provability is a weaker notion than truth."[5] The claims of truth always exceed our ability to demonstrate their necessity. Any program that seeks, like Frege's, an objectively "eternal foundation"[6] is bound to fail. Following Frege's own eventual renunciation of mathematical philosophy, Russell and Hilbert, in this respect, stand as examples of a faith misplaced or of an aximatics misfounded. Hilbert had sought an exhaustive "proof of consistency" that might cover the whole of mathematical reasoning. It was thus "almost impossible for Hilbert to accept Gödel's result," which dealt nothing less than a "death blow" to his entire project.[7] Russell, likewise, famously "wanted certainty in the kind of way in which people want religious faith."[8] Like Badiou, Russell found in mathematics a "perpetual reproof" of the confusing plurality of "opinion and private judgement," the random particularities of "taste and bias." But, unlike Badiou, he sought to ground such reproof on a strictly "nonhuman" foundation, in a "region of absolute necessity" that he imagined as a last bulwark against the dreadful sense of "human impotence, of weakness, of exile amid hostile powers."[9] Hence the "sorrow" and disarray that he said set in once "the splendid certainty which I had always hoped to find in mathematics was lost in a bewildering maze."[10] In the end, unable to find an alternative between absolute certainty and mere tautology, Russell could not resist the belittling conclusions of Wittgenstein's *Tractatus,* and came to believe that "to a mind of sufficient intellectual power, the whole of mathematics would appear trivial" (212).

Badiou's own conviction, by contrast—in mathematics as much as politics—remains essentially intact, precisely because it depends on literally nothing outside its own integrity. The only price to be paid for such axiomatic independence is the loss of any "objectively" consistent description of this integrity as such. For all its subjective power, in other words, true thought must accept a certain ignorance regarding exactly what and how it thinks. Axiomatic thought must accept a merely implicit intuition of what it does, if it is to preserve the perfect clarity of its effect. The word "set," for instance, does not figure among the axioms of set theory: "Axiomatic thought grasps the disposition of undefined terms. It never encounters either a definition of these terms, or a practicable explication of what they are not. The primordial statements of such thought expose the thinkable without thematizing it. Of course, the primitive term or terms are inscribed. But they are inscribed not in the sense of a nomination whose referent would have to be represented, but in the sense of a series of dispositions, where the term is nothing outside the regulated game of its founding connections."[11] This apparent limitation, of course, is simply the condition that axiomatic thought must meet in order to sustain its effectively absolute power. If thought engages with nothing that is fundamentally external to or enabling of its prescription, the criteria of thought must be internal to the operation of thought itself.

Beyond Historicism: Evental Time and Subjective Immortality

The self-founding validity of a truth is eternal or incorruptible in a particularly rigorous sense. Once subtracted from all that is nonthought, thought as such is invulnerable to decay. A truth—the infinite, unending deployment of an evental implication—can never be exhausted. (The same principle does not apply, clearly, to the subjects of a truth—which is why they need to draw on an *ethics* of truth.) However, we also know that every eternally valid truth begins with a precise event, just as it stems from a particular situated place. The articulation of the eternal and the historical has been, from the beginning, one of the major preoccupations of Badiou's work. This articulation is what organizes Badiou's distinctive concept of evental time.

Remember that, for the Maoist, "truth" emerges as a revolutionary Unity produced through the cumulative, historical development of the proletariat. In Badiou's later work, to an effectively timeless mathematical ontology corresponds a more strictly eternal or endless concept of truth (EE, 367). The model of this correspondence is again axiomatic. An axiom is precisely that paradoxical declaration that asserts an eternal principle because it is established "in one point." It is precisely in the wake of something that happened once, at a specific moment, that we can speak of truly eternal consequences. Only the present impact of an exception can last forever, since normality endures for merely "as long as it works," for as long as it is convenient. Mere corruption or "change is something entirely different from time. . . . Time 'begins' with subjective intervention."[12]

From the beginning, true time is diagonal to the chronological accumulation of time, that is, a time constrained by an already established measure. On the one hand, "every event constitutes its own time,"[13] such that "there is no time in general; there are *times*. Each truth carries with it its own time" (TA, 16.4.97). The time of a truth always overthrows an already established time, just as "a revolution is the closing of an era" (D, 97). On the other hand, truth is itself oriented toward the eternal, to the eternally renewable: "All truth, as generic infinity, is eternal" (PM, 28). Not only does a truth set a new beginning for time, but its validity exceeds chronological time as such. Once it has been declared, it will always have been true (scientific statements provide the most obvious examples). Truth is thus a "forgetting of time itself, the moment in which we live as if time (this time) had never existed" (D, 97). Or again, the time of truth is the time of a properly eternal present, indifferent to both the inheritance of the past and the promise of the future. The subject of fidelity lives exclusively in an unfolding present, the present of evental consequences.

Nowhere is the incisive simplicity of Badiou's orientation more apparent than in his conception of time. Whereas Sartre's philosophy is organized around the future, Bergson's around the past, and Derrida's around the deferral of presence, Badiou's subject lives in a time that is entirely saturated by the present, a time without promise, inheritance, or reserve. Where for

Heidegger temporality was the very medium of the authentic subject, in a supremely intimate relation cemented by mortality, for Badiou temporality is merely an external "environment" for the subject, in a relation exploded precisely by truth's indifference to mortality. Where, for Deleuze, time in its pure state is the very form of a fully cosmic creativity, for Badiou time is pure only in terms of the discontinuity of a present.

Framing things in the more systematic terms of his *Théorie axiomatique du sujet*, we can summarize Badiou's analysis of time as follows.

Mere being as being, mere presentation as such, is simply timeless. Only "truth is temporal," and the cut between the merely timeless and the actively temporal is marked, of course, by the event, which marks the beginning of a new time.

The evental declaration *e* is not itself locatable in this time, since it gives rise to it: *e* remains "co-present" with this time as a whole; it is the "index of the opening of a time" (TA, 16.4.97). Declaration of *e* is the pure instant from which an entire temporal universe expands. (The hysterical declarer of *e* is the person who lives in anticipation of a properly miraculous time, the literally instantaneous compression of all time into a single decisive moment, without duration.)

Affirmation of the consequences of *e* constitutes the present of time, as distinct from the instant. The subjective figure of mastery is fundamentally a master of the present as such, that is, of the ordered movement from one consequence to another. A faithful subject is nothing other than a present fragment of truth, a shifting point in its forever unfolding being-there. (If a truth could be thought of as "whole," it would be already finished.[14]) In a very general and obviously nonchronological sense, Badiou defines "modernity as the predominance of the present in the entangling of time." To be modern is to be fully contemporary with what is truly taking place in your own time, without yielding to the temptations of routine or regret (TA, 18.3.98).

The reactionary figure yields to precisely this temptation. What the reactionary denies is the distinctive urgency of the present as such, that is, the presence of the present. The reactionary recognizes only an indeterminate temporality, in which the present is either diluted in a diffuse continuity ("This is the way it's always been," "Nothing ever changes") or dissolved in a series of entirely discontinuous moments ("It all depends on the circumstances," "It's impossible to generalize"). Either way, the result undermines the possibility of radical change here and now, in favor of a cautious adherence to the past, to whatever seems "true" because "tried." The reactionary tends to privilege memory over improvisation. Every pious invocation of a "politics of memory" is reactionary by definition.

The obscurantist figure obliterates the present. The original event is all that matters, and its truth can be recovered only by escaping time altogether. The obscurantist is not oriented simply toward the past but toward death pure and simple: death in the present is the price every obscure subject must pay to rejoin his atemporal truth.

The figure of renewal revives (rather than remembers) the present. Strictly speaking, there is no "collective memory," no subjective history of truths: they exist only in the present, in their active reenactment, and it is the possibility of endless renewal that guarantees the eternity of truth. As Badiou says, "Truths are eternal because they are resubjectivizable, reexperimentable" (TA, 17.12.97). This is not to say that truth is a matter of proximity to what is timelessly correct—a criterion that concerns only knowledge. Contemporary truths are not more true than those of the past; they are simply those that remain true for us, as disruptive of our routine.

Against Constructivism

We are now in a position to follow Badiou as he distinguishes his theory of truth from its main philosophical alternatives. Badiou's closely argued readings of his more significant rivals have resulted in some of the most striking extensions and refinements of his system.

Several of the meditations that make up *L'Etre et l'événement* are devoted to a critique of constructivism, conceived as an orientation broad enough to include nominalism, Leibniz, Wittgenstein, the linguistic turn, Anglo-American analytic philosophy, and perhaps incongruously, Foucault.[15] Constructivism privileges language over being, meaning over truth, and communication over conviction. "Truth" in the constructivist sense is simply a matter of appropriate conformity to widely recognized norms, such that "to say something true is to say something correct."[16] Like the sophists before them, constructivists equate knowledge and truth, and in doing so, eliminate the possibility of an encounter with the indiscernible or undecidable. Constructivism turns on the conviction "that thought cannot think something indiscernible . . . , that there can be neither concept nor thought of that which is inaccessible to [soustrait à] language."[17] A constructivist universe is one in which every definition fits, in which everything remains in its properly recognizable place—in which the state, or re-presentation, maintains a perfect grip on what is presented in the situation. Once true meaning has been equated with habitual use, then, as Wittgenstein admits, "philosophy may in no way interfere with the actual use of language; it can in the end only describe it." Such a philosophy, very deliberately, "leaves everything as it is."[18]

Consider the case of Leibniz, who dreams of that well-made language which could articulate an absolutely discernible universe. The articulable universe would be defined as a logically consistent continuity of infinitely divided parts, conceived as so many "intrinsic denominations" or monads. "The immeasurable fineness of things"[19] would be rendered by a sort of universal calculus, justified by its presumed approximation of God's own calculation-creation. Leibniz thus posits an infinite dispersal with no "foundational" term, that is, with no chance of an encounter with the void of being. (Badiou has gone on to indicate two major problems with this arrangement. First, in the absence of any extensional difference between them, in what precise sense are monads genuinely distinct? In the end, are they not simply "an infinite collection of *names* of the void?" Second, Leibniz leaves no room for disruptive innovation: as so many intrinsic denominations, monads can do only what they are, can "experience" only what they include. As Badiou writes, "What seems to happen to them is only the deployment of their own qualitative predicates" [EE, 356–57].)

The mathematical version of constructivism—and, in particular, that branch of constructivism known as intuitionism—has its roots in the belief that meaningful statements must be confined to assertions whose validity can be directly established or produced for inspection. Associated with some of the great names of modern mathematics (Kronecker, Poincaré, Borel, Brouwer, Bishop, and others), constructivism rejects such classically acceptable means of indirect proof as *reductio ad absurdum* or the excluded middle.[20] It denies any "evidence-transcendent" notion of truth, and in particular any "reasoning which results from treating infinite collections as cases of Being rather than cases of Becoming, in other words, as if they have any existence transcending that of the rule of generation by which they are given to thought."[21] Seen from a constructivist perspective, the foundations of mathematics are derived not from exceptional axioms or inventive decisions but from certain structurally consistent rules, along with the mental or linguistic operations that give rise to them.[22] In Wittgenstein's archconstructivist view, mathematics is simply a matter of thoughtless calculation or tautology: "Proof in mathematics is exactly not a means whereby something is found out."[23]

Since constructivism requires direct evidence before it can acknowledge truth, it excludes in advance everything that Badiou associates with the subject and the event (EE, 319–20). Whereas classical reasoning invites an encounter with contradiction by means of the excluded middle or *reductio ad absurdum*, every "constructive reasoning ... simply exhibits a case according to the law."[24] Whereas each truth procedure turns on the resolution of an undecidable, the maxim of constructivism is simply "Always think and act in such a way that everything remains clearly decidable" (EE, 348). Constructivism is very precisely the spontaneous philosophy of law and order, the philosophy of the status quo as such. It is a conception of philosophy that leads, sooner or later, to the justification of what Lakatos quite accurately calls a "thought police."[25]

To be precise, constructivist and generic philosophies part company at exactly the point that Badiou identifies as the crux of every ontological orientation—the point where, given an infinite set n, set theory indicates that there is a still more infinite excess of 2^n over n. Whereas "generic thought holds the roving [errance] of the excess for the real of being, for the being of being" (MP, 61), constructivist thought is organized around the drastic specification and reduction of this excess. In a universe that recognizes the existence only of constructible sets, Cantor's continuum hypothesis—the presumption that the power set 2^n of an infinite set n is the next largest number after n itself, or that $2^{\aleph_0} = \aleph_1$—follows as a matter of course. In the constructivist universe, the state literally "*succeeds*" the situation that it governs (EE, 342). The representation of parts fits perfectly over the presentation of elements. Seen from within, the constructible universe is thus order incarnate; seen from without, however, from a perspective that tolerates no limits on $2^{\aleph_0}$, in which inaccessible cardinals abound in a mind-boggling profusion, in which the unnameable and indiscernible can be thought in a perfectly precise sense, the constructible universe is chiefly remarkable for its "stupefying poverty" (EE, 347).

If constructivist claims have never been taken very seriously by most working mathematicians,[26] it is all too easy to show that a broadly constructivist approach to language and reality today remains the "almost universally accepted" doctrine (CT, 44). As for "deconstruction," it can figure here only as a kind of constructivism turned against itself. Deconstruction preserves the constructivist coordination of language and thought intact, a position best summarized by Gadamer's famous quip "Being that can be understood is language." Derrida's insistence that "the experience of thought is also a matter of language"[27] is a quintessentially constructivist position: simply, what is again and again constructed, in Derrida's work, is the deferral or complication of any particular construction.

Subtraction and Destruction

It is easy to see how the critique of constructionism might spill over into a celebration of "destructionism" for its own sake. Every true attempt to grapple with the real of a situation must first find a way of cutting through that which passes for reality in that situation (i.e., its status quo). As Badiou has written, "It is reality that gets in the way of the uncovering of the real," and each grappling with the real presumes the penetration of every "pretension of substance, every assertion of reality," of semantic depth or cultural "thickness" in the situation (LS, 52–53).

There is an essential difference, however, between what Badiou calls the "destructive" and "subtractive" versions of this penetration. The destructive option presumes that only the full, literal elimination of reality will allow for the unqualified affirmation of the real. Only destruction of the old can make room for the new. Only the annihilation of previous notions of art can clear the way for an entirely new avant-garde practice, just as only the wholesale destruction of inherited cultural norms can enable the birth of an altogether new revolutionary Man. Needless to say, never had the appeal of the destructive option proved so strong as in the revolutionary twentieth century, which was driven from start to finish by an unflinching "passion for the real." An entirely unrestricted innovation can arise only from the ruins of an absolute destruction (LS, 38; cf. LS, 134 n. 7). The great error of the twentieth century was not its willingness to endure the violence of true innovation, but its readiness to accept the destruction that must accompany the pursuit of *definitive* forms of such innovation. The century was betrayed by its readiness to engage in the search, in each domain of truth, for some kind of "final solution"—be it another war to end all wars (Mao), or a definitive formalization of mathematics (Bourbaki), or a definitive consummation of Art in the avant-garde (with Breton or Debord). Destruction and definition are linked together as the disjunctive elements of a "fundamental couple" (LS, 31).

Badiou is the first to admit that his early work was "led astray" by the apparent necessity of "an essential link between destruction and novelty" (EE, 446: LS, 45). In all of his subsequent work he has sought to weaken this link, beginning with the realization that destruction is a merely objective category.[28] The alternative, subtractive option seeks "to purify reality, not by annihilating it, but by withdrawing it from its apparent unity so as to detect in it the minuscule difference, the vanishing term that is constitutive of it," the inconsistency that sustains it: "That which takes place differs only barely from the place," but it is in this "only barely," this rare space of "immanent exception," that everything of true value happens (LS, 53). Along with Mallarmé's poetry, Badiou's aesthetic illustrations include Anton Webern's "diamantine" work (vanishing wisps of sound woven around fragments of silence) and Malevitch's landmark painting of 1914, *White Square on a White Background* (the subtraction of pure form from color, which leaves, in the form of a geometrical allusion, the indication of "a minimal difference: the abstract difference between form and background, and in particular, the empty difference between white and white, the difference of the Same, which we might call vanishing difference"[29]).

Subtraction avoids destruction because "rather than treat the real in terms of identity, it is treated from the beginning as a gap" in the continuous fabric of determination. To treat the real as a substance or identity requires the destruction of its simulacra or false pretenders; subtraction, by contrast, presents only the minimal difference of an interval as such. Subtraction invents new means of formalization at precisely that point where recognizable difference is minimal, where there is "almost nothing," at the edge of whatever is void for that situation (LS, 54).

Subtraction is no less penetrating of reality than destruction. It is no less driven by a passion for the real. Simply, it limits its action to the strictly subjective domain (such is its *action restreinte*). That "truth is subtracted from knowledge" means precisely that "truth does not contradict it" (EE, 445). The subtractive approach understands that the operations that consolidate "reality"—representation, appearing, semblance: the state of the situation— are not simply external to the real as a cover that might be removed, but are organized as its ontologically irreducible repression. The state cannot be destroyed, but a truth can puncture its repression and suspend its domination. The very force of the state is itself derived, ultimately, from the real excess and disorder (the excess of parts over elements) that it is designed to conceal. Althusser deployed a similar logic to make sense of ideology as the symptomal re-presentation of "a real that it localizes, subjectively, as misunderstanding *[méconnaissance]*," and so did Freud to make sense of neurosis, as driven by precisely those unconscious forces it is designed to deflect (LS, 40). The attempt to destroy the symptom, in either case, solves nothing: what is required is its analysis, its disaggregation into parts, so as to subtract from it that inconsistent truth that is nothing other than a pure part as such, an any-part-whatever, an inclusion with no discernible definition (EE, 373).

A Missed Opportunity: Kant

As opposed to Badiou's void-based ontology, Kant centers his critical philosophy around the epistemological irreducibility of perception, that is, around the constituent relation between subject and object. Kant's conception of objectivity and scientific truth is grounded in the irreducible role of perspective in the formulation of knowledge: we know the world only according to a subjective perspective, but each such perspective opens onto a necessarily independent or "objective" world. Subjective experience is itself organized in the objective terms of a universal time and space, and in the firmly scientific categories of substance, causality, and so on. Against Leibniz's rationalism on the one hand and Hume's empiricism on the other, Kant insists that sensual experience and pure understanding "can make objectively valid judgments about things only in *connection* with each other."[30] So Kant, like Badiou, holds that "thought is not, indeed, in itself a product of the senses, and is to that extent also not limited by them." But unlike Badiou, Kant insists that "it does not therefore have its own and pure use forthwith, without the assistance of sensibility [i.e., intuition], since it is then without an object." As to whether there might be noumenal objects—that is, "objects wholly detached from [our] sensibility's intuition"—this is a question that "can be answered only indeterminately," something about which we must forever remain "completely ignorant."[31]

Badiou emphasizes the need, today, to "extirpate the universal from Kantianism," that is, to overcome the reduction of the universal to the form of moral judgment and empirical knowledge.[32] No philosophical adjective is likely to annoy Badiou more than "neo-Kantian." Kant's authority is invoked as much by intuitionists like Brouwer as by the contemporary advocates of human rights. But Kant needs to be taken seriously because he proposed a kind of "subtractive ontology" of his own (through the evacuation of "things in themselves") and provided access to a sort of actual infinity (grounded precisely in the purely "subjective" or *practical* awareness of moral obligation). Kant's moral philosophy rests on a kind of ultimately axiomatic prescription (or categorical imperative). Though comparable in certain respects, Badiou's conclusions are firmly opposed to Kant's in both domains. We will come to the ethical questions in chapter 12; the ontological matter must be dealt with here.

Kant is an important rival to Badiou because, breaking with Spinoza and Leibniz, he proposed for the first time a philosophy made fully autonomous of the play of *substantial* reality. He subtracted the categories of pure reason from any constituent relation with noumenal realities. Kant might seem, then, to occupy a special place in the neoplatonic campaign to isolate thought from substance, the ideal from the physical, experience from Creation, or the *réel* from reality. But no. No sooner had Kant fenced off the field of things in themselves than he subordinated the autonomy of pure reason to the bland domain of the mere object or phenomenon. Whereas Plato had looked for certainty at a level of coherence beyond the illusions of appearance and consensus, for Kant it was precisely the world of appearance that alone seemed certain and coherent. Seeking a secure foundation for reason against (Hume's) skepticism and (Swedenborg's) delirium, Kant argued that reason can be sure of itself only when it links sensory intuition and conceptual understanding in the synthetic unity of an object. Pure thought provides no knowledge. The pure concepts of the understanding have an exclusively empirical application, such that "thinking *is* the act of referring given intuitions to an object."[33] Void or "objectless" perception, then, must be simply empty or "thoughtless."

For all his obvious differences from Leibniz and Aristotle, Kant's true contribution is therefore to what Badiou characterizes as the anti-Platonic ontological tradition. Aristotle, remember, had conceived of logic as playing a secondary, clarifying role in the perception of substantial or phenomenal confusion. Kant preserves this role; he subordinates ontology to epistemology (and in doing so, confirms the foreclosure of any *actually* infinite reality as such[34]). Although Kant's categories might appear to foreground logical relations (inherence, causality, limitation, and so on) as the primordial foundation of thought, Badiou argues that such relation *(Verbindung, liaison)* presupposes the more fundamental unity *(Einheit)* of the "faculty of relating" *(lier)* itself, that form of self-consciousness that Kant calls "originary apperception." It is this synthetic faculty that first unifies or counts-as-one diverse perceptions as perceptions of a single presented object, and that ensures the corresponding unity of the subject (the "transcendental unity of self-consciousness"). Such originary apperception corresponds roughly to what Badiou calls the "structure" of a situation, that is, that which presents x and y, or counts them as elements. The logical or categorical relations linking x to y might then correspond to the metastructure or re-presentation of what is thus presented, its distribution in parts of the situation. Like Badiou, Kant thus distinguishes the "counting for one, the guarantee of consistency, the originary structure of all presentation," from "relation *[le lien]*, the characteristic of representable structures."[35] But whereas Badiou everywhere pursues the delicate subtraction of presentation from re-presentation, Kant conceives of presentation as nothing more than the raw material *for* re-presentation itself. The mind makes one or "object-ifies" the elements it perceives so as to be able to establish logical relations among phenomena. The structures presented by originary apperception are simply what the metastructural "relation of the phenomenally diverse requires" if it is to work properly, that is, if it is to operate in keeping with the apparent certainties of Euclidean mathematics and Newtonian physics (CT, 156). Kant's synthetic "one" is only thought *for* relation. His elements exist only in order to be grouped in subsets or parts. The very category of "object" can designate only that which, "of the existent, can be represented according to the illusion of relation *[du lien]*" (CT, 157).

If Badiou is to demonstrate the failure of Kant's epistemology, he must show first that the illusions of object and relation cannot eliminate the properly foundational role of that which is without object, or void, and second that this objectless reality is alone real (thereby confirming the merely illusory status of relation).

Kant says that what we can know is simply the flux of phenomena in conformity with certain consistent structures of perception. What we know is always an object. But since the concept of object is not itself empirical, it in no way answers the question of its own ontological status. The general concept of object can be only "anything at all," a kind of "object = x"[36]—that is, something whose being overlaps with what Badiou calls pure or inconsistent multiplicity. Such an empty, undetermined, or "transcendental" object = x is quite literally "nothing for us." Strictly speaking, the object = x can be nothing other than a name for the ontological void (CT, 158–59). Likewise, while any actually perceiving subject is empirical or contingent, and corresponds in its plenitude to the general flux of phenomena, nevertheless the form of the subject in general, of "originary apperception" or the transcendental "subject = x," is itself void of all empirical specification. Against Descartes, Kant famously maintains that this grammatical subject of apperception, while it organizes all possible knowledge, cannot know itself (as a phenomenon). The "I think" says nothing about what "I am." In order, then, to account for the perceptual unification of any particular object, Kant is obliged to conceive of this structuring operation as the "correlation of two voids," subjective and objective. The transcendental subject = x and the equally transcendental object = x must be posited as primitive terms prior to all intuition and experience, and act as nothing other than names of "the withdrawn void of being" itself (CT, 160). This was Kant's great opportunity. Full acceptance of this correlation as void might indeed have led to a genuinely subtractive ontology.

But, Badiou concludes, "Kant's powerful ontological intuitions" remain the prisoner of those epistemological relations whose operation they are ultimately designed to guarantee. Rather than ground his philosophy firmly on the void, "Kant assigns the foundational function to the *relation* of the two voids," objective and subjective (CT, 161), such that it is precisely the work of perception and synthesis that proceeds as primary. It is this work that ensures the smooth coordination of empirical object with empirical subject. Only such coordination guarantees that "the heterogeneity of existence" remains rational and objective (rather than delirious).[37] Against this conclusion, Badiou argues that it is precisely "the *concept* of the void itself," as deployed in the rigor of mathematical deduction, that "upholds the heterogeneously existent, once we admit, since the void is certainly not an object (even if it is perhaps a letter), that we are not restricted, in order to avoid delirium, to the phenomenal confinement of objectivity (for the void is not a phenomenon either)."[38] Because thought can deduce order directly from the void, there is simply no need for it to pass through the detour of perception and the relation of objects. What an ontology based on the void eliminates, very precisely, is any foundational role for relation as such. There can be no relation with the void. In particular, there can be no object-mediated symmetry between "the void of the count for one (the transcendental subject) and the void as name of being (the object = x)" (CT, 162). The notion of object cannot, Badiou insists, be the primary category of thought. Both object and relation must be dissolved in the austere univocity of what set theory articulates of pure multiple presentation, founded on the sole void.

The first question Badiou himself must answer is simply this: If there is to be no relation between ontology and epistemology, and if the void is to be the sole basis for the "heterogeneously existent," how exactly are we to describe the transition from void to existence? Can this transition then be anything other than purely contingent (if not indeed "delirious")? A second question concerns the indirect ontological implications of what Kant called practical reason.[39] No less than Badiou, Kant asserted the ultimate "primacy of pure practical reason" over its speculative-empirical counterpart.[40] Kant's moral philosophy is nothing other than a sustained affirmation of universally binding subjective "truth," made in the absence of any reliable knowledge as such.[41] If we are indeed finite as phenomena, as moral agents we act as infinite noumena (and, through these actions, illustrate the noumenal basis of our freedom, our immortality, and so on[42]). Precisely because practical reason is free of any "heteronomous" or "empirical motives,"[43] Kant's moral philosophy holds "firm even though there is nothing in heaven or on earth from which it depends or on which it is based."[44] Is there not, then, an important sense in which the supremely Kantian effort—"the effort to annul knowledge [Wissen] in order to make room for faith [Glaube]"[45]— anticipates, if we swap "fidelity" for "faith," the central preoccupation of Badiou's philosophy?

The obvious difference of Kant's arrangement from Badiou's is that Kant grounds his practical reason less upon the random incidence of an event than upon the constituent attribute of freedom as the property of all rational beings. Badiou sees freedom as an exceptionally fragile achievement, whereas Kant sees it as a necessary presumption. Though Kant accepts that we cannot know freedom as "something real in ourselves and in human nature," he believes we do know that "we must presuppose it" as the very environment of our action.[46] Kant thus lends the universal a deliberately lawlike character, grounded in the literally regular employment of a general faculty. In Kant's hands, moral behavior becomes the realm of a general legislation or supervision, a matter

ie: state legality..

of public "duty" and "obligation." With the evental or extralegal dimension of his work, Badiou thus has a reply of sorts to the great problem of Kant's moral philosophy: how to individuate the free or autonomous (transcendental) self, that is, how to situate this self in the empirical world in which it acts. On the other hand, by making subjectivation so radically exceptional a procedure, Badiou turns the "extraordinary" human capacity for truth into something little short of the miraculous. If thought is a capacity for truth, how does the varied employment of this capacity explain its constitution as a capacity?

Three Rivals: Spinoza, Hegel, Deleuze

Less epistemologically driven orientations pose more substantial challenges to a subtractive conception of philosophy. Like Badiou, Spinoza, Hegel, and Deleuze all claim to formulate rigorously univocal notions of being, and all accept versions of an actually infinite truth. But they collapse these two dimensions together, as One. They maintain, in their different ways (or rather, at their different speeds) the intrinsic infinity of being. They assert the coherence on a single plane of being and truth, and in doing so, they posit an effectively divine subject of Being. In the process, all three eliminate the dimension of the event, in favor of the eventual Unity of truth.

Spinoza

Like Badiou, Spinoza insists that "all truth is generic," or again, that what ultimately "can be thought of being is mathematical."[47] The problem is that he tries to make these conclusions automatic, as if based on a divinely "eternal axiomatics." For Spinoza, the notion of an actually infinite creative substance provides an ontological solution to every conceivable problem. As Badiou writes, "Spinoza is the most radical ontological effort ever made to identify structure and metastructure . . . , to indistinguish belonging and inclusion" (EE, 130). For Spinoza, to exist is simply "to belong to God," where God is both structure and state. Everything that is is to be conceived as the effect of this one cause, the expression (or explication) of a perfectly sufficient plenitude. As a direct consequence, "Spinoza attempts the ontological eradication of the void" (EE, 137), just as he "excludes any event, by prohibiting excess, chance, and the subject" (CT, 74).

In L'Etre et l'événement, Badiou's counterattack dwells on Spinoza's apparent inability to relate finite and infinite.[48] If God is purely infinite and sole cause, how can this infinity give rise to finite modes? The point where the infinite "ceases" to be infinite can be only the void of the infinite itself, and such a boundary would violate the univocity of substance. Spinoza turns here to what Badiou deems the incoherent concept of an infinite mode, something corresponding to the "totality of the universe": "We must suppose that the direct action of the substantially infinite produces in itself only infinite modes. But it is impossible to justify the existence of even one such mode." If they exist, they exist only as inaccessible, that is, as "a void *for us*" (EE, 136–37).

In a more recent article, Badiou emphasizes Spinoza's inability to sustain a fully univocal logic of Creation, one that moves directly from virtual Creator to actual creatures. Badiou detects this failure in Spinoza's confusion of two apparently incompatible modes of actualization: a logic of "causality (a thing is a set of modes that come together to produce a single effect)," and a logic of "expression (a thing bears witness to the infinite power of substance)."[49] The crux of this incompatibility concerns, again, Spinoza's attempt to resolve the relation of finite and infinite through the ambiguous mediation of the "intellect" *(intellectus)*. Like love and desire, the rational intellect is a mode of the attribute of thought. Finite human intellect is to be explained through its inclusion in the divinely infinite intellect. For this to work, however, Spinoza is obliged to complicate the supposedly inflexible rules of divine causation or expression. The intellect is both part of this substantial expressive order, and the means by which this order is itself expressed or made known. Alone among modes, the intellect has the peculiar property of grasping or conceiving the general infinity of all modes.[50] Starting out from God as supreme cause, the infinite intellect must be, like any other mode, an effect of God—but it also effectively "comprehends" God. The intellect is a modal anomaly or exception. Badiou is pleased to see in the intellect, thanks to its "undecidable" status, "a localized subject effect" (CT, 91)—an effect quite at odds with its divinely ordained causation.

In order to restrict this exceptional infinite mode to a properly finite dimension, Spinoza has to take another problematic step. All that follows from an infinite mode is itself infinite.[51] Unlike the attribute of thought, however, the attribute of extension naturally lends itself to finite division: the restriction effected upon the finite intellect, then, must come from an already restricted source in extension, namely a body. The finite intellect is precisely the idea of the body. But what this intellect can know, as Badiou points out (cutting short a long debate among Spinozists), is not the particular singularity of one such body—my body—but instead what is typical of all bodies. What can be known by the finite mind is guaranteed by "what is common to all things,"[52] that is, the famous "common notions" that account for what there is in general. And "what there is" is of course nothing other than the nature of Creation or God. The attempt to isolate finite from infinite thus comes full circle: what the finite intellect can know is necessarily infinite, or common. Spinoza's philosophy remains stuck within what Badiou calls a "closed ontology," "closed" by the "attributive identification of the divine infinity" (CT, 90).

Badiou's resistance here is not that Spinoza emphasizes the generic or mathematical aspect of thought; far from it. It is that he poses these characteristics as natural and necessary. For Spinoza, the axioms linking finite to infinite are always already established laws. He thus reduces the drama of human thought to a more or less quickly accomplished process of adequation to these eternal axioms, a matter of "coming home to God." Where Spinoza seeks to conjoin generic truth with a regime of absolute causality, Badiou insists that the generic can be reached only through subtraction from this regime, through thought characterized by "indetermination, difference, undecidability, atypicity . . ." (CT, 92).

Badiou's discussion of Spinoza is somewhat partial. He does not consider the quasi-evental dimension of Spinoza's concept of "encounters," and in particular of encounters with common notions.[53] He disregards the crucial relation between actual and virtual capability, that is, the relation whereby, through such encounters, we more fully actualize the attribute of thought we express. By thus learning to "realize our potential," so what is given as finite comes to express the infinity that it is in its being. Spinoza believes that we are created as beings that, in order to become what we fundamentally are, first need to learn how to "grow up"—to grow up out of our passive affections, our ignorance, our "sad" dependence. The properly ethical dimension of Spinoza's work thus retains some degree of active negotiation *with* worldly interests and temptations as such.

By contrast, Badiou defends a notion of the event that effectively converts the subject to be, all at once. It is not clear then, if he is any more able than Spinoza to establish a genuine "connection" between finite and infinite. The process whereby a truth induces a subject (E, 39), whereby a subject becomes the finite component of an infinite truth (MP, 75), remains curiously abrupt. There is precisely nothing between subject and truth, other than chance. Nor is it clear that his solution retains any of that "worldly" aspect of Spinoza's work so ably endorsed by Deleuze (the counting of "affects," the internal transformation of interest and passion, and so on). Arguably, Badiou's purely mathematical notion of the infinite is infinitely less inclusive than Spinoza's no less axiomatic conception of a substance expressed in an infinity of qualitatively different kinds (or "attributes") of infinity.[54] As for his critique of *intellectus*, Badiou's own conception of truth may be vulnerable to much the same sort of objection. Does not mathematics play a comparable role in Badiou's thought? On the one hand, it is one mode of truth among several, and no less evental or contingent than the others. But it is also exceptional in its provision of tools for the transmission of truth in general. Ontology is both a situation, and the means of describing all situations qua situations. Mathematics is both one of four generic procedures and the privileged medium for the portrayal of every procedure, a "guide to the consistency of thought in its entirety."[55] Set theory provides Badiou with nothing less than "the regulative idea for prescriptions" in general; if each truth procedure is sufficient in itself, what is properly "philosophical is the abstraction [of these procedures] from all speculative empiricism, and the assignation of the form of these determinations to their generic foundation: the theory of pure multiplicity."[56] Whatever the situation, "outside mathematics we are blind."[57]

Hegel

Badiou believes that Hegel writes himself into much the same impasse as Spinoza, that is, into the substantial identity of being and truth. Hegel's infinite ontology avoids the decision of the axiom of infinity. He tries to draw the infinite out of the immanent structure of being itself. However violent and disruptive the process of negation might be, he maintains a dialectical continuity between subject and object. At all costs, Badiou must demonstrate the necessary failure of this effort. Badiou's subject comes to be as an abrupt break with the regime of continuity and in the radical absence of an object. By the same token, there can be no constituent relation between the infinite per se (the multiple as such, as postulated by the axioms of set theory) and the mere diversity of worldly particularities.

Hegel is famous for his equation of reason and reality, where the truth of reality is actually, metaphysically infinite [unendlich]. Every finite thing is simply an aspect of the infinite whole, an aspect defined by its dynamic relations with other such things that negate and constrain it. Mere mathematics is incapable of describing such an infinite dynamism. Like other pre-Cantorian metaphysicians, Hegel concludes that the mathematically or potentially infinite is a "bad" or "spurious" substitute for the true concept. It is able only to suggest an endless succession of finite things, an infinitely tedious approximation of the genuinely or metaphysically infinite. Its image is a straight line, open in either direction; no particular segment of the line itself ever "approaches" the infinite. As in a world cut off from its Creator, nothing carries the linear segments toward their infinite limit, just as no particular number in the sequence of natural numbers (1, 2, 3, 4 . . .) ever approaches an actually infinite number. The bad infinite involves simply the repetition of one thing after another. The switch to a good infinity depends upon liberating the movement of repetition as such, for its own sake, as freed from any result. The repetitive moving beyond (the moving from 2 to 3 or 3 to 4, and so on) must be conceived as a purely intransitive action.[58] The good infinity thus bends its every segment toward and within the creatively infinite. As God breathes eternal life into mortal shapes, so the truly or absolutely infinite invests the finite with its infinite movement. Its image is the circle, a line "bent back into itself . . . , closed and entirely present, without beginning and end."[59] Genuine philosophy should concern itself, then, only with things "that present themselves *directly* as infinite with regard to their content" and power, things like "freedom, spirit, God"—that is, the very things that merely mathematical science fails to grasp.[60] Hegel's substantially infinite notion of "Force" compels an understanding of creation and infinite reality as "inner difference, a repulsion of the selfsame, as selfsame, from itself. . . . This simple infinity, or the absolute Notion, may be called the simple essence of life, the soul of the world, the universal blood, whose omnipresence is neither disturbed nor interrupted by any difference, but rather is itself every difference, as also their supersession; it pulsates within itself but does not move, inwardly vibrates, yet is at rest."[61] Hegel thereby inverts Aristotle's judgment, and explicitly repudiates the mathematically for the metaphysically infinite.[62]

Like Spinoza, then, in Badiou's view Hegel maintains that "there is a being of the One . . . whose counting for one the pure multiple holds in itself" (EE, 181). The difference is that Hegel believes that this effective identity of the One and the counted for one must first develop over (all of historical) time. Hegel presumes, via the interiority of the negative, an "identity in becoming" of pure presentation, on the one hand, of the "there is" (*'il y a'*) as such, and, on the other hand, the structuring or counting operation whereby "there comes to be One" (*'il y a de l'Un'*) (EE, 182; cf. TS, 37). In other words, any given element, any structured unit, has a constituent relation to its "inner" being (i.e., to what is structured or presented, to what corresponds, in Badiou's own account, to purely structureless inconsistency). This relation is something more than what Badiou conceives, in his own ontology, as a simple structural counting for one, more than the nonrelation between a count and what is counted (between consistency and inconsistency).

It is worth proceeding fairly carefully here. Remember that Badiou deems the elements presented by any situation or set different because they are counted for one *as* different ones, *a, b, c, d,* and so on. The difference between the elements is "the difference of same to same, that is, the pure position of two letters" (EE, 190). Such minimal difference is precisely what Hegel cannot admit as "real." Hegel's "law of the counting for one is that the counted term possesses in itself the other-mark *[marque-autre]* of its being" (EE, 181). Any one element is what it is only to the degree that it is not another—that is, to the degree that it exceeds itself "toward" the others it is not. The negativity that separates one element from another also sustains each element in a constant, dynamic relation, a relation that moves them toward their eventual overcoming toward the Absolute. Any particular element or one is nothing other than the movement to overcome what limits it as merely one among others. Hence there is a built-in movement from finite to infinite: being as being generates from itself and out of itself the "operator of the infinite" (*l'opérateur d'infini*). Hegel replaces the foundational decision of infinity with an inherent Law of being that ensures the intrinsic or "substantial" continuity of the one(s) and the infinite (EE, 183). This continuity is the root of what Badiou attacks as Romanticism. What he must demonstrate is the necessary incoherence of this arrangement.

Badiou looks for evidence of this incoherence in Hegel's apparent failure to derive one single definition of the infinite. The lack of such a one must violate the dialectical condition of an intrinsic continuity.[63] The merely finite "moving beyond" (*outrepassement*) of individual ones remains stuck in the bad or mathematically infinite. At no point in the endlessly repeated sequence of particular overcomings can there be a global affirmation of an infinite being as such, that is, a being immeasurably more than the cumulative repetition of ones. In Hegel's view, Badiou writes, "the going-beyond must itself be got beyond" (EE, 185). This second move defines the good or metaphysically infinite. Badiou's question, then, has to do with how we can move from the immanent repetition of the bad infinite to the global affirmation of the good, without "a disjunctive decision"—without recourse to the axiom. Hegel's answer is to distinguish between the result of the bad infinity (the objective, effectively mindless repetition of the finite) and the mechanism of the repetition itself. The fact of repetition is one thing; the power to repeat is another. This power or capacity—a kind of awareness of repetition, a repetition become conscious of itself—is itself the good or affirmative infinite (EE, 186–87). The crux of Badiou's argument is that without tacit recognition of the disjunctive decision to affirm the infinite, the good, "qualitative" infinity cannot join up with a properly quantitative notion of infinity at all. Despite Hegel's effort to maintain one dialectical continuity, the moment of this disjunction is irreducible. As Badiou writes, "Banished from representation and experience, the disjunctive decision returns in [Hegel's] text itself, through a split between two dialectics . . . , quality and quantity," both labeled "infinite."[64]

The question that might be asked of Badiou himself, at this point, is: why does such a double derivation need necessarily be inconsistent with a notion of the infinite? Badiou thinks that this duplicity—this Two-ness of the truth & knowledge, event & angel. (Kantianism &)

infinite itself—is a problem rather than an opportunity. Again, it might well be argued that this is precisely the strength of Hegel's system.[65] In declaring the unicity of the infinite—even if what is produced, through this axiomatic unicity, is an infinitely infinite multiplicity of infinities—does Badiou not accept a radical discontinuity between ontology and world, between mathematical multiplicity and dialectical moving beyond? The axiom commands everything it creates, but by the same token, it has no purchase on what it excludes. From a neo-Hegelian perspective, Badiou's philosophy must figure as a return to broadly Kantian dualisms, reworked in terms of the dichotomy of truth and knowledge or subject and object. Although Badiou's truths are too emphatically situated in a particular situation to be vulnerable to the sort of arguments Hegel marshals against Kant, still the subtractive configuration of these truths is unlikely to seduce Badiou's more conventionally dialectical or materialist critics. The most obvious question needs no further introduction: Once ontology has been confined to numbers, how is philosophy to confront the "crowned anarchy" of things?[66]

Deleuze

If, as Badiou submits, his system "is the most rigorously materialist in ambition that we've seen since Lucretius,"[67] his greatest contemporary competitor must surely be Gilles Deleuze. After Leibniz and Bergson, Deleuze is the most significant of the modern figures working in what Badiou calls the neo-Aristotelian ontological path—working, that is, from the assumed priority of a creative energy or substance. The need for some sort of comparison of Badiou with Deleuze is clear enough, and I am not the first to make it.[68]

Badiou's early opinions of Deleuze and Guattari make interesting reading today. The Maoist could not find words strong enough to deride the "pedantic" complacency of these "petty teachers of the desiring ambush," "these old Kantians," "these hateful adversaries of all organized revolutionary politics."[69] He mocked the "egoism" of "saint Gilles [Deleuze], saint Félix [Guattari], saint Jean-François [Lyotard]" (TC, 72). Deleuze's "desiring flux" was for the early Badiou nothing more than a reinvention of Stirner's petit bourgeois individualism, "the simple inversion of conservative structuralism."[70] Deleuze's "microrevolutions of the desiring individual" were for the author of Théorie du sujet limited to the elements rather than the parts of a situation, and such element-individuals always "stay in their place" (TS, 236). By definition, "there can be no molecular critique of the molar concept of politics" (PP, 16).

More recently, Badiou has recognized Deleuze as his most consequential peer, perhaps his only worthy opponent in the search for an answer to "the problem particular to contemporary philosophy: What exactly is a universal singularity?"[71] He wrote a detailed, finely balanced critique of Deleuze's *Le Pli: Leibniz et le baroque* soon after it came out in 1988;[72] a boo̶ ̶ ̶ ̶ followed in 1997. The later Badiou is prepared to recognize a ̶ ̶ ̶ gence of interests. He applauds Deleuze for his refusal to g̶ "hegemonic theme of the end of philosophy" and for his r̶ ̶ ̶ form of hermeneutics. Deleuze was the first philosopher of his generation to understand that "a contemporary metaphysics is necessarily a theory of multiplicities and a grasping [*saisie*] of singularities."[73] With their notion of a subject-monad that disconnects knowledge from all relation to an object, Leibniz-Deleuze are in line with what Badiou recognizes as the genuinely contemporary problem of a subject without object.[74]

That said, Badiou presents Deleuze's philosophy as substantially opposite to his own on every count. We know that, according to Badiou, "there have never been more than two schemas, or paradigms, of the Multiple: the mathematical and the organicist, Plato or Aristotle. . . . Number or Animal? Such is the cross of metaphysics, and the greatness of Deleuze-Leibniz . . . is to opt without flinching for the animal" ("Rev. of Gilles Deleuze: *Le Pli*," 166). Number is the domain of the abstract, the ideal, the punctual, the decisive, the discontinuous; animal is the domain of the sensual-concrete, the natural, the plane, modulation, continuity. Both Deleuze and Badiou are philosophers of the radically new, of the as yet unrepresentable, of experiences that call for genuinely creative thought—thought as opposed to the more or less habitual processes of recognition, expectation, classification, representation, comparison, manipulation. But whereas Badiou pinpoints every location of the new in an evental break and thereby ensures the radical discontinuity between truth and the situation in which it comes to pass, Deleuze conceives the new as in some sense folded within the infinite complexity of what is "already there" (D, 21). To be sure, Deleuze scans the foldings of the already there only so as to prepare the way for all that is not yet. Nevertheless, Badiou argues, the whole effort of this scanning is to demonstrate how the new or the not yet can emerge, in all its apparent aberration, in the cruel violence of its eruption, in fundamental *continuity* from the already there. Deleuze writes the realm of the continuous as such, that is, a realm in which Cantor's continuum hypothesis is taken as proved: a realm without gaps. Such continuity eliminates all *genuinely* disjunctive "break-downs in signification" in advance ("Rev. of Gilles Deleuze: *Le Pli*," 171), and thus blocks the process of subjective intervention in Badiou's sense. As Badiou reads him, Deleuze is essentially a philosopher of nature, which is to say, in the end, a philosopher of description or construction (rather than subtraction).[75] His worldly,

qualitative multiplicity excludes Badiou's deductive, mathematical multiplicity; his fold is precisely a qualitative or "antiextensional concept of the
Multiple . . . , at the opposite extreme from a resolutely set-theoretic understanding."[76] Deleuze is the presocratic to Badiou's Plato. He is the philosopher of *physis* and universal chaos, whereas his rival seeks, after Descartes, to
promote thought to a position "philosophically independent of any global
contemplation of the universe" (D, 150). In short, "Deleuze identifies, purely
and simply, philosophy with ontology" (D, 32), a move that brings him closer
to Heidegger than he might have liked to admit.

As far as Badiou is concerned, then, Deleuze's philosophy proceeds as a
misappropriation of the event.[77] Deleuze collapses the difference between
the place and the taking-place. His "event is simultaneously omnipresent
and creative, structural and unprecedented" ("Rev. of Gilles Deleuze: *Le Pli,*"
168). He presents the world itself as "a pure emission of singularities,"[78] as a
continuous stream of events, each of which is an affirmation or expression of
the one Event of life, of vital intensity as such.[79] While Badiou insists on the
punctual rarity of an event *("une grâce")* and the ontologically exceptional
status of a subject, Deleuze's philosophy concludes that *"Tout est grâce."*[80]
Very precisely, where Badiou subtracts every truth from the ordinary and the
everyday (LS, 129), Deleuze seeks a quasi-mystical equation of the two declarations "'Everything is ordinary!' and 'Everything is unique!'"[81] Precisely this
equation opens the door to a "pure contemplation, and immediately brings
about the identity of the mental and the physical, the real and the imaginary,
the subject and the object, the world and the I."[82] Deleuze thinks that what
happens is always a fold in the unique ontological continuum. He wants to
conceive the event—the very form of discontinuity—as "thinkable within
the interiority of the continuous" ("Rev. of Gilles Deleuze: *Le Pli,*" 173). By
Badiou's criteria, this effort is mistaken for much the same reason that both
Spinoza and Hegel are mistaken: it is impossible to establish "an evental
theory of the singular . . . once 'event' means: everything that happens, insofar as everything happens" (167). To Deleuze's sensual fold Badiou opposes
the ascetic rigor of the cut.

So according to Badiou—and he is undoubtedly right—the consequence
of Deleuze's philosophy is a restoration of the metaphysical One.[83] Indeed,
Badiou argues, Deleuze is "the most radical thinker of the One since
Bergson" (D, 118). Like Spinoza and Nietzsche before them, Bergson and
Deleuze understand that "intuition of the One (which can go by the name
of the Whole, Substance, Life, body without organs, or Chaos) is the intuition of its immanent creative power, or that of the eternal return of its
differentiating power as such. The goal of philosophy is then, in keeping

with Spinoza's maxim, to think adequately the greatest possible number of particular things (the 'empiricist' side of Deleuze, his disjunctive syntheses, his *petit circuit*) so as to think, adequately, Substance or the One (the 'transcendental' side of Deleuze, or of his Relation, or *'grand circuit'*)."[84] For Badiou, any such reinvestment in the One violates the post-Cantorian break with theology. The monadological formula of $1/\infty$, defended in *Le Pli*, inevitably returns us to "the snares of that Subject whose paradigm is God, or the One-infinite . . . : if 'everything is event,' then it is the Subject who must take upon himself both the One and the Infinite. Leibniz-Deleuze cannot escape this rule,"[85] no more than Hegel can. Hence Deleuze's dilemma: to the degree that he insists on the radical univocity of being as continuous with "what happens," he is forced to abandon any viable concept of the event as rupture. Or, insofar as he wishes to retain a concept of event rupture, he is forced to introduce a notion of discontinuity into the fabric of univocal being itself (virtual as distinct from actual, relations as distinct from terms, intensity as opposed to extension). Deleuze may well insist on the univocity of being, but Badiou goes one step further, to emphasize the "univocity of the *actual*" to the exclusion of any virtual One (D, 78–79; cf. CT, 57–58). A truth, in its militant fidelity, can be only actual pure and simple.

Badiou's book on Deleuze is by any standard one of the strongest and most compelling yet written. Unlike so many of Deleuze's readers, Badiou acknowledges the fundamentally univocal aspect of his work. That he remains within a vitalist paradigm, that he maintains an ultimate ontological Unity, that he assigns thought the task of thinking "one single event for all events,"[86] and so on, are indeed the deliberate and explicit goals of Deleuze in his work from start to finish. Badiou's account of his rival's conception of time, virtuality, and the eternal return is without a doubt the most lucid and incisive available.

Nevertheless, there is a significant gap in Badiou's critique. Deleuze's philosophy is certainly a philosophy of the One, so long as we remember that "the One is already in itself nothing other than the power by which its immanent modes occur." It is also true that such a philosophy must imply a fundamental continuity between being and innovation, a continuity between philosophy and ontology presupposed by the disjunctive production of differences (and it is this very continuity, of course, that the whole of *L'Etre et l'événement* is designed to interrupt). But it is a mistake to present this emphasis on the One in *competition* with an emphasis on difference and multiplicity. By adhering to this apparent dichotomy, Badiou turns what Deleuze calls "actual" beings into "equivocal simulacra," that is, essentially misleading surface delusions obscuring the virtual truth of being. It is this move that allows for the presentation of Deleuze's work as "ascetic" in a rather distorted sense: *if* actual beings are equivocal or misleading, it follows that "it is in renouncing their form and by dissolving themselves within their own (virtual) depth that beings (objects) are finally disposed, thought, imaged, according to the univocity of the One" (D, 94).

I think Deleuze's position is a little more complicated. The most important dualism in his work is not between actual and virtual so much as between what might be called "ignorant" actuals on the one hand and "knowing" actuals on the other, that is, between actual creatures who affirm their status as pure creatings, or actualizations of a virtual intensity that they embody in extension, and actual creatures who, caught up in *ressentiment* and reactive forces (the delusions of psychology, semiology, representation, and so on), deny or otherwise evade this status. The word *equivocal* should be reserved for a variant of Spinoza's use of the term: all actual creatures are fundamentally expressive of the One and therefore consistent with the univocity of being, but some of these creatures become indirectly or reactively expressive of being, mere "signs" of being. Only such creatures are in any sense deluded or misleading.

It does not follow, therefore, that actual beings must dissolve or die in order adequately to express the One. They are already expressive, through the very process of actualization itself: it is simply a matter of enhancing their expressive power or making it active, of "being all that they can be." This certainly involves the preliminary death of equivocal-signifying-psychologizing delusions, but need not involve the dissolution of actuality *tout court*. Because Badiou equates "actual" and "equivocal," he disregards or at least plays down what is arguably Deleuze's own central concern: the difficult, laborious process whereby we ourselves, in our actuality, might become maximally or actively expressive of the One. Though we are originally endowed with the power to become rational, this *becoming* is itself irreducible. All human beings must develop, through inventive experimentation, the means of transcending our initially childish passivity and ignorance. Mere reflection upon what we are capable of will remain abstract and ineffectual until we actively discover "what a body can do."[87] The difficult invention of such means of becoming active is the very substance of Deleuze's work. By failing to take it properly into account, Badiou risks equating an intuition of the One with abstraction pure and simple.

Moreover, even so lucid an account underestimates some of the fundamental ways in which Deleuze's project is at least partially consistent with Badiou's own. Both Badiou and Deleuze write against a merely specific or relational coherence in favor of an ultimately singular self-determination (of truths for the one, of creation for the other: both believe that all true creation creates its own medium of expression and existence). Both presume a "classical" or pre-Kantian equation of thought and being; both write a version of Return as the "test of ontological selection"; both insist on the eternal or untimely primacy of the Idea; both are the implacable enemies of metaphor and interpretation; both aim to write a fully literal discourse, a discourse of the ellipse and of the proper name; both rage against every invocation of community or territory; both refuse a conventional ethical framework governed by individual autonomy and responsibility for others; both discount what Deleuze calls the "Other structure"; for both, philosophy begins where mere discussion ends.

One symptom of this partial proximity is a blurring of the essential distinction of the Aristotelian (Leibniz, Bergson, Deleuze) and Platonic (Descartes, Mallarmé, Badiou) ontological paths. After confirming Deleuze's allegiance to Leibniz and Bergson, Badiou is obliged—again with good reason—to recognize the neoplatonic aspect of his rival's univocal emphasis. "Ultimately," Badiou concludes, "*le deleuzisme* is a reaccentuated Platonism" (D, 42; cf. 69, 92). The broadly "neoplatonic" task for both thinkers is not so much to relate the univocal to the equivocal—for both, this relation is essentially one of subtraction alone—as it is to provide an internally consistent account of a divided univocity (for Badiou, one divided between pure being and appearing, or between inconsistency and consistency; for Deleuze, a "difference explicated in systems in which it tends to be cancelled," a Life that "alienates itself in the material form that it creates"[88]).

Perhaps the most striking sign of convergence here is the proximity of Badiou's *soustraire* to Deleuze's *extraire*. The discontinuous logic of the one effectively inverts the disjunctive logic of the other. For Deleuze, the true—what he variously calls a Problem, an Idea, an Event, or a Concept—is itself a purely virtual entity. This virtuality may then come to be (become actual) in a material situation on the one hand and a verbal proposition on the other, but this actuality "adds" nothing to the idea or event. Conversely, we who are given in actuality and begin in it must work to extract a virtual event from what happens to us and so, on the Stoic model, become adequate to it (or expressive of it). For Badiou, on the other hand, a truth is a complete and actual part of the situation.[89] Badiou turns Deleuze's arrangement on its head: the situation precedes the truth that emerges, through subtraction, as its purified Ideal. The logic of purification or singularization itself, however, is at least roughly similar in each arrangement, and both sequences culminate in a kind of "becoming imperceptible."[90] Deleuze's Idea is Real or "true" because it is entirely independent of its merely derivative actuality; Badiou's generic procedure is true because it is entirely withdrawn from what actually governs its situation. Both

Deleuze and Badiou conceive the subject as the bearer of a truth that exceeds him. Deleuze locates this excess in terms of the virtual as distinct from the actual, while Badiou frames it in terms of the "transcendent" or infinite as opposed to the "local" or finite.[91] The role played by the virtual for the one is played by the transcendent for the other: at its limit, the difference may be less substantial than it seems.

Badiou shares, moreover, the problem Deleuze and Guattari confront in *Mille Plateaux*—the risk of that "black hole" posed by an unrestricted deterritorialization. Deleuze and Guattari know that a "too-sudden destratification may be suicidal"—hence their duly classical emphasis on "sobriety" and "moderation."[92] Badiou's ethical philosophy, as we shall see, obeys a similar structural necessity: "the ethics of a truth amounts entirely to a sort of restraint [*retenue*] with respect to its powers" (C, 194). Both Deleuze and Badiou, in order to avoid disaster, appeal to a problematic ethical power somehow above or beyond that of the truth itself.

It is not clear, finally, whether Badiou's materialism can be as inclusive as that of Deleuze. Deleuze delights in describing mechanisms of transformation between the most varied levels of ontological intensity and the most disparate registers of being (chemical, cosmic, animal, mechanical, molecular, and so on). His is a univocity that aligns these very different sorts of reality on the same "plane of consistency." Badiou's univocity operates, on the contrary, by disregarding the particularity of beings in favor of the abstract homogeneity of their being as being. When push comes to shove, Badiou's tendency is to conceive of *all* substantial reality as too much the product of illusion to be worthy of philosophical attention. His ontology cannot itself then describe the steps whereby univocity is maintained over the expansion of its field of inquiry to include the various concrete situations that compose material or historical existence. Such situations, in their materiality, retain a somewhat mysterious "supplementarity," a reliance on "something more," about which his philosophy has thus far had little to say (EE, 13). In order to match Deleuze's comprehensive embrace, Badiou will need to develop a logic of material or organic situations that demonstrates how their structurings are indeed consistent with the basic axioms of set theory.

For both Badiou and Deleuze, "relations are external to their terms."[93] For the one, the terms alone count, in a fully extensional universe of sets. For the other, it is only relations—relations made "absolute," so to speak—that become and act. While Deleuze cannot account for the individuation of his virtual relations (Problems, Event, Ideas, and so on), Badiou cannot flesh out the material, endlessly ramified identity of thought and being. In the end, both philosophers stumble over the problem of relationality in its broadest sense.

part III

The Generic Procedures

Badiou holds that the production of truth operates in four fields or dimensions: "science (more precisely, the matheme), art (more precisely, the poem), politics (more precisely, . . . of emancipation), and love (more precisely, the procedure that makes truth of the disjunction of sexual positions)."[1] He calls the operation of truth in these four fields "generic procedures" or the "conditions of philosophy"—the terms are synonymous. The generic procedures condition philosophy, because philosophy works from the production of truths and not directly from itself, not from some kind of pure contemplation. Any philosopher must "practice the conditions of philosophy. To know and study modern poetry, to work through recent mathematics, to endure and think the two of love, to be militant in political invention—such is the strict minimum to be expected of those who claim to be philosophers."[2] It is no surprise that philosophers are rare.

Why these particular four domains? Because they mark out the possible instances of the subject as variously individual or collective. Love obtains in the "situational sphere of the individual." Love affects only "the individuals concerned . . . , and it is thus for them [alone] that the one-truth produced by their love is an indiscernible part of their existence." Politics, on the other hand, concerns only the collective dimension, that is, a generic equality without exception. And in "mixed situations"—situations with an individual vehicle but a collective import—art and science qualify as generic to the degree that they effect a pure invention or discovery beyond the mere transmission of knowledges (EE, 374). In short, "there is an individual subject to the degree that there is love, a mixed subject to the degree that there is art or science, a collective subject to the degree that there is [emancipatory] politics."[3]

What about the other domains of human experience? As a general rule, they are not conceivable in terms of pure subjective conviction, that is, they cannot be fully subtracted from the operations of knowledge and re-presentation. They have no means of withdrawing from the state of the situation: "Every subject is artistic, scientific, political or loving . . . , for outside these registers, there is only existence, or individuality, but no subject" (MP, 91). There can be no subject of athletics, of agriculture, of charity, of education. The ordinary "service of goods" precludes all subjectivation. And, whatever happens, "there can be no philosophy of commerce *[philosophie commerçante]*" (EE, 375–76).

Truths are material productions because the generic procedures do indeed provide the "material, or real, basis of philosophy. . . . The generic procedures are truly the *matter* of philosophy."[4] And they are material *productions* because the labor of a truth accumulates step by step, one investigation at a time, as an experiment without any external or covering law (in the absence of any "metalanguage" [CT, 136; D, 87]). That the generic procedures condition philosophy does not mean that philosophy must itself be either mathematical, artistic, political, or romantic. Badiou has little interest in a philosophy *of* politics or of mathematics. When he says that philosophy is conditioned by politics or art, he means that a particular philosophy is conditioned by particular political movements or particular works of art, not by certain abstract considerations on political society, human cooperation, or the rationalization of public institutions, let alone by general reflections on the nature of sensation, taste, inspiration, and the like. Badiou's own philosophy, for example, is conditioned by certain political initiatives undertaken in France in fidelity to the principles of May 68, along with certain poems by Mallarmé, Celan, and Pessoa. Philosophies that claim to be conditioned only by some general ideas labeled "political thought" are in fact conditioned by the prevailing state logic of the day (in the case of much recent political philosophy, by the ideology of liberal parliamentarism).

All four generic procedures, whether individual or collective, follow the same path, which Badiou summarizes with the following adaptation of Lacan's famous diagram:[5]

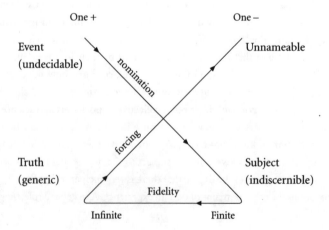

Such is the "trajectory of a truth." It begins with an event or undecidable statement, a supernumerary (One +) supplement. What it presents, ultimately, is an unnameable (One -), that is, an element in the situation about which verifiable statements cannot be "forced." Between the undecidable and the unnameable, a truth passes through those finite investigations that are decided by a subject and grouped, through the persistence of fidelity, in an infinitely accumulating indiscernible or generic set.

Over the next four chapters I consider each of the generic procedures in turn, before paying special attention, in chapter 12, to the place of the unnameable as the "highest stage" of truth.

Love and Sexual Difference

Following in Plato's footsteps, Badiou conceives of love as one of the direct conditions of philosophical thought.[1] The truth of love, like that of the other conditions of philosophy, cannot simply be deduced, abstractly, by philosophers with a romantic disposition. It must be experienced or undergone. Love involves the conversion of a "hateful self" or "dead Ego"—a being that one could not, by definition, love—into a subject. Only a subject is worthy of love, and "the subjective process of a truth is one and the same thing as the love for that truth" (SP, 95–97). In the case of love, of course, such truth is private by definition, and it will come as no surprise that Badiou has had less to say, thus far, about love than about the other generic procedures. Nevertheless, inasmuch as what motivates any subject is always a love of truth, it is appropriate to begin our review of the procedures with a brief discussion of love.[2]

It is typical of antiphilosophy to hold that "love is what is inaccessible to theory."[3] On this point antiphilosophy conforms to Romantic doxa: love is supposed to be the experience par excellence of a vague, ineffable intensity or confusion. The antiphilosopher maintains that what can be said of love is at best suggested through the imprecise and roundabout medium of art. When Badiou, by contrast, insists that love is a domain of truth, he means that it is as precise, as austere, in its operation as the domain of mathematics itself. Indifferent to all sentimental confusion, and against any merely moralistic supervision of sexual desire, the philosopher seeks "an *exact* appreciation of the disjunctive character of love."[4] In particular, Badiou says, any truly contemporary effort "to put philosophy under the condition of love is unthinkable, today . . . if we neglect the radical enterprise by which Lacan organizes, in thought, the quasi-ontological *face-à-face* of love and desire."[5]

A truth is always the truth of its situation, composed through some kind of eventual supplement to that situation. What truth, then, does love pronounce? Certainly not the truth of a romantic fusion, of two become one. Still less the truth of our "natural" disposition, via a momentary return to prelapsarian plenitude. As a rule, "no difference is natural, and to begin with not that which decrees that there are men and women" (RT, 86). On the contrary, "far from governing 'naturally' the supposed relation of the sexes, love is what makes truth of their unrelation *[dé-liaison]*. Love is the only experience that we have of a Two counted from itself, of an immanent Two."[6] Love proclaims the truth of sexual difference, or, in other words, love effects the axiomatic disjunction of sexual positions. Through love, as through every form of truth, what we normally know as related is thought as unrelated. Through love, an individual qua individual realizes (s)he is not a self-sufficient One (an ego) but a disjointed part of an original bifurcation, or Two. As Judith Butler reminds us, "There is no 'I' prior to its assumption of sex."[7]

Plato

Love is thus that contingent experience which allows access to something true about the situation of sexual differentiation and, through it, of that energy which drives our desire and so exceeds our conscious experience. The truth of sexual difference remains elusive for those who have not loved. Before love, so to speak, sexual difference is not real: a true experience of sexual difference is reserved to the sole subject of love. The sequence is not first, (biological) sexual difference, and therefore (romantic) love. Biological difference has no role to play here. In the most literal sense, "the sexes do not preexist the loving encounter but are rather its result" (B, 56). True sexual difference is not an objective domain in any sense. It is not a matter for doctors and sociologists. In everyday life, what passes for sexual difference simply reflects the current state of the situation, with its various conventions and clichés. Love is the only process through which "the difference of the sexes is not simply experienced, suffered, and articulated, but also made accessible to thought. And the difference of the sexes is not only an empirical phenomenon, but more radically the first and fundamental scene of difference *tout court*. It is in love that thought frees itself from the powers of the One, and is exercised according to the law of the 'Two.'"[8] From being counted-as-ones (ones among others), love splits us into that part of a two from which we begin an investigation of the infinite (of everything that touches our love).

Love is, first and foremost, a matter of literally unjustified commitment to an encounter with another person. Everything begins with the encounter. The encounter "is not destined, or predestined, by anything other than the haphazard passage of two trajectories. Before this chance encounter, there was nothing but solitudes. No two preexisted the encounter, in particular no duality of the sexes. Inasmuch as sexual difference is thinkable, it is so only from the point of an encounter, in the process of love, without our being able to presuppose that a primary difference conditions or orients that encounter. The encounter is the originary power of the Two, thus of love, and this power that in its own order nothing precedes is practically beyond measure."[9] The "encounter" is not properly the encounter between two individuals, two consolidated bundles of interests and identities, but instead an experience that suspends or nullifies precisely this re-presentative notion of the two, a two as one plus one. The "power of the encounter," Badiou writes, "is such that nothing measures up to it, neither in the sentiment itself nor in the desiring body."[10] Love reflects, in the private sphere, the general "evental status of the Two" (MP, 18), and every Two operates "in the element of non-rapport, of the un-related. Love is the 'approach' of the Two as such," and the truth of this approach is "obviously inaccessible to knowledge, especially the knowledge of those who love" (MP, 64; cf. PM, 173–74). The true worthiness of the beloved can never be verified or proved. A loving subject remains a subject insofar as the couple continues to draw present consequences from an original declaration that they "believe without knowing why."[11] Fidelity to love implies attestation before justification. The only serious question to be asked of love, as with Proust's Swann, is always a question about the existence of love itself: "Is it still there?" (TA, 8.4.98).

No less than any other truth, love thus testifies to "the void of relationship *[lien]*" (C, 286). Everything in Badiou's account turns on the assertion that "there can be no sexual relationship *[il n'y a pas de rapport sexuel]*."[12] Badiou adopts this idea more or less as is from Lacanian theory, where sexuality is itself defined as "the effect on the living being of the impasses which emerge when it gets entangled in the symbolic order, i.e., the effect on the living body of the deadlock or inconsistency that pertains to the symbolic order *qua* order of universality."[13] Sexual difference is nothing other than the result of incommensurate relations to the signifier, that is, differing relations to our incorporation into (or alienation by) language.[14] Man is defined as wholly determined by symbolic castration—that is, by total alienation in language—and is thus "bounded" by the symbolic system, forming a "free," exceptional, but delimited Whole within it. He is whole, yet forever cut off from the substantial Thing of his primordial (incestuous) desire. Woman, on the other hand, is defined as being only partially enveloped in the symbolic or "phallic" function; she is thus not bounded, not whole, and not limited in her enjoyment. Woman is open to an un-re-presentable *jouissance*, a *jouissance* for which there is no signifier.[15] As Žižek summarizes things, "The 'masculine' universe involves the universal network of causes and effects founded in an exception (the 'free' subject which theoretically grasps its object, the causal universe of the Newtonian physics); the 'feminine' universe is the universe of boundless dispersion and divisibility which, for that very reason, can never be rounded off into a universal Whole."[16] Badiou endorses a version of this Lacanian distribution of roles. The adopted position called "man" is "for all" *(pour tout)*, at one with the symbolic phallus of a universal mathesis. "Woman," by contrast, is "not all" *(pas toute)*; "'woman' is what punctures this totality"[17] in favor of an infinitely unbounded excess. These two positions are adopted as incommensurable responses to the event of the loving encounter: "Masculine desire is affected, infected, by the void that separates the sexed positions in the very unity of the loving process. 'Man' desires the *nothing* of the Two. Whereas the 'woman,' errant, solitary guardian of the original unity, from the pure point of the encounter, desires *nothing but* the Two."[18]

Between nothing and nothing-but, between for-all and not-all, between totality and infinity, there is no common measure. Man and woman do not, *pace* Plato's Aristophanes, fit together in a single Whole.[19] As Badiou writes, "The two positions are totally disconnected. 'Totally' must be taken in the literal sense: nothing of the experience is the same for the man position and the woman position" (C, 257; cf. B, 56). The "original discord" of sexual difference precedes any socialized conception of a familial Same.[20]

Badiou's most recent contribution to the formalization of the truth of love turns on "love as process, or as duration *[durée]*, or as the construction of a scene *[scène]*," a sustainable scene or staging of the Two.[21] This requires a preliminary admission that, although the two sexual positions are indeed incompatible, still we should not accept the "segregative thesis" whereby there would be strictly nothing in common between them. Instead of nothing, Badiou posits a nonempty but "absolutely undetermined, nondescribable, noncomposable term," which he notes as u. The new thesis is that "there is indeed something that is simultaneously in relation with the two positions, but that this something—in which we recognize the ghost of an object—is made of nothing, and can be made the object of no analytical description." This term u acts as "a punctual rapport within the nonrapport" of man and woman. Though it is in rapport with both positions, "there is nothing that enters into rapport with *it*, other than the void" (5). On this basis, Badiou can propose a more developed definition of love: "A loving encounter is what attributes, eventually, a double function to the atomic and unanalyzable intersection of the two sexed positions: that of the object in which a desire finds its cause, and that of a point from which is counted the Two, thereby initiating a shared investigation of the Universe" (6). The difficult, continuing exercise of love is the living of this irreducibly double function, the maintaining of a single split desire, the introspective sharing or "centration" of an indeterminate sexual desire the lovers can never explain, and the external elaboration, from this disjoined center, of "innumerable common practices or shared investigations of the world" (7).

We might do well, at this point, to distinguish Badiou's concept of sexual difference from the rather more familiar ideas of another of Lacan's long-standing interlocutors, the antiphilosopher Luce Irigaray. No one has done more than Irigaray to emphasize the irreducible duality of the sexes. Gendered orientations, as she has explained in book after book, "cannot be reduced to complementary functions but correspond to different identities."[22] Aware that "the truth is always produced by someone,"[23] she has an interest, like that of Badiou, not in "describing, reproducing, and repeating what exists" but in knowing "how to invent or imagine what hasn't yet taken place."[24] What she evokes as the identity of woman is an ongoing "project," an identity of the future. And among the contributions to this project, love plays a decisive role in the shift from merely parochial difference to a kind of "immortal" transfiguration.[25]

That said, Badiou is diametrically opposed to Irigaray's conception of love and sexual difference on every point. What Irigaray means by a "generic" identity is the exact opposite of Badiou's meaning: it is precisely a call for a kind of sociocultural separatism, an assertion of "women's right to their own specific culture,"[26] complete with a specifically feminine "sort of social organization, . . . , a religion, a language, and either a currency of their own or a non-market economy."[27] Whereas Badiou would subtract the truth of sexual difference from all positive or culturally validated indicators, for Irigaray the goal is "social and cultural sexualisation for the two sexes."[28] Whereas Badiou seeks, in the case of love as in that of everything else, a precise and systematic conceptual description, Irigaray embraces a typically antiphilosophical distrust of concepts and a deliberately antisystematic means of presentation.[29] Whereas Badiou reserves the truth of sexual difference to an exclusively subjective realm of thought, Irigaray anchors it in an ultimately specified physical frame of reference, the "body as primary home,"[30] as thematized by the motifs of "virginity," "maternity," "muscosity," and so on. Whereas Badiou stresses the absence and impossibility of a sexual relationship, Irigaray specifies a vague notion of "relation" as an essentially feminine disposition and the "natural" starting point for an eventual reconciliation of the sexes, as guided by woman's primordial experience of maternity. Whereas Badiou grounds his ethics of sexual difference in a positive fidelity to an ephemeral encounter, Irigaray's version leads to an ever more insistent emphasis on "the civil rights and responsibilities of the two sexes," on a legally protected right to and respect for difference as an end in itself.[31] Whereas Badiou's work, finally, is in permanent anticipation of an anarchic atheism, Irigaray's work is infused with nostalgia for a mythical age of "women's law," when "the divine and the human were not separate."[32]

So while Irigaray looks for a specifically legal codification of the ultimately natural (if not mysterious) sexual differences, Badiou insists on the radically axiomatic status of sexual differentiation as an essentially artificial and illegal process: "The two sexes differ, radically, but there is exactly nothing of substance in this difference" (RT, 86). That sexual difference is a matter of truth means precisely that it can be grounded only upon an "objective" void, as an assertion made in the absence of any cultural or biological justification. An axiom never comes with a guarantee. As (loving) subjects, we can say that there is man and woman, but we cannot infer this saying "from a description or an empirical saying" (PM, 152). Like all truth procedures, love is sited on the edge of the void, and "every love is established in the joy of the empty gap of the Two of the sexes that it founds" (NN, 200).

Again, if the two sexes are utterly disjoined, this is because this disjunction, which is to say love itself, is one. Since there are two sexes, "there is only one humanity" (C, 258). The two of the disjoined and the one of the disjoining exclude the dialectical possibility of a third position. There is no sexless angel. There is no additional position outside the Two, and "the two positions cannot be counted as two" (C, 262). The two is not reducible to the couple, and only the couple is visible to an outside observer. Badiou, like Girard, holds that desire, as desire *for* something or someone, is always the effect of a socially mediated triangulation. Such mimetic desire has nothing to do with love.[33] Love is no more a matter of interindividual negotiation or envy than it is of Romantic fusion or obsession. If love involves two individuals, the subject of love is itself, like all subjects, singular: "The subject of love is not the 'loving' subject described by the classical moralists. . . . The lovers as such enter into the composition of *one* loving subject, who exceeds them both" (E, 40, my emphasis).

Like all truth processes, love is threatened by a terrible danger or "evil"— the conversion of its own axiomatic subjectivity into a definitive objectivity. The danger threatening every love is that the medium of disjunction might itself be named and objectified, defined, and thus turned into a force of fusion. According to Badiou, this medium is sexual pleasure, "*la jouissance sexuelle.*" It is the subjective experience of this *jouissance* that makes present the void separating and joining the two sexes, the place in which their disjunction is subjectively indistinguishable from their fusion. But this indistinction must not be objectified. The subjects of love must not attempt to *know* their disjunction. A unity of fusion, "the romantic idea of full, fusional love, under the purified sign of the One, is exactly the Evil of love" (NN, 200).

True love, then, must not try to force (in Cohen's sense) everything in its situation. The sexual medium of love itself must resist the forcing of love's truth. This is what Badiou means when he says that sexual pleasure is the unnameable of love. Love as a subjective or generic procedure may eventually rename everything in its shared situation—except its unnameable medium itself.

chapter 8

Art and Poetry

If truth is a subjective composition, then of all the generic procedures, the notion of an artistic truth may for many readers be the most intuitively plausible or recognizable. Modernity has long been comfortable with versions of aesthetic defamiliarization. However, what is at issue in Badiou's own broadly modernist conception of art is not some kind of aesthetic process or faculty, but the particular consequences of certain concrete artistic events or truths. "As opposed to aesthetic speculation," what Badiou calls "inaesthetics describes the strictly intraphilosophical effects produced by the independent existence of some works of art" (PM, 7).

From the start, this sharply distinguishes Badiou's position from the more familiar orientations of his major rivals in the field of aesthetics, however radical their understanding of artistic defamiliarization might be. Where Adorno and Lyotard, for example, look to the general characteristics of an aesthetic conception of things—as a means, precisely, of "representing" the objectively unrepresentable reality of things[1]—Badiou looks for the quite exceptional consequences resulting from a fidelity to a couple of privileged artistic sequences or "configurations." In ultimately antiphilosophical style, Lyotard and Adorno pick out and celebrate instances where conceptual thought breaks down in favor of an aesthetically accessible reality beyond the concept. Since "to think is to identify," Adorno's goal is to dissolve conceptual thought in favor of the object's nonidentity, thereby gaining "insight into the *constitutive* character of the nonconceptual in the concept."[2] Badiou, by contrast, seeks to isolate the precise conceptual consequences of an encounter with art. Adorno believes that philosophy always threatens "the liquidation of the particular,"[3] and that it is the privilege of artistic perception to help "break the bonds of a logic which covers over the particular with the universal."[4] Badiou's "inaesthetics," on the other hand, is one of the conditions of philosophy, and, like all such conditions, articulates the singular directly with the universal.

Badiou distinguishes his position from three more established ways of configuring the relation of art to philosophy. The first is "didactic," and it argues that art, barred from a direct relation to truth, can only imitate certain effects of truth. Though fictional or untrue, this imitation can be highly convincing and so must be carefully controlled and supervised by extra-artistic means. Examples include the Plato of the *Republic* and Brecht (whom Badiou accuses of a "Stalinized Platonism").[5] The second position is "romantic," and it holds that "art alone is capable of truth." Romantics urge the creation of glorious art as "incarnation of the absolute, the absolute as subject" (PM, 12). Badiou calls the third position "classical," and links it to Aristotle, Descartes, Spinoza, and Lacan. For a classicist, art is not really a problem at all. It is not only incapable of truth, but incapable of providing a convincing imitation of truth. Its nature is simply therapeutic, its effect cathartic or pleasing. Art's very innocence limits it to a purely decorative role. In Lacan's psychoanalysis, for example, art allows the "unsymbolizable object of desire to approach, in subtraction, the very plenitude of a symbolization," but its "ultimate effect remains imaginary" (PM, 17–18).

Badiou argues that all three positions are today "saturated" beyond recovery. A contemporary didacticism (since Brecht) has been discredited by the prescriptions of socialist realism. Romanticism has exhausted itself (since Heidegger) in unfulfilled prophecies of a divine Return. Classicism has become cynical (since Lacan), disarmed by its own demystification of desire, by the eventual domestication of art through an ever more refined analytical mastery. This saturation of aesthetics is reflected in the poverty of the only genuinely contemporary contribution to the issue: the theme of "the end of the avant-gardes," maintained from Dada to the Situationists. Badiou dismisses this short-lived effort as a mere "didacticoromantic" melange— didactic in its "desire to put an end to art, the denunciation of its alienated and inauthentic character," and romantic in its "conviction that art would then be reborn as *absoluité*, as complete awareness of its own operation, as the immediately legible truth of itself" (PM, 18–19). Although he admires the "splendid and violent ambition" of the great avant-garde innovators themselves (LS, 122), Badiou accepts that it is impossible simply to return to their agenda. He refuses to pursue its ultimately destructive implications. In its determination to work exclusively in a forever revolutionary present, the avant-garde was ultimately unable to resist the "suicidal chimera" of a perpetual beginning. It was thus unable to move beyond an essentially "hys- terical" conception of the creative instant as such, a conception that leads only to the radical erasure, or *désoeuvrement*, of art as such, its dissolution in the unsustainable dream of a general aestheticization of everyday life (LS, 122–23). The avant-garde, in short, was unable to devise a genuinely sustain- able answer to the question What is art's *work?*

Hence the need for a new alternative, a fourth position, one able to sus- tain both the "immanence and the singularity" of art as truth. Philosophers must have the modesty to recognize that "what art teaches is nothing other than its existence. It is simply a matter of encountering this existence, which means: thinking a thought" (PM, 21). A work of art is not an object of reflec- tion or appreciation, any more than love is reducible to the couple available for external observation. The thinking of a truth must take place from within the truth procedure itself: from outside its subjectivizing effect, poetry is only wordplay, or versification, or decoration (Badiou has no distinct place for a theory of reading or interpretation as such). As with all genuinely crea- tive thought, the nature of an encounter with art cannot be simply receptive or descriptive. The relation of thought to a truly contemporary moment in art—a moment of artistic improvisation as such, when past experience and a knowledge of rules do not suffice to predict or produce a new result—can be that only of a "localized prescription, and not a description."[6] Against any notion of art as cultural therapy, as particularist, as identitarian or commu- nitarian, as "imperial" or re-presentative, Badiou affirms the production of contemporary works of art, universally addressed, as so many exceptional attempts "to formalize the formless" or "to purify the impure." The sole task of an exclusively affirmative art is the effort to render visible all that which, from the perspective of the establishment, is invisible or nonexistent.[7]

Like all truth, an artistic truth begins with an event and is sustained by a subject. As distinct from science, art is a matter of putting ultimately sensual experience into (verbal, visual, audible) form. The evental site in an artistic situation always lies on the edge of what is perceived, in that situation, as the void of form. Artistic events take place on the border of what is formless, or monstrous, the point at which the formal resources of the existing arts are overextended (for instance, chromatism as the saturation of the classical tonal system). An artistic event demonstrates that it is possible to conceive of what has hitherto been considered monstrous or formless as "formable," as the material for a new formalization or putting into form (TA, 8.4.98). An artistic event is the demonstration of this possibility, which is to say that it is not usually a single work so much as a cluster of works, all more or less unplaceable in the prevailing state of things. Further works undertaken in fidelity to such a violation or breakthrough can be thought of as so many "situated investigations [enquêtes] into the truth that they actualize locally, or of which they are finite fragments." A particular work or investigation can then be treated as "subject point of an artistic truth." The order and sequence in which successive works appear is itself a matter of chance and proceeds one step at a time. The infinite truth thus composed is what Badiou calls an artistic configuration. It is "composed of nothing but works. But it is manifest—as infinity—in none of them" in particular.[8] Badiou gives as examples: Greek tragedy, set in motion by Aeschylus and saturated by the time of Euripides; the classical style in music, beginning with Haydn and ending with Beethoven; the European novel, beginning with Cervantes and ending with Joyce.[9] Any given "configuration thinks itself in the works that compose it." It is not the business or privilege of philosophy alone to ponder the nature of art in general. Philosophers simply try to identify the configurations active in their time, always seeking in this time the things that will sustain a timeless evaluation.[10]

In close proximity to the militant though ultimately destructive legacy of the avant-garde, Badiou groups the great art events of *our* time, as you would expect, as formal variants on the general project of generic subtraction. Rather than set out to destroy the very category of the work or image, a subtractive art seeks instead "the minimal image," the simplest imaginary trait, a vanishing work, an art of "rarefaction" achieved "not through an aggressive posture with respect to inherited forms, but through mechanisms that arrange these forms at the edge of the void, in a network of cuts and disappearances," on the model of Webern's music or Mallarmé's poetry (LS, 106). The rigorously generic character of the result—of the enduring work—follows as a matter of course. In Badiou's work to date, modern poetry has taken pride of place in the field of artistic truths, while Beckett's fiction (complemented by a recent reading of Proust) has provided him with his most detailed example of a generic prose; further, somewhat scattered reflections on theatre, dance, cinema, and photography round out a varied portrait of the modes of artistic subtraction.[11]

Generic Poetry

Whereas mathematics composes the truth of "the pure multiple as the primordial inconsistency of being as being," being evacuated of all material presence or sensual intensity, "poetry makes truth *[fait vérité]* of the multiple as presence come to the limits of language. It is the song of language insofar as it presents the pure notion of 'there is' *[il y a]*, in the very erasure of its empirical objectivity" (PM, 39). Like mathematics, poetry is language reduced to the strict presentation of presentation. Simply, because this presentation takes place in words rather than in numbers, what is presented has an irreducibly sensory or qualitative component that distinguishes it from the more perfectly abstract discourse of mathematics: "The poem exhibits the generic truth of the sensible as sensible (that is to say, outside of all specification)."[12]

Although a poem is made of language, it does not operate according to the coded conventions of linguistic communication. The poem does not relate word to object or language to world. The poem, like any truth, cuts all ties and disjoins all relations: "The poem is without mediation" and "has nothing to communicate. It is only a saying, a declaration that draws its authority only from itself. . . . The singularity of what is here declared enters into none of the possible figures of interest."[13] The poem interrupts; it cuts the lines of communication with what Badiou calls a "diagonal" use of language. He gives as an example Rimbaud's line "Je navigue sur l'arc des voyages qui ne commencent jamais." A poetic truth is constituted in fidelity to such literally inconsistent perceptions, through the composition of a subjective awareness unlimited by objective constraints: "The poetic diagonal declares that a faithful thought, that is, one capable of truth, bores a hole in what significations concentrate of knowledge," thereby "enabling another current of thought."[14] (As Lacan quips: "Poets don't know what they're saying, yet they still manage to say things before anyone else" [S2, 16/7].)

A poem is the liberation of what a language can do, once freed of the existing regime of re-presentation (habits, conventions, clichés, and so on). The poem subtracts language from the world in which it is normally put to work. The poem subtracts language from the manipulations of knowledge. In the absence of any referential object, the poem thus "declares from end to end its own universe." It demonstrates that "an experience without object" must be a "pure affirmation, which constitutes a universe whose right to exist, whose mere probability, nothing guarantees. . . . The poem is, preeminently, a thought that obtains in the retreat, the breakdown, of everything that supports the faculty of knowledge."[15] Evacuated of its objects, the universe perceived by poetry is populated by "pure notions" and "autonomous prescriptions."[16]

A true poem must be addressed, like Mallarmé's *Livre,* to the universal Crowd. Like a mathematical formula, a poem is "destined for everyone" (PM, 53). Just as every scientific discovery violates established and exclusive customs and thereby invites a universal inspection or approval, so a poem, by punching a new way through the particularity of confirmed opinions and idioms, lays claim to the only true universality that ordinary language can achieve. In a sense, the more hermetic a poem might seem from within the state of a language situation, the more generic its appeal can be. Poetry does not distinguish insiders from outsiders: that any particular poem is expressed in a particular language simply confirms the invariable fact that every truth is always situated. Subtracted from all habitual familiarity, a poem leaves everyone equally confounded. Without concern for the conventional requirement of language users, poetry affirms the pure "sovereignty of language" (PM, 161). On this point, at least, Badiou is prepared to acknowledge a certain proximity to that Heidegger for whom "to gain access to the work of art, it [is] necessary to remove it from all relations to something other than itself." To "preserve the work," Heidegger continues, is not to "reduce people to their private experiences, but [to] bring them into affiliation with the truth *happening* in the work."[17]

for how long?

Badiou distinguishes two general ways in which poetic truths escape the mediation of knowledge and habit: through lack or excess. Either "the object is subtracted, withdrawn from Presence by its own self-dissolution (this is Mallarmé's method). Or it is uprooted from its domain of appearing, undone by its solitary exception, and from that moment rendered substitutable with any other object (this is Rimbaud's method). At the same time, the subject is annulled—either made absent (Mallarmé) or made *effectively* plural (Pessoa, Rimbaud)" (MP, 58). A philosophy conditioned by Mallarmé—as Badiou's has been, explicitly, since the late 1960s[18]—embraces the austerity of an ideal "Purity" distilled through its subtraction for semantic or sensual confusion.[19] Triggered by a fleeting impression or encounter (an event), composed as "the mise-en-scène of its appearing-disappearing," the poem persists in the vanishing of this impression. The event takes place in an empty, minimally specified place (the ocean, the desert). The event itself—a shipwreck, a dream, a vision, a sensation—leaves no trace: "radically singular, pure action, without the poem [it] would have fallen back into the nullity of the place" (EE, 214). The poem makes its passing persist, as the purifying passage from sensual to ideal, from known to true. The poem is the passing itself made consistent. Here, "to make something (swan, star, rose) appear that appears only so as to be canceled out is constitutive of the poetic act" (PM, 161). In Mallarmé's *L'Après-midi d'un faune,* for instance, the speaker wonders if there might exist in nature, in his surroundings, the material traces of his dream: "Might the water," Badiou asks, "bear witness to the coldness of one of the desired women? Might the wind not remember the voluptuous sighs of the other? If this hypothesis has to be put aside, it is because the water and the wind are nothing, they inexist *[inexistent]*, with respect to the power of arousal, through art, of the Idea of water and the Idea of wind. . . . Through the visibility of its artifice, which is also the thought of poetic thought, the poem surpasses in power that of which the sensible is capable. The modern poem is the contrary of a mimesis. By its operation it displays an Idea whose object, whose objectivity, are but pale copies" (PM, 38–39). As Proust was eventually to conclude, "We can only imagine what is absent," and it is on the basis of this absence that art provides access to a beauty that withstands the force of time's erosion.[20]

To put philosophy under the condition of Pessoa (and his various heteronyms, Ricardo Reis, Alberto Caeiro, and Alvaro de Campos), on the other hand, means "to open a way forward that manages to be neither Platonic nor anti-Platonic" (PM, 64; cf. LS, 92). On the one hand, much of Pessoa's work incants an anti-Platonic, quasi-Deleuzian vitalism, accompanied by the erosion of classical or bivalent logic, an almost sophistic emphasis on discursive diversity, and a characteristically presocratic search for the thing in itself in all its sensual immediacy. Hence "a poetry without aura," written to the exclusion of all conceptual idealization. This aspect of Pessoa's work links him, up to a point, with Adorno: in Caeiro's words, "A thing is what cannot be interpreted" (quoted in PM, 68). But in other respects, Pessoa adopts an essentially Platonic stance. He affirms an almost mathematical precision, and his "syntactical machination" breaks the natural continuity of sensual perception and instinctual emotion in favor of rigorously isolated "types." In Campos's *Maritime Ode,* for example, the real or manifest quay evokes the ideal Great Quay, an ephemeral smile points toward the eternal Smile, and a contingent passerby suggests the eternal Passing-by. What this particular poem declares is indeed "that *things are identical to their Idea*" (PM, 71). A philosophy conditioned by Pessoa will thus grope toward the recognition of "the coextension of the sensible and the Idea, but without conceding anything to the transcendence of the One. It will think that there are only multiple singularities, but without drawing anything from them that resembles empiricism." With a hint of self-criticism, Badiou concludes that philosophy, insofar as it continues to pit Platonism against anti-Platonism, remains "behind" Pessoa: it is time to catch up (PM, 73).

Appreciation of the more general place of poetry in Badiou's system is complicated by the strained historical relation between poetry and philosophy. This history has been punctuated, above all, by their temporary separation after the Platonic banishment of the poets, and by their temporary fusion during what Badiou, after Heidegger, calls the "age of the poets," in the later nineteenth and early twentieth centuries. Badiou's own position, in a sense, combines these two moments. He confirms the Platonic move as essential to a generalized desacralization of thought: poetry must not be placed above philosophy. But unlike Plato, he recognizes that a poetry that has escaped its mimetic function is very precisely a condition of philosophy, rather than its antithesis or rival. To the degree that the poem asserts a subject without object, or a City without community, or a being without Nature, it deserves to escape its Platonic proscription.[21] During the true age of poetry (roughly, from Rimbaud to Celan), poetry rightly took on some of the functions abandoned by a philosophy temporarily preoccupied with the sterile hypotheses of scientific positivism and historical materialism.[22] This age, however, has now passed. The poem is simply incapable of a genuinely philosophical self-awareness. The poem declares the Idea, but not the truth of the Idea. The poem can aspire to condition philosophy, not to replace it.

By the same token, no philosopher is in a position to set limits upon what poetry can do. This is why Badiou has always refused Adorno's historicizing prohibition of poetry in the wake of Auschwitz. As a matter of firm principle, Badiou refuses to accept the idea of any external limit to truth (any limit, that is, other than its own unnameable medium or source). There can be nothing in what happens, however appalling its impact, that can interrupt artistic formalization as such. Paul Celan is precisely the poet who has lent form to what happened at Auschwitz, and who has registered the brutal evacuation of eloquence that this happening entails (LS, 71). As for the necessary inhumanity of such an art, Badiou is prepared to accept this particular consequence, at least, as an instance of a more general feature of all true art. All art "testifies to what is inhuman in the human," since it is oriented solely toward the limits of what can be sensed, experienced, or endured. Poetry does nothing to satisfy human needs or comfort human sorrows. On the contrary, it gives form to the promise, from within the limits of its domain and in the radical absence of compassion, of an infinite "surhumanité." (LS, 129).

Generic Fiction: The Case of Beckett

Beckett's work is well suited to Badiou's anti-Heideggerian aesthetic. No authentic sacralization here. Beckett explores "generic humanity" (B, 24) in all its subtractive sobriety. Faithful to Descartes's premise that if you want to undertake a "serious enquiry upon thinking humanity you have first to suspend everything that is inessential or doubtful," Beckett reduces his characters to their minimal, ontologically irreducible functions (B, 19, 22). For example, he abstracts the function of movement through the progressive elimination of all moving things, means, or surfaces, until, "thus divested, the 'character' arrives at that pure moment at which movement is externally indiscernible from immobility, because it is no longer anything other than its own and ideal mobility" (B, 20–21). He likewise reduces the function of will to willing the end of will, an endless willing the disappearance of the will, just as he reduces the function of joy to its breathless affirmation. In a process of stripping down comparable to what Deleuze describes as Beckettian exhaustion *[épuisement]*, he in turn abstracts the function of being from all secondary ornamentation, until "being and nothingness are one and the same thing."[23] For Badiou's Beckett as for Heraclitus, "being is nothing other than its becoming nothing" (27). The sole foundation of being as being is the void. With Beckett, this foundation takes on the aspect of a dark gray space, "a black gray enough for it not to be in contradiction with light" (30–31).

We know that such ontological reduction serves only to isolate the truths that exceed being as being. Pursued as an end in itself, it leads to the impasse of pure solipsism. This is the root of the "crisis" that Badiou locates in the 1950 *Textes pour rien*. In an early novel like *Watt* (1942), "the place of being" stands as "absolutely closed," "complete, self-sufficient, eternal" (B, 40), pointing only to the flat redundancy of speech and the futility of any subjective existence. The Beckett of the 1950s, by contrast, realizes that "the subject must be open to an alterity, must cease to be folded inside himself in an interminable, torturous discourse *[parole]*." From *Comment c'est* (1960) in particular, the half-light of being was broken by "the voice of the other" (38). From then on, "the 'with the other' is decisive. But here again, we have to isolate its nature, set it up in a way that evacuates all psychology, all obvious, empirical exteriority" (23). The relation with the other saves the speaking subject from solipsism and mere absorption into the gray void of being—but this relation is itself utterly generic or aspecific. In the world of "executioners" and "victims" described in *Comment c'est*, for instance, the other is "an evasive circularity, since it is possible to occupy successively the position of the executioner, then that of the victim, and nothing else specifies the difference" (23). The other is not a particular being, relative to the self, but a pure "singularity," a voice confirmed by "no bodily encounter." The eventual conclusion: "The other, reduced to its primitive functions, is caught in the following tourniquet: if he exists, he is like me, he is indiscernible from me. And if he is clearly identifiable, it is not certain that he exists" (24).

As a general category, the existence of the other is undecidable. Like all undecidables, however, it can be decided eventually. The concrete existence of others may always be revealed through an event, however trivial its substance, that no ontological category can predict or induce. Simply, "it happens that something happens." It happens that the gray screen of being is occasionally punctured in a moment of miraculous clarity, lighting the way to "truth and courage" (B, 79). The essential rule in Beckett's writing is thus to "hold oneself as close as possible to that of which, at the end of the day, all existence is composed: the empty stage of being, the half-light in which everything is acted, but which, itself, acts nothing; and the events that suddenly populate it, and that are like stars in the anonymous place, holes in the distant canvas of the theater of the world."[24]

Badiou probes the example of Beckett's *Worstward Ho!* (1982) with particular attention. He reads this late work as "a recapitulative text, one that takes stock of Beckett's whole enterprise"[25]—it is another minimalist "stenography of the question of being," but one liberated, unlike most of the preceding works, from any latent dramatization or story. In *Worstward Ho!,* translated into French as *Cap au pire,* the realm of human existence is again subjected to an almost Cartesian principle of methodological "worsening" *(l'empirer)*: the reduction of all existence, all action and reaction, to an essential *"imminimisable moindre"* (PM, 177). The overwhelming experience of the text is one of radical subtraction or withdrawal in the "half-light" that defines the void of pure being. All that can be discerned in this half-light are a few fleeting shadows: a hunched-over woman, an old man with a child, a head or skull with a pair of eyes, a mouth: "The universe, or the set of that which appears, might be named by Beckett: a void infested with shadows" (142). These shadow beings are defined as what can "worsen," set against the backdrop of the ultimately unworsenable void or pure being as being: for example, we can move, in the perception of the two shadowy eyes, to the worsened perception of two black holes, the blind indication of an abstract "visibility" (162). In this as in all Beckett's later work, the properly "artistic or poetic effort is an arid working upon language so as to organize it according to the exercises of a worsening." Language begins to "ring true" in its very "break with adequation," the closer it comes to the unworsenable limit of all worsening, the void of pure being as being—the more its *dire* becomes *mal-dire* (164).

From worse, however, we never get to worst. This is an essential point of principle. It is a matter of worst-ward only. The worsening voice will never be able to dissolve itself in the unworsenable, absolute emptiness of the void itself. The effort to worsen becomes more and more demanding the closer we come to the edge of the void, but the temptation to be resisted above all is that of a definitive *mal-dire*, a missaying so mistaken as to finish the effort of speech once and for all. To escape from the painful prescription to speak through a silent reunion with the void: such is the "mystical temptation" that haunts every antiphilosophy. Beckett faces this temptation and then moves beyond it. Language can be worsened but never silenced. In other words, pure being as being or "the void 'in itself' is what cannot be poorly said [*mal dit*]. This is its definition. The void can only be said. In it, the saying and the said coincide" (PM, 167). And since, at the limit of all worsening, being and thought are one and the same, the thinking subject cannot subtract itself entirely. Eyes can become holes, but in the end, "in the skull everything disappears but the skull" (176).

In the closing pages of the text, at the summit of its worsening, a moment of truth flickers through an event that Badiou compares with the appearance of the Great Bear constellation at the end of Mallarmé's *Coup de dés*. Having said that there is nothing more to say, that "nothing has taken place but the place [*rien n'a eu lieu que le lieu*]," there occurs a "sudden adjunction," an abrupt break or metamorphosis—the appearance of three pins, perhaps corresponding to the seven stars in Mallarmé's poem.[26] These pins, however trivial in their substance, appear with a clarity quite unlike that of the shadowy beings that populate the rest of the text. Their appearance prepares the way for a subtle but decisive subjective shift in the narrative voice, an affirmation of the declaration "*plus mèche encore* [said nohow on]."[27] In other words, "The moment when there is nothing more to say than the stable figure of being [i.e., the void], there erupts with a suddenness that is grace without concept, a configuration of things in which we will be able to say '*plus mèche encore*.'" And this new assertion is a saying no longer constrained within the sole onto-logic of worsening, but one that springs out from an "event, which creates a remoteness," an "incalculable distance" (PM, 184). What remains to be said as the truth of language is now "the saying of 'again,' of '*plus mèche encore*,' the imperative of saying as such. At bottom, it is the limit of a kind of astral language, one that would float above its own ruin and from which everything can begin again, from which everything can and must begin again. . . . The good, that is the proper mode of the good in the saying, is the sustaining of the 'again.' That's all. To sustain it without naming it. To sustain the 'again' and to sustain it from that point of extreme incandescence from which its sole apparent content is '*plus mèche encore*.' For this, an event must break out of the last state of being. And then I can, I must, continue" (187).

Generic Fiction: The Case of Proust

At the thematic antipode of Beckett's subtractive prose, Badiou finds in Proust an equally uncompromising effort to "extract" a generic or universal truth from a world and a particular way of being in the world (*mondanité*) that are themselves destined to nothing more than death and oblivion.[28] What remains of this world dies and is forgotten, pure and simple—witness the fate that awaits Albertine *disparue.* The extraction of an incorruptible truth from such a world requires a dramatic revaluation of the very notion of life itself, the extraction of a truth of life that is fundamentally distinct from life as it is lived *(le vécu).* It requires, on the one hand, a long and difficult apprenticeship, an artistic initiation marked by a series of variably inspiring encounters (with Bergotte, La Berma, Elstir, and Vinteuil, as well as with those telling failures who are Swann and Charlus). On the other hand, it presumes the methodical falsification of alternative conceptions of the truth, conceptions that would preserve some link between *vérité* and *mondanité.* The narrator must learn that truth does not figure among a discernible range of logical possibilities (the truth cannot be calculated or predicted, it is always surprising, it always begins with an event); cannot be grasped through willpower alone (truth begins as involuntary, and continues as something to be undergone rather than anticipated or imposed); cannot, for the same reason, be controlled through direct action or communication (hence the essential futility of every subject of jealousy—be it Swann vis-à-vis Odette, Charlus vis-à-vis Morel, or the narrator vis-à-vis Albertine); cannot be said deliberately and explicitly (the truth is revealed only in the gaps and inconsistencies of what is said, or is evoked "through" what is said); and cannot, finally, be received as a form of immediate intuition (the truth is not simply in the experience that gives rise to its eventual evocation). Truth is not a matter of speculation, determination, communication, assertion, or revelation. On the contrary, the truth is itself one with the way to the truth. The composition of truth cannot be distinguished from the process whereby one arrives at the truth.

As narrated in the *Recherche,* this truth process has a number of clearly demarcated steps. The process begins with a variation of Badiou's own ontological presumption: a state of indifferent neutrality or emptiness, characterized by the absence of passion or love, the dominance of idle curiosity, and the free play of interests, especially social interests. The indifferent continuity of the world is occasionally interrupted, however, by the glittering promise of a proper name, or name effect (Balbec, Gilberte, Venice, Guermantes, but also the namelike bodies that are Gilberte among the hawthorn or Albertine and her friends on Balbec Beach). Unlike Lacan, for whom the name is the Symbolic entity par excellence, Proust invests his names with an entirely Imaginary plenitude. A name is whatever points toward an ineffable and essentially inaccessible transcendence. Since this transcendence is Imaginary, a name opens only onto radical and inevitable disappointment, regardless of what is named (be it La Berma, Elstir, or Venice). Such disappointment is radical because *nothing* of the reality involved can survive it. From within the process of disappointment itself there is nothing to salvage. However, from the void thus evacuated by disappointment, it is indeed possible to create, as if ex nihilo, a new Symbolic configuration, one purified of *mondanité* and undertaken, like any truth, at the level of the real as such. At this absolute distance from the *vécu*, it is possible to see how true reality can be grasped through the strictly formal operations of "thought" and "style": "We only truly know that which we are obliged to recreate in thought, that which is hidden from us by everyday life."[29] "Truth only begins," in Proust's often quoted words, when a writer is able to lend form to the strictly eternal (or otherworldly) correspondences that exist between objects and experiences.[30] It follows that "true life, life finally discovered and understood—the only life, then, that is really lived—is literature."[31] It follows, too, that every truly original artistic project is nothing less than a "re-creation" of the world itself.[32]

Generic Humanity: Theater and Cinema

Badiou has a long-standing interest in theater, and over the years has written six plays of his own, four of them since 1992.[33] Like poetry, theater in general, theater as a genre, is an occasion or at least an opportunity to think an artistic truth: "Theater, inasmuch as it thinks, is not a matter of culture, but of art. People don't come to the theater to be cultivated. They are not cabbages. . . . They come to be struck. Struck by theater ideas. They leave not cultivated but stunned, tired, thoughtful" (PM, 119). Whereas dance, for instance, produces only "the idea that the body *can* carry ideas," theater is nothing other than a machine for the actual production of generic ideas.[34]

As we might expect, untrue or "bad theater . . . is one that naturalizes differences" and translates "supposed substances into signs." Good or true theater, by contrast, is "a procedure that reveals generic humanity, that is, indiscernible differences that take place on stage for the first time. . . . The true theater makes of each performance, each actor's every gesture, a generic vacillation in which differences with no basis might be risked. The spectator must decide whether to expose himself to this void, and share the infinite procedure. He is called, not to pleasure. . . , but to thought" (RT, 91, 92). The actors' task is to evacuate themselves of all specificity (however "original" or "unique") so as to reveal an invariably singular genericity, an ongoing "evaporation of all stable essence. . . . The ethic of acting is that of an escapee."[35] Whereas the novel, Badiou claims, remains bound to its context, to the *world* it creates, "the great theatrical text, because open and incomplete, because it will be played over centuries, by people indifferent to everything concerning this text's context, . . . must have the powerful simplicity of the intemporal; it must say a generic humanity. . . . Bérénice, Titus, Hamlet, Orestes [etc.] are proper names of genericity; they belong to subject language that is spoken by nobody, being the natural inverse of every historical language. The men and women these names designate can exist at any moment."[36] As performed, moreover, theater is clearly the most evental of arts: "No other art captures in this way the intensity of what happens" (RT, 23). The ephemeral passing of the performance clears a space for the unlimited eternity of its characters and themes: "The performance encounters in the instant what the text holds in the eternal" (115), but the intemporal genericity of a character is not constrained by any given performance.

By contrast, Badiou is not entirely convinced of the artistic potential of film. Cinema is a merely "bastard art," more "artificial" than art itself—a "Saturday night art."[37] Whereas theater sets up an encounter with ideas, cinema presents only the ephemeral "passage of an idea, or of its ghost" (PM, 120). And whereas painting "is the art par excellence of the idea meticulously rendered in its entirety," cinema, as a "moving picture," as a labor of montage, allows an idea only to pass through it. Cinema "calls us to a particular idea through the force of its loss" (PM, 132).

Nevertheless, Badiou is prepared to grant cinema the task of attempting to save itself, so to speak, from its own irreducible artistic impurity. Thinking cinema—Badiou mentions the films of Oliveira, Kiarostami, Straub, Wenders, Pollet, and Godard—proceeds as the ongoing "purification" of the impure, unmastered, or unspiritualized material it inevitably contains (extraneous imagery, ambient noise, conventions of perspective, etc.).[38] The specific operations of cinema can thus be conceived as an unending sequence of evacuations, applied to its various domains—for instance, the evacuation of psychological motivation in the hyperstylized violence of John Woo, or the liberation of sound from its confinement in inane "background" music or clichéd dialogue in Godard's fragmented compositions.[39] A true film thereby seeks to "purify its (visual and auditory) materials from all that ties them to the domination of re-presentation, to the procedures of identification and realism," and in particular, from all that links these materials to the *automatic* or thoughtless "consumption of sounds and images, whose privileged mechanisms are today: pornographic nudity, cataclysmic special effects, the intimacy of the romantic couple, social melodrama, and pathological cruelty."[40] Since a film is contemporary only if the material to which its purifying operations are applied can be identified as belonging to the recognizable nonart of our time, it is the resistance of these mechanisms that now confronts any attempt to renew the art of cinema. Regarding sexual visibility, the true question remains, "What degree of 'nudity' can love endure, without inviting pornographic corruption?" Regarding cruelty, the question is "How might cinematic violence be revalued through reference to newly monstrous forms of 'tragedy'?" Regarding the recurrent theme of apocalypse (read, the consequences of Americocentric globalization), the question is: How can cinema invent, beyond the feeble ideological gestures of an *Independence Day* or *Armageddon,* a new kind of "epic"? As for social melodrama, the question is: How will cinema be able to invent, beyond what Badiou sees as the merely nostalgic innovations of a Mike Leigh or a Ken Loach, a new subjective "figure of the worker" *[figure ouvrière],* that is, one detached from any sociologizing objectivity?

That art itself is a procedure of truth means that it need no longer be considered either a rival to or an ornament of philosophy. It is no longer a rival, because it provides material *for* philosophy. It is no longer a supplement, because it carries its own self-sufficient truth.[41] The poem is a "purity folded on itself."[42] Simply, this purity is not to be confused with a neo-Romantic variation of the "literary absolute," since it stems from the exclusive process of subtraction. Purity makes no appeal to an objective plenitude. It seeks no apotheosis in the self-conscious fulfillment of art as Spirit. Just as an axiom must accept only an implicit knowledge of what it does, so the subject of art must accept a certain objective ignorance as to what it is. Art is to be distinguished from its evil simulacrum by its readiness to accept the unnameability of its formal medium. Poetry, for example, cannot name its own "consistency": there is no metalanguage with which it might name language itself. Poetry, the subjective manipulation of what language can do, cannot know what language is: "Precisely because the poem is addressed to the infinity of language . . . , it cannot determine this infinity itself."[43] Only the absence of a definitive name permits a perpetual process of autonomination.

c h a p t e r 9

Mathematics and Science

Scientific truth, as opposed to the body of currently accepted scientific knowledge, is not a matter of what can be verified through experimentation within assumed theoretical parameters. It concerns the invention of those parameters. Like any truth, scientific truth begins with an event or discovery, and is proclaimed, in the face of received wisdom, by the subject of that discovery—Galileo and Einstein are the most obvious of Badiou's main examples. The site of such discoveries is in each case a real point of impasse *events* that interrupts *la puissance de la lettre,* that is, the power of mathematical formalization, to articulate clear and distinct relationships, be they physical, geometrical, or numerical.[1] True scientific practice is what adopts this problematic point as its own experimental environment. It does not simply establish correspondences and verify what is already known; it gropes in the dark, at the frontier of uncertainty, in the uneven tension between ignorance and innovation: "We must deliver the sciences from every so-called 'theory of knowledge,'" from every "vain confrontation of language and experience. The sciences are procedures of truth. And thus they are fidelities, deductive or experimental, to unpredictable, chance events of thought."[2]

No less than its artistic counterpart, scientific truth proceeds as an effort to formalize that domain previously conceived as formless or unformable, monstrous. Cantor's project, for instance, was precisely an attempt to formalize the hitherto indeterminable formlessness of the geometric continuum. But,

209

unlike art, through which sensation is put into articulate or consistent form, literal scientific formalization transcribes "sensation inaccessible to itself, sensation as insensible (or, as the Stoics would say, as incorporeal)" (TA, 4.6.98). Access to this inaccessible sensation requires the invention of a pure form, a literality more powerful than anything contemplated by poetry. Scientific truth is certainly the truth of its situation (say, the physical, chemical, or biological situations), but the perception of this truth always requires a mathematical supplement, an evental ultra-one, in order for it to be perceived. For example, in order to confirm, after Copernicus, the as yet unperceived truth of the solar situation—that the earth indeed rotates around the sun—Galileo required the invention of something else, a purely formal supplement to that situation: differential calculus.[3] Even so "naturally" minded a scientist as Darwin needed, in order to understand the mechanics of natural selection, to connect the consequences of geographic isolation with the Malthusian mathesis of scarcity and competition.

Between Scientific Revolution and Committed Research

To begin with, a few points of reference. Anglo-American readers may find it useful to compare Badiou's conception of science with the relatively familiar positions in the philosophy of science associated with Thomas Kuhn and Imre Lakatos. Badiou's approach might be read as a blending of Kuhn's emphasis on innovation and Lakatos's emphasis on commitment.

Like Kuhn, Badiou emphasizes the properly revolutionary aspect of scientific discovery. In Kuhn's terms, established scientific knowledge is organized in a paradigm, that is, a set of expectations and assumptions. What Badiou would call a scientific truth begins with an "anomaly" that violates these expectations,[4] something unrecognizable by means of available norms or criteria. Such an anomaly is situated "on the edge of the void" of this situation, meaning that it is something whose own distinct elements are invisible or indistinguishable from the perspective of that situation's preconceptions. There then follows the growth of confusion and the accumulation of contradictory evidence; the incoherence of Ptolemaic astronomy, for instance, was widely recognized as a problem well before Copernicus developed his theory.[5] Such confusion threatens the current state of scientific procedure and suspends what Kuhn calls normal problem solving activity. It exposes what Badiou calls an evental site, that is, a site from which the entire situation can be transformed. But, as Kuhn insists, confusion and anomaly alone are not enough to motivate a rejection of the prevailing paradigm: "The decision to reject one paradigm is always simultaneously the decision to accept another" (77). The revolutionary shift is not "cumulative" but discontinuous. It requires a "whole reconstruction of the field from new fundamentals" (85), a process analogous to those "political revolutions [that] aim to change political institutions in ways that those institutions themselves prohibit" (93). The new theory or discovery, in other words, forces scientists to take sides in the most literal sense. There is no real space for compromise here: the theory of evolution replaces the assumption of species rigidity, heliocentrism replaces geocentrism, oxygen replaces phlogiston. Acceptance of Einstein's theory implies that Newton was wrong. And since "there is no standard higher than the assent of the relevant community" (94), the conflict is as much a subjective as an objective one, as much a matter of persuasion as of pure evidence or logic. The transition between paradigms "cannot be made a step at a time, forced by logic and neutral experience," but rather is made "all at once (though not necessarily in an instant) or not at all" (150). It requires something of a leap of "faith," a complete "conversion experience" (151, 159). In the light of the new theory, objectivity itself has to be rethought.

Badiou's notion of science, however, cannot simply be identified with Kuhn's. Kuhn's epistemological relativism goes so far as to remove, in effect, any reference to truth from science.[6] Like Kuhn's critic Lakatos, Badiou is careful to insist on the reasoned integrity of a new scientific truth, what Lakatos calls a "research programme." Wary of Kuhnian references to faith and conversion—which imply, he suggests, a conception of change pushed by "contagious panic," "a matter for mob psychology"[7]—Lakatos emphasizes the active, historically specific process of argument and counterargument, the process of "struggle" at work in the elaboration of a new scientific theory.[8] Any particular "research programme" (examples include Newtonian mechanics, Marxism, psychoanalysis, relativity) advances a core hypothesis (the laws of mechanics and gravitation, the logic of class struggle, the topology of the unconscious, the essential unity of matter and energy, etc.), supported by a "vast protective belt of auxiliary hypotheses" and a heuristic or problem-solving machinery able to tackle and reduce apparent anomalies. Program by program, the criteria of truth are established neither in conformity with an eternally transcendent objectivity nor by a purely contingent experimental confirmation, but carried by what Lakatos describes as a sustained creativity or "resourcefulness."[9] Rather than celebrate the accumulation of internally consistent certainties, Lakatos emphasizes a kind of "permanent revolution" driven by suspicion of all established knowledge.[10] Merely isolated "refutations, however, are not the hallmark of empirical failure, as Popper had preached, since all programmes grow in a permanent ocean of anomalies. What really count are dramatic, unexpected, stunning predictions."[11] Such predictions, maintained in militant fidelity to a research program, correspond closely to what Badiou calls the investigations of an active truth procedure. And, as with any truth procedure, there is a range of possible orientations within a given research program ("conservative, rationalist, anarchist"). What Badiou would identify as the truth of the program is sustained so long as it remains able to innovate and create; its persistence requires a tenacity and resourcefulness that must long outlast the initial discovery or hypothesis that inspired it.[12] It took a full eighty years, for instance, before Darwin's theory of natural selection gained widespread acceptance among biologists—and this thanks to the persistence of those few disciples (after Wallace and Huxley, Weismann, Simpson, Mayr, and others) who forced its adoption and generalization.[13] In the end, a program "degenerates" or becomes "saturated" not so much when it is proved wrong as when its ability to predict new facts begins to dry up.[14]

Badiou's notion of fidelity is very close to the commitment and subjective investment at the heart of Lakatos's account, and it sharply distinguishes his conception of scientific truth from the well-known extremes represented by Karl Popper on the one hand and Thomas Feyerabend on the other. Popper's hostility to theoretical commitment as such is explicit. A theory is scientific, Popper says, only if it foregrounds its always imminent falsification. The scientific attitude, by these criteria, demands a minimum of preconceptions and a maximum sensitivity to change, an "openmindedness" generally venerated as the very essence of the discipline. Feyerabend's scientific anarchism, for all its thematic radicalism, actually privileges quite similar values. Feyerabend certainly rages against "the chauvinism of science that resists alternatives to the status quo."[15] He extends his critique, however, to the point where the privilege of science over "myth" is greatly reduced if not eliminated altogether.[16] Unlike Badiou's militant scientist, Feyerabend's epistemological anarchist has "no everlasting loyalty" to any principle and "is against all programmes . . . ; his aims remain stable or change as a result of argument, or of boredom, of a conversion experience, or to impress a mistress, and so on." Indeed, the "one thing he opposes positively and absolutely are universal standards, universal laws, universal ideas such as 'Truth,' 'Reason,' 'Justice,' 'Love. . . .'"[17] Both Popper and Feyerabend, in short, are radically suspicious of everything Badiou associates with conviction and fidelity.

It is this fidelity, combined with a revolutionary or evental insight, that Badiou privileges in his favorite illustrations of scientific truth—the programs of Copernicus, Galileo, and Einstein. Badiou is certainly no specialist in the philosophy of science, and his references to these and other equally familiar sequences do not yet add up to a fully fledged theory. Badiou's priorities, thus far, have pulled him in other directions. "My silence about science is entirely temporary and contingent," he explains. "There's absolutely no principle involved."[18]

What does involve a far-reaching matter of principle is his close conjunction of science in general with mathematics in particular. Badiou has never strayed from Lacan's neo-Cartesian prescription, that (modern) scientific thought begins at an absolute distance from any knowledge acquired through sensory or imaginary "intuition."[19] The direct implication is that only pure mathematics—as distinct from the necessarily inconclusive practice of experimental falsification—can provide science with its true methodological foundation. Just as Badiou firmly dissociates political conviction from anything relating to administration, so too does he divide the subjective aspect of science from any constituent relation with an object as such. In order to preserve an effectively unlimited creativity in science, he must restrict the scientific truth process to matters of pure formalization alone, that is, to matters involving the confrontation of form with its real limit or impasse. And since every real zone of formlessness is by definition internal to the existing means of formalization, Badiou's treatment of scientific truths effectively equates them with innovations undertaken in their mathematical foundation pure and simple. One implication seems to be that biology, say—or indeed any observation-dependent science—is effectively less scientific than the more mathematized science of physics.

In more empirical terms, the issue turns on the eventually necessary inclusion of any science of particular beings within the (mathematical) science of being-as-being. That science here defers to mathematics is not simply a reflection of the need for objective accuracy in measurement. Equations of "scientific" with "quantifiable" can, by definition, concern only the realm of knowledge, not truth. What Badiou suggests, at this point in his research, is that mathematics constitutes the internal limit and tendency of science, to the degree that science will be ever more driven toward mathematics the closer it comes to isolating things in their being as being: "In the final analysis, physics, which is to say the theory of matter, is mathematical. It is mathematical because, as the theory of the most objectified strata of the presented as such, it necessarily catches hold of being-as-being through its mathematicity. . . . The physical situation will then be a very powerfully mathematised situation and, in a certain sense, more and more so, the closer it comes to apprehending the smallest, most primordial elements of reality."[20] Beyond the smallest elements of existence or reality, beyond every quantum paradox, beyond the sway of the uncertainty principle, there is the subjective certainty or truth of mathematics as the science of being as being, or ontology. All scientific roads, it seems, eventually lead to Badiou's mathematical Rome.

Since we considered the properly ontological dimensions of mathematics in chapter 3, the goal here is to consider, again briefly and with a minimum of technical jargon, the characteristic features of mathematics as a truth procedure, that is, as distinct from all merely statistical knowledge.[21]

Mathematical Thought

As Badiou often says, there is no surer way to distinguish a philosophy of truth from the sophistry of opinion or from an antiphilosophy of the ineffable than by asking the question "Is mathematical thought really thought at all?" We know that Wittgenstein and Heidegger agreed on this point: "Mathematical propositions express no thoughts."[22] Both thinkers reduce mathematics to a matter of essentially blind calculation and manipulation. Alfred Ayer's positivist method for reaching the same conclusion may be more familiar. As a conscientious empiricist, Ayer insists that there can be no meaning independent of experience: "A sentence says nothing unless it is empirically verifiable."[23] And since mathematics must indeed be acknowledged independent of both experience and verification, mathematical statements are no less necessarily true than they are inevitably meaningless (77). Mathematical statements, so conceived, are merely "analytic judgments" in Kant's sense; they contribute nothing to the concepts they presuppose, and function purely by formal manipulation of "the definitions of the symbols [they] contain," thereby telling us "only what we may be said to know already" (78, 80).

Nothing, clearly, could be further from a philosophy conditioned by mathematical *truth*, a philosophy that already sees in the (historically complex) affirmation of the number zero—a number that cannot be said to "exist," and yet that provides the whole decimal organization of number with its operative foundation—proof of an irrefutable capacity for invention.[24] That mathematics is indeed a matter of thought becomes clearly apparent, Badiou argues, when it is obliged by some sort of evental disruption to determine just what sort of practice it is. Mathematics thinks when, in a moment of epistemological crisis, it is required to make a decision "without guarantee or arbitration." There are, Badiou notes, three especially famous examples of such a decision (CT, 46–49). The first occurred when the Pythagoreans, convinced that all relationships could be expressed in ratios of whole numbers, discovered that the diagonal of a square (the hypotenuse of a right triangle) could not be so expressed: the diagonal of a square with a side measured as 1 is the square root of 2, an "irrational" number. This discovery may have provoked an "existentialist crisis in ancient Greek mathematics."[25] A second case is the challenge to Frege's theory of numerical classes, which was raised by Russell's famous paradox concerning classes belonging to themselves. A third example is the axiom of choice widely used in modern set theory: it is difficult to defend this axiom on philosophical grounds—its operation is undefinable, its results unconstructible—yet it appears to be a necessary tool for many of the demonstrations and results deemed essential to the field in general.[26]

In each case, resolution of the crisis required an active intervention or decision—in other words, creative and resourceful thought. The resolution of the Pythagorean problem required a different way of conceiving the relation between number and being, between arithmetic and geometry (a decision taken by Eudoxus and his followers). Frege himself lacked the means or the will to overcome Russell's paradox, but set theory was reestablished on secure foundations thanks to the axiomatic decisions taken by Zermelo (1904–1908), Fraenkel (1922), Von Neumann (1925), and their followers—decisions that dramatically restricted the powers of language in the determination of pure multiplicity. The crucial axiom of choice, proposed in defense of Cantor's theory by Zermelo in 1904, itself remains very much a matter of choice and requires, each time it is used, a decision as regards the existence of an actual but indeterminate infinity (an existence intuitionists still deny).[27]

Deciding the Truth of Mathematical Continuity

If we accept the reality of mathematical invention or thought, we still have to ask how such thought can be composed as truth, that is, as a truth process. Like any truth, Badiou explains, mathematics is sparked by an event, is established by a decision made with respect to that event, and continues through fidelity to that event. And, like any other truth, it must guard itself against an evil self-objectification; mathematical truth is every bit as subjective as that of love or art.

Common sense, of course, suggests that nothing is more certain than quantitative measurement and the "hard facts" of scientific knowledge. But common sense is ill equipped to consider in what exactly this objectivity consists. What *is* a number? What are we doing when we use numbers? Numbers can certainly be applied more or less indifferently to quantifiable reality, in perfect ignorance of what is involved in such application. But the reality of number itself, Badiou insists, is accessible only as truth, not as knowledge. For Badiou as for Lakatos and Gödel, the fact that logic cannot "automatically" found and confirm the practice of mathematics proclaims the irreducibly subjective bias of mathematical creativity.[28]

The main decisions taken by modern mathematics are, in the first, most literally fundamental sense, the axioms proclaimed by elementary set theory.

On the basis of these axioms, set theory derives the structural core of mathematics as a whole, the transfinite succession of ordinal numbers. The undecidable event that prompted these axiomatic decisions was Cantor's invention of transfinite numbers, and his consequent suggestion of what is known as the continuum hypothesis (CH).[29] As we saw in chapter 3, CH implies a perfectly measurable relation between a set of elements and the possible ways of arranging those elements in parts, that is, a perfectly natural "succession" of state over situation, of re-presentation over presentation (EE, 342). By contrast, to acknowledge a radically immeasurable excess of an infinite power set 2^n over any set n would be to accept a kind of intrinsic "undecidability" within the very fabric of number, that is, the lack of any continuity between the realm of whole numbers (the domain of denumerability) and the realm of real numbers (the domain of geometric or nondenumerable division).

The implications of CH are so vast as to justify Badiou's distinction of the three main orientations of ontology—constructivist, transcendent, and generic—in terms of their responses to this single controversy, the nature of the disjunction of membership $\in$ and inclusion $\subset$, the measurement of this excess of parts over elements.[30]

Constructivists generally attempt to prove the truth of the continuum hypothesis by imposing drastic restrictions on what qualifies as a legitimate part or subset (as only that which can be constructed from previously definable subsets). This is to decide the issue in some sense from below. The resulting mathematical universe is very limited, indeed the smallest possible universe (NN, 43; EE, 344–46). It is a universe patterned on a numerical version of the Great Chain of Being, in which any particular being has its docile and appropriate place.[31] In philosophical terms, we know that Badiou associates this orientation with Aristotle and Kant, as much as with the more generous or exuberant constructions of Leibniz and Deleuze.

What Badiou labels the transcendent orientation attempts to force the decision from above, through the introduction of ever more infinite infinities, an "endless enlarging of the universe, under the idea of a dominating 'great infinity,' or an altogether-Other"—under the idea, that is, of a kind of metamathematical God.[32] The names proposed to describe such numbers point to their antiphilosophical implication: inaccessible cardinals, hyperinaccessible cardinals, eventually ineffable cardinals, and beyond. Defenders of such an absolutely unconstructible and inconceivable transcendence reject the continuum hypothesis definitively, in the interests of a redemptive logic beyond all possible calculation. The spontaneous philosophy of this orientation is hermeneutic, or Heideggerian.

The generic orientation, of course, underlies Badiou's own ontological perspective. After results achieved by Gödel and Cohen, it accepts that the continuum hypothesis cannot be proved one way or the other.[33] The axioms do not suffice to decide the issue. Once we are willing to tolerate the existence of purely extensional or nonconstructible sets, the power set of an infinite appears to evade every predictable application of measure.[34] The independence of CH from the axioms of set theory introduces an element of numerical anarchy into the very foundations of mathematics. Thus "linked to the undecidable, mathematics must constantly be *redecided*," and "since the decision is primary, and continually required, it is vain to try to reduce it to constructive or externally normed protocols."[35] The generic orientation, in other words, disproves CH without recourse to a transcendent Altogether Other. It argues that "the realm of Number admits, as much in the infinitely large as in the infinitely small, and without breaking the total order, a proliferation that exceeds any intuition of continuity."[36] What *is* is the purely uncountable or inconsistent multiplicity of being as being, an absolute excess beyond any conceptual construction or mastery. Such inconsistent multiplicity is what Badiou calls the domain of Number. Particular numbers (the numbers 1, 2, and 3, as much as fractions, negative numbers, irrational numbers, infinitesimals, inaccessible cardinals, and so on) are then the products of precise mathematical interventions whereby a particular slice of this multiplicity is counted as one, that is, is made to consist in a thought or concept. Number with a capital *N,* the pure "stuff" of numbers in its inconceivable multiplicity, "ek-sists" above and beyond them "as the latency of their being."[37] And the actual "history of mathematics . . . is precisely the history, interminable in principle, of the relation between the inconsistency of multiple being, and of what our finite thought can make consistent of this inconsistency" (NN, 262; cf. CT, 151).

Between these three orientations, constructivist, transcendent, and generic, there can and should be no possible agreement. It is not a matter of interpreting what exists, but of asserting (incompatible) notions of existence. This is why "no real conflict in the realm of thought can be solved; consensus is the enemy of thought" (CT, 54). Translated into political-philosophical terms, constructivism posits a kind of liberal parliamentarism: it assumes that all existents are so many cases of a particular protocol of construction, or representatives of particular places and interests. The transcendent orientation, privileging the absolute totality of an existence beyond the actual universe, corresponds to a kind of Stalinism. The generic orientation, finally, might be associated with a kind of disciplined anarchism. It "privileges the undefined zones, the multiples subtracted from all predicative recollection, the points of excess [or] wandering *[errance]*." It affirms the political primacy of all that "exists solely on account of its not being countable" (CT, 53).

(Remember, however, that when it comes to the [metaontological] question of truth per se Badiou affirms a fourth way, a fourth orientation of thought, which he traces to Marx and Freud. This, of course, is the way of the Subject, and it turns precisely on the recognition that the truth of CH, the "truth of the ontological impasse itself," cannot be properly grasped from within the ontological situation as such [EE, 314–15]. The impasse of being can be thought only through a process that breaks with being as being. It is this break, in the end, that distinguishes Badiou's position from that of Hegel on the one hand and that of Deleuze on the other.)

Numbers as Truths

What numbers are and how they are used are clearly two quite different issues. Numbers are used, obviously, to quantify knowledge. The entire realm of the statistical—of opinion polls, prices, measurements, and so on—however ramified, however complex its manipulations, belongs to what Badiou calls the realm of knowledge. Since all knowledge is devoid of truth, Badiou always laments the "ruinous image" of mathematics as mere calculation or technique (CT, 38; NN, 264).

What, then, is the truth of number? If it is to be consistent with Badiou's prescriptions, it must combine the notions of event, decision, fidelity, and the unnameable. Like all truth, a consistent number is, in itself—as opposed to its application or objectification—a subjective production: "Number is not an object, or an objectivity. It is a gesture *[geste]* in being" (CT, 149). A particular number (small n) is, in its truth, a "thought multiplicity" (NN, 261), that is, a particular slice made in the unlimited proliferation of Number. The mechanics of just how a number is cut out of this inconsistent proliferation, how a slice of inconsistency is made to consist, are too complex to summarize here. Roughly speaking, Badiou's "evental definition of number," building on John Conway's celebrated contributions to number theory, shows that any particular cut selects one and only one possible number between two limits, a "high" and a "low," which circumscribe an infinitely dense field of numbers.[38] "Every number is the place of a cut" (NN, 176; cf. 276 n. 2).

The next question is whether, given the proliferation of different kinds of numbers obeying different kinds of logics (natural integers, ordinals, negative and rational numbers, real numbers, complex numbers, infinite and infinitesimal numbers, and so on) there can be a single generic definition for Number in general.[39] "Neither Frege's logicist perspective, nor Peano's axiomatics, nor even the set-theory framework conceived by Dedekind and Cantor" can provide such a unified concept of number. But in his book *On Numbers and Games* (1976), Conway proposed a definition broad enough to include all of these varieties of number, and, more particularly, an infinite number of as yet unthought numbers. Conway's definition established what Badiou paraphrases as an "organized macrobody" of Number, the body of "'surreal' numbers" (CT, 143). This is "a configuration in which a total order is defined, where addition, subtraction, multiplication, and division are universally possible," and in which we can situate not only rational, irrational, and ideal numbers, but also a "still unnamed infinity of kinds of numbers, in particular infinitesimals, or numbers situated 'between' two adjacent and disconnected classes of real numbers, or infinite numbers of all kinds, beyond the ordinals and the cardinals."[40] The macrobody is "the generic, inconsistent place in which the numerical consistencies coexist" as so many aspects of a single concept, the concept of Number as such.

Within this generic field, any particular number is designated as a pair of variables or coordinates: "A Number is a set with two elements, an ordered pair, composed, in order, of an ordinal and a part of this ordinal. Its notation is: (α, X), where X is a part of the ordinal α (where $X \subseteq \alpha$)."[41] You may recall from chapter 3 that an ordinal is defined (by Von Neumann) as a transitive set whose elements are all transitive, that is, whose elements are also parts or subsets of that set (cf. NN, 86–87). The ordinals are all deduced from the empty set, through the operation of the axiom of subsets. They succeed each other in an infinitely stable continuity, and thereby demonstrate a kind of intrinsic homogeneity and coherence that allows them to be designated "the primordial material of Number." The second element in the pair, X, is much more variable. In a sense, it has "pulled itself away from the first." It tends to be unstable, perhaps discontinuous or incalculable (CT, 146). If the ordinal α is the stable matter of a number, its part X determines that number's "form." It is the defining or "cutting" edge of the number.

Some examples may make this a little less abstract. (a) In the simplest case, the ordinal (or natural) numbers themselves (first, second, third, and so on) are defined by an "empty gesture." Their matter coincides with their form. The cut that defines them cuts away or includes everything from the ordinal matter. Any ordinal α is written (α, α). (b) Negative numbers are, in a sense, the inversion of an ordinary ordinal. Rather than an empty gesture or immaterial cut (a cut that includes everything), a negative ordinal is defined by a "nongesture," one that includes nothing, that cuts away nothing at all from the ordinal matter. Its form is void. The negative of an ordinal α is written $(\alpha, \emptyset)$. (c) The number zero itself is both without matter and without form, or $(\varnothing, \varnothing)$—Badiou defines it as an "impossible gesture." (d) The real numbers—the numbers that "enumerate" the infinitely divisible geometric continuum—include all the numbers whose matter is the first infinite ordinal ω and whose form is infinite (CT, 148). (e) Numbers whose ordinal matter is larger than ω can be thought of as "not yet studied numbers"—proof that "what we use in the realm of numbers is only a tiny part of what resides in being under the concept of Number."[42] (f) An infinitesimal, finally, is a number whose matter is ω and whose form is finite, for example, $(\omega, 1)$. Such a number is smaller than any real number, however close that real number may be to zero; it belongs to an altogether different (or "nonstandard") order of dimension.

We might say that all of these forms of number are like so many discontinuous evental productions, so many punctual illuminations, within a field of endlessly inconsistent Numerical obscurity. The consistent numbers are like the points of light cast in the dark sky of Beckett or Mallarmé. The only difference is that the mathematical invention of new numbers is even less constrained than is poetry by any order of substantial or empirical existence. A particular number *is* simply if its distinction, within the infinite inconsistency of Number, is internally consistent.

Conway's configuration, in short, allows Badiou to present numerical productions in conformity with the other generic procedures. As in each case, the subject points of a truth (the numerical cuts made in the fabric of being) are undertaken as so many finite investigations that contribute to its infinite (Numerical) accumulation. As in each case, the evental origins of these investigations will forever belie their subsequent application or re-presentation. And, as in each case, what a truth comes to pronounce is indeed the truth of its situation ("all the Numbers are already there" [NN, 178]), but this pronouncement is itself the result of an irreducibly active or decisive operation. As subjects, we add nothing to being. Nevertheless, the isolation of any particular number still requires an invention in thought. Simply, at this unique level of absolute abstraction that defines ontology or the thought of being as be-ing, these two operations, be-ing and thinking, are indistinguishable. Such is the true Platonic prescription. Numbered beings are not constructed by a thinking subject. Rather, through the thinking subject, being articulates its own truth. Mathematics is nothing other than "being thinking itself."[43]

It is relatively easy now to pick out the necessarily unnameable dimension of mathematical truth. If mathematics thinks the rigor of a self-constituent, axiomatic deduction, its unnameable limit must be the objective integrity of its own medium or foundation. The mathematician must not objectify the field of numbers as a definitive continuum, but preserve it as an infinitely discontinuous realm of punctual operations. These operations take place, certainly, within a single field of being, but they do not succeed each other in a single deductive movement. As we have known since Gödel's famous demonstration, "it is not possible, for a mathematical theory, to establish as verifiable the statement of its own consistency."[44] Mathematics can persevere as subject only if it remains forever unfinished as object. Mathematical truth is the interminable effort to explore and enlarge that small fraction of consistency that inventive thought is able to discern from within the unlimited dissemination of pure Numerical inconsistency.

chapter 10

Politics: Equality and Justice

Politics is truth in the collective, by the collective. Though all generic procedures are addressed to everyone, only in the case of politics does this universality characterize both import and operation. Badiou writes, "Politics is the only truth procedure that is generic not only in its result, but in the local composition of its subject." Though every situation is ontologically infinite, "only politics summons up, immediately, as subjective universality, this infinity." Hence a certain pride of place for politics in a fully generic philosophy. Badiou knows perfectly well that, just as love relates only two people, so does a mathematician, in order to complete a proof, need only one other competent colleague to recognize its validity. Science, art, and love might be called "aristocratic" procedures, whereas "politics can only think as the thought of all" (AM, 156–57). Politics is organized around the Real of a radical fraternity before it is drawn to the Imaginary pursuit of equality or the Symbolic presumption of liberty. True politics begins with an exposure to "the real violence of fraternity" and is sustained in the practical present of its "demonstration" *(manifestation)*.[1] As with every truth procedure, this real "manifests itself, constructs itself, but never represents itself": fraternity is no more representable than is an insurrection or a demonstration.

Badiou's conception of political truth has nothing to do, then, with bland speculations concerning civic responsibility or liberal "communication." Badiou knows that only a "militant conception of politics . . . can link

223

politics and thought" (AM, 22); in particular, only such a conception can avoid recourse to the false dichotomy of theory and practice: "There is certainly a 'doing' *[faire]* of politics, but it is immediately the pure and simple experience of a thought, its localization. It cannot be distinguished from it" (AM, 56). The philosophical or metapolitical problem is simply one of understanding how politics *thinks,* according to what mode of thought and through what categories—the categories of Virtue and Corruption for Saint-Just, for instance, or revolutionary consciousness for Lenin. True political thought is a matter neither of judicious deliberation (Arendt) nor of anguished choice (Sartre), and still less of expert social engineering (Rorty) or procedural notions of justice (Rawls). Badiou, like Lenin, like Fanon, like all great revolutionary thinkers, maintains a strictly classical form of political logic: either p or not p, with no possible compromise in between. Badiou conceives of politics precisely as a matter of what Rimbaud called "*logical revolt,*" a matter of clearly stated principle—the sort of principle incarnated by the great intellectual *résistants,* Jean Cavaillès and Albert Lautman.[2] The political subject acts or resists as a matter of course, and not thanks to a reasoned affiliation with a particular group, class, or opinion. He resists, not as a result of communication or consensus, but all at once, to the exclusion of any "third way."[3]

We know that the sole criterion of true political engagement is an unqualified equality (EE, 447; cf. DO, 15). It is a rudimentary principle of Badiou's ontology that all elements that belong to a situation belong (or are presented in, or exist, or count) in exactly the same way, with exactly the same weight. Politics is the process whereby this simple belonging is abstracted from all defining conditions or re-presentations. The criteria of equality establish a radical but fully abstract logic of the Same, whose precise tactical "advantage is its abstraction. Equality neither supposes closure nor qualifies the terms it embraces, nor prescribes a territory for its exercise." Equality is both "immediately prescriptive" yet "free of any program" (C, 247–48). Like any criterion of truth, this equality is by definition a purely subjective quality.[4] In the absence of any one transcendent Truth and in the suspension of objective criteria, political subjects are equal "co-workers" in truth, caught up in the "equality of a common sharing in work."[5]

So, as much as love or art, true politics is exceptional, an exception to the contemporary cliché that "everything is political."[6] Politics proceeds as indifferent to "dialectic of the objective and the subjective . . . ; the deployment of subjective thought should take place from within the subjective itself, through the hypothesis of the foundation of the subjective in the subjective and not in the confrontation of the subjective to the objective," let alone in "reference to the economy, the state, alienation, etc."[7] The kind of subject-object coordination proposed by Habermas's increasingly state-centered conception of politics, for instance, serves only to block the necessary violence of political presentation within the legal norms of re-presentation.[8] As far as Badiou is concerned, socioeconomic "analysis and politics are absolutely disconnected"[9]: the former is a matter for "expertise" and implies hierarchy; the latter is not. A generic or axiomatic politics affirms the "political capacity of all people," the principle that "everyone can occupy the space of politics, if they decide to do so."[10] Whereas the sort of sociology practiced by Badiou's contemporaries Balibar and Bourdieu can only "discuss" political issues, evental political sequences transform the objects of such discussion into militant subjects in their own right.[11]

That everyone can join in a political process means that the Two of political antagonism is not to be thought in terms of a purely destructive competition. A political process does not pit two well-defined antagonists against each other in a life-and-death struggle for supremacy. There is, strictly speaking, only one political actor, namely the we that comes out or demonstrates in the real of fraternity (i.e., in the element of pure presentation as such). What resists the organized political we is not an alternative political subject so much as the brute inertia of re-presentation, which is nothing other than the inertia of the status quo itself. Politics thus proceeds through the invention of new subtractive mechanisms of formalization that can confront and transform this formless resistance to change (LS, 89).

Like any truth, a political sequence can begin only when business as usual breaks down for one reason or another. This is because what ensures submission to the status quo is "submission to the indetermination of power, and not to power itself" (TA, 8.4.98). Under normal circumstances, we know only that the excess of the static re-presentation over elementary presentation is wildly immeasurable (corresponding to the infinite excess of $2^\aleph$ over $\aleph$). Today's prevailing economic regime indeed dominates its inhabitants absolutely, precisely because we can hardly imagine how we might limit or measure this regime. The first achievement of a true political intervention is thus the effective, "distanced" measurement of this excess. Intervention forces the state to show its hand, to use its full powers of coercion so as to try to restore things to their proper place. Every political sequence worthy of the name proceeds in keeping with the combative principle maintained, in Badiou's native France, by the leaders of the *chômeurs* (unemployed) movement of 1997–98: "We act according to what is right, not what is legal."[12] Political truth always begins in "trial and trouble," in social "rupture and disorder" (AM, 114). This is a price that those who seek after justice must be prepared to pay: "We have too often wanted justice to establish the consistency of social bonds, whereas it can only name the most extreme moments of inconsistency. For the effect of the egalitarian axiom is to undo the bonds, to desocialize thought, to affirm the rights of the infinite and the immortal against the calculation of interests. Justice is a wager on the immortal against finitude, against 'being for death.' In the subjective dimension of the equality we declare, nothing now is of any interest other than the universality of this declaration, and the active consequences that follow from it" (AM, 118).

The instances or modes of so exalted an understanding of politics are rare by definition. Badiou's friend Sylvain Lazarus has devoted much of his energy to their formulation and classification.[13] Four stand out. First, the revolutionary or Jacobin mode, operative from 1792–94 and conceived in particular by Saint-Just. The Jacobins understood the revolution in purely political terms, and not as a historical category or moment of transition. They believed that the revolution is an instance of collective decision and struggle that pits Virtue against Corruption. Second, the Marxist or "classist" mode, mainly operative from 1848 through 1871. The Marxists believed that the subjective orientation of class struggle itself serves to guide a "naive" international revolutionary movement; the defeat of the Commune demonstrates its failure and the need for more disciplined means. The third, Bolshevik, mode (1902–17) was organized as a response to this need, as a campaign against opportunism, spontaneity, reformism, and trade unionism. It insisted upon the integrity of the party and its prescriptions. Lenin recognized that the mere existence of a popular movement is no guarantee of victory. Radical political change must be channeled through "militant figures of consciousness, or more precisely, through *thought,* and not through the movement of History or the representation of social groups."[14] The fourth mode is Maoist (dated either from the struggle to liberate China in the 1920s, or from the Cultural Revolution in the 1960s): its characteristic feature was popular mobilization on a scale never attempted by Lenin, the direct empowerment of the people in an ongoing, permanent revolution (AM, 49–51). Each mode presents a certain version of political truth, as constrained by the circumstances of the time. They are all subjective, all egalitarian, but they do not add up to a single narrative. They do not culminate in One apocalyptic Truth. They represent so many efforts to do what could be done in the situation at hand. What they have in common is a revolutionary commitment to the dissolution of the state.

Today, however, now that the "age of revolutions is over," Badiou admits, "I have been obliged to change my position as regards the state. The guiding principle can no longer be, in a unilateral way, 'destatification.' It is a matter more of prescribing the state, often in a logic of reinforcement. The problem is to know *from where* politics prescribes the state."[15] Recent political sequences—the Palestinian Intifada, the uprisings in East Timor and Chiapas, the student mobilization in Burma in 1988—have proceeded in large part as attempts to answer this question, in terms most appropriate to the situation as it stands. Among the most consequential ongoing efforts is the massive Landless Workers Movement (MST) in Brazil: rather than persist in the futile pursuit of land reform through established re-presentative channels, the MST has organized the direct occupation of farmland by the landless poor themselves, allowing some 250,000 families to win titles to over fifteen million acres since 1985. What the MST has understood with particular clarity is that legal recognition can be won only as the result of a subjective mobilization that is itself indifferent to the logic of recognition and re-presentation as such. The remarkable gains of the MST have been won at what Badiou would call a "political distance" from the state, and depend upon its own ability to maintain a successful organizing structure, develop viable forms of nonexploitative economic cooperation, and resist violent intimidation from landowners and the state police.[16]

Badiou's own Organisation Politique (OP) was conceived as part of an answer to much the same question: From which precise points is it possible, in today's "democracies," to force change upon the state of our situation?[17] How is it possible to organize an effective political force without reliance upon the institutional re-presentation of a party (liable to corruption) on the one hand, or the pseudospontaneity of a mass movement (liable to fatigue) on the other? Though it remains something of an organizational experiment, the OP is testimony to what even a handful of committed militants are able to achieve. The OP intervenes only on particular questions, raised by specific confrontations or events, always guided by the strict, axiomatic assertion of subjective equality: political equality for everyone living in the national community, residence papers for the *sans-papiers*, political empowerment of all workers *as* workers, equal universal access to health and education, and so on. Badiou insists that these interventions do not add up to a general program or party line: "God protect us from 'sociopolitical programmes'! The essence of modern politics is to be nonprogrammatic. Politics, as we conceive it in the OP, promises nothing. It is both without party and without program. It is a prescriptive form of thought, discerning possibilities entirely inaccessible to parliamentarism, and one that works entirely independently for their realization."[18] If politics has taken up a position distant from rather than simply antithetical to the state, it remains committed to a homogeneously subjective orientation.[19]

Axiomatic Politics

The OP is conditioned by four distinctive principles: the first two are essentially formal, concerning the nature of politics as prescription and as justice; the other two are more emphatically concrete, concerning the subjective status of workers and immigrants under conditions that have become increasingly hostile since the late 1970s.

1. The status of universal political principles, like the status of all forms of truth, is necessarily axiomatic (or nondefinitional). Because equality is subjective, justice—the political principle par excellence—can be only prescriptive. Justice cannot be defined; it is a pure "affirmation without guarantee or proof." Rather than an ideal state that any given situation can only approximate, "justice indicates a subjective figure that is effective, axiomatic, immediate [. . . ; it] necessarily refers back to an entirely disinterested subjectivity." We are either subjectively disinterested, or objectively interested, with nothing in between; we either think (in justice), or avoid thought (in interest) (AM, 112–13). That politics is thus axiomatic or "thought" means that it is not a representation or a reflection of something else (the economy, the state, society, etc.).[20] When the enslaved call for freedom, for instance, or the colonized for liberation, or women for equality, the declaration of freedom or liberation or equality is itself primary or unconditioned, and not a matter of investigation or confirmation. Equality is not something to be researched or verified but a principle to be upheld. The only genuinely political question is What can be done, in the name of this principle, in our militant fidelity to its proclamation? This question can be answered only through a direct mobilization or empowerment that has nothing to do with the condescendingly "compassionate" valorization of certain people as marginal, excluded, or *misérables*.[21]

  The prescriptions of the OP are invariably simple, minimally theoretical principles—for example, that every individual counts as one individual, that all students must be treated in the same way,[22] that "everyone who is here is from here," that factories are places of work before they are places of profit, and so on. A political situation exists only under the prescription of such transparent statements, whose universality is as clear as it is distinct.[23] Pressure, resistance, or outrage, even mobilized or organized outrage, is not enough. The OP is adamant that only political organizations, not movements, can sustain prescriptions (which may then be presented or carried by movements).[24] In this respect, the OP remains true to its Leninist roots: the formulation of a true consciousness is a quite separate operation from the spontaneous development of a movement.[25]

2. All genuine politics seeks to change the situation as a whole, in the interest of the universal interest. But this change is always sparked by a particular event, one located in a particular site and carried by a particular interest (the *sans-culottes,* the soviets, the workers, the *sans-papiers,* and so on). 1792 in France, 1917 in Russia, 1959 in Cuba, 1988 in Burma: each time, the event opposes those with a vested interest in the established state of the situation to those who supported a revolutionary movement or perspective from which the situation was seen as for all. Other, more narrow, principles and demands, however worthy their beneficiaries might be, are merely a matter of syndicalism or trade union–style negotiation, that is, negotiation for an improved, more integrated place within the established situation. Clearly, what goes under the label of politics in the ordinary day-to-day sense amounts only to "revendication and resentment . . . , electoral nihilism and the blind confrontation of communities" (AM, 110).

The very notion of identity politics is thus an explicit contradiction in terms. The OP regularly condemns the articulation of a "'French' identity that authorizes discrimination or persecution" of any kind; the only legitimate national unit is one that counts all of its elements as one, regardless of ethnocultural particularity.[26] The left-liberal insistence on the vacuous "right to remain 'the same as ourselves' has no chance against the abstract universality" of contemporary capital, and does nothing more than "organize an *inclusion* in what it pretends to oppose."[27] Of course, it has often been argued that if we are oppressed *as* Arab, *as* woman, *as* black, *as* homosexual, and so on, this oppression will not end until these particular categories have been revalued.[28] Badiou's response to this line of attack is worth quoting at length:

> When I hear people say, "We are oppressed as blacks, as women,"
> I have only one problem: what exactly is meant by "black" or
> "women"? . . . Can this identity, in itself, function in a progressive
> fashion, that is, other than as a property invented by the oppressors
> themselves? . . . I understand very well what "black" means for those
> who use that predicate in a logic of differentiation, oppression, and
> separation, just as I understand very well what "French" means when

Le Pen uses the word, when he champions national preference, France for the French, exclusion of Arabs, etc..... Negritude, for example, as incarnated by Césaire and Senghor, consisted essentially of reworking exactly those traditional predicates once used to designate black people: as intuitive, as natural, as primitive, as living by rhythm rather than by concepts, etc.... I understand why this kind of movement took place, why it was necessary. It was a very strong, very beautiful, and very necessary movement. But having said that, it is not something that can be inscribed as such in politics. I think it is a matter of poetics, of culture, of turning the subjective situation upside down. It doesn't provide a possible framework for political initiative.

The progressive formulation of a cause that engages cultural or communal predicates, linked to incontestable situations of oppression and humiliation, presumes that we propose these predicates, these particularities, these singularities, these communal qualities, in such a way that they become situated in another space and become heterogeneous to their ordinary oppressive operation. I never know in advance what quality, what particularity, is capable of becoming political or not; I have no preconceptions on that score. What I do know is that there must be a progressive meaning to these particularities, a meaning that is intelligible to all. Otherwise, we have something that has its raison d'être, but that is necessarily of the order of a demand for integration, that is, of a demand that one's particularity be valued in the existing state of things....

That there is a remnant or a support of irreducible particularity, is something I would acknowledge for any kind of reality.... But in the end, between this particularity present in the practical, concrete support of any political process, and the statements in the name of which the political process unfolds, I think there is *only* a relation of support, but not a relation of transitivity. You can't go from the one to the other, even if one seems to be "carried" by the other.... It is not because a term is a communal predicate, or even because there is a victim in a particular situation, that it is automatically, or even easily, transformed into a political category.[29]

In a situation like that of the former Yugoslavia, for instance, Badiou maintains that a lasting peace will come not through external intervention, and still less through a carving up of territory according to ethnic states, but instead through a concerted, popular movement against all ethnic, linguistic, and religious essentialisms, in a common state that counts all people as one.[30] Likewise, there can be genuine peace in the Middle East only with the end of an Israel specified as a Jewish state, and the establishment, in keeping with the original demands of the Palestine Liberation Organization, of a single, ecumenical Palestine, open to all without discrimination.[31] In short, an egalitarian state can exist only when its universality is prescribed by those who make up the "country" *(pays)* itself. And any such country, Badiou goes on to argue, can exist only when its workers exist, as empowered political subjects confronting and prescribing the objective inertia of capital: "Without its workers, there can be no country."[32] At this point, the abstract principle of equality becomes insistently concrete.

3. Perhaps the most contested of all contemporary political prescriptions concerns the simple existence of what Badiou and the OP call a "figure of the worker" or "working figure" *(figure ouvrière)*: "By 'figure of the worker' we mean a political subjectivity constituted in the factory, in an ability to make declarations about the factory and the worker that are different from those of management, the unions, . . . and the state. This intrication between the figure of the worker and the capacity to make declarations concerning the factories and the workers is essential. It alone puts an end to the classist figure that founded trade unionism, and alone allows 'worker' to be something other than an expressive, circulating figure."[33] A *figure ouvrière* is the worker become subject; the phrase, awkward to translate into English, connotes the militant empowerment of the workers. It is not a matter of asking employers for respectful appreciation, or for a more or less condescending acknowledgment of their importance in the productive process. It is a matter of truth and power, the power to keep managerial supervisors at a distance.[34] Acknowledgment of the statement that "at the factory there are workers" means that "at the factory the worker exists as subjectivity, as political capacity," that the factory is not simply a place of production; conversely, "to destroy the figure of the worker is to destroy people, to reduce workers, subjectively, to nothing."[35]

This unfashionable importance accorded to the workers—the very word now has an anachronistic ring to it—is not merely proof of Badiou's lingering Maoist commitment. By "workers" Badiou means something almost as broad as "people," insofar as they cannot be reduced to units of capital. In the subjective absence of the worker, there persists only the values of capital (production, competition, consumption). Clearly, work here includes intellectual as much as physical work. If physical work, above all factory work, nevertheless remains preeminent in Badiou's account, it is because it is obviously the least counted, the most vulnerable to exclusion from the criteria of our prevailing social count. Because the factory (and its analogs) is thus on the edge of the void, or in the least protected part of our political-economic situation, "all contemporary politics has the factory as its place" (AM, 59). By not counting its workers, a factory becomes nothing more than a place of industrial production regulated by managerial decisions. By not counting its workers, a country becomes nothing more than a balance sheet writ large, a set of capital flows and statistics, a purely objectified (i.e., thoughtless) realm. In this sense, "the word 'workers' is a condition of the freedom of thought," Badiou says. "Look at how political thought has become inert, unified, in short totalitarian, since the term disappeared."[36]

The void left by the disappearance of the term "workers," of course, has been filled by the obscure category of "immigrants." Badiou has little trouble showing that "the hatred of immigrants was established massively, consensually, at the level of the state, from the moment when we began, in our representations of the world, to omit the workers, the figure of the workers."[37] It is obvious that "the immense majority of immigrants are workers or people looking for work"[38]—hence the absurdity of current distinctions between "asylum seekers" and "economic migrants." It is no less obvious that the invention, as pseudopolitical labels, of the terms "immigrant," "foreigner," "étranger," "clandestin," and so on, coincides with the swing in the global political economy over the 1980s against organized labor and popular movements generally.[39] In France, Badiou points out, this movement can be dated quite precisely. One of Mittérand's first prime ministers, Pierre Mauroy, justified the repression of a strike at Renault-Flins in 1983 on the grounds that the striking workers were "foreign to the social reality of France."[40] The violent repression of another strike at Talbot later the same year confirmed the trend.[41] Two years later, the socialist Laurent Fabius confessed that it was "Le Pen [who] is posing the real questions,"[42] an admission effectively confirmed by Michel Rocard ("France cannot open its doors to the misery of the world") and Mittérand ("We must struggle firmly against illegal immigration").[43] The resulting consensus is indeed consistent, as the OP is at pains to stress, with the general approach of the Front National (FN). On the issues of economic liberalism, immigration, crime, drugs, and the *banlieues* (roughly equivalent to "inner cities"), the FN is "*internal* to the consensus" established over two decades of *Mittérandisme*.[44] Hence the conclusion "Strengthen the workers, and thus limit Lepenism."[45] Without a strong figure of the worker there can be no effective response to the so-called immigrant question.

4. The fourth and most currently pressing axiom, connecting the universality of the state with the subjective presence of the workers, thus concerns the status of the *sans-papiers*. That "everyone who is here is from here" *(tous les gens qui sont ici sont d'ici)* is no doubt the most frequently printed slogan of *La Distance politique*. Nothing could be simpler, yet nothing could be more contentious in today's political situation. The state campaign against immigrants is already two decades old (in 1977, the end to family reunification; in 1982, a freeze on work permits and immigrant visas). Its contemporary strategy, however, dates from the notorious Pasqua laws of 1993, which established a special status for "clandestine" foreigners living in France. Among other things, these laws oblige a mayor to refuse to marry an undocumented couple; they authorize Social Security to refuse health care and welfare benefits to "illegal" immigrants; they allow the police to expel foreign parents of French children if they commit drug-related offenses. All in all, these laws amount to what the OP calls a general "law of persecution,"[46] the first step in the official "Lepenization of the state."[47] The Pasqua laws were quickly confirmed, in the face of vocal protest and a massive petition campaign, by the Debré laws,[48] and their essential purpose has survived Jospin's recent (1997–98) reformulations, known as the Weil-Chevènement laws.[49] All of these "national" laws are peculiar in that they concern only particular sectors of the population. Their very purpose is to divide the political community into re-presented parts rather than to apply the same formal criteria to its members. Confronted with this legislative onslaught, the OP's prescriptions are unequivocal: they call for the immediate restoration of the *droit du sol* (i.e., automatic citizenship for all children born in France), the legalization of all *sans-papiers,* an end to the expulsions and detention centers, and explicit protection of workers and their families.[50] In short, the OP calls for an end to the entire immigrant lexicon,

and with it an end to the emphasis put on integration via a particular set of privileged cultural norms.[51]

Concretely, this has meant lending significant organizational assistance to a growing mobilization of the *sans-papiers* since the summer of 1996, when hundreds of African immigrants occupied the Saint Bernard church for several months, thereby refuting their official characterization as "clandestine" in the most convincing terms. After these immigrants were expelled from the church by force in August 1996, and again evicted from the town hall of the eighteenth arrondissement in Paris in June 1997, the Saint Bernard campaign organized, with the help of the OP, a series of major Paris rallies (15 and 22 November 1997, 6 December 1997, and 7 February 1998). Throughout this campaign, the emphasis has been on the militant subjective presence of the *sans-papiers* themselves—demonstrating that they are not somehow alien or invisible, but are simply *there* as ordinary workers under extraordinary pressure. "Saint Bernard is proof," says the OP, "of a strong principle of autoconstitution, in the sense that people decided one day to come out from their homes and to constitute themselves collectively in their demand for residence papers."[52]

Practical Politics

As the Saint Bernard campaign suggests, the work of the OP is anything but abstract or academic, and if there is no space here for anything like a proper history of the organization, it is important, in a study of Badiou's philosophy, to give some idea of the concrete, day-to-day activism of this the most pressing of its conditions. Here I can at least mention the OP's two most intensive campaigns of recent years: the campaign for workers' compensation during the closure of the Renault factory at Billancourt in 1992, and the campaign against the demolition of the *foyers ouvriers* (workers' hostels) in the Paris suburb of Montreuil (1996 through 1998). If these issues seem far removed from the lofty plane of philosophical speculation, we must remember that for Badiou—the most rigorous contemporary philosopher of truth—truth has nothing at all to do with speculation. If truth exists, it is *en acte,* in the detail of an ongoing commitment or campaign. Philosophy as such always comes after the act.

Billancourt

The history of the OP has always been tied up with factory politics. In part, this reflects their continuation of the tradition established by May 68—the tradition of discussion and mobilization outside factory doors, which for many *soixante-huitards* received a fatal blow with the murder of Pierre Overney in front of the Renault factory at Billancourt in 1972. Among groups claiming a fidelity to May 68, the OP is unique in its persistence. The OP divides factory politics into three sectors or modes.[53] (a) The state or managerial mode, oriented to the pressures of economic competition, encourages, with the occasional support of the conservative trade union, the CFDT (Confédération Française Démocratique du Travail), the familiar package of layoffs, downsizing, early retirement, and other forms of "flexibility" that strip the workers of any security or autonomy. The result: a working factory "without workers."[54] (b) The old communist or classist mode, preserved by what is left of the more militant unions, is of course hostile to the layoffs and retirement plans, but is unable to do anything about it. *La Distance politique* is consistent in its denunciation of the "impotence and passive complicity" of the CGT (Confédération Générale du Travail), their *"discours misérabiliste de victimes."* (c) On something closer to the old anarchist model, reminiscent of Catalonia's POUM (Partido Obrero de Unificación Marxista), the OP itself supports the direct mobilization of the workers in their own name, organized into small, close-knit groups or *Noyaux.*

When Renault decided to close their massive plant at Billancourt in March 1992, it was heralded in the press as the end of an era, the surrender of the workers' "fortress," a break with the legacy of industrial confrontation rooted in 1968. After some initial negotiations, the Renault management agreed to a paltry 80,000F (c. $12,000) compensation package for the workers left jobless, many of whom had worked at the plant for twenty or thirty years. What was peculiar about this arrangement was that the workers would receive this money only if they signed an agreement to accept early retirement. The actual, confrontational situation—mass firings and layoffs—was to be turned into a situation of apparently voluntary redundancy, in which the workers were literally to write themselves out of existence. The money was paid not to acknowledge decades of toil on the assembly line, but as a reward for accepting managerial priorities. As far as the OP was concerned, what was at issue were two incompatible conceptions of the factory, two incompatible prescriptions: "There is here a merciless conflict between two notions of politics. The pressure put on the workers to sign this paper in which they declare themselves to be 'leaving,' when they are actually being kicked out, has no economic significance. It aims to destroy the subjective rapport of the workers with themselves, as workers, and to count for nothing the years spent on the assembly line."[55] When 130 workers were fired in

March 1991 after refusing to sign the retirement agreement, tensions became acute and conflict persisted for more than a year. The OP held rallies at the Place Nationale in Billancourt every Wednesday afternoon over the first six months of 1992, both before and after the plant closure in March. While "the unions did all they could so that everything ended quietly at Billancourt," the OP published militant bulletins and tracts and had them distributed through the *Noyaux* in the factory.[56] The *Noyaux* encouraged random work stoppages and constant confrontations with the supervisors, and maintained consistent pressure on the management. In the end only a minority of workers signed the retirement plan, and most received their 80,000F one way or another.

Montreuil

La Distance politique first began reporting on the campaign to block demolition of the *foyers ouvriers* (workers' hostels) in Montreuil in July 1995 (in issue 14). Montreuil is a mainly working-class suburb of Paris. Many of its current residents came from Mali, often two or three decades ago. The foyers provide collective, inexpensive housing, mostly to single men who sleep as many as six to a small room. They are organized on a semicommunal basis, preserve some of their old village-related customs, and generally help their members to survive on their ever more inadequate wages. In March 1995 the left-wing, integrationist mayor of Montreuil, Jean-Pierre Brard, with the support of the prefect of Bobigny, began the destruction of the Nouvelle France foyer, and completed its demolition by force in July 1996—before finding suitable substitute housing for its occupants. The CRS (Compagnie Républicaine de Sécurité) simply threw the 336 foyer inhabitants into the street. African families were simultaneously blocked from renting homes previously occupied by "French" families through a policy of residential apartheid aimed at a systematic expulsion of the "nomads."[57] Offered only dubious proposals of relocation scattered across the general Parisian area, the former residents of the Nouvelle France began a campaign, with the OP, to have their foyer rebuilt in Montreuil. The campaign has been running since March 1995.[58]

Like the Saint Bernard movement, with which it is now connected, the mobilization of Montreuil is proof of what the OP has discerned as a new political mode after the major public sector and student strikes of December 1995. These widely supported "popular strikes" made explicit, for the first time in recent memory, a link between an actively democratic prescription upon the state and a popular mobilization in the workplace.[59] Today, in the aftermath of December 1995, the OP looks to the Saint Bernard movement, the foyers campaign, and the recent *mouvement des chômeurs* as so many examples of (still partial and fragmentary) political subjectivation. In each case, "people are gathering together, demonstrating that they have their own political capacity, which the state must take into account."[60]

Political Implications

Where does all this leave Badiou on the broader, more theoretical questions of the economy, the state, and the status of a contemporary Marxism?

Politics against Economics

Badiou and the OP have long maintained that "the only kind of economy is capitalist," which is to say that "there is no socialist economy" as such.[61] What is known in France as *la pensée unique* adopts this economy as its sole principle, a principle of apparent "necessity" driven by global competition and European monetary union.[62] The OP seeks to articulate a viable refutation of this "*politique unique* whose present form is the declaration that the economy decides everything." True politics can begin only at a distance from the economy, and policies supposedly justified by economic necessity are for the OP simply synonymous with reactionary politics.

On the other hand, there can be no political retreat from the challenge posed by an ever more global, ever more triumphant capitalist economy. According to Badiou,

> Emancipatory politics must be at least equal to the challenge of capital. That is Marx's idea. When Marx says that capital destroys all the old ties, all the ancient sacred figures, that it dissolves everything in the frozen waters of selfish calculation, he says it with a certain admiration.[63] Marx had already distinguished himself from those who dreamed nostalgically of a resistance to capital rooted in the ancient customs and territories. He called this reactive phenomenon "feudal socialism." Marx was radically critical of this idea, and it's because he accepted that there were formal similarities between the ambitions of emancipatory politics and the workings of capital. Because we can never go back on universalism. There is no earlier territoriality calling for protection or recovery.[64]

Progressive politics as Badiou understands it must both operate at a level of universality that can rival that of capital itself and ensure that this rivalry unfolds on a plane other than that dominated by capital. He writes, "I think what is Marxist, and also Leninist, and in any case *true*, is the idea that any viable campaign against capitalism can only be political. There can be no economic battle against the economy."[65] Should politics try to confront capitalism on its own economic terrain, the eventual result will be capitalist every time. Any political subject must constitute itself, out of itself, in the inviolable sufficiency of a *distance politique*. Whether this position, and the vehement anti–trade unionism it implies, is of much practical help in confronting the immediate political consequences of ongoing corporate globalization is a question to which I will return in chapter 13.

Politics and the State

We know that Badiou's early and unequivocally hostile attitude to the state has considerably evolved. Just how far it has evolved remains a little unclear. His conception of politics remains resolutely anticonsensual, anti–"re-presentative," and thus antidemocratic (in the ordinary sense of the word). Democracy has become the central ideological category of the neo-liberal status quo, and any genuine "philosophy today is above all something that enables people to have done with the 'democratic' submission to the world as it is."[66] But he seems more willing, now, to engage with this submission on its own terms. *La Distance politique* again offers the most precise *points de repère*. On the one hand, the OP remains suspicious of any political campaign—for instance, an electoral contest or petition movement—that operates as a "prisoner of the parliamentary space."[67] It remains "an absolute necessity [of politics] not to have the state as norm. The separation of politics and state is foundational of politics." On the other hand, however, it is now equally clear that "their separation need not lead to the banishment of the state from the field of political thought."[68] The OP now conceives itself in a tense, nondialectical "vis-à-vis" with the state, a stance that rejects an intimate cooperation (in the interests of capital) as much as it refuses "any antagonistic conception of their operation—a conception that smacks of classism." There is no more choice to be made between the state and revolution; the "vis-à-vis demands the presence of the two terms and not the annihilation of one of the two."[69] Indeed, at the height of the December 1995 strikes, the OP recognized that the only contemporary movement of *"déstatisation"* (destatification) with any real power was the corporation-driven movement of partial destatification in the interests of commercial flexibility and financial mobility. Unsurprisingly, "we are against this withdrawal of the state to the profit of capital, through general, systematic, and brutal privatization. The state is what can sometimes take account of people and their situations in other registers and by other modalities than those of profit. The state assures from this point of view the public space and the general interest. And capital does not incarnate the general interest."[70] Coming from the author of *Théorie de la contradiction,* these are remarkable words.

The next question is whether the very possibility of such prescription according to the general interest does not itself presuppose that same liberal-parliamentary realm upon whose systematic vilification its own critical distance depends. What kind of state can respond "responsibly" to political prescriptions, if not one responsive to electoral pressure? Badiou maintains that the old socialist states, as states, were more sensitive to workers' strikes than are today's parliamentary states—the great example being the *Solidarnosc* campaign in Poland.[71] But when the OP ventures into the vexing domain of constitutional reform, it is to propose very explicitly parliamentary procedures: an end to a separately elected president (and so an end to the possibility of cohabitation), a purely cosmetic head of state, only one major forum for elections (a legislative chamber of deputies), assurance that the head of government is always the head of the dominant party, and finally, a guarantee "that there *is* always a dominant party," thanks to some kind of first-past-the-post electoral system. The whole package is to be softened with calls for more open government and the rule of law.[72] The once Maoist Organisation Politique now recommends something very like the British Constitution!

At this point, the reader has to wonder if the OP's policy of strict nonparticipation in the state really stands up. The OP declares with some pride, "We never vote," just as "in the factories, we keep our distance from trade unionism."[73] The OP consistently maintains that its politics of prescription requires a politics of "nonvote." But why, *now*, this either/or? Once the state has been acknowledged as a possible figure of the general interest, surely it matters who governs that figure. Regarding the central public issues of health and education, the OP maintains, as do most mainstream socialists, that the "positive tasks on behalf of all are incumbent upon the state."[74] That participation in the state should not replace a prescriptive externality to the state is obvious enough, but the stern either/or so often proclaimed in the pages of *La Distance politique* reads today as a displaced trace of the days when the choice of "state or revolution" still figured as a genuine alternative.

Marxist or Post-Marxist?

If Badiou both rejects any direct articulation of politics with economics and tolerates a certain degree of reliance on the state, in what sense does his project still merit the Marxist label? Badiou recognizes no single subject of History, no global historical movement, no priority of the mode of production—not even the ultimate political primacy of class struggle per se. Judged by the relatively orthodox criteria of an Aijaz Ahmad, for instance, there is little doubt that Badiou's work must figure as part of the "eclectic," antisystemic trend characteristic of much Western social and cultural theory since the early 1970s.[75] The dominant feature of Ahmad's Marxism is precisely its perception of a systematic coherence governing historical change, and its consequent characterization of the "universal" as an effect of "the global operation of a single mode of production."[76] Badiou, by contrast, is certainly "not a historicist," he says, "in that I don't think events are linked in a global system. That would deny their essentially random character, which I absolutely maintain."[77]

The OP has itself adopted at various times the adjectives "post-Leninist"[78] and "post-classist."[79] It certainly accepts that the strict Marxist Leninism of the Khmers Rouges and the Shining Path is "historically dead,"[80] just as it renounces as "classist" a historical materialism that presumes some kind of dialectical relation between political subjectivity and the objectivity of class relations. Equally classist and "trade unionist" is the "obsolete" idea that the state is the creation, effect, and tool of the ruling class. Badiou "think[s], to put it quite abruptly, that Marxism doesn't exist" (AM, 67). Badiou's ramified conception of praxis certainly subtracts it from every vulgar Marxist instance of the One—the one of the party and its theoretical authority as much as the one of the historical or social totality. But he refuses the term "post-Marxist" (in Laclau's sense) as a description of his work.[81] The OP's practice and priorities are proof of how far Badiou is from joining Laclau, along with André Gorz and Alain Touraine, as they bid "farewell to the working class." He writes, "In camouflaged form, the abandon promoted by Gorz and others in fact shows that they have been won over, politically, to the established order. It leaves the properly political sphere untouched. It represents a kind of idealisation of a self-regulating social movement of capital itself. It is a vision of the affluent. The rich societies' dream of a maximum possible comfort. And so we are to busy ourselves with the environment, with development, with the reduction of the working week, with recreation, with training for all."[82] Against this postpolitical vision, Badiou stresses the continuing relevance and accuracy of Marx's general diagnosis of the capitalist economy:

> I think that global trends have essentially confirmed some of Marx's fundamental intuitions. There is no going back on this; there is no need for a revision of Marxism itself. It is a matter of going beyond the idea that politics *represents* objective groups that can be designated as classes. This idea has had its power and importance. But in our opinion, we cannot today begin from or set out from this idea. We can begin from political processes, from political oppositions, from conflicts and contradictions, obviously. But it is no longer possible to code these phenomena in terms of representations of classes. In other words, there may exist emancipatory politics or reactionary politics, but

these cannot be rendered immediately transitive to a scientific, objective study of how class functions in society.... The realization of the world as global market, the undivided reign of great financial conglomerates, etc., all this is an indisputable reality and one that conforms, essentially, to Marx's analysis. The question is, where does politics fit in with all this?[83]

It is not yet clear that the Organisation Politique provides a fully convincing answer to this question. Nor is it clear in what sense their answer to this question can still be called "Marxist," if politics is not articulated in *some* kind of relation with changes in the mode of production and attendant class antagonisms. In what sense can a politics that defines itself as a prescription upon the state afford to remain indifferent to global economic trends whose direct effect is to undercut and limit the functions of a prescribable state? Can Badiou affirm both the fully "random" distribution of events and the structural regularity of "global trends"—without, at least, relating the one to the other?

Badiou's politics have always been about "collective emancipation, or the problem of the reign of liberty in infinite situations" (DO, 54; cf. TC, 60). His political goals have remained consistent over the years, since "every historical event is communist, to the degree that 'communist' designates the transtemporal subjectivity of emancipation, the egalitarian passion, the Idea of justice, the will to break with the compromises of the *service des biens,* the deposition of egoism, an intolerance of oppression, the wish to impose a withering away of the state. The absolute preeminence of multiple presentation over representation."[84] What has changed is communism's mode of existence. In Badiou's earlier work, the practical (if ultimately unattainable) goal was always to effect the actual, historical achievement of stateless community. Today, in order to preserve politics' "intrinsic relation to truth" (DO, 48), Badiou has had to let go of almost any sort of political engagement with the economic and the social. He continues to declare a wholly egalitarian politics, but as reserved for a strictly subjective plane. The unqualified justice of a generic communism, first proposed in Marx's *1844 Manuscripts* and conceived in Badiou's own terms as the advent of "pure presentation," as the "undivided authority of the infinite, or the advent of the collective as such" (AM, 91), remains the only valid subjective norm for Badiou's political thought. This subjective norm has become ever more distant, however, from the day-to-day business of "objective" politics: the programmatic pursuit of the generic ideal is itself now dismissed as a "Romantic" dream leading to "fraternity terror" (AM, 101). It is as if Badiou's recent work positively embraces a version of what Hegel dubbed the unhappy consciousness—the stoical affirmation of a worthy ideal or subjective principle, but as divorced from any substantial relation to the material organization of the situation. It seems that the Maoists' mistake was not their emphasis on the generic, or even their understanding of what was required to make it a historical reality, but simply their determination to apply this understanding to the world (cf. E, 75).

A certain self-restraint is thus the condition politics must fulfill if it is to respect its own unnameable. Since "true politics is the collective brought to its immanent truth," the "collective as commensurable with thought,"[85] politics must never try to define or institutionalize what this collectivity might be. The "community, the collective, are the unnameables of politics: every effort to name 'politically' a community induces a disastrous Evil," on the model of Nazism or the National Front (E, 77). A political or generic community is a community that exists for as long as it is able to resist naming itself. Every subject persists insofar as it resists its conversion into an object.

chapter 11

What Is Philosophy?

This is now a relatively simple question to answer, and it is no accident that this should be among the shortest chapters of the book. All truths are matters of thought, and thought is not the special prerogative of philosophy. Philosophy is thought thinking itself. Badiou defines philosophy as "the apprehension in thought of the conditions under which thought is exercised, in its different registers" (AM, 99). Truths occur regardless of philosophy, and "eternity" takes place without consulting a philosopher; philosophy is simply that discipline which "pays attention to the conditions whereby eternity comes to pass" (TA, 17.12.97). This paying attention, however, is itself an entirely inventive, fully specific dimension of thought. A truth must find its philosopher, in whatever guise, in order to be identified and affirmed *as* truth. There is nothing in the truth procedures themselves that performs this function, since a truth procedure need not be conscious of itself in order to proceed (anyone who has been in love can confirm the point).

The truths invented in love, art, science, and politics are the conditions rather than the objects of philosophy. Strictly speaking, philosophy has no distinct object. The history of philosophy is precisely the history of its de-objectivation, its subtraction from the myriad empirical domains initially claimed by Aristotle's encyclopedic embrace.[1] Today, cognitive science claims to explain the processes of understanding and knowledge, mathematics has absorbed logic, and the study of morality is caught up with anthropology and sociology, while matters of judgment and aesthetics have been subsumed by the disciplines of art history or semiotics. Modern philosophy, especially in the wake of Kant and Heidegger (after the final "encyclopedic" efforts of Hegel and Comte) has renounced its ancient proximity to knowledge. Without a distinctive object of its own, philosophy cannot be identified through reference to any previously constituted domain. Instead, no less than the procedures that condition it, philosophy is a kind of act, an "intervention," which takes place.

The nature of this intervention varies. Nietzsche developed a form of genealogical intervention, which his recent French successors have extended to analyze the structures of power and normalization. Heidegger was obsessed with the intervention of a question, the question of Being recovered from our forgetful fascination with beings. Deleuze defended a purely creative form of intervention, philosophy as the autonomous creation of concepts. Each such intervention is an act that takes place locally, as an encounter with forms of thought that resist any merely objective description—that is, as an encounter with active truths. The conditions of philosophy thus provide philosophy with the proper "places" for its performance—for instance, poetry as the place of philosophical questioning for Heidegger, or mathematized logic as the place from which Frege and Russell reintroduced the priority of clarity and precision, or cinema as a spur to conceptual creation for Deleuze. Other places of philosophy might include music (as for Rousseau or Adorno), religion (as for Malebranche or Corbin), or psychoanalysis (as for Milner or Jambet). As for the history of philosophy, it provides philosophy with an "indirect" place, that is, a "place for the places of philosophy." In each case, "philosophy thinks only thought," but it thinks this thought under the peculiar circumstances determined by its place.[2]

The place itself is worked by the philosopher, but no philosophy can ever "incorporate" its place. It is rather the philosopher who must submit to the demanding "preexistence of the place."[3] Christian faith, for instance, the place of philosophy for Malebranche or Pascal, remains fully independent of the reason it inspires, just as Deleuze insists that the cinematic folding of percepts and affects spurs the philosophical creation of concepts, without cinema's being in any sense "conceptualized" in the process. As a matter of principle, in order better to resist the temptation of incorporation (in order to avoid resurrecting a new One), every philosophy should explore several places at once. Deleuze's work is as exemplary, in this regard, as that of Plato or Sartre. Even Comte, though drawn to the apparent sufficiency of science, nevertheless pursued a quasi-political project (the creation of a new "church") and was marked by the experience of love (the encounter with

Clotilde de Vaux). Every genuine "philosophy is multilocal," and philosophical specialization is no less a contradiction in terms for Badiou than it was for Socrates.

What, then, does philosophy actually contribute to truth itself? The philosopher has no way of answering this question. As Badiou writes, "The effects of philosophy outside of itself, its effects in reality, remain entirely opaque for philosophy itself. . . . The impossible of thought proper to philosophy, which is thus its real, lies in the effect that it produces on its conditions."[4] But there may at least be circumstances where this uncertain contribution counts, strategically, for a great deal. As a rule, truths do not "indicate themselves from the outside." Nothing in mathematical discourse itself, to take the most obvious case, indicates its ontological status. All truths exist in the "form of works, efforts, and experiences in the extraordinarily confused totality of human activity. . . . Certainly, there are truths, but it is up to philosophy to declare their existence."[5] It has for centuries fallen to philosophy to isolate and analyze the particular truths of art, for instance, just as it was the *philosophes* who distinguished the secular certainties of science from superstition and myth. After every pious Newton, there is a Voltaire.

Nevertheless, the order of priority is clear: first the conditioning, then the conditioned: "Philosophy is in no way 'first' or foundational" with respect to its conditions, the generic procedures. On the contrary, "they must all be fully fulfilled for there to be philosophy."[6] This, by itself, is enough to ensure that philosophy is not restricted to the particular field presumed by any one of these conditions. We know that "there is no and cannot be any philosophy *of* mathematics," for instance, any more than there can be a philosophy of art or of politics.[7] If nothing in mathematical discourse itself declares its ontological status, if only philosophy can identify math as ontology, this is on the condition that philosophy rigorously distinguish itself from ontology, just as it once distinguished itself from cosmology, physics, religion, and so on (CT, 55). Philosophy is the most generic of all discourses, more so even than mathematics, because it is not specified by any particular domain or dimension.

What a particular philosophy does is put together in some kind of systematic shape those contemporary truths it is able to recognize and affirm. Philosophy demonstrates the "compossibility" of its current conditions. In more evocative terms, philosophy arranges a liaison or rendez-vous with truth—"philosophy is the *madam [maquerelle]* of truth. And just as beauty is a requirement of the woman encountered, but is not at all required of the madam, so too are truths artistic, scientific, amorous, or political, but not philosophical."[8] Philosophy does not determine the general or transcendent criteria of truth; rather, "the most singular and most characteristic effort of philosophy is that of the compossibilization [of its conditions]."[9] Descartes's effort, for instance, organized the truths of mathematics and theology around the central notion of the singular subject, while Heidegger linked the affirmation of poetic insight, the critique of instrumental reason, and a reconceptualization of the history of philosophy to the central question of ontology. Today's compossibilization, we know, turns around the concept of the generic. The conditions of a truly contemporary philosophy have been marked out, in their various domains, by Cohen, Lacan, Celan, and activists inspired by mobilizations ranging from May 68 to the Intifada: ultimately, Badiou writes, "our time will be representable as the time in which these events, in thought, *took place*" (MP, 69).

"Formalization at the Level of the Real": A Philosophy for the Twentieth Century

Badiou's recent meditations on the twentieth century, *Le Siècle,* make up his most elaborate effort to explore the philosophical compossibility of the great truths of our time. Based on a series of lectures given at the Collège International de Philosophie (1998–2001), *Le Siècle* is an attempt to make sense of how the twentieth century thought itself, that is, from within distinctively twentieth-century forms of subjectivation rather than more recent, literally fin-de-siècle, forms of reaction or resignation. The philosophical twentieth century opened with the extraordinarily innovative generation of 1890 (1890–1914), a virtually unprecedented "period of polymorphous creativity"—the generation of Mallarmé, Frege, Einstein, Poincaré, Hilbert, Freud, Schoenberg, Lenin, Conrad, Proust, Joyce, and Picasso, among others (LS, 5–6). The century began with a period that was as "inventive" as it was "disparate." This period was brought to an end by the First World War and a generalized militarization of thought, beginning with the thought of politics itself, as was confirmed in the wake of October 1917. The distinctively twentieth-century project remained one of pure innovation or invention, but over the course of the 1930s this project became a programmatic one, organized around a "final" or definitive solution. Lenin was replaced by Stalin, Mandelstam by Brecht, Sigmund Freud by Anna Freud.

In both its inventive and its programmatic moments, the twentieth century was driven by an urgent "passion for the real" in every domain. Exposure to the real is exposure to the violence of pure decision as such in a space inaccessible to the prevailing norms of re-presentation and in a time devoted entirely to the "here and now" of a new beginning, a present stripped—always at the risk of undiluted horror—of all reserve, deferral, inheritance, or illusion

(LS, 17–18). The true subjects of the twentieth century accepted without reservation that "the real is antagonism" or revolt, *en acte,* and that every real struggle proceeds without reference to the moralizing categories of good and evil, or to the "realistic" categories of compromise and consensus.[10] What philosophy can identify in the twentieth century is its unprecedented determination to endure the trial of this real in the absence of any comforting mediation or critical distance. The century demands that its passion for the real be thought in terms that yield nothing to interpretation or equivocation—in terms, that is, that most nearly approximate a purely literal formalization: "Formalization, in the end, is the great unifying power behind the century's great initiatives: from mathematics (formal logics) through politics (the Party as the a priori form of all collective action) via art, both prose (Joyce and the Odyssey of forms), painting (Picasso, confronted with any visual challenge, as the inventor of an adequate formalization), or music (the formal, polyvalent construction of Alban Berg's *Wozzeck*). But in 'formalization' the word 'form' is not opposed to 'matter' or 'content'; it is coupled with the real of the act."[11] "Form" is of course to be understood here in its Platonic rather than its Aristotelian sense: form is nothing other than the process whereby an idea is subtracted from the substantial confusion of appearance and reality. Formalization is the vehicle of thought driven solely by a passion for the real, that is, thought that refuses the luxury of approximation or verification. If Freud, Lenin, and Cantor remain the great inaugural thinkers of the century, it is because they each invented new, purely formal means for thinking an encounter with the real (respectively: the real of sex, the real of politics, and the real of infinity). Freud, for instance, understood that our relation to sexuality "is not of the order of knowledge, but of the order of a naming, or an intervention"—that is, of an analysis, which seeks to subtract it from the blind power of knowledge and norms (LS, 58). Against Jung, Freud's achievement was successfully to resist any confusion of analysis with (cultural) interpretation. Freud ensured that the "naked truth" of sex would remain accessible only through strictly formal methods of analysis, that is, methods sensitive to the symptomal disruption (displacement, condensation, and so on) of normal subjective "content," methods whose articulation was to culminate with the hermetic mathemes of Lacan. Lenin, likewise, would seek to ensure that politics remained a matter of real antagonism and subjective commitment pure and simple; the only vehicle of such commitment is the formal integrity of political organization itself (the party), in the absence of any fundamental reference to a particular policy agenda or social program.

Formalization finds its only foundation in an encounter with the real, just as it finds its exclusive address through the evacuation of all particularity (all interpretatibility). Badiou refuses to make any concession on this point: "If a work must be interpreted, can be interpreted, it is because there still subsists in it too much particularity, it has not attained the pure transparency of the act, it has not exposed, naked and bare, its real." Bauhaus, abstract expressionism, minimalism, formalist axiomatics, the architects of socialism—all seek to formalize, *au ras du réel*, "a universality without remainder, without adherence to particularity of any sort" (LS, 130). No less than Deleuze, Badiou fully accepts that ordinary humanity cannot endure this evacuation (the evacuation of its every satisfaction). "Man" cannot survive the advent of a purely formal univocity. Humanity is equivocal, only "superhumanity is univocal," and "all univocity stems from a formalization whose act determines its localizable real *[dont l'acte est le réel localisable]*."[12] Only a superhuman or immortal coherence indicates a destination or address worthy of humanity.

The last decades of the twentieth century, of course, witnessed the exhaustion of programmatic fidelity to such formal univocity. The present moment is almost entirely dominated by a reactionary denial of the real and a generalized suspicion of formalization. At every point we are urged to busy ourselves with the interpretation of reality, the thick description of cultures, the negotiation of identities, the articulation of discourses, the translation of differences, and so on. Does this mean that the philosopher's job is to explore the contours of a new, fin-de-siècle compossibility? Not at all: since the present moment is characterized by the denial or exhaustion of truth, then the only compossibilization consistent with this denial is that presumed by versions of the "end of philosophy." To treat contemporary denials of truth as if they were truths is simply to abandon philosophy altogether. The fact that Badiou's own reaffirmation of philosophy took on its distinctive shape during precisely this period of reactionary denial conditions nothing other than his denial of the denial. The properly philosophical project remains oriented around the robust renewal of formalization, the invention of new axioms, new logics. Since "the essence of thought always rests in the power of forms," our task is to renew, suitably reworked, the essential wager of the twentieth century. Our task is "to declare again, and this time around, perhaps, who knows, to win, that war in thought that was the century's own, but that also already opposed Plato to Aristotle: the war of formalization against interpretation. . . . The war of the Idea against reality. Of freedom against nature. Of the event against status quo. Of truth against opinions. Of the intensity of life against the insignificance of survival. Of equality against equity. Of rebellion against acceptance. Of eternity against History. Of science against technology. Of art against culture. Of politics against the management of business. Of love against the family" (LS, 132).

The Universality of Philosophy

The fact that every philosophy is fully conditioned by the generic procedures of philosophy in no way qualifies the "irreducible autonomy" of philosophy. That philosophy is conditioned by the evental truths operative in its time does not mean that it simply reflects them in a kind of passive determination. If philosophy does not express a truth, then, this is because what it does express, with respect to its own time, is nothing less than the "unity of thought" as such, the singular compossibility of truths, or what Badiou sometimes calls "the Truth" *(la Vérité)* (C, 65). Philosophy cannot itself know anything of its "effects" upon the truths that condition it, but since "history and epistemology do not establish, in themselves, any philosophical pertinence,"[13] philosophy itself has to evaluate the ultimate importance of an event. Only philosophy can clarify and distinguish what, in its own time, is of eternal value. Only philosophy can align a sense of the actively contemporary with "what Plato called the 'forever of time' *[le toujours du temps],* toward the intemporal essence of time" (C, 80). Only philosophy, in other words, can begin to make sense of the question "What is our particular historical era worth?"[14]

Philosophy can continue its engagement with this question, moreover, only if it resists its own version of objectification. Philosophical disaster strikes when philosophy is "captivated" or "fascinated" by something outside its domain, either by one of its own conditions—as when Stalin sutured philosophy to politics, or when Heidegger subordinated philosophy to poetry, or when Carnap declared that "philosophy is to be replaced by the logic of science"[15]—or by something wholly external to it, as when Hegel annexed philosophy to the mediations of History and the State.[16] Such subservient philosophies are "sutured" to a logic literally beneath their station. In the hands of a pragmatist like Richard Rorty, for instance, philosophy effectively disappears altogether: once thought has been reduced to social engineering and governmental problem solving on the one hand and to a merely private irony or idiosyncrasy on the other, what passes for philosophy is left, in duly post-Wittgensteinian fashion, merely to supervise this division.

A distinctive discourse called philosophy can exist only in the conceptual medium of an unqualified universality. There can be no limits to philosophy other than those that constrain the truths that condition it. Badiou's work is one of the most inventive answers to perhaps the most far-reaching question to have preoccupied French philosophy after Sartre: "What exactly is a universal singularity?"[17] Or: How exactly might the universal be sub-tracted from a merely relational—or dialectical, intersubjective, interactive—mediation? The many rival answers to this question include (however eclectic this collection might seem) Blanchot's solitude, Bataille's sovereignty, Girard's truth, Deleuze's virtual, Nancy's plural singular, and Henry's autoaffection, along with the singular One beyond being of Levinas and Corbin, or the one beyond doubling or beyond difference of Rosset and Laruelle.[18]

With his own recent "Huit Thèses sur l'universel" (Eight theses on the universal), Badiou provides a concise overview of his philosophy as a whole.[19] As we might expect, he firmly distinguishes the universal from merely "ency-clopedic regularities." The biological, mental, and social structures that char-acterize homo sapiens, "the invariants that can be identified in the human animal, are verifiable empirical generalities," he says, and for that very rea-son, "obviously contingent." Certainly, "the truths that we produce and know are dependent upon this contingency, which frames them all. Nevertheless, their universality as such is not affected by this contingency, no more than by the fact that an event is always an event for a situation, and not 'in itself.'"[20] Truth subtracts itself from the circumstances in which it is produced, be they social, psychological, or cognitive, and only a truth can be called universal in a strictly unqualified sense.

Badiou's eight theses are as follows:

"Thesis 1: The proper element of the universal is thought," and all true thought operates at the limits of available knowledge. Nothing objective is universal.

"Thesis 2: Every universal is a singularity." The universal cannot be directly articulated with any recognizable particularity, grouping, or identity.

"Thesis 3: Every universal has its origin in an event, and the event is in-transitive to the particularity of the situation." A universal is always unpre-dictable, incalculable, and so in a certain sense "unconscious."

"Thesis 4: A universal appears at first as the decision of an undecidable or the valorization of something without value," that is, as a decision concerning the reality of those elements collected in a situation's evental site.

"Thesis 5: The universal has an implicative or consequential structure." The universal is the consequence of a decision, visible only to those who share in making the decision.

"Thesis 6: The universal is univocal." The universal is a matter of fidelity to the consequences of a truth, and not of the interpretation of its meaning(s).

"Thesis 7: Every universal singularity is unfinishable, or open." The uni-versal is indifferent to our mortality or fragility.

"Thesis 8: Universality is nothing other than the faithful construction of an infinite generic multiplicity." Universal is properly an adjective that applies to a certain "status of *being*" (being assembled according to the criteria of its pure being as being, i.e., through the mechanics of a truth procedure) rather than to a category of judgment or knowledge.[21]

In brief, universality is a result. Every universal is exceptional, has its origin in one point, is assembled step by step, is the consequence of a decision, is a category of the subject, is a matter of being-true rather than of knowing. Philosophy consists of the analysis and articulation of such universalities.

part IV

Complications

These last chapters are slightly different in nature from the others in the book. If up to this point we have mainly pursued a straightforward exposition of Badiou's philosophical system, here we will begin to consider a number of different problems or complications arising from this system. Chapter 12 tackles the most obvious such problem, the problem that defined much of Badiou's work in the years immediately following the publication of *L'Etre et l'événement*. This is the problem of ethics and evil, the problem of truth gone wrong. What is to stop a truth from asserting an effectively dictatorial power? Chapter 13 moves into more varied problematic territory, and brings together my own questions regarding certain aspects of Badiou's system, most of which turn on the problem of relationality, broadly understood. I suggest that, to some degree at least, Badiou evades the question of dictatorship only by recourse to an approximately absolutist logic. The last chapter summarizes Badiou's own very recent and still tentative investigation of the whole question of relation and logical possibility, his elaboration of a domain of "appearing" or "being there" to complement that of pure being as being.

chapter 12

Ethics, Evil, and the Unnameable

There is today no question more topical in philosophy and in the humanities generally than the question of ethics, understood as a kind of reflective sensitivity to matters of cultural difference and civic responsibility. And there is probably no assertion of Badiou's more shocking than his summary pronouncement "The whole ethical predication based upon recognition of the other must be purely and simply abandoned."[1] Very much against the contemporary grain, Badiou's ethics is an ethics of the Same. Since difference or multiplicity is very literally what *is*, what *should be* is a matter of how such difference is transcended in favor of something else—in favor of the generic equality asserted by a truth.

From Morality to Ethics

As Žižek reminds us, "There is ethics—that is to say, an injunction which cannot be grounded in ontology—insofar as there is a crack in the ontological edifice of the universe: at its most elementary, ethics designates fidelity to this crack."[2] The question of ethics arises only, beyond being as being, with truth and the subject. Outside a truth procedure there are only moral norms and customs, as regulated by the state of the situation. The ethical perspective shared by Lacan, Žižek, and Badiou is one that breaks sharply with the long tradition, reaching back to Aristotle, that attempts to ground ethical practice in some substantial or extrasubjective good (pleasure, virtue, civic

255

harmony, and so on).[3] True ethics must instead be internal to a truth procedure, and consequently indifferent to all objective goods or differences.

Not for the first time, Badiou finds himself in a dramatically exceptional position here. For not only have the austere declarations of Althusser and Foucault recently been swapped for the neo-Kantian and neo-Tocquevillian slogans of liberal individualism and *la nouvelle philosophie,* but much of the original force of what has been widely attacked as *la pensée soixante-huit* was itself diluted years ago by its own major proponents. In the late 1970s, Foucault and Lyotard both moved toward a dialogue with Kant and a direct engagement with explicitly ethical questions. Derrida has become more and more interested in matters of cultural diversity and ethical responsibility. Over the last decade, interest in Levinas's work has seen a spectacular revival.[4] An affirmation of difference and a respect for "otherness" have become virtually definitive characteristics of the Anglo-American cultural studies that derives so much of its theoretical inspiration from these same thinkers. Whereas Badiou accepts the unpleasing fact that there can be no respect but only struggle between "really different" positions—and prepares his positions accordingly—today's sophists insist that "no one can enter the public arena without declarations of the rights of others on their lips."[5]

The two major inspirations behind this resurgence of ethics are precisely those two great authorities invoked in Lyotard's supremely sophistic text, *Le Différend* (1983): Kant and Wittgenstein. From Kant we have adopted the notion of an absolute moral imperative transcending all matters of mere political circumstance, and the notion of a "radical Evil, identified as indifference to the suffering of the other."[6] A "return to Kant," Badiou notes with acid distaste, is always "a sign of closed and morbid times."[7] From the later Wittgenstein we have learned to accept the principle that there is "nothing more primitive than our disposition to agree."[8] How "we" agree to go about things, justified on the shared basis of habit, utility, and conformity, has become the sole standard of value for judging what "we" do. How we play a particular language game cannot be measured by anything other than the rules of that particular game. Philosophy can ensure only that we play by the rules in each case.[9] Where these two approaches can most comfortably coincide is clearly where we agree to organize ethics around the prevention of suffering and death. Thinkers as different as Rorty and Levinas can concur with Ricoeur's principle that *"la souffrance oblige"* (suffering obliges).[10] An emphasis on the management of human rights follows more or less as a matter of course, and with it a strictly negative conception of ethics: ethics, and the humanity it affirms, is defined indirectly, in terms of protection from the evils of suffering or misrecognition (E, 10–16).

This is a point of departure that Badiou cannot accept. "The status of victim, of suffering beast, of emaciated dying individual," Badiou points out,

> reduces man to his animal substructure, to his pure and simple identity as dying. . . . Neither mortality nor cruelty can define the singularity of the human within the world of the living. As torturer, man is an animal abjection. But we must have the courage to say that as victim, he is not generally worth much more. All the narratives of the tortured and the survivors demonstrate the point: if the torturers can treat their victims as animals, it is because the victims have indeed become animals. The torturer has done what needed to be done for this to be the case. Some of them, however, are still human, and testify to the fact. But precisely only through extraordinary effort, and thanks to a resistance in them, thanks to what does not coincide with the victim identity.[11]

Any genuine ethics is from the beginning antihumanist inasmuch as it implies the preliminary, inaugural affirmation of a "superhuman, or immortal, dimension of the human."[12]

Though left-hanging intellectuals are obviously reluctant explicitly to defend today's prevailing regime of capitalist exploitation, many happily agree that the supposedly "real Evil is elsewhere," for instance, in ethnic fundamentalism, totalitarian violence, or religious terrorism. Enthusiastic denunciation of these crimes encourages us to make believe that we ourselves enjoy "if not the Good then at least the best possible state of affairs"—and helps us forget that nothing about such denunciation actively "leads in the direction of the real emancipation of humanity."[13] Badiou is one of very few contemporary thinkers prepared to accept the certainty of violence and the risk of disaster implicit in all genuine thought, that is, in any compelling break with the prevailing logic of re-presentation. As far as the established order is concerned, every "Idea is cruel" by definition, and there is no guarantee against this cruelty other than the devastating imperative so typical of our times: "Live without Idea" (LS, 95). Badiou is a thinker for whom the question of terror remains a genuine *problem*, rather than an essentially unproblematic instance of barbaric evil or crime. Since thought is grounded only in the real and proceeds purely as an "unjustifiable" affirmation, it is always vulnerable to a form of paranoid insecurity. There can be no evading the fact that "the real, conceived in its contingent absoluteness, is never so real that it cannot be suspected of being fictitious *[semblant]*. Nothing can testify to the fact that the real is real, other than the fictional system in which it will come to play the role of the real" (LS, 43). And since the real is fundamentally indifferent to the moral categories of good and evil, there is no built-in mechanism to prevent this fictional system from drawing upon terror as its ultimate means of distinguishing false from truthful testimony. There is, in particular, no blandly "humanizing" mechanism adequate to this purpose. Since every truth springs from an exception to the rules, we must refuse, in principle, the idea of any automatic or inherent rights of Man.[14] No less than Lacan and Žižek, Badiou displaces the facile emphasis on human rights from the center of ethics by accepting that fidelity to truth need have "nothing to do with the 'interests' of the animal, is indifferent to its perpetuation, and has eternity as its destiny."[15] Human rights, if they exist at all, can be only *exceptional* rights, asserted and affirmed in their positivity rather than deduced, negatively, from the requirements of survival. Failure to make this distinction simply confuses human and animal rights in a single calculus of suffering.

Any given question of rights, then, is always particular to a truth procedure. The multiplicity of procedures rules out in advance the possibility of a single, transcendental morality. Badiou refuses to subordinate the particularity of political sequences, say, to universal moral judgments of the kind "violence is always wrong." Since any political truth is an effort to realize the universal within the particularity of a situation, the pursuit of means appropriate to this universality must be internal to that situation. The unity of theory and practice in Badiou's concept of truth compels the foreclosure of any abstract notion of morality per se (any deliberation as to what I should do). However transcendent its authority, mere morality remains a matter of the world. Morality calculates interests and benefits. What Badiou defends as ethics always involves, one way or another, a decision to forego the world, that is, to forego calculation—and so to accept a fully logical obligation, though one *based* only on chance. Unsurprisingly, Pascal's analysis of choice is for Badiou an exemplary piece of true ethical reasoning.

The obvious question that arises is this: Does this amoral refusal of calculation imply the refusal of all notions of moderation and restraint? What happens if a truth runs out of control? How can Badiou's philosophy of effectively sovereign truths guard against their despotic corruption? If there is no moral "outside" to a truth, what can limit its effective jurisdiction? These are the questions Badiou tackles with his notion of the unnameable.

The Unnameable

A truth is founded on an unnameable in somewhat the same way that a situation is founded upon its evental site. Every truth, in other words, includes one subset or part whose own elements it cannot distinguish or analyze, one point where its powers of discernment are interrupted. Remember that truth begins with a name or implication, and proceeds by testing the various elements of a situation against this implication. What Badiou calls an unnameable is thus a part of the truth that must ultimately be spared this confrontation, in order that the truth might continue as an infinite or unending process. That there is at least one element that remains, as far as a truth procedure is concerned, "neutral, immobile, logically invariable, atemporal, unincorporable," ensures that truths do not proceed as a complete "refoundation of the world" but happen in one and the same world, which they alter but do not reinvent ex nihilo (TA, 4.6.98).

In other words, in order for a truth to continue as the truth of its situation the subject of that truth must stop short of investigating everything within the situation.[16] The lover must stop short of a jealous possession of the beloved; political subjects must resist the temptation to define the boundaries and characteristics of their egalitarian community; the scientist must accept an essential uncertainty principle, in nature as much as in mathematics. Recognition of the unnameable ensures that a truth can never be total or definitive, can never be reincorporated into the realm of knowledge and objectivity. For if everything could be named or said, its saying would simply express Totality itself, and the truth of this saying could be derived from a kind of universal grammar. There would then be no difference between a true statement and a grammatically correct statement. Such a statement would not "think" in Badiou's sense of the word, that is, it would no longer be conditioned by an event that exceeds it. Badiou writes, "That truth and totality are incompatible is no doubt the decisive—or post-Hegelian—teaching of modernity." Or, as Lacan used to put it: "The truth cannot say 'everything' about itself; it can only 'half' say itself [elle ne peut que se mi-dire]."[17]

It would be misleading, however, to think of the unnameable in the essentially negative terms that the word implies. That the truth is founded upon (and oriented toward) the unnameable puts only a very particular sort of limit on its power. Remember that for Badiou, the critic of linguistic constructivism, there is nothing restrictive or debilitating about unnameability as such. On the contrary: with respect to the prevailing state of the situation, every part included in a true generic set is unnameable, since "every nameable part of a situation, discerned and classified by knowledge, relates not to being in situation as such, but to the ways in which language is able to distinguish identifiable particularities in that situation" (EE, 374). The subjectively unnameable enjoys roughly the same kind of subtractive distance from a truth that a truth enjoys with respect to the state of the situation in which it takes place.

We would do better to think of the unnameable as a kind of autopurification of the name, an ascesis of the name itself. If the subject connects, in the insignificance of a proper name, the implication of the event with the process of fidelity, "the unnameable is the proper of the proper. So singular that it does not even tolerate having a proper name. So singular in its singularity that it is the only thing not to have a proper name" (C, 186). In other words, the unnameable is the real of a truth itself; it is that which remains impossible for a truth. Every subjective "real indicates itself by a term, one single point, at which the power of a truth is interrupted . . . ; no nomination fits this term of the situation."[18] This is why "every regime of truth founds itself, as real, on its own unnameable [se fonde en réel sur son innommable propre]," and it is this real point that ensures that a truth "is *this* singular truth, and not the self-awareness of the Whole" (PM, 41–42). Love of the unnameable is thus still more true than a love for the generic itself: "However powerful a truth might be . . . , this power comes to fail on a single term, which in a single movement tips the all-powerful over into the vanity of power, and transports our love of the truth from its appearance, the love of the generic, to its essence, love of the unnameable. . . . For in matters of truth, it is only by enduring the test of its powerlessness that we find the ethic required for the adoption of its power" (C, 211).

We know from the preceding chapters that Badiou identifies the "unique unnameable" term in each of the four generic procedures as, respectively, sexual pleasure (in love), the community (in politics), language as such (in poetry), and consistency (in mathematics).[19] The case of mathematics is perhaps particularly striking. As Weyl reminds us, "Pure mathematics acknowledges but one condition for truth, and that an irremissible one, namely consistency."[20] But we must not make this condition itself the substance or object of truth. Mathematical truth can develop its internal consistency, step by logically deducible step, because mathematical "substance," so to speak—the pure multiplicity of what is counted—is entirely inconsistent. Given any infinite set, the excess of parts ($2^{\aleph_0}$) over elements ($\aleph_0$) is immeasurable. The "stuff" of mathematical infinity is thus "absolutely open, embedded [scellé] in the point of the impossible, thus of the real, which renders it inconsistent: that is, there cannot exist a set of all sets."[21]

As foundation of the inconsistent stuff or be-ing of a truth, the unnameable is testimony to a truth's fully axiomatic status. The communal or collective will, for instance, is the very "substance" of a political procedure, and for that reason, it is precisely what its subject cannot name or define. Again, language is the very substance of poetry, and consistency the very substance of mathematics, but a truth is precisely that process which conceives of its substance exclusively as process, never as object or referent. If what can be collected of a truth is accessible to ontology as a generic set, nevertheless the

---

analysis of this set *as a set* (as a collection) is secondary to the process: what a truth is, is essentially the active collecting of itself. The being of a truth is subordinate to its doing, and it is precisely the being of this doing, this doing that begins with an interruption of the very laws of being, that cannot be named. (This is why truth and being can never be said in one and the same discourse [EE, 391]). Thinking as collective is what a political subject does; it cannot at the same time suspend this doing so as to name or define it. The demonstration of what language can do (language as subtracted from the constraints of communication) is simply what poetry itself does, and its every naming is internal to this doing. Being what it does, the unnameable point of a subtractive truth is the necessary point of its own subtraction from itself.

It is the precise status of the unnameable that again distinguishes Badiou's ethics from the firmly antiphilosophical positions of Lacan's most influential disciple, Žižek. Like Badiou, Žižek acknowledges the "ultimately unnameable" status of a "Real act"[22]—not, however, as the foundation of a truth or the basis of its continuation, but simply as an indication of the ultimate truthlessness of human finitude itself. Žižek's unnameable turns out to be another name for death:

> The whole of Lacan's effort is precisely focused on those limit-experiences in which the subject finds himself confronted with the death drive at its purest, prior to its reversal into sublimation. . . . What "Death" stands for at its most radical is not merely the passing of earthly life, but the "night of the world," the self-withdrawal, the absolute contraction of subjectivity, the severing of its links with "reality"—*this* is the "wiping the slate clean" that opens up the domain of the symbolic New Beginning, of the emergence of the "New Harmony" sustained by a newly emerged Master-Signifier. Here, Lacan parts company with St Paul and Badiou. . . . (160, 154)

The remainder of Žižek's argument suggests that the strictly Lacanian alternative can culminate only in a radical obscurantism, a morbid fascination with the abject, inarticulable realm of the corpse as such—the "undead" that is Oedipus after his mutilation, or Antigone reduced to her "living death."[23] Žižek accepts this reduction without flinching: "Modern subjectivity emerges when the subject perceives himself as 'out of joint,' as excluded from the order of things, from the positive order of entities"; "for that reason, the ontic equivalent of the modern subject is inherently excremental. . . . There is no subjectivity without the reduction of the subject's positive-substantial being to a disposable 'piece of shit'" (157). What thus "remains beyond Badiou's reach," Žižek concludes, is "this domain 'beyond the Good,' in which a human being encounters the death drive as the utmost limit of human experience, and pays the price by undergoing a radical 'subjective destitution,' by being reduced to an excremental remainder."[24]

Badiou would no doubt plead guilty as charged. For the great virtue of his system, compared with Lacan's, is surely its separation of the merely ineffable, in-significant horror of death from the generic destitution demanded by any subjectivation. It is Badiou's achievement to have subtracted the operation of truth from any redemption of the abject, and to have made the distinction between living and unliving, between finite and infinite, a matter of absolute indifference. The emergence of "the undead-indestructible object, [of] Life deprived of support in the symbolic order,"[25] is simply incapable of provoking the slightest reaction from within either the domain of purely multiple being as being on the one hand, or the domain of an immortal subjectivization on the other.

In the Face of Evil: What Restrains the Truth?

If the unnameable is not unnameable in itself but only for the subject of a truth, it follows that the only force able to restrain a truth is its own subject. Though it is truth that induces a subject, it is the subject who regulates the operation of a truth.

We know that an event exposes the void of the situation, and "love of the unnameable" is nothing other than a love of the void as void, a willingness to think in the element of an empty inconsistency as such. What Badiou calls evil *(le Mal)* is always the effort to specify and fill out what is void in the situation. Or again, evil is the effort, internal to a subjective truth, to name the unnameable.

This can happen in one of two symmetrically opposite (and thus perhaps ultimately indistinguishable) ways. In the first case, it is evil "to consider the void, which is the very being of the situation, as something formless," to specify the void as something unformed, something monstrous or revolting that does not properly belong in the situation. It is evil to "empty" a particular part of the situation or to deny it form, that is, to attribute to it precisely the name of "unnameable" or "untouchable." Every true subject remembers that "to suture a situation to its pure multiple being, through the subject and by the void, is not, is never, to 'void' the situation."[26] But whereas all true politics acts as "guardian of the void," of "what is not counted in the situation" (NN, 200), an evil politics seeks to specify and eliminate precisely those outsiders who elude the count. The canonical example is the Nazi identification of the Jews as the void of the German situation, that is, the attribution of "Semitic" qualities to this void, or, since it amounts to the same thing, the voiding of the Jewish part of that situation. Nazism specifies the void as Jew, and itself as the "full" community (E, 64–65). Remember that belonging to a situation means that a multiple is counted or identified as one within the situation—without this identification's implying anything about what this multiple *is*, in its being. What any multiple is, is simply pure inconsistency. The evil specification of the void is thus a specification of the very "stuff" of that which belongs. The Nazi specification of Aryan and Jew concerns the substance of these elements. Jews are condemned by Nazism in their very being, rather than in their qualities, actions, opinions, loyalties, and so on. This is evil as the brutal antithesis of a truth.

In the second case, it is evil to monumentalize the void as such: this is evil as the sinister corruption of a truth. For although an event exposes the void of the situation and "undoes the appearance of plenitude" in the situation, no sooner has it done so than it fades away, leaving only its name in its place. The only truthful way of dealing with the void, in the reconstituted situation, is through fidelity to this new name. Nevertheless, there may "remain a nostalgia for the void itself, as it was summoned forth in the flash of the event, a tempting nostalgia for a void that would be full, of an inhabitable void, a perpetual ecstasy" (PM, 203–4). This is a temptation the subjects of truth must overcome at all costs. The temptation can take several forms. Whereas the place of truth must always be "the place of an absence, or a naked place, the mere taking place of a place," evil asserts the exceptional majesty of its place—the Third Reich, the Bastion of Socialism, the Land of Freedom and Democracy, etc. (PM, 78; cf. LS, 83–84). Whereas the true name of the event is always a variant of the *quelconque*, of the any-name-whatever, evil affirms "the sacred quality of the name."[27] And whereas every truth takes place as something unrepeatable, evil strives to repeat and control what is portrayed as the holy experience of the event. Since an event can only be named, since it cannot properly be remembered or narrated at all, it is always evil to commemorate the experience of the event in terms of "plenitude and the sacred."[28]

Heidegger is not the only philosopher to have succumbed to such temptations. Where Nietzsche affirms the vitality of life, Husserl the rigor of his science, and Pascal or Kierkegaard the intensity of their authentic experience, Badiou sees so many examples of a philosophical disaster, all driven by a substantialization of truth, by the "filling-in of the void that supports the exercise of Truth" (C, 64–70, 72). Though truths are resolutely opposed to the regime of opinion, they must not seek to abolish that regime by creating a situation in which only the truth might speak. The final stages of Mao's Cultural Revolution demonstrated the consequences of such an abolition

(E, 74). Even Plato lurches toward evil when, rather than refute the sophist, he eliminates him altogether. The ethics of philosophy itself requires us "to maintain the sophist as its adversary, to preserve the *polemos,* the dialectical conflict. The disastrous moment comes when philosophy declares that the sophist should not exist."[29] Disaster follows upon the total or exclusive imposition of a truth.

The logical relation between truth and evil is thus perfectly clear: first a truth, *then* the possibility of its corruption. Evil cannot be something radically other than the good that enables it. There is, in Badiou's philosophy, no place for a "radical Evil" in the neo-Kantian sense (i.e., some kind of innate, anthropologically constant propensity to evil). Evil is something that happens either to a truth procedure, as its corruption, or in a way that resembles a truth procedure, as its simulacrum. Evil, where it exists, can be only a "disturbed effect of the power of truth itself. . . ."[30] As Heidegger himself recognized, "untruth must derive from the essence of truth" and not the reverse.[31] Hitler's own advent, Badiou accepts, was "formally indistinguishable from an event—it is precisely this that led Heidegger astray."[32] Nazism must be taken seriously as a political (rather than simply an irrational or malevolent) sequence, as "a simulacrum of truth." And because it took place as the simulacrum of a true political sequence, Badiou refuses to accept the notion, suggested by Adorno and Lyotard, that Auschwitz marks a unique "interruption of thought." There is no evading the fact that Auschwitz was itself an expression of political thought, and must be confronted as such.[33]

Since evil is something that happens to a truth or in proximity to truth, there can be no fail-safe defense against evil that does not simultaneously foreclose the possibility of truth. Preoccupied with the catastrophic effects of an absolute Evil (Auschwitz, the Gulag, the Killing Fields), radical anti-philosophers from Adorno and Lyotard to Rancière and Lardreau have made a virtue of the political self-emasculation of philosophy. No assertion of principle is acceptable, it seems, if it does not defer, suspend, or otherwise subvert the very mechanics of assertion or judgment. Confronted with the many evils of this most violent century, Badiou refuses to go along with the consequent renunciation of organized politics *tout court.* In each case, he argues, it was "not politics that turned against itself as barbarism, but rather the end [or corruption] of a given political sequence that opened the way for the state to pursue a course of pure banditry."[34] It is essential that each sequence be considered as such, in its complexity and essential "discontinuity," rather than explained by a more or less instinctive reference to a general diagnosis (communism, totalitarianism, fundamentalism, ethnic hatred, tribalism, and so on).[35] It is essential that philosophy provide reasoned grounds for the risk of truth.

Badiou's Ethics

Since evil is the determination to impose the total power of a truth, to name everything in its situation, "the ethics of a truth derive entirely from a sort of restraint *[retenue]* with respect to its powers."[36] The truth cannot and must not try to say everything. It must content itself with a form of what Mallarmé called "restrained action" *(l'action restreinte)*. Only such restraint allows it to persevere in its forever ongoing self-elaboration (PM, 56; SP, 99).

The principal inspiration here is again Lacan. His famous command, "Do not give up on your desire *[ne pas céder sur son désir]*,"[37] the essential principle of an ethics of psychoanalysis, provides Badiou with the closest contemporary approximation of an ethics of truth in general. To be thus faithful to the peculiarity of your desire first requires "a radical repudiation of a certain ideal of the good" (Lacan, S7, 270/230), that is, the repudiation of all consensual social norms (happiness, pleasure, health, etc.) in favor of an essentially asocial, essentially traumatic exception. Lacanian ethics is first and foremost the ethics of a properly superhuman tenacity: examples from the Lacanian pantheon include Antigone in her cave, Oedipus in his pursuit of the truth, Thomas More in his fidelity to Catholicism, and Geronimo in his refusal to yield to an inevitable defeat.[38] The pursuit of our desire cares nothing for our happiness. Beckett's stubborn persistence ("I can't go on, I will go on") is for Badiou exemplary of an ethics of perseverance.[39]

Building on Lacan's inspiration and Beckett's example, Badiou's ethical maxim is simply "Keep going!" or "Continue!" regardless of the circumstances or cost[40]: "Every ethics centers on the negation of the negation, on not denying [the event]," that is, on "holding to the present" of its consequences (TA, 14.5.97). But whatever your truth, Badiou adds, one should not go all the way. One should continue in such a way as to be able to continue to continue. And since evil is always an interruption or perversion of the truth, ethics enables this continuation by strengthening a subject's resistance to evil. To the risk of evil as betrayal, or the renunciation of a difficult fidelity, ethics opposes courage and endurance ("Do not give up on the truth"). To the risk of evil as delusion, or the confusion of a genuine event with its false simulacrum, ethics opposes a sense of discernment ("Do not confuse the true and the false"). To the risk of evil as terror, or the effort to impose the unqualified power of a truth, ethics opposes the ancient virtues of moderation and restraint ("Resist the idea of total or 'objective' truth") (E, 77).

There can be no general principle of human rights, therefore, for the simple reason that what is universally human is always rooted in particular truths, particular configurations of active thought—configurations whose continuation may well require the "disqualification" if not the "sacrifice" of certain individual humans.[41] Every subject is constituted as an exception to prevailing conceptions of natural or human rights, and ethics is simply what helps a subject remain a subject. To be in love, to be a revolutionary, to be a truly creative artist or scientist, is in each case to be indifferent to "what most people think"; what inspires these subjects to continue their elaboration of a truth and defend this truth from corruption varies, in each case, with the truth in question. Though not necessarily ascetic—the imperative to continue is as much an imperative of power and joy as it is of austerity and faith—the ethics of truth is thus as "asocial" as the truth itself: "The ethic of a truth is absolutely opposed to opinion" (E, 48), just as it is indifferent to the comfort, satisfaction, and even the life of the individual who affirms it. Subjectivation always begins with fear and loss—the loss of identity, of approval, of security, of "the little you have...." Neither social nor moral nor psychological nor biological, ethics turns always on one and only one question: "How will I, as someone, continue to exceed my own being?... Which might also be said as: How will I continue to think?" (E, 45; cf. LS, 100).

Back to Kant?

The essential difference between Badiou's ethics and Kant's categorical imperative should now be clear enough. As I suggested in chapter 6, there are indeed strong grounds for comparison here. Like Badiou, Kant abstracts questions of ethics from all "sensibility," and, also like Badiou, he posits the universal as the sole legitimate dimension for subjective action.[42] Insofar as Badiou's approach is one that acknowledges the ability of everyone to become subject, it is consistent with Kant's refusal to treat people as means rather than ends. It was Kant who first evacuated the ethical command of any substantial content, so as to ground ethical fidelity in nothing other than the subject's own prescription. "The unique strength of Kant's ethics," as Žižek explains, "lies in this very formal indeterminacy: moral Law does not tell me what my duty is, it merely tells me that I should accomplish my duty. That is to say, it is not possible to derive the concrete norms I have to follow in my specific situation from the moral Law itself—which means that the subject himself has to assume the responsibility of 'translating' the abstract injunction of the moral Law into a series of concrete obligations.... The only guarantor of the universality of positive moral norms is the subject's own contingent act of performatively assuming these norms."[43] Kant's very procedure—the evacuation of all heteronomous interests and motives, the suspension of all references to psychology and utility, the refusal of any calculation required to obtain happiness or welfare[44]—bears some resemblance to Badiou's. What remains paramount for both is a specifically subjective (and explicitly "infinite") power, the force of our will. When Kant says, "I ought never to act except in such a way that I could also will that my maxim should become a universal law" (402), the active willing is an essential component of the criterion (424). Moreover, Badiou is no less incapable than Kant of providing an "objective" explanation of the noumenal basis of this subjective capacity (i.e., a definition or description of what the subjective axiom prescribes). We might say that from the Kantian perspective, ethics must accept as its own unnameable "the subjective impossibility of *explaining* the freedom of the will" (459–60).

However significant this rapprochement might seem, what sets Badiou's ethics clearly apart from Kant's is his unwavering insistence on the singular and exceptional character of every ethical imperative. What Badiou objects to in Kant is not, of course, the association of truth with an infinite reality "independent of animality . . . and the whole world of sense," but the association of this reality with a categorical, transcendental normality. Kant grounds the authority of the moral law in the *fact* of freedom and the faculty of reason.[45] Having banished the transcendent One from his ontology, Kant resurrects it in his morality.[46] By contrast, Badiou argues that only ontological infinity is "normal"; every subjective (i.e., ethical) infinity is an exception to the rules, including moral rules. Badiou's ethics is incommensurable with the whole Kantian register of legality, duty, obligation, and conformity. Nothing is less typical of Badiou's ethics than a prescription to act "for the sake of the law" as such,[47] and nothing is more foreign to his notion of the subject than the idea of a will determined by purely a priori principles.

At least three questions might be asked of Badiou's ethics. The first concerns the relative contingency of ethical deliberation. In his discussion of the *Social Contract*, Badiou notes that Rousseau was never able to resolve the question of "how the generic character of a political sequence can endure should it fail to solicit unanimity" (EE, 385). However fragmentary its institutional base, his own post-Party conception of politics cannot avoid a version of the same problem. If anything resembling "universal suffrage" or majority rule is to be excluded from the field of true politics (since the discernment of countable opinions runs counter to the indiscernible universality of the general will [386–88]), how exactly are profound or genuine disagreements to be decided? Insistence that "the subject is not consciousness of the truth," that no (finite) subjects can know or direct the (infinite) truth that sustains them (EE, 435), does not so much resolve this problem as shift it toward the essentially nonnegotiable domain of conviction or "confidence." To be sure, there can be no justification for dogmatic ownership of a truth. But since it is undertaken in the absence of any falsifying or verifying reference to a shared knowledge, participation in a truth procedure does not itself offer any clear indication of how we are to cope with the conflict of rival configurations of confidence.

Precisely because engagement in truth is always an axiomatic intervention, Badiou's approach excludes any merely moral or critical distance (in which one might ask, "What *should* I do?"). Nevertheless, Badiou naturally wants to avoid a simply dictatorial model of subjective engagement, however logical its dictation. His response is to accept *some* sort of deliberative procedure, while insisting that such a procedure arises in each case as fully internal to its situation:

> As a general rule, every generic procedure is in reality a process that can perfectly well be deliberative, as long as we understand that it invents its rule of deliberation at the same time as it invents itself. It is not constrained by a pre-established norm that follows from the rule of deliberation. You only have to look at how the rule of deliberation in different organisations, in different political sequences, and in different political modes, is entirely variable. . . . Every time a plurality of individuals, a plurality of human subjects, is engaged in a process of truth, the construction of this process induces the construction of a deliberative and collective figure of this production, which is itself variable.[48]

But the whole question is precisely whether such deliberation is variable, in the sense of so many variations on some kind of minimally invariant process, or forever different, in the sense of so many inventions ex nihilo, each one literally peculiar to a given procedure. This is where Badiou might have to engage with Habermas's elaboration of a "quasi-transcendental" schema of communicative rationality—the minimum upon which we must all agree, so as to be able to disagree (in any particular case). Where exactly are we to draw the line between the sort of strictly subjective deliberation that is internal to the elaboration of a truth, and a merely external or ideological opposition? Both of Badiou's preferred examples, Leninist and Jacobin, testify to the uncertainty of such a line as much as they illustrate an inventive approach to the resolution of differences.[49] Moreover, though we know that truth "induces a subject" and not the reverse (E, 39; EE, 444), we know, too, that only the subject is capable of restraining truth. By introducing subjects capable of restraining the truth that induces them, does not Badiou effectively concede some sort of ethical supervision of the truth?[50]

My second question concerns Badiou's essentially instrumental understanding of violence. His strict separation of true subjects from merely objective "individuals" allows him to consider violence as essentially external to any truth process, and there is certainly a compelling strategic case to be made for this position. But how exactly then are we to acknowledge the potential of any individual to become a subject? What precise circumstances justify the suppression of this potential? For it might well be argued that the last century, driven by that "passion for the real" which by Badiou's own admission excludes the luxuries of critical distance or reserve, demonstrated more than once the inadequacy of an ethics based on an appreciation of these very luxuries. It might be more consistent, and arguably more courageous, to insist that the true break with our established order will come, not through recourse to alternative forms of violence, but with the organized, uncompromising imposition of a radical nonviolence. Only a precisely axiomatic commitment to nonviolence offers any hope of a lasting break in the futile recycling of violences. Only such a principled commitment can both respond to the violent re-presentation of the state and, once this re-presentation has been suspended, block the creation or reassertion of new forms of violence.

In the absence of such a commitment, the appeal to philosophical "restraint" is ultimately unconvincing. We know that "the ethics of a truth is absolutely opposed to opinion" and communication, but at the same time "we must communicate, we must have our opinions" (E, 48, 75). It is only by preserving the very opinions it penetrates that a truth avoids its disastrous totalization. But what is the precise mechanism of this preservation? This gives rise to my third question. If the only relation between truth and knowledge is one of subtraction, how can the one preserve the other? How are we to coordinate the imperative to maintain this relation—to maintain the sophist, maintain opinions, maintain the dialogue—with that more insistent imperative, prescribed by every generic procedure, to act in the singular absence of relation, to pursue a radical *déliaison?* If "philosophy ultimately has no relation other than to itself,"[51] if philosophy is conditioned by nothing other than truth, it is difficult to see how it might regulate its relations with its nonphilosophical counterpart, be it sophist, citizen, or opinion.

In the end, the question of ethics turns on the preservation of a viable relationship *between* knowledge and truth, opinion and subject—but it is precisely this relationship that Badiou's philosophy has yet to express in other than mainly subtractive terms.

chapter 13

Generic or Specific?

In one of his recent books Badiou develops a comparison that may serve to illustrate the central dilemma of his philosophy. The comparison is between Mallarmé's poem *Un Coup de dés* and a pre-Islamic Arabian ode by Labîd ben Rabi'a, whose title translates as *The desert and its code.*[1] In the French poem, an anonymous Master hesitates to throw the dice as he sinks slowly under the surface of the sea; reality dissolves, nothing takes place, but then suddenly, mysteriously, at the very moment of absolute dissolution, there appears the flashing glimpse of a constellation in the night sky, portent of a truth on the horizon of our awareness. The Arabic poem begins with an evocation of the empty desert. Driven on by nostalgia for ancestral authority, it culminates in a celebration of the wise and virtuous leader, the glorification of a lawful mastery adequate to the austerity of nomadic life (PM, 76–77).

Badiou's comparison dwells on the antithetical figures of mastery presented by each poet. In Mallarmé's poem, the master is sacrificed to the void of a more than human truth, and this sacrifice is the price paid for its own poetic preservation. In the poem of Labîd ben Rabi'a, the master emerges as triumphant over the void of his surroundings, and the poem's affirmation of this triumph is conditioned by its own subordination to this authority. Such is, Badiou suggests, the impossible choice forced upon us by our modernity itself: either the inhuman anonymity of a socioscientific or technical truth, indifferent to and transcendent of all personal mastery (this Badiou associates with the realm of capitalist pseudo-democracy, where the desacralization of political leaders goes hand in hand with a blind obedience to the imperatives of capital and technology); or, as the only apparent alternative, the constitution of an authoritarian exception to this regime, held together by collective veneration of a charismatic leader and reinforced more or less directly by terror (this Badiou associates with Stalin).

Badiou's way out of this impasse is to go back a step, "toward what Mallarmé and the pre-Islamic ode have in common, namely, the desert, the ocean, the naked place, the void. We have to recompose for our time a thought of truth that is articulated on [sur] the void without passing through the figure of the master" (PM, 87). Such is certainly the task that Badiou has set for his own project, along each of the ramified lines of enquiry he has pursued. It is the peculiar orientation of his project from and toward the void that I want to explore in more systematic detail here. It is this orientation that ensures the alignment of Badiou's thought along paths of subtraction rather than (liberal-democratic) communication on the one hand or (authoritarian) destruction on the other. Only the void, Badiou insists, can provide the medium of a collective affirmation that cannot be mastered, an unmasterable subjective equality that resists any transcendent alignment (SP, 63–64). Only the void provides the basis for that radically ungovernable assembling of indifferent particularities accomplished by a truth procedure. It is the orientation of Badiou's project toward the void, I think, that will eventually come to be seen as its most fundamental, most distinctive, most rigorous—and no doubt most enigmatic—aspect.

Let's review the basic logic at issue here. That every truth is articulated from a void does not mean that truths are empty, pure and simple.[2] Badiou's approach is firmly situation specific. The void is that particular situation's "suture" to the inconsistency of being. The void is pure inconsistency according to a situation, or again, the void is all that can be presented, in a situation, of pure inconsistent being as such (EE, 68–69). And in every situation other than the strictly ontological situation—in every situation, that is, that is at least partly substantial, material, or historical—the void of that situation is never emptiness pure and simple. As situated, the void has an edge and a name. The edge of the void (or evental site) is composed of elements that its particular situation cannot discern or distinguish. A situation, remember, is made up of an infinity of different and mutually indifferent elements. A situation is a collection of pure singularities, each of which belongs to the situation "on its own terms," without any reference to any of the other elements. But in every situation, the pure anarchy of this collection is overlaid with and dominated by the distinguishing, organizing mechanisms of the state of the situation. The state is what classifies and separates the elements of its situation, arranges them into groups, distributes them in an order that suits the logic of domination prevalent in that situation. Located at the edge of its void, the eventual site is that element which, having no elements that the situation can discern (no elements in common with the situation), appears empty within the situation, and consequently cannot be grouped or arranged with other elements. There is no way of knowing "what" would be thus grouped. The void's edge is composed of elements that do not relate to the rest of the situation, and that thus remain indiscernible to that situation. The void is not so much verifiably "empty" as demonstrably impervious to or devoid of *relations*. Universally included in its every part, the void of a situation is bordered, or "edged," by a place that is impervious to the relational mechanisms devised by its state—and thus impervious to relationality *tout court*, since the elements of a situation, subtracted from the mechanisms of the state, exist independently of interelemental relations, as a purely disordered collection of singularities. In short, the void is nonrelational and without place; it is nothing yet is included in all things; it is located nowhere yet scattered everywhere.

What a truth then assembles, from the bias of the void, is a mass of unrelated singularities, a collection of "extreme particularity." Since the relational consistency of a situation is simply an illusion maintained by its state, a truth breaks this illusion down so as to "deploy all that the multiple presents, on the edge of the void, in the way of affirmative singularity" (AM, 83). By investigating these singularities with respect to an event that once exposed, for an instant, the void of a situation, a truth assembles its elements solely in terms of their pure being in situation. A truth considers these elements solely insofar as they are present in the situation. The consequent emergence of a set of extreme particularity or pure multiplicity, whose sole organizing principle is the haphazard series of investigations maintained by the subjects of a truth procedure, is properly dubbed "generic, because, if we want to describe it, we will simply say that its elements *are*," in the absence of all differentiating relations (EE, 373). To consider elements in truth is the only way of considering them that is not mediated by the prevailing mechanisms of distinction, relation, or representation that define the state of the situation. In each case, the redemptive force of a truth thus "depends on separation and isolation," operations that deliver the lacunary multiple from the "tenacious illusion of relation and rapport" (C, 128–29). Strictly speaking, this rule applies as much to enthusiastic relations of solidarity and reciprocity as it does to enforced relations of supervision or domination.[3] As we have seen, the goal of truth is always a self-sufficient "purity," where "purity is the composition of an Idea such that it is no longer retained in any relation *[lien]*"

(C, 120). True thought is itself nothing other than "thought without rapport [rapport], thought that relates [rapporte] nothing, that puts nothing in rapport" (PM, 105).

That every truth is "articulated from the void" means, in short, that the articulation of truth is subtracted from relationality. The aim of this penultimate chapter of my book is to consider the implications of this subtraction in a more systematic manner than the constraints of the preceding exposition have allowed, as much at their ontological roots as in their epistemological, political, and cultural consequences. The reader already knows that I think the question of relation is the most significant question that Badiou's philosophy has to answer. As we shall see in the next and final chapter, Badiou has begun to put together the pieces of a detailed response. But, as things stand, he has yet to address in fully convincing detail a whole cluster of broadly relational issues, ranging from the nature of relations between situations to the nature of relations between subjects, or between truths, or between knowledges and truths. Many of the more intransigent problems raised by these relations are effectively dismissed in advance by the relatively simplistic configuration of the two decisive operations that dominate Badiou's system: state-driven operations of inclusion or classification, and truth-driven operations of separation or subtraction. Badiou's determined resistance to any broadly dialectical articulation of the relation between knowledge and truth or between subject and object (or indeed between subject and subject) automatically blocks any productive exploration of relationality, that is, an exploration that is able to conceive of relations in terms more nuanced than those of inclusion or subtraction, on the one hand, or (in Badiou's most recent work) of mathematical equivalence (=), nonequivalence (≠), and order (> or <), on the other.[4]

I begin this chapter with a return to Badiou's antirelational ontology and its implications for his understanding of knowledge and opinion. I then review the consequences of his refusal of a relation between politics and economics in the first place, and between truth and culture in the second place, before ending the chapter with an assessment of the degree to which some of the components of Badiou's philosophy might be considered singular or nonrelational in an approximately "absolutist" sense.

At each point, the alternative to Badiou's strictly generic conception of things is a more properly *specific* understanding of individuals and situations as conditioned by the relations that both enable and constrain their existence. In order to develop this alternative, it is essential to distinguish scrupulously between the specific and what might be called the specified (Badiou's "objectified").[5] Actors are specific to a situation even though their actions are not specified by it, just as a historical account is specific to the facts it describes even though its assessment is not specified by them. The specific is a purely relational subjective domain. The specified, by contrast, is defined by positive, intrinsic characteristics or essences (physical, cultural, personal, and so on). The specified is a matter of inherited "instincts" as much as of acquired habits. We might say that the most general effort of philosophy or critique should be to move from the specified to the specific—without succumbing to the temptations of the purely singular. Badiou certainly provides a most compelling critique of the specified. But he has—at least thus far—inadequate means of distinguishing specified from specific. The result, in my view, is an ultimately unconvincing theoretical basis for his celebration of an "extreme particularity" as such.

The Ontological Suspension of Relation

As Badiou reminds us, "It is when you decide what exists that you tie your thought to being" (CT, 54). By tying the nature of existence to the axioms of set theory, Badiou has decided, very simply, that relations between elements or between situations do not exist. Badiou's ontology recognizes no constitutive role for relationality in the broadest sense. The multiples governed by set theory are prescribed (by the axiom of replacement) to be mutually substitutable, that is, "specifically indistinguishable."[6] It is a cardinal point of ontological principle that "the true infinity of being, although it is related [se rapporte] to the multiple, is not caught up in relations [liens] of calculation, and does not tolerate relation [le rapport]" (C, 128). Within this presumed infinity, existence is a function of belonging alone: an element exists (in a set) if and only if it is counted as one by the structure of that set. As regards what Badiou calls its being as being, the fact that any such one may be one among others is of no consequence. This for two reasons. First, because the founding axiom of extensionality defines a set in terms of its elements alone, regardless of the relations that might obtain among them. The only sorts of differences between sets that Badiou is willing to recognize are punctual rather than global or qualitative. The second reason, of course, is that all of the elements generated by set theory are founded directly on the empty set. Set theory "pulls from the sole void a Universe" (CT, 74), and if we are clearly obliged to recognize the physical reality of "'atoms,' these are not, as the materialists of Antiquity believed, a second principle of being, i.e., the one after the void, but compositions of the void itself" (EE, 71). We know that according to Badiou, "The void, rigorously (mathematically) subsumed under a concept, is precisely what sustains the heterogeneously existent" and grounds its exclusively actual univocity.[7] There is thus nothing "in" the elements that might form the basis of some kind of relationship between them.

Elements are as indifferent to each other as are different slices of empty space. Or—and it is the same thing—they are so different from each other as to preclude any sort of merely relative similarity or continuity: "*In the situation* (let's call it: the world) . . . there are *only* differences" (SP, 105, my emphasis). And between situations, it seems, there can be nothing but more of the same discontinuity.[8]

The compelling force of Badiou's position here speaks for itself. But there are, it seems to me, three general sorts of questions that need to be asked of this antirelational ontology, all of which concern, one way or another, its deliberate abstraction. First of all, by separating so decisively the ontological from the material or the physical, Badiou introduces a new dualism at the heart of his radically univocal arrangement. That mathematics provides the only rigorous means of describing the physical is uncontroversial. But short of endorsing a doctrine of creation ex nihilo, the precise derivation of the heterogeneously existent from the mathematically void remains something of a mystery (or, at the very least, simply "contingent"). I have already quoted (in chapter 3) Badiou's disclaimer, early in *L'Etre et l'événement:* "Mine is a thesis about discourse, not about the world. It affirms that mathematics, in all their historical development, declare what is sayable of being as being."[9] We know that this thesis serves to preserve the dimension of thought—the thought of ontology as much as the thought of intervention and fidelity—from any mediation through the object. It is not clear, however, that a radical (and materialist) univocity can survive this dualism. Nor is it clear just what sort of difference the vague concept of "world" can oppose to the discourse of ontology, given that, "like Lacan, [Badiou is] inclined to think that the idea of the world is itself in the final analysis a phantasy."[10] Since Badiou's system is explicitly designed to equate being and what can be thought of being, it is hard to know what sort of authority his distinction of discourse and world might have, ultimately, other than that of illusion pure and simple. For example, if "infinite alterity is quite simply everything there is"—such that "there is as much difference between a Chinese peasant and a young Norwegian professional as between myself and anybody at all, including myself" (E, 26)—this assertion is clearly not justified by an exploration of the "world" but presumed as a consequence of his founding axioms. It is this presumption that lends Badiou's work both its trenchant, exhilarating certainty, and its troubling inconsistency: having denied that "impure" being is mathematical, he proceeds as if it was. Since a mathematical ontology cannot itself justify this move, Badiou will need to provide other kinds of argument in order to justify this "as if."

Just how inclusive, in any case, can this mathematized materialism be?

This is my second question. The content of particular nonontological situations is clearly not to be derived from mathematics itself. Since ontology is itself a situation, "any kind of transcendental deduction of situations from the intelligible schema of being as being is obviously impossible."[11] What is singular about the ontological situation is that it prescribes the rules that describe situational form itself, that is, the form of all situations qua situations. However, even if we suppose that indifferent matter, abstracted from all qualities and predicates, does indeed conform to the mathematical prescription of existence—if only because existence itself is not a predicate—it clearly does not follow that the qualities thus abstracted conform, themselves, to this mathematical prescription. It is not just the "soft," qualitative aspects of experience, the things that make up what Davis and Hersh call the "inner world of human life," that seem resistant to mathematization.[12] There is good reason to suppose, for example, that biological (let alone social, cultural, or psychological) systems are irreducible, in their most *elementary* materiality, to the basic principles of set theory—in particular the principle of extensionality. In what precise sense is the being of even the most rudimentary organism (or cell, or organelle) abstractable from its environment and relations with other organisms?

To put this point another way, since we know that the axiomatic foundations of modern mathematics begin with the suspension of all reference to extramathematical forms of intuition and experience, is it possible to defend both a fully axiomatic orientation and a wholly univocal conception of being? If not, Badiou's ontology cannot, from within its axioms, provide a compelling answer to Heidegger's quintessentially Romantic question: "Is the manifest character of what *is* exhausted by what is demonstrable?"[13]

Finally, does the sole operation recognized in this nonrelational conception of being—the operation of belonging ($\in$)—allow us to explain rather than simply redescribe the way different situations are structured, and consequently differentiated? Remember that the "structure" of a situation (the rules by which certain elements are presented in that situation) is determined solely by the elements that belong to it, according to an extensional logic designed to refute the dialectical truism that the whole is more than the sum of its parts. The way these elements are then classified and re-presented, the "metastructure" of the situation, is of course the business of the state of the situation and the knowledges it has at its disposal.[14] In the strict ontological situation, however, "both the notion of set and the notion of membership are taken as primitive (i.e., unanalyzed and undefined),"[15] and it is not clear in what precise sense an unanalyzable term can structure something else. It is no accident that a leading philosopher of mathematics presents the concept of set as "completely structure free,"[16] or that one of the great authorities on Cantorian set theory concludes that a fully extensional approach is directly at odds with any "structuring" or "unifying" conception of set.[17]

In nonontological situations, the mechanics of belonging presumably vary from situation to situation, but Badiou generally pays little attention to these mechanisms. If a situation or set is nothing other than the "collection" or "counting for one of its elements," do analogies with the simple process of counting elements help us to understand the sorts of structuring at work in the differentiation of even very simple material or social situations, say? Consider again the "extraordinarily vague" notion of a situation. Badiou says that its elements may include "words, gestures, acts of violence, silences, expressions, comings together, corpuscles, stars, etc."[18] But what distinguishes one word or gesture from another in the first place? Certainly not the situation itself: if belonging is our only ontological verb, we must stick to a purely combinatorial rather than properly structuring notion of situation, that is, we must equate "situation" with "collection" pure and simple, and leave the problem of how the elements thus collected are themselves structured or differentiated aside. A set-theoretic situation collects or selects a particular arrangement from among "already" distinct elements.[19] On the other hand, to introduce another ontological action would be to violate the strict univocity of Badiou's set-theoretical approach, and with it the generic homogeneity of being as being.

The alternative is indeed to accept an ultimately equivocal notion of ontological inconsistency or infinity, and with it a constituent role for relation at the heart of being—including a role for relation *between* being and thought. Being embodies us before we found being on the empty set, and it is because we are embodied that we must abstract quality and matter before we can conceive of mathematics and the void. If Badiou would proclaim mathematics to be ontologically primary, this proclamation is itself epistemologically secondary. Where Badiou says things exist in their extreme and isolated particularity and accede to truth in their subtraction from relation, I would argue that nothing exists outside of its relations with other beings. Relation is the true medium of being as being. Relations should be recognized as co-implied with their terms, at the same level of ontological primacy. There is no more actual independence "before" relation than there can be a genuine autonomy after subtraction from relation. A relational perspective, in other words, cannot accept the strict distinction of consistent from inconsistent multiplicity: how we are structured is not indifferent to what we are, and the latter cannot be sustainably characterized in terms of pure indetermination or abstract freedom.

Subtracting Society

Like his friend Sylvain Lazarus, Badiou rejects the very category of "society," and with it every reference to a social "'totality,' 'world,' or 'historical world.'"[20] Why? Because the concept of society—in particular the variant known as "civil society"—articulates the subjective and the objective together, as components of a single dialectic. Society implies some sort of interconnection of "politics and History, the subjective and the state." And "social analysis" is nothing other than an attempt to relate the subjective and the objective through the mediation of something like class, disposition, behavior, consciousness, representation, or mentality.[21] To dwell on the forms of such mediation is by Badiou's criteria simply to depoliticize the situation in advance.

In his insistence upon an exclusively universal, exclusively subjective commitment, Badiou preserves the militant integrity of a vanguard interventionism in an age otherwise remarkable for its cynicism, defeatism, and managerial pessimism. He does so, however, by reinforcing a debatable line between "true" political action and the systematic or "administrative" engagement with irreducibly structural forms of injustice and exploitation, by which I mean precisely the sorts of issues generally grouped under the label of "social" work—poverty reduction and the provision of housing, welfare, education, public services, and so on. It is one thing to recognize that these two forms of engagement never amount to the same thing and cannot be analyzed in the same way; it is something else to insist upon the strict subtraction of the former from the latter. Progressive social institutions (schools, hospitals, trade unions, and so on) have a direct impact on the environment in which any political movement takes place and are themselves surely among the most valuable—and often most acutely contested—achievements of popular mobilization. In our contemporary situation, the very existence of public services has become an irreducibly political question.

Deprived of any reference to social mediation, moreover, Badiou's emancipatory project simply confronts an inflated model of the state as its sole and exclusive adversary. Since there is nothing between subject and state, so on issues ranging from poverty and unemployment to chauvinist bigotry, "the state is responsible."[22] End of discussion. Badiou lacks, in other words, a developed notion of hegemony, as proposed by Gramsci and as pursued, in different ways, by Raymond Williams and Ernesto Laclau. He also lacks, for the same reason, a nuanced appreciation of the technologies of power in Foucault's sense, understood as those productive, locally effective procedures (governing individuation, production, reproduction, punishment, education, etc.) that enable the consolidation of centralized power as their effect.

Badiou might no doubt argue that his concept of the state of the situation is sufficiently broad to include what Gramsci and Foucault analyze in terms of hegemony and power, but it is not obvious that reference to a single term helps account for the variety of mechanisms at issue.

Consider the relation of nation and state. We know that Badiou conceives of the only legitimate state as one expressly designated for all, open to people from everywhere. However we define a nation, it must not be through the distinction of insiders and outsiders. It is certainly true that "any state that founds itself on ethnic or communal characteristics is in effect a state of civil tensions and war."[23] The problem, then, is how, with the operation of the state as our sole explanatory principle, to account for the particularity of France, say, as a country among others. We clearly cannot invoke some sort of intrinsically specified Frenchness. But Badiou and *La Distance politique* are not quite prepared to abandon the concept of a national specificity altogether: "What constitutes unity among the people who live in the same country is neither culture, nor religion, nor customs, which are most often varied. It is common values. These values are formed through school, the workplace, and as far as it goes, the army. We can add today that, whatever one thinks about it, they are also formed through television, consumption, and sport."[24] Many readers are likely to find this distinction of "common values" from "culture" unconvincing.

What is missing, again, is an account of national identities in terms of their constituent relations. Cultural nationalism is one thing when it expresses the relation of a dominant power to those it dominates, and quite another thing when it expresses the opposite relation. Badiou would no doubt agree that when or if national values or forms are worth defending it is not because of their intrinsic merit but because their defense is part of a universalizable struggle for justice—for example, against an invasive or oppressive force, against divisive particularisms or special interests, and so on. But his strictly asocial and acultural conception of politics prevents him from acknowledging that, under the constraints of such a struggle, a strictly subtractive approach to cultural or national predicates may not always work in this universal interest. "What do identitarian and communitarian categories," Badiou asks, "have to do with the procedures of truth, for example political procedures?" His answer is categorical: "These categories must be withdrawn *[absentées]* from the process."[25] Badiou's antirelational orientation obliges the prescription of a general principle where a strategic flexibility would be more appropriate. As Fanon and Cabral remind us, it may be that a beleaguered national cause must draw on and reinforce its "particular" cultural integrity if it is even to become able to develop a genuinely interactive relationship with other nations.[26] Those fighting for indigenous or aboriginal empowerment in places like Australia and the Americas might make a similar point. Can the "communitarian categories" of such situations simply be withdrawn, without fundamentally changing their very structure? In what sense, indeed, can some of these categories be called communitarian at all? Do they not rather appeal to a different kind of universality, to an alternative conception of the generic place of humanity—albeit a universality that remains irreducibly specific to certain distinct ways of life?[27]

Such questions point directly to the problematic universality of philosophy itself. Badiou accepts, today, that the kind of role philosophy plays in identifying truths and demonstrating their compatibility is "still open."[28] But what is clear is that its four conditions "must all be fully met if philosophy is to exist," and it follows as a matter of course that philosophy "doesn't exist in all historical configurations."[29] The absence of mathematics alone would seem to condemn entire cultures to a prephilosophical untruth. Indeed, since it is only subjectivation through truth that allows us to transcend the merely animal "substratum" of our existence, might Badiou's conception of philosophy not imply that certain cultures are rather more animal than others? The evidence of a long and vigorous debate as to the status of African philosophy, to take only one of several obvious examples, demonstrates that it can be as difficult to draw a firm line between culture and philosophy as it is to preserve the more or less self-sufficient "immanence" of a situation.[30]

Subtracting Economics

We know that any genuine political sequence must, as Badiou prescribes it, take place at a principled distance from the economy. The whole effort of L'Organisation Politique (OP), in its prescription of a new figure of the worker, is to "distinguish, isolate, in some sense, a politics from the demands of the economy, the laws of capital." This means, very concretely, refusing to accept a merely economic justification for the sorts of policies now associated with commercial "flexibility" (layoffs, unpredictable schedules, reduced time for meals and breaks, etc.): "It is not a matter of the needs or constraints of how the factory works (as an objectivity prescribed by the imperatives of capital or the economy or 'competition') but of a political prescription made upon how the factory works."[31] This is not to say that Badiou denies the fact of global economic homogenization. Simply, he maintains that only a purely political campaign can offer any genuine resistance to economic exploitation. After Marx, after Lenin, his question remains: "What kind of politics is *really* heterogeneous to what capital demands?"[32]

Badiou's answer to this question is a politics based on prescriptive principles, articulated by small, tightly knit groups of workers *(Noyaux)* independent of any large-scale institutional support, be it political party or trade union. Adamant opposition to unionization has been one of the constants of Badiou's political career, from his uncompromising early Leninism to the polemics of *La Distance politique:*

> If the unions direct things, the workers will be betrayed.[33]

> The unions have always been against the figure of the worker . . . , encircling and repressing it each time it appears.[34]

> The slightest workers' action always exists at principled distance from the union. Since 1968, it has become obvious that a strong factory presence of the CGT [Confédération Générale du Travail] and a constituted figure of the worker are mutually exclusive propositions.[35]

The unions, according to the OP (in line here with a long tradition of Leninist criticism), are nothing but the lackeys of the capitalist state. Unions are "statelike organizations within factories."[36] They seek only their own institutional expansion, and offer only an improved form of integration into the established order of things. What does the OP offer in their place? Their "politics is not that of strikes. . . . The *Noyaux* believe that we should create small, closely united groups of workers in the workplace, that the bosses and unions cannot penetrate, and that these groups should be constituted directly through the political discussions proposed by the *Noyaux*." If a problem should arise, they say, "we stop working" and talk directly with the employer.[37] Just how effective these tactics are likely to prove against a fully "flexible" employer like Ford or General Motors is a question I leave to the reader's own judgment.

Another question, however, is unavoidable: what exactly is the OP after, that unions cannot provide? To date, their main factory prescriptions include fair compensation packages when a plant closes, better job security, more regular schedules, better salaries and working conditions, more time for relaxation during the working day, better support for the unemployed. All of these could have been drawn from any number of trade union campaigns. *La Distance politique* derides the unions for saying to the workers, "If you are with us, we will work to make sure that the state protects you," your salaries and the length of your working day—but now the OP, at least in its post-Maoist mode, seeks to prescribe the state to do very much the same thing.[38] The OP makes much of its refusal of broad institutional power. Nevertheless, its aim, naturally, is to "extend the politics of the *Noyaux*" in the factories.[39] Should this extension succeed, it will be interesting to see how it avoids recourse to the sorts of institutional backup that most unions have found essential to the maintenance and coordination of large campaigns. The main difference between OP and union, in short, now seems to be that between organized mass mobilization on the one hand, and the isolated affirmation of principle on the other.

In my view, Badiou's antiunionism is mainly inconsistent with the evolution of his thought since the late 1970s. Unlike Badiou, though without wanting to deny the relatively state-centered orientation of France's trade unions, I would insist that at least in today's situation, organized labor remains one of the essential components of any progressive politics; that it is no accident that unions are always and everywhere among the first targets of any "modernizing" government; that the only medium-term response to pressure for ever more flexible means of exploitation is to strengthen and develop properly international unions, not weaken them still further.

The more general danger is that Badiou's firm isolation of politics from economics may reduce at least some of his prescriptions to rather hollow declarations of principle. Take, for instance, the medical situation, as analyzed in *L'Ethique*. A doctor's only clinical rule, Badiou maintains, must be to treat any particular patient "as thoroughly as he can, using everything he knows and with all the means at his disposal, without taking anything else into consideration" (E, 17). Adherence to this otherwise uncontroversial principle becomes difficult, however, at precisely the point where Badiou's analysis comes to an end. Hospital emergency rooms are *systematically* overextended. Doctors are constantly faced by the need to decide whether to continue treating a particular patient or to attend to the no less pressing needs of other patients. For precisely the reasons Badiou deplores, waiting lists have become a feature of the clinical situation as much as of the hospital managerial situation. To pretend it is not so is to avoid the actual structural constraints of the clinical situation as such.[40]

Badiou's principled divorce of politics and economics is usefully contrasted with Bourdieu's recent contribution to much the same sort of problem.[41] Like most critics, both Badiou and Bourdieu attribute our contemporary "neoconservative revolution" to the consolidation of the market and the law of profit maximization as "the sole defining standard for all practices."[42] Like Badiou, Bourdieu castigates those intellectuals who "restrict themselves to a verbal defence of reason and rational dialogue or worse still, suggest an allegedly postmodern but actually radical-chic version of the ideology of the end of ideologies." But Bourdieu sees as the main bulwark against this conservative revolution those trade unions and that "social state" (127) which Badiou so insistently keeps at a distance. Following Ernst Bloch, he seeks to revive a "considered" or "reasoned utopianism," that is, an engagement both informed by an expert "knowledge of the *objective* trend" and committed to its active, political transformation (128, my emphasis). Building on a truly European network of alliances, the sociologist hopes to "launch realistic projects and actions closely matched to the objective processes of the order they are meant to transform." Unlike Badiou, Bourdieu sees the "creation of institutions—parliaments, international federations, European associations . . . within which some common European programmes can be discussed and elaborated"—as an urgent priority (128–29). Again unlike Badiou, Bourdieu makes a direct connection between political disempowerment and economic circumstance. He investigates the "*social* costs of economic violence" and "the different forms of social misery" in our societies; tracing their causes "back to economic decisions" and neo-liberal policies, he suggests means for the realization of "an economics of well-being."[43]

It would be hard to imagine a more comprehensive program for what Badiou would no doubt denounce as the corruption of any genuine (or antiprogrammatic) politics. The dangers of the top-down, essentially administrative orientation to any such scheme are obvious enough. The advantage of Bourdieu's approach, however, is that it acknowledges the inevitable and necessary relation of politics and economics as basic to the very *structure* (and not simply the metastructure) of our situation. Badiou's determination to pursue an essentially isolated if not intermittent politics—a politics that now bears more than a passing resemblance to the later Sartre's politics of isolated subjective praxis performed by a "group in fusion," at an absolute distance from the deadening objectivity of the practico-inert—may mean that his commitment has little chance of forcing the internal transformation of this particular situation.

Badiou *Absolutiste?*

In somewhat the same way, Badiou's firm dissociation of the process of subjectivation from its enabling "natural" or "psychological" conditions may do more to simplify our understanding of that process than explain it. He defines the human in terms of our exceptional "capacity for thought," but shows little interest in the origin and nature of that capacity—not least because to do so might undercut his argument that "the individual as such is not endowed with a nature that automatically warrants our working to preserve it" (LS, 81). No amount of insistence upon the exceptional or nonnatural status of the subject, however, accounts for or justifies dismissal of the nature of that being which is uniquely able to *become* exceptional, any more than it helps us understand how and why certain individuals actually become subjects. Badiou effectively reduces this process to an inaccessible moment of decision: "The evental nomination has always already taken place . . . , and this 'already' is our only guarantee. The rest is a matter of faith. . . ."[44] The process of a subsequent coming to resolution figures, then, as a more or less instantaneous conversion: an event takes place; an undecidable is decided; an axiom comes into effect.

The most obvious problem with this configuration is analogous, up to a point, to the one that Hegel famously found at work in the French Revolution: by literally cutting its links with the situation, by subtracting itself from the order of relations operative in the situation, it moves too quickly to affirm an ultimately abstract freedom.[45] Given the uncertain structuring resources deployed by the concept of set, Badiou's insistence on the fully situational, fully immanent development of a truth is not likely to convince his more dialectically minded critics. To be sure, freedom is nothing other than an abstraction from the prevailing regime of specification and automation: the essential question is simply how we are to distinguish a merely abstract abstraction from a more effectively *concrete* abstraction, that is, one that works through these relations, qua relations, in order to transform them. Badiou's procedures certainly proceed point by subtractive point, but the accumulation of their truths remains a punctual or extensional process, a matter of points, never of relations—or rather, of relations defined simply as collections of points (EE, 483–86). Indeed, at each decisive moment in the elaboration of Badiou's philosophy, everything turns on the assertion of a properly "unconditional point"—unconditional, precisely, because conditioned by nothing other than itself, and punctual, because subtracted from any dialectic or relationality: "All that is conditional, in this world, falls under the law of the circulation of objects, moneys, and images." Consequently, the "radical demand of contemporary philosophy [is for] the interruption of this circulation"; its task is to "announce or assume that there is an unconditional limit or 'fixed point'" (DP, 21; cf. SP, 7). Every singular configuration has its basis in the exceptional assertion of such a point: "For singularity, if we think the matter through, is properly always a matter of decision, and every decision, ultimately, to the degree that it is a real decision, is a singular decision. . . . To the degree that what a truth commits, or what commits one to a truth, or what is upheld by a fixed point, is of the order of a decision, so it is also of the order of the singular" (DP, 27–28).

The issue that then arises is less the charge of an irresponsible "decisionism" levied by Lyotard[46] than that of the roughly absolutist dimension of Badiou's work. Remember that absolutism defines sovereignty as singular and univocal—in Bodin's terms, as "perpetual," self-coincident, a pure disinterest[47] beyond all particular interests. Absolutism affirms the unqualified subtraction of the sovereign from the specified social field. True sovereign power is founded less in the plenitude of the situation (i.e., justified by the history or organization of the realm) than in the void presumed by its axiomatic self-proclamation. The sovereign has no constituent relation with its subjects. The sovereign is very exactly a subject without object; it is that which has, as its only being, the being of its decision to be. The simple existence of the sovereign confirms it as legitimate: sovereign legitimacy and sovereign power are one and the same thing.[48] The logic of sovereignty is an exemplary version of the general logic of actively nonrelational singularity. Since true sovereignty is "no more divisible that a geometric point,"[49] through the sovereign exception, "a Multitude of men are made One Person," united in a single political determination.[50] The sovereign resolves every conflict between interests by establishing a power beyond interest. Its decisions, finally, are regulated only by that sort of enlightened self-restraint characteristic of what Badiou calls "the ethics of a truth" (C, 194; cf. E, 78; SP, 99).

Needless to say, I do not want this provocative analogy to be misunderstood. I do not mean to suggest that Badiou's position is in any sense authoritarian or solipsistic, let alone despotic. A procedure qualifies as true only if it is a free and open appeal to the universal interest, and every such procedure certainly proceeds *through* the ramified, "impure" fabric of particular interests, opinions, and so on. The cumulative growth of the generic set that it assembles is painfully slow and laborious. The truth thereby assembled, however, is as pure as its evental affirmation is immediate or instantaneous. This is the one and only point that my reference to the logic of sovereignty is designed to reinforce. A truth bores a hole through the tangled, impure fabric of opinions and circumstances that define the prevailing state of its situation, but the hole-boring mechanism itself is and cannot be not so tangled. In every case, *"The truth is not said of the object, but says itself only of itself."*[51] Though it moves through circumstantial impurity, every truth affirmation is itself pure or nonrelational from the outset.

The mistake, then, would be to suggest that the subject of truth itself somehow moves, slowly and progressively, from a situation of relational impurity to one of singular purity. Subjectivation is not a learning process. A subject is, from the beginning, induced by a truth, and a truth is, from the beginning, qualitatively distinct from the impurity of opinions and interests. From the beginning, "subjective thought is to be strictly established from the subjective itself, without passing through any kind of objective mediation" (AM, 36). The affirmation or commitment that carries a truth along is no more caught up in dialectical interaction with the circumstances of the situation than it is supervised by general criteria of judgment or procedure; it is not bound up in relations of proof or argumentation, and it is not a negotiation or an interpretation in any sense of the word. It is purely a matter of decision and conversion. This is why what Badiou calls ethics has to kick in after the fact of truth, precisely as a regulative mechanism to stop the process from getting out of hand.

Bruno Bosteels will no doubt prove to be one of Badiou's most able advocates on this point, and it is well worth anticipating his rebuttal here. Objecting to my association of Badiou and sovereignty, Bosteels defends a reading of the truth procedures as dialectical "movements through the pure and towards the pure, movements which are never complete." The unlinking pursued by a truth process is a "step-by-step process and for this very reason is relative, impure and always precarious." In particular, Bosteels holds that Badiou problematizes the "move from the purely mathematical to the various heterogeneous qualitative situations" at work in his many historical examples, as if there was some fundamental shift in level or register when we move from ontological to extraontological situations (with the consequent implication that if this shift could be accentuated we might be able to step back from the more abstract speculations of *L'Etre et l'événement* to recover the more concretely situated orientation of *Théorie du sujet*).

I concede that this is certainly the best way of defending Badiou as a rigorously "specific" interventionist thinker. But if Bosteels's suggestion is taken to mean that Badiou's approach, when it shifts from the mathematical to the historical, is in some sense changed by the recognition of material complexity or sociohistorical opacity, then it is quite misleading. There is no more place for objective mediation (meaning the mediation of thought through an object) in Badiou's mature understanding of history than there is in his understanding of science or love. True thought is always unequivocally subtractive; Badiou makes no concessions on that score. On the other hand, if what Bosteels has in mind is simply Badiou's conviction that the impasse of ontology, if it is to be thought at all, requires a decisive break with the domain of ontology per se, of course he is quite right. Only on this condition, however: that we recognize that this break as such, which is nothing other than the subject's intervention, makes absolutely no detour at any stage through the domain of objectivity, a domain that is never anything other than (sensual or social) illusion pure and simple. The path of the subject, which breaks with the pure thought of being as being, is no less a matter of pure thought, that is, of thought subtracted from any object, any relation of adequation or interpretation. To be sure, the path is made up of an endless series of investigating steps: nevertheless, Badiou's whole effort is to withdraw each such step, along with the collection of every such investigation, from anything resembling dialectical mediation through what is investigated. Connection itself, which is the only active operator at work in the entire sequence, is as bivalent as it is abrupt. The logic of connection is classical (or non-Hegelian) through and through. That the sequence of connections proceeds one element at a time is simply an obvious aspect of its existence as a generic (i.e., unconstructible) set. That this sequence itself might have any sort of constituent relation with the substantial individuality or complexity of what it investigates, on the other hand, is precisely what a set-theoretic understanding of the being of truth definitively proscribes in advance. Since they approach the situation from the exclusive bias of its void, subjects "relate" to the elements they investigate solely in terms of their inconsistent multiple being—which is to say, solely from the perspective in which their "objective" being is indistinguishable from their "subjective" thinking, in the absence, again, of any discernible in between, of any dialectical mediation of the two.[52]

Bearing these provisos in mind, I think we can reasonably make cautious use of the analogy with absolutism to emphasize the nonrelational or self-regulating quality of a number of Badiou's concepts.

1. We know that his ontology is built entirely upon the self-grounding decisions that are the axioms of the infinite and the void. The void itself, sole foundation of being in general, is that most sovereign of existences, a self-founding name: "Its inaugural advent is a pure act of nomination.... The name of the void is a pure proper name; it is self-indicating" (EE, 71–72). More to the point, any axiomatic operation is effectively "sovereign" as a matter of course. An axiom creates the field of its effects ex nihilo, a field in which existence itself is a function of conformity to the rule that it declares (EE, 38). An axiom cannot know what it prescribes any more than it might relate to what it excludes. The criteria of an axiomatized procedure are entirely immanent to its performance. Only this ensures that an axiomatized multiplicity remains absolutely pure, beyond empirical qualification of any sort.

2. The event is of course an element that belongs, with its site, to itself (EE, 212). And if "Chance *[le Hasard]* is the pure thought of the event," it is because "Chance is the self-realization of its Idea, in every act in which it is at stake, such that it is a delimited affirmative force, and in no sense a correlation with the world."[53]

3. As a figure of pure affirmation or conviction, the subject can also be described as responsible only to itself: "The subject is confidence in

itself."[54] It is not the content of what is asserted but the fact that it is asserted as unqualified that lends the evental statement its subjective force: "It is not the statement that brings a subject into being, but the *saying [dire]* of this statement," its effective declaration. The subject is nothing other than the "there is *['il y a']* of a statement" (TA, 5.3.97), so long as the statement cuts through all merely interpretative relations.

Does this declaration allow, then, for the existence of one subject, or many subjects? The early Badiou held that "there is only one subject, whose existence always makes for an event."[55] The later Badiou recognizes that "there is not, in fact, one single Subject, but as many subjects as there are truths."[56] To be sure, any one individual belongs to a vast number of situations, and subjective participation in any one procedure need not block other sorts of commitment: unlike the Marxism that sutures philosophy to politics, Badiou has no concept of total or exclusive commitment. All the same, "there is only one situation once we grasp it in truth" (C, 264), and to any one truth, there seems to correspond only one subject. The subject is "always singular," always "without vis-à-vis," and if every "generic procedure of fidelity concerns the *one* of the situational being," there is no obvious way that a situation might tolerate more than one subject.[57] In any case, since "a truth is as such subtracted from every position," the components of subjectivation (event, nomination, intervention, fidelity, and so on) do not themselves provide any developed means for the individuation or differentiation of distinct subjects.[58] Badiou's position on this point, in particular, is in marked contrast with that of his master Lacan, who admits "an original intersubjectivity ..., intersubjectivity at the beginning," deployed in the mechanics of speech and the subject's pursuit of recognition.[59]

What, then, is the status of the other in Badiou's work? Only in his recent book on Beckett (1995) has Badiou directly addressed the question "Who am I, if the other exists?"[60] Here, indeed, "the 'with the other' is decisive. But again, we have to isolate its nature, set it up in a way that evacuates all psychology, all obvious, empirical exteriority" (B, 23). What remains of the other in this empiricopsychological vacuum? It is hard to say. Whatever it is, it is not a primarily relational or at least not a "directional" category.[61] Always, Badiou writes, "Beckett's characters are those anonymous figures of human toil whose comic aspect renders them both interchangeable and irreplaceable" (B, 75),

a collection of pure singularities. We know that in the world of victims and executioners of *Comment c'est*, for example, the other is "an
evasive circularity, since it is possible to occupy successively [the position of either], and only the position specifies the difference" (23). At
best, relation with the other is thus restricted to sharing a truth: "We
must experiment to see if a truth can at least be shared" (46). But even
in the case of a loving relationship—the only case developed from
Beckett himself—we know there is just one subject proper, not two:
"The lovers as such enter into the composition of *one* subject of love,
who exceeds them both," just as "the subject of a revolutionary politics is not the individual militant; . . . it is *one* singular production" (E,
40, my emphasis).

In short, subjective singularity, or operational self-regulation—
they amount to the same thing in practice—is characteristic of each
generic procedure: "The poem is accessible only in its act,"[62] just as
"politics has no end other than itself. . . . A political sequence must
be identified and thought from the perspective of the sequence itself, as a homogeneous singularity, and not from the heterogeneous
nature of its empirical happening."[63]

4. Philosophy, finally, proceeds through its history as "nothing other
than a desubstantialization of the Truth, which is also the auto-
liberation of its act" (C, 82). Badiou's ultimate goal can be quite accurately described as a declaration of the sovereignty of "philosophy
itself, in its singular delimitation" (C, 76–77). He writes always in
search of the "proper place" of philosophy, against "its delegation to
something other than itself."[64] Badiou opposes all forms of pseudophilosophical speculation that delegate its autonomy to a relation
with another dimension—the historical, the transcendent, the linguistic, the poetic, the communal or cultural. Just as only the sovereign can judge the sovereign, so too "there are no criteria of truth"[65]
external to the affirmation of that truth's existence: once philosophy
"breaks with the order of representations, it has no other guarantee
of reality other than its own experience" (C, 57–59; PP, 90).

I have already suggested that since his explicitly Maoist days, Badiou has
in some ways moved to a more rather than a less "absolutist" position. He
has moved forever further from any approach mediated by the activity of
interpretation, broadly understood.[66] In place of a partisan truth carried
to some extent by a dialectical process of historical change, Badiou's work
now affirms a subject whose very existence is "maintained only by his own

prescription."[67] Though always sited in terms that reflect the current state of the situation, the subject is no more bound up in a process of dialectical interaction with a sociohistorical "outside" than it is endowed with a private "interiority . . . , in which might be generated a question of self. The subject is even, properly, the unquestionable, since it is that by which proceeds a response."[68] The unquestionable is invulnerable to all interpellation. Though it may serve to protect him from any confusion of the subjective with the ideological, Badiou has yet to provide a fully convincing way of distinguishing such recourse to the unquestionable from its sovereign avatar.[69]

Of course, Badiou is not about to let an accusation like this go unchallenged. For almost a decade now, he has focused much of his attention on precisely relational questions—questions concerning the nature of logic, knowledge, and the internal organization of a situation. It will be another year or two before he has finished the second volume of *L'Etre et l'événement*, in which he promises to integrate the answers to these questions within his philosophical system as a whole. But in the next and final chapter of the present book we can look briefly, in anticipation, at the tentative outlines of the argument to come.

chapter 14

Being-there: The Onto-logy of Appearing

We turn now, in closing, to the matter of Badiou's challenging and remarkable work in progress, which promises to renew, if not transform, several
of his most fundamental concepts. This renewal may in time amount to a
shift as considerable as that which distinguishes (without separating) *L'Etre
et l'événement* from *Théorie du sujet*. The full implications of this revision
have yet to be fully integrated into the systematic order of his philosophy as
a whole. Although Badiou has published much of what I will cite here, all of
this material remains somewhat speculative or prospective, and should be
treated as such.

Perhaps the most striking general development is a shift from a previously disjunctive approach organized essentially around the dichotomy of
either-or to a more inclusive position arranged in terms of and-and. Where
before the subtractive ontology of pure being qua being was emphatically
opposed to more continuous or constructivist conceptions (say, Leibniz-
Bergson-Deleuze, for short), the two approaches are now arranged as thoroughly distinct yet compatible or perhaps even complementary angles. Now
nonrelational abstract being is itself endowed with a more relational, more
emphatically situated onto-logical dimension: the dimension of its appearing or being-there. As Badiou writes, "Being is essentially being-there *(Dasein)*," and "being-there is conceivable only in terms of relation" since every
"there" is the product of a particular set of differential relations that flesh out

a situation in a particular way.[1] There is thus less of a stark choice between disjunction and relation, between *déliaison* and *liaison*, than there is a recognition of the apparent paradox that "being is multiple, in radical disjunction [*déliaison*], and yet at the same time everything is in relation" (TA, 6.11.96). To some extent at least, Badiou has incorporated the relational alternative his philosophy, thus far, had always sought to exclude.

In a letter dated 1996, Badiou outlined "four problems" to be addressed in the forthcoming second volume of *L'Etre et l'événement*.[2] (1) He will include "an acceptable foundation for the language of the situation, and thereby for knowledge," whereby, considered as a logical Category, "each term of the situation can be grasped (identified) only through the 'logical' network (non-existent, in a certain sense) of its relations to others." (2) He will consolidate the "theory of the evental site, in its role both as 'material' of the event and as local origin of the truth procedure. . . . The arbitrary (random) quality of the subject's trajectory is limited by the 'attractive' power of the site. You don't 'set out' from just anywhere, nor in any old direction." (3) He will reconsider the "rapport *'en torsion'* between a truth and the knowledge it deposes, [. . . whereby] knowledge is properly the exclusive material of a truth. Not in the sense, as you suggest, of a 'compactification' in one point, but in the sense of an attentive, complex refolding [*re-pli*] of the logical relations constitutive of knowledge, a refolding that establishes, step by step, the generic subset." And (4) he will reconsider "the unnameable as the unique instance of the One, but not as the *'réel'* of the procedure. It belongs rather to its symbolic aspect. This symbol positions the procedure 'outside the Whole' [*hors-Tout*]. But it is quite a complicated business!"

In this chapter I will present Badiou's development of the first point, the only one of the four to have received much published attention thus far. As Badiou said in a recent interview, "The reworking I'm engaged in at the moment consists of giving both a legitimacy and a much greater consistency to this double question of the language of the situation and the existence of knowledges. This has naturally led me to rethink the most basic concept of my thinking, which is precisely the notion of 'situation.'"[3] As tentative as they are, his comments are worth quoting at some length:

> In reality, the concept of situation is reduced, in *L'Etre et l'événement*, to the purely multiple, to which is added, slightly from the outside, the language of the situation and its predicates. Setting out from a study of what determines the particularity of a situation, I hope to show that there is necessarily in every situation a predicative universe, which I will call its being-there [*être-là*]. I will

try to distinguish the being of the situation, which refers back to ontology, from its being-there, that is, the necessity for every situation to be not simply a being but, coextensive with that being, an appearing *[apparaître]*. It is a doctrine of appearing, but of a non-phenomenal appearing. It's not a matter of an appearing for a subject, but of an appearing as such, as localisation. It is a localisation that doesn't itself refer back to any particular space or geography, but is rather an intrinsic localisation. It is a supplementary ontological property, in addition to pure multiplicity.

In other words, I'm going to tackle the problem of the distinction between a possible and an effective situation, between possible situation and real situation, since I'll go back over the fact that ontology doesn't settle this question, that it is beneath this point of distinction. Hence the effectivity of a situation, its appearing, can't be deduced from its configuration of multiplicity. There is no transitivity between the one and the other.

At this point we'll have to ask about the laws of appearing. I think that we can maintain the idea that mathematics still explains some of what happens, that we aren't absolutely obliged to leave the realm of the mathematical. Simply, we'll need a slightly new form of mathematicity, one that requires a minimal theory of relation, a *logic*. I call "logic" that which is a theory of relation as relation, relation between elements, between parts, etc. I will argue that being-as-being, that is as beneath the relation between being and being-there, is a pure multiplicity. But I will show how this pure multiplicity is always attached to, distorted by, or reworked by, a universe of relations, which will define the logic peculiar to the situation, and not merely its being displayed in its multiplicity, or its network of belongings.[4]

The main methodological inspiration for Badiou's own logic of relation and appearing is provided by that branch of mathematical logic known as category theory: "The logic of appearing, once you push it toward the dialectic of relations, requires an engagement with categorial mathematics, just as pure ontology is unthinkable without mathematical set theory" (EL, 98). In what follows I will review what Badiou takes to be the essential insights of this theory, after considering some of the wider issues associated with a truly mathematized logic as the basis for any general theory of appearance and relation.

Being and Appearing: Reworking the Concept of Situation

We know that Badiou's ontology presumes the elimination of any primordial One or Totality. There is no possible set of all sets that could be studied in its own right. So even if we invest a univocal mathematics as sole ontological discourse, we must realize that any particular "ontological investigation is ir-remediably local" (CT, 190). We cannot study being in general, in its totality; we can study only particular localizations or situations of being. This is why all being is essentially being *there*, and also why ontology is itself a situation. Or again, what can be consistently thought of being is what, in a particular situation, appears to thought.

It remains the case, Badiou insists, that "a being qua being *[l'étant en tant qu'étant]* is, itself, absolutely unrelated. It is a fundamental characteristic of the purely multiple, as thought in the framework of a theory of sets. There are only multiplicities, nothing else. None of these are, by themselves, linked to any other. In a theory of sets, even functions should be thought as pure multiplicities, which is why we identify them with their graph. . . . Which excludes that there be, strictly speaking, a being of relation. Being, thought as such, in a purely generic fashion, is subtracted from all relation" (CT, 192). What Badiou calls "the world of appearances" or phenomena, by contrast, "is always given as solid, related *[lié]*, consistent. It is a world of relation and cohesion, in which we have our points of reference and our habits, a world in which being is, in sum, captive of being there."[5] (Throughout Badiou's current work, "appearing" seems to obey quasi-Kantian rules of intelligibili-ty, compatibility, and coherence.) The goal now is to understand "how it is possible that any situation of being is both pure multiplicity on the border of inconsistency, and intrinsic, solid relation *[liaison]* of its appearing" (CT, 200). Whereas the pure being of being is inconsistent—and thus wildly an-archic, disordered, free . . .—the appearing of being is itself a certain order-ing of being (LM, chap. 1, p. 2). We might say that the shifting of Badiou's attention from the being of being to the appearing of being already implies a shift in priorities that brings him closer to Deleuze than ever before: from now on, the ultimate reference to ontological inconsistency or "chaos" will always be mediated by the exploration of precise ontic strata or "complexity," in roughly the sense made current by complexity theory.

What does Badiou mean by "appearing," exactly? He proposes to "call the appearing *[apparaître]* of a being that which, of a being *[étant]*, is linked to the constraint of a local or situated exposition of its multiple being *[être-multiple]*," that is, its "being-there *[être-là]*." Appearing appears here neither in Heidegger's phenomenological sense nor as a function of time, space, or the constituent subject. It appears as an "intrinsic determination of being" (CT, 191–92), a direct consequence of the impossibility of any totalization (or all-inclusive set) of being. In the absence of any Whole, "appearing is that which ties or reties a being to its site. The essence of appearing is relation."[6]

Though it is an intrinsic determination of being that it be there (that it appear), nevertheless it is not exactly pure being qua being as such that appears: what appears of pure being is a particular quality of being, namely existence. Thanks to the equation of ontology and set theory, pure being qua being is essentially a matter of quantity and univocal determination: something either is or is not (with no intermediary degree). Existence, by contrast, is precisely a "quality" of being, a matter of intensity and degree. Something is if it belongs to a situation, but it exists (in that situation) always more or less, depending on how clearly or brightly it appears in that situation (EL, 3–5). We might say, for instance, and very crudely, that while a great many things belong to the American situation, that situation is arranged such that certain characteristic things (free speech, pioneers, private property, baseball, freeways, fast food, mobile homes, self-made men, and so on) appear or exist more intensely than other, dubiously "un-American," things (unassimilated immigrants, socialists, opponents of the National Rifle Association, etc.).

How something appears is not deducible from its ontological profile. Always, Badiou (like Sartre and Lacan before him) is determined to sever any analysis of how we behave from presumptions about how or what we *are:* our nature, our identity, our roots, and so on (LM, chap. 1, p. 19; LM, chap. 2, p. 21). To take the most obvious case: though the numbers used to identify the pages in this book are ontologically the same as those used to distinguish prices in a supermarket or the results of football games they *appear* differently in each situation (cf. LM, chap. 1, pp.15–16). How we appear, in any given situation, is determined by the established ordering and organizing procedures internal to that situation. What Badiou calls *le transcendantal* (a phrase that I translate here as "the transcendental regime") of a situation is that statelike part of the situation which measures the degrees of self-identity that distinguish particular existences. It is the transcendental regime of a situation that determines the degree to which things belong to that situation, the intensity of their appearing in it (in our American situation, the degree to which things are worthy of patriotic veneration and cultural approval). Unlike Kant's idealist conception of the transcendental (attributed to the structural, a priori operation of a subject), Badiou's transcendental regime is entirely a function of the objective world it governs and in which it is itself included; it is part of the sphere occupied, in symmetrical opposition to the sphere of truth, by an "object without subject" (LM, chap. 2, p. 3). A large part of Badiou's recent teaching has been devoted to what he calls the "mathematics of the transcendental." This is not the place to hazard a proper summary of this new teaching, since it is both partially incomplete and highly technical (and, at least in the view of this reader, considerably more resistant than set theory to simplified analogical explanation[7]). Nevertheless, the two or three main developments of this teaching are well worth mentioning at this stage.

The conceptual core of Badiou's whole understanding of the transcendental dimension of a situation is provided by an analysis of the mathematical relation of order (as opposed to equivalence). Order is what relates smaller quantities to larger ones. Unlike the relation of equivalence, it is obviously nonsymmetrical ($p < q \neq p > q$), and Badiou thus treats it as the most primitive logical expression of comparative difference, the "very first inscription of an exhortation [exigence] of the Other" (EL, 9–10). What a transcendental regime does, essentially, is order the various elements of its situation in terms of their existential intensity. These degrees of intensity (the brightness of their appearing) are themselves determined by a set of "identity functions," written Id (A) for any element A. These functions first measure the degree of self-identity of any element A, ranging between a degree of maximum intensity (whereby the existence of A appears absolutely certain) and a degree of minimum intensity (such that A appears altogether nonexistent). By contrasting these degrees of self-identity, the identity functions can subsequently measure the degree of identity between two elements, across degrees of resemblance ranging from "exactly the same" to "entirely different" (EL, 59). The basic idea is that A "has all the more phenomenal existence in the situation, the more vigorously it affirms its identity in the situation" (EL, 60). The transcendental regime of a situation can then be defined as a set that is at least partially ordered (i.e., most of its elements can be related in terms of $>$ and $<$); that contains a minimum and a maximum degree of recognizable intensity; that, given an element A, can measure the "opposite" or obverse [l'envers] of that element; that, given two elements A and B, can describe the multiple that these elements have in common (the "largest inferior element" that they share) along with the "global" multiple just large enough to envelop them both; and so on.[8]

The theory further allows for the decomposition of each appearing element, or "object," into ultimately nondecomposable parts or "atoms," each of which appears more or less strongly in its turn (i.e., belongs more or less significantly to its object). At this atomic or literally elemental level, degrees of existence or appearing are directly determined by pure ontological being: the relative appearing of an atom effectively "expresses" the being of the particular element (belonging to the situation) to which it corresponds. This is what Badiou calls the "first principle of materialism."[9] At the atomic level, then, it remains the case that, against any Deleuzo-Bergsonian investment in the virtual, "every object, and thus every appearing, is determined by its [actual] ontological composition" (EL, 65). It is the atomic level, likewise, that provides the basis for a "connection between the logic of appearing and the mathematics of being" as such (EL, 79). This connection further allows, very roughly speaking, for an analysis of the "compatibility" of various objects appearing in a situation, along with their "localization" and atomic "decomposition"—all of which enables a description of "what happens to a multiple *insofar as* it is objectified in a situation," and not simply insofar as it *is* (EL, 70). In *Logiques des mondes* Badiou gives the example of a political demonstration in which various groupings of elements (unions, political parties, anarchists, *lycéens*, passersby, etc.) appear more or less distinctly (powerfully, uniformly, insistently) and more or less compatibly according to the criteria that come to govern the logic of this demonstration. Each group, insofar as it remains a distinctive group, will flaunt certain irreducibly characteristic or "atomic" features that serve to differentiate its being-there (as opposed to its generic, indifferently-different being as being) from that of the other groups (LM, chap. 2, pp. 6–9, 18). But again, should something then happen to unite the participants in an exceptional unanimity, the demonstration will cease to be a mere compilation of allied groups and become part of the mobilization of a true political subject—as happened, for instance, to the various groups of actors involved in the making of the French Revolution.

What this complex and highly abstract configuration provides is a considerably more nuanced definition of a situation or "world," which now includes the following onto-logical features (EL, 96):

1. Every situation S is made up of a collection of multiples (sets, or elements, noted A, B, C . . .), which compose the "stable being" of any such situation. Nothing new here.

2. Any S also includes a particular multiple T, "the transcendental regime *[le transcendantal]*" of S, whose structure is generally uniform (characterized by an at least partial order ranging between a minimum and a maximum degree of intensity, a largest inferior element common to any pairing of elements, etc.) but whose sophistication or range of degrees is infinitely variable. T is what accounts for the structuring principle of a situation (as distinct from its state, or representing principle), a point that was left more or less unexplained in *L'Etre et l'événement*.

3. Any particular multiple A of the situation can be "indexed" against T according to its particular identity function or "function of appearing" (Id), and the result of this indexing is what determines an "object" A for the situation, written (A, Id).

4. Any such object A is, in turn, made up of atomic components that can be noted Id *(a, x)*, where *a* is a minimal element of A and *x* is a degree of self-identity measurable in T. Every element *a* of an object A is distinguishable according to its degree of existence in A and is also localizable by an element of T.

5. Between two objects A and B there can exist relations (i.e., variations on the relation of order, or > and <), on condition that these relations "preserve the essential characteristics of their regime of appearing: localizations, and intensities of existence." Or again: a relation between two objects preserves the atomic logic of these objects.

6. Insofar as they appear in the situation, the multiples that belong to it are thus structured by their "apparent" objectivation (their incorporation into objects), meaning arrangements of similarity, difference, compatibility, enveloping, order, and so on, which are preserved by the relations operative in the situation. In short, a situation can be defined as "a universe of objects and relations that makes a collection of pure multiples appear" (EL, 96). What Badiou now calls a "world" is just a situation in this newly ramified sense, that is, considered in terms of its being-there. A world is a coherent set of innumerable appearings governed by an infinitely ramified transcendental regime (this regime is what category theory will label the "central object" of a topos; more on this below). A discrete world exists insofar as it holds together a certain "configuration of multiple-beings which appear 'there,' along with a certain range of transcendentally regulated relations between these beings" (LM, chap. 3, p. 2). In the third chapter of *Logiques des mondes* Badiou develops in particular detail the example of Québec, as the "world" whose historical development runs from Cartier's initial voyages in the 1530s through the recent referenda on national sovereignty, and in which "appear," more or less intensely, an infinite multiplicity of things including the voyageurs, the Inuit, Neil McKenty, hydroelectric power, Laval University, maple syrup, ice hockey, Saint-Saveur, and so on. The unlimited dissemination of the elements of its elements reconfirms in onto-logical terms the presumption of *L'Etre et l'événement* that "every world is ontologically infinite, and the order of this infinity is properly inaccessible."[10]

A *Truly* Mathematized Logic

It is the fact that being must appear somewhere, Badiou continues, "that ensures that there is logic . . . ; appearing is nothing other than the logic of a situation." The word "logic," of course, sounds somewhat out of place in Badiou's philosophy. Certainly, "that mathematics is a form of thought means, first of all, that it is not a logic."[11] For a long time, Badiou admits, he had believed that a Platonic reversal of Aristotelianism required the "destitution of formal logic" as the privileged means of access to rational thought. He is now confident, however, that logic can be accounted for, not as an empty syntactical construction, but as an effect of mathematical prescription itself (CT, 188). A logic will always be particular to a decided mathematical universe, and "logic" will mean the principles of coherence operating in such a universe. Logic will describe the domain of appearing, leaving pure mathematics to describe the domain of being as being. But inasmuch as appearing or relation is now perceived as an intrinsic constraint upon being, logic or "the science of appearing must itself be a component of the science of being, and thus of mathematics. It is necessary that logic be mathematical logic. But inasmuch as mathematics apprehends being in its being, beyond its appearance, and thus in its fundamental *déliaison*, it is also necessary that mathematics be in no way confused with logic" (CT, 194).

(It also remains the case, as you might expect, that when something *happens*, when in the wake of an event "being seems to displace its configuration under our eyes, it is always at the expense of appearing, through the local collapse of its consistency, and so in the provisional cancellation *[résiliation]* of all logic. Because what comes then to the surface, displacing or revoking the logic of the place, is being itself, in its fearsome and creative inconsistency, or in its void, which is the without place of every place."[12])

We have, then, a double imperative. We must conceive of logic as mathematical logic, but without confusing mathematics with logic. Neither imperative is surprising. If Badiou is prepared to import a logical theory of relation into his ontology, this can only be a logic that recognizes its ultimate subordination to mathematics (as opposed to an allegiance to language or some vaguely defined faculty of judgment). The problem—and hence the importance of the second imperative—is that the kind of mathematized logic we have inherited from the pioneering efforts of Boole and Frege is a logic that was mathematized in the wrong way, according to a mistaken understanding of mathematics itself. Such logic remains, consistent with what Badiou terms the Aristotelian ontological tradition, a (more formalized) kind of clarifying language applied to an otherwise confused material. The entire effort of this mathematized logic, beginning with "Frege's ideography, has been to constitute logical languages as formal objectivities *[objectités]*."[13] The mathematical aspect of such logic is thus "derivative and external" (CT, 196), and Badiou sees the whole enterprise as simply one aspect of that linguistic turn promoted, in other domains, by Heidegger, Wittgenstein, and analytical philosophy generally.[14] "Between Aristotle and Hegel," Badiou writes, "logic was the philosophical category in which ontology maintained its ascendancy over language. The [Fregean] mathematization of logic, on the other hand, authorizes the seizure of philosophy by language. And the price paid for this seizure has been the destitution of ontology in general; either as according to Wittgenstein, the statements of ontology have no meaning—or, as according to Heidegger, the statements of metaphysics have reached the moment of their closure in nihilism" (CT, 123–24). The first thing Badiou needs to do, then, is reconceptualize the mathematization of logic in keeping with his own ontological prescriptions. We know that from a true Platonic perspective, the essence of mathematics is not its merely formal clarity but its capacity to think and transcribe being as being.[15]

That logic can be properly understood as mathematical requires a conception of logic that allows it to emerge from within the movement of mathematics itself, rather than from the application of a linguistic frame to mathematics. So the real question is "What event of thought, with regard to logic, enables philosophy to evade the hold of grammar and logic?" Badiou's answer is the development, begun in the 1940s by Eilenberg and Mac Lane, and subsequently continued by Groethendieck, Freyd, and Lawvere, of what is known as category or topos theory.[16] Badiou writes triumphantly, "I have been able to solve at least partially my problem"—the problem of the relation between logic and mathematics—"by putting philosophy under the condition of the theory of toposes" (CT, 125). Topos theory establishes the desired conclusion that "logic is a local dimension of possible mathematical universes" (CT, 129):

> As soon as logic is mathematized in the form of a syntax, or a formal theory, its connection to language is primordial. . . . The theory of Categories proposes a complete reversal of perspectives. Whereas the syntactical presentation of logic as formal language disposes its universes, or models, as semantic interpretations, in the categorial presentation what exist are Universes, of which logic is an internal dimension. . . . Logic now appears as an immanent constraint enveloped by mathematics. And above all, logic is localized. It is a presented, *situated* dimension of universes whose possibility mathematics describes. The problem of the delimitation of mathematics and logic thus takes on a completely different turn. This delimitation no longer lets itself be decided by linguistic criteria that would exhaust its power. It is referred back to distinctions, themselves ontological, that are far more fundamental, and that concern two conceptual pairs: that of the real and the possible, and that of the

global and the local. It marks out what we might call an essential ontological geometrization of the relationship between logic and mathematics. (CT, 128)

What complicates any discussion of this localization is the obviously double use of the word "logic"—on the one hand, as logic in general, that is, global, descriptive of what holds for any possible universe, and, on the other hand, as a local logic, that is, determined by the orientation of a particular mathematical universe (classical, modal, intuitionist, etc.). The theoretical inclusion of mathematics in logic is thus preserved, in a sense, but the practical force of this "priority" in any given localization of logic is denied: "If set theory is an ontological decision, the theory of Toposes is a logical description of possible ontologies," and thus prior to and "larger" than any particular ontology.[17] But it is also, by the same token, a merely possible dimension, and thus empty of any real prescriptive force. The deciding of one universe among others—and this is where Badiou still differs from Leibniz—cannot be deduced from or calculated with the tools that describe the empty structure of all possible universes (CT, 197–98). Although these tools allow for a description of the decision and its consequences after the fact, any such decision is itself fully primary or self-foundational. Though logic may encompass mathematics, it cannot found it, and as soon as we begin speaking of the real rather than the merely possible, we speak from the practical priority of mathematics over logic. (The essential opacity of the decision taking is thereby preserved intact.)

Elements of Category Theory

Even the most rudimentary review of how category theory actually works would triple the size of this chapter.[18] With the space available we should still be able, however, to get a sense of the basic principles involved and appreciate a couple of its more significant implications.

Like set theory, category theory presents itself as an "exposition of ontology (of mathematics) as a whole," but from a completely different angle.[19] Category theory and set theory offer opposing approaches to "all the decisive questions of the thought of being (acts of thought, forms of immanence, identity and difference, logical framework, admissible rationality, relation of experience and existence, infinity, unity or plurality of universes, etc.)" (T, 5). They are, in short, different ways of conditioning philosophy. If the first volume of *L'Etre et l'événement* was written under the sole mathematical condition of set theory, the second volume will be written under the double condition of both theories, suitably integrated so as to ensure the ontological priority of set theory.

Where set theory directly articulates being-as-being, category theory is "the science of appearing, the science of what signifies that every truth of being is irremediably a local truth" (CT, 199). A set-theoretic ontology declares being before relation, whereas in categorial logic "relation precedes being" (CT, 168). Where set theory configures being in terms of a purely inconsistent multiplicity without-one "the ontology prescribed by category theory determines being as act, relation *[rapport]*, movement" (T, 1). Where set theory recognizes only actual forms of being, category theory, oriented only by the logical characteristics of any possible universe, illustrates "the primacy of the virtual over the actual, of construction over decision."[20] Set theory is rigorously univocal, founded on the strict unicity of the void or empty set; in category theory, even the void is made "equivocal," meaning that in certain categories there may be many objects without elements yet distinct from zero. The spontaneous logic of a set-theoretic ontology is classical (because it accepts the unrestricted use of the law of double negation), whereas the natural logic of categories is intuitionist (because it refuses the indirect proofs of double negation, and must show or construct an object in order to be able to say that it exists). Set theory asserts a rigorous faith in the reality of what cannot be seen; category theory complies, so to speak, with the maxim that seeing is believing. The identity of a set is extensional (or combinatorial); the identity of a category is intensional (or conceptual): whereas a set is nothing but what belongs to it, an "object" in category theory is "a simple point (i.e., a simple letter) without a determined inside." In Desanti's terms, a set-theoretic ontology is "intrinsic" and a categorial ontology "extrinsic," meaning that its "determination of an object is achieved exclusively by relations, or movement, of which this object is the source or target."[21] If Badiou himself can claim to have written a philosophy adequate to the prescriptions of set theory, he associates the philosophical bias of category theory with Bergson and Deleuze.[22]

The most basic tools of category theory are not complicated; indeed, their very simplicity is part of what makes the theory hard to grasp. The theory offers "a highly formalized language especially suited for stating abstract properties of structures."[23] The sort of actual mathematical structures that correspond to particular categories include things such as sets, groups, or topological spaces. The theory is designed to allow for the most general possible description of logical relations or operations between such structures or entities (for example, their equation or negation, their product or sum, the exponentiation of one by another, etc.), and the more operations a category can recognize, the richer is the conceptual universe it formalizes. Methodologically, the way these structures are represented is essentially geometric[24]: isolated, manageable parts of a category are expressed in diagrams (though the more complex the diagrams, the more algebraic the geometry becomes). These diagrams are made up of objects, on the one hand, and of arrows or "morphisms," on the other. Arrows are "oriented correlations between objects; an arrow 'goes' from object a (its source) to object b (its target)." For example, such objects might designate mathematical structures and the arrows relationships (say, functions) between these structures.[25]

The single most important principle of category theory is that all individuating power or action belongs to these dynamic arrows alone. In category theory, an object is "'without interior,' and is exclusively identified by the arrows of which it is the source or the target" (CT, 171). Its nature is "entirely derivative" of the operations performed on it and the relations it supports.[26] One implication is that what defines any object a as this particular object is itself an arrow, known as its identity arrow, written Id(a): "The identity arrow *is* the object a, considered as 'stopping time' within the action. The underlying, fairly Bergsonian (or Deleuzian) idea is that an identity is never anything other than an arrest of movement, a null movement" (T, 8). Because no identity is intrinsic, two nominally distinct objects are the "same" if they are the source and target of the same kinds of movements.

The axiomatics governing categorial configurations are equally sparse. They are, as Badiou summarizes, "associative and identitarian; it is required that the compositions of arrows be associative (so that we can 'link' without ambiguity the correlations between objects), and that each object be linked to itself by an 'identical' arrow, which identifies that object as itself.... The size of a universe thus generated depends on the correlations possible within it. These operations are uniformly defined as 'limits' of certain configurations (of certain finite diagrams engaging a certain number of objects and arrows)."[27] These limits include, among others, the initial object (noted "O") and the terminal object (noted "1"), sums and products (of two objects), their exponentiation (object a to the power of object b) the "pull-back" of two arrows to the same target. The terminal object of a category envelops what I have described earlier in this chapter as the transcendental regime T of any situation S, and corresponds roughly to the structuring operation of the situation: it is what counts as one every object in the situation, in the sense that "every object has one and only one relation with a terminal object, a relation that ensures that the object is indeed *an* object" (EL, 100). This is why the terminal object can be considered as the object One, and noted "1." The One can effectively count all the elementary (atomic) components that belong "absolutely" to the object, that are most remarkable or distinctive about that object (EL, 101). The initial object of a topos, or Zero, further corresponds to the minimum degree of existential intensity recognized by T. Whatever exists as Zero in a situation is what cannot be counted as one, that is, what cannot enter into a relation with One. "Zero" is whatever is empty of one-ifiable elements. In the category defined by set theory, Zero and the empty set are clearly one and the same (meaning that there is only one object, in the set-theoretic situation, that "counts" as Zero). This coincidence need not apply in other sorts of category, however, where it may happen that quite different things appear as empty or minimally existent.

Within a category, finally, the functions of syntax and semantics cannot be clearly distinguished. Logical operators such as verification, negation, disjunction, conjunction, implication, and so on, are all arrows or operations of the same kind as semantic values such as true or false (CT, 198). The values (arrows) of true and false are thus "active affirmations" in an almost Nietzschean sense (T, 64).

Diagrams of a category are "structured" or "consistent" (as opposed to merely indefinite or arbitrary) if arrows that define one half of a diagram have the same effect as (and are thus identical with) the arrows defining its other half. For example—and purely for the sake of literal illustration— given a triangular diagram with vertices a, b, and c, the diagram is consistent if it "commutes," that is, if the arrows that go from a to b to c add up to the same arrow that goes directly from a to c. Such a diagram would be drawn something like this:

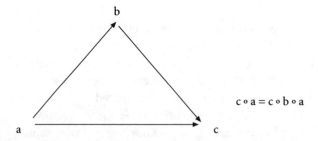

$$c \circ a = c \circ b \circ a$$

A diagram of this sort might be used, to give a somewhat arbitrary example, to express the symmetrical relations of support and condemnation that a typical progressive French citizen might feel, during the showdown at the Saint Bernard church, toward the *sans-papiers* on the one hand and the police on the other:

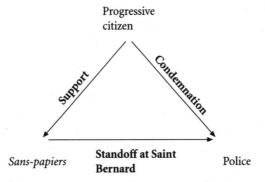

That such a diagram (or its reactionary inverse, or any diagram linking progressive and reactionary citizens, and so on) commutes, means that whatever might increase this citizen's support for the *sans-papiers* would simultaneously increase his or her disapproval of the police (cf. LM, chap. 3, pp. 10–12).

The specific kinds of categories Badiou is mainly interested in are known as toposes.[28] A topos is a category whose every diagram is consistent, each of which has a "limit" in the sense described earlier (a kind of universally valid concept: more technically, such categories are characterized by what is known as "Cartesian closure" [T, 70]). A "world" as defined earlier in this chapter—that is, as a collection of multiples whose appearing or being-there is governed by a transcendental regime—is a topos. Every topos includes a central object, or C, which acts as its "classifier of subobjects"; a world's transcendental regime, that is, what Badiou described in *L'Etre et l'événement* as the "encyclopaedia" of a situation, corresponds to this central object C.[29] A topos is further endowed with arrows, called "truth arrows," directed from the terminal object (1) to the central object (C), and includes the pull-back of these truth arrows (meaning that such arrows are monomorphisms or "conservers of difference": if arrows f and g are different, f + m and g + m are also different). A topos is a centered universe. Its arrows converge on C, and the relation of truth is established as "a singular connection between two objects of the universe."[30] As a truth procedure progresses it "bores a hole in the [transcendental regime or] encyclopaedia as a trajectory between the set-theoretic (decisional) and the categorial (definitional or relational) aspects of the axiomatic. It refolds *[repli]* (as Subject) the relations into the pure presentation of elements."[31]

Whereas the basic axioms of set theory themselves generate and order a large part of the set-theoretic universe, the nature of any particular category cannot be deduced from category theory itself. Each investigation can proceed only "empirically," as an inspection of what it contains. There would be little to gain, at this point, from any sort of detailed inventory of the different kinds of categories.[32] The essential thing, for Badiou's purposes, is what categorial description has to say about set-theoretic categories (i.e., toposes in which set theory or something like set theory determines what exists). The great value of category theory is that it makes explicit in any particular mathematical universe logical operations that otherwise remain implicit. For example, we know that set theory demands a form of classical logic, that is, the validity of indirect proof. But set theory itself cannot articulate this logic as a justifiable principle; it cannot demonstrate the necessary connection between its ontological assumptions and this logical consequence. For set theory is first and foremost a decision or choice, and "an ontological choice erases at the same time the system of possibilities in which it is decided." Once the axioms have been decided, this system is no longer accessible: "Nothing else was possible, for here holds a truth," in all its consequent necessity.[33]

In other words, category theory is useful not because it informs and clarifies an ontological decision qua decision (i.e., not because it provides access to the "taking" of the decision, but because it allows, retrospectively, for an understanding of what was thereby decided or refused). It allows us to represent the founding ontological decision "as a singular choice, including the choice of a logic."[34] Because it is itself committed to no particular orientation, category theory can describe logical connections that any given ontological commitment can no longer discern, since it is "blinded" by the import of its decisions. It provides, after the fact, a comfortable or critical distance with respect to a decision. As you might expect, mere knowledge of such a theory decides nothing at all, and "sophistry begins when we start to believe that the investigation of logical possibilities is itself an ontological decision, or—which means the same thing—when we conclude that any decision is arbitrary (or that there is no ontology of truth)" (T, 45).

Badiou's Onto-logy: Logic under Ontological Prescription

Badiou's interest in category theory, then, should not be seen in any sense as a qualification of his commitment to set theory. "For me," he insists, "set theory is still today the only consistent ontology that I know of" (T, 76). An axiomatic ontology alone decides, it alone prescribes what is real, and the real alone "matters." If category theory describes possible universes, "real mathematics is not a mathematized inspection of possible mathematical universes. Real mathematics *decides* a universe" (CT, 134). What Badiou now calls onto-logical is the domain described, by category theory, of the logical consequences of an ontological decision (CT, 129). In other words, given a particular decision concerning what exists—for example, the decision to recognize either punctual or qualitative differences—onto-logy can spell out the local logical implications of that decision. Badiou's particular interest, of course, is in the logical implications of a set-theoretic ontology. We know that set theory links together a concept of radical immanence (whereby any multiple is defined by what belongs to it), a concept of punctual difference (whereby all differences are local, or "in one point"), and an exclusive concept of the void (as unique and sole foundation). None of these concepts or proposals constrain the general categorial conception of all possible universes (or even a sizeable fraction of these universes). The set-theoretic universe, then, is a dramatically "singular" configuration within category theory. The great advantage of seeing it in this categorial setting (i.e., as itself situated, as a situation among others) is that its precise logical characteristics emerge as explicit and distinctive (T, 77–78).

Three such onto-logical characteristics or correlations (meaning three theorems of category theory) stand out as especially important in Badiou's account thus far. These theorems link logical properties of appearing or existence to strictly ontological characteristics. In each case, what the theory demonstrates—contrary to the principles of a more conventionally mathematized logic—is that "we go from the manifestation of being to the principles of language, and not the reverse" (CT, 131).

1. If what exist in a topos are only punctual differences (i.e., if the topos is what is known as a well-differed or "well-pointed" topos), category theory tells us that this topos recognizes one and only one object as zero, or void.[35] A well-pointed topos is one in which the difference between two distinct relations j and k linking the same two objects x and y is based on an element in at least one of those objects x or y that is itself fully distinct, such that this element "points" to the difference (T, 78; EL, 107). Among the range of possible categorial features this is an exceptional characteristic, and its equally exceptional consequence is the unicity of the void.[36] Badiou writes, "The key question, with regard to the void, is that of its unicity. If an ontological description establishes the unicity of the void, it assumes, in the Parmenidian tradition, a certain reversibility of being, as subtraction from the count and the One. If it admits the multiplicity of the void, or its absence, it pluralizes the foundation itself, and, in the Heraclitean tradition, institutes it as alteration, or becoming" (CT, 131). Deleuze, for example, working

in this Heraclitean tradition, refuses to recognize the ontological priority of the void. The same can be said for Leibniz and Bergson. Badiou's own position, then, might be described as a "Parmenidian principle applied to Parmenides' negation. Parmenides' negation amounts to the assertion: the nothingness of every presentation *is* (there is the void). The Parmenidian principle amounts to the assertion: everything that is, inasmuch as it is, is One. The combination of the two amounts to this: inasmuch as it is, the void is One" (T, 134).

2. If a topos is well pointed, its logic is necessarily bivalent, or classical. Or, a topos that acknowledges only punctual differences is one whose "central object C has only two elements: the true and the false."[37] It is the ontological trait (punctual difference) that compels the logical characteristic (bivalency), and not the other way around. Combining this result with the first theorem, we can conclude that the unicity of the void prescribes application of the law of double negation: not-false equals true; not-not-true equals true (rather than "partly true" or "not-altogether-false"). This is something set theory (and Badiou's philosophy as a whole) presumes in practice, without managing explicitly to explain why. Category theory demonstrates that the co-implication of these two ontological characteristics is indeed "a universal law (a law of possible universes)" (T, 97, 128).

   Conversely, then, "if a topos is not well pointed, and thus if there exist, as with Leibniz, Bergson, or Deleuze, intensive, qualitative, or global differences . . . then your logic cannot be classical," but rather intuitionist or modal (CT, 132). With Leibniz, for example, we know that between p and not-p, there will be an infinity of intermediary states, just as, with Deleuze, we know that negation has no power of implication, and what matters is a syntax of AND AND AND, of *et* over *est*.[38] In other words, "the Two is classical" in its exclusive recognition of p and not-p, whereas, as we have known since Hegel, "the overcoming of classicism requires the Three."[39] If not-not-p is to be something more (or less) than p, we need a third position that is that of the time of creative negation or transcendence. Nonclassical logic, in other words, presumes a genuine mediation of p and not-p as a relation over time (the disjunction of outcome from origin), whereas classical logic presumes the immediate identity of p and not-not-p (the identity of outcome and origin).[40]

3. If a topos admits the axiom of choice, its logic is bivalent or classical.[41] The axiom of choice implies, in other words, the legitimacy of
indirect proof and the law of the excluded middle. This is perhaps
the most striking of the three theorems. You may recall that the
axiom of choice asserts the possibility, given an infinite number of
sets, of creating an infinite subset composed of one element ran-
domly chosen from each of these sets; this choice is effected as if
automatically, without a criterion of selection. The resulting subset
is made up of a truly haphazard collection of more or less "typical" elements, brought together by purely arbitrary means. Within
mathematics considered as an active truth procedure, we know that
the axiom of choice is a clear sign of subjective "intervention" (EE,
254). Moreover, the axiom of choice "has the following ontological
implication: there exists an infinite, anonymous and lawless representation, for every infinite situation," in keeping with the ontological presumptions of concepts like Descartes's divine freedom
or Rousseau's general will.[42] What is remarkable is that a topos that
accepts the legitimacy of this anarchic procedure—in keeping with
most of mainstream mathematics, but in sharp contrast to intuitionist principles—must also accept the implacable rigor of classical
logic. The generic, in other words, is indeed logically compatible
with the austerity of the truth as *opposed* to the false.

Taken together, these three theorems reconfirm the "two possible lines of
thought," the two ontological traditions associated with Plato and Aristotle,
outlined at the opening of my third chapter:

1. Unity (ontological, of the void), localization (of difference), classicism (of logic).
2. Plurality (of voids), globalization (of differences), intuitionism (of
logic).[43]

For the first orientation, all differences are elementary in the most literal
sense, and concern effectively independent entities. For the second orientation, difference figures as "the difference of two arrows, two oriented actions,
and not as the difference of two objectivities, or two multiples. Rather as in
the physical universe according to Aristotle, the first 'differencing' is that of
movements."[44] Difference here results from action, and results as "general,
global, or qualitative." Leibniz's monads, for example, although they include
the whole universe and have no extension (they cannot be defined exten-
sionally), "see" the universe in a different way and express it according to a

distinct modality—the elementary ontological relation being, for Leibniz, precisely one of inclusion rather than belonging.

The Primacy of Decision

What Badiou is at pains to emphasize, in his several discussions of category theory and the new conditions it establishes for his philosophy, is its ultimate subordination to the earlier ontological condition prescribed by the axioms of set theory in particular, and the principles of axiomatic decision in general. Set theory and category theory stand opposed on almost every point, and "the discord between set theory axiomatics and categorial description establishes mathematical ontology in the constraint of options of thought whose choice no purely mathematical prescription can norm" (PM, 37). This does not mean, however, that Badiou's philosophy now wavers in some uncertain hesitation between these two options. As a general rule, "the real is encountered only under the axiomatic imperative," and it is just mere possibility that "can be described under the regime of definitions and classifications" (CT, 135). Badiou's commitment to a set-theoretic or axiomatic orientation is no less strong today than it was when he wrote the first volume of *L'Etre et l'événement*. The sign of his fidelity is precisely the fact that such an orientation rests upon an absolute decision or choice (a choice without criteria—a "choice no purely mathematical prescription can norm") (PM, 37). There is no way to calculate the "correct" choice of a set-theoretic as opposed to an intuitionist or Aristotelian ontological orientation, for example. The choice is not between set theory and category theory. Category theory simply provides Badiou with tools to describe the choices made by set theory.

If category theory has become one of the conditions of Badiou's recent philosophy, his commitment to an axiomatic ontology remains properly unconditional. How this ontology conditions his philosophy remains absolute. *Nothing* informs the ontological choice. What any such choice or decision chooses is a certain way of conceiving or "fixing" the infinite *("une fixation de l'infini")*. "This fixation cannot be preliminary, transcendental, or linguistic, because it depends on an event, an Act," which is the axiomatic declaration itself. "Thought is thereby under the condition of a pure eventual addition, and it is for this reason that it produces an implacable logic. This logic stems from what thought exposes of itself by admitting the Act, by being faithful to the event. This fidelity, in turn, arranges a truth that is necessary for no one other than its Subject. Necessity is always a result" (CT, 138). Badiou has thus faced, head on, the "transcendental" challenge posed to his philosophy by logic. He has accepted the condition imposed by a duly mathematized logic, but in such a way as to make this condition itself subordinate to the more fundamental condition of mathematics itself (i.e., of mathematics as a truth procedure). Rather than simply ignore logic's claims to priority over mathematics (as he did, in effect, in *L'Etre et l'événement* itself), Badiou now has an elaborate and convincing way of dealing with this claim. Thought is not logic, "but it is no less true that there *is* always a logic of thought. To think mathematics as thought means, from within this thought, to forget the logic, to the advantage of a fidelity to the decisions."[45]

Badiou now knows, so to speak, "what" exactly his fidelity forgets. Having confronted the question of logical priority, he is in a position to propose a "modern pact ... between a Platonic orientation assumed as dominant, and an Aristotelian (Leibnizian) orientation providing a mechanism of control *[de contrôle]*," a mechanism that allows, from within the "after-effect of the real," for the retrospective exploration of the forgotten possibilities from which this real was decided and subtracted.[46] Although the mechanism of control seems to presume a degree of theoretical transcendence, nevertheless "the existence of *a* logic depends only on a process of truth, itself hanging on the chance of an eventual condition, and on a decision concerning this chance." In this way, the hierarchy of decision over logic and truth over language is preserved and reinforced. Every truth procedure demonstrates that "there is a logic of truth, but no truth of logic" (CT, 137).

Badiou sums up his current agenda in a four-point program, which I quote almost in full:

1. Logic is not a formalization, a syntax, a linguistic apparatus. It is a mathematized description of possible mathematical universes, under the generic concept of Topos. A mathematical universe, a Topos, localizes its own logic.

2. A possible mathematical universe establishes constraining correlations between certain ontological features and certain features of its immanent logic. The study of these correlations is the fundamental content of logic itself. Logic thus thinks its own subordination to ontology. It is because it thinks this subordination that it can be mathematized, since mathematics is ontology itself.

3. Mathematics operates through axiomatic decisions that arrange in the real a possible universe *[disposent en réel un univers possible]*. Logical constraints follow as a result. The constraints are thought logically by the logic of possible universes. They are practiced, but not thought, by real mathematics.

4. Consequently, the irreducible gap between logic and mathematics stems from the blind point of a thinking decision, which is that every decision of this type installs a logic that it practices as necessary [although ...] it is a consequence of the decision. Mathematized logic is a clarification of

this blindness, since it thinks the onto-logical correlation. But to do this, it must regress from the real, which is encountered only under the axiomatic imperative, to the possible, which can be described only under the regime of definitions and classifications. (CT, 134–35)

All of this defines, Badiou says, a "program of thought," one that turns on the determination "to think the possible from the point of the real. Or, to invest definitions from axioms, and not the reverse." As much as at any point in the evolution of his thought, Badiou remains committed, today, to the fundamental principle that "philosophy is essentially axiomatic, and not definitional or descriptive" (CT, 137).

With his onto-logy, his onto-logic, Badiou believes he has discovered what it is "that ensures that, however inconsistent their being, all worlds or situations are implacably related [liés]" (CT, 177). It is a brilliant extension of a philosophical system already extraordinary in its range and ramification. Its full integration into the concrete mechanics at work in what Badiou describes as the generic procedures promises to be a quite remarkable work of adjustment and synthesis.

It is of course too early to submit this extension to rigorous evaluation. Two points about Badiou's new conception of relation, however, may be worth making at this initial stage of its development. Both are obvious, and both are unlikely to change very much in future versions of the argument. The first is that relation remains a clearly derivative category. As we have seen, Badiou is very insistent about this. Relation is still denied any properly ontological status, and its strict equation with logic ensures that it will always play second fiddle to the true moving force of Badiou's philosophy. An axiom relates nothing, whereas interelemental relation itself "appears" only insofar as it leaves untouched the self-identical degrees of intensity of the apparent elements, or objects, it relates. As a result, no relation can increase or diminish "the degree of identity between two terms." In other words, "a relation creates neither existence nor difference" (EL, 94; LM, chap. 3, p. 7). Relation always comes after its terms. Relations of solidarity or antagonism, for instance, still play no constitutive role in the shaping of the individuals they mobilize, connect, or divide.[47]

The second point is that the kind of relation articulated by pure logic is itself a relation made "absolute," so to speak. What any one relation relates is here exclusively a matter of other relations. Categorical elements themselves are nothing but "relations" of self-identity, expressed by a function of appearing or measure of existential intensity (Id). If relation does not create difference, we might say, it is because it creates identity itself.[48] It is as if Badiou has gone from one extreme to another, from an ontology determined solely by elements subtracted from all relations to an onto-logy determined solely by relations abstracted from all elements. For we know that in category theory, as one textbook introduces it, "objects are not collections of 'elements'" but simply compositions of arrows or morphisms, that "all properties of objects must be specified by properties of morphisms," and that "morphisms cannot be applied to 'elements' but only composed with other morphisms."[49] Identity and difference are here conceived exclusively as the effects of actions performed upon empty carriers of these effects (and consequently identified or differed). An element is intrinsically differed, never differing.

This is why relations between elements remain derivative, even if relations "in themselves" are effectively absolute. An element is first determined by its own degree of identity to itself, and only then differs from others by comparison with their own degrees of self-identity.[50] As a result, interelemental relations can really be analyzed with the new "transcendental" machinery only as variations on the comparative relation of order itself (as relations of larger than or smaller than), which, as we know, provides Badiou with the "very first inscription of an exhortation [exigence] of the Other" (EL, 9–10). Some readers, however, may well object to this very restriction right from the start. Is not this primacy itself, once again, the result of its abstraction? In terms of what appears, blue is perhaps different from orange, or John different from Jane, or mine different from yours, without these differences' being, in the first instance, a matter of quantity or degree at all. In any case, relations in this configuration are not, strictly speaking, relative to their terms at all, which they either compare or identify pure and simple. Deleuze has already anticipated the necessarily anti-dialectical conclusion: such "relations are external to their terms."[51]

This is a conclusion any philosophy of the specific must reject. Badiou's acceptance of a categorial conditioning of philosophy may well have brought him closer to his ontologically opposite number, Deleuze. But it has not encouraged him to consider the alternative to either of these two singular positions, namely, that both elements and relations can be accounted for only together, as co-implied in a single process that maintains the elementary integrity of what is related, precisely insofar as it is related. If the "abstract types" isolated by category theory clearly have their uses in the rarefied domain of pure logic, Badiou is too quick to conclude that they hold the key to relationality as such. He is too quick to associate the relational so firmly with the realm of mere possibility. Category theory describes only what can be abstracted of relation. Actual relations themselves, however, exist between, rather than after or above, what they relate.

Conclusion

Since there should be no need to repeat here the kind of summary of Badiou's philosophical system provided in my introduction, I will conclude with an effort to situate this system in terms deliberately foreign to its own orientation—the terms of its limit.

There are at least two simple limits to any philosophy, which we might call "lower" and "upper." The lower limit would concern what philosophy conceives as beneath its dignity (what Badiou, for instance, associates with the animal, the worldly, the interested, the ephemeral, and so on); in crossing this limit, philosophy would cease to be philosophy, and would become something else (opinion, common sense, communication, tradition, ideology, etc.). The upper limit would concern what philosophy is unable to analyze or account for, yet must presume as essential to its practice (typically, Thought, Being, God, the Infinite, the Outside, the Inconsistent, and so on). By trying to cross this limit, philosophy risks its paralysis in a silent veneration of what exceeds rational articulation.

Thematic differences aside, most philosophies might be crudely divided into two broad tendencies as regards their own situation within these limits. Some philosophies tend to confirm and perhaps reinforce the lower limit, while struggling to blur the upper limit. At its most extreme, this tendency will culminate in what Badiou calls antiphilosophy or mysticism (a full participation or "extinction" in the limit). The more a philosophy can penetrate

317

its upper limit, the more vigorously it can defend its less noble frontier underneath. However variously it is pursued, this effort, I think, links (without in any way identifying) philosophies as diverse as those of Hinayana Buddhism, Plotinus, Saint Paul, al-Hallâj, Spinoza, Heidegger, Levinas, and Deleuze. These projects are all oriented by their upper limit or origin, by what lies beyond merely actual being (sunyata, the One beyond being, God, *Sein*, the virtual, etc.). We might call these "redemptive" philosophies. They all seek to "wake up," in Buddhism's phrase, from the slumbering illusions of worldly specifications and distinctions. They die to the world as world, so as to embrace a purer life above or beyond it. The goal of such a philosophy is to become, through a more or less traumatic process of despecification, (newly) immediate to its primordial, singular condition. Satori, Resurrection, Eternal Return, ethics, *aletheia*, becoming-imperceptible, and so on, are so many rituals of initiation or criteria of selection by which the properly despecified can escape mediation and rejoin their true state.

Other philosophies, however, cultivate a certain skeptical distance as regards knowledge of their upper limit, so as to concentrate more on the extension of their worldly frontier. Such philosophies accept that their upper limit is indeed inaccessible or unthinkable, that this limit is banal in its inaccessibility, and thus busy themselves with what can actually be thought. They acknowledge, for instance, that it is impossible, from within thought, to think fully and adequately the thoughtless conditions that give rise to our thinking— just as it is impossible, using language, to "say" silence except by breaking it.[1] Unless we presume that thought engenders itself in a quasi-miraculous confusion of cause and effect, we accept that what enables thought is indeed effectively "transcendental" to thought itself. From this transcendental condition spreads the full and unlimited mediation, in thought, of an always relational specificity. Philosophies as diverse as those of Mahayana Buddhism, Montaigne, Kant, Merleau-Ponty, Foucault, and even (the earlier) Lacan, might be read as contributions to this alternative. From this perspective, the experience of a self is always mediated by the experience of others—but not by an inaccessibly or absolutely Other (which instead ensures or provides, we might say, the medium of this mediation). The inaccessible is indeed the condition of mediation as such. Because the inaccessible is indeed inaccessible, what is conditioned is unlimited by its condition and constitutively related to others conditioned in the same way. Any philosophy of the specific, I think, will have to develop at least some of the lines of enquiry explored by this tendency, one way or another.

To be sure, to conceive of the inaccessible as in any way "substantial"—as noumenal, secret, or ineffable—can produce only a form of antiphilosophy.

The alternative is to acknowledge the inaccessible as such—not as any kind of pregnant secret or noumenal plenitude, but simply as a limit or horizon. The inaccessible is void, pure and simple, but as Badiou reminds us, a void is always void *for* a situation. A horizon is not an objective structure of the world or the universe, but a limit specific to a particular perception or conceptualization, however inclusive or abstract. Even the mathematical demonstration of an unending sequence of ever larger infinite numbers, while it certainly establishes the banal and numerically limitless dimension of all number, is nevertheless obliged to acknowledge a kind of specifically numerical "horizon," that is, an unreachable limit that no numbering operation can cross and within which every feasible numbering operation takes place: this is the limit indicated, as we know, by the impossibility of a single set of all sets. Such an impossible set would precisely be a set without horizon in this sense, that is, a set that excludes anything inaccessible.

One of the remarkable things about Badiou's generic philosophy is that it refuses to recognize this distinction of tendencies as a real distinction at all. On the one hand, we know that Badiou conceives of any particular philosophy as the effort to demonstrate the internal compossibility of those truths contemporary with it. Badiou's radical immanentism commits him to the principle that truth is always the truth of its situation, that it is collected as a subset within this situation. A philosophy simply identifies and connects such truths. The active components of a truth procedure are always militant interventions within the concrete limits of the situation. Anticipating Badiou's future work, we might say that a truth always "appears" as specific.

But on the other hand, and perhaps more fundamentally, Badiou's axiomatic orientation presumes the singular autoconstitution not only of the subject and truth but of the medium of this very autoconstitution itself, that is, thought as such. Thought—the stuff of philosophy in general, the Thought that stands to *a* thought somewhat as the logic of possibility stands to a "local" or decided logic—is precisely that which decides itself into existence, all at once, in the element of pure subtraction. Thought is what lacks any upper limit, and for that reason, it is effectively cut off from its lower, worldly (or animal) contamination. Thought, as decided by a subject, as proclaimed by an axiom, is at once immediate to the truth (of being, of politics, of sensation, and so on) that it articulates. And so thought is from the beginning withdrawn from relation in the most general sense, and especially from a relation with what lies "beneath" it.

As regards what other philosophers have conceived as inaccessible, then, Badiou's position is very simple: *"There is nothing inaccessible."* He writes:

Every atheist philosophy posits that nothing, in principle, is inaccessible. Hegel is decisive on this point: the whole of the real is rational. My own thesis is not that the Inaccessible is accessible. It is that *there is nothing inaccessible*. Neither the event, which has vanished, but remains as named and active as truth procedure, nor the unnameable (which is accessible to knowledge, and inaccessible only to truth), is inaccessible. As Mao used to declare: "We will come to know everything that we did not know before." It is, in any case, one of the implications of the laicization of the infinite . . . . At the moment, I am the only atheist around![2]

This refusal of the inaccessible is what enables Badiou's commitment to an eternal notion of truth as proclaimed on earth. A truth is neither limited by a worldly corruption that will eventually absorb it nor blocked by an unsayable beyond that must ultimately exceed it.

I have two questions to ask of this refusal and its consequences. The first concerns, predictably, the status of relation. Is it possible to relate (to be relative, rather than absolute), in the absence of something ultimately inaccessible, or at least whose effective access is forever deferred? For the inaccessible is precisely "something" toward which we can *only* relate, because it is necessarily beyond absorption or negation. To recognize something ultimately inaccessible is to characterize our existence, from the beginning, as essentially relational. Is the refusal of an inaccessible not the same thing, in the end, as a refusal of relation itself? It is telling, in this respect, that Badiou's recent admission of logical relation into his philosophy is achieved precisely through acknowledgment of an effectively inaccessible domain—the domain of purely logical possibility that frames any given ontological choice. However virtual or empty, this is indeed a domain that no particular ontology or philosophy can get "behind" and explain. Might it not be considered as the horizon of ontology?

In the second place, to what degree might Badiou's refusal more rightly be called a *denial* of the inaccessible? For instance, can his decreed "laicization" of the infinite fully resolve the matter of an infinitely infinite number? His relegation to mere "nonbeing" of what Cantor saw as the inaccessible upper limit of inconsistent multiplicity—the infinite extension of infinite number with no possible largest number or set of all sets—does not fully dispel the indication of a domain that is ultimately inaccessible to number.[3] That this domain cannot be coherently thought in terms of a (divine) "One" will not trouble those theologically minded philosophers for whom the ultimate "One beyond being" is equally a "One beyond Unity," that is, the indication, precisely, of a pure inaccessibility in which any distinction of the one, the multiple, and the void is inadequate by definition.[4] More important, if Badiou's axiomatic model of truth can account for the effectively sovereign exercise of any particular instance of thought, to what degree can it account for the general existence of thought itself? Does an axiomatic thought not presuppose, at least, the medium of its assertion? Does a decision not presume, as Nietzsche might say, the "one that decides"? To the degree that Badiou can proceed only from the assumed sovereignty of thought, his orientation must eventually compete, in my view, with the first of the two tendencies described in this conclusion. The subject of a thought is always the "induced" effect of that thought itself. A thought is the result of something that happens, that is, of a particular truth procedure. But thought itself, the medium of any particular thinking, cannot be so derived from what happens, since it enables it to happen.

Hence the necessary ambiguity of the term "thought" in Badiou's philosophy. On the one hand, Badiou writes that "with the word 'thought' I designate any truth procedure taken in subjectivity. 'Pensée' is the name of the subject of a truth procedure" (AM, 155). In this sense, thought is axiomatic, exceptional, rare, and thus "unnaturalizable" (LS, 81–82). On the other hand, Badiou is sometimes obliged to define thought almost as an anthropological attribute, a natural or structural constant of that age-old hybrid the "thinking animal": "The exclusively human capacity is thought" (AM, 111). Though Badiou, of course, seeks to maintain a strictly evental definition of the human, nevertheless our "singular human capacities"[5] (the ability to use mathematics, to love, and so on) make up an effectively general domain of thought as such. Such capacities are employed in particular instances of truth (any particular mathematical invention), but cannot themselves, as capacities, be fully generated by them. Thought in this general sense is indeed irreducible to its particular configuration in truths. Badiou's axiomatic procedures cannot "explain" what they do. Nor do they tolerate enquiry into what enables their doing: axiomatic thought encounters nothing but more axiomatic thought.

The transcendental regime presumed by any conception of the specific, by contrast, acknowledges certain specified (i.e., thoughtless) conditions of thought. We cannot get outside thought to think these conditions as they are "in themselves," and whether they are attributed to a divine providence or a mechanical evolution is not, in the first instance, particularly important. Our reconstruction of these conditions will always be just that, a reconstruction. By the same token, they do not intervene "in" thought to determine what thought thinks. It is all of thought, thought as an open whole, that is conditioned by its specified conditions; this is why these conditions do not themselves specify any particular thoughts. No rational theology, no evolutionary psychology, no cognitive science or neurology, will ever be in a position to specify the direction of particular thoughts.

Badiou is certainly right to agree, with Parmenides, that thought and being are one and the same. Simply, Badiou's ontology prescribes the nature of being directly, without any dialectical intermediary, and his conception of thought is essentially linear (the step-by-step composition of a subset). Specific thinking, by contrast, can never be fully immediate to being as being. On the contrary, thought is nothing other than being-mediated. Specific thought folds itself over concrete being, distances itself from it, in such a way that there can be no direct or unmodulated transition from the one to the other. The relation is irreducible. This is the banal reason both for our freedom "within" being (what we do is never specified by the general structures of being) and for our frustration "outside" it (whatever we do, we cannot rejoin or consume being).

Badiou's guiding assumption is that the be-ing of an individual or a situation is a matter of inconsistent multiplicity, an inconsistency that is accessible only once that individual has been subtracted from the regime of relations it has with other individuals; my guiding assumption is that an individual has no being outside of its relations with other individuals, so what matters is the conversion of oppressive relations into liberating ones.

By any criteria, Badiou's project is one of the most remarkable, most original, and most powerful contemporary efforts to renew an engaged, progressive conception of philosophy. His is certainly the most rigorous and most inspiring assertion of a subject-based or conviction-driven philosophy since Sartre. To my mind his philosophy is much the most inventive, the most thought-provoking, of his generation. It is "limited," if that is the word, only by its refusal to grant relation any properly constituent force. As long as philosophy is defined as singular rather than specific, as long as it preserves itself in its pure *déliaison,* as long as it retains a strictly axiomatic integrity, it will not be able to provide a fully convincing account for the shift from withdrawal to intervention, from subtraction to transformation, from prescription to production. Though it will have long since ceased merely to describe the world, its promise to change this world will always remain unduly abstract.

On the Development of Transfinite Set Theory

Set theory is one of the most significant conditions of Badiou's philosophy, and it provides the formal framework for his ontology. This appendix is designed to offer, independently of Badiou's unique application of the theory, some elementary background information concerning its history, purpose, and broad philosophical significance. The reader will find summary explanations of a number of concepts and terms referred to at various points during the main text, including actual and potential conceptions of the infinite, denumerable and nondenumerable sets, Cantor's continuum hypothesis, Russell's paradox, the Zermelo-Fraenkel axioms, Gödel's incompleteness theorem, and (in a little more detail) Cohen's generic sets and concept of forcing. All are presented with the strict minimum of technical complication and intimidation.[1]

What the great German mathematician Georg Cantor (1845–1918) called "transfinite" or "suprafinite" set theory is clearly a theory that aims to combine a conception of the infinite with a conception of set (or number).[2] Its revolutionary innovation concerns the mathematical status of the "actual," or completed, infinite—the infinite conceived, precisely, as a *set*, that is, as an embraceable collection or whole. This appendix begins, then, with the general context in which this innovation took place. Subsequent sections look at the various components of the theory, and at perhaps the two most important moments (associated with Gödel and Cohen, respectively) of its post-Cantorian evolution. The principle guiding the whole of this presentation is that of a shameless simplification throughout.

Infinity before Cantor

Before Cantor's dramatic invention, most philosophers had agreed that application of the concept of actual, or self-embracing, infinity should be reserved for an entity more or less explicitly identified with God (the One of Plotinus, Descartes's idea of God, Spinoza's substance, Hegel's Absolute or "good" infinite, and so on). The most that mathematics could do, it seemed, was describe something *potentially* infinite, the sort of thing illustrated by unending numerical succession: 1, 2, 3 . . . *n*. Only this concept of the infinite as potential or neverending was deemed worthy of scientific status. Indeed, the idea of a completed infinite provided many classical philosophers with the supreme example of an idea exceeding the powers of human thought.[3] On the one hand, the possibility of an actually infinite division of time or quantity into ever smaller quantities appeared to suggest the impossibility of motion itself (Anaxagoras, Zeno); on the other hand, the possibility of an actually infinite number, a number such that $n = n + 1$, appeared to defy the principles of arithmetic themselves (Galileo, Leibniz). Real or actual infinity seemed forever destined to belong to a realm beyond number and thus beyond measurement—doomed to remain, in short, an essentially indefinite, if not frankly religious, concept.[4]

Perhaps the most significant moment in this metaphysical consensus can be traced to Aristotle. Confronted with Zeno's famous paradoxes concerning motion and division, Aristotle set a trend that would hold good for the next two thousand years: even if physical bodies might in principle be infinitely divided, he argued, they never are so divided. Nothing existent is actually made up of infinitely small parts. As a result, if the infinite can be said to exist at all, it must have an exclusively "potential existence."[5]

The story of the actually infinite in modern mathematics, then, is the story of the slow subversion of this eminently sensible Aristotelian approach. Most histories of mathematics distinguish three or four central episodes in this story: the discovery of irrational numbers; the algebraicization of geometry; the discovery of calculus and the controversial status of "infinitesimals"; the discovery of non-Euclidean geometries, and the consequent search for a new arithmetic foundation for mathematics. The last of these four episodes determines the immediate context for Cantor's set theory.

Incommensurable Magnitudes

One of the first great mathematical encounters with the infinite is associated with the apparent discovery, a century or two before Aristotle's own intervention, of incommensurable magnitudes or ratios.[6] Pythagoras and his followers had maintained that all of reality could be described in terms of commensurable magnitudes, that is, in terms of the whole numbers or ratios of whole numbers. It may, then, have come as quite a shock to discover that the diagonal of a square could not be expressed as a ratio at all. If we consider such a diagonal as the hypotenuse of a right triangle whose two equal sides are measured as one unit, the familiar formula $a^2 = b^2 + c^2$ gives the diagonal's length as $\sqrt{2}$ units. The square root of 2 (or of any other prime number) is irrational, meaning that it cannot be expressed as a fraction or ratio of two whole numbers (however large).[7] Its decimal expansion, beginning $1.4142135\ldots$, is endlessly unrepeating. It is thus a literally infinite number—not, of course, because the quantity it represents is infinitely large, but because any finite representation of it can be only approximate. In a sense, the existence of such irrational numbers provided the first mathematically irrefutable proof of the inexhaustible wealth of the "number line" or geometric continuum: it would seem that there is no obvious way to count all the possible numbers between any two whole numbers, just as there is no obvious way to count all the extensionless geometric points in a given stretch of space. Even to pose such questions in this way would seem to be incoherent.[8]

Descartes and the Algebraicization of Geometry

The ancient promise of an exact and universal measurement was reasserted centuries later by Descartes and the thorough algebraicization of geometry, but this new effort also led to another paradoxical encounter with the actually infinite. Before Descartes came along, geometry was essentially the stuff of ruler-and-compass manipulations of the kind still taught in primary school—a matter of graphic, intuitive representation or spatial modeling. What Descartes did was to begin to eliminate the intuitive aspect of geometry, in favor of a purely numerical description of forms and curves, that is, a description that allows us to reduce the expression of a form to the calculus of its coordinates.[9] As Mary Tiles puts it:

> Prior to the algebraicisation of geometry the classical [i.e., Aristotelian] finitist could stand his ground without suffering mathematical penalties. So long as geometry (the science of continuous magnitudes) and arithmetic (the science of discrete magnitudes) remained separate and largely independent branches of mathematics, the infinite inherent in the continuum remained internal to the notion of continuity which was taken as a primitive notion grounded in geometric intuition. In this context the question "How many points are there in a line?" has no mathematical sense . . . , because a line as a continuous magnitude

does not form the sort of whole to which a number, other than a measure of length, is assignable. . . . The situation changes, however, with the algebraicisation of geometry. . . . With the introduction of an algebraic notation there is immediately a tension between the view of a continuous curve as a whole given before its parts and as a whole composed of discrete entities—given *as* its parts.[10]

In other words, the numerical description of the hitherto purely spatial or intuitive notion of a linear continuum had become a genuine conceptual possibility.

Calculus

The calculus invented independently by Newton and Leibniz took partial advantage of this possibility. Calculus describes forms of continuous variation (curves or motions) in precise numerical terms. To do so it had recourse to what Leibniz called the "useful fiction" of infinitesimal numbers—ideal or imaginary numbers infinitely smaller than any conceivable real number (and thus adequate to represent the "lengths" of the infinitely short line segments that make up a curve). With calculus, the possibility of an arithmetic description of the continuum became a reality of sorts. The question remained: "What sort of reality?"[11] At the end of the seventeenth century, mathematicians such as De l'Hospital and Fontenelle were indeed confident of the actually infinite dimension of the infinitesimals. But the next century was to see a gradual reaction against this actuality, however, spurred in part by Berkeley's famous critique of the infinitesimals as the "ghosts of departed quantities." Over the early decades of the nineteenth century, thanks to the cumulative work of Cauchy, Bolzano, and Weierstrass, the apparently incoherent notion of an actually infinitesimal number was at last replaced by the more easily acceptable idea of a numerical "limit" toward which an infinite series tends. In other words, rather than conceive of the gradient of a curve as the ratio of two infinitely small quantities dy/dx, this ratio is conceived as "the limit of an infinite sequence of ever closer approximations to a given quantity."[12] The exclusive existence of the potential infinite was thereby reestablished, and discussion of the actually infinite was once again presumed to refer to nothing more than what Gauss called (in 1831) a "manner of speaking."[13]

What this theory of limits required in its turn, however, was an account of its own now exclusively numerical foundation, and in particular an arithmetic basis for the so-called real numbers (i.e., infinitely continuing or irrational numbers).[14] The need for such a foundation became all the more urgent with the discovery, also made over the first decades of the nineteenth century, of alternative forms of geometry itself.

Non-Euclidean Geometries

According to some accounts, the discovery of non-Euclidean geometries was "the most consequential development" of nineteenth-century mathematics.[15] Euclid's geometry had been premised on the idea that what it described in the idealized terms of points and lines was ultimately the very reality of space and physical extension themselves. Descartes's innovations had done nothing to challenge this idea, and it remained a basic assumption for the entire rationalist tradition no less than for Galileo, Newton, and the scientific revolution as a whole. Writing at the end of the eighteenth century (and somewhat behind the mathematical trends of his day), Kant still stuck to firmly Euclidean principles in his description of a priori space. Euclid's famous postulate that parallel lines never meet, for instance, was held to express an obvious fact of the physical universe as much as an intuitively demonstrable principle of ruler-and-compass geometry. After many attempts, however, it turned out to be impossible to develop a conclusive proof of the postulate's necessary truth (and the impossibility of its direct derivation from Euclid's other and less controversial axioms was finally confirmed in 1868). At the same time, a number of mathematicians (Lobachevsky, Bolyai, and Riemann are the most celebrated) managed to demonstrate the existence of perfectly coherent but thoroughly counterintuitive, non-Euclidean geometries comprising any number of theoretical dimensions. In the light of their discoveries, a conception of space in which the parallel postulate holds true now appears to be one rather limited conception among a multitude of others. For example, the non-Euclidean configuration of two-dimensional space as mapped onto the surface of a sphere asserts either a plurality of lines through a certain point P parallel to a certain line L (Lobachevsky), or the absence of any such lines (Riemann).[16]

In other words, geometric axioms could no longer be understood as the transcription of certain elementary, self-evident aspects of homogeneous physical space, but were recognized to be irreducibly relative to a particular *model* of space. More than any other modern mathematical discovery, the elaboration of new geometries at a level of complexity far beyond the limits of any conceivable physical existence (let alone any merely graphic representation) served to undermine the idea, so widely accepted in the seventeenth century, that mathematics was ultimately grounded in its correspondence with the innately mathematical structure of the universe itself. One consequence was the need to clarify the now unavoidable fact of mathematical autonomy. If not material reality, what was to secure the foundation of mathematical truths?[17]

The attempt to answer this question led to a newly rigorous investigation of the properly numerical foundations of arithmetic itself. Only the natural number system based on the elementary succession of units (1, 2, 3, 4 . . .) appeared invulnerable to skeptical relativism, an attitude summed up by Leopold Kronecker's quip, "The whole numbers are the work of God. All else is the work of man," and therefore doubtful.[18]

Even here, however, paradox remains close at hand. If number is to be the sole basis of mathematics, is number itself an ultimately coherent notion? Long before the invention of non-Euclidean geometries, Galileo had realized that if we order sets of numbers on the basis of an (unending) one-to-one correspondence, "there are as many squares as there are numbers" (see the figure in the next section of this appendix)—a result that encouraged him to conclude that the very notion of number loses its coherence as it approaches infinity. Hobbes's presumption remained the typically pre-Cantorian view: "When we say any thing is infinite, we signify only that we are not able to conceive the ends and bounds of the things named; having no conception of the thing, but of our own inability."[19] Above all, the mathematicians of the mid–nineteenth century still upheld the commonsense empiricist notion, that the idea of "one infinite infinitely bigger than another" is an "absurdity too gross to be confuted."[20] The concept of an actual, measurable infinity—and thus the possibility of different "sizes" of infinity, of different infinite numbers—seemed to be forever resistant to precise mathematical description. Such was the situation in which Cantor set to work, with Dedekind's help, in the 1870s.

Cantor's Theory of Transfinite Numbers (1880–97)

What Cantor did, then, was provide precisely what previous mathematicians and philosophers had almost unanimously declared impossible: a mathematically precise description of infinite numbers qua numbers. Of course, an infinite number is not measurable in terms of finite quantities: nevertheless, Cantor established that the concept of numerical order or succession is every bit as coherent in the realm of the actually infinite as it is in the realm of the obviously finite. He showed that it made perfect sense to speak of the size (or "cardinality") of different infinite quantities, conceived as completed wholes or sets.[21]

Cantor's definition of a set was simplicity itself: "By a set S we are to understand any collection into a whole of definite and separate objects m of our intuition or our thought."[22] In order to conceive of any such collection as a collected whole, Cantor realized that there was no need actually to count out how many elements were collected (although, significantly, he did cling fast to the idea that all such collections could be enumerated in principle, that is, by some sort of infinitely powerful counting agent). Actually to enumerate a given quantity is, as Russell put it, a "very vulgar and elementary way of finding out how many terms there are in a calculation."[23] What mathematicians call ordinal numbers are determined through such enumeration, by counting their elements up from zero. Cardinal numbers, by contrast, are compared in terms of a one-to-one correspondence quite independent of the ordinal counting or ordering process.[24] For instance, we can easily compare the number of teacups to that of saucers on a tray, and determine whether there are as many cups as saucers, without having to enumerate either quantity up from zero. In other words, cardinality refers to the relative size or "power" of a set, while ordinality refers to the way it is ordered or counted (up from zero). The ordinal numbers provide what we might call an absolute scale of numerical succession; cardinality measures the effectively relative size of sets. So long as we limit ourselves to finite quantities, ordinal and cardinal numbers clearly amount to one and the same thing: any finite number can be ordered or counted in only one way (and thus coincides with its cardinality). When it comes to infinite quantities, however, it is a different story. An infinite set of a particular cardinality may well be ordered in many different ways, which means that the relation between its ordinal value and its cardinal value is not obvious. Indeed, what distinguishes an infinite quantity (by the definition that Dedekind proposed and Cantor refined, and that Galileo had anticipated but dismissed as nonsensical) is precisely the fact that it can be put into a one-to-one correspondence with one of its own subsets or parts.[25] An infinite number, in other words, violates Euclid's postulate that the whole is necessarily larger than the part.

Natural Numbers	Odd Numbers	Squares
1	1	1
2	3	4
3	5	9
4	7	16
5 ...	9 ...	25 ...

Since the sequence of natural or "counting" numbers is itself infinite, it is perfectly true that there are as many odd numbers as there are both odd and even numbers.

More remarkable still is the fact that, as one of Cantor's earliest articles showed, the set of numbers that includes all of the fractions conceivable between any two whole numbers is itself no "more" infinite than the set of whole numbers on their own. Though there are infinitely many rational numbers or fractions between any two whole numbers—since between any two fractions we can always add another fraction—this infinitely dense abundance of the rational numbers adds no discernible quantity to the already infinite wealth of the natural numbers. Cantor (eventually) confirmed this counterintuitive result by perfectly intuitive means: all that needs to be done is to show, once again, that the endless sequence of fractions can be put into a countable, one-to-one correspondence with the natural number sequence:

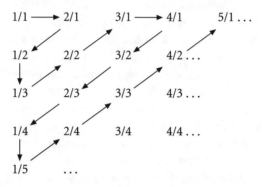

By following the arrows we come up with a "number line" that will come to include every possible fraction, a line whose elements can in principle be paired off, with some repetitions, with the natural or counting numbers:

1	2	3	4	5	6	7 ...	n.
1/1	2/1	1/2	1/3	2/2	3/1	4/1 ...	n.

In other words, any set (finite or infinite) whose elements might be paired with the natural or counting numbers can thereby be considered denumerable, and all infinite denumerable sets have the same cardinality or size, regardless of how large a part of the "whole" infinitely denumerable set they include. Cantor chose to represent this first or smallest infinite cardinal number, representing the size of the set to which belong all natural and rational numbers, with the first letter of the Hebrew alphabet, subscripted with a zero: $\aleph_0$.[26]

Does the denumerability of even the set of all possible fractions mean that all (infinite) sets are denumerable? Are there infinite sets other than this $\aleph_0$? Were Hobbes and Locke right in thinking that there can be only one order of infinity? For the first time in history, Cantor was able to give firmly negative answers to these questions. After all, the discovery of irrational numbers had already demonstrated the existence of numbers no fraction could translate—numbers representing so many "holes" on the numerical continuum, holes that no ratio of whole numbers could represent or "fill in." The problem Cantor had inherited from previous attempts to complete the arithmetization of geometry was precisely the one posed by the fact that the ordered, denumerable body of rational numbers does not produce an exhaustive numerical description of a linear continuum (i.e., it cannot count out all the conceivable geometric points belonging to a line). His initial goal, then, was to arrive at an arithmetic definition of the set of numbers required to represent or index this elusive number. His great achievement was to show that this set, the set of real numbers required to describe the uninterrupted continuum of a line segment, is not denumerable at all. The real numbers are of an entirely different order of infinity from that of the denumerable, rational numbers; they are, precisely, infinitely more numerous than the infinite set of denumerable numbers.

Cantor's most famous demonstration of this point is indirect. Imagine a line segment measured as one unit, that is, as a segment running from 0 to 1 on a number line. Now suppose that it were denumerable, and suppose that all the numbers between 0 and 1 could be listed as indefinitely proceeding decimals, in the form $d = 0.x_1,x_2,x_3,x_4 \ldots x_n$, where each x stands for one digit in the decimal sequence. This would generate an endless listing of these decimals that would include, to choose some arbitrary examples,

$$0.\textbf{1}111111111\ldots$$
$$0.1\textbf{6}87923982\ldots n$$
$$0.36\textbf{7}8945983\ldots n$$
$$0.695\textbf{9}234054\ldots n$$
$$0.8238\textbf{9}78453\ldots n$$
$$0.n_1,n_2,n_3,n_4\ldots n_n$$

We might expect that this kind of list should eventually cover every possible decimal number between 0 and 1. Nevertheless, Cantor could easily show that it is possible to construct endless further numbers between 0 and 1 that could *not* be included in any such list, simply by performing some arbitrary operation on a number generated diagonally down the list (here, the digits in bold type). Say we construct a number that differs, in every digit, by one (or two, or three . . .) from the "diagonal" number $0.16799\ldots n$ that can be put together in this way, thus yielding $0.27800\ldots$ or $0.38911\ldots$. The result will certainly be a number that is between 0 and 1, yet different from any of the numbers in the original list, if only in the nth place. In this way Cantor confirmed by arithmetic means the ancient geometric understanding that, though infinitely dense, the collection of rational numbers does not form a continuum: however fully this collection is enumerated, it is punctured by infinitely many irrational holes.[27] The cardinality of the continuum as such, this nondenumerable set that includes all the real numbers, Cantor called c. By another counterintuitive demonstration, he showed that this cardinality applies to any segment of a continuum, no matter how large in conventional terms—one inch as much as a trillion miles, a line as much as a plane or cube. Even the $\aleph_0$-dimensional continuum is of the same size (or cardinality) as the one-dimensional continuum.[28]

There are thus at least two different orders of mathematical infinity, the second (c) infinitely larger than the first ($\aleph_0$). From $\aleph_0$, moreover, the elementary procedures of set theory can easily generate an infinite succession of further infinite numbers or sets, most obviously by means of the axiom of the power set. Once we have a established a set of a given cardinality n, finite or infinite, we can create a new, much larger set by bringing together all of its possible subsets, all of the possible ways of combining its elements into parts. As we saw in chapter 4, given a set n, the total number of parts or subsets thus collected together will form a set with 2^n elements. When n is a finite number, however large, this excess of the power set over the set itself (or of parts over elements) is easily measured. When n is infinite, however, the excess is itself infinitely larger than the set's own infinity. Hence an unending sequence of infinite numbers, each infinitely larger than its predecessor:

$$\aleph_0, 2^{\aleph_0}, 2^{2^{\aleph_0}} \ldots$$

Cantor was able to show that the second number in this sequence, the power set of $\aleph_0$, could be put in a one-to-one correspondence with the nondenumerable cardinality of the continuum itself, c: $2^{\aleph_0} = c$.

Cantor's next and abiding question, formulated as the famous "continuum hypothesis" (CH), was this: What sort of relationship is there between the first and smallest infinite cardinal $\aleph_0$ and its power set $2^{\aleph_0}$ (or c)? Might the power set be proven to be the "successor" to $\aleph_0$, that is, the next largest cardinal on the transfinite numerical scale, written $\aleph_1$? In other words, might the power set follow immediately after the denumerable infinity of the natural numbers, with no distinct number between the two? CH is the presumption that $2^{\aleph_0} = \aleph_1$ (or that $c = \aleph_1$).

Cantor was convinced that this seemingly plausible hypothesis was true, and that it provided the basis for a kind of order and stability in the realm of the transfinite: in a universe in which a generalized CH held true, every infinite set could be thought of as "well ordered."[29] The potentially anarchic concept of a nondenumerable set would be defined as following immediately from the cardinality of the denumerable set of natural numbers.[30] To Cantor's great consternation, however, he was unable to prove the point. As Cohen was eventually able to establish, the derivation of a successor cardinal simply bears no obvious relation to the operation of the power set axiom. It cannot be determined that the sequence of infinite cardinals $\aleph_0, \aleph_1, \aleph_2 \ldots$ is identical with the exponential series $\aleph_0, 2^{\aleph_0}, 2^{2^{\aleph_0}} \ldots$. To this day, CH remains one of the great bones of mathematical contention: more than any other issue, it indicates the differences between the various ways of thinking (which Badiou distinguishes as intuitionist, transcendent, and generic) about the nature and reality of mathematics (see chapter 9).

We should address one further point before moving on. Cantor's definition of set left undecided the question of whether a set is what Russell was to call "intensional"—that is, the collection of objects corresponding to a predicate or concept (the set of all nations, all Cubans, all abstract ideas, all natural numbers, etc.)—or extensional, that is, the result of a simple collecting together of previously existent elements, which may or may not share any unifying properties (the set of all things lying on my desk, the set of all things caught in a fisherman's net, etc.).[31] The intensional, or rule-governed, conception of set—first defended by Frege and in a later version by Russell himself—presumes the logical priority of the concept over its application. The concept of fourness, for example, is what will allow the gathering together of any number of sets of four (four people, four apples, four zeros, etc.) into a set defined as one whose elements all have four elements. The extensional, or "combinatorial," conception of set proceeds instead from the bottom up; such a set is simply a result, the result of collecting together a certain bundle of elements.

In contemporary set theory (and in Badiou's ontology), the extensional approach prevails, largely because Russell's famous paradox concerning sets' belonging to themselves demonstrated the vulnerability of any set theory that tries to *define* the notion of set. For if sets are to be thought of as intensional, it makes sense to distinguish between properties that include themselves within their intensional grasp and those that do not. Some sets will include themselves (the set of abstract objects will be an abstract object, the set of all collections of paintings will itself be a collection of paintings), but others will not (the set of all women is not a woman, the set of all stars is not a star). The question then arises: Is the set of all sets that are not members of themselves a member of itself? Consider, for instance, the analogy of a village barber who shaves only those people in the village who do not shave themselves. Does the barber, then, shave himself?[32] We must conclude that there can be no straightforward answer. But the fundamental assumptions of intensional set theory seem to bar us from saying that there can be no such paradoxical set.

The immediate effect of the paradoxes was devastating for Frege and the intensional concept of set, and had, according to his great contemporary David Hilbert, a "downright catastrophic effect" on mathematics in general.[33] The debates concerning the nature and reality of mathematics that developed in the early years of the twentieth century arose as so many responses to this new crisis in its foundations. The intuitionist school, led by Brouwer, simply refused to acknowledge anything whose existence could not be directly demonstrated (or constructed), including actually infinite sets.[34] Russell's own solution was to reformulate Frege's logicism—the attempt to reduce mathematical expressions to elementary principles of logic—by defining the notion of set in terms of hierarchical types, in such a way as to exclude the possibility of sets that include themselves (since the including set would always belong to a higher type). In this approach, sets do not provide the most elementary "stuff" of thought but are perceived instead as constructs manipulated by still more basic logical operations. The more distinctively mathematical way of handling sets, finally—an approach initiated by Zermelo and pursued by Fraenkel, Hilbert, and most other working mathematicians—applies axiomatic principles "directly to the sets themselves, rather than to logic as an intermediary."[35] This enables a more intuition-free foundation for geometry and number theory. Only what came to be known as axiomatic set theory provided a way of avoiding the logical paradoxes without sacrificing the many achievements made by classical (i.e., nonintuitionist) mathematics.

Why There Can Be No Definition of "Set"

Not only was Cantor unable to prove his precious continuum hypothesis, but hardly had he put his ideas in their final, finished form than he became aware of another problem, comparable to the one later indicated by Russell's paradox. Even before Cantor, Galileo and Leibniz had already realized that "the number, or set, of all numbers entails a contradiction if one conceives of it as a completed whole."[36] Cantor's theory led to a similar conclusion: any attempt to define the ultimate set of all sets leads immediately to paradox. For there can be no such set without immediately accepting the existence of its power set (since, as a set, it must be included in the set of *all* sets). But one of Cantor's own fundamental theorems established that the power set $p(x)$ of the set x must always be larger than x. Hence a set apparently "larger" than the set of all sets. This contradiction led Cantor to distinguish strictly between ordinary or "consistent" infinities (the transfinite per se), capable of numerical treatment, and an "inconsistent" infinity (the Absolutely infinite), which remains beyond the realm of number altogether and forever out of human reach.[37] Whereas the transfinite is essentially like the finite in that it is both "fixed and definite in relation to all other numbers" and "increasable," that is, part of an unending numerical succession or hierarchy, the absolute is itself defined as "unincreasable" or "unapproachable."[38] At this unincreasable limit, number ceases to be consistent. In other words, the "set of all sets" is not a set and fails even Cantor's "naive" definition: it cannot be coherently collected into a whole.[39]

The devoutly pious Cantor himself had no difficulty in attributing this Absolute infinity to a divine transcendence.[40] His followers, however, wanted a more precise explanation of how exactly to set this inconsistent limit, how to situate the place where number gets too big for set theory to handle. What is known as the "limitation of size hypothesis" (versions of which were proposed by Jourdain, Russell, Zermelo, Fraenkel, and Von Neumann, among others) attempted to specify precisely that place.[41] But, despite several heuristic advances, none of these attempts have fully succeeded. The exact demarcation of consistent and inconsistent sets remains unclear, and has given rise to an abundance of theories concerning more or less strongly "inaccessible" cardinals, larger than anything Cantor would have recognized as consistent.[42] These attempts to establish a clear limitation of size fail, it seems, for the same reason that the continuum hypothesis itself cannot be confirmed: it has not proved possible to put effective limits on the (impredicative) operation of the power set axiom. The consequences of the power set axiom, that is, the generation of new orders of infinite power or cardinality, simply cannot be aligned in any clear way with the ordinal or countable number sequence.

It is crucial for an evaluation of Badiou's philosophy to consider the fairly subtle ontological implications of this outcome. Why, you might ask, did Cantor feel compelled to introduce this vexing power set axiom at all? Indeed, it was not part of his own initial theory of transfinite numbers. Cantor understood that there was no need actually to enumerate the elements of a set in order to establish its cardinality (or size). Nevertheless, he initially believed that he might be able to map out the transfinite domain by assuming that it could, in principle, be counted out as a well-ordered (rather than an exponential) succession. What is distinctive about Cantor's initiative is precisely his "ordinal theory of cardinality," that is, his belief that all the transfinite cardinals (or powers) "are capable of being ordinally numbered," or counted up from zero: first, second, third, and so on.[43] Hallett calls this "dominance of the ordinals perhaps the most striking feature of Cantor's work," the basis for its fundamental "finitism."[44] It is striking because there is no clear reason to believe that infinite sets even should be countable in this way. Rather than accept that infinite collections cannot actually be counted—and thus look, as did Frege, for another definition of number altogether, one based on purely relative ("one-to-one") correspondences between sets—Cantor persisted in trying to treat the transfinite as the finite, that is, as countable or orderable. This implies that the counting mechanism presumed by Cantor's transfinite ordinals must itself be actually infinite.

There is a very real sense, then, in which "for Cantor, much more important than our ability to conceive of a collection as 'one' was God's ability to do so.... It is really God who has put elements together to form sets, not we."[45]

Now we know that a fairly conventional notion of counting or ordering allowed Cantor to define his first, "denumerable" infinite number, $\aleph_0$. It was when he tried to count the set of all real numbers (the geometric continuum) that he was obliged—and obliged against his will—to introduce the power set axiom. Only this axiom allowed him to collect the real numbers together in an apparently "definite" set (the set whose cardinality is indeed $2^{\aleph_0}$). But it did not allow him to *count* them. Even if we attribute quasi-divine ordering powers to some hypothetical counting agent, we still cannot count out this new power set. In other words, counting or ordering could no longer be considered the basic mathematical principle behind both finite and transfinite sets. And Cantor could not propose any viable new principle in its place.[46]

As Lavine and Hallett argue in convincing detail, the post-Cantorian axiomatization of set theory that began with Zermelo's once controversial axiom of choice (1904) was less a response to the familiar logical problems associated with Russell's paradox concerning sets that are members of themselves than an effort to enable Cantor's fundamental "ordering" project to succeed. The price to be paid for Cantor's ordinal approach—unlike Frege's cardinal theory—is that in order to preserve set-theoretic consistency from contradiction, the uncountable limit to all possible countings or sets must be explicitly barred from inclusion in the theory.[47]

Axiomatization was first proposed largely in order to locate this limit and ensure the "order" of the whole transfinite realm. In the process, it also had the effect of blocking the specifically logical difficulties that Russell associated with unrestricted application of the "comprehension theory" of set, that is, the paradoxes concerning sets of things that are members of themselves. Axiomatization prescribes—in particular through the axiom of foundation— means for avoiding these paradoxes. But the essential thing to understand is that this axiomatic advance was achieved at the cost of any explanation of the most basic concept involved, that of set itself. As Von Neumann put it, "In the spirit of the axiomatic method one understands by 'set' nothing but an object of which one knows no more and wants to know no more than what follows about it from the postulates."[48] Set theory was axiomatized, Hallett explains, precisely "because we do not understand the set concept well."[49] Indeed, in a fully axiomatic set theory the notion of "sethood" is "not just unexplained but inexplicable" (37). Once we embrace a fully extensional theory of set (whereby a set is defined solely by what belongs to it), there is no obvious sense in which a set retains any distinctive unity at all.

This is where, for many philosophers of mathematics, the ontological chickens come home to roost: because it is not able to say what its elementary concept *is*, axiomatic set theory is generally refused any properly ontological authority. This is why Hallett, for instance, is doubtful that set theory can legitimately be applied to the real domain of the continuum at all. For, since the axiomatic system as a whole cannot be proved consistent (if only, even before Gödel's famous incompleteness theorems, because of the anarchic consequences of the power set axiom), we cannot say why all of mathematics should be embraced by the concept of set. In particular, we cannot say why the continuum (i.e., the power set of $\aleph_0$) should be embraced by it.[50]

Badiou takes exactly the opposite view: it is precisely because the theory prescribes (rather than describes) the most basic predicates of existence that it can be held to be the sole truly ontological discourse, the discourse where be-ing and thought are actively indistinguishable. And nowhere does this discourse ring more true than at its "real" point of impasse, that is, the point where we attempt the impossible measurement of the power set of $\aleph_0$.[51] This point is the *"passe"* of the subject, because it indicates the exact point where we cannot know (in Hallett's sense) the consistency of mathematics— the point where we are forced to make a choice.

The Axiomatization of Set Theory

We can go back now to review what is actually involved in this axiomatization. Thanks largely to the discovery of non-Euclidean geometries, axioms are no longer generally understood in modern mathematics as self-evident truths or idealizations of empirical behavior. The truth of mathematics is no longer ensured through its correspondence to observable reality; for most mathematicians, "propositions are true at best insofar as they follow from assumptions and definitions we have made."[52] An axiom, in the modern sense, is indeed something we *make*, something artificial or postulated. It is simply a rigorous convention accepted on the basis of its utility and its compatibility with other similarly accepted conventions.

In a sequence of steps published between 1908 and 1925, a group of mathematicians including Zermelo, Fraenkel, Skolem, and Von Neumann put Cantor's still partly intuitive theory of sets on a secure axiomatic (or nonintuitive) footing.[53] The result became known as the Zermelo-Fraenkel axiom system (ZF), and is widely held to provide the "the most natural version of set theory."[54] Rather than conceive of a set as a collection of objects according to a conceptual definition or rule, the new "iterative" conception of sets as cumulative hierarchies assumes that any collection or whole is always generated from or after its parts or elements. This iterative concept of a set foregrounds the procedures by which all the sets recognized in the ZF universe are formed out of smaller, simpler sets. As we saw in some detail in chapter 4, all such sets are constructed by the combination of axiomatically prescribed procedures (principally those prescribed by the power set and union axioms) in successive steps from an assumed foundational empty set $\emptyset$, such that any given set is precisely formed at one "stage" in this succession: $\emptyset$, $\{\emptyset\}$, $\{\emptyset, \{\emptyset\}\}$, $\{\emptyset, \{\emptyset, \{\emptyset\}\}\}$ ... ω_0—or 0, 1, 2, 3 ... ω_0.[55] The transfinite ordinals are generated in exactly the same way, founded on omega (ω_0), the axiomatically asserted "limit ordinal," or largest countable (i.e., smallest infinite) number, whose cardinality is equal to $\aleph_0$. The only primitive relation presumed in the entire system is that of belonging, $\in$ (for inclusion can be described in terms of belonging).

There are nine basic axioms in the ZF system.[56]

1. Axiom of extensionality: "If two sets have the same elements, then they are identical; in other words, a set's identity is determined entirely by its elements."

2. Null-set axiom: "There is a set that contains no elements, written $\emptyset$." This is "the only set whose existence is directly asserted. Every other set is constructed in some way or other from this set."[57] (Given the axiom of extensionality, the *uniqueness* of the empty set follows as an obvious theorem.)

3. Subset axiom, or power set axiom: "Given a set α, there is another set, written $p(\alpha)$, the power-set of α, whose elements are the subsets or parts of α." The collecting together of the subsets of α provides Badiou with his definition of the *state* of α.

4. Union axiom, or sum set axiom: "If x is a set, then there is a set denoted $\cup$, the union of all the elements of x, whose elements are all the elements of the elements of x." For example, if x is a set with two elements, y and z, where y = {a, b, c} and z = {a, c, d, e}—in other words, such that x = {{a, b, c}, {a, c, d, e}}—then the union of the (two) elements of x is simply the set {a, b, c, d, e}. If the axiom of subsets is what groups together all the possible groupings of a set's elements, the axiom of union has the opposite effect, enabling the decomposition or "dissemination" of elements into their own multiple elements.

5. Axiom of infinity. This axiom declares the existence of a "limit ordinal," that is, a set that, though not empty, nevertheless does not succeed another ordinal. It guarantees the existence of at least one infinite set, from which endless others can be generated.

6. Axiom of foundation (or regularity): "If α is a nonempty set, then there is an element b of α such that there are no sets that belong both to α and b." This axiom explicitly outlaws the paradoxical situation of sets' belonging to themselves. It ensures that, given a certain set, it is impossible to count down indefinitely from the set to a member of that set and then to a member of that member. Eventually, we reach something that belongs to the set but that itself has no member: an "urelement," or the empty set, which is thus "foundational" of all the other sets.[58]

7. Replacement axiom: "If a set α exists, there also exists the set obtained by replacing the elements of α by other existent elements." This axiom allows us to conceive the consistency of a set as "transcendent of the particularity of its elements" (EE, 537).

8. Axiom of separation: "Given a set α, on the one hand, and a well-defined property b, on the other, there exists the set of those elements of α for which b is true." The predication of this property "separates" this particular part of α. This means, roughly speaking, that any recognizable property that can be stated in the formal language of the theory can be used to define a set (the set of things having the stated property). As far as Badiou is concerned, this axiom confirms that "being is anterior to language," since we can use language to isolate a set only if we first presume the existence of that set (EE, 79; cf. 538).

9. Axiom of choice: "If α is a set, all of whose elements are nonempty sets no two of which have any elements in common, then there is a set c that has precisely one element in common with each element of α." Russell's illustration is well known: if we have infinitely many pairs of shoes, we do not need the axiom of choice to pick one shoe from each pair: we can just pick the left shoe, say. But if we have infinitely many pairs of socks and want to pick one sock from each pair, we need the axiom of choice. Zermelo first proposed this axiom in 1904, in order to prove Cantor's belief that every set can be well ordered.[59] It has remained controversial ever since, because it defies all construction: it is impossible to specify any rule that might guide an infinite set of arbitrary choices. Once we accept a purely extensional or combinatorial notion of set, however, this axiom follows as a matter of course. Badiou himself associates this axiom with the possibility of a purely generic or "anarchic representation," a "principle of infinite liberty."[60] It provides him with the precise concept of the being (as opposed to the act) of subjective intervention (EE, 251–52).

The axiomatization of set theory as the foundation for mathematics completed the process begun by Descartes and the arithmetization of geometry, namely, the liberation of mathematics from all spatial or sensory intuition. Numbers and relations between numbers no longer need be considered in terms of more primitive intuitive experiences (of objects, of nature) or logical concepts. The whole of mathematics could now be thought to rest on a foundation of its own making, grounded on its own internally consistent assertion.

Thus axiomatized, Cantor's set theory appeared secure from paradox and internal contradiction. By 1925 David Hilbert felt confident enough to declare, famously, "No-one will succeed in driving us from the paradise Cantor created for us."[61] And, in a sense, this assertion still stands, despite two major further blows to its optimism: one to the apparently unshakeable integrity of axiomatic systems themselves, the other to Cantor's own continuum hypothesis.

Gödel, Cohen, and the Mathematically Undecidable

Hilbert had believed that the thoroughgoing axiomatization of mathematics would resolve the question of its foundations once and for all, and securely establish "the certitude of mathematical methods."[62] In books such as his landmark *Foundations of Geometry* (1899) he maintained that the key to mathematics lay in a "complete mastery of the axioms" and a rigorous fidelity to what logical deduction might derive from them. In order to prove a particular conclusion, there was no need to construct an answer; it was enough to "show that the solution, as a matter of Logical necessity, must exist, since any other conclusion would result in a contradiction."[63] The essential thing, then, was that the system of posited axioms be "complete" and "consistent."[64] In 1925, Hilbert looked forward to the possibility of a complete axiomatization that would guarantee the many results of mathematics threatened by intuitionist skepticism—the existence of irrational numbers, of functions, of transfinite numbers; the law of the excluded middle; and so on.[65]

Kurt Gödel's celebrated incompleteness theorem, published in 1931, dashed Hilbert's hopes once and for all.[66] Gödel proved the inherent limits of any axiomatic method. Using methods acceptable within any of the dominant approaches to mathematics, Gödel showed that "it is impossible for a sufficiently rich formalized deductive system, such as Hilbert's system of all classical mathematics, to prove the consistency of the system by methods belonging to the system."[67] There will always remain the possibility of constructing "undecidable" statements—that is, apparently true statements that cannot be proved true or false by the system's own resources. In other words, any fully consistent axiomatic system will be inadequate even to establish the elementary principles of arithmetic, while any system rich enough for the job cannot be proved, within that system, to be consistent.

Gödel's theorems are too technical to discuss in any detail here; what he did, in brief, was to use number theory to "talk about" number theory, to make the theory reflect upon itself. Gödel made number theory "introspective," to use Hofstadter's phrase, by assigning numbers (the famous "Gödel numbers") to the various parts of number theory itself.[68] He then demonstrated that it is possible to formulate, in a kind of reworking of Epimenides' paradox, an obviously true statement in number theory that number theory itself cannot confirm—that is, a statement that asserts its own unprovability.[69] In short, Gödel's result established that "there are questions of mathematics that mathematics cannot answer; one of these undecidable questions is whether set theory itself is consistent."[70] The foundations of mathematics were thus shown to include, for all their logical necessity, an element of rigorous faith; the adoption of axiomatic methods was henceforth to be more a matter of "belief" than of certainty per se.[71]

It should be stressed that Gödel himself did not interpret his result as implying the end of certainty and a crisis in mathematics. On the contrary, he remains the most celebrated contemporary advocate of a mathematical Platonism in the familiar sense, one that affirms the independent reality and existence of mathematical truths. Unlike more formalist thinkers, Gödel saw the axioms of set theory as self-evident and immediately accessible: they "force themselves upon us as being true," he believed, in much the same way that physical objects force themselves upon sense perception.[72] More to the point, a further result of Gödel's went some way toward restoring confidence in the consistency of set theory itself. He demonstrated the internal coherence of the "constructible" or well-ordered universe, the universe established in a series of clearly defined steps from the succession of ordinal numbers, and showed that within this constructible universe both the axiom of choice (AC) and the continuum hypothesis can be proved consistent with the ZF axioms. In other words, "If A is any infinite constructible set, then there is no constructible set 'between' A and 2^A."[73] Since all the sets manipulated in mathematical calculations (the natural numbers, real and complex numbers, functional spaces, and so on) are constructible, since any "working mathematician" will directly "*encounter* only constructible sets" (EE, 336–37), part of Cantor's dream had come true.

However, in 1963 Paul Cohen established that set theorists would indeed have to settle for this small part of the dream alone. If Gödel had shown that CH and AC could be consistent with the other ZF axioms, Cohen confirmed that CH and AC could not be *proved* consistent from these same axioms. After Cohen, it had to be accepted that Cantor's precious continuum hypothesis was simply "independent" of the basic axioms of set theory. Cohen thus showed CH to be "a very dramatic example of what might be called an absolutely undecidable statement (in our present scheme of things)."[74]

Without a doubt, this result is itself the single most important postulate in the whole of *L'Etre et l'événement*, and the means of its verification require a considerably more involved survey than did the other topics mentioned in this appendix. As you might expect, the crux of the matter concerns the nature of a nonconstructible, or "generic," set. Cohen's own procedure is again too technical to summarize properly in so brief a presentation, but the gist of it is as follows.[75]

Gödel demonstrated the consistency of CH with ZF by tolerating only constructible sets. Remember that a universe populated exclusively by constructible sets is one in which explicit definition maintains a perfect grip on the multiplicity of being. In the constructible universe every name fits its referent, every quantity can be ordered, and every excess can be measured. In Badiou's terms, it is precisely a universe in which, since CH holds true, the state of a situation directly "succeeds" the situation itself, without any numerical gap between presentation and representation.[76] Cohen's argument thus begins by rejecting the "unreasonable" requirement that "a set must be constructed according to any prescribed formula in order to be recognized as a genuine set."[77] After all, the axiom of extensionality (which defines a set exclusively in terms of what belongs to it) suggests that a purely random collection of elements, though lacking any principle of construction, nevertheless qualifies as a perfectly acceptable ZF set. If a set is simply "any collection of previously given objects," it seems plausible to assume that "the power set of $\aleph_0$ should include *all* possible collections of elements of $\aleph_0$ whether there is a defining condition or not."[78] A generic subset will be one that is organized so as to reflect something of this all-possibility, that is, a little of everything that happens to be available in the set. So while every "constructible set has a special character—the steps by which it can be constructed," a generic set will "lack any such individuality."[79] By contrast with a constructible set, a generic set is one characterized by "the least possible information"[80]: as a result, the gap between presentation and re-presentation in such a set will prove to be literally immeasurable.

In order to formulate a model of set theory in which CH does *not* hold, we begin by positing a constructible "ground model" M that reflects the characteristic features of the theory, where M includes a denumerably infinite set (i.e., one whose members include all the natural numbers up to and including the limit ordinal ω_0, along with its constructible subsets), where M is transitive (i.e., if x belongs to a member of M and y belongs x, then y will belong to M), and in which CH is presumed to be true. As it is a denumerable model, we know that its elements, that is, the elements of ω_0, can be counted out in a one-to-one correspondence with the unending sequence of whole numbers.[81] The "actual" counting out of this denumerable infinity, however—the operation that collects ω_0 as a set—is possible only from a perspective outside M, a perspective that embraces the broader universe of set theory as a whole.

As a constructible set, M includes a very limited selection of the possible subsets of ω_0. If (as is customary) we represent the whole universe of sets as an infinite cone spreading up from the empty set along a vertical "backbone" defined by the succession of ordinal numbers $(0, 1, 2, 3 \ldots \omega_0, \omega_0+1 \ldots \omega_0+\omega_0 \ldots \omega_1 \ldots)$, such that the width of the cone at any particular ordinal level indicates the number of subsets of that ordinal, the shaded area M will include only a narrow section of the whole cone. We know that the number of subsets of ω_0 will be infinitely larger than ω_0 itself, and so long as we recognize only the constructible subsets of ω_0, Gödel's result implies that this number will correspond to ω_1 (or $\aleph_1$).

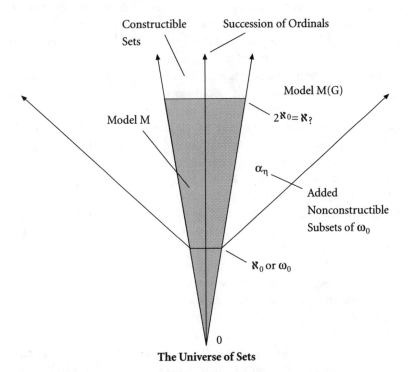

The Universe of Sets

Adapted from Tiles, *The Philosophy of Set Theory,* 186, and Crossley, *Logic,* 74.

The goal is now to enlarge and widen the minimal model M to form an extended model—call it M(G)—by "forcing" M to include a certain number k of nonconstructible subsets, written $\alpha_1, \alpha_2, \alpha_3, \ldots \alpha_\eta$. Since all finite sets, along with ω_0 or $\aleph_0$ itself, are constructible, the first point where it may be possible to introduce nonconstructible sets and thus widen our cone is where we come to consider infinite subsets of $\aleph_0$: all our α_η will thus be infinite subsets of $\aleph_0$, and if M(G) can be "fleshed out" in such a way that each α_η is distinct, in M(G) the set of all subsets of $\aleph_0$, or $2^{\aleph_0}$ will be larger than or equal to k.

Nonconstructible sets, remember, take full advantage of the axiom of extensionality, and cannot be defined in terms of any overarching principle; in order to collect them into a coherent group or set at all, their infinite contents will simply have to be read out, element by element, one at a time.[82] In order to talk about these new subsets α_η before we have thus read them out, that is, before we know what exactly they will consist of, all we are able to do is name what they will become. To do this we can set up a language L of the model M of ZF that will allow us to name every sort of set that ZF can recognize: this language will include labels for every element smaller than k, along with the logical signs for existence, membership, and negation, and so on. We want to make sure that no statements in L will be true of any added α_η that are not directly required to be true, in keeping with the axiom of extensionality, by the members of that α_η. We can arrange things in such a way that the verification of statements about any α_η in M(G) will be "forced" by a finite amount of information about the members of that α_η. We encode such information in groups of finite "conditions" that will serve to approximate descriptions of α_η. These conditions are individually discernible in M and ordered in such a way that "extended" or more inclusive conditions give more information about the set being approximated. If M(G) is to remain a coherent model of ZF, all these conditions will have to fit in one consistent infinite subset of M, written "G" (for "generic"). Inspection of the conditions belonging to G will then allow us to determine in advance all the statements that will be true in M(G), even though we cannot yet inspect M(G) itself. Rather, we will use G to give an interpretation to each of the terms in the language L of M, such that our new extended set M(G) can be defined precisely as the set of these interpretations. In short, any sentence λ of the language L of ZF will hold true in M(G) if there is some condition P belonging to G that forces the sentence λ.

What Cohen calls "forcing" thus defines the relation between finite groups P of conditions and verifiably true statements λ formulated in L to describe the newly added infinite subsets α_η. Any formula in the language of ZF, no matter how complex, will be forcible if there is some condition in G that ensures that the formula is satisfied in the model. (The term "forces" is simply Cohen's jargon for "satisfaction in the model.") Conditions correspond to what Badiou himself calls "investigations" (EE, 376), that is, the finite stages of a truth, or generic, procedure. The set G of conditions is what Badiou opts to label ♀: it collects as one the being of such a procedure, that is, the being of a truth.

Since any given condition P gives only a finite and thus incomplete amount of information about newly specified infinite subsets α_η, we must make provision for the extension (or, as Badiou says, the "domination") of these conditions that will allow them to embrace, again one at a time, all the elements of any infinite α_η. In particular, we need to show that any condition P might force the negation of a statement λ about any α_η if and only if, for all conditions Q that extend P, it is not the case that Q forces λ itself (for example, P can negate the statement "$\alpha_1 = \alpha_2$" only if there is no extension Q of P that forces its affirmation). In other words, we cannot simply presume, as classical logic might suggest, that if P does not force λ it must force the negation of λ, since it could be that this particular P simply does not yet contain enough information to settle the question of λ one way or the other: we want P to force the negation of λ only when, no matter how much further information we acquire, λ is still not forced.[83] As a result, although we cannot say, given any condition P and any statement λ about the newly added subsets α_η, that P must either force λ or the negation of λ, we can at least assume that for every P and λ there must be a further condition Q extending P that forces either λ or the negation of λ. This will mean that, in our extended model M(G), each and every statement λ about the newly added sets can indeed be verified or disproved by a finite amount of information about their membership, that is, by some Q extending P. Since M is denumerable, it can be shown that such a complete and consistent sequence of conditions—that is, a coherent generic subset G of M—must indeed exist.

To make this a little less abstract, imagine that the conditions belonging to G consist merely of sequences of 0s and 1s, along the lines of <0, 1, 0> or <0, 1, 0, 0>. Each such condition encodes a simple piece of information—say, the property of "containing at least one 1"—and the second sequence "extends" the first by including a little more information ("containing at least three 0s"). Any particular condition can be extended in one of two incompatible ways, so each time we move up the chain of extensions we need to choose between two mutually exclusive possible extending conditions—<1,1,1>, for instance, can be extended by either the condition <1,1,1,1> or the condition <1,1,1,0>, but not by both. Any discernible set formed in keeping with a finite condition P will thus remain distinct from at least one extension that negates it (EE, 406). The property of "having only 1s," for example, exhibited by the infinite sequence of conditions <1>, <1, 1>, <1,1,1> . . . , is in turn extended by a condition that exhibits the property of "having at least one 0"—this because, however large a finite sequence of 1s we read out, we can always stick a 0 on the end of it. <1,1,1,0> "extends" <1,1,1>. On the other hand, a subset formed in keeping with an infinite set of conditions that intersects *every* consistent extension (i.e., that has at least one element in common with every mutually compatible extending condition) will be indiscernible according to the criteria of discernment available in M. In our example, these are the criteria that can distinguish sequences of 0s and 1s. All that can be said about such a set G is that it is vaguely "typical" of M, since in the end, the only condition that might consistently include or extend every other condition M will exhibit a property that is precisely *not* distinguishable in terms of 0s and 1s—namely, the property of "having any number of 0s and 1s." The set of conditions that exhibit this property will extend all more specific conditions of the type "having at least four billion 0s" or "having ten trillion 1s in a row." On the other hand, G will not include every possible condition in M, since sequences defined as "beginning with 0" and "beginning with 1," for instance, are not compatible: such conditions cannot be put into one in the same set. Our most inclusive condition G, at the summit of the chain, will thus emerge through the sequence of preliminary decisions or exclusions—or, as Badiou would say, through the pursuit of militant investigations.

In Cohen's own version of the sequence, the conditions belonging to the generic subset G of M are sets of triples of the form $<n, \eta, i>$, where n is some number smaller than ω_0, η is a number that indexes some newly specified subset included in k, and i is variable, taking either 0 or 1 as value. What such a condition will tell us is whether any number n actually belongs to any subset α_η, depending on whether i is 0 ("yes") or 1 ("no"). If a given triple $<n, \eta, 0>$ belongs to G, this will *force* the belonging of n to α_η. A given condition P forces n to belong to α_η if and only if the sequence $<n, \eta, 0>$ is included in or extended by P.

We are now in a position, at last, to demonstrate the independence of CH from the model M(G) of ZF. In fact, the final move is very simple. All we need do is show that the language of ZF allows us to force a measurement of $2^{\aleph_0}$ in M(G) that corresponds to some cardinality other than the next largest set directly after $\aleph_0$, that is, some cardinality other than $\aleph_1$.

By building up our generic set G, we know we can force the distinction in M(G) of an infinite number k of nonconstructible subsets α_η of $\aleph_0$. Remember that, as seen from outside M (from the perspective that embraces the general universe of set theory), M is defined as a denumerable set, so the set G of conditions that determine whether any given number n belongs or does not belong to any given subset α_η added to M will also be denumerable or "complete": no condition P can force the equation of two newly specified subsets α_x and α_y if $x \neq y$, since there will always be a condition Q extending P such that, for any number n, the further condition whereby "n belongs to α_x but not α_y," or vice versa, is included in Q. This is simply what it means to be a *generic* set (i.e., a set of conditions that includes at least one element from every consistent extension), and this is what ensures that all our subsets α_η are genuinely distinct. Clearly, whatever the size of $2^{\aleph_0}$, it must be at least as big as k.[84]

It turns out that, once we are able to demarcate infinitely many distinct though nonconstructible subsets of $\aleph_0$ in this way, there is simply nothing in the language of ZF to stop us from setting the value of k at just about *any* infinite cardinality. The conditions enumerated in G will allow for the distinction of $\aleph_2$, $\aleph_3$, or even $\aleph_{102}$ worth of new subsets α_η. As far as we can tell from the model M, the value of the continuum might be $\aleph_{\omega_0}$.

Though it might seem more of a sleight of hand than a genuine "proof," this result is altogether less magical than it might first appear. It doesn't imply that we thereby somehow "create" all these non-denumerably many new subsets out of thin air. By definition, all our newly distinguished subsets were already *included* in the set of all subsets of $\aleph_0$, they just couldn't be distinguished in a universe that recognized only constructible sets. Tacitly included in M, these newly distinguished subsets didn't yet *belong* to M. The essential thing is simply that our infinitely extended sequence of conditions in G will allow us to distinguish or "read out," element by element, a truly *immeasurable* number of subsets of $\aleph_0$. Cohen shows that G can easily be arranged so as to force the equation $2^{\aleph_0} = k$ where k amounts to $\aleph_2$ or $\aleph_{102}$. The resulting model M(G) will thus be a model of set theory in which CH is untrue.

Again, there is certainly nothing about ZF that directly authorizes this demonstration: the point is simply that there is nothing in ZF to prevent it, either. Cohen's proof does not establish the actual value of the continuum: it does not actually measure $2^{\aleph_0}$; it just establishes the independence of this measurement from the statements that can be verified in the language of ZF. The ZF axiom system simply does not tell us enough about the mathematical universe it creates for us to be able to measure the consequences of the power set axiom. In the wake of Cohen's result, it is possible, as Hallett notes, that just one application of the power set axiom to an infinite set might be enough to "exhaust the whole universe" of number.[85] In Badiou's terms,

Cohen proved that the laws of being (the axioms of ZF) set no clear limit on either the normal unthinking domination of the state or the exceptional capabilities of true subjective thought: confined by definition to the static analysis of being as being, ontology offers a single "measure" for both sorts of excess, in the form of an immeasurably infinite power set.

The general implications of Cohen's result are often compared to those of the invention of non-Euclidean geometries. Both Cantor and Gödel had assumed that the continuum had an objective, definite structure that might one day be fully determined or described, as a construction built upon a numbered collection of points (or real numbers). It appears now that a unique continuum of real numbers could not be numbered or well ordered even in principle.[86] Cohen's truly post-Cantorian set theory is one in which there is "not one but many models, each constructed with a particular purpose in mind."[87] Many mathematicians thus interpret Cohen's result as implying a new pluralism or relativity at the foundations of set theory, as suggesting that "there is simply not one set theory but several . . . ; in some set theories the continuum hypothesis will be true, in others it will be false."[88] Which theory we adopt and consequently what sort of mathematical reality we recognize remains a matter of genuinely fundamental choice, a function of "what is to be done."

We know that Badiou, far from seeking to limit the radicality of this choice, invokes it in order to situate the irreducible decision that distinguishes the three fundamental orientations of ontology (constructivist, transcendent, and generic). And rather than seek to evade its implications, he embraces it as the unique point from which it is possible, with all the rigor of a subject's indiscernment, to explore the anarchic *being* of a truth.

Notes

Where two page numbers are given, the first refers to the original work, the second to its English translation.

Introduction

1. Badiou is not even mentioned in either of the two most substantial recent English surveys of French philosophy in the twentieth century (Eric Matthews, *Twentieth Century French Philosophy* [1996]; Gary Gutting, *French Philosophy in the Twentieth Century* [2001]), and the *Philosopher's Index* through 1998 lists no articles referring to Badiou—as compared with 106 on Deleuze and 656 on Foucault. Along with my own "Generic Sovereignty" (1998), Slavoj Žižek's article "Psychoanalysis in Post-Marxism: The Case of Alain Badiou" (1998) was one of the first substantial engagements with Badiou to appear in English; a longer version appears in his recent *The Ticklish Subject: The Absent Centre of Political Ontology* (1999), and much of Žižek's work provides a highly pertinent point of comparison with that of Badiou. Jean-Jacques Lecercle's article ("Cantor, Lacan, Mao, Beckett, *même combat:* The Philosophy of Alain Badiou" [1999]) provides an especially accessible overview. See the bibliography for a list of current and forthcoming English translations of Badiou's work. Unsurprisingly perhaps, it is in Latin America that Badiou's philosophy has had the greatest immediate impact thus far. In addition to publishing translations and original contributions by Badiou, the Argentinian journal *Acontecimiento* has, for more than a decade now,

developed his political thought in directions as diverse as the movement of the Madres de Plaza de Mayo in Buenos Aires and the Zapatistas in Chiapas. A forthcoming work by Bruno Bosteels (tentatively titled *Badiou and the Political*) will make some of this material available to anglophone readers. *Think Again: Alain Badiou and the Future of Philosophy* (ed. Peter Hallward, forthcoming) collects critical responses to Badiou's work by Ernesto Laclau, Alenka Zupančič, Jean-Luc Nancy, Etienne Balibar, Jacques Rancière, Jean-Toussaint Desanti, Daniel Bensaïd, and several others.

2. See in particular Agnes Heller and Ferenc Feher, *The Grandeur and Twilight of Radical Universalism* (1991).

3. What Badiou calls a generic truth is acultural by definition: "The same in its sameness need not be cultivated" (C, 250; cf. SP, 117, E, 27).

4. S3, 59 / 48; cf. 163 / 143.

5. Cf. EE, 245; LS, 136–37 n. 15.

6. Karl Marx, *Second Thesis on Feuerbach*, in *Early Writings*, 422.

7. SP, 6. Badiou adheres firmly to Lacan's maxim "Nothing fruitful takes place in man save through the intermediary of a loss of an object" (S2, 165 / 136).

8. E, 47. As exposure of the void, an event corresponds roughly to what Lacan calls that "fertile moment," that burst of anxiety when "the non-integrated, suppressed, repressed looms up" (S1, 292 / 188), breaking the delusions of our everyday routine and enabling a difficult articulation of its truth: "The end of the symbolic process is that non-being [i.e., the repressed, the void of the situation] comes to be, because it has spoken" (S2, 354 / 308).

9. Alain Badiou, "Politics and Philosophy," 124. As Deleuze puts it, "Something in the world forces us to think. This something is an object not of recognition but of a fundamental encounter" (Gilles Deleuze, *Différence et répétition*, 182 / 139).

10. Frantz Fanon, *Les Damnés de la terre*, 66 / 36.

11. Slavoj Žižek, *The Sublime Object of Ideology*, 64.

12. Alain Badiou, "L'Impératif de la négation," 9.

13. EE, 9; E, 10; cf. TS, 203–4.

14. TA, 6.11.96. Always, "psychology is the enemy of thought" (Alain Badiou, "Saisissement, dessaisie, fidélité," 14).

15. "The Subject that concerns us today cannot be the subject of history. The idea of a historical totalization is not coherent" (Alain Badiou, *Jean-Paul Sartre*, 8).

16. Compare with Jacques Derrida, *Donner la mort: L'Ethique du don, Jacques Derrida et la pensée du don*, 67 / 67, 101–2 / 108–9.

17. Alain Badiou, "L'Entretien de Bruxelles," 23.

18. Alain Badiou, "Dix-neuf réponses à beaucoup plus d'objections," 263.

19. MP, 60–69; cf. Alain Badiou, *Une Soirée philosophique*, 22–23.

20. I am referring to Hegel's celebrated analysis of the French Revolution as an experiment in abstract decisionism; I take up this point in chapter 13.

21. Jean-Paul Sartre, *La Transcendence de l'ego,* 79 / 98–99.

22. C, 119–20; cf. Alain Badiou, Rev. of Gilles Deleuze, *Le Pli: Leibniz et le baroque,* 182.

23. Alain Badiou, "Les Langues de Wittgenstein," 2.

24. Badiou, "L'Entretien de Bruxelles," 25; cf. CM, 22.

25. Alain Badiou, "Being by Numbers," 85.

26. Gilles Deleuze and Félix Guattari, *Qu'est-ce que la philosophie?* 143.

27. Alain Badiou, "On ne passe pas," 1, 3.

Part I. Matters of Principle

1. Taking Sides

1. TA, 4.12.96. "There can be a subject only in the absence of god," that is, in the absence of eternal necessity (TA, 26.11.97).

2. Badiou, "L'Entretien de Bruxelles," 13; cf. EE, 14, C, 165, MP, 15, 21–22. Badiou is part, here, of a revival whose other members include Henri Corbin, Christian Jambet, and Guy Lardreau.

3. Alain Badiou, "Entretien avec Alain Badiou" (1999), 5.

4. Cf. D, 149; Alain Badiou, "Platon et / ou Aristote-Leibniz: Théorie des ensembles et théorie des Topos sous l'oeil du philosophe," 67; PM, 63–64.

5. Badiou, "Politics and Philosophy," 123.

6. CT, 99; cf. Plato, *Phaedo,* 66d and *Phaedrus,* 250c, in *The Collected Dialogues.*

7. PM, 69. For Plato, the study of mathematics was "the easiest way for [the soul] to pass from becoming to truth and being" (Plato, *Republic,* vii, in *The Collected Dialogues,* 525).

8. Badiou, "Platon et / ou Aristote-Leibniz," 62–63. Badiou thus sets himself the task of debunking that prevailing conception of mathematical Platonism "promoted, in particular, by Anglo-Saxon commentary," which identifies it with a belief in the independence, exteriority, or transcendence of mathematical objects (see for instance, Paul Benacerraf and Hilary Putnam, introduction to *Philosophy of Mathematics: Selected Readings,* 17–18; Paul Bernays, "On Platonism in Mathematics," 259).

9. Badiou, "Politics and Philosophy," 124.

10. Badiou, "Entretien avec Alain Badiou" (1999), 2.

11. Alain Badiou, "Dieu est mort," in CT, 22. A living God is "always *someone's* God," the God of Abraham and Jacob, of Pascal or Kierkegaard (12–13).

12. Badiou, "Saisissement, dessaisie, fidélité," 19; cf. NN, 86.

13. There can be no such all-inclusive set, no mathematical One-All, since any attempt to enclose or measure such a set will immediately allow for the creation of an even larger set—for instance, its power set—and this precisely ad infinitum. There will be more on this in chapter 4.

14. NN, 86; cf. TS, 295, EE, 164, MP, 86.

15. Badiou, "Being by Numbers," 86.

16. Galileo, *The Assayer*, sect. 6, in Michael Sharratt, *Galileo*, 140. Newton likewise ensures that the study of "attraction" or gravity is purely mathematical, and proceeds in deliberate ignorance of its physical mechanism (Isaac Newton, *Principia*, definition viii, 6–7).

17. Cf. Morris Kline, *Mathematical Thought from Ancient to Modern Times*, 334.

18. The canonical reference here is Alexandre Koyré, *From the Closed World to the Infinite Universe* (1957); see, for instance, EE, 163, NN, 75 n. 2.

19. Descartes reserves the term "infinite" for the "positively" unlimited plenitude of God, and the term "indefinite" for merely mathematical possibilities or magnitudes (René Descartes, *Principles of Philosophy*, part 1, sect. 27, in *Philosophical Writings*, vol. 1, 202).

20. EE, 471. It is the radically axiomatic status of Badiou's conception of the subject—as distinct from Descartes's still semi-intuitive cogito—that escapes, at least up to a point, Kant's famous objection to Descartes' direct deduction of being from thought (Immanuel Kant, *Critique of Pure Reason*, B422–23).

21. Badiou, "Dix-neuf réponses," 261–62.

22. Martin Heidegger, "Modern Science, Metaphysics, and Mathematics," in BW, 300–301.

23. Badiou, "Dix-neuf réponses," 259.

24. Alain Badiou, "Réponses écrites d'Alain Badiou" (1992), 68.

25. Alain Badiou, letter to the author, 19 June 1996.

26. C, 302. The word "real" here preserves its Lacanian connotations, while describing those numbers whose (actually infinite) decimal expansion is beyond all merely rational reduction (i.e., reduction to the ratio of two whole numbers, however large). The set of real numbers includes irrational numbers like π and $\sqrt{2}$.

27. Badiou, "L'Entretien de Bruxelles," 5–6.

28. Badiou, "Politics and Philosophy," 120.

29. PP, 87: "Nor do I have much of a taste for proofs of the existence of the proletariat" (88).

30. Badiou, *Sartre*, 3–4.

31. Alain Badiou, "Qu'est-ce que Louis Althusser entend par 'philosophie'?" 34; AM, 71.

32. Badiou, "De la Langue française comme évidement," 3–5.

33. C, 196; cf. EE, 474. In *Théorie du Sujet*, "Lacan is the Lenin of psycho-analysis" (TS, 144) to Badiou's "Mao," and "our Hegel" to Badiou's "Marx" (264).

34. S1, 104/62; S2, 59–60/44. Badiou shares Lacan's scorn for everything associated with the *"le service des biens"* and the "American way of life" (S7, 350/303; *Ecrits*, 245–46/37–38).

35. See especially Lacan, *Ecrits*, 634/269, 693/288, 835.

36. S1, 301/194. Lacan's (early) conception of the subject depends, at a maximum distance from Badiou, on the fact of deceit as an irreducible dimension of speech.

37. AM, 68–69 (my emphasis); cf. S20, 114. Except where noted, as here, all emphases in quotations are those of the authors quoted.

38. Lacan, *Ecrits*, 831, 858; S11, 143/126.

39. Lacan, *Ecrits*, 302/88; cf. C, 205.

40. Lacan, *Ecrits*, 808/306.

41. S20, 108, quoted in C, 322: "The only [true] teaching is mathematical; the rest is a joke ... " (Jacques Lacan, ... *ou pire*, quoted in C, 292). Again, "there is no such thing as a truth which is not 'mathematized,' that is ..., which is not based, qua Truth, solely upon axioms. Which is to say that there is truth but of that which has no meaning" (Jacques Lacan, "Le Séminaire XXI," 11 Dec. 1973, in Bruce Fink, *The Lacanian Subject: Between Language and Jouissance*, 121). On Lacan's mathematics, see Alain Juranville, *Lacan et la philosophie*, 305–18, Roudinesco, *Lacan*, 360.

42. The mathemes are "the indices of an absolute signification" (Lacan, *Ecrits*, 816/314; cf. S7, 276–77/236). Familiar examples include the mathemes for fantasy, metaphor and metonymy, and the four discourses; the graph of desire; the schemas L and R; the formulae of the phallic function; the Borromean chain linking R, S, and I, and so on. More precisely, explains Badiou, a matheme indicates a "point of impasse" in mathematics (TA, 13.11.96).

43. Alain Badiou, "Lacan et les présocratiques" (1990), 3–4. Even Badiou's most Lacanian book, *Théorie du sujet*, bears little resemblance to the often wild ramblings of Lacan's most "mathematized" seminar, ... *ou pire*.

44. S11, 188/167; S17, 143.

45. Badiou, "Politics and Philosophy," 124. "Thought is not a relation to an object, it is the *internal* relation of its real *[rapport interne de son réel]*" (AM, 37; cf. TS, 146–47).

46. See in particular S17 and S20; cf. Gilbert D. Chaitin, *Rhetoric and Culture in Lacan*, 217.

47. Badiou, "Politics and Philosophy," 124.

48. See in particular EE, 472–74, along with TS, 247–49, 262. Crucially, "Lacan remains pre-Cantorian. ... Lacan does not see any contradiction between a

recourse to infinity and the recourse to intuitionist logic. For his purposes Lacan has no need of the existence of an infinite set. All he needs is the operation of a point which is inaccessible from the finite," in the way that, for instance, "feminine jouissance is a point of inaccessibility for phallic jouissance" (C, 298). If Badiou aims to move beyond Lacan, it is mainly because the psychoanalyst remains committed to the structural sufficiency of *language* or the symbolic (however disruptive its impact upon the imaginary ego), rather than open to the rare, contingent universality of the event. Lacan is too preoccupied with the "algebraic" domain of structural repetition to be able to affirm the "topological" torsion or "excess" of the subject (TS, 255). Badiou's Lacan remains, in short, too complicit with that contemporary linguistic turn he everywhere denounces as antithetical to the affirmation of exceptional truths (Badiou, "L'Entretien de Bruxelles," 22; cf. EE, 472–73). Lacan maintains that it is only with language that "the dimension of truth emerges" (Lacan, *Ecrits*, 524/172; cf. S17, 70): Lacan's "man is the subject captured and tortured by language" (S3, 276/243), and outside language he finds only horror, never truth.

49. Bruno Bosteels, "Vérité et forçage: Badiou avec Heidegger et Lacan," in *Badiou: Penser le multiple*, ed. Charles Ramond. In his important article "Por una falta de política" Bosteels extends a version of Badiou's argument to include Žižek, Laclau, and the proponents of radical democracy (see chapter 5).

50. S11, 208/186. "The event is coextensive with its real, which is why its coming is heralded by anguish, which is the subjective signal of the real's excess" (TA, 23.4.97). In the terms of *Théorie du sujet*, the real is the always sudden and necessarily ephemeral uprising of the "masses," an abrupt break in the historical continuum, a vanishing cause that consists (through the logical mediation of the party) only in the proletarian subject that affirms its consequences (TS, 244–45; cf. 81–82, 154).

51. DP, 15–18; C, 63–64; cf. Alain Badiou, "Silence, solipsisme, sainteté: L'antiphilosophie de Wittgenstein," 46.

52. Badiou, "L'Entretien de Bruxelles," 21; cf. EE, 321–25, CT, 121.

53. Badiou, "Réponses écrites" (1992), 67.

54. Badiou, "Les Langues de Wittgenstein," 8; cf. Ludwig Wittgenstein, *Tractatus Logico-Philosophicus* 4.115.

55. DO, 47; cf. DP, 13 Badiou, "Silence, solipsisme, sainteté," 33, 44.

56. Alain Badiou, "Un, Multiple, Multiplicité(s)," 16 n. 2.

57. Badiou, letter to the author, 19 June 1996.

58. Alain Badiou, "Philosophie et poésie au point de l'innommable," 93.

59. Martin Heidegger, *On Time and Being*, 74 (my emphasis).

60. Martin Heidegger, "Only a God Can Save Us."

61. Martin Heidegger, "Letter on Humanism," in BW, 253; "Being Is the *Transcendens* Pure and Simple" (Martin Heidegger, *Being and Time,* 62).

62. MP, 52; Martin Heidegger, "On the Essence of Truth," in BW, 129, 131.

63. Martin Heidegger, "The Origin of the Work of Art," in BW, 196, 162–63.

64. Martin Heidegger, "What Is Metaphysics?" in BW, 97.

65. Heidegger, "On the Essence of Truth," 125.

66. Heidegger, "The Origin of the Work of Art," 206.

67. Heidegger, "On the Essence of Truth," 125, 129, 138.

68. EE, 34–35. If both Badiou and Heidegger seek to deconstruct the ontic privileging of the One, they do so to opposite ends. Heidegger wages a campaign against the One of an *existent* being, a being (God, reason, or "Man") whose metaphysical supremacy blocks any genuine access to that fragile open space or "clearing" in which any particular being can simply *be* the one that it is. For Heidegger, it is precisely that Platonic or metaphysical privileging of "the Idea as singular presence of the thinkable, [that] establishes the existent *[étant]* as predominant over the initial or inaugural movement, of the opening up of being." Against Heidegger's return to the presocratics, Badiou thus proposes a return to "the magnificent figure of Lucretius," who, rather than orient the poem to the Open and divine, "strives to subtract thought from any return of the gods, and to establish it resolutely in the multiple" as such, as an "inconsistent infinity, which nothing gathers together" (CT, 28).

69. Heidegger, "The Origin of the Work of Art," 198. Heidegger thereby "sutures" philosophy to its poetic condition. Badiou's conclusion: "There can be no fundamental critique of Heidegger other than this: that the age of the poets is finished." Which is to say that, rather than essentially mysterious or elusive, today's ongoing "disorientation" is indeed *"conceptualizable"* (MP, 55), that is, accessible to a philosophy conditioned by contemporary mathematics.

70. Heidegger, "The Origin of the Work of Art," 202, 159.

71. EE, 144. See the comments of François Regnault, in Alain Badiou, Christian Jambet, Jean-Claude Milner, and François Regnault, *Une Soirée philosophique,* 36.

72. Blaise Pascal, *Pensées,* sect. 24 (4), in *Oeuvres complètes,* 1095.

73. Ibid., sect. 267.

74. Heidegger, "Letter on Humanism," 258.

75. Badiou, "Les Langues de Wittgenstein," 10.

76. Badiou, "Silence, solipsisme, sainteté," 17.

77. Saint Paul, 1 Cor. 1:15; SP, 18.

78. Cf. Chaitin, *Rhetoric and Culture in Lacan,* 9, 244.

79. Badiou, "Politics and Philosophy," 124. Like most antiphilosophers, Lacan associates philosophy with totalization and closure (cf. S1, 190–91 / 118–19; S11, 90 / 77). He links philosophy with the master's discourse (in S17), that is, with the

inversion of psychoanalytic discourse: rational philosophy can know nothing of the fleeting, *real* intensity of desire or jouissance.

80. Badiou, "Silence, solipsisme, sainteté," 43; cf. CT, 121.

81. Badiou, "Les Langues de Wittgenstein," 7.

82. CD, 10–11; cf. SP, 65, 76.

83. Cf. Russell Nieli, *Wittgenstein: From Mysticism to Ordinary Language* (Albany: State University of New York, 1987).

84. Wittgenstein, *Notebook* of 1916; *Tractatus,* 6.432. "What is good is also Divine; this summarizes my ethics" (*Notebook* of 1930, quoted by Badiou in "Silence, solipsisme, sainteté," 49).

85. Badiou, "Silence, solipsisme, sainteté," 22–23, 29. "What *can* be shown *cannot* be said" (*Tractatus,* 4.1212), or as Jaspers will put it: "the ultimate in thinking is silence" (*Reason and Existenz,* 106).

86. Badiou, "L'Impératif de la négation," 14.

87. Ibid., 4–8; cf. Lardreau, *Véracité,* 96.

88. Badiou would no doubt include the "non-philosophy" of François Laruelle among the contemporary variants of antiphilosophy: for Laruelle, "access to the real is blocked by the philosophical decision to establish being as its central concept," and a non-philosophy begins with the suspension of this decision, so as to open the way for an absolutely immanent "vision as One" (LS, 143 n. 51; for a sustained comparison of Badiou and Laruelle, see Tristan Aguilar, "Badiou et la Non-Philosophie: Un parallèle," 37–46). Jacques Rancière, another former *soixante-huitard,* provides Badiou with a further example. Archivist of populist resistance and proletarian rebellion, chronicler of the episodic history of egalitarian anarchy, Rancière proclaims a blanket hostility to all figures of philosophical "mastery." Believing that the politics conceived by philosophers is "necessarily nondemocratic" (AM, 129), he turns philosophical weapons against philosophy itself so as to guard against every dangerous pronouncement of "premature conclusions." Rancière writes the "suspension of prescription" (AM, 125) through the elaboration of paradoxical, self-disarming arguments. The result, Badiou argues, is simply the permanent suspension of political intervention itself (122).

89. SP, 117–18; C, 217 (referring to Maurice Blanchot, *La Communauté inavouable;* Jean-Luc Nancy, *La Communauté désoeuvrée;* Giorgio Agamben, *The Coming Community*). See Todd May's useful article "The Absence of Community in the Works of Lyotard, Nancy, and Lacoue-Labarthe," *Philosophy Today* 37:3 (1993), 275–84.

90. Badiou, "L'Entretien de Bruxelles," 19; AM, 82–83.

91. C, 245, 250. For instance, should you argue the case "for African-Americans, women and others having the same rights as anyone else, it's absolutely indis-

pensable to support that on other grounds than the existence of a community of African-Americans or women. The theme of equal rights is really progressive and really political, that is, emancipatory, only if it finds its arguments in a space open to everyone, a space of universality" (Badiou, "Being by Numbers," 123).

92. E, 25. *"Pire que la méconnaissance est la reconnaissance"* (Worse than misunderstanding is recognition) (PP, 16).

93. PP, 18, 19. Marx provides the model: he "sets out, absolutely, not from the social architecture . . . , but from the interpretation-cut of a hysterical symptom of the social: riots and the workers' political parties" (PP, 20).

94. Badiou, Rev. of Gilles Deleuze: *Le Pli,* 184.

95. As Derrida observes, "The way (be it central or peripheral to their work) that a thinker or science speaks of animality constitutes a decisive symptom as regards the essential axiomatics of the discourse they propose" (Jacques Derrida, "La Main de Heidegger," in *Psyché: Inventions de l'autre,* 428; cf. Jacques Derrida, *De l'esprit: Heidegger et la question,* 28, 79–80).

96. Badiou, "Saisissement, dessaisie, fidélité," 15; E, 13–14.

97. Alain Badiou, "Qu'est-ce qu'un thermidorien?" 57. Like Badiou, Žižek freely accepts that "there is no effective freedom without 'terror'—that is, without some form of unconditional pressure that threatens the very core of our being" (*Žižek Reader,* ix).

98. Badiou, "Qu'est-ce qu'un thermidorien?" 56–60.

2. From Maoism to L'Organisation Politique

1. EE, 446; MP, 57; DO, 43; LS, 45–46. "What Althusser failed to grasp, what I failed to grasp between 1968 and, let's say, the beginning of the 1980s, and what I can see today, was the need fully to recognize the immanence in thought of *all* the conditions of philosophy" (C, 233).

2. DI, 22; Alain Badiou, "Le Flux et le parti (dans les marges de *L'Anti-Oedipe*)," 40.

3. See CM, 52; Alain Badiou, "La Subversion infinitésimale" (1968) and "Marque et manque: À propos du zéro" (1969).

4. Anglophone readers may have to wait for Bruno Bosteels's forthcoming *Badiou and the Political* for a sustained engagement with *Théorie du sujet;* my own brief remarks here make no claim to be anything like an exhaustive account.

5. Alain Badiou, "L'Etre, l'événement et la militance," 13.

6. For background to the history of Maoism in France, see Christophe Bourseiller, *Les Maoïstes: La folle histoire des gardes rouges françaises* (1996); Patrick Kessel, ed. *Le Mouvement maoïste en France* (1972 and 1978); Robert Linhart, *L'Etabli* (1981); Pierre Saunier, *L'Ouvriérisme universitaire* (1994). I owe these references to Sebastian Budgen.

7. Groupe Yenan-Philosophie, "Etat de Front," in *La Situation actuelle sur le front de la philosophie,* ed. Alain Badiou and Sylvain Lazarus (1977), 5–6.

8. Alain Badiou, H. Jancovici, D. Menetrey, and E. Terray, *Contribution au problème de la construction d'un parti marxiste-léniniste de type nouveau,* 47.

9. Some of the most important features of Badiou's mature ontology—the axioms of infinity, the nature of the void—are first approached in the difficult articles he published in the *Cahiers pour l'analyse* of the Ecole Normale Supérieure (written 1966–67).

10. Alain Badiou, "L'Autonomie du processus esthétique," 77.

11. Badiou, "Marque et manque," 163.

12. Ibid., 156–57, 161.

13. Ibid., 162.

14. Ibid., 163. Or again, "Science is the Subject of philosophy, and this precisely because there is no Subject of science" (163).

15. Badiou, *Contribution au problème,* 4; cf. TC, 9. Badiou's assessment of the primary evental occasion of his own subjectivation has not changed much over the years. Looking back at May 1968 thirty years later, he remembers feeling "that the uprooting of my previous life (that of a small-time provincial functionary, married, head of a family, with no other vision of Redemption than that of writing books) and the departure for a new life subjected, ardently subjected, to militant obligations in previously unknown places, hostels, factories, housing projects, suburban marketplaces, and with this, confrontation with the police, being arrested in the early hours of the morning, being on trial—that all this sprang not from a lucid decision but from a special sort of passivity, that of a total abandonment to what was taking place" (LS, 102).

16. Badiou, *Contribution au problème,* 15, 26, 39.

17. TS, 205; cf. 25; TC, 82; DI, 14. Badiou: "We are not *ouvriéristes,* in any sense of the term (*Contribution au problème,* 42).

18. Alain Badiou, "Custos, quid noctis?" (1984), 862.

19. TS, 62; cf. Badiou, *Sartre,* 6.

20. Badiou, *Sartre,* 7; cf. Alain Badiou, *Le Mouvement ouvrier révolutionnaire contre le syndicalisme,* 34.

21. TS, 62; cf. Badiou, *Contribution au problème,* 27.

22. DI, 98, 96. The properly "modern philosopher" is "a systematic proletariat" (TS, 11); the proletariat is first and foremost "a logical power" (DI, 108).

23. Badiou, *Contribution au problème,* 44, 47.

24. See in particular TS, 156–58.

25. TS, 149; TC, 102. "Without destruction, no construction, this is a principle of Mao Zedong's thought" (Badiou, *Le Mouvement ouvrier révolutionnaire,* 29).

26. Badiou, *Le Mouvement ouvrier révolutionnaire,* 29, 32.

27. Alain Badiou, La *"Contestation" dans le P.C.F.*, 11; Badiou, *Contribution au problème*, 46; Badiou, La *"Contestation" dans le P.C.F.*, 15–16.

28. Badiou, "Le Flux et le parti," 30.

29. Ibid., 33; cf. TS, 263.

30. TS, 338. Hence the essential lesson of May 68: "Those who, like us, looked first to what was missing (subjective political precarity, the absence of a party) rather than to what appeared full (the revolt, the masses in the street, liberated speech) had what they needed to nourish their confidence *[confiance]*, while the others were left only to betray their belief *[croyance]*" (TS, 342). If Badiou and his friends are the last of the *soixante-huitards* to be found campaigning outside factory doors, he writes, this is "not because we're saying and doing the same things as we did twenty years ago." On the contrary, it is because "the 'others' failed to make and endure the necessary transformation, that they have dropped out" ("Réponses écrites" [1992], 66).

31. TS, 327, 337; DI, 128; cf. Badiou, *Le Mouvement ouvrier révolutionnaire*, 30.

32. Alain Badiou, "1977, une formidable régression intellectuelle," 78.

33. Badiou, "Réponses écrites" (1992), 67. The first issue of *La Distance politique* compares the collapse of Stalinism and the simultaneous triumph of capital's new world order with the fall of Napoleon in 1815. An end to a viciously aggressive regime—but to the profit of the Bourbon restoration, the White Terror, and the Holy Alliance and to the attendant vilification of the revolutionary tradition (*La Distance politique* 1 [Dec. 1991], 10).

34. Badiou, "1977, une formidable régression intellectuelle," 78.

35. Alain Badiou, "Six Propriétés de la vérité, *Ornicar?* 33, 142.

36. PP, 52. Up to a point, Badiou reconfigures this destruction as the preliminary to a kind of a *resurrection* of Marxism: "To be the subject of the crisis of Marxism is not the same as being its object" (PP, 54).

37. Badiou, *Jean-Paul Sartre* (1981), 5. Subsequent quotations are taken from this pamphlet.

38. Badiou, "L'Etre, l'événement et la militance," 13.

39. Badiou, "Politics and Philosophy," 114.

40. Ibid., 114–15.

41. Alain Badiou, "Nous pouvons redéployer la philosophie," 2.

42. S20, 90, quoted in TS, 131.

43. "This question of the thought of the two has as its horizon the destiny of dialectical thought: in the end, is the category of contradiction in the Hegelian, Marxist, and Sartrean inheritance still pertinent or not to the conceptualization of difference? . . . I think the question is still open" (Badiou, "L'Entretien de Bruxelles," [1990], 15).

44. Alain Badiou, "La Scène du Deux" (1998), 1.

45. TS, 42. "Every Marxist statement is, in a single self-dividing movement, constative and directive . . . ; every [Marxist] description is a prescription" (TC, 16).

46. MP, 71– 72; cf. PP, 107, 114; EE, 353.

3. Infinite by Prescription

1. Alain Badiou, "Les Lieux de la vérité," 116; cf. DI, 52–55; "Dix-neuf réponses," 254.

2. Such, we might say, is Badiou's single concession to the postmodern turn: from now on, the analysis of what happens will presume the integrity of fully discrete temporal sequences, however little these might resemble what Lyotard famously dubbed "small narratives *[petits récits]*" (cf. Jean-François Lyotard, *La Condition postmoderne* [1979], chap. 14). Daniel Bensaïd is no doubt not the only critic to think that there is more of a resemblance here than Badiou might want to admit (Bensaïd, "Alain Badiou et le miracle de l'événement," 163).

3. It should be stressed that Badiou's interest in mathematics is as long-standing as his interest in politics. In one of his first published works he developed a general "concept of model" based on set theory (CM, 52), and many of the components of his mature system (Cantor's multiple of multiples, the excess of parts over elements, Cohen's generic subset, and so on) are all present in *Théorie du sujet*—deprived, simply, of a properly ontological authority.

4. Badiou, "Politics and Philosophy," 127.

5. Badiou, "La Subversion infinitésimale," 136. Thirty years later, Badiou divides twentieth-century French philosophy into two similar groups. One follows Bergson in pursuit of the concrete, the vital, the Total, the dynamic, the Open. The other follows Brunschvicg and the Cartesian tradition, celebrating mathematical *idéalité*, the axiom, the clear and distinct, refusing to trust anything that is not "specifiable as a closed set whose signature is a concept" (D, 144). Badiou presents himself as the current champion of the mathematizing option, and acknowledges Deleuze as his most illustrious opposite number, working to achieve the "complete laicization of Bergsonism" (D, 145).

6. Why? Because, as we shall see, if mathematical consistency defines the unnameable of the ontological situation, there is no comparable Real for the "human" situation as such. In other words, there is nothing analogous in Badiou's philosophy to Žižek-Lacan's Real qua incestuous Thing, where this Thing is not merely repressed but "foreclosed or 'primordially repressed' *(ur-verdrängt),*" such that its repression is not a historical variable but is constitutive of the very order of symbolic historicity" in general (Slavoj Žižek, *The Metastases of Enjoyment: Six Essays on Woman and Causality,* 199).

7. S3, 168 / 148; D, 94.

8. S2, 130 / 104. As is well known, in the decade following his famous first

seminar at the Ecole Normale Supérieure (1964–65) Lacan's own thinking moved ever closer toward the ideal of pure mathematization. Unlike Badiou, however, Lacan never ceased to believe that "the notion of being, as soon as we try to grasp it, proves itself to be as ungraspable as that of speech" (S1, 352/229)—if only because "the unconscious does not lend itself to ontology" (S11, 38/29).

9. CT, 92; cf. Badiou, "Marque et manque," 164.

10. Cf. Morris Kline, *Mathematics and the Search for Knowledge,* 196–220.

11. Léon Brunschvicg, *La Modalité du jugement,* 221; cf. D, 144.

12. Hao Wang, *Computation, Logic, Philosophy,* 48.

13. NN, 11, 261. Badiou's position is thus far removed from what remains today perhaps the most familiar view of mathematical objects, the view associated with Frege and Russell whereby "a number is something that characterises certain collections," or "classes"—that is, collections of twos, threes, fours, and so on (Bertrand Russell, *Introduction to Mathematical Philosophy,* 12). Thus defined, "numbers do not have being—they are, in fact, what are called 'logical fictions'" (132).

14. "I've always thought that any other conception than mine makes of the general consonance of physical experimentation and actually existing mathematics a mystery pure and simple" (Alain Badiou, letter to the author, 9 Dec. 1998).

15. In this Badiou essentially follows Cantor's lead: given the independence of mathematics "from any constraints imposed by the external reality of the spatial-temporal world," its "freedom [is] its essence. . . . This distinguished position differentiates mathematics from all other sciences" (Georg Cantor, "Foundations of the General Theory of Manifolds," 79).

16. Theodor Adorno, "The Actuality of Philosophy" (1931), 120.

17. Martin Heidegger, "Modern Science, Metaphysics, and Mathematics," in BW, 277.

18. Ibid., 302.

19. Badiou, "Politics and Philosophy," 127.

20. From a broadly Heideggerian or Deleuzian perspective, of course, Badiou's approach can for this reason only be a dramatic impoverishment of ontology: from such a perspective, mathematics articulates only one of many "regions" of Being (alongside the regions articulated by physics, biology, art, and so on), and a genuine ontology must remain "the science of Being as a whole, not the science of a region or aspect of Being" (Dan Smith, letter to the author, 11 June 2001; Smith mounts a compelling neo-Deleuzian critique of Badiou's ontology in his contribution to *Think Again,* ed. Hallward).

21. More technically, mathematical set theory is arranged in such a way as to consider any particular existence from a purely conditional angle. *If* a certain set of elements exists, the basic rules of set theory make it possible to isolate or

manipulate certain parts of that set in certain ways—in particular, in the ways prescribed by the axioms of union, of separation, of the power set, and of choice (EE 75–79). In most such cases, however, the actual existence of the set to be manipulated is purely and simply taken for granted. Set theory offers nothing resembling the deduction of types of existences from the general category of being.

22. Badiou, "Politics and Philosophy," 127–28.

23. Badiou, "Un, Multiple, Multiplicité(s)," 8.

24. See in particular Heidegger, "On the Essence of Truth," 125.

25. Sartre, *L'Etre et le néant,* 51.

26. Badiou, "Saisissement, dessaisie, fidélité," 19.

27. C, 159; cf. E, 73; TS, 171; NN, 263.

28. See, for example, NN, 77, 99, 127, 257–58.

29. Alain Badiou, untitled response, (1989), 113.

30. See Joseph Warren Dauben, *Georg Cantor: His Mathematics and Philosophy of the Infinite,* 147, 294–97; cf. EE, 53–54.

31. EE, 551. As one textbook puts it, set theory is a theory of distinction presented at the highest possible level of "generality and abstractness, such [that] further analysis is clearly impossible. When a theory is ultimate in this sense, it can only be based on a postulated domain of objects, the essential properties of which are embodied in formal axioms." By contrast, a theory based on more familiar or "imaginable" objects, such as the integers of arithmetic or points of space in geometry, might be regarded—at least for "normal" use—as the "mathematical idealisation of more intuitive knowledge" (B. Rotman and G. T. Kneebone, *The Theory of Sets and Transfinite Numbers,* 1).

32. Although this position is relatively orthodox in the philosophy of mathematics, it is naturally resisted by philosophers who put things before numbers—philosophers such as Deleuze (for whom pure intensity is irreducible to any metric quantification) and Merleau-Ponty (for whom any formalization always follows an act of imaginative and embodied perception not essentially different from any other perception [cf. Maurice Merleau-Ponty, *Phénoménologie de la perception,* 441 / 385; Maurice Merleau-Ponty, *La Prose du monde,* 173]). Badiou would no doubt dismiss Merleau-Ponty's perception-dependent approach to mathematics as an impoverished variant of intuitionism, itself the prisoner of a misplaced belief in the empirical representation of mathematical objects: axiomatic set theory reveals such things to be nothing more than configurations of the void. Genuine mathematical thought can proceed, to the exclusion of any sort of perception or imagination, only as the deductive supervision of coherent relations between empty forms of pure multiplicity (EE, 277). All of Badiou's work takes place at a maximum distance from what Merleau-Ponty was eventually to call a "perceptual faith" in the sheer presence of the sensual world.

33. Cf. Eli Maor, *To Infinity and Beyond: A Cultural History of the Infinite*, 135–37.

34. Hence Cantor's conclusion: given the coherence of transfinite mathematics, "the only correct thing to do ... is to grant the human understanding the predicate 'infinite' in certain respects" (Cantor, "Foundations," 76).

35. Plotinus, *The Aenneads*, VI, 9, 6; cf. Proclus, *The Elements of Theology*, Prop. 8, 9.

36. René Descartes, *Principles of Philosophy*, part 1, sect. 26, in *Philosophical Writings*, vol. 1, 202; cf. Pascal, *Pensées*, sect. 84 (348, 352), in *Oeuvres complètes*, 1107–8.

37. Bertrand Russell, *Our Knowledge of the External World*, 169.

38. Bertrand Russell, *Mysticism and Logic*, 85; Russell, *Our Knowledge of the External World*, 164.

39. Russell, *Mysticism and Logic*, 64, 81; cf. Bertrand Russell, *The Autobiography of Bertrand Russell*, 335.

40. Penelope Maddy, *Realism in Mathematics*, 125; Penelope Maddy, "Believing the Axioms," 486.

41. José A. Bernadete, *Infinity: An Essay in Metaphysics*, 29; cf. A. S. Moore, *The Infinite*, 112; Dauben, *Cantor*, 4, 118.

42. Roitman, *Introduction to Modern Set Theory*, 73. As Cantor's translator notes, "The philosophical revolution brought about by Cantor's work was even greater, perhaps, than the mathematical one" (Philip Jourdain, preface to Georg Cantor, *Contributions to the Founding of the Theory of Transfinite Numbers*, vi).

43. David Hilbert, "On the Infinite" (1925), in *Philosophy of Mathematics*, ed. Benacerraf and Putnam, 191.

44. Georg Cantor, "On Linear Aggregates" (1883), in Bernadete, *Infinity*, 28; cf. Dauben, *Cantor*, 124–25.

45. Maddy, "Believing the Axioms," 761.

46. Cf. Keith Devlin, *Fundamentals of Contemporary Set Theory*, 150.

47. The power set of $\aleph_0$ is in Cohen's account "an incredibly rich set given to us by one bold new axiom [the power set axiom], which can never be approached by any piecemeal process of construction" (Paul J. Cohen, *Set Theory and the Continuum Hypothesis*, 151).

48. See EE, 22–23, 309–12, 376–77. Badiou is hardly alone in singling out Cohen's landmark result. Gödel called it "the most important progress in set theory since axiomatisation" (in *Companion Encyclopaedia of the History and Philosophy of the Mathematical Sciences*, ed. Ivor Grattan-Guinness, 642).

49. Cohen, *Set Theory*, 1; cf. Mary Tiles, *The Philosophy of Set Theory: An Introduction to Cantor's Paradise*, 193.

50. Michael Hallett, *Cantorian Set Theory and Limitation of Size*, 205 (my emphasis).

51. Ibid., 208, my emphasis; cf. 236.

52. Friedrich Nietzsche, "In the Horizon of the Infinite," in *The Gay Science*, sect. 124, 180.

53. Karl Jaspers, *Reason and Existenz*, 104–6.

54. Cf. CT, 35. For "despite its total abstraction, the infinite is a world of great simplicity.... By going to the infinite, the complexity of the large finite is lost" (Keith Devlin, *Mathematics: The New Golden Age*, 41).

55. Maddy, *Realism*, 4.

56. Weyl, quoted in Constance Reid, *Hilbert*, 218, 274; Kline, *Mathematics and the Search for Knowledge*, vi.

57. Hilbert, "On the Infinite," 195; cf. Abraham Robinson, "Formalism 64," in *Selected Papers*, ii, 507, 512.

58. Philip J. Davis and Reuben Hersh, *The Mathematical Experience*, 226. In Hilbert's axiomatized geometry, for example, points and lines are not ideal approximations to objects in physical space but undefined terms that conform to procedures governing their manipulation. Rather than persist in the conception of the ancient Euclidean axioms as self-evident truths, formalist geometry accepts the strictly relative validity of multiple (non-Euclidean) geometries, each based on its own, internally consistent, axiom system. Cf. Reid, *Hilbert*, 77–79.

59. Davis and Hersh, *Experience*, 340.

60. Gödel admits that "the objects of transfinite set theory ... clearly do not belong to the physical world," yet maintains that we have a reliable intuitive perception of them (Kurt Gödel, "What Is Cantor's Continuum Problem?" 483–84).

61. Mathematicians customarily distinguish four or five schools of constructivism, ranging in degrees of severity from a strict finitism that denies even potential infinity, to the relatively permissive orientation of André Weyl and Solomon Feferman. Intuitionism proper occupies something of an intermediate position between these extremes.

62. André Weyl, *Philosophy of Mathematics and Natural Science*, 51. As the canonical account has it, "The only thing which can make a mathematical statement true is ... an intuitively acceptable proof, that is, a certain kind of mental construction" (Michael Dummett, *Elements of Intuitionism*, 7; cf. Michael Dummett, *Truth and Other Enigmas*, xxv).

63. Thomas Hobbes, *Leviathan*, 99.

64. Dummett, *Elements of Intuitionism*, 55–56.

65. Ludwig Wittgenstein, *Remarks on the Foundations of Mathematics*, 56.

66. Robinson, "Formalism 64," 505–6.

67. Devlin, *Mathematics*, 41.

68. Hallett, *Cantorian Set Theory*, 303.

69. Hilbert (1928), quoted in Kline, *Mathematical Thought*, 1208.

70. NN, 106. As François Châtelet observes, "It is the great merit of Badiou to think through all the relative failures of Frege and Dedekind," so as to conclude that "the infinite can be decided but not deduced" (Gilles Châtelet, rev. of *Le Nombre et les Nombres*, 121–22).

71. Moore, *The Infinite*, xi, 11, 218.

72. Kline, *Mathematical Thought*, 1028.

73. Kline, *Mathematics and the Search for Knowledge*, 215.

74. Kline, *Mathematical Thought*, 1029, 1035. The fact that physics, for instance, in Einstein's wake, has occasionally been able to make good use of these apparently fanciful constructions in no way limits their constitutive autonomy.

75. Maor, *Infinity*, 256. Maor compares Gödel and Cohen's work to Heisenberg's famous uncertainty principle.

76. Maor, *Infinity*, 255; Abraham Robinson, "Some Thoughts on the History of Mathematics," in Selected Papers, vol. 2, 572; cf. Wilder, *Introduction to the Foundations of Mathematics*, 283–84.

77. Weyl, *Philosophy of Mathematics*, 20; cf. Maddy, "Believing the Axioms," 481, 761. As Maddy's title suggests, commitment to the axioms of set theory is indeed a matter of "belief" in the strong sense.

78. Bernadete, *Infinity*, 114.

79. Kline, *Mathematical Thought*, 1035.

80. Badiou, "Dix-neuf réponses," 267.

81. Philip J. Davis and Reuben Hersh, *Descartes' Dream: The World according to Mathematics*, 43 ff.

82. Badiou, "Saisissement, dessaisie, fidélité," 15. "With Number thus entrusted to being, we can turn our attention to the nonnumerable effects of the event" (NN, 140).

83. NN, 264. "Politics will be conceivable only as delivered from the tyranny of number" (PP, 68).

84. NN, 264; D, 116; cf. NN, 12. "*Il n'y a de chiffrage que de la mort*" (SP, 88).

85. Badiou, "Les Lieux de la vérité," 113.

Part II. Being and Truth

4. Badiou's Ontology

1. Badiou, untitled response (1989), 109.

2. SP, 82. In the absence of any immanent limit to the multiple, "there is no original principle of finitude"; "infinity is another name for multiplicity itself" (CT, 34).

3. Howard Eves, *An Introduction to the History of Mathematics*, 462. Of course Badiou is not the first to pose the question of the "'ontological commitments' of

set theory" (see, for instance, Benacerraf and Putnam, introduction to *Philosophy of Mathematics*, 30–33; Dauben, *Cantor*, 171).

4. "Philosophie et mathématiques," in C, 165; EE 20–21. Cf. EE, 12, 78; John Horton Conway, *On Numbers and Games*, 7.

5. By general—though not universal—agreement, "set theory provides a unified framework for the whole of pure mathematics" (Devlin, *Fundamentals of Contemporary Set Theory*, 35).

6. Readers unfamiliar with the axioms are advised to check the full list in my appendix (or the dictionary that supplements *L'Etre et l'événement*). Briefly, the axiom of the void provides the sole existential basis of the theory, and the axiom of infinity ensures the *actually* infinite expansion of this existence. The axiom of extensionality prescribes how existing sets differ. The axioms of subsets, of union, of separation, of replacement, and of choice all perform particular operations upon a certain preexisting set x that yield another set y (cf. EE, 75).

7. The canonical reference is to Cantor, "Foundations," 93. Gödel explains the basic concept of set by comparison with Kant's categories of pure understanding: "The function of both is 'synthesis,' i.e., the generating of unities out of manifolds (e.g., in Kant, of the idea of one object out of its various aspects)" (Gödel, "What Is Cantor's Continuum Problem?" 484 n. 26).

8. Devlin, *Fundamentals of Contemporary Set Theory*, 2.

9. Weyl, *Philosophy of Mathematics*, 47; cf. Dauben, *Cantor*, 176.

10. Zermelo's second axiom (which he calls the "Axiom of Elementary Sets") refers to the empty set as "fictitious," that is, a fabrication required by the theory (Ernst Zermelo, "Investigations in the Foundations of Set Theory" [1908], in *From Gödel to Frege*, ed. Jan Van Heijenoort, 202).

11. As Cohen puts it, "In our system, all objects are sets. We do not postulate the existence of any more primitive objects. To guide his intuition, the reader should think of our universe as all sets which can be built up by successive collecting processes, starting from the empty set" (Cohen, *Set Theory*, 50).

12. Badiou, "Politics and Philosophy," 130.

13. Of course, in this as in any other-than-ontological example, determining the precise criteria of this particular belonging, or counting as one, or structuring, will in turn certainly involve the discernment of features we consider peculiar to or typical of galaxies—galaxies as distinct from large groups of stars, sections of empty space, and so on.

14. Russell, *Introduction to Mathematical Philosophy*, 12.

15. Moore, *The Infinite*, 129.

16. T, 42.

17. T, 76–77.

18. Cantor, *Contributions*, 86; cf. Gödel, "What Is Cantor's Continuum Problem?" 470.

19. Charles Parsons, "What Is the Iterative Conception of Set?" in *Philosophy of Mathematics*, ed. Benacerraf and Putnam, 509; Maddy, *Realism in Mathematics*, 134.

20. This controversial axiom, first proposed by Zermelo in 1908, asserts the possibility, given an infinite number of sets, of selecting without any explicit protocol or criteria a "representative element" from each set, so as to compose a new infinite subset. The selection is "produced without any kind of law of construction. The axiom thus affirms a pure infinite existence. . . . It has the following ontological implication: there exists an infinite, anonymous and law-less representation, for every infinite situation" (Badiou, "Logique et philosophie" [1994], 10). As you might expect, constructivists deny the legitimacy of the axiom of choice.

21. Tiles, *The Philosophy of Set Theory*, 147.

22. For instance, Dummett writes: "Infinite sequences must be regarded as intensional in character: they are given by means of a particular process of generation, and are therefore not uniquely determined by their terms" (Dummett, *Elements of Intuitionism*, 63). However, "most set theorists find [this principle of] constructibility an artificial restriction" and accept the "combinatorial idea" that *any* possible collection can be considered a set (Maddy, *Realism in Mathematics*, 134–35).

23. Cf. NN, 93; EE, 154, 203, 206–9. Cantor's inconsistent "set of all sets" is itself excluded from the theory by this axiom of foundation, since any such set would have to belong to itself.

24. EE, 113; cf. NN, 82–84; TS, 235.

25. We must "hold the *errance* of the excess to be the real of being" (MP, 61); Easton's theorem confirms the point (EE, 308–9).

26. Badiou, "Un, Multiple, Multiplicité(s)," 11.

27. Slavoj Žižek, *The Plague of Fantasies*, 82.

28. Slavoj Žižek, *For They Know Not What They Do: Enjoyment As a Political Factor*, 44.

29. A "symptom turns a dispersed *collection* into a *system*" (Žižek, *Plague*, 128).

30. Slavoj Žižek, *Tarrying with the Negative: Kant, Hegel, and the Critique of Ideology*, 124.

31. Žižek, *Plague*, 76.

32. Ibid., 217.

33. EE, 53. "Every effort to conceptualize inconsistency produces a pure theory of 'minimal' consistency, the local consistency of sets, which refers inconsistency to the dimension of the Whole (there is no set of all sets). Let's say that ontology (mathematics) 'touches' the inconsistency of the multiple at its totalizing edge, with the statement: 'The Whole inconsists'" (Badiou, letter to the author, 9 Dec.

1998). And Žižek: "Badiou's inconsistent pure multiple is Lacan's Real as *pas-tout* . . . , that X that precedes the Kantian transcendental synthesis" (Žižek, *The Ticklish Subject*, 166).

34. PM, 57. Justice, for example, is the "philosophical name of the inconsistency of the state and society [declared by] all egalitarian politics" (AM, 118).

35. Moore, *The Infinite*, 186, 126.

36. Moore, *The Infinite*, 198; cf. Rudy Rucker, *Infinity and the Mind*, 47, 191–205.

37. The "One" of Plotinus shares with Badiou's multiplicity the attribute of being "under no limit either in regard to anything external or internal" (Plotinus, *Aenneads*, v, 5, 11).

38. EE, 409; cf. E, 6, 9; C, 199.

39. Badiou, "Six Propriétés de la vérité," *Ornicar?* no. 32, 41; cf. EE, 67. Elsewhere, Badiou identifies this *présentation simple* with "whatever people are thinking" in a given situation ("Un, Multiple, Multiplicité(s)," 11).

40. PP, 76. An event is always, "one way or another, a break-down of the count" (Badiou, "Politics and Philosophy," 129).

41. MP, 89. Verifiability is "a convention—a consensus—attached to the statements of the language of the situation" (Badiou, "Six Propriétés de la vérité," 42; cf. EE, 366).

42. Badiou, "Le Flux et le parti," 33–34.

43. EE, 113: In set-theoretical terms, the operation of the state coincides with the power set axiom.

44. Alain Badiou, "Ta Faute, ô graphie!" 261. Hegel's *Philosophy of Right* remains the preeminent philosophical engagement with a strictly re-presentational conception of the State.

45. Badiou, "Un, Multiple, Multiplicité(s)," 12. In 1917, for instance, the state power of the czar was demonstrated to be not only measurable and fragile but even weaker, thanks to the war with Germany, than "the power of the simple collective presentation" itself (AM, 162–63).

46. Badiou, "Les Lieux de la vérité," 114.

47. Badiou has always considered the state the "objective" and "violent core of legal domination." He believes that "its effect is to nullify antagonistic subjective force" (TS, 190; cf. DO, 57).

48. Badiou, "Platon et/ou Aristote-Leibniz," 72; cf. EE, 270; CT, 74. Badiou prefers the term "void" *[vide]* over "nothing" *[rien]* because, whereas "nothing" is global (in relation to the "all" that is counted), the "void" is always local, indicating a (precise) gap or breakdown in the count (EE, 69).

49. E, 25; cf. EE, 45, 70–71; C, 177.

50. EE, 81. Any nonaxiomatic derivation of the void will always be vulnerable

to Bergson's famous critique of the nothing as a nonsensical affirmation of mere absence as "something" in its own right (Henri Bergson, *L'Evolution créatrice*, 274–75).

51. Since the void can never belong to a set (i.e., can never exist), it is itself a multiple "subtracted from the primitive Idea of the multiple" (EE, 81; cf. Châtelet, Rev. of *Le Nombre et les nombres*, 121–22).

52. CT, 36. The pure (algebraic) letter is the vehicle of that "integral transmission" effected by the matheme (cf. Lacan, S7, 276–77 / 236; S20, 100). What might be called Badiou's epistemological optimism—his faith in the literal sufficiency of truth, and the consequent redundancy of epistemology as such—is rooted in the several forms of his appreciation of the letter: "Only the letter effects but does not discern. . . . The letter, which carries the murmur of the indiscernible, is addressed without division. Every subject is traversable by the letter, every subject is transliterable. This would be my definition of freedom in thought, an egalitarian freedom: a thought is free as soon as it is transliterated by the little letters of the matheme, the mysterious letters of the poem, the taking of things by the letter *[à la lettre]* in politics, and the love letter" (PM, 57).

53. Badiou, "Un, Multiple, Multiplicité(s)," 14–15 (my emphasis).

54. Lacan, *Ecrits*, 392.

55. NN, 84. Cf. EE, 100: Of course, inclusion of the void does not in any sense "fill out" the sets in which it is included. The empty set itself, which like every set includes the empty set (itself) as a subset, remains no less empty for this inclusion. What such inclusion points to is rather the haunting indication of the utterly insubstantial "stuff" that makes up the very be-ing of whatever belongs to the situation.

56. Badiou, "Platon et / ou Aristote-Leibniz," 72. "Unicity" here means that, given a certain property, only one being can be conceived as having that property. As Badiou notes, this applies to $\emptyset$ and ω_0 as much as to a monotheistic notion of God (EE, 560).

57. Keith Devlin, *The Axiom of Constructibility*, 12.

58. John N. Crossley et al., *What Is Mathematical Logic?* 65–66.

59. EE, 107. It may be worth paraphrasing Badiou's own slightly more technical version of this derivation, since it is liable to intimidate some readers of *L'Etre et l'événement* (105–7). Set theory begins with the axiom of the void: it declares that *there is* an empty set, $\emptyset$. What is known as the axiom of subsets further declares that if a set α exists, so does the set of its subsets or parts (i.e., all the different combinations of its elements). This set is noted as $p(\alpha)$, the "putting into one *[mise-en-un]* of the multiple α" (EE, 106). By definition, the empty set $\emptyset$ itself has no elements. But like all sets, it does have a subset or part, the universally included part $\{\emptyset\}$ (cf. EE, 151). This is clearly nothing but the void itself,

considered *as* a subset. So given Ø, asserted by the axiom of the void, we also have p(Ø), asserted by the axiom of subsets, and this new set p(Ø) or {Ø} *does* have an element, namely Ø itself. Universal inclusion of the void thus generates a new element in the set of its own subsets. The process can be repeated again and again, each time adding a new "successor" subset, so as to produce the full set of natural or "counting" numbers, 1, 2, 3, 4 ... ω_0. The argument can be repeated indefinitely into the transfinite, for, given ω_0, there also exists p(ω_0), that is, the set of its subsets, from which can be derived the smallest infinite cardinal larger than ω_0. Hence the "total dissemination, disunification, of the concept of the infinite." Which is to say, again, that "God does not exist" (EE, 305–6).

60. NN, 86–87. We can define any transitive integer *n* as the set of all the smaller or preceding integers: $n = \{0, 1, 2, 3 \ldots, n-1\}$. As one textbook explains: "Roughly speaking, a transitive set keeps no secrets from itself. It knows all there is to know about its elements; what you see is what you get" (Roitman, *Introduction to Modern Set Theory*, 49; cf. EE, 210).

61. EE, 152. At the opposite end of the ontological spectrum from Bergson or Heidegger, say, Badiou maintains that "number is the medium in which Nature, grasped in its being, opens itself to our thought" (NN, 162; cf. 227).

62. Russell, *Introduction to Mathematical Philosophy*, 77.

63. EE, 178. The point is formalized with Easton's theorem: given ω_0, the excess of p(ω_0) over ω_0 is strictly incalculable (EE, 312, 309).

64. Davis and Hersh, *Experience*, 340.

65. Badiou, "Silence, solipsisme, sainteté," 45.

66. Badiou, "L'Etre, l'événement et la militance," 19.

67. Alain Badiou, "Objectivité et objectalité" (1991), 9 (my emphasis); cf. EE, 71.

68. Merleau-Ponty, *Phénoménologie de la perception*, ii–iii / viii–ix.

5. Subject and Event

1. EE, 197. And Lacan: "The dimension discovered by analysis is the opposite of anything which progresses through adaptation, through approximation ...; it is something which proceeds by leaps, in jumps" (S2, 108 / 86).

2. Quoted by Badiou, EE, 235.

3. EE, 237; cf. TS, 33–34.

4. EE, 238–44; cf. 363; "Dix-neuf réponses," 252; TS, 317.

5. Saint Paul, Gal. 3:28.

6. DO, 34; cf. C, 136.

7. Maor, *Infinity*, 55. For an especially concise account, see Joseph Warren Dauben, "Conceptual Revolutions and the History of Mathematics," 49–71.

8. Dauben, *Cantor*, 66–67.

9. Cantor, "Foundations," 75.

10. Georg Cantor (1888), quoted in Dauben, *Cantor,* 230–36. Dauben documents his "unwavering conviction" in the face of every obstacle (Dauben, *Cantor,* 298 ff.).

11. Gottlob Frege, quoted in Dauben, *Cantor,* 225.

12. Henri Poincaré, *Oeuvres,* vol. 5, 19–23, in Kline, *Mathematical Thought,* 1003.

13. Dauben, *Cantor,* 270.

14. See Deleuze, *Différence et répétition,* 267 / 207.

15. "Chance *[le Hasard]* is the pure thought of the event," because "chance is the self-realization of its idea [. . .] and in no way a correlation with the world" (Badiou, Rev. of Gilles Deleuze: *Le Pli,* 181–82). By thus consigning the determination of an event to the exclusive disposition of chance, however, Badiou risks an equation of the exceptional with the inexplicable. His philosophy effectively proscribes thought from considering the *production* of an event—the very consideration which, in a sense, defines the entire field of Deleuze's own philosophy.

16. Badiou, Rev. of Gilles Deleuze: *Le Pli,* 180.

17. Cf. SP, 70, 89; D, 143; Badiou, "Politics and Philosophy," 125. "When I use the metaphor of grace," Badiou writes, "I do so only to indicate the radical contingency, with respect to the parameters of a situation, of what happens to it eventually *[événementiellement].* But *what* happens is simply indifferent multiplicity" (Badiou, letter to the author, 9 Dec. 1998).

18. SP, 119: "I am convinced that nothing acts as the sign" of an imminent event (CT, 69). Hence at least one point of convergence with Bergson: it is the actual happening of the event that subsequently indicates its "previous" "possibility": it will have been possible in the situation only *after* it has taken place (Henri Bergson, "Le possible et le réel," in *La Pensée et le mouvant,* 111).

19. Badiou, "Politics and Philosophy," 120; cf. SP, 29.

20. Badiou, "Being by Numbers," 87. The event is not itself void, but there is nothing, other than its naming, between it and the void: "The event is not nonbeing [but] transbeing, . . . an ultra-One" (NN, 264–65; cf. EE, 203).

21. Alain Badiou, "L'Age des poètes," 31; PM, 58; AM, 118.

22. Devlin, *Fundamentals of Contemporary Set Theory,* 43.

23. Alain Badiou, letter to the author, 17 June 1996.

24. TA, 18.3.98. To give some further examples: "At the heart of the baroque style come to its virtuoso saturation, there was the void (as unperceived as it was decisive) of a genuine conception of musical architectonics. The Haydn event happens as a kind of musical 'nomination' of this void.... The event names the void insofar as it names the unknown of the situation" (E, 61). The event of Greek tragedy is named Aeschylus, and "this name, like every eventual name, is ... the index of a central void in the earlier situation of chanted verse" (PM,

26). Drawing on Badiou's terminology, Žižek offers a comparable analysis of the "Schumann event" (Žižek, *Plague*, 199 ff.).

25. EE, 195. Located by its site at the edge of the void in a situation, all that separates the event from the void is itself: to the elements of its site, the event adds its own self-presentation. Hence the formal definition: an event e_x of a site X will be the multiple that counts together the elements (x) of this site X, and itself, e_x. So $e_x = \{x \in X, e_x\}$ (cf. EE, 200).

26. In the terms that Badiou develops toward the end of the third chapter of *Logiques des mondes,* the inhabitants of an evental site are those elements that have a minimal or invisible existence according to the rules that regulate how things appear in a world, and thus entertain no observable relationship with the other elements of that world. The dominant logical structure of a situation ensures that the appearing or "being-there" of such elements is indistinguishable from mere "non-being" (LM, chap. 3, pp. 19–20).

27. TS, 149. This example allows us to pinpoint very concisely the main difference between Badiou's earlier and later conceptions of the subject. In his early work, the proletariat, insofar as it becomes subject, figures *both* as the void of the capitalist situation and as the group that is situated along its edge. In the later work he has been careful to sever this connection, which invites the (invariably disastrous) structural presentation of the void. Even if every subjectivation is a naming of the void according to a situation, under no circumstances should we seek to make the void itself subject.

28. LS, 47. As Alexander García Düttmann puts it, every new idea "marks a caesura and a discontinuity in the discursive continuity, a chance for change and transformation, a blind spot one cannot remove with cognitive means, a vacant space to which one can only relate by recognising it or not recognising it. . . . Perhaps thought must relate to a vanishing point of its time if it is to open up a new perspective" (Alexander García Düttmann, *Between Cultures: Tensions in the Struggle for Recognition,* 28–29).

29. As Feltham observes, since the immigrant nation that is Australia is "founded upon the dispossession of indigenous peoples," so "any prolonged investigation of the content of the multiple 'aboriginals' with reference to what it is to be Australian actually causes the unity of the situation to dissolve" (Oliver Feltham, "As Fire Burns: Of Ontology, Praxis, and Functional Work," 132).

30. Badiou, "Politics and Philosophy," 129. The Israeli Refusniks' startling decision to refuse military service in the occupied territories in the wake of Sharon's assaults during the spring of 2002 illustrates this same evental logic: at a time when most "predictable" peace activists remained spectacularly silent, it was precisely a few of those most committed to the defense of Israel who were prepared to "stand up and be counted," and in so doing to establish an uncondi-

tional point of principle that may, in time, come to justify the transformation of the situation as a whole. (For details consult http://www.seruv.org.il.)

31. Lacan, S3, 22 / 13: "That which has not emerged into the light of the symbolic appears in the real" (Lacan, *Ecrits*, 388).

32. Badiou, "Untitled Response," 112–13.

33. Badiou, *"N'est universel que ce qui est en exception immanente"* (SP, 119).

34. Rosa Luxemburg, "The Mass-Strike, The Political Party, and the Trade Unions," in her *Rosa Luxemburg Speaks*, 172.

35. Likewise Castro: "With the collapse of Battista, the seizure of power, and that extraordinary, very slow march of Castro towards Havana, the Cuban people as a whole were seized by something that . . . marked an absolute change of scale with respect to the disembarkation of some twenty people in the hills of the Sierra Maestra . . ." (Badiou, "Politics and Philosophy," 125–26).

36. Walter Benjamin, "Theses on the Philosophy of History," theses VI and XVII, in *Illuminations: Essays and Reflections*, 255, 263.

37. The name is "a 'presentable' multiple that is not presented" in the situation as it stands (Alain Badiou, letter to the author, 16 Nov. 1996).

38. E, 38; EE, 363. As Žižek puts it in similarly antidescriptivist terms, "It is the name itself, the signifier, which supports the identity of the object" (Žižek, *Sublime Object*, 95).

39. TA, 23.4.97. In a recent seminar, Badiou criticizes the "slightly magical" operation implied in *L'Etre et l'événement*, whereby the naming subject draws the name directly "from the void," in a process that seems to "eventalize" the very being of the subject—thereby confusing the naming subject, who operates as if from "inside" the event, with the affirming subject, who operates in its wake (TA, 16.4.97).

40. This clarifies a possible confusion encouraged by the terminology of *L'Etre et l'événement*: since an event is an ultra-one, its effect cannot be measured ontologically so much as logically. Ontologically, an event simply disappears; logically, it "appears" as a revolutionary implication.

41. Badiou, "Dix-neuf réponses," 257; EE, 224. The mathematical form of intervention is formalized as what Zermelo called the "axiom of choice": "The axiom of choice tells us: there is intervention" (EE, 254).

42. TS, 187; cf. DI, 33. Vladimir Lenin, "The Crisis Has Matured" (29 Sept. 1917), in *Selected Works*, ii, 348–50. Ed Pluth and Dominiek Hoens discuss this logic of reasoned anticipation in their compelling essay "What If the Other Is Stupid? On Badiou's Critique of Lacan's 'Logical Time,'" in *Think Again*, ed. Hallward.

43. Alain Badiou, "Philosophy and Justice," lecture given at the University of Essex, March 1998.

44. For example, inspired by Rousseau, we know that "the political decision boils down to deciding whether or not a statement is political, and in no way whether we are for it or against it" (EE, 384). Why? Because identification of a statement as political itself eliminates the entire dimension of opinion at a stroke.

45. E, 39; cf. EE, 257. Hölderlin's poetry provides L'Etre et l'événement with its major figure of artistic fidelity, conceived as a determination fully to inhabit the eventual site Hölderlin imagines as that elusive German "homeland" whose very essence is loss, migration, and wandering. Located at the edge of the unpresentable "storm" of being, only such a site is worthy of the transformative event Hölderlin names the "return of the Gods," just as it is only through fidelity to the consequences of this return that the poet, in permanent exile or embarkation, can sustain a journey through the violent intensity of the present (EE, 283–89).

46. Alain Badiou, "Custos, quid noctis?" 863.

47. Žižek, The Ticklish Subject, 136.

48. For François Furet and his conservative disciples, for instance, the task of "thinking the French Revolution" amounts essentially to a denial of its eventual status—on the one hand, following Tocqueville, by dissolving its punctual coherence across the longue durée of incremental change; on the other hand, by compressing its advent and its corruption together in a single inevitability, such that the Terror is already implicit in the assembly of 1789 (cf. François Furet, Penser la révolution française [1978]).

49. EE, 269. Mathematical deduction is adventurous, Badiou notes, because of the wholly unconstructible leaps authorized by the laws of classical logic or indirect proof, and the consequently "extreme uncertainty of the criterion of connection" (EE, 278).

50. Badiou, "Philosophie et poésie," 95.

51. EE, 314. A generic approach to this impasse, in other words, seeks not to "reduce but to rejoin . . . the mysterious excess of the state"—simply, in such a way as to release the anarchic indifference of indiscernible subsets from any organization that would ensure the domination of other, more discernible subsets (313).

52. EE, 377; cf. 24. Any political process, for instance, results ultimately in the assembly of a "people," that is, a situated grouping of generic or universal humanity (383).

53. Lucas, Conceptual Roots of Mathematics, 333.

54. EE, 365. The failure to acknowledge precisely this difference between truth and knowledge, says Badiou, was the great mistake of "vulgar Marxism" and "vulgar Freudianism." Since it never clearly distinguished the true (proletarian) subject of truth from the nameable, classifiable object that is the working class, vulgar Marxism confused the necessarily militant truth (a matter of struggle)

with a merely scholarly knowledge of History or Society (a matter of research). The same goes for American ego psychology, which is why Lacan, in militant fidelity to the Freud event, had to reassert the radical disjunction between subjective truth and mere knowledge (of the ego) (EE, 368–69).

55. Badiou, "Being by Numbers," 87.

56. Badiou, "Platon et / ou Aristote-Leibniz," 79.

57. Alain Badiou, "D'un sujet enfin sans objet," 22. Lacan's subject likewise "announces himself—he will have been—only in the future perfect" (*Ecrits*, 808 / 306), for, as he says, what is truly "realised in my history is not the definite past of what was, since it is no more, or even the present perfect of what has been in what I am, but the future anterior of what I shall have been for what I am in the process of becoming" (*Ecrits*, 300 / 86; cf. S1, 251 / 159).

58. Cf. Žižek, *The Ticklish Subject*, 137.

59. This list is compressed from EE, 429–30, 434.

60. PM, 88. Badiou writes, "Subjectivation is the proper name, in situation" of that *general* proper name that is "the" void; it is an "occurrence of the void" (EE, 431).

61. Badiou, "D'un sujet enfin sans objet," 17.

62. "It is often said," notes Badiou, "that the external world is properly the place of precision, and our internal worlds the place of imprecision. I argue exactly the opposite. A subject is a machine for producing determination, under conditions that can be largely undetermined or indeterminable" (TA, 20.11.96). The only subject of indetermination, despite the pretensions of deconstruction, is the nonsubject of opinion, habit, or consciousness.

63. "There is no One," Badiou writes, "except inasmuch as it is for all . . . , the only possible correlate to the One is the universal" (SP, 80).

64. De Beauvoir, *Le Deuxieme sexe*, vol. 2, 557 / 793.

65. Žižek, *For They Know Not What They Do*, 25; Žižek, *Sublime Object*, 208.

66. EE, 472. As Žižek puts it, "An analysand becomes an analyst upon assuming that his desire has no support in the Other, that the authorisation of his desire can come only from himself" (Žižek, *Metastases of Enjoyment*, 72–73).

67. Jacques-Alain Miller, "Commentary," in *Reading Seminars I and II*, ed. Bruce Fink, Richard Feldstein, and Maire Jaanus, 425–26; cf. S11, 304 / 273.

68. No one emphasizes this aspect of Lacan's teaching more gleefully than Žižek himself. See also Bruce Fink, *The Lacanian Subject: Between Language and Jouissance*, 95; Bruce Fink, *A Clinical Introduction to Lacanian Psychoanalysis: Theory and Technique*, 208–15.

69. Badiou appears to reject as invalid an intermediary figure, a position between the hysteric and the Master—the figure of the "apostle." The apostle would be the one who bore witness to the declaration, yet remains able to teach its

implications (TA, 9.1.97). It might be argued that such a figure would describe Badiou's own position with respect to May 68.

70. Badiou writes, "The family is to love what the State is to politics" (TA, 4.3.98).

71. Žižek, *The Ticklish Subject*, 141, 128.

72. Badiou, "La Subversion infinitésimale" (1968), 136; cf. D (1997), 144–45.

73. Žižek, *The Ticklish Subject*, 228.

74. Badiou, "Dix-neuf réponses," 249.

75. Žižek, *The Ticklish Subject*, 143–44.

76. Oliver Feltham develops a compelling response to Žižek along similar lines, accusing him of confusing Badiou's notion of truth with the ideological perversion of a truth (Feltham, "As Fire Burns," 184–91).

77. Badiou, "Politics and Philosophy," 124.

78. Louis Althusser, *Philosophy and the Spontaneous Philosophy of the Scientists*, 13.

79. Louis Althusser, *Reading Capital*, 59; cf. 27.

80. Louis Althusser, *Lenin and Philosophy*, 171.

81. Žižek, *Tarrying*, 4; Slavoj Žižek, *The Indivisible Remainder: An Essay on Schelling and Related Matters*, 5.

82. Slavoj Žižek, *Žižek Reader*, ix.

83. Žižek, *Plague*, 222. Indeed, Badiou deals with the fact that "an ideological identification exerts a true hold on us precisely when we maintain an awareness that we are not fully identical to it, that there is a rich human person beneath it" (Žižek, *Plague*, 21), in very much the same way as Žižek himself: Badiou's subject, by definition, is deprived of precisely this delusion. When Žižek suggests that it is indeed "possible to assume a place that enables us to maintain a distance from ideology, but this place from which one can denounce ideology must remain empty, it cannot be occupied by any positively determined reality," he is redescribing the very space Badiou reserves for the subject (Slavoj Žižek, "The Spectre of Ideology," in *Žižek Reader*, 70).

84. Žižek, *Plague*, 227.

85. Žižek, *For They Know Not What They Do*, 68.

86. Žižek, *Sublime Object*, 180–81.

87. Cf. Bruno Bosteels, "Por una falta de política: Tesis sobre la filosofía de la democracia radical," 63–89; see also his "Travesías del fantasma: Pequeña metapolítica del '68 en México' (1999) and his "Vérité et forçage: Badiou avec Heidegger et Lacan." Bosteels extends his argument to include Laclau's radical democratic project: "For lack of a true political sequence, the philosophy of radical democracy limits itself to assuming, as a kind of death drive, the inherent impossibility of the symbolical order of a society. Even if it does not want to reduce itself to a mere becoming conscious [*toma de conciencia* or *prise de conscience*],

which would be an obvious way of contradicting its critique of the ideology of the subject, the project nonetheless seems to be able to formulate itself only in terms of a categorical imperative that obliges us to recognize the intrinsic negativity of the social, as if the task consisted always only in coping with the impasse—without passing through it, let alone forcing a way out" (Bosteels, "Por una falta de política," 77). The difference between the post-Marxism of Laclau and Žižek and what Bosteels analyzes as Badiou's post-Maoism is the topic of his forthcoming book *Badiou and the Political*, in which he seeks to retrieve more fully Badiou's *Théorie du sujet* and its reelaboration in *Logiques des mondes*.

88. Žižek, "The Undergrowth of Enjoyment," in *Žižek Reader*, 17–19. Analysis ends when "the subject fully assumes his or her identification with the sinthome, when he or she unreservedly 'yields' to it" (Žižek, *Tarrying*, 60).

89. Žižek, *Sublime Object*, 124. It is no coincidence that this identification with the sinthome "involves the acceptance of a radical ontological closure," that is, the "tragic" rejection of any (comfortably messianic) "notion of the universe as not-yet-fully ontologically constituted" (Žižek, *Plague*, 31; cf. *Metastases of Enjoyment*, 184). By contrast, Badiou *philosophe* finds in Cantor's theorem a perfectly clear ontological reason for the impossibility of closure, without justifying any sort of tragic posture.

6. The Criteria of Truth

1. Maddy, *Realism in Mathematics*, 16.

2. Dummett, "Realism," in *Truth and Other Enigmas*, 146.

3. Michael Dummett, "Realism," in *Truth and Other Enigmas*, 146; cf. Michael Dummett, "Realism and Anti-Realism," in *The Seas of Language*, 465.

4. Badiou, "Réponses écrites" (1992), 70.

5. Robert Hofstadter, *Gödel, Escher, Bach: An Eternal Golden Braid*, 19; cf. Weyl, *Philosophy of Mathematics*, 219.

6. Gottlob Frege, *The Foundations of Arithmetic*, vol. 1, xvi.

7. Reid, *Hilbert*, 177; 197–98.

8. Bertrand Russell, *My Philosophical Development*, 260.

9. Bertrand Russell, "The Study of Mathematics" (1907), quoted in Russell, *My Development*, 211.

10. Russell, *My Development*, 73, 212.

11. CT, 32. Politics, likewise, "identifies itself as politics (and so as a singular figure of thought) without passing through a definition of politics" (Badiou, "L'Etre, l'événement et la militance," 15).

12. Badiou, "Dix-neuf réponses," 255–56; cf. EE, 232. "The singularity of politics," for example, "does not as such have a relation to historical time, for it constitutes its own entirely separate time" (AM, 132).

13. Badiou, "Being by Numbers," 118.

14. The notion of an integral truth (a complete and sufficient revelation) is necessarily a reference to the *past*. The paradigm here is mystical Islam (cf. Henri Corbin, *Histoire de la philosophie islamique,* 26, 99).

15. EE, 320. As far as Badiou is concerned, "Foucault is a theoretician of encyclopaedias. He was never really interested in the question of knowing whether, within situations, anything existed that might deserve to be called a 'truth.' . . . He wasn't interested in the protocol of either the appearance or the disappearance of a given epistemic organisation. As long as you don't have an immanent doctrine of what in the situation exceeds the situation, you can't be concerned about answering the question of how we pass from one system to another" (Badiou, "Being by Numbers," 123). Badiou's philosophy of the subject sets him sharply apart from Foucault's investigation of how individuals are *made* subject—constituted as both subject and subjected, through the human sciences, through social institutions, through "technologies of power" and "techniques of the self"—through everything, that is, short of an immediate autoconstitution. Badiou refers on several occasions to "Foucault's thorough-going nominalism" (MP, 76; cf. EE, 320), to his alleged "*idéalinguisterie 'fixiste'* [that] excludes any subject" (TS, 204), in favor of the excavation of merely static or truthless constructions. In my own view, however, if there is undeniably a nominalist dimension to Foucault's archaeological work in particular, the guiding effort of his project from start to finish is precisely one of radical despecification—a matter, precisely, of approaching that pure "limit" that is the void of all classification, that is inaccessible to any normalization.

16. Dummett, *Elements of Intuitionism,* 375–77, 401; Dummett, *The Seas of Language,* 48.

17. MP, 76. Cf. EE, 317–25; C, 60–61; DO, 47; DP, 13.

18. Ludwig Wittgenstein, *Philosophical Investigations* I, sect. 124, p. 49.

19. Gottfried W. Leibniz, *Philosophical Works: New Essays,* 57.

20. CT, 45, 52. Cf. Luitzen Egbertus Jan Brouwer, "Historical Background, Principles and Methods of Intuitionism," in *Collected Works,* vol. 1, 511.

21. Grattan-Guinness, ed., *Companion Encyclopaedia,* 656–57. These are the two key ideas that Dummett identifies with a contemporary intuitionism: the commitment to an exclusively potential conception of the infinite (the infinite as "never completed"), and the presumption that meaning depends on "the mental constructions which may serve to prove the statement" (Dummett, *Elements of Intuitionism,* v, 4–6). Dummett argues that "intuitionism represents the only sustained attempt by the opponents of a realist view to work out a coherent embodiment of their philosophical beliefs" (ix).

22. In Brouwer's classic though somewhat dated account, mathematics is based on "an essentially languageless activity of the mind having its origin in

the perception of a movement of time, i.e., of the falling apart of a life moment into two distinct things, one of which gives way to the other, but is retained by memory. If the two-ity thus born is divested of all quality, there remains the empty form of the common substratum of all two-ities. It is this common substratum, this empty form, which is the basic intuition of mathematics" (Brouwer, "Historical Background," 510; cf. Luitzen Brouwer, "Consciousness, Philosophy and Mathematics" (1948), in *Collected Works*, vol. 1, 482). Brouwer's intuitionism thus tends toward a domain of "psychology," that is, an elucidation of the laws of thought or intuition (128–29). In Dummett's more recent version of intuitionism he was careful to restrict the issue to more strictly operational or linguistic matters (Dummett, *Elements of Intuitionism*, 7; Michael Dummett, "Language and Truth," in *The Seas of Language*, 118; Michael Dummett, *The Origins of Analytic Philosophy*, 15).

Badiou's vehement opposition to intuitionism obscures the several things he has in common with Brouwer's original orientation. Like Badiou, Brouwer insists that "there are no non-experienced truths" (Brouwer, "Consciousness, Philosophy and Mathematics," in *Collected Works*, vol. 1, 488). Like Badiou, Brouwer firmly "separates mathematics from mathematical language, in particular from the phenomena of language which are described by theoretical logic" ("Historical Background," 509–10). Like Badiou, Brouwer conceives of genuine thought as subtraction from the petty negotiation of mundane interests. He seeks "liberation from participation in cooperative trade and from intercourse presupposing *plurality of mind*" (487, my emphasis). Also like Badiou, Brouwer pronounces the worldly calculation of "security" to be unworthy of thought, and argues that any genuine philosophy works against "cooperation" with the way of the world: "In particular, [philosophy] should not communicate with the state" (487).

23. Crispin Wright, *Wittgenstein on the Foundations of Mathematics*, 240; cf. Wittgenstein, *Tractatus*, 6.21; Wittgenstein, *Philosophical Investigations* I, sect. 124. Wittgenstein's "resolute opposition to set theory" in particular is well documented (Pasquale Frascolla, *Wittgenstein's Philosophy of Mathematics*, 97 ff.).

24. PP, 113, my emphasis; cf. TS, 284–85.

25. Cf. Imre Lakatos, *Philosophical Papers*, vol. 2, 235.

26. If they do not find intuitionist limitations "outright devastating" (Von Neumann, "An Axiomatisation of Set Theory," in *From Frege to Gödel*, ed. Van Heijenoort, 395), most "uncommitted mathematicians believe that the constructivists are wasting their time by tying their hands with unnecessary restrictions" (Robinson, "Concerning Progress in the Philosophy of Mathematics," in *Selected Papers*, vol. 2, 559). Gödel is just one of many classically minded mathematicians who find that "Brouwer's intuitionism is utterly destructive in its results" (Gödel, "What is Cantor's Continuum Problem?" 473).

27. Derrida, *Points de suspension*, 388.

28. As Badiou writes, "A destruction is not true, it is knowing *[savante]*." Strictly speaking, a truth can "disqualify *[déqualifier]* a term" of the situation, but "it cannot suppress it in its being." Since every truth is egalitarian, only pre-evental hierarchies can be disqualified (EE, 446, 466).

29. LS, 142 n. 44; 46; 106. Along the same lines, Badiou privileges the hesitant path of Celan's subtractive *Anabase* (1963) over the violently destructive fraternity of Saint-John Perse's 1924 epic of the same name (LS, 66–79).

30. Kant, *Pure Reason*, A271 / B327.

31. Ibid., A287 / B343–A288 / B344. Badiou's critique of Kant bears some resemblance to Žižek, *Tarrying*, 17–20.

32. Alain Badiou, "Huit Thèses sur l'universel" (1998), tapescript.

33. Kant, *Pure Reason*, A247 / B303–304, my emphasis; cf. Badiou, "Objectivité et objectalité" (1991), 6.

34. Kant, *Pure Reason*, A432 / B460–A433 / B461.

35. Alain Badiou, "L'Ontologie soustractive de Kant," in CT, 155.

36. Kant, *Pure Reason*, 109A.

37. Badiou, "Objectivité et objectalité" (1991), 6.

38. Ibid., 9.

39. Similar questions have been raised by Monique David-Ménard and Etienne Balibar (at the Forum sur l'universel, Collège International de Philosophie, 4 Nov. 1998). Žižek likewise refers to (and perhaps exaggerates) Badiou's "hidden Kantianism" (Žižek, *The Ticklish Subject*, 166).

40. Immanuel Kant, *Critique of Practical Reason*, 120–22.

41. Ibid., 47, 49. The convergence of expression is itself striking: Badiou writes, "The subject is maintained in the process only by his own prescription" (Badiou, "L'Etre, l'événement et la militance," 21), and Kant, "The subject feels himself necessitated through his own reason" (Immanuel Kant, *Opus Postumum*, 129).

42. Kant, *Practical Reason*, 126, 146.

43. Immanuel Kant, *Groundwork of the Metaphysics of Morals*, 390.

44. Ibid., 425–26.

45. Kant, *Pure Reason*, Bxxx.

46. Kant, *Groundwork*, 449.

47. Alain Badiou, "L'Ontologie fermée de Spinoza," in CT, 91.

48. EE, 132–33. Cantor, among others, had raised a similar question (Cantor, "Foundations," 76).

49. Badiou, "Un, Multiple, Multiplicité(s)," 13–14.

50. Badiou, "L'Ontologie fermée de Spinoza," 79–80. See Baruch Spinoza, *Ethics* I, theorem 16.

51. Spinoza, *Ethics* I, props. 22, 23, 28.

52. Spinoza, *Ethics* II, prop. 44, cor. 2.

53. This is one of the aspects emphasized in Deleuze's reading of Spinoza (Gilles Deleuze, *L'Idée d'expression dans la philosophie de Spinoza*, 260–61 / 282 and passim).

54. "If a thing is only infinite in its kind," Spinoza argues, "one may deny that it has infinite attributes" (*Ethics* I, def. 6). Badiou's mathematical infinity is limited in precisely this sense.

55. Badiou, "Dix-neuf réponses," 259; Badiou, "Un, Multiple, Multiplicité(s)," 12–13.

56. Badiou, "Un, Multiple, Multiplicité(s)," 12–13.

57. CT, 92.

58. Badiou illustrates the point with a reference to serial forms in modern art (cubism, collage, serial music, and so on) as so many attempts to invent an art that would be visible only in its act as such, without regard for its results, or "works" (LS, 127).

59. Georg W. F. Hegel, *The Science of Logic*, 149.

60. Georg W. F. Hegel, *The Encyclopaedia Logic*, sect. 8.

61. Georg W. F. Hegel, *The Phenomenology of Spirit*, sect. 161–62.

62. Hegel, *Encyclopaedia Logic*, sect. 94, sect. 104.

63. Badiou is referring here primarily to Hegel, *Encyclopaedia Logic*, sect. 93–95.

64. EE, 189–90. In an earlier reading, by contrast, Badiou had found Hegel "altogether right" in demonstrating how "the becoming real of the One guaranteed the transition of quality to quantity," that is, the shift from the merely "many ones" of the multiple to the truly unique one One *[das Eine Eins]* (TS, 228–29). Badiou returns to his critique of Hegel in LM, chap. 1, pp. 36–44.

65. As Juliette Simont argues, "Badiou, in order to preserve the pure *errance* of the multiple . . . fixes its apprehension in one discipline, mathematics," whereas Hegel "multiplies the multiple and augments its profusion" in infinities both quantitative and qualitative (Juliette Simont, "Le Pur et l'impur [sur deux questions de l'histoire de la philosophie dans *L'Etre et l'événement*]," 51). By Simont's reading, Spinoza's infinite modes and Hegel's multiple infinities, far from being the impasse or "fault" diagnosed by Badiou, constitute the "internal and positive mobility" of their work (48–49).

66. "Univocal Being is at one and the same time nomadic distribution and crowned anarchy" (Deleuze, *Différence et répétition*, 55 / 37).

67. Badiou, "Being by Numbers," 123.

68. See, for instance, Pierre Verstraeten, "Philosophies de l'événement: Badiou

et quelques autres," 262–63, 275; Eric Alliez, "Badiou / Deleuze," 49; Ray Brassier, "Stellar Void or Cosmic Animal? Badiou and Deleuze," 200–217. Wahl has written the most thorough comparison with Deleuze, which organizes much of his detailed introduction to Badiou's work (François Wahl, "Le Soustractif" [1992]).

In their *Qu'est-ce que la philosophie?* Deleuze and Guattari provide a compressed and somewhat incomprehensible summary of Badiou's "particularly interesting" and "extremely complex" system before suggesting that it is, "in the guise of the multiple, the return to an old conception of transcendent *[supérieure]* philosophy. It seems to us," they continue, "that the theory of multiplicities does not support the hypothesis of a generic multiplicity (even mathematicians themselves have had enough of set theory). There must be at least two multiplicities, two types, from the outset [i.e., virtual and actual, and so on, and] multiplicity is precisely what happens between the two" (144 / 152, trans. modified). Badiou himself, after declaring himself baffled by this depiction of his project, emphasizes his "frontal opposition" to Deleuze (D, 11): "There is no possible compromise between Deleuze's vitalism and Mallarmé's subtractive ontology" (109).

69. Badiou, "Le Flux et le parti" (1977), 25, 40, 41.

70. TC, 75; cf. DI, 8. For Deleuze, meanwhile, Badiou's philosophy is "reflexive, negative, analogical, and transcendent" (D, 116).

71. Badiou, "Un, Multiple, Multiplicité(s)," 15.

72. Badiou, Rev. of Gilles Deleuze: *Le Pli.* It is not an accidental choice: as a neo-*Leibnizian,* Deleuze inherits all the loaded constructivist connotations this label carries for the author of *L'Etre et l'événement.*

73. Badiou, "Un, Multiple, Multiplicité(s)," 1.

74. As Deleuze writes: "Every perception is hallucinatory because perception has no object" (Gilles Deleuze, *Le Pli: Leibniz et le baroque,* 125 / 93).

75. "Deleuze wants and creates a philosophy of Nature, or rather, a philosophy-nature" (Badiou, Rev. of Gilles Deleuze, *Le Pli,* 177), a philosophy of "movement and description," rather than decision and prescription (C, 103).

76. Badiou, Rev. of Gilles Deleuze, *Le Pli,* 162–63. In his most recent contribution to the debate, Badiou develops this central point in still more convincing detail: "The Deleuzian elaboration of multiplicities requires the preliminary deconstruction of *sets,* as closed, static, immobilizing, rather than open, dynamic, and alive" (Badiou, "Un, Multiple, Multiplicité(s)" [1998], 4). To which Badiou makes three counterobjections: (a) Deleuze's "external," "experimental" conception of multiplicity remains pre-Cantorian. That is, this distinction between the finite (the closed, the numbered, the static) and the infinite (the open, the living, the multiple) is no longer tenable; we know that the contemporary notion of set demands precisely that "the opposition of the closed and the open be put entirely aside" (6). (b) Deleuze's conception of the multiple, "including its qualitative de-

terminations, remains inferior to the concept of the Multiple that can be drawn from the contemporary history of sets" (4). The realm of the spatially intuitable is a tiny fraction of the infinitely larger horizons of pure mathematics, as post-Euclidean geometries demonstrate with such reckless exuberance. Deleuze's frequent recourse to Riemannian analogies, moreover, though nicely illustrative of the dizzying variety of post-Kantian spaces and more than metric extensions, works directly against his own vitalist-materialist agenda. Far from exploding the Cartesian restriction of thought in favor of qualitative multiplicity and anarchic difference, "the power of Riemann's thought lies entirely in the neutralization of difference," that is, in the indifferent configuration of numbers, points, lines, functions, and spaces as so many nonintuitable forms of multiplicity (10). (c) Deleuze's reliance on the *figural* (on "descriptive Ideas—the Fold, the Rhizome, the Throw of the dice . . .") means, ultimately, that he cannot "attain a univocal determination of the multiple without one" (5). In the end, his position culminates in a kind of *"mystique naturelle"* (14).

77. "The list of thinkers of the event according to Deleuze (the Stoics, Leibniz, Whitehead . . .) contains only names that we could just as well cite in reason of their opposition to every concept of the event: the declared adversaries of the void, of the clinamen, of chance, of disjunctive separation, of radical rupture, of the Idea" (Badiou, Rev. of Gilles Deleuze, Le Pli, 173).

78. Deleuze, Le Pli, 81 / 60.

79. Deleuze writes, "Being is the unique event in which all events communicate," the "position in the void of all events in one, the expression in non-sense of all senses in one" (Deleuze, Logique du sens, 211 / 179).

80. D, 142. For example, Deleuze's repeated emphasis on the essential unicity of the "dice throw," the gesture that affirms the One of chance, ensures the basic "indiscernibility of the dice throwers (of events, of bursts of virtuality)." Such an apparent "plurality of events is purely formal" (111). Badiou, on the other hand, insists that every event is "absolutely distinct, not formally (on the contrary, the form of all events is the same) but ontologically" (114).

81. Deleuze, Le Pli, 121 / 91.

82. Gilles Deleuze, Cinéma 2: L'Image-temps, 30–31 / 19–20.

83. If anything, Badiou does not go far enough in this direction, toward a fully "creationist" (or nonrelational) reading of Deleuze. See Peter Hallward, "Deleuze and Redemption from Interest," "Deleuze and the 'World Without Others,'" and "The Limits of Individuation, or How to Distinguish Deleuze from Foucault."

84. Badiou, "Un, Multiple, Multiplicité(s)," 3.

85. Badiou, Rev. of Gilles Deleuze, Le Pli, 183. Badiou decided early in his career that Deleuze's "multiplicity . . . is merely the semblance of the multiple, for the position of the multiple requires the presupposition of the One as substance. . . .

For me," he wrote, "this 'process without a subject' of the multiple is the very summit of the One" (TS, 40–41).

86. Deleuze, *Logique du sens*, 211 / 180.

87. Cf. Deleuze, *L'Idée d'expression*, 199–200 / 219; *Mille plateaux*, 314 / 257.

88. Deleuze, *Différence et répétition*, 293 / 228, Gilles Deleuze, *Bergsonisme*, 108 / 104; cf. Deleuze, *L'Idée d'expression*, 195–96 / 214–15.

89. Badiou, "D'un sujet enfin sans objet," 18.

90. "The imperceptible is the immanent end of becoming, its cosmic formula" (Gilles Deleuze and Félix Guattari, *Mille Plateaux*, 342 / 279).

91. Badiou, "D'un sujet enfin sans objet," 19.

92. Deleuze and Guattari, *Mille Plateaux*, 628 / 503; cf. 231 / 188, 198 / 160, 278–81 / 227–29, 412 / 334.

93. Gilles Deleuze, *Empirisme et subjectivité*, 122–23 / 108–9.

Part III. The Generic Procedures

1. C, 79. Badiou has yet fully to explain these *"plus précisément."* In *L'Etre et l'événement*, which predates the more detailed investigations collected in *Conditions* (1992) and his subsequent books, the four procedures are listed simply as "love, art, science, and politics" (EE, 23).

2. Badiou, "Nous pouvons redéployer la philosophie," 2.

3. EE, 430. Badiou does not pretend to deduce these four categories from some kind of transcendental structure of Truth. It all depends, to use his rather vague phrase, on the "'contingency of humanity'" (TA, 16.4.97), that is, on the kinds of truth that human animals are capable of (by analogy with Spinoza's admission that, although God is no doubt expressed in an infinity of attributes, we ourselves are immanent to only two of these attributes: extension and thought [TA, 8.4.98]).

4. Badiou, "Réponses écrites" (1992), 70.

5. C, 187; I follow the slightly more recent version, used in a lecture given at the Centre for English Studies in London, March 1998.

7. Love and Sexual Difference

1. According to Plato, love orients the lover toward beauty in itself, and thus to truth and purity, the perception of "pure light" (*Phaedrus*, 250c; cf. *Symposium*, 206b).

2. Philosophy is first and foremost the literal "love of truth" (C, 196).

3. "La Scène du Deux" (1998), 2.

4. Ibid., 4 (my emphasis).

5. AM, 64. If, as Lacan claimed in a late seminar, "the only thing that we do in the analytic discourse is speak about love" (S20, 77), what Badiou draws from

this discourse is not, of course, the aspect of love whose "duplicity" and narcissistic "deception" Lacan so often condemns (S11, 282 / 253–54, 298 / 268; cf. S20, 44, 46).

6. C, 261; Badiou, "La Scène du Deux," 8.

7. Butler, *Bodies that Matter*, 99. (The question of how far Badiou's adaptation of Lacanian theory—or indeed, any such adaptation—must remain wedded to an ultimately heterosexual conception of sexual difference is one I will leave the reader to decide.)

8. Badiou, "Nous pouvons redéployer la philosophie," 2; cf. C, 304.

9. Alain Badiou, "L'Ecriture du générique," in C, 357. Love is the supreme example of what Žižek calls a "forced choice." In order to remain a matter of choice, it must certainly be free. But this is not the sort of freedom involved in consumer choice, say: calculating the best of a range of eligible candidates is unlikely to coincide with "real love": "The paradox of love is that it is a free choice, but a choice which never arrives in the present—it is always already made. At a certain moment, I can only state retroactively that *I've already chosen*" (Žižek, *Sublime Object*, 166).

10. B, 55. Paraphrasing Plato, Iris Murdoch puts it in suitably dramatic language: "'Falling in love' . . . is for many people the most extraordinary and most revealing experience of their lives, whereby the centre of experience is suddenly ripped out of the self, and the dreamy ego is shocked into awareness of an entirely separate reality" (Iris Murdoch, *The Fire and the Sun: Why Plato Banished the Artists*, 36).

11. In his novel *All the Names* (1995), Portuguese novelist José Saramago has written one of the most remarkable explorations in recent fiction of a pure "decision to love." Saramago's story *The Unknown Island* (1997) might even be read, up to a point, as an allegory of Badiou's philosophy in general.

12. S20, 17.

13. Žižek, *Tarrying*, 56.

14. Essentially, "men" *have* the symbolic phallus *(ils ne sont pas sans l'avoir)*; "women" do not (S20, 73). As a result, "there is no symbolisation of woman's sex as such . . . , the phallus is a symbol to which there is no correspondent, no equivalent" (S3, 198 / 176).

15. Fink, *The Lacanian Subject*, 107–8.

16. Žižek, *Tarrying*, 58. Adapting Kant's analytic of the sublime, Žižek helpfully refers to sexual difference as the "'ontological scandal' of two types of antinomies"—mathematical (feminine, implying the necessary incompletion of the Whole, the unbounded openness of the universe) and dynamic (masculine, implying that the logical connection of all phenomena requires an "exception,"

a "freedom" that "sticks out" as self-moving [God, soul, free will, phallus], as the basis for a new causal series).

17. RT, 70–71. See S20, 13, 61–71.

18. B, 58–59; cf. C, 270.

19. Plato, *The Symposium*, 190–94.

20. Badiou, "Lacan et les présocratiques" (1990), 5–6.

21. Badiou, "La Scène du Deux" (1998), 2.

22. Luce Irigaray, *Je, Tu, Nous: Pour une culture de la différence*, 58 / 48.

23. Luce Irigaray, *Temps de la différence: Pour une révolution pacifique*, 47 / 30.

24. Irigaray, *Je, Tu, Nous*, 60 / 49.

25. Luce Irigaray, *Ethique de la différence sexuelle*, 33 / 28.

26. Irigaray, *Temps*, 16 / xvi.

27. Luce Irigaray, *Sexes et parentés*, 93 / 79.

28. Irigaray, *Temps*, 32 / 14.

29. See Margaret Whitford, *Irigaray: Philosophy in the Feminine*, 36. As Irigaray writes: "In a woman('s) language, the concept as such would have no place" (Luce Irigaray, *Ce Sexe qui n'en est pas un*, 122 / 122–23; cf. *Speculum*, 177–78 / 142–43). What women *are* is here associated with typically antiphilosophical themes (divine, angelic, ethereal, liminal, aesthetic, and so on).

30. Irigaray, *Ethique*, 123 / 128.

31. Irigaray, *Temps*, 79 / 67 ff. As Irigaray wrote: "We need laws that valorise difference" (Irigaray, *Je, Tu, Nous*, 25 / 22).

32. Irigaray, *Temps*, 28 / 10. The assertion of a newly specified women's culture turns in part on new forms of "divine representation," female gods' affirming women as women, as "beautiful and slim," and so on (Irigaray, *Je, Tu, Nous*, 135 / 111).

33. See René Girard, "Le Désir triangulaire," in *Mensonge romantique*, 15–67.

8. Art and Poetry

1. For Lyotard, a genuinely postmodern art provides fragile means for the representation of the irreducible "incommensurability" of phrases and events. Any work of art worth the name points to the real "absence of criteria" applicable across different phrase regimes or language games (Jean-François Lyotard and Jean-Loup Thébaud, *Au juste*, 30 / 14; *Le Différend*, sect. 34); all singular occurrences are to be "judged in [their] incomparability" alone (*Le Différend*, sect. 264). In the end, only the sublime can represent such incomparability, precisely because an experience of the sublime makes present "the incommensurability of reality to concept" (Jean-François Lyotard, "Réponse à la question: qu'est-ce que le postmoderne?" 364 / *Postmodern Condition*, 79; cf. Jean-François Lyotard, *Léçons sur l'analytique du sublime*, 71 / 52, 190–91 / 155–56).

2. Adorno, *Negative Dialectics*, 5, 12 (my emphasis). Bruno Bosteels makes a compelling case for proximity between Badiou and Adorno for precisely this reason: since "Adorno always seeks to track down the non-conceptual content within the concept, he too would have nothing but scorn for the quasi-mystical nonsense of modern-day aestheticians or neo-Heideggerian philosophies of art and poetry" (Bruno Bosteels, letter to the author, 27 April 2000). In my view, however, the sharing of certain anti-Heideggerian and pro-minimalist sympathies counts for less than Adorno's "affinity for things," his critique of abstraction as the "liquidation" of the object, his condemnation of the totalitarian pretensions of reason, his ultimately antiphilosophical investment in aesthetics over metaphysics, his eventual affectation of a tragic intellectual isolation, and so on. Adorno's insistence that epistemology should "be driven at every stage by its inadequacy to the things themselves" (Theodor Adorno, *Against Epistemology*, 25) is blocked in advance by Badiou's equation of ontology and mathematics, as is any "groping for the preponderance of the object" and any recognition of "all that is heterogeneous to concepts" (Adorno, *Negative Dialectics*, 183, 4). Between Badiou's subtractive conception of a subject without object and Adorno's strained conceptual dialogue between concept and object—where "if the thought really yielded to its object . . . the very objects would start talking under the lingering eye" (27)—there can be no real compromise. Adorno's vision of a philosophy that "truly gives itself" to the "diversity of objects that impinge upon it" (13), his belief that if thought can "press close to its object, seek to touch it, smell it, taste it, so thereby [it may] transform itself" (Theodor Adorno, *Prisms: Cultural Criticism and Society*, 240), is cut brutally short by Badiou's literal evacuation of any notion of the object. Adorno's "incommensurability" has little to do with Badiou's axiomatic "inconsistency": the latter testifies to the very identity in truth of being and thought, whereas the former appeals to their constituent dislocation, to thought's own "giving itself over to the object" (Adorno, *Prisms*, 240; cf. Theodor Adorno, *Dialectic of Enlightenment*, 12).

By the same token, if both Adorno and Badiou can be read as resisting any "liquidation of the particular" (Theodor Adorno, *Minima Moralia: Reflections from a Damaged Life*, 17), it is certainly Adorno and not Badiou who affirms an explicitly relational or antiextensional understanding of particularity. Individual particularity "does not exist utterly by itself but is in itself 'other' and linked with otherness. What it is, is more than what it is" (Adorno, *Negative Dialectics*, 161). Badiou would have to condemn this approach for the same reason that he condemns the Hegelian logic that inspired it (EE, 180–81). In doing so, Badiou deprives himself of any *ontological* defense to the most predictable Adornian countercharge, of complicity in the abstractions imposed by the modern primacy of exchange value. Badiou's strictly subtractive conception of art, moreover, deliberately invites the accusation that he "capitulates before the problem of the relationship between art and the social"—and that his position may thus leave untouched that "most real of dependencies, the dependence on society" (*Aesthetic Theory*, 236; Adorno, *Negative Dialectics*, 164).

3. Adorno, *Minima Moralia*, 17.

4. Theodor Adorno, "A Portrait of Walter Benjamin," in *Prisms*, 230.

5. PM, 15–16 (cf. Plato, *Republic*, 398a, 607b). In *Le Siècle*, Badiou qualifies his critique with an appreciation of Brecht as the greatest and most "universal" of all communist artists (LS, 36). Badiou's own plays certainly owe rather more to the didactic simplification of Brecht than to, say, the complex reveries of Pessoa (cf. LS, 93).

6. Alain Badiou, "Considérations sur l'état actuel du cinéma, et sur les moyens de penser cet état sans avoir à conclure que le cinéma est mort ou mourant," 1.

7. Alain Badiou, "Esquisse pour un premier manifeste de l'affirmationisme," 13–19.

8. PM, 24. Any truth is infinite, but as the "subject-point" of a truth each "work of art is essentially finite," in the triple sense that it is exhibited as "a finite objectivity in space and / or time," that it is finished once and for all, and especially, that it proclaims itself as its own end: it is the "convincing procedure of its own finitude" (PM, 23).

9. Badiou draws here on Charles Rosen, *The Classical Style: Haydn, Mozart, Beethoven* (1976).

10. PM, 28–29. That a configuration becomes saturated means that it "no longer gives rise to clearly perceptible works, or to decisive investigations of itself." Any configuration, however, can unexpectedly be renewed and so remains "intrinsically infinite," unlike the necessarily finite works that "constitute its matter" (PM, 27).

11. This is not to say, of course, that the other arts—painting, sculpture, architecture, music, and so on—are devoid of truth; Badiou has simply yet to consider them in any detail.

12. Badiou, "Dix-neuf réponses," 266.

13. Alain Badiou, "Que pense le poème?" 214–15. As Badiou writes, "Beauty comes when the poetic nomination of events grasps thought at the edge of the void" (Alain Badiou, "Ce qui arrive," 2).

14. Badiou, "L'Age des poètes," 32. With Saint-John Perse, for instance, Badiou celebrates the poetry of *errance* as such, of movement for its own sake, "independent of any destination," and thus a poetry of pure *dé-liaison*, "of the end of relations *[liens]*, the absence to self of the unrelated" (LS, 75).

15. Badiou, "Que pense le poème?," 221.

16. PM, 52, 154. This is a universe that bears more than a passing resemblance to the sphere of ideal (or non-"existent") aesthetic purity and necessity champi-

oned in Sartre's earliest works (cf. Sartre, *La Nausée*, 40–42; Sartre, *L'Imaginaire*, 369–71).

17. Heidegger, "The Origin of the Work of Art," in BW, 165, 193 (my emphasis). According to Badiou, "Heidegger very legitimately restored the autonomous function of the poem. . . . He subtracted the poem from philosophical knowledge, so as to return it to truth" (Alain Badiou, "Le Statut philosophique du poème après Heidegger," 265). Heidegger rightfully debunked the neo-Aristotelian reduction of poetry to the mere object of the aesthetic "branch" of philosophy. But Heidegger further restored "the sacred authority of poetic proferation, and the idea that the authentic lies in the very flesh of language." The goal, then, is to "emerge from Heidegger, without going back to Aesthetics" (266–67).

18. See especially Alain Badiou, "La Méthode de Mallarmé," in C, 117–18; Badiou, "Que pense le poème?" 220; EE, 240; TS, 90. Badiou writes, "For some twenty years now, Mallarmé has been for me emblematic of the relation between philosophy and poetry" (CS [1992], 108 n.16).

19. TS, 92; cf. 128; C, 118–19, 154.

20. Marcel Proust, *Le Temps retrouvé*, 262.

21. Badiou, "Philosophie et poésie," 88, 96.

22. Badiou, "L'Age des poètes," 22–23; Badiou, "Le Statut philosophique du poème après Heidegger," 265.

23. B, 21, 37. Cf. Gilles Deleuze, *L'Epuisé* (1992).

24. B, 77–78. In a suggestive variant on this generic formula, Badiou reads the baroque proliferation of Severo Sarduy's prose as a writing founded only on "emptiness" and *"non-sens"* (Alain Badiou, "Vide, séries, clairière: Essai sur la prose de Severo Sarduy" [1998], 2). The Cuban novelist's "strategy is, starting out from this . . . primordial vacuity, to saturate it with disciplined semantic fields, with an entirely *phrased [phrasée]* cosmology," one populated with the most varied assortment of animals, plants, environments, places, and happenings. Then, in a second moment, Sarduy moves to "undo this saturation," to demonstrate its artifice—not so as to return to "the initial void," but so as to attain a state of tranquility, a "center of peace" that lends things and names their stable, measured coherence. After all manner of narrative commotion, Sarduy's fiction moves toward that calm in which "thought decides to enjoy what comes to pass" (2–3).

25. Alain Badiou, "Etre, existence, pensée" [1992], in PM, 139.

26. "Enough. Sudden enough. Sudden all far. No move and sudden all far. All least. Three pins. One pinhole. In dimmest dim. Vasts apart. At bounds of boundless void" (Samuel Beckett, *Worstward Ho!* 46–47; cf. PM, 183).

27. With this closing line Beckett echoes the beginning of the text: "On. Say on. Be said on. Somehow on. Till nohow on. Said nohow on" (Beckett, *Worstward Ho!* 7).

390 / Notes to Chapter 8

28. What follows is a reconstruction of Badiou's "Proust et la vérité," an unpublished lecture given at Maison Française, Oxford (14 Oct. 2000).

29. Marcel Proust, *Sodome et Gomorrhe I*, 252.

30. Proust, *Le Temps retrouvé*, 283.

31. Ibid., 289.

32. Marcel Proust, *Le Côté de Guermantes II*, 67.

33. Badiou's plays are *L'Echarpe rouge* (1978), "L'Incident d'Antioche" (unpublished), *Ahmed le subtil* (1994), *Ahmed se fâche* (1995), *Ahmed philosophe* (1995) and *Citrouilles* (1995).

34. As a purely physical, corporal activity, dance remains necessarily preconceptual. In displaying the body mastered to such a point that all physical routine is carried by the apparently effortless flight of pure improvisation or inspiration, the dancing body points to the possibility of a disciplined movement beyond the corporal; it points to "thought as event, but before it has its name . . . , in its own fading away" (PM, 92, 97). Drawing on Mallarmé and Nietzsche, Badiou draws up six principles of dance, which serve to distinguish it from theatrical thought. Dance requires a pure space (rather than a theatrical set), that is, a space situated on the edge of the void of space; it is anonymous (it deploys no characters); it asserts the "erased omnipresence of the sexes" (it demonstrates the two sexual positions even as it de-differentiates them); it effects a "subtraction from self" (the dancer does not so much dance, does not know or perform a dance, as is danced); it requires and reveals the necessary nudity of the dancing body (it is without costume); and it requires a rigorously impersonal spectator, that is, a spectator at a distance from emotional identification or desiring investment. Theater, by contrast names its place, identifies its characters, exaggerates sexual difference, exceeds rather than subtracts itself, denies radical nudity, and calls the spectator to participate (100, 107).

35. RT, 94. Badiou's position here is close to a method long championed by theatre director Peter Brook: "An actor takes a part [and asks himself] 'What can I do with this part?' . . . If the actor does that, he is working from himself as he knows himself, and he believes himself superior to the part. But if you take the opposite view then whatever the part is, when you start, that part is greater than you, otherwise it isn't worth playing. If you're playing a fool, he is more richly foolish than you; if you're playing a mean person, he is more intensely mean than you. . . . If you believe that, then you are experimenting all the time, going towards the character, realizing that you can't reach the character. And then the character comes towards you and says: 'There is something that you thought you could never understand but you're beginning to find it'" (Peter Brook, *Platform Papers*, 10; cf. Peter Brook, *Between Two Silences: Talking with Peter Brook*, 59–60).

36. RT, 112. According to Badiou, "Swann, Goriot, Saint-Preux or Don

Quixote" can exist only "in the text"—that is as "immortal" but not "eternal" (RT, 112).

37. Alain Badiou, "Le Plus-de-Voir," 5.

38. We might say that fully animated or computer-generated films, on the model of *Toy Story,* attest precisely to the fact that a *thoroughly* "purified" film can be achieved only in the realm of pure fantasy.

39. Badiou, "Considérations sur l'état actuel du cinéma," 2–3.

40. Ibid., 4.

41. Alain Badiou, "Art et philosophie," 163.

42. Badiou, "Que pense le poème?" 215.

43. Badiou, "Philosophie et poésie," 94.

9. Mathematics and Science

1. In every case, it is "at the point where something is not literalizable that there intervenes a new power of literalization" (TA, 4.6.98).

2. Badiou, "Nous pouvons redéployer la philosophie," 2.

3. Cf. Badiou, "Objectivité et objectalité" (1991), 11.

4. Thomas Kuhn, *The Structure of Scientific Revolutions,* 52.

5. Kuhn, *Structure,* 67–74.

6. See Kuhn, *Structure,* 170; cf. 176, 210.

7. Lakatos, *Philosophical Papers,* vol. 1, 91.

8. Imre Lakatos, *Proofs and Refutations,* 3, 142.

9. Lakatos, *Philosophical Papers,* vol. 1, 70–71, 111–12.

10. Ibid., vol. 2, 29–30.

11. Ibid., vol. 1, 6.

12. Ibid., vol. 1, 50–51.

13. See Ernst Mayr, *One Long Argument: Charles Darwin and the Genesis of Modern Evolutionary Thought,* 132–34.

14. Lakatos, "Falsification," in *Philosophical Papers,* vol. 1, 49 (Lakatos himself gives the example of Marxism after 1917). For one program to be replaced by another it need not be falsified in Popper's sense of the word but simply surpassed in terms of predictive or interpretative power. This rise and fall of rival programs is itself neither predictable or inevitable; "one can be 'wise' only after the event" (Lakotos, *Philosophical Papers,* vol. 1, 113; ibid., vol. 2, 60).

15. Paul Feyerabend, *Against Method,* 47.

16. Ibid., 171, 295–96.

17. Ibid., 189.

18. Badiou, "Being by Numbers" (1994), 123.

19. Lacan, *Ecrits,* 831.

20. Badiou, "Politics and Philosophy" (1997), 127.

21. The dual status of mathematics in Badiou's system—its implication in

both being and truth—is liable to cause some initial confusion. Inventive mathematical or ontological research is itself an ongoing field of truth (EE, 20–21), but the elementary ordinal structure of mathematics formalizes precisely that "normality" which any active truth procedure must interrupt.

22. Both quoted in "Logic, Philosophy, and the 'Linguistic Turn,'" 2.

23. Alfred Jules Ayer, *Language, Truth and Logic,* 73; see also Carl Hempel, "On the Nature of Mathematical Truth," in *World of Mathematics,* ed. James R. Newman, vol. 3, 1621–31.

24. See Robert Kaplan's thorough and accessible study *The Nothing That Is: A Natural History of Zero.*

25. Davis and Hersh, *Experience,* 180; cf. Dauben, "Conceptual Revolutions," 52–57; see also David Fowler, *The Mathematics of Plato's Academy: A New Reconstruction,* 356 ff.

26. Another example is provided by the controversy surrounding the foundations of mathematical analysis or calculus, that is, the precise ontological status of what Leibniz called "infinitesimal" numbers—a controversy first resolved in a firmly arithmetic fashion by Cauchy and Weierstrass in the first decades of the nineteenth century, and then redecided in the 1960s, in more Leibnizian fashion, by Abraham Robinson's invention of "nonstandard analysis."

27. As Badiou writes, "The axiom of choice formalizes, in ontology, the predicates of intervention" (EE, 251); cf. Lavine, *Understanding the Infinite,* 103–16.

28. Lakatos, *Philosophical Papers,* vol., 19–23; cf. 64–65; cf. also Philip Kitcher, *The Nature of Mathematical Knowledge* (1984).

29. For details, see the second and third sections of the appendix.

30. NN, 39; EE, 311–15. Many mathematicians or metamathematicians agree that CH (which concerns the status of real numbers) is the most highly charged point of quasi-"ontological" disagreement separating one orientation from another. See, for example, Abraham Robinson, "Concerning Progress in the Philosophy of Mathematics," in *Selected Papers,* vol. 2, 565; Weyl, *Philosophy of Mathematics,* 50; Dummett, *Truth and Other Enigmas,* 208; Benacerraf and Putnam, eds., *Philosophy of Mathematics,* vii.

31. NN, 43; cf. Tiles, *The Philosophy of Set Theory,* 183.

32. Badiou, "Platon et / ou Aristote-Leibniz," 80.

33. Ibid., 72 n. 14; Cohen's own view is that CH is "obviously false" (Cohen, *Set Theory,* 151).

34. It is for precisely this reason that one of the great authorities on Cantorian set theory concludes, contrary to the whole spirit of Badiou's ontology, that we simply should not "expect a theory of sets to answer the deepest analytic questions about the continuum" at all (Hallett, *Cantorian Set Theory,* 305). Precisely because "it is strong enough to render the classical theory of the continuum," that is, the set of real numbers or "points on a line," the consequences of the

power set axiom escape any axiomatic determination or "limitation." But rather than insist (with Badiou) on the undecidability of this size as the condition for its truthful decision, Hallett instead suggests that it points to an ontological limitation of set theory itself. Why, he asks, should we expect all of mathematics to be embraced by the concept of set at all? In particular, why should we assume that the continuum (i.e., the power set of $\aleph_0$) is embraced by it? In Hallett's effectively antiphilosophical view, our inability to reconcile the power set axiom with the other axioms, our inability to explain how the axioms hold together as a system, seems to suggest that we are bound to accept some version of Cantor's "Absolute" incomprehensibility at the higher end of the numerical scale (xiii).

35. Badiou, "Platon et / ou Aristote-Leibniz," 66.

36. Alain Badiou, "L'Etre du nombre" (1994), 12. By contrast, Lavine seeks to ground our understanding of the infinite in a smooth derivation from our more intuitive, more everyday understanding of the "indefinitely large," that is, in "intuitions that we have as a matter of actual psychological fact" (Lavine, *Understanding the Infinite,* 249, 9–10).

37. CT, 149–50; cf. NN, 175.

38. NN, 180–93. For useful overviews, see John Conway, "The Surreals and the Reals," and Philip Ehrlich, "General Introduction," both in *Real Numbers,* ed. Philip Ehrlich (1994).

39. This problem arises only because of the collapse of the "intuitive" notion of number as a "multiplicity composed of unities" (Euclid, *Elements,* vol. 2, 277). For Euclid, the question "What is a number?" could be comfortably referred back to the founding certainty of the One. This framework collapsed, as Badiou explains, under the combined impact of three facts: "the Arabic introduction of zero, the calculation of infinity, and the crisis of the metaphysical ideality of the One." Zero introduced the void into the heart of number, and infinity pushed mathematics beyond combinational logic toward topology, while the "death of God" enabled the conception of pure multiplicity as without One (CT, 141).

40. CT, 143–44; cf. Harry Gonshor, *Introduction to the Theory of Surreal Numbers,* 1–2.

41. CT, 145; cf. NN, 128.

42. Badiou, "L'Etre du nombre" (1994), 11.

43. Cf. NN, 77, 99, 127, 257–58.

44. Badiou, "Philosophie et poésie," 94.

10. Politics

1. LS, 83. As Badiou argues in dialogue with Brecht's didactic play *The Decision* (1930), "As soon as it's a matter of creative action, the real is only accessible through the subsumption of an 'I' by a 'we'" (LS, 99).

2. AM, 12; cf. Georges Canguilhem, *Vie et mort de Jean Cavaillès,* 39. Cavaillès's

insistence upon the historically situated yet irreducible *creativity* of mathematics as a formal discipline, a creativity independent of all cultural or physical mediation, suggests an especially fruitful point of comparison with Badiou's later philosophy (see in particular Jean Cavaillès, *Sur la logique et la théorie de la science*, 1947). The executions of Cavaillès and Lautman, founders of a "modern Platonism" and the inspiration for a contemporary conjunction of mathematics and philosophy, left the field of French philosophy open, Badiou suggests, to German Romanticism and the linguistic turn (AM, 13). Badiou's own project, in politics as much as in philosophy, takes up largely where they left off.

3. AM, 15. Those who chose not to resist, Badiou concludes, quite simply chose not to think: "They didn't think according to the real of the situation of the moment. . . . Not to resist is not to think" (AM, 17).

4. As Badiou writes, "It is very important to notice that here, 'equality' signifies nothing objective. It is not at all a matter of the equality of status, of earnings, or functions. . . . Political equality is not what we want or what we project [for the future]; it is what we declare in the heat of the moment, here and now, as what is, and not what should be" (AM, 111–12). Badiou cites Breton with approval: "Rebellion carries its justification in itself, altogether independently of the chances it has of changing, or not, the state of affairs that provokes it," since what matters is "living as intensely as possible" (André Breton, *Arcane 17,* in LS, 114).

5. SP, 63–64. In *Théorie du sujet*, Badiou picks out of French history "three figures of a possible universality": the Commune, the Resistance, and May 1968 (TS, 13).

6. *La Distance politique* 1 (Dec. 1991), 6. See note 17 for more on this publication.

7. Ibid., 7.

8. Cf. Jürgen Habermas, *Between Facts and Norms;* LS, 140 n. 37.

9. As Badiou writes, "The great novelty and the great power of the Organisation Politique is to maintain absolutely the separation" of science and politics, of analytic description and political prescription (*La Distance politique* 28 [May 1998], 2).

10. *La Distance politique* 28 (May 1998), 3.

11. Badiou writes, "The 'social sciences,' in my view, are not sciences at all, and have no place in the distribution of truth procedures." While left-leaning social scientists like Balibar and Bourdieu may certainly analyze important themes (the *sans-papiers,* feminism, the labor movement, poverty, and so on), they are "politically very weak, for the simple reason that they do not break with parliamentarism, with 'democratic' consensus." They can contribute only to an "oppositional" stance, that is, a position of protest from *within* the state-sanctioned structures and rules (parties, elections, trade unions, constitutional amendments, etc.).

But "unfortunately, the category of 'opposition' is precisely a central category of parliamentarism, of 'democracy.' No genuine break can be made from within this category. The social sciences thus remain dependent upon the state, and are consequently without truth" (Badiou, "Entretien avec Alain Badiou" [1999], 6).

12. Charles Hoareau, "Chômeurs rebelles: Chef-lieu Marseilles," *Le Nouvel Observateur* 8 (Jan. 1998), 26–27.

13. As regards the analysis and identification of political sequences, Badiou freely admits, "My thinking on this point is sustained, purely and simply, by that of Lazarus" (AM, 62–63). Badiou's glowing review of his friend's *L'Anthropologie du nom* (1996) makes up one of the most important chapters of his *Abrégé de métapolitique*. In equal measures post-"historicist, classist, dialectical, or positivist," in his book Sylvain Lazarus "eliminates the category of the object" altogether, so as to privilege the purely subjective naming of a political sequence as that which can never be defined, only thought (AM, 36; cf. Lazarus, *L'Anthropologie*, 52). Badiou's sole reservations concern the limited status left to philosophy per se in Lazarus's configuration.

14. *La Distance politique* 2 (Feb. 1992), 9.

15. Alain Badiou, letters to the author, 17 June 1996 and 13 Oct. 1997; cf. Badiou, "Politics and Philosophy," 114–15; TA, 26.11.97. Badiou explains that China's Cultural Revolution (May 1966 through September 1967) was the last of the great revolutions because it marked the culmination, and the "saturation," of the long effort to pursue a genuinely inventive political sequence *within* the space of the party-state (Alain Badiou, *La Révolution culturelle*, 4, 9).

16. For more information go to http://www.mstbrazil.org.

17. Along with Badiou, the major figures of the OP are his long-standing friends and fellow *soixante-huitards* Sylvain Lazarus and Natacha Michel. The operation of the OP in its current form and under its current name dates from 1984 (cf. "Histoire de L'Organisation politique," *La Distance politique* 30–31 [March 1999], 17–19). Between 1983 and 1992, the OP published their first *journal d'opinion*, called *Le Perroquet*. Since 1991, they have made their positions known through *La Distance politique*. *La Distance politique* is a relatively short bulletin (usually between six and fifteen pages in length), published on average four times a year, with articles and editorials detailing particular demonstrations and rallies, interviews with workers or immigrant groups, discussions of electoral campaigns and results, and general analyses of "what is to be done." The first three issues included brief reviews of major works by Marx, Lenin, and Mao, in that order; issue 5 carried an article on Althusser. Since then the emphasis has been almost exclusively practical, and *La Distance politique* has remained much more of an organizing tool than a contribution to "political theory." In addition to the issues and *cahiers* published by *La Distance politique*, the OP has published

three books written by the *Noyaux* of workers they help organize in various factories: one on the relation between workers and their supervisors, another on the Bourogne strike of 1994, and another on the history of Billancourt from 1968 to 1992. Finally, starting in July 1995, following the racist murder of Brahim Bouarram in May by members of the National Front, the OP began to help organize "Associations pour la paix civile et l'amitié entre les familles" (cf. *La Distance politique* 14 [July 1995], 7–16); as of September 1997, such associations were up and running in Montreuil, Lille, Reims, and Toulouse. It should be stressed that the articles in *La Distance politique*, although sometimes written in the first person, are always anonymous and should be treated as such. Although it would be fairly easy to pick out at least some of the pieces by Badiou himself, there is little to be gained in doing so. The OP operates through strict collective responsibility, and as a rule the positions expressed by *La Distance politique* can be taken as fully consistent with Badiou's own. Badiou is categorical on this point: he insists that the OP is, with all the rigorous implications of the term, a "subjective condition of my philosophy" (AM, 117).

18. Badiou, "Réponses écrites" (1992), 70.

19. Any political mode, Badiou concedes, has its objective "places" as well as its purely subjective categories (for example, in the Revolutionary mode, the places indicated by the Convention, the *sans-culottes* clubs, the revolutionary army, and so on). But the point is not to relate, in a dialectic of "heterogeneous multiplicities," the institutional materiality of a place to the subjective reality of their actors. By "thinking together the mental (the ideas and convictions of the revolutionaries) and the material (the Convention, the *sans-culottes* clubs, etc. . . .), you sacrifice the name of the mode (which disappears, as a singularity, within the dialectical totality), and in the end you make politics as thought disappear as well: the thought becomes unthinkable. If on the contrary you consider the Convention, etc., as places of the name, as processes that are themselves prescriptive, and which are made of the same stuff as subjective politics, then you keep the name and, preserving the investigation within a homogeneous multiplicity, you can, from the inside, think the thought *[en intériorité penser la pensée]*" (AM, 42–43).

20. *La Distance politique* 2 (Feb. 1992), 4.

21. *La Distance politique* 19–20 (Apr. 1996), 9; *La Distance politique* 17–18 (Oct. 1996), 13.

22. *La Distance politique* 21 (May 1997), 4.

23. *La Distance politique* 7 (July 1993), 8; see, in particular, *La Distance politique* 13.

24. *La Distance politique* 17–18 (Oct. 1996), 3, 4.

25. *La Distance politique* 2 (Feb. 1992), 9; cf. *La Distance politique* 15 (Dec. 1996), 4.

26. Badiou, "Le Pays comme principe" (1992), 135.

27. Alain Badiou, letter to the author, 11 June 1996.

28. See, for example, Terry Eagleton, "Nationalism: Irony and Commitment," 23–26; Toril Moi, *Sexual/Textual Politics*, 13.

29. Badiou, "Politics and Philosophy," 118–19; cf. Badiou, "Le Pays comme principe" (1992), 135. As Badiou writes, "The existence of victims cannot by itself found a political process—this is a principle I firmly maintain" (Badiou, letter to the author, 9 Dec. 1998).

30. *La Distance politique* 6 (May 1993), 8.

31. *La Distance politique* 4 (Oct. 1992), 6; Badiou, "Le Pays comme principe" (1992), 135.

32. *La Distance politique* 4 (Oct. 1992), 7.

33. *La Distance politique* 26–27 (Feb. 1998), 8.

34. Ibid., 15.

35. Ibid., 8–9.

36. *La Distance politique* 1 (Dec. 1991), 3. The OP adds a certain moralizing flavor to its campaign: "The question of knowing whether there are factories in our cities (factories, and not supermarkets) is decisive. Because if it isn't the figure of work that socializes people, that guides their exchange, that leads them out of their homes, then it will be another figure: that of drug trafficking, theft, gangs, and mafias" (*La Distance politique* 22 [June 1997], 2).

37. *La Distance politique* 1 (Dec. 1991), 3.

38. Ibid., 3.

39. The obscene "debate" on asylum seekers that so clearly characterizes the prevailing re-presentation of the British situation would provide Badiou with perhaps the most telling contemporary illustration of his point. The very name (the characterization as passive "applicants" and the consequent distinctions between "justified" and "unjustified" applicants, between political "victims" and economic "swindlers," between desirable migrants and undesirable parasites) is testimony to the fact that the belligerent preservation of First World privilege has become, in denial of precisely that economic aggression which creates it, the perfectly explicit rather than merely effective goal of state policy.

40. *La Distance politique* 3 (May 1992), 12.

41. *La Distance politique* 26–27 (Feb. 1998), 18.

42. *La Distance politique* 19–20 (Apr. 1996), 2.

43. *La Distance politique* 7 (July 1993), 6.

44. *La Distance politique* 22 (June 1997), 3. *Mittérandisme* connotes "the denial of all free and critical thought." Mittérand's political career demonstrated, as its sole working principle, maximum approximation with the prevailing opinion of the day, successively Pétainiste, *résistant*, colonialist, conciliator, socialist, free

marketeer—each time because *"c'est comme ça"* (*La Distance politique* 9 [Oct. 1994], 3–4; *La Distance politique* 14 (July 1995), 1–3).

45. *La Distance politique* 1 (Dec. 1991), 3.

46. *La Distance politique* 10 (Nov. 1994), 2.

47. *La Distance politique* 7 (July 1993), 5–6.

48. *La Distance politique* 19–20 (Apr. 1996), 1–4. Outrage against the Debré laws—sparked by an appeal made by filmmakers and intellectuals and culminating in major demonstrations in February 1997—was an important factor in the defeat of the Juppé government and Chirac's surprise parliamentary dissolution of May 1997.

49. The Weil-Chevènement project differs from Pasqua-Debré only in that it divides the category of "foreigner" in two: on the one hand, admissible professionals and students, on the other, inadmissible poor and working people (*La Distance politique* 25 [Nov. 1997], 6).

50. *La Distance politique* 25 (Nov. 1997), 3, 7.

51. *La Distance politique* 23–24 (Sept. 1997), 6. The very concept of integration, of course, works against all distance prescription (7). In this sense, the OP's position is quite distinct from that taken by the once-significant lobby SOS-Racisme and like-minded *beur* movements. *La Distance politique* presents these groups as part and parcel of Mittérandisme and its antiworker campaign, as part of a new generation's "denial of working fathers" (*La Distance politique* 14 [July 1995], 2–3). SOS-Racisme and other antiracist groups, says the OP, preoccupy themselves with youth and the youth culture, celebrating an "ethnicity of the young" in the belief that "integration" is to be achieved through "rap and fashion," in the absence of any political principle (*La Distance politique* 17–18 [Oct. 1996], 12; cf. *La Distance politique* 19–20 [Apr. 1997], 8–9).

52. *La Distance politique* 19–20 (Apr. 1997), 7.

53. *La Distance politique* 8 (July 1994), 7–10.

54. *La Distance politique* 7 (July 1993), 10.

55. Badiou, "Réponses écrites" (1992), 70; cf. *La Distance politique* 1 (Dec. 1991), 13–16.

56. *La Distance politique* 23–24 (Sept. 1997), 14; cf. *La Distance politique* 3 (May 1992), 10.

57. *La Distance politique* 14 (July 1995), 13–14.

58. *La Distance politique* 17–18 (Oct. 1996), 16–17; *La Distance politique* 23–24 (Sept. 1997), 10–13. The OP helped organize major demonstrations in June and September of 1996, and more than a thousand people turned out for meetings held in and around Paris on 15 November and 6 December 1997 and on 7 February 1998. Mass delegations were sent to the police stations of Bobigny and Nanterre in March 1998 and that of Créteil in April 1998.

59. *La Distance politique* 26–27 (Feb. 1998), 13. Under the new slogan *"tous ensemble,"* this was a "strikers' strike" that nevertheless exceeded mere trade union maneuverings: "The December strikes put forward demands, but nevertheless, the demands were subordinated to the subjectivity of the strikers, and not the reverse" (4).

60. *La Distance politique* 26–27 (Feb. 1998), 19.

61. *La Distance politique* 2 (Feb. 1992), 2.

62. *La Distance politique* 17–18 (Oct. 1996), 5.

63. Here Badiou is quoting Karl Marx and Friedrich Engels, *The Communist Manifesto,* 82.

64. Badiou, "Politics and Philosophy," 120–21.

65. Ibid., 117. Badiou writes, "All the efforts to construct an alternative economy strike me as pure and simple abstractions, if not driven by the unconscious vector of capital's own reorganisation. We can see for example, and will see more and more, how so many environmentalist demands simply provide capital with new fields of investment, new inflections and new deployments. Why? Because every proposition that directly concerns the economy can be assimilated by capital. This is so by definition, since capital is indifferent to the qualitative configuration of things" (117).

66. Badiou, "Entretien avec Alain Badiou" (1999), 2; cf. Alain Badiou, "Highly Speculative Reasoning on the Concept of Democracy," 28–43; Alain Badiou, "Le Balcon du présent," 8–11.

67. *La Distance politique* 19–20 (Apr. 1996), 2.

68. *La Distance politique* 6 (May 1993), 1. By 1996, the OP was ready to admit that their previous "indifference to the state remained classist" (*La Distance politique* 19–20 (Apr. 1996), 14).

69. *La Distance politique* 11 (Jan. 1995), 3–4.

70. *La Distance politique* 15 (Dec. 1996), 11.

71. Badiou, letter to the author, 9 Dec. 1998. Comparable examples in the capitalist bloc would include those episodes famously analyzed by Frances Fox Piven and Richard A. Cloward in *Poor People's Movements* (1977).

72. "Proposition de réforme de la Constitution," *La Distance politique* 12 (Feb. 1995), 5–6.

73. *La Distance politique* 12 (Feb. 1995), 1: "A vote is an anti-declaration organized by the State" (*La Distance politique* 8 (July 1994), 3).

74. *La Distance politique* 10 (Nov. 1994), 1. As Bensaïd asks, "Isn't a politics without party simply a politics without politics?" (Daniel Bensaïd, "Alain Badiou et le miracle de l'événement," 157–58).

75. Aijaz Ahmad, *In Theory: Classes, Nations, Literatures,* 5, 70–71.

76. Ahmad, *In Theory,* 103; cf. Fredric Jameson, *Postmodernism, or the Cultural*

Logic of Late Capitalism, 380; Neil Lazarus, *Nationalism and Cultural Practice in the Postcolonial World*, 16–19.

77. Badiou, "Being by Numbers," 118.

78. *La Distance politique* 2 (Feb. 1992), 9; cf. EE, 443.

79. *La Distance politique* 19–20 (Apr. 1996), 2.

80. *La Distance politique* 4 (Oct. 1992), 5; cf. PP, 52; EE, 368.

81. Alain Badiou, conversation with the author, 12 March 1998.

82. Badiou, "Politics and Philosophy," 121.

83. Ibid., 117.

84. DO, 12–14; cf. DI, 55–56, 61, 67.

85. Badiou, "Philosophie et poésie," 88.

11. What Is Philosophy?

1. Alain Badiou, "Les Lieux de la philosophie," 2–3. This important text, read to the philosophy department of the Ecole Normale Supérieure in the autumn of 1998, is the closest thing to an inaugural lecture that Badiou has yet written.

2. Badiou, "Les Lieux de la philosophie," 4–6.

3. As for the "choice" of place, Badiou goes on, this is grounded ultimately in a pure "decision" or "conceptless axiom" that the criteria of no particular place can justify (Badiou, "Lieux de la philosophie," 8).

4. Badiou, "Qu'est-ce que Louis Althusser entend par 'philosophie'?" 37–38.

5. Badiou, "Nous pouvons redéployer la philosophie," 2.

6. Ibid.; cf. AM, 63.

7. Badiou, "Platon et / ou Aristote-Leibniz," 61.

8. PM, 21. Badiou's definition leaves the status of his own philosophy somewhat uncertain, since is it both conditioned by various particular procedures (named Cohen, Mallarmé, Lenin) and equipped to provide the general theory for *any* such conditioning. When pressed, Badiou provides a second definition: "Philosophy is the general theory of being and the event, as linked by truth" (PM, 45–46). It is not clear how *this* philosophy is itself conditioned, if not indeed by the event of his own work.

9. Badiou, "L'Entretien de Bruxelles," 11, 10; cf. C, 74; EE, 10. It is thus also up to philosophy to help clarify the complex interconnections that may link the various procedures. This is a problem that Badiou has only begun to address, beginning with the most canonical examples: the interconnection of politics and science in Engels's historical materialism and Marxist scientism, or again in today's managerial approach to politics (i.e., economics); the interconnection of art and love, as exemplified by the proximity of the novel and romance, or conversely, an understanding of love as a kind of "aestheticization of existence" (TA, 4.6.98).

10. LS, 32; 116. Badiou's approach might be usefully supplemented by Denis

Hollier's reading of Bataille, Malraux, and their contemporaries in *Absent without Leave: French Literature under the Threat of War* (1997).

11. LS, 128. Obvious differences aside, Badiou sees a similar "passion for the real" at work in the formalist projects of what is generally labeled "high structuralism"—the projects of Jakobson, Benveniste, Mauss, Dumézil, Koyré, Marc Bloch, and Moses Finley (LS, 141 n. 42).

12. LS, 130. The more purely axiomatic the project, the more purely univocal its dimension: Badiou's model example here is the attempt, from Hilbert to Grothendieck and *Bourbaki,* to pursue the complete and thoroughgoing formalization of mathematics, culminating in a general theory of the Universes of pure thought. Such a theory would have made all previous theories redundant, and allowed for the equation of mathematics with the pure "act" of its coded inscription, that is, with pure formalization as such (LS, 130).

13. Badiou, "Logique et philosophie" (1994), 1.

14. Badiou, "Nous pouvons redéployer la philosophie," 2; cf. AM, 116.

15. Rudolph Carnap, *The Logical Syntax of Language,* xiii.

16. Badiou, "Nous pouvons redéployer la philosophie," 2.

17. Badiou, "Un, Multiple, Multiplicité(s)," 15.

18. A fairly systematic study of these and other related projects is the stuff of my own current work in progress.

19. Alain Badiou and Etienne Balibar, "Forum sur l'universel," organized by the Collège International de Philosophie in Paris, 4 Nov. 1998.

20. Badiou, letter to the author, 9 Dec. 1998.

21. Badiou, "Huit thèses sur l'universel" (1998), tapescript.

Part IV. Complications

12. Ethics, Evil, and the Unnameable

1. E, 25; PP, 16; Badiou, "Dix-neuf réponses," 263; SP, 117.

2. Žižek, *Plague,* 214.

3. See in particular Lacan S7, 20–21/11, 85/70, 218/185; Jacques Lacan, "Kant avec Sade," in *Ecrits,* 767.

4. Levinas's work, as Badiou reads it, is essentially nothing other than the wholesale destitution of "philosophy to the profit of ethics" in this pejorative sense (E, 19). The essential principle behind Levinas's conception of an unconditional responsibility for the other is that "there is no Other except to the degree that he is the immediate phenomenon of the Wholly Other," that is, the Other as God or pure infinite transcendence. Philosophy, in short, is here silenced by theology (E, 23). In my introduction to the English translation of Badiou's *Ethics,* I distinguish in more detail Badiou's difference-indifferent approach to ethics from the Other-oriented approach of Levinas and Derrida. The differend

is perhaps especially striking with Derrida—the Derrida who conceives of ethics in terms of a divine or inaccessible secrecy, who invests every power of decision in the other qua other, who insists upon the fundamental finitude of human reality, who equates the experience of thought with the experience of language, and whose practice of deconstruction is ultimately nothing other than a version of constructivism turned around against itself.

5. AM, 28; Badiou, "L'Impératif de la négation," 12. As Žižek puts it, "The fundamental lesson of postmodernist politics is that *there is no Event*, that 'nothing really happens'. . . . Is not the ultimate deconstructionist lesson that every enthusiastic encounter with the Real Thing . . . is a delusive semblance?" (Žižek, *The Ticklish Subject*, 135, 133).

6. Badiou, "L'Impératif de la négation," 7.

7. Ibid., 14.

8. Wright, *Wittgenstein on the Foundations of Mathematics*, 371.

9. Cf. Wittgenstein, *Philosophical Investigations* I, sect. 124, p. 49.

10. Paul Ricoeur, quoted in Alain Badiou, "Ethique et psychiatrie" (1995), 3.

11. Badiou, "Ethique et psychiatrie" (1995), 6.

12. Badiou, "L'Impératif de la négation," 6; cf. Alenka Zupančič, *Ethics of the Real*, 95–96.

13. Badiou, "On Evil," 69.

14. SP, 81. Sam Gillespie points out that Badiou's critique of human rights fails to address the reconceptualization of the political proposed by Claude Lefort and Etienne Balibar, among others, in terms that "resonate with Badiou's own work: the predicatelessness of the subject, the preference for universalism over globalism, a critique of the 'bad universalism' of identity politics, the heteronomy of the political, etc." (Sam Gillespie, letter to the author, 5 Feb. 1999).

15. E, 44; Badiou, "Entretien avec Alain Badiou" (1999), 3.

16. Žižek makes much the same point: "One is faithful to one's desire by maintaining the gap which sustains desire" (Žižek, *Plague*, 239), meaning the gap on account of which the desired Thing remains forever out of reach. "If the subject is to survive his act," Žižek maintains, "he is compelled to organize its ultimate failure . . . , to avoid totally identifying with it" (Žižek, *Tarrying*, 32; cf. Žižek, *Metastases*, 33, 50).

17. PM, 41; cf. Lacan, S17, 39.

18. C, 209. Badiou writes, "The unnameable is unnameable *for* the subject-language. Let's say that this term is not susceptible of being made eternal, or is not accessible to the Immortal. In this sense, it is the symbol of the pure real of the situation, of its life without truth" (E, 76). Despite obvious differences, Badiou's unnameable invites some comparison with Derrida's recent insistence on political principles ("a messianism without religion, an idea of justice, an idea

of democracy") that must remain forever in the "spectral" form of a promise, "never 'ontologized' into a positive agency" or substance (Jacques Derrida, *Spectres de Marx*, 102).

19. C, 208; cf. E, 77; MP, 90.

20. Weyl, *Philosophy of Mathematics*, 27.

21. Thus is accomplished "Lucretius's acosmism" (CT, 36).

22. Žižek, *The Ticklish Subject*, 167; cf. Žižek, *Sublime Object*, 4–5 and passim.

23. Lacan, S2, 270–71 / 232–33, in Žižek, *The Ticklish Subject*, 155, 160. Like Badiou after him, Lacan insists that "behind what is named, there is the unnameable"; but for the analyst as opposed to the philosopher, the "quintessential unnameable [is] death" (S2, 247 / 211). From a Lacanian perspective, "the function of desire must remain in a fundamental relationship to death" (S7, 351 / 303), that is, it must remain within a properly tragic dimension (S7, 361 / 313). A (Lacanian) emphasis on the structural "regularity" of the subject, in other words, orients it toward the mere cessation of that structure—whereas Badiou's "exceptionality" makes a break with mortality altogether.

24. Žižek, *The Ticklish Subject*, 161.

25. Ibid., 155.

26. Badiou, letter to the author, 17 June 1996.

27. C, 72. Agamben pursues a comparably generic approach to political nomination in *The Coming Community* (1993).

28. PM, 210, 215. It is important to stress that genuine evil, far from violating the principles of an essential "community" or "being together," stems rather from a being together made absolute. After all, "nobody more than Hitler desired the being together of the Germans" (E, 58). As a rule, "every real figure of Evil presents itself not as a fanatical nonopinion attacking being-with, but as a politics striving on the contrary to establish an authentic being-with—against which there exists no 'common sense,' but only another politics" (AM, 30).

29. C, 75. Badiou is referring to Plato, *The Laws*, book 10.

30. E, 54–55; 60. Badiou's ethics is his response to Lacan's question "How can we be sure that we are not impostors?" (S11, 293 / 263).

31. Martin Heidegger, "On the Essence of Truth," in BW, 128.

32. E, 65; cf. Žižek, *Tarrying*, 222.

33. Badiou, "Les Lieux de la vérité," 117; E, 58–59, 65. The same argument must apply to that pseudoevent whose injustice is sometimes justified as a response to the radical evil of Auschwitz: the creation of a Zionist state in the Middle East. Ben Gurion's unilateral declaration of the state of Israel in 1948 can be understood only as the simulacrum of an event, for rather than affirming what was least represented or most "generic" in the situation, this declaration instead divided it in favor of one particular group. The declaration did not subtract itself

404 / Notes to Chapter 12

from the power of the state, but simply established a new state with new powers of aggression. A true declaration, in the same situation, would have been more in line with the original demand of the Palestine Liberation Organization for a single, ecumenical state for *all* the inhabitants of Palestine, regardless of ethnicity or faith.

34. Badiou, "L'Impératif de la négation," 13. The case of Yugoslavia after the end of Tito's political sequence provides Badiou's most telling example. See Badiou, "Le pays comme principe" (1992), 134–35; Alain Badiou, "La Sainte-Alliance et ses serviteurs" (on Kosovo). Gourevitch's compelling account of the Rwandan genocide likewise explains it, not as the incomprehensible symptom of ancient and intractable ethnic conflict, but as deliberate state policy, a program ruthlessly planned and implemented by Hutu Power precisely as a form of "bringing people together," "an exercise in community building." Whereas the Rwandese Patriotic Front has sought to subtract a political field from the question of ethnicity and thereby recognize the genocide as what Kagame rightly calls "the defining *event* in Rwandan history," Hutu Power has always sought to "make its crime a success by making it indistinguishable from the continuum of Rwandan history" (Philip Gourevitch, *We Wish to Inform You That Tomorrow We Will Be Killed with Our Families,* 95–96, 221, my emphasis). Again, only the adoption of similar principles offers any chance of justice in Palestine. So long as we understand the situation in terms of ethnic hatreds or "clashes of civilizations," rather than in terms of those fundamental *breaks* dated 1948 and 1967, we do nothing but adhere to an essentially Israeli perspective.

35. Badiou, "Le pays comme principe" (1992), 134.

36. E, 63; C, 194. The assumption that all elements of the situation depend on the event defines a "dogmatic" operation of connection (EE, 263).

37. Lacan, S7, 362–68 / 314–19.

38. See Žižek, *Tarrying,* 97; Žižek, *Metastases,* 201.

39. Samuel Beckett, *L'Innommable,* 213. With Beckett, Badiou points out, "nothing begins that is not in the prescription of the again or of the rebeginning" (PM, 140).

40. E, 47, 78. Badiou's subjectivation, Lacanian "desire and Kantian ethical rigour [all] coincide in their disregard for the 'demands of reality': [none] of them acknowledge the excuse of circumstances or unfavourable consequences . . ." (Žižek, *Metastases,* 68).

41. E, 18. Badiou writes, "If you think that the world can and should change absolutely, that there is no more an order of things to be respected than there are preformed subjects to maintain, then you will acknowledge that the individual may be sacrificed" (LS, 81).

42. Kant, *Groundwork,* 443, 438. For a brilliant Badiou-influenced reading of

Kant, see Zupančič, *Ethics of the Real*. Zupančič offers an unusually sophisticated analysis of precisely how a true ethics turns on "the gesture by which every subject, by means of his action, posits the universal, performs a certain operation of universalization," such that "the subject is nothing other than this moment of universalization" (Zupančič, *Ethics of the Real*, 61; cf. 34–36, 163–64).

43. Žižek, *Plague*, 221; cf. Lacan, S7, 364 / 315.

44. Kant, *Groundwork*, 391, 394.

45. Kant, *Practical Reason*, 91–92.

46. Kant, *Critique of Pure Reason*, Bxxx, A641–42 / B669–70, A828 / B856.

47. Kant, *Groundwork*, 390.

48. Badiou, "Politics and Philosophy," 122 (my emphasis). As Badiou writes, "A singular truth is always the result of a complex process, in which discussion is decisive. Science itself began—with mathematics—by renouncing all principles of authority. Scientific statements are precisely those exposed, naked, to public criticism, independently of the subject of their enunciation." Against Arendt, Badiou insists that discussion can be privileged *over* truth only if a "right to discussion" is a right reserved for "falsehood and lies" (AM, 24).

49. For Badiou a Truth is worth the risk of Terror. "Disaster is less worthless than mere non-being *(mieux vaux un désastre qu'un désêtre)*. The philosopher—and with him, over the span of time, *humanity as a whole*—will always prefer, to a 'politics' withdrawn from all thought, to a politics that convokes to its sprawling management only the petty exacerbation of interests, a politics sutured to philosophy, however terrorist, sacralized, and ecstatic it becomes, because it is at least under the sign of the Idea" (C, 230).

50. Again, Badiou concludes that "there is only one maxim in the ethics of a truth: do not subtract the last subtraction" (C, 195). Clearly, however, this maxim cannot itself be derived from the practice of subtraction as such. What is its source, if not the altogether classical philosophy of the subject as subject of moderation? Of mastery and self-control? Or even, of *"calcul"*?

51. Badiou, "Qu'est-ce que Louis Althusser entend par 'philosophie'?," 37, 38.

13. Generic or Specific?

1. Stéphane Mallarmé, "Un Coup de dés," in *Oeuvres complètes;* Labîd ben Rabi'a, "Le Désert et son code," in *Du Désert d'Arabie aux jardins d'Espagne: Chefs-d'oeuvre de la poésie arabe classique*, ed. André Miquel, 21 ff.

2. As Badiou has warned on several occasions, it is essential not to confuse the apparent or "logical" void of truth—a void that appears as empty from within a particular situation—with the ontological void, the void of being as being. A truth exposes the link between the elements of a situation and their pure generic being, but it does not articulate this being as such (which remains

the exclusive prerogative of mathematics). As postevental, "the process of a truth entirely escapes ontology" (EE, 391), and thereby puts an end to Heidegger's dream of an original union of being and truth as much as to Hegel's anticipation of their eventual reconciliation. If Cohen's work shows that ontology can indeed conceptualize the being of a truth process, that ontology is "compatible" with truth, that it is possible to establish the existence of a generic or "indiscernible" set—nevertheless a truth and the being of that truth are radically distinct (EE, 391). What a truth does and what a truth is are not to be confused, and, as a doing, truth builds *from* the void, not in the void. "It is this radical distinction of being and truth," Badiou notes, "that my critics seem to have the most trouble grasping, especially when taken to the point where it assumes a complex conception of the being of truths" (Badiou, "Dix-neuf réponses" 253; cf. EE, 451–70).

3. What orients a political movement toward truth, for example, are not the relations of solidarity or organization that hold its elements together as part of a movement per se, but rather its power to dissolve *all* interelemental relations: "If it is obvious that relations are constitutive of a mass movement . . . , politics only makes sure of the enduring meaning of an event by breaking the presumed relation in which the mass movement is effected. Even at the heart of a mass movement, political activity is an unrelating *[déliaison]*," that is, something that considers the "masses" as an "infinity of singularities." Whereas the state deals always with elements "tied" together as parts or groups, true politics deals with the masses, because the mass as such is inaccessible to the discriminating operations of the state: "The 'masses' is thus a signifier of extreme particularity, of the *non-lien,* and this is what makes it a political signifier" (AM, 83).

4. There is more than a passing resemblance between Badiou's subtractive tenacity and Sartre's essentially tragic confrontation, in the *Critique de la raison dialectique,* of true subjective praxis with the deadening accumulation of the practico-inert. The obvious alternative would be to pursue a line closer to Merleau-Ponty's articulation of subject and object together as part of a single dialectic of being in the world, or *"intermonde."* It remains to be seen if such a line can be as politically incisive as its neo-Sartrean rival.

5. I have begun to outline what is at stake with this distinction in "The Singular and the Specific: Recent French Philosophy" (2000).

6. EE, 55. Badiou writes, "The consistency of a multiple [i.e., a set] does not depend on the particular multiples" that it groups (78). And elsewhere, "An element is not algebraically distinguished by its location in the set. It is enough that it belongs to it" (TS, 226).

7. Badiou, "Objectivité et objectalité" (1991), 9; D, 81, 88. Badiou writes, "I acknowledge only one type of reality: indifferent multiplicity, or *multiple de*

multiple. For everything else, the void is all I need" (Badiou, letter to the author, 9 Dec. 1998).

8. For example, any new artistic event "generally renders an earlier artistic configuration obsolete" (PM, 25); there seems to be room, in any situation, for only one truth at a time.

9. EE, 14; cf. Badiou, "Being by Numbers," 85. But elsewhere, emphasizing his strict materialism, Badiou goes on to note that only idealists "distinguish between thought and matter . . . , between pure thought and empirical thought," and insists that "none of these distinctions function in the system I propose" (123).

10. Badiou, "Being by Numbers," 85.

11. Badiou, letter to the author, 17 June 1996.

12. Davis and Hersh, *Descartes' Dream,* 13–14; 279–82.

13. Martin Heidegger, "The End of Philosophy and the Task of Thinking," in BW, 448.

14. Badiou defines knowledge as a "classifier of subsets" (C, 201; cf. EE, 362–66; Badiou, "Being by Numbers," 87).

15. Rotman and Kneebone, *Sets and Transfinite Numbers,* 57; cf. Alexander Abian, "Sets and the Elementhood Predicate," in *The Theory of Sets,* 3.

16. Maddy, "Believing the Axioms," 484. The concept of a generic set in particular rests on "a purely extensional interpretation of the notion of 'set' (a set is just a collection of elements into a whole, without there being any implication about the existence, or the possibility, of a principle of selection)" (Tiles, *The Philosophy of Set Theory,* 191).

17. For the sake of those readers familiar with the ordinal-based orientation of Cantor's theory (cf. the third section of my appendix), we can be a little more precise about this. Cantor based his notion of transfinite sets on the idea that they could, in principle, be counted out from zero, or "ordered" in a clear numerical succession. (By "counting" Cantor meant something like "putting many into one," or the "aggregation of manifolds into unities"). Of course, we ourselves can actually count only finite numbers, which means that Cantor's theory must presume some sort of infinite counting agent. A quasi-divine counting mechanism could certainly "see each of the members of a set individually, all in one glance of the infinite mind," but in the absence both of such a mechanism and of any intensional principle of set, the "unity" of a set is difficult to grasp (35–37). Moreover, once we apply the power set axiom—in order to measure the size of c, or the set of real numbers—even a divine notion of counting or "aggregation" cannot serve to describe the basic collecting principle involved. At this point, Hallett continues, "we must give up the idea that our use of sets is anything like a Kantian 'synthesis of manifolds into unities'" (303). The question is then: Can *any* notion of structuring survive this giving up? Does not thorough

axiomatization make the structuring principle implied in the concept of set, as Hallett suggests, effectively "inexplicable"? (303).

18. Badiou, "Six Propriétés," 41; cf. C, 199.

19. This principle is precisely the foundation of a set-theoretic realism (cf. Hallett, *Cantorian Set Theory,* 237).

20. Lazarus, *L'Anthropologie du nom,* 193, quoted in AM, 52.

21. AM, 53. Althusser's mistake, for instance, was to relate political thought to the objectivity of socioscientific laws, expressed as a "complex whole structured in dominance." Likewise, Lazarus suggests, Foucault's emphasis on the objectivity of epistemic structures supposedly prevented him from formulating a true "prescriptive, or subjective, core" (Lazarus, *L'Anthropologie du nom,* 105–6, quoted in AM, 54–55).

22. *La Distance politique* 14 (July 1995), 9.

23. Ibid.

24. *La Distance politique* 23–24 (Sept. 1997), 7.

25. SP, 12. Some readers may well recognize this very distinction of spheres, this very subtraction of politics from culture, as characteristic of a particular culture. Others might well see in Badiou's own essentially modernist emphasis on the new and the exceptional further proof of his allegiance to this same culture. In any case, it would be easy to demonstrate that not all transformative ways of thinking are equally amenable to the concept of an eventAl origin for truth. Buddhism, for instance, certainly proclaims a radically generic truth, the absolute subtraction of *sunyata,* and proclaims it precisely through its indifference to all established distinctions—but this truth is neither eventAl (the example of Buddha being precisely that, an *example,* a demonstration of "how it is done") nor immanent to any distinct situation (other than that of the universe itself). And Islam? Though Muhammad's revelation certainly broke with the prevailing state of the situation, it was anything but an ephemeral anomaly whose very lack of definition would allow for the elaboration of an open-ended fidelity. On the contrary, his words settled (in principle) every philosophical issue in advance. Islamic philosophy is generally not oriented toward the future composition of a still unknown truth, so much as "back-up" to an originally definitive (and subsequently obscured) sufficiency. On this point, see Henri Corbin, *En Islam iranien,* vol. 1, 46; Corbin, *Histoire de la philosophie islamique,* 129, 138, 299.

26. See, for instance, Amilcar Cabral, "National Liberation and Culture," in *Return to the Source: Selected Speeches of Amilcar Cabral,* 39–56. For Cabral, fighting against specifically cultural as well as political forms of imperialism, national mobilization requires a preliminary "reconversion of minds," a "re-Africanization," to be consolidated through the "communion of sacrifice required by the struggle" (58).

27. Badiou goes a long way toward answering such questions when he writes, pressed on this point, that "the generic character of a truth is not an abstraction. It often implies that the multiple composition of this truth can be subtracted from the linguistic and cultural predicates [of the situation in which it takes place] only by incorporating local 'representatives' of all these predicates (for if one of these predicates is radically excluded, then the corresponding *negative* predicate changes the genericity of the truth). This presumes, then, that we defend the real and active aspect of these predicates. It is entirely possible that, as the condition of a universal construction, we must affirm the absolute necessity of defending the rights of minorities, of protecting threatened languages, etc. We [the OP] have maintained that politics is the business of 'people from everywhere.' And 'everywhere' really means everywhere! We insist only that all political use of 'cultural' predicates be able to prove that this use accords with a universal process, and not to a strictly particularist prescription." How might this apply, say, to the apparently particularist demands of the Parti Québécois in Canada? "To defend the use of French in Quebec is universal in a precise sense: a Canadian anglophone who opposes it effectively desires, consciously or unconsciously, the absorption of Canada by the United States. And *this* absorption, in the current circumstances, would be a bad thing for humanity as a whole." As a rule, we need not "look for 'intrinsic' reasons to support the autonomy of Québec, or the Indians of the Amazon. I am bound *[requis]* by what they do and declare. I joined with the FLQ (Front de Libération du Québec) at the time of the national liberation struggles, and the singularity of the process was internal to this time. Which is why the Québécois militants of the day were fully sympathetic with Castro and Vietnam. That the general target was then American imperialism was obvious to everybody, even if the local singularity of the FLQ's statements applied to Canada's federal government, Québécois traitors, etc. . . . It is in such conditions that there is a basis for the universal, and never in the structure of particularity" (Alain Badiou, letters to the author, 9 and 30 Dec. 1998; cf. LM, chap. 3).

28. Badiou, "Politics and Philosophy," 131.

29. Badiou, "Nous pouvons redéployer la philosophie," 2; MP, 13. As Badiou writes, "There can be no philosophy, neither ancient nor contemporary, that doesn't take into account the mathematical events of its time" (Badiou, "Entretien avec Alain Badiou" [1999], 1).

30. See, for instance, V. Y. Mudimbe, *The Invention of Africa: Gnosis, Philosophy, and the Order of Knowledge* (1988); Emmanuel Chukwudi Eze, ed., *Postcolonial African Philosophy: A Critical Reader* (1996).

31. *La Distance politique* 7 (July 1993), 11; cf. *La Distance politique* 23–24 (Sept. 1997), 19.

32. Badiou, "Politics and Philosophy," 117.

33. *La Distance politique* 23–24 (Sept. 1997), 15. According to the early Badiou, the CGT (Confédération Générale du Travail) and the PCF (Parti Communiste Français) were nothing less than "social fascists" (Badiou, *Le Mouvement ouvrier révolutionnaire contre le syndicalisme*, 26–27).

34. *La Distance politique* 26–27 (Feb. 1998), 12.

35. *La Distance politique* 13 (Mar. 1995), 10, 12. More specifically, the OP attacks the centrist CFDT (Confédération Française Démocratique du Travail) for its close cooperation with Mittérand and with business interests generally, while it pours scorn on the obsolete "old labor" principles of the mainly communist CGT: "The CGT, clinging to the last tatters of a miserable *classisme,* perseveres in a politics of complete powerlessness, of bluff, which it tries pitifully to present as a politics of principle" (*La Distance politique* 8 [July 1994], 6).

36. *La Distance politique* 12 (Feb. 1995), 7; cf. TS, 253.

37. *La Distance politique* 17–18 (Oct. 1996), 32.

38. *La Distance politique* 26–27 (Feb. 1998), 12.

39. Ibid., 16.

40. A further simplification vitiates Badiou's alternative to "medical ethics." He maintains that "chance, the circumstances of life, the tangle of beliefs, combined with the rigorous and impartial treatment without exception of the clinical situation, is worth a thousand times more" than the pompous recommendations of state-sponsored commissions (E, 35–36). But once again, actual clinical choices are not so much determined by random accidents and emergencies as by their structural regularity (among relatively well-defined sectors of the population) and by their endless accumulation: there is simply no escaping the need for some sort of procedure for the determination of clinical priorities.

41. Pierre Bourdieu, "A Reasoned Utopia and Economic Fatalism." See also Pierre Bourdieu, *Contre-feux: Propos pour servir à la résistance contre l'invasion néo-libérale* (1998).

42. Bourdieu, "A Reasoned Utopia," 125.

43. Ibid., 129; cf. Pierre Bourdieu, ed., *La Misère du monde* (1993).

44. Badiou, "L'Etre, l'événement et la militance," 21. This is where Badiou's Heideggerian critics are likely to focus their attention. There is very little in Badiou's account to take the place of those transformative and "individualizing" operations that Heidegger analyzes, however abstractly, in terms of "anxiety" and "resolution." Both Heidegger and Badiou understand that it is essentially what can be done to change a situation that defines it as this particular situation. Resoluteness, summoning "us to our potentiality-for-Being, does not hold before us some empty ideal of existence, but calls us forth into the Situation," that is, into "taking action" within that situation (Heidegger, *Being and Time,* 347). But whereas Heidegger's resolution comes about as a radical transformation of

everyday *relations* to others and the world (344–45), Badiou's subject arises as a subtraction from these relations qua relations. Badiou's refusal to engage in any existential way with finitude or mortality raises a further question: Can we account for the exceptional assumption of a subjective "immortality" without relating this immortality to the merely individual mortality it transcends? It is precisely this question that prompts Žižek's most telling critique of Badiou: "Against Badiou, one should insist that only to a finite / mortal being does the act (or Event) appear as a traumatic intrusion of the Real. . . . Badiou remains blind to how the very space for the specific 'immortality' in which human beings can participate in the Truth-Event is opened up by man's unique relationship to his finitude and the possibility of death" (Žižek, *The Ticklish Subject,* 164, 163).

45. In the revolutionary affirmation of its "absolute freedom," as the canonical text puts it, spirit presents itself as "self-consciousness which grasps the fact that its certainty of itself is the essence of all the spiritual 'masses,' or spheres, of the real as well as of the supersensible world, or conversely, that essence and actuality are consciousness' knowledge of itself. . . . It comes into existence in such a way that each individual consciousness raises itself out of its allotted sphere, no longer finds its essence and its work in this particular sphere, but grasps itself as the Notion of will, grasps all spheres as the essence of this will, and therefore can only realise itself in a work which is a work of the whole. In this absolute freedom, therefore, all social groups or classes which are the spiritual spheres into which the whole is articulated are abolished; the individual consciousness that belonged to any such sphere, and willed and fulfilled itself in it, has put aside its limitation; its purpose is the general purpose, its language universal law, its work the universal work." Crucially, "in absolute freedom there was no reciprocal action between a consciousness that is immersed in the complexities of existence, or that sets itself specific aims and thoughts, and a valid external world, whether of reality or thought" (Hegel, *Phenomenology of Spirit,* sect. 585–88, 594; the importance of this whole compressed section of Hegel's book for Badiou's project speaks for itself). To quote Taylor's gloss: "The society of absolute freedom must be entirely the creation of its members. First, it must be such that everything in it is the fruit of human will and decision. And secondly, the decisions must be taken with the real participation of all" (Taylor, *Hegel,* 403–4). As Hegel understood with particular clarity, there is no obvious way that any political *institution* can be made "compatible with the abstract self-consciousness of equality" (Hegel, *Philosophy of Right,* sect. 5). The demands of absolute freedom are indifferent, precisely, to all re-presentation.

Now Badiou himself can easily show, in reference to precisely this Hegelian analysis, how the objectifying or "destructive" version of subjectivation leads to universal "suspicion" and terror (LS, 44–45). The question is then: in defending itself against this outcome while remaining fully axiomatic and subtractive, to what extent does the redoubled abstraction of Badiou's project undercut its practical political force? Rather than endure an ever more absolute subtraction from relations—and thereby rely on an ever more critical (and ever more obscure) operation of *restraint*—would we not be better advised to rethink the whole dimension of relationality as such?

46. Referring to Carl Schmitt's "state of exception" ("the sovereign is he who decides in and from the state of exception"), Lyotard retorts that "the notion that authority consists of deciding of and from the state of exception is exactly what you describe with regard to the [evental] site" (Jean-François Lyotard, Untitled discussion of *L'Etre et l'événement*, 242; see also note 68 to this chapter). The pure decision has no self-reflexive reserve, no awareness of what it is deciding. Badiou provides three answers to the charge. First, he says, "I've never said: you *have* to name [the event]. There is no purity of the decision," but only the laborious preservation of a fidelity to its consequences (Badiou, "L'Etre, l'événement et la militance," 21). Second, Badiou has always campaigned against the "authentic" plenitude preached by Heidegger, Junger, and Schmitt, and in favor of an empty mathematical rigor (Badiou, "Dix-neuf réponses," 249). Third, he counters with the accusation that Lyotard's own "passibility" provides no effective defense against fascism. In the absence of any precise criteria of judgment, there is nothing to stop its affirming "the most detestable significations." Badiou opts rather for the strict criterion of the "altogether neutral" (258–59).

47. Jean Bodin, "De la souveraineté," in *La République* (1576), book 1.

48. Hobbes, *Leviathan*, 252; cf. Jacques Bossuet, *Politique tirée de l'écriture sainte par ses propres paroles*, 56; Armand Jean du Plessis, duc de Richelieu, *Testament politique*, 265, 340–42. The deduction of sovereignty, Spinoza explains, "requires no belief in historical narratives of any kind," but is rather "self-validating and self-evident" (Baruch Spinoza, *Tractatus theologico-politicus*, in *The Political Works*, 73, 75).

49. Cardin Le Bret, *De la souveraineté du Roy* (1632), in Gilbert Picot, *Cardin Le Bret*, 29.

50. Hobbes, *Leviathan*, 220.

51. Badiou, "Saisissement, dessaisie, fidélité," 21.

52. See, in particular, MP, 90; PM, 57; CT, 200. As for the (explicitly knowledge-mediated) relation of forcing, it too is determined in a rigorously punctual, thoroughly antidialectical fashion. Once established as a "condition" (i.e., once connected to the event), the simple membership of an element in a generic set will automatically force the eventual verification of statements referring to that element. All such statements will take a flatly bivalent form, as answers

to the question: Is there or isn't there (a new form of poetry, a militant factory movement, a still-undiscovered planet, etc.)? (On this point see chapter 5.)

53. Rev. of Gilles Deleuze: *Le Pli*, 181–82. There is no relation, moreover, between the event and its site: "It is indeed a matter of a Two (the site as counted for one, and the multiple put into one), but the problem is that between these two terms there is no relation *[rapport]*" (EE, 230).

54. Badiou, "D'un sujet enfin sans objet," 21.

55. TS, 160; cf. 148. Badiou writes, "Marxist truth is not a conciliatory truth. It is, in itself, dictatorship, and if necessary, terror" (TC, 17). The author of *Théorie de la contradiction* still preserves a qualified support for the "strong thought of Joseph Stalin" (TC, 39), and a rather less qualified support for the still stronger proposals of the Khmer Rouge (TC, 85–89). Badiou's early enthusiasm for the Cambodian "dustbins of history" makes for painful retrospective reading.

56. E, 28; cf. Badiou, "Politics and Philosophy," 122–23.

57. Badiou, "L'Etre, l'événement et la militance," 19; MP, 74; EE, 374 (my emphasis).

58. C, 260. Badiou's recent reading of Brecht's didactic play *The Decision* (1930) addresses this question directly. The individual militant who disagrees with the party's strategy is entitled to say only, "I am right, but my being right is only real insofar as it yields, if only provisionally, to the 'we' that alone confers it a political existence. The singularity of this we is a condition of its practical force. The partisan we proceeds not through the strict *elimination* of disagreement but by preserving an 'inseparation' between the individuals who compose it, and who, even if they disagree, nevertheless agree to disagree *within* the party that provides the only forum in which their disagreement may, eventually, have real (active, consequential) significance" (LS, 99).

59. Lacan, S1, 335/217. Lacan writes, "Analysis consists in getting the subject to become conscious of his relations, not with the ego of the analyst, but with all these Others who are his true interlocutors, whom he hasn't recognised. It is a matter of the subject progressively discovering which Other he is truly addressing, without knowing it ... " (S2, 288/246).

60. B, 12, 61; cf. 38; C, 346.

61. See chapter 8.

62. Badiou, "L'Age des poètes," 23; cf. Badiou, "Art et philosophie," 164. This, too, has always been the condition of a properly sovereign power—as Bossuet puts it, "The king's designs are only well understood through their execution" (Bossuet, *Politique tirée de l'écriture sainte*, 114).

63. AM, 103; Badiou, "Les Lieux de la vérité," 116; Badiou, "Qu'est-ce qu'un thermidorien?" 55; cf. EE, 381–82. In *Le Siècle*, a work shot through with the vocabulary of the "absolute" and its cognates, Badiou refers interchangeably to

"revolutionary" or "absolute" politics, meaning a politics inspired by a subjective passion for the real (LS, 44). Indeed, since "the privileges of knowledge are not what command political access to the real," since "politics, when it exists, founds its own principle with respect to the real, and thus needs nothing other than itself," Badiou does not hesitate to approve the principle of Fouquier-Tinville's notorious Revolutionary judgment: "The Republic has no need of scholars [savants]" (LS, 52).

64. Badiou, "L'Entretien de Bruxelles," 2.

65. Badiou, "Six Propriétés de la vérité," Ornicar? no. 32, 64, and Ornicar? no. 33, 121.

66. For example, in 1992 Badiou was critical of the notion of "interprétation-coupure" advanced in Peut-on penser la politique? (1985)—prototype of the concept of "intervention"—because it "was not yet totally dissociated from a hermeneutic orientation" (C, 112 n.17).

67. Badiou, "L'Etre, l'événement et la militance," 21.

68. Badiou, "Saisissement, dessaisie, fidélité," 20.

69. To push this line of the argument to its limit, it would be worth drawing, in more detail than present constraints allow, on the terms developed in Giorgio Agamben's remarkable study of the logic of sovereignty (Homo Sacer: Sovereign Power and Bare Life, 1995). Agamben's thesis, in a nutshell, is that the progressive consolidation of sovereign political power over the entire course of Western history has as its symmetrical consequence the reduction of those governed by such power to their mere biological existence, that is, a purely mortal existence that, when "necessary," can be terminated without committing either legal murder or religious sacrilege. Of course, Badiou's strict disjunction of subject from state absolves him in advance from anything resembling complicity in this development. Nevertheless, is there not at least a danger that those who become subjects in Badiou's radically exceptional sense—and thereby subtracted from any merely moral interaction with the other members of that situation—might assume a position with respect to which some other members of the situation would effectively become homo sacer, that is, "disposable without guilt"? Does not the radically exceptional status of the subject at least make possible a situation in which, considered from the subject's effectively sovereign point of view, certain nonsubjects could in principle be eliminated without committing either murder on the one hand (since the real is illegal and immoral) or sacrifice on the other (since there is nothing about the individual as such that warrants preservation [LS, 81])? Furthermore, is it not from the subjective or immortal perspective that what Agamben would call the "bare life" of the human animal, the animal as mortal nonsubject, itself takes on its distinctive character—that is, as a set of essentially passive attributes exposed to the decisive actions of the subject? See,

in particular, Agamben, *Homo Sacer,* 83; cf. Giorgio Agamben, *Potentialities: Collected Essays in Philosophy,* 221.

14. Being-there

1. EL, 3–4; TA, 12.11.97. Badiou can now endorse Hegel's emphatically anti-subtractive (if not "ideological") assertion, that "the essence of essence is to show itself."

2. Badiou, letter to the author, 19 June 1996.

3. Badiou, "Politics and Philosophy" (1998), 130.

4. He goes on, still more tentatively: "I think I'll be able to draw most of the argument from the relation of order, from the elementary relation of order, order being defined simply as the first asymmetrical relation [i.e., essentially the relation of "precedence," where x < y means that x precedes y]—of course the didactics of the thing, the way of presenting it, is very important to me, and as long as I haven't fully discovered it I'm not entirely at ease. I'm going to try to solve the problem—and you see that I've read your work and am sensitive to what you've said—by injecting something like dissymmetry into the general edifice, without in any way renouncing it. In other words, it will mean something to say that *a* is in relation with *b,* in a relation which is something other than the strict relation of equivalence or equality. I'll take up the relation of order because it is, in the end, mathematically, the most primordial, most abstract, non-symmetrical relation" (Badiou, "Politics and Philosophy," 130–31). In his most recent work, Badiou writes that "a relation between singularities is always antisymmetrical, which means, in keeping with Nietzsche's intuition, that it is always a relation of power." No two singularities can "trade places." In other words, "no singularity is indifferent to its place in a rapport" (Badiou, "La Scène du Deux," 3–4). (It remains the case, however, that "the sexed distribution of human animals *is not inscribed in a rapport,*" that is, we can say neither that man is equal to or less than woman, nor vice versa, but only that they are "without rapport, or incompatible" [4].)

5. Badiou writes, "It is much rather being in itself, thought as the mathematicity of the purely multiple, or even as the physics of quanta, which is anarchic, neutral, inconsistent, unrelated *[délié]* . . ." (CT, 193).

6. CT, 192. Predictably, Kant remains *the* example of a philosopher who annexes being entirely to appearing, and therefore consigns being as being to the realm of the unknowable (193).

7. Badiou is guided here, in part, by algebraic methods devised by Brouwer's disciple Arend Heyting; the recourse to intuitionist methods may itself be a significant symptom of the shift in Badiou's orientation.

8. EL, 9–20. In *Logiques des mondes* Badiou develops the example of a tranquil rural scene suddenly interrupted by the sound of a motorcycle. The "envelope" of this particular situation is not some vague global space called "society"

or "nature," let alone a "clearing" in the ontological complexity of beings, but refers simply to the minimal "value of appearing" that is large enough to include the various elements it presents: the country house, the color of the leaves, the shadow of the trees, the sound of the motorcycle, and so on—but not, say, the appearance of a revolutionary militia (cf. LM, chap.1, p. 26).

9. LM, chap. 2, p. 21; chap. 3, pp. 16–17.

10. LM, chap. 3, p. 4. Badiou is careful to dispel a possible ambiguity here. Obviously any human world will have a finite number of elements or inhabitants; around 7.5 million people currently belong to the world of Québec, for instance. The point is that to each of these people there belongs an infinite number of further elements—possessions, personal experiences, thoughts, impressions, and so on, each of which can be said to include or relate to an innumerable dissemination of further subelements—which in turn all belong to their world. There is simply *nothing* beneath such subelements, no "ultimate formless matter," that might limit their possible variety or provide the raw material of a world (ibid., 5). A world incorporates the full dissemination of its constituent elements, just as it includes every re-presentation of its parts, that is, every configuration of its state. It is this fully immanent configuration of a world, the fact that it allows no unformed substance to subsist beneath it and no transcendent principle to hover above it, that "leads eventually to the *necessity* that every world be ontologically infinite" (6, my emphasis). That this infinity is inaccessible (i.e., corresponds to what mathematicians call an inaccessible cardinal) means that it cannot itself be measured by any intraworldly operation: "The extension of a world remains inaccessible to the operations that open up and disperse its multiplicity. Like the Hegelian Absolute, a world is the unfolding of its own infinity, but unlike this Absolute, a world cannot measure from within, or provide the concept for, the infinity that it is" (6).

11. Badiou, "Platon et / ou Aristote-Leibniz," 81.

12. CT, 200. Or again: "If we assume the equation of logic = appearing then we can say that what an event can do is change that which appears (rather than that which is) locally. It modifies the local conditions of appearing," in which an emergent subjective space will unfold (TA, 23.4.97).

13. CT, 126; cf. D, 146; cf. Lacan, *Ecrits*, 855–57.

14. Badiou writes, "The linguistic turn is ultimately authorized by the mathematization of logic" (CT, 125; cf. Dummett, *Origins of Analytic Philosophy*, 128–29).

15. Mathematical "formality" is itself a result. Its "formal transparency follows directly from the fact that being is absolutely univocal. Mathematical writing is the transcription, the inscription, of this univocity" (CT, 196).

16. A topos is a particular, restricted (and exemplary) kind of category.

17. Badiou, "Platon et / ou Aristote-Leibniz," 76, 81. From the perspective of categorical algebra, "set theory appears to be an unnaturally restrictive and inflexible language" (William S. Hatcher, *The Logical Foundations of Mathematics*, 238).

18. Readers interested in the technical procedures will have to tackle the textbooks on their own: Colin McLarty's *Elementary Categories, Elementary Toposes* is one of the most comprehensive. The most accessible of such surveys is Badiou's own unpublished introduction, entitled "Topos, ou Logiques de l'onto-logique: Une introduction pour philosophes" (1993, 153 typescript pages).

19. As one summary account puts it, "Category theory permits a uniform handling and formulation of problem statements that occur universally across the most varied fields of mathematics. It works directly with the mathematical objects (sets, groups, topological spaces, K-modules, and so forth) without resort to the level of their elements," considering only their "characteristic mappings" or "morphisms" (Grattan-Guinness, ed., *Companion Encyclopaedia*, 757). Common categories include sets (with sets as objects, and functions as morphisms), topological spaces (as objects, with continuous functions as morphisms), vector spaces (with linear transformations as morphisms), groups (with group homomorphisms as morphisms) (Andrea Asperti and Guiseppe Longo, *Categories, Types and Structures*, 4).

20. Badiou, "Platon et / ou Aristote-Leibniz," 75–76.

21. T, 2. It was Desanti's critique of *L'Etre et l'événement* that first led Badiou to a detailed engagement with category theory. Cf. Jean-Toussaint Desanti, "Quelques Remarques à propos de l'ontologie intrinsèque d'Alain Badiou" (1990).

22. Badiou writes, "Category theory is especially suited to the examination of 'dual' ontological situations, that is to say reversible correspondences, ambiguities of position, identities turned on their head, effects of symmetry and mirroring. In this sense, its spontaneous philosophy is Deleuzian, and it narrows the gap between the symbolic and the imaginary as much as possible" (T, 26). As one textbook puts it, the key to the "topos theoretic outlook consists in the rejection of the idea that there is a fixed universe of 'constant' sets within which mathematics can and should be developed. . . . Topos theory makes every notion of constancy relative, being derived perceptually or conceptually as a limiting case of variation" (P. T. Johnstone, *Topos Theory*, xvii [quoting William Lawvere]).

23. Asperti and Longo, *Categories, Types and Structures*, 3.

24. Badiou writes, "A category must always be thought as a geometric universe" (T, 40).

25. Badiou, "Platon et / ou Aristote-Leibniz," 74.

26. T, 3. In category theory, an "element is nothing more than a particular case of a sub-object" (T, 44).

27. Badiou, "Platon et / ou Aristote-Leibniz," 73.

28. "Toposes are categories which allow the constructions used in ordinary mathematics"; they have "set-like properties" (McLarty, *Elementary Categories,* 6).

29. More precisely, as Badiou explains, "The central object or 'classifier of sub-objects' of a topos is a Heyting algebra, and the transcendental regime of a world is what mathematicians call a complete Heyting algebra, which in my terms means one in which the 'envelope' always exists. What I call an 'object' corresponds with what mathematicians call an omega-set, and given a complete Heyting algebra we can demonstrate that the corresponding category of omega-sets is a topos" (letter to the author, 11 July 2002).

30. Badiou, "Platon et / ou Aristote-Leibniz," 75.

31. Badiou, letter to the author, 19 June 1996. A truth then proceeds in the familiar way: "The truth procedure bores a hole in the encyclopedia as a trajectory between the set-theoretic (decisional) and the categorial (definitional or relational) aspects [faces] of the axiomatic. It 'refolds' *[repli]* (as Subject) the relations onto the pure presentation of elements (an operation that Deleuze, as you have shown, poses as impossible, and that is the real reason for our differences)" (ibid.).

32. Among other things, category theory allows Badiou to reformulate his notion of the subject, conceived as a group in the mathematical sense (CT, 165–77). In categorial terms, "a group is a category that has one single object, and whose arrows are all isomorphisms" (172). This sole object provides the name of the group, its "instituting letter." Call it "G." Its arrows all go from G and end in G, and these provide its "operative substance." They emphasize the fact that what makes a group *a* group, what makes G, *G,* is "the set of different ways in which the object-letter G is identical to itself." Any such "group-Subject is infinite," that is, the number of ways it has of being identical to itself is inexhaustible (CT, 176).

33. Badiou, "Platon et / ou Aristote-Leibniz," 80.

34. Ibid., 81.

35. Ibid., 82; cf. T, 79 ff.; McLarty, *Elementary Categories,* 145–47.

36. The proof of this first theorem is fairly straightforward, and gives some indication of the categorial method (I follow the account in Badiou, "Platon et / ou Aristote-Leibniz," 82 n. 18). Elementary topos theory tells us that:

1. In a topos, for every object *a,* there is one and only one arrow that goes from the initial object 0 to *a,* and this arrow is a monomorphism (i.e., an arrow that conserves or "carries" differences).

2. In every "real" Topos—that is, one that has not "degenerated" and been reduced to only one object—this object 0 is empty (i.e., there is no arrow from the terminal object 1 to 0).

3. Every monomorphic arrow possesses a "centration" (an arrow that goes from the target of the monomorphism to the central object, in a commutative square; two different monomorphisms have different centrations).

4. Every object *a* has a self-identical arrow, going from *a* to *a;* this arrow is also a monomorphism.

That the void is unique means that every empty object *y* is the "same" as 0, and that every object different from 0 has an element (and thus an arrow from 1 to it). Take an object *b*, different from 0. There is necessarily an arrow from 0 to *b* (a monomorphism), and we can construct its centration, an arrow from *b* to the central object C (call it arrow f). We further construct the identity arrow from object *b* back to itself, and the centration of this arrow (again *b* to C, call it arrow g). Since we presume that 0 and *b* are really different, f and g must be different arrows. If this topos is well pointed, there must be an element x of *b* such that f to x is different from g to x. Clearly, *b* cannot be empty, as x is an element of *b*. Therefore, every object *b* different from 0 cannot be empty. In other words, 0 is the only empty object in the topos.

37. T, 93; Badiou, "Platon et / ou Aristote-Leibniz," 82. Such truth values—the arrows "true" and "false"—exist in every topos as arrows from 1 to C. In a well-pointed topos, these two arrows are the only elements the central object (the classifier of subobjects) admits. This (rare) kind of topos is known as "Boolean."

38. Gilles Deleuze and Claire Parnet, *Dialogues,* 71 / 57.

39. T, 139. The usual French expression for the law of the excluded middle is precisely *le tiers exclu.*

40. Badiou relates such modal or nonclassical logic to Kripke's semantics, read as the subordination of categories of true and false to time. For Kripke, statements are only "sometimes" true (T, 144–45) whereas for Badiou himself, of course, a truth is properly eternal (or creative of its own time).

41. Badiou, "Logique et philosophie" (1994), 10; Badiou, "Platon et / ou Aristote-Leibniz," 83. This is known as Diaconescu's theorem, and dates from 1975. Cf. McLarty, *Elementary Categories,* 162–64.

42. Badiou, "Logique et philosophie" (1994), 10.

43. T, 134; cf. D, 144–45; Badiou, "La Subversion infinitésimale" (1968), 136.

44. Badiou, "Platon et / ou Aristote-Leibniz," 76.

45. Ibid., 81.

46. Ibid., 83.

47. Badiou illustrates his position through discussion of a landmark moment in the recent history of Québec, the Oka Crisis of 1990, when a land dispute led to a long and eventually violent standoff between a group of Mohawks and the

province's armed forces. Badiou argues that the relations of solidarity and antagonism at issue here did nothing to alter the actual individuals they affected. Relations of this kind certainly clarify the prevailing logic of the transcendental regime operative in the situation, but for reasons fundamental to Badiou's entire enterprise, it remains the case that "a relation as such is not an event. A relation doesn't alter the transcendental evaluations operative in a world, it presumes them, insofar as it too appears in this world. The Mohawk revolt then, strictly conceived as a relation between the object 'the Mohawks' and the object 'the Québecois administration,' simply allows already existent objectivities to appear, even if—and this was one of the reasons for the revolt—one of these existences was minimised, or scorned, by officials of the state." The incident at Oka thus "activated but did not produce" the relations of solidarity among the Mohawks it mobilized. In this as in any such case, what Badiou calls the logic of appearance, and with it the logic of relations between appearings, concerns the "localisation of beings *[étants]* according a transcendental being-there, and not the coming to be of the very being of these beings *[l'étantité des étants]*" (TM, chap. 3, pp. 8 –9). This arrangement allows Badiou to continue to subtract a fully affirmative conception of truth (for instance, the political assertion of civic equality) from a dialectical conception that might seek to link such assertion with the negation of previous inequalities or injustices. But it also complicates the discernment of a genuine event from its relational conditions of possibility, and presumes distinctions that may defy generalization (for instance, across scenarios concerned with biological evolution or psychological development).

48. Since relations identify their object, "taken in similar networks of relations and external actions, 'two' objects are indiscernible—except as pure empty letters" (T, 2–3). "It is the essence of category theory that isomorphic objects can be treated as practically identical" (Hatcher, *The Logical Foundations of Mathematics,* 248).

49. Asperti and Longo, *Categories, Types and Structures,* 3.

50. As a result, "the force of a relation cannot prevail over the degree of existence of the related terms," or again, "an element cannot be 'more identical' to another element than it is to itself" (EL, 61).

51. Deleuze, *Empirisme et subjectivité,* 122–23 / 108–9.

Conclusion

1. Of course, the inaccessible need not have any religious or even any strictly ontological significance. Evolution ensures that the experience of other species is inaccessible to us (i.e., is "untranslatable"), just as the temporality of the universe implies limits (beginnings, endings, boundaries) that will remain forever inaccessible to its inhabitants.

2. Badiou, letter to the author, 19 June 1996. Like Cantor, Badiou could just

as well have quoted another of his allies: "The time will come when these things that are now hidden from you will be brought into the light" (Saint Paul, 1 Cor., in Cantor, *Contributions*, 85).

3. EE, 53; cf. letter from Cantor to Dedekind (1895), in *From Frege to Gödel*, ed. Van Heijenoort, 114; Moore, *The Infinite*, 186, 198.

4. I am thinking in particular of Corbin and Jambet.

5. Badiou, "Politics and Philosophy," 128.

Appendix

1. I should stress again that in providing this appendix I do not myself claim *any* expertise in these matters, and have drawn as closely as possible on well-known surveys of the field. I have found four such books of particular value: John N. Crossley et al., *What Is Mathematical Logic?* (1972), Mary Tiles, *The Philosophy of Set Theory* (1989), Michael Hallett, *Cantorian Set Theory and Limitation of Size* (1984), and Shaughan Lavine, *Understanding the Infinite* (1994). I am grateful to Keith Hossack, John Collins, and Gilbert Adair for their comments on draft versions of the text; I alone am responsible, of course, for any errors that may remain.

2. Cantor, "Foundations," 76.

3. See, for instance, Hume, *Treatise of Human Nature*, book I, part 2, sect. 1, "On the infinite divisibility of our ideas of space and time," 23–24.

4. Cf. Boyer, *A History of Mathematics*, 611.

5. Aristotle, *Physics*, III, 4 and 5, in *The Complete Works of Aristotle: The Revised Oxford Translation*; cf. Cantor, "Foundations," 75.

6. See Dauben's concise account in "Conceptual Revolutions and the History of Mathematics," 52–57. Recent research has cast doubt on the historical circumstances of this discovery (David Fowler, *The Mathematics of Plato's Academy: A New Reconstruction*, 356 ff), but I retain an outline of the traditional story here because of its relatively straightforward illustrative value—and because Badiou himself refers to it on several occasions.

7. With any isosceles right triangle, the square of the hypotenuse is twice the square of one of the other (equal) sides, but the square of one whole number only ever approximates twice the square of another: for instance, 7 squared gives 49, while twice 5 squared gives 50; 17 squared is 289, and twice 12 squared is 288, and so on.

8. As Wittgenstein scoffs, to ask how many points there are on a line is like asking, "How many angels can dance on a needlepoint?" (Wittgenstein, *Remarks on the Foundations of Mathematics*, 59).

9. Evert W. Beth, *Mathematical Thought: An Introduction to the Philosophy of Mathematics*, 7, 22, 175.

10. Tiles, *The Philosophy of Set Theory*, 209–11.

11. Leibniz himself insisted on the necessary existence of the actually Infinite in the metaphysical sense (God), but excluded the idea from mathematics in general and calculus in particular. Cf. Abraham Robinson, *Non-Standard Analysis,* 280.

12. Tiles, *The Philosophy of Set Theory,* 70–72.

13. Carl Gauss, quoted in Maor, *Infinity,* 54; cf. Robinson, "The Metaphysics of the Calculus" (1967), in *Selected Papers,* vol. 2, 547.

14. Cf. Maddy, *Realism in Mathematics,* 22–23. "One of the most surprising facts in the history of mathematics is that the logical foundation of the real number system was not erected until the late nineteenth century. Up to that time not even the simplest properties of positive and negative rational numbers and irrational numbers were logically established, nor were these numbers defined" (Kline, *Mathematical Thought,* 979).

15. Kline, *Mathematical Thought,* 1023.

16. Davis and Hersh, *Experience,* 217–23.

17. Lakatos, *Proofs and Refutations,* 139.

18. Leopold Kronecker, quoted in Kline, *Mathematical Thought,* 1197.

19. Hobbes, *Leviathan,* 99.

20. Locke, *Essay Concerning Human Understanding,* book 2, chap. 17, sect. 20.

21. See, in particular, Philip Jourdain, "Preface," in Cantor, *Contributions,* 79; Dauben, *Cantor,* 124–25. Important preliminary steps were taken, as Cantor acknowledged, in Bolzano's *Paradoxes of the Infinite* (1851).

22. Cantor, *Contributions,* 85.

23. Russell, *Mysticism and Logic,* 80; cf. Frege, *Foundations of Arithmetic,* 53–54.

24. Cantor, "Foundations," 78; cf. Hallett, *Cantorian Set Theory,* 151–52.

25. Cf. Dauben, *Cantor,* 79.

26. Cantor, *Contributions,* 103–5. The letter aleph, used in Hebrew to represent the number one, conveys a sense of the transfinite numbers as "infinite unities" (Dauben, *Cantor,* 179). The subscript zero identifies $\aleph_0$ as the foundation for all the succeeding alephs or transfinite cardinals, just as the empty set $\emptyset$ serves as the immediate foundation for all the finite successor ordinals.

27. See Cohen and Hersh, "Non-Cantorian Set Theory," 104–5; Dauben, *Cantor,* 166–67. A constructivist would argue that such an indirect demonstration proves only the possibility of constructing an infinite sequence of "new" numbers. It is the demonstrable existence of irrational and transcendental numbers—numbers like π (3.14159 . . .), e (2.71828 . . .) and ϕ (phi), the so-called "golden ratio" (1.61803 . . .)—that guarantees Cantor's conclusion, and that gives "to the real number system the 'density' that results in a higher power" (Boyer, *A History of Mathematics,* 614).

28. Cantor, *Contributions,* 95.

29. Ibid., 169–70. In a well-ordered set F, its "elements f ascend in a definite succession from a lowest f_1" (Cantor, *Contributions,* 137).

30. Dauben, *Cantor,* 172–73.

31. This distinction is based on Russell, *Introduction to Mathematical Philosophy,* 12 ff.

32. Cf. Eves, *Introduction,* 476.

33. Reid, *Hilbert,* 98.

34. To this day intuitionists accept only potential infinities, that is, those "in process of generation" (Dummett, *Elements of Intuitionism,* 32).

35. Rotman and Kneebone, *Sets and Transfinite Numbers,* 57.

36. Leibniz, letter to Bernoulli, *Math. Schriften,* vol. 3, 536, quoted in Weyl, *Philosophy of Mathematics,* 48.

37. Cantor, letter to Dedekind (1895), in *From Frege to Gödel,* ed. Van Heijenoort, 114; cf. Dauben, *Cantor,* 192–93.

38. Cantor, letter to Eulenberg, 28 Feb. 1886, quoted in Hallett, *Cantorian Set Theory,* 41; Cantor, "Foundations," 94.

39. As Hallett and Lavine point out, because Cantorian theory applies only to collections or sets considered as wholes or "countable" collections (and not every collection, as Cantor knew very well, can be so considered), it is not immediately vulnerable to the paradoxes that vitiate the unrestricted application of the "comprehension theory" of set (Hallett, *Cantorian Set Theory,* 38, 74; Lavine, *Understanding the Infinite,* 76).

40. See, in particular, Cantor, "Foundations," 94.

41. Von Neumann's answer is the simplest: "A set is 'too big' if and only if it is equivalent to the set of all things" (Von Neumann, letter to Zermelo, 15 Aug. 1923, quoted in Hallett, *Cantorian Set Theory,* 288).

42. Such inaccessible numbers were first proposed by Zermelo in 1930 and Tarski in 1938.

43. Hallett, *Cantorian Set Theory,* 164.

44. Ibid., xiv.

45. Ibid., 35, 301.

46. Lavine, *Understanding the Infinite,* 95–97; 245; 290; cf. Devlin, *The Axiom of Constructibility,* 27.

47. Hallett, *Cantorian Set Theory,* 151–53; Lavine, *Understanding the Infinite,* 55–60.

48. John Von Neumann, "An Axiomatisation of Set Theory," in *From Frege to Gödel,* ed. Van Heijenoort, 395.

49. Hallett, *Cantorian Set Theory,* 300.

50. According to Hallett, we should simply not "expect a theory of sets to

answer the deepest analytic questions about the continuum" (Hallett, *Cantorian Set Theory*, 305).

51. Cf. EE, 469.

52. Benacerraf and Putnam, eds., "Introduction," *Philosophy of Mathematics*, 18.

53. Cantor's own position was positively antiaxiomatic. He refused the notion of mathematical "hypothesis" altogether, holding that the basic laws of arithmetic, like those of the transfinite numbers, are eternally "immutable," "simply absolute" (Dauben, *Cantor*, 237–38).

54. Cohen and Hersh, *Set Theory*, 51.

55. George Boolos, "The Iterative Conception of a Set," in *Philosophy of Mathematics*, ed. Benacerraf and Putnam, 491–93.

56. I present them as glossed in Cohen and Hersh, "Non-Cantorian Set Theory," 114, Tiles, *The Philosophy of Set Theory*, 121–23, and EE, 536–38.

57. Tiles, *The Philosophy of Set Theory*, 124.

58. Jean-Louis Krivine, *Introduction to Axiomatic Set Theory*, 35.

59. Lavine, *Understanding the Infinite*, 104–9; cf. Maddy, *Realism in Mathematics*, 120 ff.

60. Badiou, "Logique et philosophie" (1994), 10.

61. Hilbert, "On the Infinite" (1925), in *Philosophy of Mathematics*, ed. Benacerraf and Putnam, 191.

62. Hilbert, "On the Infinite," 184; cf. Weyl, *Philosophy of Mathematics*, 22.

63. Reid, *Hilbert*, 77–79, 33.

64. Ibid., 60–61.

65. Ibid.,155–56.

66. Kurt Gödel, "On formally Undecidable Propositions of *Principia Mathematica* and Related Systems," in *Collected Works*, vol. 1, 145–95; cf. Reid, *Hilbert*, 197–98. For brief, relatively accessible accounts of Gödel's incompleteness theorem, see James Robert Brown, *Philosophy of Mathematics: An Introduction to the World of Proofs and Pictures*, 71–77, Crossley, *Logic*, 45–58, Rudy Rucker, *Infinity and the Mind*, 267–94, or Raymond L. Wilder, *Introduction to the Foundations of Mathematics*, 256–60.

67. Eves, *Introduction*, 483.

68. Hofstadter, *Gödel, Escher, Bach*, 17–19.

69. Kurt Gödel, "On Formally Undecidable Propositions," in *Collected Works*, vol. 1, 149.

70. Roitman, *Introduction to Modern Set Theory*, 32; cf. Tiles, *The Philosophy of Set Theory*, 181.

71. Cf. Maddy, "Believing the Axioms," 482; Devlin, *Fundamentals of Contemporary Set Theory*, 63.

72. Gödel, "What Is Cantor's Continuum Problem?," Benacerraf and Putnam, eds., *Philosophy of Mathematics*, 483–84.

73. Davis and Hersh, *Experience*, 231. In other words, this "constructible universe is, in a certain sense, the smallest universe of sets we can have" (Tiles, *The Philosophy of Set Theory*, 183).

74. Cohen, *Set Theory*, 1. Cohen himself believes that "CH is obviously false," that is, that c, the power set of $\aleph_0$, is "an incredibly rich set given to us by one bold new axiom [the power set axiom], which can never be approached by any piecemeal process of construction" (151).

75. This is the point where my own account becomes entirely reliant upon a handful of secondary sources: I have drawn mainly on the abridged reviews in Cohen and Hersh, "Non-Cantorian Set Theory," 115–16, Crossley, *Logic*, 73–77, and Tiles, *Philosophy of Set Theory*, 185–91, along with Badiou's own more involved account in meditations 33, 34, and 36 of *L'Etre et l'événement*. For a more substantial overview, see Raymond Smullyan and Melvin Fitting, *Set Theory and the Continuum Problem* (1996). As suggested in chapter 5, Cohen's work amounts to a "blind recognition," on the part of ontology, of the "possible being of truth" (EE, 425).

76. EE, 342. It can also be shown that in a universe governed by the presumption that all sets are constructible, the decision to impose the axiom of foundation (which alone blocks, in general set theory, the paradoxical existence of sets belonging to themselves—i.e., the existence of events) is no longer a decision at all but a simple theorem, one that follows naturally from the other axioms of ZF. The same applies to the "anarchic" axiom of choice.

77. Cohen, *Set Theory*, 112.

78. Tiles, *The Philosophy of Set Theory*, 186.

79. Cohen and Hersh, "Non-Cantorian Set Theory," 116.

80. Cohen, *Set Theory*, 112.

81. What is known as the "downward Löwenheim-Skolem theorem" establishes that any axiom system, even if it gives rise to nondenumerably many things, has a denumerable model that faithfully reflects the working of those axioms.

82. As Cohen suggests, "The crucial idea [involved in 'forcing'] will be the preferential treatment of the universal quantifier [∀ 'for all . . .'] over the existential quantifier [∃ 'there exists . . .']" (Cohen, *Set Theory*, 112).

83. As Badiou puts it, "Once we are not obliged to affirm, it becomes possible to negate" (EE, 454).

84. As seen from inside M, however, the values of both $\aleph_0$ and $2^{\aleph_0}$ are nondenumerable; from within M, the value of $2^{\aleph_0}$ appears entirely "speculative," a sort of conjecture about what lies beyond the limits of the universe.

85. Hallett, *Cantorian Set Theory*, 208; cf. 236.

86. Tiles, *The Philosophy of Set Theory,* 220–21; cf. Hallett, *Cantorian Set Theory,* 303–5.

87. Cohen and Hersh, "Non-Cantorian Set Theory," 116.

88. Devlin, *Mathematics,* 46; cf. Davis and Hersh, *Experience,* 236. To this day, "there is certainly no consensus on whether or not CH should be accepted"; it remains a matter of decision and "assumption" (H. Garth Dales and Gianluigi Oliveri, "Truth and the Foundations of Mathematics," in *Truth in Mathematics,* ed. Dales and Oliveri [1998], 19).

Bibliography

Works by Alain Badiou

Books of Philosophy, Politics, and Criticism

Le Concept de modèle: Introduction à une épistémologie matérialiste des mathématiques. Paris: Maspéro, 1972.

Théorie de la contradiction. Paris: Maspéro, 1975.

De l'idéologie. Paris: Maspéro, 1976.

Théorie du sujet. Paris: Seuil, 1982.

Peut-on penser la politique? Paris: Seuil, 1985.

L'Etre et l'événement. Paris: Seuil, 1988. Trans. Oliver Feltham as *Being and Event.* London: Continuum Press, forthcoming. The chapters on Hegel and on Descartes/Lacan were translated, respectively, by Marcus Coelen and Sam Gillespie and by Sigi Jöttkandt with Daniel Collins in *Umbr(a)* (Buffalo: State University of New York Press) 1 (1996).

Manifeste pour la philosophie. Paris: Seuil, 1989. Trans. Norman Madarasz as *Manifesto for Philosophy.* Albany: State University of New York Press, 1999.

Le Nombre et les nombres. Paris: Seuil, 1990.

Rhapsodie pour le théâtre. Paris: Le Spectateur français, 1990.

D'un désastre obscur (Droit, Etat, Politique). Paris: L'Aube, 1991.

Conditions. Paris: Seuil, 1992. Two chapters ("The (Re)turn of Philosophy *Itself*" and "Definition of Philosophy") are included in Madarasz's translation of the *Manifesto for Philosophy* (Albany: State University of New York Press, 1999). Two other chapters ("Psychoanalysis and Philosophy" and "What is Love?") appeared in *Umbr(a)* (Buffalo: State University of New York) 1 (1996). Another two chapters, "Philosophy and Art" and "Definition of Philosophy," are included in *Infinite Thought*, ed. Clemens and Feltham.

L'Ethique: Essai sur la conscience du mal. Paris: Hatier, 1993. Trans. Peter Hallward as *Ethics: An Essay on the Understanding of Evil.* London: Verso, 2001.

Beckett: L'incrévable désir. Paris: Hachette, 1995. Ed. and trans. Nina Power and Alberto Toscano with Bruno Bosteels as *Beckett.* Manchester: Clinamen Press, forthcoming. The translation includes, as appendices, "Etre, existence, pensée" [on Beckett's *Worstward Ho!*] from *Petit manuel d'inesthétique,* and "L'Ecriture du générique" from *Conditions.*

Gilles Deleuze: "La clameur de l'Etre." Paris: Hachette, 1997. Trans. Louise Burchill as *Deleuze: The Clamor of Being.* Minneapolis: University of Minnesota Press, 2000.

Saint Paul et la fondation de l'universalisme. Paris: Presses Universitaires de France, 1997. Trans. Ray Brassier as *Saint Paul: The Foundation of Universalism.* Stanford, Calif.: Stanford University Press, 2003.

Abrégé de métapolitique. Paris: Seuil, 1998. Trans. Jason Barker. London: Verso, forthcoming.

Court traité d'ontologie transitoire. Paris: Seuil, 1998. Trans. Norman Madarasz as *Briefings on Existence: A Transitory Ontology.* Albany: State University of New York Press, 2003.

Petit manuel d'inésthétique. Paris: Seuil, 1998. Trans. Alberto Toscano as *Handbook of Inaesthetics.* Stanford, Calif.: Stanford University Press, forthcoming.

Badiou: Theoretical Writings. Ed. Alberto Toscano and Ray Brassier. London: Continuum Press, forthcoming.

Infinite Thought: Truth and the Return to Philosophy. Ed. Justin Clemens and Oliver Feltham. London: Continuum, forthcoming.

Logiques des mondes. Paris: Seuil, forthcoming. [My references are to the typescript versions of chapters 1, 2, and 3, respectively entitled "Le Transcendental," "L'Objet," and "Le Monde."]

Le Siècle. Paris: Seuil, forthcoming. [Bilingual edition, with translation and commentary by Alberto Toscano.]

Novels and Plays

Almagestes [novel]. Paris: Seuil, 1964.

Portulans [novel]. Paris: Seuil, 1967.

L'Echarpe rouge [play]. Paris: Maspéro, 1979.

Ahmed le subtil [play]. Arles: Actes Sud, 1994.

Ahmed se fâche, suivi par Ahmed philosophe [plays]. Arles: Actes Sud, 1995.

Citrouilles [play]. Arles: Actes Sud, 1995.

Calme bloc ici-bas [novel]. Paris: P.O.L., 1997.

Shorter Works

"Matieu." In *Derrière le miroir: 5 peintres et un sculpteur*, 24–31. Paris: Maeght Editeur, 1965.

"L'autonomie du processus historique." *Cahiers Marxistes-Léninistes* (Paris: Ecole Normale Supérieure) 12–13 (1966): 77–89.

"L'Autorisation" [short story]. *Les Temps modernes* 258 (1967): 761–89.

"Le (re)commencement du matérialisme dialectique" [rev. of Althusser, *Pour Marx*, and Althusser et al., *Lire le Capital*]. *Critique* 240 (May 1967): 438–67.

"La Subversion infinitésimale." *Cahiers pour l'analyse* (Paris: Ecole Normale Supérieure) 9 (1968): 118–37.

Contribution au problème de la construction d'un parti marxiste-léniniste de type nouveau. Paris: Maspéro, 1969. [Written with H. Jancovici, D. Menetrey, and E. Terray.]

"Marque et manque: À propos du zéro." *Cahiers pour l'analyse* 10 (1969): 150–73.

Le Mouvement ouvrier révolutionnaire contre le syndicalisme [pamphlet]. Marseilles: Potemkine, 1976.

"Le Flux et le parti (dans les marges de *L'Anti-Oedipe*)." In *La Situation actuelle sur le front de la philosophie*, ed. Badiou and Lazarus, 24–41.

La Situation actuelle sur le front de la philosophie. Cahiers Yenan No. 4. Paris: Maspéro, 1977. [Coedited with Sylvain Lazarus.]

La "Contestation" dans le P.C.F. [pamphlet]. Marseilles: Potemkine, 1978.

Le Noyau rationnel de la dialectique hegelienne. [Text by Zhang Shiying; translation and commentaries by Alain Badiou, Joel Bellassen, and Louis Mossot.] Paris: Maspéro, 1978.

Jean-Paul Sartre [pamphlet]. Paris: Potemkine, 1981.

"Custos, quid noctis?" [rev. of Lyotard, *Le Différend*]. *Critique* 450 (Nov. 1984): 851–63.

"Poème mise à mort, suivi de 'L'ombre où s'y claire.'" In *Le Vivant et l'artificiel*, 19–23. Sgraffite: Festival d'Avignon, 1984.

"Six propriétés de la vérité." *Ornicar?* 32 (Jan. 1985): 39–67; continued in *Ornicar?* 33 (Apr. 1985): 120–49.

Est-il exact que toute pensée émet un coup de dés? [pamphlet]. Paris: Conférences du Perroquet, 1986.

"Les Noeuds du théâtre." *L'Art du théâtre* 7 (1987), 83–88 [reprinted in *Rhapsodie pour le théâtre*].

"L'Enjeu éthique du jeu." *L'Art du théâtre* 9 (1988), 129–37 [reprinted in *Rhapsodie pour le théâtre*].

"L'Etat théâtral en son Etat." *L'Art du théâtre* 8 (1988), 11–28 [reprinted in *Rhapsodie pour le théâtre*].

Une Soirée philosophique [pamphlet]. Paris: Potemkine/Seuil, 1988. [Written with Christian Jambet, Jean-Claude Milner, and François Regnault.]

"Dix-neuf réponses à beaucoup plus d'objections." *Cahiers du Collège International de philosophie* 8 (1989): 247–68.

"D'un sujet enfin sans objet." *Cahiers Confrontations* 20 (1989): 13–22. Trans. Bruce Fink as "On a Finally Objectless Subject." In *Who Comes after the Subject?* ed. Eduardo Cadava, Peter Connor, and Jean-Luc Nancy, 24–32. London: Routledge, 1991.

Samuel Beckett: L'Ecriture du générique [pamphlet]. Paris: Editions du Perroquet, 1989. Abridged trans. Alban Urbanas. *Journal of Beckett Studies* 4:1 (1994): 13–21.

Untitled response. In *Témoigner du différend: Quand phraser ne peut: Autour de Jean-François Lyotard,* ed. Francis Guibal and Jacob Rogozînskî, 109–13. Paris: Osiris, 1989.

"Lacan et les présocratiques." Typescript [1990].

"L'Entretien de Bruxelles." *Les Temps modernes* 526 (1990): 1–26.

"Objectivité et objectalité" [rev. of Monique David-Ménard, *La Folie dans la raison pure: Kant lecteur de Swedenborg* (Paris: Vrin, 1990)]. Typescript [1991].

"Pourquoi Antoine Vitez a-t-il abandonné Chaillot pour le Français?" *L'Art du théâtre* 10 (1990): 143–45.

Rev. of Gilles Deleuze, *Le Pli: Leibniz et le baroque.* In *Annuaire philosophique 1988–1989,* 161–84. Paris: Seuil, 1990. Trans. Thelma Sowley as "Gilles Deleuze, *The Fold: Leibniz and the Baroque,*" in *Gilles Deleuze: The Theatre of Philosophy,* ed. Constantin Boundas and Dorothea Olkowski, 51–69. New York: Columbia University Press, 1994.

"Saisissement, dessaisie, fidélité" [on Sartre]. *Les Temps modernes* 531–33, vol. 1 (1990): 14–22.

"Ta Faute, ô graphie!" In *Pour la photographie III,* 261–65. Paris: Germs, 1990.

"L'Etre, l'événement et la militance" [interview with Nicole-Edith Thévenin]. *Futur antérieur* 8 (1991): 13–23.

"L'Age des poètes." In *La Politique des poètes: Pourquoi des poètes en temps de détresse,* ed. Jacques Rancière, 21–38. Paris: Albin Michel, 1992.

Casser en deux l'histoire du monde? [pamphlet]. Paris: Le Perroquet, 1992.

"Les Lieux de la vérité" [interview with Jacques Henri]. *Art Press spécial: "20 ans: l'histoire continue,"* hors série no. 13 (1992): 113–18.

Monde contemporain et désir de philosophie [pamphlet]. Reims: Cahier de Noria, no. 1, 1992. Trans. Justin Clemens and Oliver Feltham as "The Contemporary World and the Desire for Philosophy," in *Infinite Thought*, ed. Clemens and Feltham.

"Le Pays comme principe." *Le Monde: Bilan économique et social 1992*: 134–35.

"Réponses écrites d'Alain Badiou" [interview with student group at the University of Paris VIII (Vincennes/Saint-Denis)]. *Philosophie, philosophie* 4 (1992): 66–71.

"Le Statut philosophique du poème après Heidegger." In *Penser après Heidegger*, ed. Jacques Poulain and Wolfgang Schirmacher, 263–68. Paris: L'Harmattan, 1992.

"Y-a-t-il une théorie du sujet chez George Canguilhem?" In *Georges Canguilhem, Philosophe, historien des sciences*, 295–304. Bibliothèque du Collège International de la Philosophie. Paris: Albin Michel, 1992. Trans. Graham Burchell. *Economy and Society* 27:2–3 (1998): 225–33.

"L'Impératif de la négation" [rev. of Guy Lardreau, *La Véracité* (Paris: Verdier, 1993)]. Typescript [1995].

"Nous pouvons redéployer la philosophie" [interview with Rober-Pol Droit]. *Le Monde*, 31 Aug. 1993,: 2.

"Que pense le poème?" In *L'Art est-il une connaissance?* ed. Roger Pol Droit, 214–24. Paris: Le Monde Editions, 1993.

"Qu'est-ce que Louis Althusser entend par 'philosophie'?" In *Politique et philosophie dans l'oeuvre de Louis Althusser*, ed. Sylvain Lazarus, 29–45. Paris: Presses Universitaires de France, 1993.

"Philosophie et poésie au point de l'innommable." *Po&sie* 64 (1993): 88–96.

"Sur le livre de Françoise Proust, *Le Ton de l'histoire*." *Les Temps modernes* 565–66 (1993): 238–48.

"Topos, ou Logiques de l'onto-logique: Une Introduction pour philosophes, tome 1." Manuscript, 1993.

"Art et philosophie." In *Artistes et philosophes: Éducateurs?* ed. Christian Descamps, 155–70. Paris: Centre Georges Pompidou, 1994.

"Being by Numbers" [interview with Lauren Sedofsky]. *Artforum* 33.2 (Oct. 1994): 84–87, 118, 123–24.

"L'Etre du nombre." Typescript (partially published in *Court traité*) [1994].

"Logique et philosophie." Typescript [1994].

"1977, une formidable régression intellectuelle." *Le Monde 1944–1994*. Le Monde, SARC (Nov. 1994), 78.

"L'Ontologie implicite de Spinoza." In *Spinoza, puissance et ontologie*, ed. Myriam Revault d'Allonnes and Hadi Rizk, 54–69. Paris: Kimé, 1994. [Reprinted in *Court traité*.]

"La Question de l'être aujourd'hui." Lectures (partially published in *Court traité*) given at the Ecole Normale Supérieure, Paris (my references are to the typescript) [1994].

"Silence, solipsisme, sainteté: L'antiphilosophie de Wittgenstein." *BARCA! Poésie, Politique, Psychanalyse* 3 (1994): 13–53.

"Ethique et psychiatrie." Typescript [1995].

"Il faut descendre dans l'amour." Preface to *Heureux les déliants: Poèmes 1950–1995,* by Henry Bauchau, 7–16. Brussels: Labor, 1995.

"Logologie contre ontologie" [rev. of Barbara Cassin, *L'Effet sophistique* (1995)]. *Poë&sie* 78 (Dec. 1996), 111–16.

"Platon et/ou Aristote-Leibniz: Théorie des ensembles et théorie des Topos sous l'oeil du philosophe." In *L'Objectivité mathématique: Platonismes et structures formelles,* ed. Marco Panza, 61–83. Paris: Masson, 1995 (partially published in *Court traité*).

"Qu'est-ce qu'un thermidorien?" In *La République et la terreur,* ed. Cathérine Kintzler and Hadi Rizk, 53–64. Paris: Kimé, 1995 [reprinted in *Abrégé de métapolitique*].

"Jean Borreil: Le style d'une pensée." In *Jean Borreil: La raison de l'autre,* ed. Maurice Matieu and Patrice Vermeren, 29–35. Paris: L'Harmattan, 1996.

"Les Gestes de la pensée [on François Châtelet]." *Les Temps modernes* 586 (1996): 196–204.

"Penser la singularité: Les noms innommables" [rev. of Sylvain Lazarus, *Anthropologie du nom* (1996)]. *Critique* 595 (Dec. 1996): 1074–95 [reprinted in *Abrégé de métapolitique*].

"Vérités et justice." In *Qu'est-ce que la justice? Devant l'autel de l'histoire,* ed. Jacques Poulain, 275–81. Paris: Presses Universitaires de Vincennes, Dec. 1996.

"L'Insoumission de Jeanne." *Esprit* 238 (Dec. 1997): 26–33.

"Lieu et déclaration." In *Paroles à la bouche du présent: Le Négationnisme: histoire ou politique?* ed. Natacha Michel, 177–84. Marseille: Al Dante, 1997.

"Logic, Philosophy, and the 'Linguistic Turn.'" Typescript [1997].

"Ce qui arrive" [on Beckett]. Typescript [1997–98].

"Le Dépli du désert." Preface to *Le Voyageur sans Orient: Poésie et philosophie des Arabes de l'ère préislamique,* by Salam al-Kindy, 11–15. Arles: Sindbad/Actes Sud, 1998.

"On ne passe pas" [on Badiou's own practice of writing]. *Théorie, littérature, enseignement* (revue du Departement de Lettres, Université de Paris VIII) 16 (Autumn 1998), 17–20 [my references are to the typescript].

"Paul le saint" [interview with Jacques Henric]. *Artpress* 235 (May 1998): 53–58.

"Penser le surgissement de l'événement" [interview with E. Burdeau and F. Ramone]. *Cahiers du Cinéma,* numéro spécial (May 1998).

"Le Plus-de-Voir" [on Godard's *Histoire(s) du cinéma*]. *Artpress*, hors série 1998.

"Politics and Philosophy" [interview with Peter Hallward]. *Angelaki* 3:3 (1998): 113–33.

"Théâtre et politique dans la comédie." In *Où va le théâtre?* ed. Jean-Pierre Thibaudat, 17–24. Paris: Hoëbeke, 1998.

"Théorie axiomatique du sujet: Notes du cours 1996–1998." Typescript [1998].

"Considérations sur l'état actuel du cinéma, et sur les moyens de penser cet état sans avoir à conclure que le cinéma est mort ou mourant." *L'Art du cinéma* 24 (Mar. 1999), 7–22.

"De la Langue française comme évidement." Typescript [1999].

"Entretien avec Alain Badiou" [interview with N. Poirier]. *Le Philosophoire* 9 (1999): 14–32.

"Les Langues de Wittgenstein." *Rue Descartes* 26 (Dec. 1999), 107–16 [my references are to the typescript, 1999].

"La Sainte-Alliance et ses serviteurs" [on Kosovo]. *Le Monde,* 20 May 1999 (available at http://www.lemonde.fr/article/0,2320,6246,00.html).

"La Scène du Deux." In *De l'Amour,* ed. L'Ecole de la Cause Freudienne, 177–90. Paris: Flammarion, "Champs." 1999 [my references are to the typescript]. [With other contributions by Roger Dragonetti, Alain Grosrichard, Brigitte Jaques, Charles Méla, and Jacques Roubaud.]

"Vide, séries, clairière: Essai sur la prose de Severo Sarduy." In Severo Sarduy, *Obras completas,* ed. François Wahl, vol. 2: 1619–25. Madrid: Galaxia Gutenberg, 1999 [my references are to the typescript].

"Art and Philosophy" [extract from *Petit manuel d'inesthétique*]. Trans. Jorge Jauregui. *lacanian ink* 17 (Autumn 2000): 51–67.

"L'Etre-là: Mathématique du transcendental." Typescript [2000].

"L'Existence et la mort." In *Philosopher T2: Les Interrogations contemporaines, matériaux pour un enseignement,* ed. Christian Delacampagne and Robert Maggiori, 293–302. Paris: Fayard, 2000. Trans. Alberto Toscano and Nina Power as "Existence and Death." *Discourse: Journal for Theoretical Studies in Media and Culture,* special issue titled *Mortals to Death* (forthcoming).

"Frege" and "On a Contemporary Usage of Frege" [extracts from *Le Nombre et les nombres*]. Trans. Justin Clemens and Sam Gillespie. *Umbr(a)* (Buffalo: State University of New York) *2000: Science and Truth* (2000): 99–113.

"Highly Speculative Reasoning on the Concept of Democracy." Trans. Jorge Jauregui. *lacanian ink* 16 (Spring 2000): 28–43.

"Huit thèses sur l'universel." In *Universel, singulier, sujet,* ed. Jelica Sumic, 11–20. Paris: Kimé, 2000 [my references are to the tapescript, held at the Collège International de Philosophie, Rue Descartes, Paris].

"Les Lieux de la philosophie." *Bleue: Littératures en force* 1 (Winter 2000): 120–25 [my references are to the typescript].

"Metaphysics and the Critique of Metaphysics." Trans. Alberto Toscano. *Pli (Warwick Journal of Philosophy)* 10 (2000): 174–90.

"Of Life As a Name of Being, or Deleuze's Vitalist Ontology" [translation of *Court traité d'ontologie transitoire,* chap. 4]. Trans. Alberto Toscano. *Pli (Warwick Journal of Philosophy)* 10 (2000): 191–99.

"Psychoanalysis and Philosophy." Trans. Oliver Feltham. *Analysis* (Melbourne) 9 (2000): 1–8.

"Saint Paul, fondateur du sujet universel." *Etudes Théologiques et Religieuses* 75 (Mar. 2000): 323–33.

"Sur *La Parole muette* de Jacques Rancière." *Horlieu-(x)* 18 (2000): 88–95.

"Une Tâche philosophique: Être contemporain de Pessoa." In *Colloque de Cerisy: Pessoa,* ed. Pascal Dethurens and Maria-Alzira Seixo, 141–55. Paris: Christian Bougois, 2000.

"Théâtre et philosophie." *Frictions* 2 (Spring 2000), 131–41.

"Un, Multiple, Multiplicité(s)" [on Deleuze]. *Multitudes* 1 (Mar. 2000): 195–211 [my references are to the typescript].

"Esquisse pour un premier manifeste de l'affirmationisme." Typescript [2001].

"Le Gardiennage du matin" [on Lyotard]. In *Jean-François Lyotard: L'Exercise du différend,* ed. Dolorès Lyotard, Jean-Claude Milner, and Gérard Sfez, 101–11. Paris: Presses Universitaires de France, 2001.

"On Evil: An Interview with Alain Badiou" [interview with Christoph Cox and Molly Whalen]. *Cabinet* 5 (Winter 2001): 69–74.

"The Political as a Procedure of Truth." Trans. Barbara P. Fulks. *lacanian ink* 19 (Fall 2001): 70–81.

"Who Is Nietzsche?" Trans. Alberto Toscano. *Pli (Warwick Journal of Philosophy)* 11 (2001): 1–11.

"Le Balcon du présent." Lecture given at the French Institute in London, 31 May 2002. Typescript [2002].

"The Caesura of Nihilism." Lecture given at the University of Cardiff, 25 May 2002. Typescript [2002].

"Depuis si longtemps, depuis si peu de temps" [on Françoise Proust]. *Rue Descartes* 33 (2002): 101–4.

"The Ethic of Truths: Construction and Potency." Trans. Thelma Sowley. *Pli (Warwick Journal of Philosophy)* 12 (2002): 245–55.

La Révolution culturelle: La dernière révolution? [pamphlet]. Paris: Les Conférences du Rouge-Gorge, Feb. 2002.

"Que penser? Que faire?" [on the French presidential elections of April 2002]. *Le Monde* 28 (April 2002). Trans. Norman Madarasz as "What Is to Be

Thought? What Is to Be Done?" *Counterpunch* 1, May 2002: http://
counterpunch.org/badiou0501.html. [Written with Sylvain Lazarus and
Natacha Michel.]

Works on Alain Badiou

Aguilar, Tristan. "Badiou et la Non-Philosophie: Un parallèle." In *La Non-
Philosophie des Contemporains*, ed. François Laruelle, 37–46. Paris: Kimé,
1995.

Alliez, Eric. "Que la vérité soit." In *De l'Impossibilité de la phénoménologie: Sur la
philosophie française contemporaine*, 81–87. Paris: Vrin, 1995.

———. "Badiou/Deleuze." *Futur antérieur* 43 (1998): 49–54.

———. "Badiou/Deleuze (II)." *Multitudes* 1 (2000): 192–94.

———. "Badiou: La grâce de l'universel." *Multitudes* 6 (2001): 26–34.

Barker, Jason. *Alain Badiou: A Critical Introduction*. London: Pluto, 2002.

Bensaïd, Daniel. "Alain Badiou et le miracle de l'événement." In *Résistances: Essai
de taupologie générale*, 143–70. Paris: Fayard, 2001.

Bosteels, Bruno. "Por una falta de política: Tesis sobre la filosofía de la democracia radical." *Acontecimiento: Revista para pensar la política* 17 (1999): 63–89.

———. "Travesías del fantasma: Pequeña metapolítica del '68 en México.'"
Metapolítica: Revista Trimestral de Teoría y Ciencia de la Política 12 (1999):
733–68.

———. "Alain Badiou's Theory of the Subject, Part I: The Re-commencement
of Dialectical Materialism." *Pli (Warwick Journal of Philosophy)* 12 (2002):
200–29.

———. "Alain Badiou's Theory of the Subject, Part II." *Pli (Warwick Journal of
Philosophy)* 13 (2002).

———. "Vérité et forçage: Badiou avec Heidegger et Lacan." In *Badiou: Penser le
multiple*, ed. Charles Ramond, 259–93. Paris: L'Harmattan, 2002.

———. *Badiou and the Political*. Durham, N.C.: Duke University Press,
forthcoming.

Brassier, Ray. "Stellar Void or Cosmic Animal? Badiou and Deleuze." *Pli (Warwick
Journal of Philosophy)* 10 (2000): 200–17.

Burchill, Louise. "Translator's Preface: Portraiture in Philosophy, or Shifting
Perspective." In Alain Badiou, *Deleuze: The Clamor of Being*, vii–xxiii.
Minneapolis: University of Minnesota Press, 1999.

Châtelet, Gilles. Rev. of *Le Nombre et les Nombres*. In *Annuaire philosophique
1989–1990*, 117–33. Paris: Seuil, 1991.

Clemens, Justin. "Platonic Meditations: The Work of Alain Badiou." *Pli (Warwick
Journal of Philosophy)* 11 (2001): 200–229.

Clucas, Stephen. "Poem, Theorem." *Parallax* 7:4 (2001): 48–65.

Critchley, Simon. "Demanding Approval: On the Ethics of Alain Badiou." *Radical Philosophy* 100 (2000): 16–27.

Desanti, Jean-Toussaint. "Quelques Remarques à propos de l'ontologie intrinsèque d'Alain Badiou." *Les Temps modernes* 526 (May 1990): 61–71.

Dews, Peter. "Uncategorical Imperatives: Adorno, Badiou, and the Ethical Turn." *Radical Philosophy* 111 (Jan. 2002): 33–37.

Feltham, Oliver. "As Fire Burns: Of Ontology, Praxis, and Functional Work." Ph.D. diss., Deakin University, May 2000.

Fink, Bruce. "Alain Badiou." *Umbr(a)* (Buffalo: State University of New York) 1 (1996): 11–12.

Gil, José. "Quatre méchantes notes sur un livre méchant." Rev. of Badiou, *Deleuze: Futur antérieur* 43 (1998): 71–84.

Gillespie, Sam. "Hegel Unsutured (An Addendum to Badiou)." *Umbr(a)* (Buffalo: State University of New York) 1 (1996): 57–69.

———. "Neighborhood of Infinity: On Badiou's *Deleuze: The Clamor of Being.*" *Umbr(a)* 2001: 91–106.

———. "To Place the Void: Badiou on Spinoza." *Angelaki* 6:3 (Dec. 2001): 63–67.

———. Rev. of Alain Badiou, *Ethics. Pli (Warwick Journal of Philosophy)* 12 (2002): 256–65.

Hallward, Peter. "Generic Sovereignty: The Philosophy of Alain Badiou." *Angelaki* 3:3 (1998): 87–111.

———. "Ethics without Others: A Reply to Simon Critchley." *Radical Philosophy* 102 (July 2000): 27–31.

———. Translator's introduction to Badiou, *Ethics*, vii–li.

———, ed. *Think Again: Alain Badiou and the Future of Philosophy.* London: Continuum Press, forthcoming. [With contributions by Etienne Balibar, Daniel Bensaïd, Bruno Bosteels, Ray Brassier, Jean-Toussaint Desanti, Peter Dews, Alex García Düttmann, Ernesto Laclau, Jean-Jacques Lecercle, Todd May, Jean-Luc Nancy, Ed Pluth and Dominiek Hoens, Jacques Rancière, Daniel Smith, Alberto Toscano, Slavoj Žižek, and Alenka Zupančič.]

Hyldgaard, Kirsten. "Truth and Knowledge in Heidegger, Lacan, and Badiou." *Umbr(a)* 2001: 79–90.

Ichida, Yoshihiko. "Sur quelques vides ontologiques" [on Badiou and Negri]. *Multitudes* 9 (May 2002): 49–65.

Jambet, Christian. "Alain Badiou: *L'Etre et l'événement.*" In *Annuaire philosophique 1987–1988*, 141–83. Paris: Seuil, 1989.

Kouvélakis, Eustache. "La Politique dans ses limites, ou les paradoxes d'Alain Badiou." *Actuel Marx* 28 (2000): 39–54.

Lacoue-Labarthe, Philippe. Untitled discussion of *L'Etre et l'événement. Cahiers du Collège International de philosophie* 8 (1989): 201–10.

———. "Poésie, philosophie, politique." In *La Politique des poètes: Pourquoi des poètes en temps de détresse,* ed. Jacques Rancière, 39–63. Paris: Albin Michel, 1992.

Laerke, Mogens. "The Voice and the Name: Spinoza in the Badioudian Critique of Deleuze." *Pli (Warwick Journal of Philosophy)* 8 (1999): 86–99.

Lecercle, Jean-Jacques. "Cantor, Lacan, Mao, Beckett, *même combat:* The Philosophy of Alain Badiou." *Radical Philosophy* 93 (Jan. 1999): 6–13.

Lyotard, Jean-François. Untitled discussion of *L'Etre et l'événement: Cahiers du Collège International de philosophie* 8 (1989): 227–46.

Madarasz, Norman. Translator's introduction to *Manifesto for Philosophy,* by Alain Badiou. Albany: State University of New York Press, 1999.

Ophir, Adi, and Ariella Azoulay, "The Contraction of Being: Deleuze after Badiou." *Umbr(a)* 2001: 107–20.

Pesson, René. Rev. of *Manifeste pour la philosophie.* In *Annuaire philosophique 1988–1989,* 243–51. Paris: Seuil, 1989.

Ramond, Charles, ed. *Alain Badiou: Penser le multiple* [papers given at the international conference on Badiou, Bordeaux, 21–23 Oct. 1999]. Paris: L'Harmattan, 2002.

Rancière, Jacques. Untitled discussion of *L'Etre et l'événement. Cahiers du Collège International de philosophie* 8 (1989): 211–26.

Riera, Gabriel, ed. *Alain Badiou: Philosophy under Conditions.* In preparation.

Simont, Juliette. "Le Pur et l'impur (sur deux questions de l'histoire de la philosophie dans *L'Etre et l'événement).*" *Les Temps modernes* 526 (May 1990): 27–60.

Terray, Emmanuel. "La Politique dans *L'Etre et l'événement.*" *Les Temps modernes* 526 (May 1990): 72–78.

Toscano, Alberto. "To Have Done with the End of Philosophy" [rev. of Badiou's *Manifesto* and *Deleuze*]. *Pli (Warwick Journal of Philosophy)* 9 (2000): 220–39.

Toscano, Alberto, and Ray Brassier, eds. Introduction to *Badiou: Theoretical Writings.* London: Continuum, forthcoming.

Verstraeten, Pierre. "Philosophies de l'événement: Badiou et quelques autres." *Les Temps modernes* 529–30 (Aug. 1990): 241–94.

Villani, Arnaud. "La Métaphysique de Deleuze" [critique of Badiou's *Deleuze*]. *Futur antérieur* 43 (1998): 55–70.

Wahl, François. "Le Soustractif." Preface to *Conditions,* by Alain Badiou, 9–54. Paris: Seuil, 1992.

Žižek, Slavoj. "The Politics of Truth, or, Alain Badiou as a Reader of St. Paul." In *The Ticklish Subject,* 127–70. [An abridged version of this essay appeared as "Psychoanalysis in Post-Marxism: The Case of Alain Badiou" in *South Atlantic Quarterly* 97:2 (Spring 1998): 235–61.]

———. "Political Subjectivization and its Vicissitudes." In *The Ticklish Subject*, 171–243.

Other Works Cited

Abian, Alexander. *The Theory of Sets*. Philadelphia: Saunders, 1965.

Adorno, Theodor. "The Actuality of Philosophy" [1931]. Trans. Benjamin Snow. *Telos* 31 (Spring 1977): 120–33.

———. *Prisms: Cultural Criticism and Society*. Trans. Samuel and Shierry Weber. London: Neville Spearman, 1967.

———. *Negative Dialectics*. Trans. E. B. Ashton. London: Routledge, 1973.

———. *Minima Moralia: Reflections from a Damaged Life*. Trans. E. F. N. Jephcott. London: New Left Books, 1974.

———. *Against Epistemology*. Trans. Willis Domingo. Oxford: Blackwell, 1982.

———. *Dialectic of Enlightenment*. Trans. John Cumming. New York: Continuum, 1993.

———. *Aesthetic Theory*. Trans. and ed. Robert Hullot-Kentor. London: Athlone Press, 1997.

Agamben, Giorgio. *The Coming Community*. Trans. Michael Hardt. Minneapolis: University of Minnesota Press, 1993.

———. *Homo Sacer: Sovereign Power and Bare Life*. Trans. Daniel Heller-Roazen. Stanford, Calif.: Stanford University Press, 1998.

———. *Potentialities: Collected Essays in Philosophy*. Ed. and trans. Daniel Heller-Roazen. Stanford, Calif.: Stanford University Press, 1999.

Ahmad, Aijaz. *In Theory: Classes, Nations, Literatures*. London: Verso, 1992.

Althusser, Louis. *Pour Marx*. Paris: Maspéro, 1965. Trans. Ben Brewster. London: Verso, 1979.

Althusser, Louis. *Lenin and Philosophy*. Trans. Ben Brewster. London: New Left Books, 1971.

———. *Philosophy and the Spontaneous Philosophy of the Scientists*. Ed. Gregory Elliott. London: Verso, 1990.

Althusser, Louis, et al. *Reading Capital*. Trans. Ben Brewster. London: Verso, 1977.

Anderson, Benedict. *Imagined Communities* [1983]. London: Verso, 1991.

Aristotle. *The Complete Works of Aristotle: The Revised Oxford Translation*. 2 vols. Revised by Jonathan Barnes. Princeton, N.J.: Princeton University Press, 1984.

Asperti, Andrea, and Longo, Guiseppe. *Categories, Types and Structures*. Cambridge, Mass.: MIT Press, 1991.

Ayer, Alfred Jules. *Language, Truth, and Logic* [1936]. London: Victory Gollancz, 1958.

Balibar, Etienne. "Ambiguous Universality." *Differences* 7:1 (1995): 48–74.

———. *La Crainte des masses*. Paris: Galilée, 1997.

Beckett, Samuel. *L'Innommable*. Paris: Minuit, 1953.

———. *Comment c'est*. Paris: Minuit, 1960.

———. *Worstward Ho!* London: John Calder, 1982.

Benacerraf, Paul, and Hilary Putnam, eds. *Philosophy of Mathematics: Selected Readings*, 2nd ed. Cambridge, U.K.: Cambridge University Press, 1983.

Benjamin, Walter. *Illuminations: Essays and Reflections*. Trans. Harry Zohn. New York: Schocken Books, 1969.

Bergson, Henri. *La Pensée et le mouvant* [1938]. Paris: Presses Universitaires de France, 1990.

———. *L'Evolution créatice*. Paris: Presses Universitaires de France, 1941.

Bernadete, José A. *Infinity: An Essay in Metaphysics*. Oxford: Oxford University Press, 1964.

Bernstein, Richard J., ed. *Habermas and Modernity*. Cambridge, U.K.: Polity, 1985.

Beth, Evert W. *Mathematical Thought: An Introduction to the Philosophy of Mathematics*. Dordrecht, the Netherlands: Reidel, 1965.

Blanchot, Maurice. *La Communauté inavouable*. Paris: Minuit, 1983. Trans. Pierre Joris. Barrytown, N.Y.: Station Hill Press, 1988.

Boolos, George. *Logic Logic and Logic*. Cambridge, Mass.: Harvard University Press, 1998.

Bossuet, Jacques. *Politique tirée de l'écriture sainte par ses propres paroles*. In *Oeuvres choisies*. Paris: Hachette, 1865, vol. 2.

Bourdieu, Pierre. "Universal Corporatism: The Role of Intellectuals in the Modern World." *Poetics Today* 12:4 (1991): 655–69.

———. *Les Règles de l'art: Genèse et structure du champ littéraire*. Paris: Seuil, 1992. Trans. Susan Emanuel. Stanford, Calif.: Stanford University Press, 1996.

———. *Raisons pratiques*. Paris: Seuil, 1994. Trans. Randal Johnson and Gisela Sapiro. Stanford, Calif.: Stanford University Press, 1998.

———. *Méditations pascaliennes*. Paris: Seuil, 1997.

———. *Contre-feux: Propos pour servir à la résistance contre l'invasion néo-libérale*. Paris: Liber-Raisons d'Agir, 1998.

———. "A Reasoned Utopia and Economic Fatalism." *New Left Review* 227 (Jan. 1998): 125–30.

Bourdieu, Pierre, ed. *La Misère du monde*. Paris: Seuil, 1993.

Bourseiller, Christophe. *Les Maoïstes: La folle histoire des gardes rouges françaises*. Paris: Plon, 1996.

Bowie, Malcolm. *Lacan*. London: Fontana, 1991.

Boyer, Carl Benjamin. *A History of Mathematics*. New York: Wiley, 1968.

Brook, Peter. *Platform Papers* 6. London: Royal National Theatre, 1994.

———. *Between Two Silences: Talking with Peter Brook*. Ed. Dale Moffitt. London: Methuen, 2000.

Brouwer, Luitzen Egbertus Jan. *Collected Works*. 2 vols. Amsterdam: North Holland, 1976.

Brown, James Robert. *Philosophy of Mathematics: An Introduction to the World of Proofs and Pictures*. London: Routledge, 1999.

Brunschvicg, Léon. *La Modalité du jugement*. Paris: Presses Universitaires de France, 1964.

Butler, Judith. *Bodies That Matter: On the Discursive Limits of "Sex."* London: Routledge: 1993.

Cabral, Amilcar. *Return to the Source: Selected Speeches of Amilcar Cabral*. New York: Monthly Review Press, 1973.

Canguilhem, Georges. *Vie et mort de Jean Cavaillès*. Ville-franche, France: Pierre Laleur, Les Carnets de Baudasser, 1976.

Cantor, Georg. *Contributions to the Founding of the Theory of Transfinite Numbers*. Trans. Philip Jourdain. Chicago: Open Court, 1915.

———. "Foundations of the General Theory of Manifolds." *The Campaigner (The Theoretical Journal of the National Caucus of Labor Committees)* 9 (Jan.–Feb. 1976): 69–96.

Carnap, Rudolph. *The Logical Syntax of Language*. New York: Kegan Paul, 1937.

Cavaillès, Jean. *Sur la logique et la théorie de la science* [1947]. Paris: Vrin, 1997.

Chaitin, Gilbert D. *Rhetoric and Culture in Lacan*. Cambridge, U.K.: Cambridge University Press, 1996.

Chévallier, Jean-Jacques. *Histoire de la pensée politique*, vol. 1. Paris: Payot, 1979.

Cohen, Paul J. *Set Theory and the Continuum Hypothesis*. New York: W. A. Benjamin, 1966.

Cohen, Paul J., and Reuben Hersh. "Non-Cantorian Set Theory." *Scientific American* 217 (Dec. 1967): 104–18.

Comte, Auguste. *Auguste Comte and Positivism: The Essential Writings*. Ed. Gertrud Lenzer. Chicago: University of Chicago Press, 1975.

Conway, John Horton. *On Numbers and Games*. London: Academic Press, 1976.

Copjec, Joan. *Read My Desire: Lacan against the Historicists*. Cambridge, Mass.: MIT Press, 1994.

Corbin, Henri. *Histoire de la philosophie islamique* [1964, 1974]. Paris: Gallimard, Folio, 1986.

———. *En Islam iranien*, vol. 1. Paris: Gallimard, 1971.

Crossley, John N., C. S. Ash, A. C. Brickhill, J. C. Stillwell, and N. H. Williams. *What Is Mathematical Logic?* [1972]. New York: Dover, 1990.

Dales, H. Garth, and Gianluigi Oliveri, eds. *Truth in Mathematics*. Oxford: Oxford University Press, 1998.

Dauben, Joseph Warren. *Georg Cantor: His Mathematics and Philosophy of the Infinite*. Cambridge, Mass.: Harvard University Press, 1979.

———. "Conceptual Revolutions and the History of Mathematics" [1984]. In *Revolutions in Mathematics*, ed. Donald Gillies, 49–71. Oxford: Oxford University Press, 1992.

Davis, Philip J., and Reuben Hersh. *The Mathematical Experience*. Harmondsworth, U.K.: Penguin, 1980.

———. *Descartes' Dream: The World according to Mathematics*. New York: Harcourt Brace Jovanovich, 1986.

de Beauvoir, Simone. *Le Deuxième sexe*. Paris: Gallimard, 1949. 2 vols. Trans. H. M. Parshley. New York: Vintage, 1974.

Deleuze, Gilles. *Empirisme et subjectivité*. Paris: Presses Universitaires de France, 1953. Trans. Constantin Boundas. New York: Columbia University Press, 1991.

———. *Nietzsche et la philosophie*. Paris: Presses Universitaires de France, 1962. Trans. Hugh Tomlinson. Minneapolis: University of Minnesota Press, 1983.

———. *Le Bergsonisme*. Paris: Presses Universitaires de France, 1966. Trans. Hugh Tomlinson and Barbara Habberjam. New York: Zone, 1988.

———. *Différence et répétition*. Paris: Presses Universitaires de France, 1968. Trans. Paul Patton. New York: Columbia University Press, 1994.

———. *L'Idée d'expression dans la philosophie de Spinoza*. Paris: Minuit, 1968. Trans. Martin Joughin. New York: Zone, 1990.

———. *Logique du sens*. Paris: Minuit, 1969. Trans. Mark Lester with Charles Stivale. New York: Columbia University Press, 1990.

———. *Cinéma 2: L'Image-temps*. Paris: Minuit, 1985. Trans. Hugh Tomlinson and Robert Galeta Habberjam. Minneapolis: University of Minnesota Press, 1989.

———. *Le Pli: Leibniz et le baroque*. Paris: Minuit, 1988. Trans. Tom Conley. Minneapolis: University of Minnesota Press, 1993.

———. *L'Epuisé*. Paris: Minuit, 1992.

Deleuze, Gilles, and Félix Guattari. *Mille plateaux*. Paris: Minuit, 1980. Trans. Brian Massumi. Minneapolis: University of Minnesota Press, 1986.

———. *Qu'est-ce que la philosophie?* Paris: Minuit, 1991. Trans. Hugh Tomlinson and Graham Burchell. New York: Columbia University Press, 1994.

Deleuze, Gilles, and Claire Parnet. *Dialogues* [1977]. Paris: Flammarion, "Champs," 1996. Trans. Hugh Tomlinson and Barbara Habberjam. New York: Columbia University Press, 1987.

Derrida, Jacques. *Psyché: Inventions de l'autre*. Paris: Galilée, 1987.

———. *De l'esprit: Heidegger et la question*. Paris: Galilée, 1988.

———. *Spectres de Marx*. Paris: Editions Galilée, 1993.

———. *Donner la mort: L'Ethique du don, Jacques Derrida et la pensée du don*.

Ed. Jean-Michel Rabaté and Michael Wetzel. Paris: Transition, 1992. Trans. David Wills. Chicago: University of Chicago Press, 1995.

———. *Points de suspension: Entretiens.* Ed. Elisabeth Weber. Paris: Editions Galilée, 1992.

Descartes, René. *Philosophical Writings.* 2 vols. Ed. and trans. John Cottingham, Robert Stoothoff, and Dugald Murdoch. Cambridge, U.K.: Cambridge University Press, 1985.

Devlin, Keith. *The Axiom of Constructibility.* New York: Springer-Verlag, 1977.

———. *Fundamentals of Contemporary Set Theory.* New York: Springer-Verlag, 1979.

———. *Mathematics: The New Golden Age.* Harmondsworth, U.K.: Penguin, 1988.

Dews, Peter. *Logics of Disintegration.* London: Verso, 1987.

Dirlik, Arif. *After the Revolution: Waking to Global Capitalism.* Hanover, N.H.: Wesleyan University Press, 1994.

Dummett, Michael. *Elements of Intuitionism.* Oxford: Oxford University Press, 1977.

———. *Truth and Other Enigmas.* London: Duckworth, 1978.

———. *The Seas of Language.* Oxford: Oxford University Press, 1993.

———. *The Origins of Analytic Philosophy.* London: Duckworth, 1994.

Düttmann, Alexander García. *Between Cultures: Tensions in the Struggle for Recognition.* London: Verso, 2000.

Eagleton, Terry. "Nationalism: Irony and Commitment." In Terry Eagleton, Fredric James, and Edward Said, *Nationalism, Colonialism, and Literature.* Minneapolis: University of Minnesota Press, 1990.

Ehrlich, Philip, ed. *Real Numbers, Generalisations of the Reals, and Theories of Continua.* Dordrecht, the Netherlands: Kluwer, 1994.

Euclid. *Elements.* Ed. Thomas L. Heath. 3 vols. New York: Dover, 1956.

Eves, Howard. *An Introduction to the History of Mathematics.* New York: Holt, Rinehart and Winston, 1975.

Eze, Emmanuel Chukwudi, ed. *Postcolonial African Philosophy: A Critical Reader.* Oxford: Blackwell, 1996.

Fanon, Frantz. *Les Damnés de la terre* [1961]. Paris: Gallimar, "Folio," 1991. Trans. Constance Farrington. New York: Grove Press, 1991.

Feyerabend, Paul. *Against Method.* London: New Left Books, 1975.

Fields, A. Belden. *Trotskyism and Maoism: Theory and Practice in France and the United States.* New York: Praeger, 1988.

Fink, Bruce. *The Lacanian Subject: Between Language and Jouissance.* Princeton, N.J.: Princeton University Press, 1995.

———. *A Clinical Introduction to Lacanian Psychoanalysis: Theory and Technique.* Cambridge, Mass.: Harvard University Press, 1997.

Fink, Bruce, Richard Feldstein, and Maire Jaanus, eds. *Reading Seminars I and II: Lacan's Return to Freud.* Albany: SUNY Press, 1986.

Fowler, David. *The Mathematics of Plato's Academy: A New Reconstruction.* Oxford: Oxford University Press, 1999.

Fraenkel, Abraham A. *Set Theory and Logic.* Reading, Mass.: Addison-Wesley, 1966.

Fraenkel, Abraham A., and Yehoshua Bar-Hillel. *Foundations of Set Theory.* Amsterdam: North Holland, 1973.

Frascolla, Pasquale. *Wittgenstein's Philosophy of Mathematics.* London: Routledge, 1994.

Frege, Gottlob. *The Foundations of Arithmetic.* Trans. J. L. Austin. Oxford: Blackwell, 1950.

Furet, François. *Penser la révolution française.* Paris: Gallimard, 1978.

Girard, René. *Mensonge romantique et vérité romanesque.* Paris: Grasset, 1961.

Gödel, Kurt. "What Is Cantor's Continuum Problem?" In *Philosophy of Mathematics,* ed. Benacerraf and Putnam, 470–85.

———. *Collected Works.* Ed. Soloman Feferman. 2 vols. Oxford: Oxford University Press, 1986.

Gonshor, Harry. *Introduction to the Theory of Surreal Numbers.* Cambridge, U.K.: Cambridge University Press, 1986.

Gourevitch, Philip. *We Wish to Inform You That Tomorrow We Will Be Killed with Our Families.* New York: Picador, 1998.

Grattan-Guinness, Ivor, ed. *Companion Encyclopaedia of the History and Philosophy of the Mathematical Sciences.* 2 vols. London: Routlege, 1994.

Gutting, Gary. *French Philosophy in the Twentieth Century.* Cambridge, U.K.: Cambridge University Press, 2001.

Habermas, Jürgen. *The Theory of Communicative Action,* vol 1. Trans. Thomas McCarthy. Boston: Beacon Press, 1984.

———. *The Philosophical Discourse of Modernity.* Cambridge, Mass.: MIT Press, 1987.

———. *Between Facts and Norms: Contributions to a Discourse Theory of Law and Democracy.* Trans. William Rehg. Cambridge, Mass.: MIT Press, 1996.

Hallett, Michael. *Cantorian Set Theory and Limitation of Size.* Oxford: Oxford University Press, 1984.

Hallward, Peter. "Deleuze and the Redemption from Interest." *Radical Philosophy* 81 (Jan. 1997): 6–21.

———. "Deleuze and the 'World without Others.'" *Philosophy Today* 41 (Winter 1997): 530–44.

————. "The Limits of Individuation, or How to Distinguish Deleuze from Foucault." *Angelaki* 5:2 (Aug. 2000): 93–112.

————. "The Singular and the Specific: Recent French Philosophy." *Radical Philosophy* 99 (Jan. 2000): 6–18.

Hatcher, William S. *The Logical Foundations of Mathematics.* Oxford: Pergamon Press, 1982.

Hawking, Stephen W. *A Brief History of Time.* New York: Bantam Books, 1988.

Hegel, Georg W. F. *The Science of Logic.* Trans. A. V. Miller. London: Allen and Unwin, 1969.

————. *The Phenomenology of Spirit.* Trans. A. V. Miller. Oxford: Oxford University Press, 1970.

————. *Elements of the Philosophy of Right.* Ed. Allen W. Wood. Cambridge, U.K.: Cambridge University Press, 1991.

————. *The Encyclopaedia Logic.* Trans. T. F. Geraets. Indianapolis: Hackett, 1991.

Heidegger, Martin. *Being and Time.* Trans. John Macquarrie and Edward Robinson. New York: Harper and Row, 1962.

————. *Discourse on Thinking.* Trans. J. M. Anderson and E. H. Freund. New York: Harper and Row, 1966.

————. *On Time and Being.* Trans. Joan Stambaugh. New York: Harper and Row, 1972.

————. "Only a God Can Save Us" [the *Spiegel* interview]. Trans. William J. Richardson. In *Heidegger: The Man and the Thinker,* ed. Thomas Sheehan, 45–67. Chicago: Precedent, 1981.

————. *Basic Writings.* Ed. David Farrell Krell. London: Harper Collins, 1993.

Heller, Agnes, and Ferenc Feher. *The Grandeur and Twilight of Radical Universalism.* New Brunswick, N.J.: Transaction Publishers, 1991.

Hobbes, Thomas. *Leviathan.* Ed. C. B. Macpherson. Harmondsworth, U.K.: Penguin, 1968.

Hofstadter, Douglas R. *Gödel, Escher, Bach: An Eternal Golden Braid.* London: Harvester Press, 1979.

Hollier, Denis. *Les Dépossédés (Bataille, Caillois, Leiris, Malraux, Sartre).* Paris: Minuit, 1993. Trans. Catherine Porter as *Absent without Leave: French Literature under the Threat of War.* Cambridge, Mass.: Harvard University Press, 1997.

Hrbacek, Karel, and Thomas Jech. *Introduction to Set Theory.* New York: Marcel Dekker, 1978.

Hume, David. *A Treatise of Human Nature.* Ed. David Fate Norton and Mary J. Norton. Oxford: Oxford University Press, 2000.

Inwood, Michael. *Hegel.* London: Routledge, 1983.

Irigaray, Luce. *Ce Sexe qui n'en est pas un.* Paris: Minuit, 1977. Trans. Catherine Porter with Carolyn Burke. Ithaca, N.Y.: Cornell University Press, 1985.

—. *Ethique de la différence sexuelle.* Paris: Minuit, 1984. Trans. Carolyn Burke and Gillian C. Gill. London: Athlone Press, 1993.

—. *Sexes et parentés.* Paris: Minuit, 1987. Trans. Gillian C. Gill. New York: Columbia University Press, 1993.

—. *Le Temps de la différence: Pour une révolution pacifique.* Paris: Librarie générale française, 1989. Trans. Karin Montin. London: Athlone Press, 1994.

—. *Je, Tu, Nous: Pour une culture de la différence.* Paris: Grasset, 1990. Trans. Alison Martin. London: Routledge, 1993.

—. *Irigaray Reader.* Ed. Margaret Whitford. Oxford: Blackwell, 1991.

—. *J'aime à toi: Esquisse d'une félicité dans l'histoire.* Paris: Grasset, 1992. Trans. Alison Martin. London: Routledge, 1994.

—, ed. *Sexes et genres à travers les langues: Éléments de communication sexuelle.* Paris: Grasset, 1990.

Jameson, Fredric. *Postmodernism, or the Cultural Logic of Late Capitalism.* Durham, N.C.: Duke University Press, 1991.

Jaspers, Karl. *Reason and Existenz.* Trans. William Earle. London: Routledge, 1956.

Johnstone, P. T. *Topos Theory.* London: Academic Press, 1977.

Juranville, Alain. *Lacan et la philosophie.* Paris: Presses Universitaires de France, 1988.

Kant, Immanuel. *Opus Postumum.* Trans. Eckhart Forster and Michael Rosen. Cambridge, U.K.: Cambridge University Press, 1993.

—. *Critique of Pure Reason.* Trans. Werner S. Pluhar. Indianapolis: Hackett, 1996. [The page references to this and all other references to Kant's works are, as is customary, to the standard German edition.]

—. *Critique of Practical Reason.* Trans. Mary Gregor. Cambridge, U.K.: Cambridge University Press, 1997.

—. *Groundwork of the Metaphysics of Morals.* Trans. Mary Gregor. Cambridge, U.K.: Cambridge University Press, 1997.

Kaplan, Robert. *The Nothing That Is: A Natural History of Zero.* London: Penguin, 2000.

Kessel, Patrick, ed. *Le Mouvement maoïste en France.* 2 vols. Paris: Union Génerale d'Editions, 10/18, 1972 and 1978.

Kirk, G. S., and J. E. Raven, eds. *The Presocratic Philosophers.* Cambridge, U.K.: Cambridge University Press, 1957.

Kitcher, Philip. *The Nature of Mathematical Knowledge.* Oxford: Oxford University Press, 1984.

Kitcher, Philip, and William Aspray, eds. *History and Philosophy of Modern Mathematics*. Minneapolis: University of Minnesota Press, 1988.

Kline, Morris. *Mathematical Thought from Ancient to Modern Times*. Oxford: Oxford University Press, 1972.

———. *Mathematics and the Search for Knowledge*. Oxford: Oxford University Press, 1985.

Koselleck, Reinhardt. *Critique and Crisis*. Cambridge, Mass.: MIT Press, 1988.

Koyré, Alexandre. *From the Closed World to the Infinite Universe*. Baltimore: Johns Hopkins University Press, 1957.

———. *Galileo Studies* [1966]. Trans. John Mepham. Atlantic Highlands, N.J.: Harvester Press, 1978.

Krivine, Jean-Louis. *Introduction to Axiomatic Set Theory*. Trans. David Miller. Dordrecht, the Netherlands: Reidel, 1971.

Kuhn, Thomas. *The Structure of Scientific Revolutions*. Chicago: University of Chicago Press, 1970.

Lacan, Jacques. *Ecrits*. Paris: Seuil, 1966. Abridged trans. Alan Sheridan. London: Tavistock, 1977.

———. *Le Séminaire XI*. Ed. Jacques-Alain Miller. Paris: Seuil, 1973. Trans. Alan Sheridan. New York: Norton, 1988.

———. *Le Séminaire I*. Ed. Jacques-Alain Miller. Paris: Seuil, 1975. Trans. John Forrester. New York: Norton, 1988.

———. *Le Séminaire XX*. Ed. Jacques-Alain Miller. Paris: Seuil, 1975.

———. *Le Séminaire II*. Ed. Jacques-Alain Miller. Paris: Seuil, 1978. Trans. Sylvana Tomaselli. New York: Norton, 1988.

———. *Le Séminaire III*. Ed. Jacques-Alain Miller. Paris: Seuil, 1981. Trans. Russell Grigg. London: Routledge, 1988.

———. *Le Séminaire VII*. Ed. Jacques-Alain Miller. Paris: Seuil, 1986. Trans. Denis Porter. London: Routledge, 1988.

———. *Le Séminaire XVII*. Ed. Jacques-Alain Miller. Paris: Seuil, 1991.

Laclau, Ernesto, and Chantal Mouffe. *Hegemony and Socialist Strategy*. London: Verso, 1985.

Lacoue-Labarthe, Philippe. *La Fiction du politique*. Paris: Christian Bourgois, 1990. Trans. Chris Turner. Oxford: Blackwell, 1990.

Lacoue-Labarthe, Philippe, and Jean-Luc Nancy. *Le Mythe nazi*. Paris: L'Aube, 1991.

Lakatos, Imre. *Proofs and Refutations*. Cambridge, U.K.: Cambridge University Press, 1976.

———. *Philosophical Papers*. 2 vols. Cambridge, U.K.: Cambridge University Press, 1978.

Lardreau, Guy. *La Véracité*. Lagrasse, France: Verdier, 1993.

Lardreau, Guy, with Christian Jambet. *L'Ange*. Paris: Grasset, 1976.

Lavine, Shaughan. *Understanding the Infinite*. Cambridge, Mass.: Harvard University Press, 1994.

Lazarus, Neil. *Nationalism and Cultural Practice in the Postcolonial World*. Cambridge, U.K.: Cambridge University Press, 1999.

Lazarus, Neil, Steven Evans, Anthony Arnove, and Anne Menke. "The Necessity of Universalism." *Differences* 7:1 (1995), 75–145.

Lazarus, Sylvain. *L'Anthropologie du nom*. Paris: Seuil, 1996.

Leibniz, Gottfried W. *Philosophical Works*. Ed. and trans. R. S. Woolhouse and Richard Franks. Oxford: Oxford University Press, 1998.

———. *New Essays*. Trans. Peter Remnant and Jonathan Bennett. Cambridge, U.K.: Cambridge University Press, 1981.

Lenin, Vladimir. *Selected Works*. 3 vols. Moscow: Progress Publishers, 1967.

Levinas, Emmanuel. *Totalité et infini* [1961]. Paris: Librairie Général Française, "Livre de Poche," 1990. Trans. Alphonso Lingis. Pittsburgh, Pa.: Duquesne University Press, 1969.

———. *Basic Philosophical Writings*. Ed. Adriaan T. Peperzak, Simon Critchley, and Robert Bernasconi. Bloomington: University of Indiana Press, 1996.

Linhart, Robert. *L'Etabli*. Paris: Minuit, 1981.

Locke, John. *Essay Concerning Human Understanding*. Ed. Roger Woolhouse. London: Penguin, 1997.

Lucas, John Randolph. *Conceptual Roots of Mathematics*. London: Routledge, 2000.

Luxemburg, Rosa. *Rosa Luxemburg Speaks*. Ed. Mary Alice Waters. New York: Pathfinder Press, 1970.

Lyotard, Jean-François. *La Condition postmoderne*. Paris: Minuit, 1979. Trans. Geoff Benington and Brian Massumi. Minneapolis: University of Minnesota Press, 1984.

———. "Réponse à la question: qu'est-ce que le postmoderne? *Critique* 419 (April 1982): 357–67.

———. *Le Différend*. Paris: Minuit, 1984. Trans. George Van Den Abbeele. Minneapolis: University of Minnesota Press, 1988.

———. *Leçons sur l'analytique du sublime*. Paris: Galilée, 1991. Trans. Elizabeth Rottenberg. Stanford, Calif.: Stanford University Press, 1994.

Lyotard, Jean-François, and Jean-Loup Thébaud. *Au juste*. Paris: Christian Bourgois, 1979. Trans. Wlad Godzich. Minneapolis: University of Minnesota Press, 1985.

Maddy, Penelope. "Believing the Axioms." *Journal of Symbolic Logic* 53:2 and 53:3 (1988): 481–511, 736–64.

———. *Realism in Mathematics*. Oxford: Oxford University Press, 1990.

Mallarmé, Stéphane. *Oeuvres complètes.* Paris: Gallimard, Pléiade, 1950.

Malraux, André. *L'Espoir* [1937]. Paris: Gallimard, Folio, 1995.

Maor, Eli. *To Infinity and Beyond: A Cultural History of the Infinite.* Boston: Birhäuer, 1987.

Marini, Marcelle. *Lacan: The French Context* [1986]. Trans. Anne Tomiche. New Brunswick, N.J.: Rutgers University Press, 1992.

Marx, Karl. *Early Writings.* Trans. Rodney Livingstone and Gregor Benton. New York: Vintage Books, 1975.

———. *Capital,* vol. 1. Trans. Ben Fowkes. New York: Vintage, 1977.

Marx, Karl, and Friedrich Engels. *The Communist Manifesto.* Trans. Samuel Moore. Harmondsworth, U.K.: Penguin, 1967.

Matthews, Eric. *Twentieth Century French Philosophy.* Oxford: Oxford University Press, 1996.

Mayr, Ernst. *One Long Argument: Charles Darwin and the Genesis of Modern Evolutionary Thought.* Cambridge, Mass.: Harvard University Press, 1991.

McLarty, Colin. *Elementary Categories, Elementary Toposes.* Oxford: Oxford University Press, 1992.

Merleau-Ponty, Maurice. *Phénoménologie de la perception.* Paris: Gallimard, 1945.

———. *La Prose du monde.* Paris: Gallimard, 1969.

Miller, Jacques-Alain. "Suture: Eléments de la logique du signifiant." *Cahiers pour l'analyse* 1 (1966): 37–49.

Milner, Jean-Claude. "Lacan and the Ideal of Science." In *Lacan and the Human Sciences,* ed. Alexandre Leupin, 27–42. Lincoln: University of Nebraska Press, 1991.

Miquel, André, ed. and trans. *Du Désert d'Arabie aux jardins d'Espagne: Chefs-d'oeuvre de la poésie arabe classique.* Paris: Sindbad, 1992.

Moi, Toril. *Sexual/Textual Politics.* London: Methuen, 1985.

Moore, A. W. *The Infinite.* London: Routledge, 1990.

Mudimbe, V. Y. *The Invention of Africa: Gnosis, Philosophy, and the Order of Knowledge.* Bloomington: Indiana University Press, 1988.

Murdoch, Iris. *The Fire and the Sun: Why Plato Banished the Artists.* Oxford: Oxford University Press, 1977.

Nancy, Jean-Luc. *La Communauté désoeuvrée.* Paris: Christian Bourgois, 1986.

———. *Etre singulier multiple.* Paris: Galilée, 1996.

Newman, James R., ed. *World of Mathematics.* 4 vols. New York: Simon and Schuster, 1956.

Newton, Isaac. *Principia.* Trans. Motte-Cajori. Berkeley: University of California Press, 1947.

Nietzsche, Friedrich. *The Gay Science.* Trans. Walter Kaufmann. New York: Vintage, 1974.

Pascal, Blaise. *Oeuvres complètes*. Paris: Gallimard, Pléiade, 1954.

Picot, Gilbert. *Cardin Le Bret*. Paris: Hachette, 1948.

Piven, Frances Fox, and Richard A. Cloward. *Poor People's Movements*. New York: Pantheon, 1977.

Plato. *The Collected Dialogues*. Ed. Edith Hamilton and Huntington Cairns. Princeton, N.J.: Princeton University Press, 1961.

Plotinus. *The Aenneads*. Trans. Stephen Mackenna. London: Faber and Faber, 1969.

Proclus. *The Elements of Theology*. Ed. and trans. E. R. Dodds. Oxford: Oxford University Press, 1963.

Proust, Marcel. *Le Temps retrouvé*. Ed. Jean Milly. Paris: GF Flammarion, 1986.

——. *Le Côté de Guermantes II*. Ed. Jean Milly. Paris: GF Flammarion, 1987.

——. *Sodome et Gomorrhe I*. Ed. Jean Milly. Paris: GF Flammarion, 1987.

Reid, Constance. *Hilbert*. London: Allen and Unwin, 1970.

Renaut, Alain. *L'Ere de l'individu*. Paris: Gallimard, 1989.

——. *L'Individu*. Paris: Hatier, 1995.

Richelieu, Armand Jean du Plessis, duc de. *Testament politique*. Paris: L. André, 1947.

Robinson, Abraham. *Non-Standard Analysis*. Amsterdam: North Holland, 1966.

——. *Selected Papers*, vol. 2. Ed. H. Jerome Keisler and S. Korner. New Haven, Conn.: Yale University Press, 1979.

Roitman, Judith. *Introduction to Modern Set Theory*. New York: Wiley, 1990.

Rosen, Charles. *The Classical Style: Haydn, Mozart, Beethoven* [1976]. New York: Norton, 1997.

Rotman, B., and G. T. Kneebone. *The Theory of Sets and Transfinite Numbers*. London: Oldbourne, 1966.

Roudinesco, Elisabeth. *Jacques Lacan*. Trans. Barbara Bray. Cambridge, U.K.: Polity Press, 1997.

Rucker, Rudy. *Infinity and the Mind*. Brighton, U.K.: Harvester, 1982.

Russell, Bertrand. *Our Knowledge of the External World* [1914]. London: Allen and Unwin, 1922.

——. *Mysticism and Logic*. London: Longmans, 1918.

——. *Introduction to Mathematical Philosophy*. London: Allen and Unwin, 1920.

——. *History of Western Philosophy*. New York: Simon and Schuster, 1945.

——. *My Philosophical Development*. London: Allen and Unwin, 1959.

——. *The Autobiography of Bertrand Russell*. New York: Bantam, 1968.

Russell, Bertrand, and Alfred Whitehead, *Principia Mathematica*. Cambridge, U.K.: Cambridge University Press, 1910–12.

Sapir, Edward. *Selected Writings in Language, Culture, and Personality.* Ed. D. G. Mandelbaum. Berkeley: University of California Press, 1947.

Sartre, Jean-Paul. *La Transcendence de l'ego.* 1937. Reprint Paris: Vrin, 1988. Trans. Forrest Williams and Robert Kirkpatrick. New York: Noonday Press, 1957.

———. *La Nausée* [1938]. Paris: Folio ed.

———. *L'Imaginaire* [1940]. Paris: Folio ed.

———. *L'Etre et le néant.* Paris: Gallimard, 1943. Trans. Hazel Barnes. New York: Philosophical Library, 1956.

———. *Critique de la raison dialectique, vol. 1: Théorie des ensembles pratiques* [1960]. Ed. Arlette Elkaïm-Sartre. Paris: Gallimard, 1985. Trans. Alan Sheridan-Smith. London: New Left Books, 1976.

———. *Critique de la raison dialectique, vol. 2: L'intelligibilité de l'histoire* [unfinished]. Ed. Arlette Elkaïm-Sartre. Paris: Gallimard, 1985.

Saunier, Pierre. *L'Ouvriérisme universitaire.* Paris: L'Harmattan, 1994.

Schmitt, Carl. *Political Theology: Four Chapters on the Concept of Sovereignty* [1922]. Trans. George Schwab. Cambridge, Mass.: MIT Press, 1985.

Scholem, Gershom G. *Major Trends in Jewish Mysticism* [1941]. New York, Schocken Books, 1961.

Shapiro, Stewart. *Philosophy of Mathematics: Structure and Ontology.* Oxford: Oxford University Press, 1997.

Sharratt, Michael. *Galileo.* Cambridge, U.K.: Cambridge University Press, 1994.

Smullyan, Raymond, and Melvin Fitting. *Set Theory and the Continuum Problem.* Oxford: Oxford University Press, 1996.

Sokal, Alan, and Jean Bricmont. *Intellectual Impostures: Postmodern Philosophers' Abuse of Science.* London: Profile, 1998.

Spinoza, Baruch. *The Political Works.* Trans. A. G. Wernham. Oxford: Oxford University Press, 1958.

———. *Ethics.* Trans. Samuel Shirley. Indianapolis, Ind.: Hackett, 1992.

Taylor, Charles. *Hegel.* Cambridge, U.K.: Cambridge University Press, 1975.

———. "The Politics of Recognition." In *Multiculturalism,* ed. Amy Gutmann, 25–73. Princeton, N.J.: Princeton University Press, 1994.

Tiles, Mary. *The Philosophy of Set Theory: An Introduction to Cantor's Paradise.* Oxford: Blackwell, 1989.

Troelstra, A. S. *Principles of Intuitionism.* Berlin: Springer, 1969.

Van Heijenoort, Jean, ed. *From Frege to Gödel.* Cambridge, Mass.: Harvard University Press, 1967.

Verstraeten, Pierre. "Philosophies de l'événement: Badiou et quelques autres." *Le Temps modernes* (Aug. 1990): 241–94.

Wang, Hao. *Computation, Logic, Philosophy.* Dordrecht, the Netherlands: Kluwer Academic Publishers, 1990.

Weyl, André. *Philosophy of Mathematics and Natural Science.* Princeton, N.J.: Princeton University Press, 1949.

Whitford, Margaret. *Irigaray: Philosophy in the Feminine.* London: Routledge, 1991.

Wilder, Raymond L. *Introduction to the Foundations of Mathematics.* New York: John Wiley, 1952.

Wittgenstein, Ludwig. *Tractatus Logico-Philosophicus* [1921]. Trans. C. K. Ogden. London: Routledge, 1981.

————. *Philosophical Investigations.* Oxford: Blackwell, 1958.

————. *Remarks on the Foundations of Mathematics.* Oxford: Blackwell, 1967.

————. *Philosophical Remarks.* Ed. Rush Rhees. Oxford: Blackwell, 1975.

Wright, Crispin. *Wittgenstein on the Foundations of Mathematics.* London: Duckworth, 1980.

Žižek, Slavoj. *The Sublime Object of Ideology.* London: Verso, 1989.

————. *For They Know Not What They Do: Enjoyment As a Political Factor.* London: Verso, 1991.

————. *Tarrying with the Negative: Kant, Hegel, and the Critique of Ideology.* Durham, N.C.: Duke University Press, 1993.

————. *The Metastases of Enjoyment: Six Essays on Woman and Causality.* London: Verso, 1994.

————. *The Indivisible Remainder: An Essay on Schelling and Related Matters.* London: Verso, 1996.

————. *The Plague of Fantasies.* London: Verso, 1997.

————. *The Ticklish Subject: The Absent Centre of Political Ontology.* London: Verso, 1999.

————. *The Žižek Reader.* Ed. Elizabeth Wright and Edmond Wright. Oxford: Blackwell, 1999.

Zupančič, Alenka. *Ethics of the Real: Kant, Lacan.* London: Verso, 2000.

Index

Finley, Moses, 401n.11
Fontenelle, Bernard, 326
forcing, 135–39, 191, 344–45, 412n.52, 425n.82
formalization, xxx–xxxi, 246–48, 401n.12; artistic, 195–96; mathematical, 53, 60–61, 209–10, 213, 362n.32, 416n.15; political, 225
formalism, 71–72
Foucault, Michel, xxviii, 5, 150, 153, 159, 255, 279–80, 318, 408n.21; as nominalist, 378n.15
Foundation: axiom of, 88, 116, 339, 367n.23
foundational element of a situation, 83–84, 87–88, 119. *See also* evental site; urelement; void, the
Fouquier-Tinville, Antoine, 414n.63
Fowler, David, 392n.25, 421n.6
foyers ouvriers (workers' hostels), 234, 236
Fraenkel, Abraham, 215, 334, 337
Frankfurt School, xii
freedom, xxxi, xxxii, 285
Frege, Gottlob, xxii, 77, 86, 155, 215, 218, 244, 301, 333, 334, 335, 361n.13
French language: characteristics of, 11
French Revolution, 111, 118, 123, 126, 129, 285, 299, 374n.48, 396n.19; Hegel's interpretation of, 411n.45
Freud, Anna, 246
Freud, Sigmund, xxx, 5, 24, 113, 142, 163, 218, 246, 247
Front de Libération du Québec, 409n.27
Furet, François, 374n.48

Gadamer, Hans-Georg, xxiv, 153, 161
Galileo, Galilei, 7–8, 138, 142, 209, 210, 324, 328, 329

Gauche prolétarienne, 37, 49
Gauss, Carl, 326
generic, the, xxiii, xxvii, xxix, xxxi, 107, 129, 273, 311; generic communism, 44; as ontological orientation, 217–18
generic procedures, xxvii, xxxiv, 108, 134, 154, 181–83, 384n.1; interconnections between, 400n.9. *See also* conditions: of philosophy; truth
generic set theory, 127–28, 130–34, 342–48
Gillespie, Sam, 402n.14
Girard, René, 250; and mimetic desire, 190
Glucksmann, André, 40
God: death of, 6–7, 18, 62, 81, 101, 146, 320, 351n.11, 393n.39. *See also* One, the
Godard, Jean-Luc, 206
Gödel, Kurt, xxii, 55, 69, 70, 72, 153, 155–56, 215, 221, 336, 341, 343, 348; and definition of set, 366n.7; and incompleteness, 340–41, 424n.66; refusal of intuitionism, 379n.26
Gorz, André, 240
Gourevitch, Philip, 404n.34
grace: as metaphor for an event, 110, 115, 371n.17
Gramsci, Antonio, 279–80
Grosrichard, Alain, x
Grothendieck, Alexandre, 302, 401n.12
Guattari, Félix. *See* Deleuze, Gilles

Habermas, Jürgen, 225, 268
Hallâj, Hussein ibn Mansur al-, 318
Hallett, Michael, 75, 93, 334, 336–37, 347, 392n.34, 407n.17

Peter Hallward is a lecturer in the French department at King's College London. His previous publications include *Absolutely Postcolonial: Writing between the Singular and the Specific* and a translation of Alain Badiou's *Ethics: An Essay on the Understanding of Evil.*

Slavoj Žižek, philosopher and psychoanalyst, is senior researcher at the University of Ljubljana, Slovenia. His recent books include *On Belief, Did Somebody Say Totalitarianism?* and *The Fright of Real Tears.*